Experimental Multimedia Systems for Interactivity and Strategic Innovation

Ioannis Deliyannis
Ionian University, Greece

Petros Kostagiolas
Ionian University, Greece

Christina Banou
Ionian University, Greece

A volume in the Advances in Multimedia and
Interactive Technologies (AMIT) Book Series

An Imprint of IGI Global

Managing Director:	Lindsay Johnston
Managing Editor:	Keith Greenberg
Director of Intellectual Property & Contracts:	Jan Travers
Acquisitions Editor:	Kayla Wolfe
Production Editor:	Christina Henning
Development Editor:	Caitlyn Martin
Typesetter:	Kaitlyn Kulp; Tucker Knerr
Cover Design:	Jason Mull

Published in the United States of America by
Information Science Reference (an imprint of IGI Global)
701 E. Chocolate Avenue
Hershey PA, USA 17033
Tel: 717-533-8845
Fax: 717-533-8661
E-mail: cust@igi-global.com
Web site: http://www.igi-global.com

Library of Congress Cataloging-in-Publication Data

Experimental multimedia systems for interactivity and strategic innovation / Ioannis Deliyannis, Petros Kostagiolas, and Christina Banou, editors.
    pages cm
 Includes bibliographical references and index.
 ISBN 978-1-4666-8659-5 (hardcover) -- ISBN 978-1-4666-8660-1 (ebook) 1. Interactive multimedia--Design. I. Deliyannis, Ioannis, 1975- II. Kostagiolas, Petros. III. Banou, Christina, 1971-
 QA76.76.I59E98 2015
 006.7--dc23
                            2015015841

This book is published in the IGI Global book series Advances in Multimedia and Interactive Technologies (AMIT) (ISSN: 2327-929X; eISSN: 2327-9303)

British Cataloguing in Publication Data
A Cataloguing in Publication record for this book is available from the British Library.

All work contributed to this book is new, previously-unpublished material. The views expressed in this book are those of the authors, but not necessarily of the publisher.

For electronic access to this publication, please contact: eresources@igi-global.com.

Advances in Multimedia and Interactive Technologies (AMIT) Book Series

Joel J.P.C. Rodrigues
Instituto de Telecomunicações, University of Beira Interior, Portugal

ISSN: 2327-929X
EISSN: 2327-9303

Mission

Traditional forms of media communications are continuously being challenged. The emergence of user-friendly web-based applications such as social media and Web 2.0 has expanded into everyday society, providing an interactive structure to media content such as images, audio, video, and text.

The **Advances in Multimedia and Interactive Technologies (AMIT) Book Series** investigates the relationship between multimedia technology and the usability of web applications. This series aims to highlight evolving research on interactive communication systems, tools, applications, and techniques to provide researchers, practitioners, and students of information technology, communication science, media studies, and many more with a comprehensive examination of these multimedia technology trends.

Coverage

- Digital Communications
- Multimedia Streaming
- Mobile Learning
- Audio Signals
- Multimedia technology
- Gaming Media
- Digital Images
- Internet technologies
- Digital Games
- Social Networking

IGI Global is currently accepting manuscripts for publication within this series. To submit a proposal for a volume in this series, please contact our Acquisition Editors at Acquisitions@igi-global.com or visit: http://www.igi-global.com/publish/.

Titles in this Series

Design Strategies and Innovations in Multimedia Presentations
Shalin Hai-Jew (Kansas State University, USA)
Information Science Reference • copyright 2015 • 590pp • H/C (ISBN: 9781466686960) • US $225.00 (our price)

Cases on the Societal Effects of Persuasive Games
Dana Ruggiero (Bath Spa University, UK)
Information Science Reference • copyright 2014 • 345pp • H/C (ISBN: 9781466662063) • US $205.00 (our price)

Video Surveillance Techniques and Technologies
Vesna Zeljkovic (New York Institute of Technology, Nanjing Campus, China)
Information Science Reference • copyright 2014 • 369pp • H/C (ISBN: 9781466648968) • US $215.00 (our price)

Techniques and Principles in Three-Dimensional Imaging An Introductory Approach
Martin Richardson (De Montfort University, UK)
Information Science Reference • copyright 2014 • 324pp • H/C (ISBN: 9781466649323) • US $200.00 (our price)

Computational Solutions for Knowledge, Art, and Entertainment Information Exchange Beyond Text
Anna Ursyn (University of Northern Colorado, USA)
Information Science Reference • copyright 2014 • 511pp • H/C (ISBN: 9781466646278) • US $180.00 (our price)

Perceptions of Knowledge Visualization Explaining Concepts through Meaningful Images
Anna Ursyn (University of Northern Colorado, USA)
Information Science Reference • copyright 2014 • 418pp • H/C (ISBN: 9781466647039) • US $180.00 (our price)

Exploring Multimodal Composition and Digital Writing
Richard E. Ferdig (Research Center for Educational Technology - Kent State University, USA) and Kristine E. Pytash (Kent State University, USA)
Information Science Reference • copyright 2014 • 352pp • H/C (ISBN: 9781466643451) • US $175.00 (our price)

Multimedia Information Hiding Technologies and Methodologies for Controlling Data
Kazuhiro Kondo (Yamagata University, Japan)
Information Science Reference • copyright 2013 • 497pp • H/C (ISBN: 9781466622173) • US $190.00 (our price)

www.igi-global.com

701 E. Chocolate Ave., Hershey, PA 17033
Order online at www.igi-global.com or call 717-533-8845 x100
To place a standing order for titles released in this series, contact: cust@igi-global.com
Mon-Fri 8:00 am - 5:00 pm (est) or fax 24 hours a day 717-533-8661

List of Reviewers

Spyros Sioutas, *Ionian University, Greece*
Panos Kourouthanasis, *Ionian University, Greece*
Andreas Giannakoulopoulos, *Ionian University, Greece*
Panayotis Ioannou, *University of Crete, Greece*
Ioannis Karydis, *Ionian University, Greece*
Soultana Tsiridou, *Ionian University, Greece*

Table of Contents

Detailed Table of Contents

Chapter 1
Sonia Ferrari, University of Calabria, Italy

This chapter is focused on the elements that, in post modern era, have greatly changed our society, both in terms of buying and consumption habits and, more generally, in terms of lifestyles. This is mainly due to the Internet, which provides low cost, faster and interactive information and communication. As described in detail in the chapter, companies have been forced to adopt new marketing strategies and, thanks to the spread of social media and viral marketing, tools such as word of mouth and storytelling have become even more effective than in the past. But today companies need to use them in a different way, actively involving the consumers, because they attribute a greater value to a product if they participate in the process of creation of its image and elements of differentiation. If managed in an innovative way, focusing on sensory and transmedia aspects, storytelling becomes a very powerful Customer Relationship Marketing and image building medium and, above all, a source of enduring competitive advantage.

Chapter 2
Eleanor Dare, University of Derby, UK
Elena Papadaki, University of Greenwich, UK

This chapter examines the current state of digital artworks, arguing that they have not yet made a groundbreaking impact on the cultural landscape of the early 21st century and suggesting that a reason for this lack of notoriety is the obsolete model of agency deployed by many digital artists. As an alternative to what is framed as out-of-date forms of interactivity, the chapter highlights evolving research into interactive systems, artists' tools, applications, and techniques that will provide readers with an insightful and up-to-date examination of emerging multimedia technology trends. In particular, the chapter looks at situated computing and embodied systems, in which context-aware models of human subjects can be combined with sensor technology to expand the agencies at play in interactive works. The chapter connects these technologies to Big Data, Crowdsourcing and other techniques from artificial intelligence that expand our understanding of interaction and participation.

Chapter 3

Panagiota Stellaki, Independent Researcher, Greece

The purpose of the current article is to present the results of a survey conducted in 2010 in an exhibition at "Hellenic Cosmos", the Cultural Centre of the Foundation of the Hellenic World in Athens, Greece. The title of the exhibition was "Is There an Answer to Everything? A journey to the world of Greek mathematics". The survey was a part of the writer's dissertation at Panteion University at the MA Program "Cultural Management", Department of Communication, Media and Culture. The survey focuses only in families and it gives insight about important aspects regarding exhibition spaces such as the use of multimedia before entering the exhibition space, the relation of visitors towards multimedia exhibits and the role of the museum as an alternative place for learning, especially with the use of innovative interactive multimedia.

Chapter 4

Ioannis Deliyannis, Interactive Arts Research Lab, Greece
Dalila Honorato, Interactive Arts Research Lab, Greece

In this chapter, we present the main interaction design issues that arise during the development of edutainment scenarios through the use of branded augmented reality (AR) authoring environments. Most proprietary AR systems offer limited interaction features within their entry-level version, while licensing unlocks the desired advanced features. In order to overcome this problem we employ experimental multimedia development methods for the design of content for those platforms, enabling the development of fully featured case studies where interaction is implemented both physically and virtually. The introduction and literature research sections are complemented by selected experimental case studies that explore the interaction capabilities. It is shown how these may be implemented using limited AR resources. The chapter concludes with the presentation of the social software perspective of the communication process, as the application areas and the content domain presented in this work feature clear collaborative potential that needs to be addressed by system design.

Chapter 5

Charilaos Lavranos, Ionian University, Greece
Petros Kostagiolas, Ionian University, Greece
Joseph Papadatos, Ionian University, Greece

Music information seeking incorporates the human activities that are carried out for the search and retrieval of music information. In recent years, the evolution of music technology holds a central role affecting the nature of music information seeking behavior. The research area that deals with the accessibility and the retrievability process of music information is known as Music Information Retrieval (MIR). This chapter focuses on the presentation of MIR technologies which has a direct impact in the way that individuals, as well as different music communities such as composers, performers, listeners, musicologists, etc., handle and utilize music information. The aim of this chapter is to investigate the way different music communities interact with MIR systems. Our approach is based on a selected literature review regarding the MIR systems and the information seeking behavior of the musicians.

Chapter 6

Konstantinos Drossos, Ionian University, Greece
Maximos Kaliakatsos-Papakostas, Aristotle University of Thessaloniki, Greece
Andreas Floros, Ionian University, Greece

With the advances of technology, multimedia tend to be a recurring and prominent component in almost all forms of communication. Although their content spans in various categories, there are two protuberant channels that are used for information conveyance, i.e. audio and visual. The former can transfer numerous content, ranging from low-level characteristics (e.g. spatial location of source and type of sound producing mechanism) to high and contextual (e.g. emotion). Additionally, recent results of published works depict the possibility for automated synthesis of sounds, e.g. music and sound events. Based on the above, in this chapter the authors propose the integration of emotion recognition from sound with automated synthesis techniques. Such a task will enhance, on one hand, the process of computer driven creation of sound content by adding an anthropocentric factor (i.e. emotion) and, on the other, the experience of the multimedia user by offering an extra constituent that will intensify the immersion and the overall user experience level.

Chapter 7

May Kokkidou, University of Western Macedonia, Greece
Zoe Dionyssiou, Ionian University, Greece

This work focuses on the application of experimental multimedia in the field of music education. The end-system produced is a multimedia service designed to support music teachers who wish to generate and implement teaching scenarios, during their singing teaching session, as this progresses and evolves dynamically. The system allows them to adjust on the fly their educational content, in order to cover their classroom needs that evolve continuously during practice. The end-system combines a fully searchable multimedia database complemented by an access process designed to serve constantly changing content requirements. Most importantly, the system is designed to provide meaningful teaching-learning scenarios with the appropriate content on demand, through the implementation of a task-specific system-as-a-service access method. This chapter provides a walk through the most important characteristics of the process from the content expert perspective. This information was actively employed by developers enabling the system parameterization to cover the functional requirements of the teaching-learning process.

Chapter 8

Stelios Zimeras, University of the Aegean, Greece
Petros Kostagiolas, Ionian University, Greece
Charilaos Lavranos, Ionian University, Greece

The meaning of customer satisfaction has introduced many research analyses in many scientific fields during the recent years. Customer satisfaction represents a modern approach for evaluating quality in any kind of organizations. Customer satisfaction provides a useful and objective feedback about preferences and expectations. This can be particularly important for the design of services based on multimedia and interactive technologies, which are novel to most users. During the evaluation process, surveys analysis must be applied with main task to understand customer satisfaction. For that reason questionnaires have been proposed to reflect the previous analysis. Many times in that process, individuals that participate in the interviewing process misunderstand the pose questions leading to false answers and error results, without evaluating all recourses during the interview. The aim of this chapter is to analyze a statistical modeling of that false answers considering categorical data analysis through a digital music library case study. This chapter focuses on a proposed method which is based on the probabilities of the positive or negative TRUE and FALSE answers, with main task to reduce the variability of the errors during the survey.

Chapter 9

The chapter focuses on the aesthetic-artistic identity of the book nowadays with the aim to discuss patterns of publishing, and more specifically of the aesthetics in publishing. The chapter takes as key elements that A. the values and strategies of our age are in use for centuries, and B. the aesthetic identity of the book is still essential in its production, promotion and marketing. After a short overview of the publishing industry nowadays, the past of the publishing activity since Renaissance is studied so as to provide, through common features and values, a theoretical background and explanation of publishing strategies. Thereafter, patterns of illustration of the printed book and of gamification / use of multimedia in publishing are provided; the illustration chain is proposed as part of the publishing one. Conclusions regarding the proposed methodological framework and the opportunities of the publishing industry may enlighten issues and challenges of our era and offer to the publishing studies a specific point of view.

Chapter 10

For quite a while now there is an ongoing and fueled debate about the future of the book, the implications of the eBook, the act of reading and reading habits and so on and so forth. An eBook is primarily a piece of software, an application. And with that said, a huge world of possibilities opens up. The question that we should try to answer then, is, what exactly is the purpose of an eBook, what should it do, how should it be designed, used or consumed. Integration of multimedia, in a meaningful and practical way, gamefication, non-linearity, design and usability are a few of the concepts that are explored in relation to the eBook and how they can add value to a medium that has been significantly underexploited.

The practical training of students and employees in laboratories containing scientific instruments constitutes an educational challenge. Laboratory equipment is by definition sensitive, costly and requires specific safety rules for its use. Therefore, students do not have the opportunity to make improper use of the equipment and get trained by "trial-and-error". The educational process becomes even trickier when students are many and training takes place simultaneously within the same laboratory; damages to instrumentation and accidents are possible and as a consequence, the effectiveness of learning is greatly limited. For such purposes, an adventure-style computer game -Onlabs- has been developed to provide an interactive simulation environment of a biology laboratory where students may experiment and make several harmless mistakes and where no time or space restrictions are imposed on them. This chapter describes how Onlabs was developed to serve a real need for a remote tool for familiarization and safe experimentation within the laboratory space.

Antonia Plerou, Ionian University, Greece
Elena Vlamou, Democritus University of Thrace, Greece
Basil Papadopoulos, Democritus University of Thrace, Greece

The fusion of Artificial Neural Networks and Fuzzy Logic Systems allows researchers to model real world problems through the development of intelligent and adaptive systems. Artificial Neural networks are able to adapt and learn by adjusting the interconnections between layers while fuzzy logic inference systems provide a computing framework based on the concept of fuzzy set theory, fuzzy if-then rules, and fuzzy reasoning. The combined use of those adaptive structures is known as "Neuro-Fuzzy" systems. In this chapter, the basic elements of both approaches are analyzed while neuro-fuzzy networks learning algorithms are presented. Here, we combine the use of neuro-fuzzy algorithms with multimedia-based signals for training. Ultimately this process may be employed for automatic identification of patterns introduced in medical applications and more specifically for analysis of content produced by brain imaging processes.

Chapter 13

Anna Sołtysik-Piorunkiewicz, University of Economics in Katowice, Poland
Małgorzata Furmankiewicz, University of Economics in Katowice, Poland
Piotr Ziuziański, University of Economics in Katowice, Poland

This publication consists three main areas of interest: management of patient information in Polish health care system, novel ideas and recent trends on healthcare Web-based applications in Poland and healthcare information behavior of users of self-diagnosis and self-treatment systems in Poland. The methodology adopted includes a literature review for the utilization of Web-based healthcare applications in Poland as well as the trends of medical information systems and healthcare system in Poland. Furthermore the results of a survey research for the management of patient information in Poland are provided. Respondents have been asked about their interested and experiences on the new Polish information electronic health record system or others information systems dedicated to the management of the healthcare processes in Poland. Also another survey researches are presented. Respondents have been asked which internet tools they use for self-treatment and self-diagnosis and are also asked to rate their credibility.

Chapter 14

Antonia Plerou, Ionian University, Greece
Panayiotis Vlamos, Ionian University, Greece

During the last decades, the interest displayed in neurocognitive and brain science research is relatively high. In this chapter, the cognitive neuroscience field approach focuses in the aspect of the way that cognitive functions are produced by neural circuits in the brain. Within this frame, the effects of impairment to the brain and subsequent changes in the thought processes due to changes in neural circuitry resulting from the ensued damage are analyzed and evaluated. All cognitive functions result from the integration of many simple processing mechanisms, distributed throughout the brain. Brain cortex structures, linked with cognitive disorders, are located in several parts like the frontal, the parietal, the temporal, the occipital lobe and more are analyzed and specified. A critical topic of this chapter in the evaluation of brain operations is mapping regions that control cognitive and mathematical concepts functions. Dyscalculia, in this chapter, is described as a specific disorder of managing and conceiving mathematical concepts. Dyscalculia could be identified by difficulties in visual perception, in spatial number organization, in basic mathematical operations and in mathematical induction logic. Moreover, people who deal with dyscalculia present problems, in Euclidean and Non-Euclidean Geometry concepts perception, in Calculus aspects as well as in solving algorithmic problems where the design, the description and the application of algorithmic steps are required. In order to enhance cognitive brain functions perception, the use of EEG brain imaging is proposed measuring cerebral activity and event-related potentials. The procedure described in this chapter is about the comparison and contrasts EEG brain imaging patterns of healthy volunteers to EEG samples taken of adults considered being at risk of mathematics learning disabilities such as Dyscalculia and algorithmic thinking difficulties. EEG interpretation analysis is to follow where the deviation of a normal and an abnormal range of wave's frequency are defined. Several visualized EEG patterns in relevance with specific abnormalities are presented while several neurocognitive generated disorders could be identified with the use of EEG Brain-imaging technique. The electroencephalogram EEG brain imaging procedure, in order to evaluate problems associated with brain function, is to be further analyzed in this chapter as well. The EEG is the depiction of the electrical activity occurring at the surface of the brain. The recorded waveforms reflect the cortical electrical activity and they are generally classified according to their frequency (Delta, Theta, Beta, Alpha, Beta, and Gamma) amplitude, and shape. EEG Implementation with the use of 10/20 system of the standardized position of scalp electrodes placement for a classical EEG recording is described as well. The EEG implementation objective is to identify, classify and evaluate those frequencies and regions in the brain that best characterize brain activity associated with mathematical learning disabilities. Mapping the brain with non-invasive techniques based on trigger and sensing/evaluation experimental multimedia methods similar to those used in computer games and applications are expected to provide relevant results in order to enhance and confirm theoretical cognitive aspects. At that point, a cognitive and mathematical perception evaluation is to follow and specifically the assessment of the relation of difficulties in mathematics with particular parts of the human brain. EEG wave data visualization is contacted with the use of Acknowledge an interactive, intuitive program which provides data analysis instantly. At the end of this chapter EEG computational evaluation with the use of pattern recognition methods as well as the intuition of author's future work in relevance with the use of experimental multimedia technologies to enhance the dynamic recognition and evaluation of user cognitive responses during EEG implementation are noted.

Chapter 15

Ioannis Deliyannis, Ionian University, Greece
Georgios Papaioannou, Ionian University, Greece

In this chapter we discuss the development of edutainment systems supported by augmented reality applications, in order to enable augmented reality technologies for archaeology within the so-called communication engine for museums and cultural tourism. The task in hand is interdisciplinary and its successful implementation relies heavily on information technology as a detailed analysis of content-user needs and sound interaction design capable to support edutainment scenario is needed. This work identifies the role of each building component, describes their interrelationship within the wider context and adopts a suitably designed framework in order to develop multiple guided-tour types. Real-life case study scenario on a specific case, that of the Old Fortress in the UNESCO-listed Old Town of Corfu, Greece, are used to demonstrate the adaptive nature of content and how the system and developers handle different uses. The proposed approach offers new narration tools for content experts while it may be used to support personalised visitor experiences.

Foreword

In the decades since the first appearance of Multimedia as a distinct discipline of Information Technology, several key technologies have impacted its development: The Web 1 and 2, Big Data and Reactive Web applications, smart mobile devices, the Internet of Things, Ubiquitous Computing and Physical Computing are amongst the prominent ones. These new ways to deploy and utilize digital media are affected by the increase storage capacities and processing speeds and by the appearance of new technologies for media delivery, interaction and sensing as well as by a plethora of new software technologies: After Object Oriented Programming, functional programming is experiencing a comeback, and no-sql databases are now a regular partner to SQL in the world of data management. More importantly perhaps, the worlds of software development, digital content and social interaction between humans and between humans and machines are converging: Social media and locative media, virtual social networks and communities are weakening and blurring the boundaries between the purely technical and the human or social. The present volume contains contributions that deal with issues arising from these changes. It is addressed to readers that wish to gain an understanding of how new developments in information technologies affect the face of interactive multimedia. It reports on experiments conducted and methodologies used in the quest to develop new types of interactive multimedia applications, or to improve the effectiveness and to enhance the usefulness of existing applications. Predicting future trends and understanding the nature of the current interdependencies of multimedia technologies and human society is a difficult and challenging task. The present volume provides useful insights in this field by researchers and practitioners who have made this task the center of their concern. As such, it is a value contribution to the discourse about the nature of innovation in interactive multimedia and its role in society.

Iannis Zannos
Ionian University, Greece

Foreword

Iannis Zannos *has a background in music composition, ethnomusicology and interactive performance. He has worked as Director of the Music Technology and Documentation section at the State Institute for Music Research (S.I.M.) in Berlin, Germany, and Research Director at the Center for Research for Electronic Art Technology (CREATE) at the University of California, Santa Barbara. He has taken part at numerous international collaborative Media Arts projects and has realized multimedia performances both alone and in cooperation with other artists. He is teaching audio and interactive media arts at the Department of Audiovisual Arts and at the postgraduate course in Arts and Technologies of Sound of the Music Department at the Ionian University, Corfu. Publications include: "Ichos und Makam" (Comparative Studies on the Modal systems of Greek and Turkish Music, 1994), "Music and Signs" (edited proceedings of the 1997 conference on Music Semiotics and Systematic Musicology), and a number of articles on Music Technology and Media Arts. Participation in artistic collaborations include with Martin Carlé (2000) programming of interactive sound for Eric Sleichim / Bl!ndman Quartet, and Ulrike and David Gabriel; Cosmos-X - Multimedia installation with multiple audio and video projections based on the work of Iannis Xenakis, with Efi Xirou (2005-2006); and with Jean-Pierre Hébert real-time sound programming for the installation series on "Sand" (2004-2005). Currently Iannis Zannos is focusing on how environmental issues as well as problems of multiculturality are reflected in media-art terms.*

Preface

Our lives are dramatically affected by Information Society (IS) technologies today. It is hard to find an area where technology has not yet infiltrated. Software and hardware infrastructures are employed for multiple purposes including both interpersonal and work-based interaction, collaboration and communication. In the hardware forefront, mobile communication devices such as laptops, mobile phones and tablets are replaced at a high pace, a process driven by the need for faster and fuller information access. New devices are multimedia enabled and their increased processing and sensing capabilities allow users to access and contribute content to media-rich environments. As a result, from the software perspective, both the volume and complexity of applications increase at a high rate.

Interestingly, the most evolutionary aspect of IS today is how developers choose to innovate through this technological reality. A typical smartphone is considered a fully featured computer, as it combines multi-core processing power, fast-access memory, high-resolution monitor, multiple modes of networking, microphone, speakers, GPS, compass, multi-touch screen, orientation sensors, high-resolution camera, led light and runs on open-access software. In addition it is easier today than ever before to design and build new applications and services as the open access movement is supported globally by a large number of users, new technological hardware/software solutions and open access software that includes programming and development environments. Therefore it can clearly be employed as a hardware platform for the development of new experimental multimedia applications.

In fact, users have today moved beyond technological experimentation with new forms of communication, participation, collaboration and creativity. Their new phase is clearly more dynamic as they take up an active role in the software and hardware development processes. It is interesting to observe the diversity of ways in which existing technologies are being recycled or re-used by different user groups that extend their functionality and transform them in order to cover their particular requirements. *Experimental Multimedia Systems* are characterised by this particular developmental approach, where older systems are being re-engineered in order to cover the demands of new application domains and content. In that sense *Interactivity* and *Strategic Innovations* are both valued characteristics introduced at various levels: within the experimental multimedia system itself, and throughout the content. For instance, the book as physical and intellectual object is constantly being transformed due to a number of reasons among which the use of new information and communication technologies prevails. Within that context, the publishing industry faces significant challenges redefining thus values, redeveloping strategies, reinventing methods and re-creating taste. In a globalized world, innovation and risk go hand in hand. The exploitation of new information and communication technologies was and is one of the peak points for the publishing industry altering book production and distribution, promotion methods, marketing, advertisement, bookselling as well as reading and communicating. The role of multimedia is inevitably significant in the publishing value chain from the author to the publishers and to the reader; publications can be printed or electronic, and we read on printed books, e-books, tablets, mobile phones and other devices. Meanwhile, social media create communities of readers while direct communication between publisher and reader is among the key points for the publishing activity of our era. Furthermore, the transformations of the book through the experimentation with multimedia (for example, gamification) bring about new forms of texts as well as new reading and aesthetic experiences.

This book is a collection of carefully selected state-of-the art theoretical and applied research chapters in the field of "Experimental Multimedia Systems", with special focus on Interactivity and Strategic Innovation. The presentation of interdisciplinary case studies is of particular importance for experimental multimedia systems, as it proves their wide applicability in various domains of interest. Ultimately, readers should be able to identify innovation at different levels within systems and fields of application. In order to view this through an example, one may wish to consider the field of New Media Art. From the developer's perspective it is clearly an interdisciplinary creative & research area directly affected by technological developments where each and every creation is unique. Here, artists and technologists cooperate in order to create artwork featuring extended interaction and presentation requirements via the extension of the limitations of technology. Depending on the task in hand, artists have to develop technologies that often exploit the human sensing limitations in order to create new experiences. Clearly, this particular area of application is aided by technological developments and increased user-proficiency in new technologies, while the developments implemented during this process, can then be applied within other areas of interest.

On the other hand, this book can be used as roadmap for augmented reality technological investments. It is in fact true that the availability of a technology does not necessary imply its immediate utilisation in organizations and enterprises. The concept of supplementing reality in various settings through computer-generated information needs to further mature within the management decision-making mechanisms. This book also attempts to contribute to this discussion of reassessing already existing services. Then novel services are developed by embedding into the existing services artificial information related to the environment and its physical objects. Obviously museums, libraries, publishers and other information organizations could more straightforwardly be involved and a new window of opportunity is opening for them in developing innovative services. However, in other settings beyond the creative industry, the top management requires comprehension for the value created by such technological applications. In healthcare, for example, augmented reality applications are gradually developed for assisting the diagnoses and the therapeutic interventions. In education, applications for enhancing the learning process are progressively become available and such brilliant applications are put in use into the classrooms. We also trust that market driven forces may come to liberate a wide array of opportunities for augmented reality applications adoption, for instance in retail, branding, and in many (if not all) industries.

Then again, the management operations themselves can employ the augmented reality prospect for leadership and for other organizational processes related to human resource management. Moreover, sharing organizational aims, communication and information exchange within business networks will certainly be benefited by augmented reality experiences. Other augmented reality organization-based applications could be developed in order to increase the quality and the effectiveness of staff education programs and at the same time reducing the cost when compared to the conventional methods. Furthermore, new job descriptions are developing or existing ones are redefined in order to include staff with skills in augmented reality technologies. The technological innovation does not only affect life, as we know it, but also have an impact on the way businesses are run, management operations are taking place and management decisions are made. This is certainly a fruitful area for research for augmented reality technological applications.

Institutions and universities targeting new-media art research need to frequently adapt their curriculum in order to cover the dynamically changing research demands that evolve. As a result, interactive multimedia-based art utilises multimedia technologies clearly capable to trigger all senses, in an attempt to transfer to the audience emotions and create new user experiences.

The content structure is designed to offer the reader a scalable introduction that focuses on experimental multimedia from different perspectives. It combines state of the art research on innovative trans-media storytelling and narrative social-media-based marketing, while the role of the consumer in the process is highlighted; presentation of a number of high-profile artworks, which are analyzed in terms of their interactive aspects; real-life museum-based and open-space case studies; music information retrieval; audio emotion recognition; dynamic music teaching; evaluation of the multimedia experience; the evolution of books; and applications in museums featuring edutainment, health and medical research.

The Editors

Acknowledgment

The research on "Experimental Multimedia Systems", as on any other field, is usually developed, established, and finally made available after engaging in an active dialog with colleagues, researchers, and students. Apart from colleagues in Greece from the Ionian University, and other Universities and research institutions, who have shared with us certain issues on augmented reality applications at times, our students have heavily contributed to the promotion of the main book idea and we would like to thank them wholeheartedly.

We would also like to acknowledge the significant help of peer reviewers for achieving the required high quality manuscript standards. The peer reviewers include scholars with significant merit and it was a great honor working with them over the review process.

We would also like to thank the IGI Global team members for their excellent cooperation and continuous support.

Chapter 1
Storytelling and Narrative Marketing in the Era of Social Media

Sonia Ferrari
University of Calabria, Italy

ABSTRACT

This chapter is focused on the elements that, in post modern era, have greatly changed our society, both in terms of buying and consumption habits and, more generally, in terms of lifestyles. This is mainly due to the Internet, which provides low cost, faster and interactive information and communication. As described in detail in the chapter, companies have been forced to adopt new marketing strategies and, thanks to the spread of social media and viral marketing, tools such as word of mouth and storytelling have become even more effective than in the past. But today companies need to use them in a different way, actively involving the consumers, because they attribute a greater value to a product if they participate in the process of creation of its image and elements of differentiation. If managed in an innovative way, focusing on sensory and transmedia aspects, storytelling becomes a very powerful Customer Relationship Marketing and image building medium and, above all, a source of enduring competitive advantage.

INTRODUCTION

Stories are an effective way to communicate and involve people. Storytelling is an important part of human culture in the field of entertainment and education (Zhou, Cheok, Pan & Li, 2004). It has always been a way to fascinate the public and has been used for many years in marketing and management (Mossberg, 2008). Through it companies create stories about products and brands in order to differentiate their offerings, make stronger and long lasting ties with their customers, and improve their images.

Storytelling can be defined as the "sharing of knowledge and experiences through narrative and anecdotes in order to communicate lessons, complex ideas, concepts, and causal connections" (Sole & Gray-Wilson, 1999, p. 6). It is a marketing tool with an increasing success; since the mid-90s it has been no longer just a communication instrument dedicated to children and an object of literary studies

DOI: 10.4018/978-1-4666-8659-5.ch001

used only for leisure (Salmon, 2008). In fact, thanks to the turn of marketing from a mass instrument to a rising attention towards the relationship marketing, today firms are more and more interested in creating strong and direct connections with every consumer, to facilitate the reciprocal generation of value and encourage customers' loyalty (Agren & Ölund, 2007). Very often for the customers the value and meaning of a brand are based on one or more stories (Aaker, 1991; Escalas, 2004; Keller, 1993).

In the last few years the success and popularity of social networks and all kinds of virtual communities, together with the wide popularity of Internet, the spread of communication, information and digital technologies and the increasing use of mobile media, have caused dramatic changes in business models in terms of communication strategies and decision-making processes (Garrigos-Simon, Lapiedra Alcami & Barbera Ribera, 2012; Hagel & Armstrong, 1997). In fact, the audience is now not a passive recipient of information and communication but an active creator of media content. Besides, because of the growing importance of social media, traditional advertising is every day becoming less important in marketing strategies. For companies it is increasingly relevant to dialogue with customers, even informally, through social networks; it is a means to know better their target market and interact with them, but also a way to create a different image from the traditional and institutional one.

As it will be illustrated in this chapter, the new ways to communicate is based on the Internet, the virtual reality, the augmented reality, the trigging of all senses, and the use of multiple media platforms. *Narrative marketing* becomes a better way to involve the audience and add value to products/services and brands. In fact, through it customers can know the story of the company and other background information about its offers and its social and environmental impact (Mödinger, 2011), being more and more engaged in the creation and spreading of fascinating plots, themes and characters.

Besides the social media has effects also on the value chain and structure of enterprises, creating new forms of competition. In fact, they are precious sources of information and knowledge sharing, but also sources of creativity and innovation. Through them people can add value to firms' offers, adapting them to new trends in market preferences, tastes and needs, fashion and styles, changes in social patterns, etc. They can become also powerful promotional vehicles.

STORYTELLING AND MARKETING IN POST-MODERN SOCIETY

During the so-called *narrative turn* storytelling became a very effective communication, control and power technique (Salmon, 2008), also thanks to the Internet. As just described, it gave life to the narrative marketing, which is a way to increase customer awareness and trust, together with companies' sales, but also a tool to immerse the consumer in atmospheres and feelings with a strong emotional involvement. The stories can strengthen ties with market and stakeholders, convey ideas, create and exploit brands and improve products/services/ companies' images. Storytelling is related to *word of mouth*, since a good story can generate a positive word of mouth for a company, especially in the field of services, where expectations' formation and performances' evaluations are more difficult processes.

There are advertising stories, as well as stories about products/services, brands, tourist destinations, companies, and also consumer stories (Escalas, 2004; Mossberg, 2008). They have to meet customers' expectations and preferences to generate a feeling of compatibility with the firms, their offers and their brands (Jensen, 1999). Frequently these stories are based on fiction, films, myths, legends, and/ or historic events.

Storytelling can trig and touch people emotionally, intellectually, spiritually, and physically (Agren & Ölund, 2007; Gabriel, 2000; Gummesson, 2004), entertaining and becoming an effective instrument of communication thanks to a high impact on individual memory. It is, together with dramaturgy, a way to offer experiences to customers, stimulating their imagination, entertaining them (Escalas, 2004; Mossberg, 2008) and satisfying their desire to live trigging holistic and unique experiences.

Referring to storytelling it is possible to talk of *immersion* and *absorption* in the experience. In fact, according to Pine and Gilmore (1999) the parameters used to identify the areas of experience are two: the type of guest participation (active or passive) and the kind of relationship between the customers and the environmental experience (immersion or absorption). In the immersion the person is mentally involved, while in the absorption the involvement is physical or virtual. The first situation occurs when the person lives the experience with the mind (e.g. in reading), while the second case involves the physical (or virtual) presence of the client, with a real access inside the experience. As described later, thanks to virtual reality and augmented reality today the recipient of storytelling initiatives can live even absorption experiences with multisensory stimulations. It means that the storytelling will not give just visual stimuli but also odours, sounds, music, touch and/or taste inputs to enjoy a stronger and memorable experience.

Therefore, storytelling becomes an instrument always more used by companies, which are trying to maximize their efforts to offer products and services able to provide emotionally, physically, mentally, socially, and spiritually engaging experiences (O' Sullivan & Spangler, 1998; Pine & Gilmore, 1999). The aim of these efforts is to differentiate their offerings and increase customers' loyalty, creating emotional bonds with the market and satisfying a greater need for enjoyment and fun.

To be unique and difficult to imitate, the story must have a strong connection with the life of the firm and its organization (Mossberg, 2008; Rosen, 2000). Advertising stories could be of different types. They suggest models to use the products and in the same time entertain the audience. In same case, the advertising narrative is a starting point for customers' self-generated stories, because it becomes a way to remember and relive personal experiences. The companies can encourage the rediscovery of memories, directly with specific instructions or indirectly by means of sound, music, images, smells, fragrances and photos; it is a way of influencing the audience through a new active narrative role connected to the product / service use (Escalas, 2004; Sujan, Bettam & Baumgartner, 1993).

WEB 2.0 AND WEB 3.0 ERAS: HOW COMMUNICATION IS CHANGING

Nowadays, thanks to the Internet, that is a source of cheap and easily accessible information and also an instrument of socialization and learning, consumers have a level of freedom not previously imaginable. As a consequence, consumers, highly active and participatory, have become more informed and more demanding than ever before, reducing the information asymmetry between supply and demand of goods and services.

After the stages of *information only* (Web 1.0) and *relational marketing* (Web 2.0, the era in which companies mainly sought to contact the users of their Websites), the Internet has now entered the period of the collaborative or semantic marketing (the Web 3.0). Supply and demand can meet in an interactive way and companies and their stakeholders seek to acquire knowledge not about the client but from the client and work with him/her to strengthen their images and brands. The Internet is no longer just an information tool: it has become a new dimension, allowing the firms to know better their customers and communicate more effectively, as well as to promote and market products, services, companies, and brands.

For this reason, today digital marketing is rapidly transforming the way companies communicate. A characteristic of the Web 2.0 is the *microcontent*, created by the Internet users, which put the consumer in a central location. Microcontent and social media have synergic and viral effects (Alexander & Levine, 2008), thanks to the spreading of content in different web platforms and with the continuous insertion of new elements added to the content by every new user and conversation.

The *open source content management system* connects people within communities that share interests, facilitating the dissemination of information and the collaboration between different subjects. In the beginning of the Web 3.0 era this gave rise to forms of communication that are no longer *one to one* or *one to many*, but rather *many to many* (Kotler, Kartajaya & Setiawan,2010; Rincon, 2012). In some cases, the customer can become the creator of a myth or a story about a product/service, a company, a brand or a tourist destination. If the firms are able to adequately address and enhance the user generated content these stories could represent out-and-out tools for storytelling, and the starting point of very effective advertising campaigns. Thanks to user-generated content the roles of those who exercise authority and who control have changed and innovative languages and new forms of storytelling have emerged (Sassoon, 2012).

Besides, the easy access to information and search makes researching for related content on the web effortless for the writers and readers of stories; for this reason the sharing and enriching of stories becomes easer and storytelling can be seen as a more and more powerful communication instrument for companies.

Ultimately the availability of innovative tools, such as platforms for the sharing of digital content, social commerce, blogs, social networks, forums, newsgroups and communities, that are independent information networks, enables the consumer to become a co-producer of communication, adapting it to her/his own tastes and needs (Escalas, 2004; Hagel & Armstrong, 1997).

In this new situation, marketing strategies are above all direct marketing initiatives, which act through personal not through mass media and consumers can provide companies an active feedback by means of co-produced communication (Bacile, Ye & Swilley, 2014). For the customer it is a way to live an interactive experience, creating a value for him/her and for the organization it is a competitive advantage. The consumer, now a *prosumer,* becomes a co-creator of value (Erragcha, 2014; Prahalad & Krishnan, 2008).

As a consequence, costumers have a greater power and companies no longer have control of their brands. The importance of advertising is decreasing and the influence, already very high, of the word of

Box 1. Tuscany Faces: How to represent a place on the Web through its people

Would you like to put your work story and your picture on the Internet? It is possible thanks to www.tuscanyfaces.com, the website that collects the faces of the Tuscan people, by birth or adoption, immortalized during their daily activities. The project, conceived and edited by the Social Media Team of the Tuscany Region, intends to introduce the excellence and the peculiarities of the region through the faces of the people who live there. It is not an accident that the project began during the Feast of Tuscany: it wanted to be an homage to the original Tuscany, a tradition that marks the landscape, architecture, food and everything you see, not a natural beauty but the result of man's work.

There are people of all types in over 100 photos collected by the Social Media Team; next to each of them a brief caption (in Italian and English) summarizes the name, the craft and the history of the protagonists. "We want to tell the stories of people who somehow embody the 'Tuscany', of those who represent excellences in all areas: artistic, scientific, crafts, food and wine sectors. They are not necessarily people born in Tuscany, but people who have chosen to live there and be inspired by this land," said the team of the project.

Everyone can send his/her face, a photo and a story! In the Web they say: "You are Tuscany! If you're Tuscan by blood or soul, if you live in Tuscany or if you're an ambassador of the tuscan spirit in the world, tell us your story and send us your most bizarre photo (in the foreground or from the waist up)."

Source: adapted from: www.tuscanyfaces.com.

mouth is growing. For the companies, having their own website is not enough to maximize the results. It is essential, in fact, to be easily reached, communicate effectively with the target markets and create a trustful and interactive relationship with the market by means of a right Web Marketing strategy. The Web 3.0 is the era of the *collaborative marketing* (Kotler et al., 2010), in which firms need to cooperate with their shareholders, clients, employees, and partners and invite customers to participate in the development of products and communication. In Box 1 you can read about a promotion campaign of Tuscany Region based on the inputs of local people and residents.

EXPERIENTIAL AND MULTISENSORY TRANSMEDIA MARKETING

In the light of the foregoing, it appears that in the Web 3.0 age (in which the interaction is between computers and the aim is to process large quantities of data and information to obtain targeted knowledge) the consumer is no longer a passive recipient of one-sided communications and the storytelling has become digital (Barassi & Treré, 2012; Carbone, Contreras, Hernandez & Gomez-Perez, 2012; Eftekhari & Zeynab, 2008; Garrigos-Simon et al., 2012; Mistilis, 2012). On the network the social media are means that consumers use to convey their stories that may include products and brands. These stories, because they have been generated by customers, are more credible, effective and engaging and can be used by companies as promotional tools, creating forms of communication based on storytelling (Alexander & Levine, 2008; Brake, 2014; Sassoon, 2008).

Another important aspect of the evolution of the web is the *social media* spread. Social media are the interactions among people in which they create, share, or exchange information and ideas in virtual communities and networks, creating forms of *viral communication.* Social media are instruments to create *modern tribes* or communities of fans of a product, a brand or an experience (Cova, 1995; Cova & Cova, 2002; Maffesoli, 1996). To get in touch with these groups, companies have to offer them elements that contribute to the rites of the tribe, creating myths, magic content, stories and more (Sassoon, 2012).

Studies on the evolution of communication in recent years pay particular attention to social media and virtual communities. They provide an interesting and fascinating environment in which every user can interact with others, together with highly enriching experiences; these experiences go far beyond the desire to exchange information about products/services, brands, and consumer experiences (Hagel III & Armstrong, 1997). Members of virtual communities seek, in fact, emotions and satisfaction of intrinsic needs. The community offers a trigging environment in which they can share experiences, memories, passions and / or consumption rituals, reliving memories of past experiences, being reassured, creating social bonds, daydreaming, receiving stimuli and experiencing moments of anticipation about future experiences, as well as enjoying their leisure time (Cova, 1995; Jansson, 2002; Maffesoli, 1996; Stamboulis & Skayannis, 2003; Tussyadiah & Fesenmaier, 2009). As a consequence, the Internet has become a virtual place in which to live and share experiences and emotions, a real *experientialscape*.

The *self-generated narrative*, thanks to the shared participation of social media members and the support of multimedia web instruments (such as sounds, music, videos, photos, etc.), can create more interesting and engaging stories. They are very important in the *experience society*, in which consumers are looking for products and services that intrigue and stimulate them; in effect, they are interested in emotionally and mentally enriching goods that grant holistic, unique and memorable consumption experiences (Addis & Holbrook, 2001; Holbrook & Hirschman, 1982; Schmitt, 1999).

As Pine and Gilmore (1999) state in their studies on this phenomenon, today the firms not only offer goods and services, but also emotions and unforgettable experiences (Ferrari, 2006; Pine & Gilmore, 1999). In fact, in their approach to marketing the companies have switched in recent decades from a focus on attributes / benefits sought by consumers to a higher concentration on brand policies (an approach in which the brand determines the image and has a symbolic value) and, finally, on aesthetic marketing (Schmitt & Simonson, 1997). This includes companies' marketing activities based on providing multi-sensory experiences, which aim to meet hedonistic needs. It is precisely the emotional aspect of contacts among companies, goods, services and customers that represents the challenge of *experiential marketing* (Schmitt, 1999, 2003). It has been neglected until few years ago and rediscovered today in the purchasing and consumption processes, mainly due to the contributions of Holbrook and Hirschman (1982),

Furthermore, companies can encourage consumers to "experience the experience" (Morgan, Lugosi & Ritchie, 2010, p. 130), creating stories that allow them to relive the moments of consumption; these stories can be the base of targeted storytelling activities. The case in Box 2 shows an example of storytelling of this type.

Experiential marketing aims to deliver memorable experiences of consumption and / or purchase primarily through sensory stimulation, not only visual but also the other senses, which today call for increased attention. These stimuli should aim to intensify the sensory interaction between enterprise and customer. In fact, according to Pine and Gilmore (1999), each product and service can be *sensorized*, as to say it is possible to increase the sensory stimuli perceived during its use or consumption, increasing the emphasis on the most important sense for every consumer.

Multisensory perceptions aim to transform the experience into a global and significant event for all the senses. In fact, by "multisensory experience we mean the receipt of experience in multiple sensory modalities including tastes, sounds, scents, tactile impressions and visual images" (Hirschman & Holbrook, 1982, p. 92).

The multi-sensory experiences can be developed by means of virtual reality, multimedia presentations, interactive techniques, fire-wire connections, haptic experiences, olfactory pathways, forms of sound art and other instruments. Information and communication technologies make it possible to use tools such as virtual and augmented reality, digital reproductions of objects, reconstructions of buildings and environments, which allow the users to immerse themselves in the atmosphere, feeling stronger and trigging sensory stimuli. These are very effective tools of communication, because they are not based on language codes but on interactivity, therefore on sensory stimuli (such as sounds, images, haptic experiences, etc.). The emergence of new media environments is the result of the spread of smart phones and

Box 2. How to tell in a multimedia way the traditional Italian ice cream: The experience of Sammontana's #sedicogelato

In 2013 the Italian historic producer of ice cream Sammontana invented a type of storytelling, called *#sedicogelato* (*#ifIsayicecream*), based on consumers' images, videos and texts, which were shared by social media. The communication project is based on the transmedia and social storytelling. The begging is a video, which tells the history of the family and the company. The short film *"La storia di un sorriso"* (The history of a smile), by Virgilio Villoresi, tells with images, leafing through the pages of an imaginary book, the seventy year old story of the firm that has started from a dairy shop. The smile is the main sign of the brand of Sammontana, the producer of the first family pack ice cream in the middle fifties. In the website they trigger the users' interactivity by means of the contest *"Se dico gelato"*, specially addressed to the young. In a multimedia platform the consumers are invited to share a brief text, an image or a video about their ice cream experience, through a mobile App, the website *"Se dico Gelato"* or FB *"Facebook del Gelataio"* (Facebook of the ice cream maker).

Source: adapted from www.sammontana.it.

tablet connected to the network, accessing multimedia innovative services and applications, favoured by the spread of wireless networks. Also the miniaturisation of augmented reality technologies, the availability of augmented reality on mobile devices and the augmented reality applications easy to use have helped the extensive utilization of augmented reality in the communication area (Pavlik & Bridges, 2013).

So innovative ways to immerse the user in storytelling, transforming it from a bi-dimensional to a three dimensional perspective, can be achieved through virtual and augmented realities. Through the use of these technologies, in fact, the recipient can experience the story in a real environment or in a virtual world but with the support of physical objects and with sensory stimuli, living it through the narrative (Bimber, Encarnacao & Schmalstieg, 2003). The AR-enhanced experience becomes more funny, trigging and interactive, adding the spatial dimension to the oral and written ones (Zhou et al., 2004).

STORYTELLING TOWARDS THE FUTURE

In this context, storytelling is more and more used by organizations as a tool to emotionally involve existing and potential customers. In fact, the power of emotional engagement may not lie in the object itself but in the drama and romance of the story of the encounter with the object (Picard & Robinson, 2012).

The Internet, a multimedia instrument, can be used to communicate in an innovative and more effective way, and is especially suited to experiential products and services, e.g. tourism or leisure (Ferrari, 2012). In fact, by means of video, audio, photos, augmented reality, three-dimensional and interactive maps, virtual tours, Webcams, GIS, Tags, printed materials downloaded, geological sites, online sale, GPS and smart phones, etc., the communication changes from unilateral push tools to interactive multiple channels. Besides, the contents of communication are becoming more and more complex and specific, depending on the identity and the character of the receiver and the context of the communication itself (Stavrakantonakis, Gagiu, Toma & Fensel, 2013).

With all these innovations, the Internet has also become a tool for a strong emotional involvement on the part of the potential customer, who, through it, can imagine and create her/his own consumer experience. In fact, the new web tools allow people to share the experience of consumption in real-time with other consumers, making their stories much more engaging, especially if they are inserted in the web during the experience, often with the support of photos, audios and/or videos.

Today people use multiple digital and no digital devises on different media, sometimes in the same moment. For this reason, and also because thanks to the web customers search for interactive and bidimensional dialogues, companies have to communicate in an innovative way. More and more the companies try to reach the customer through multiple communication media, adapting the message to their different characters. So the stories can be told by television, cinema, radio, books, interactive web sites, but also by alternate reality games, social media, and QR codes that allow to connect with web sites and download, for example, audios. In this way communication and storytelling become transmedia, because they use different media with various messages and stories. The same way of communicating is, in fact, impossible to adapt to a transmedia strategy that needs a specific message for every platform.

An instrument that leads in this direction is the *transmedia storytelling* (Jenkins, 2003; Scolari, 2009), which uses multiple new and traditional channels to spread the several components of a story across time. Every component tells a unique story in itself, which has been designed adapting it to the specificity of the medium used; all together these different parts create a more complete and fascinating story. Besides, every user can enrich the whole, adding elements such as new characters, a secondary plot, a contextualization, etc.

Usually the companies' storytelling is part of a creative project and it is difficult to distinguish promotion and marketing from artwork and creativity (Dena, 2009). The carrying on of entertainment projects for marketing scopes is called *content marketing* or *branded entertainment*.

Many important transmedia projects have been realized in occasion of the launch of a product or service (a film, a book, etc.) with the aim to promote it. See in Box 3 the case of the promotion of a tourist destination, Elba Island in Italy, by means of a transmedia storytelling initiative.

Really interesting is the case of transmedia storytelling of Harry Potter, the bestseller book character. Today there are different media and products on the theme of the books: films, video games, an interactive web site, the cinematographic studio tour, a theme park, social networks, web communities, merchandising, etc. The case of Harry Potter is not just a narrative series: it is now a *narrative brand* that expresses itself in different languages and business areas (Scolari, 2009). It is an example of business diversification started thanks to the storytelling that allowed the organization to reach new segments of the market. Besides, the studios and the theme park represent cases of *brandscapes*; they are themed immersive environments dedicated to a specific brand, that strengthen in sensory terms the brand and

Box 3. The case of #elbamovie: A transmedia storytelling project to promote a tourist destination

---

#elbamovie is an innovative cross-media storytelling project for an experiential tourist promotion of the Italian Elba Island. The main aim of the project is to reinforce the image of Elba, bringing together, in a new way, the expertise of storytelling and film production with the design of tourist experiences.

2014 is the Bicentenary Year of Napoleon at Elba, where he was exiled for one year. For this reason VisitElba decided to make a short artistic film to reappraise Napoleon from a modern point of view, underlining the beauty and the rich tourist amenities of the island, with a narrative slant that differs from a traditional publicity style. The film will be divided into four episodes, each eight minutes long, forming a web-series published on YouTube and Vimeo to be used for the Web communication of the island.

To increase the degree of involvement in the initiative, the entire process of production of the film will be published on the Elbamovie site, where you can find: videos of interviews to the producers, director and actors; images of the making of the film; photographs of the actors and the scenes; materials about the life experiences of the friends of the characters in Elbamovie.

As Maurizio Goetz, Destination Manager of Elba, points out, "We really believe a lot in this project. We decided to work together with independent video makers, to promote a story of independence, in harmony with the positioning chosen for communication regarding the island of Elba, which is based on an 'independent lifestyle'". Andrea Rossi, Social Media & Marketing Manager for Elba, adds, "It's a new approach to tourism storytelling, in which the destination is the hub of an experiential narrative, which we believe will engross adventure lovers. We wanted to unite a strong tourist promotion asset with the creativity that a personality like Napoleon can unleash in the imagination of people all round the world. The goal is to do high profile, captivating and fascinating promotion – aimed at a very attentive audience – while at the same time highlighting the resources and great professional skills of this territory."

The project is based on four elements that characterises the experience: the story (that is set between the past and the present, allowing the audience to live a Napoleonic experience in a modern setting); the suspension between reality and fiction (which enables Elba's visitors to see the places where the film was made and enjoy all the experiential elements included in the narration that can be discovered on the island); the depth and variety of the transmedia storytelling experience (which can be lived uninterruptedly on various media and in the territory of Elba); the evolution of the narration project (which develops like a living organism through the nutrition supplied by the contribution of the audience. The characters in Elbamovie are imaginary, but their life experiences and friends are real).

The plot.

The Tyrant, a Spirit blinded by the desire for conquest, who wanted to conquer the entire Universe, is defeated and trapped in space and time. From that moment the Tyrant waits…

Elba – June 2014: Sara, impetuous and ambitious, is having a tough time with her boyfriend Leonardo. She helped a private French collector win an old artefact from Elba at an auction, an object of very ancient origin cast in iron from the mines.

Elba – June 1814: Napoleon has recently landed on the island. In the hall of his new residence, a shady character approaches him to pay his homage to the Emperor with a gift: an ancient iron medallion. The medallion creates a temporal bridge across this two-hundred-year gap.

The entire island, in 2014 and 1814, freezes while the Tyrant, from the depths of the earth, begins to struggle to free himself from his prison. Sara and Napoleon – in the body of Leonardo – have a few precious hours to try and save Elba and accidentally, the Universe as well.

Source: partially adapted from www.elbamovie.com. See also https://www.youtube.com/user/visitelbait.

---

the relationship with the company. For the opening of the theme park: The Wizarding World of Harry Potter in Florida, the newspaper USA Today created an augmented reality communication tool, printing a map of the world of the fictional character. In front of a webcamera Internet connected and with a specific software, this map became interactive and three dimensional on the computer screen.

So the transmedia storytelling can use the web, with the company website, but also different platforms, such as social networks, blogs, wikis, etc. The content must be visible not only on personal computers but also on tablets and smart phones. By means of QR codes users can be linked to online content to enrich their experiences, for example downloading sounds or music files. Other media can be comics, video games, mobile apps, books, e-books, newspapers, films, radio, and television. Companies must use different points of entry to reach various market segments and communicate in heterogeneous ways to exploit every sensory aspect of the story that they are telling to their customers. A well-known case of transmedia storytelling is that of the film The Matrix. In fact, the world of The Matrix comprises three franchise films, a series of comics, a series of anime movies, and a video game.

A hypothetical example of transmedia storytelling is described below (see Box 4). The story of a product is widespread on the web and its users can add their content by an interactive website. They can discuss and share the story on social media, enriching it with their photos, videos, comments, and reviews related to the consumer experience. In the product's package they can find a QR code that linked to the web provides auditory stimuli; a video game appeals to younger people and in magazines' advertising there is a fragrance that reinforces the brand image. The customers see the story in a video on YouTube;

Box 4. I love bees: A case of successful storytelling transmedia marketing

In 2004 the members of a videogame community received in their mail boxes a honey jar from someone that has to do with a web site: *I love bees.com....*

This was the beginning of *I love bees*, the core element of one of the most successful examples of viral marketing based on storytelling. *I love bees* is a transmedia story based on an alternate reality game; it was created by the 42 Entertainment for the viral advertising campaign commissioned by Microsoft to promote the videogame *Halo 2*, the sequel of the Xbox game *Halo*. *I love bees* was a web-based interactive fiction that used websites, blogs, Mp3 recordings, emails, jpegs, and other platforms with the aim to create an immersive storytelling for *Halo 2*. The plot of the story was about the life of five people who live in the year 2552, before the invasion of the Covenant.

"The distributed fiction of I love bees was designed as a kind of investigative playground, in which players could collect, assemble and interpret thousands of different story pieces related to the Halo universe. By reconstructing and making sense of the fragmented fiction, the fans would collaboratively author a narrative bridge between the first Halo videogame and its sequel" (McGonigal, 2007, p.7). As the project's lead writer Sean Stewart explains: "Instead of telling a story, we would present the evidence of that story, and let the players tell it to themselves" (McGonigal, 2007, p.7). The players did not know the promotional scope of the game.

I love bees was launched in 2004. In the same year the first trailer of *Halo 2* briefly showed the alternate reality game's website, www. ilovebees.com. It seemed the modest blog of the beekeeper Dana, but soon it was possible to notice that it has been hacked by an artificial intelligence and showed strange messages, corrupted data and countdowns. Later the players discovered that the goal of the game was to find payphones, indicated by GPS coordinates on the website all across the United States, and wait for a call. These phones rang at certain times and a pre-recorded voice required to answer questions through numerical codes. The more the game went on the more the requests became strange: to make human pyramids, tell jokes, sing one's own favourite songs. As a reward to players who had arrived at the end of the game they were allowed to play *Halo 2* preview inside the cinema.

I love bees was based on the *Halo* fiction and was a radio drama delivered to users by means of an innovative medium for narrative marketing and storytelling: ringing payphones. It was not the first alternate reality game, but it is the most well-known, also because of the popularity of *Halo*. The alternate reality game was a great success in marketing terms and obtained great attention by the traditional media.

The participants trying to solve the mystery of the story have been about 750,000 and casual participants have been about 2.5 million. More than three million people visited the site during the 3 months of play. It won several awards and helped to raise awareness of the alternate reality game throughout the world. *I love bees* was a predecessor for *Iris,* the alternate reality game of *Halo 3*.

Its success is due to the players' curiosity about the backstory of the *Halo* universe and the immersive and funny experience offered to participants. "The main goal in producing the project as a commercial game was, of course, exciting entertainment through immersive storytelling" (McGonigal, 2007, p. 9).

it is periodically changed according to the inputs of the users themselves through an app. The story is then narrated in an interactive comic e-book intended for the most loyal customers. The characters in the comic are also used for merchandising inspired by the theme of the story.

Every medium has its own narrative form, language and content. The use of different media platform makes the storytelling more interesting, fun, and easy to remember, and, if in line with the client's attitudes, also useful to create a strong and lasting relationship with the company.

But to be really involving the story must be immersive and participatory. Referring to these concepts, Rose (2011) speaks of *deep media* that offer experiences in which the users immerse themselves taking part in the stories. Rose refers especially to the Internet; it, while in the beginning was a new platform for old ways of telling stories, today represents an instrument for popularising an innovative type of storytelling. He explains that under the influence of the web "a new type of narrative is emerging – one that's told through many media at once in a way that's nonlinear, that's participatory and often gamelike, and that's designed above all to be immersive" (Rose, 2011, p. 18).

Some of the recipients, the fans of the product/ brand/ film etc., are more active than others and share the story, enriching it with their content. Therefore, the companies when conceiving a story must leave room for the fans' and users' generated content, to encourage the *fanfiction* (as to say the practice of adding elements to the story) (Bourdaa, 2012). Of course the content generated by consumers and fans is no more under the control of companies and it can represent a problem and a danger, but also a challenge.

In the Box below is described the case of *I love bees*, one of the more interesting examples of transmedia storytelling based on the launch of an alternate reality game and created to promote a videogame. An Alternate Reality Game (ARG) is an interactive story that links the web to the real word through transmedia storytelling (Sassoon, 2012). The players can change the game, which is normally based on a mystery, interacting directly with the game characters. For this reason the plot and the end of the story are just in part pre-programmed: in some way the users influence them. The alternate reality game uses different media, such as emails, blogs and telephone, but the core is that of the Internet; however the storytelling is partially fiction and partially real life. Characters and clues are distributed on and off line. Normally it has a promotional scope.

CONCLUSION AND FUTURE RESEARCH DIRECTIONS

In conclusion, today thanks to user-generated content platforms such as social networks and blogs, there is no longer on the web a boundary between stories producers and those who benefit from them; besides, the roles of the subjects that exercise authority and those that control have changed and new languages and forms of storytelling have emerged (Sassoon, 2012).

The user-generated content, even if it reduces the organizations' ability to control, increases the creative potential of storytelling. Companies must, therefore, program specific and innovative marketing initiatives to stimulate these processes, trying to keep them, directly or indirectly, under control, in order to obtain valid and long lasting results.

Besides, the fast spread of multiple communication media needs greater attention in the planning of marketing strategies and the adoption of a transmedia approach, especially in storytelling. Today companies can no longer use in the same way the different communication platforms and need to adopt forms of transmedia marketing and storytelling. They have to plan strategically, taking into account the fact that the communication world is changing every day.

However, the idea of transmedia storytelling is an evolving concept; nowadays companies rarely understand its value and only few use it in order to reach its full potential. In the future, academic research could devote a greater commitment in studying this phenomenon, which is still poorly analysed in terms of its evolution and its implications in the management and marketing fields.

REFERENCES

Aaker, D. A. (1991). *Managing brand equity: Capitalizing on the value of a brand name*. New York: The Free Press.

Addis, M., & Holbrook, M. B. (2001). On the conceptual link between mass customisation and experiential consumption: An explosion of subjectivity. *Journal of Consumer Behaviour*, *1*(1), 50–66. doi:10.1002/cb.53

Agren, M., & Ölund, M. (2007). *Storytelling. A Study of Marketing Communication in the Hospitality Industry* [Master's Thesis]. Jönköping International Business School, Jönköping University.

Alexander, B., & Levine, A. (2008). Web 2.0 Storytelling. Emergence of a New Genre. *EDUCAUSE Review*, *43*(6), 41–56.

Bacile, T. J., Ye, C., & Swilley, E. (2014). From Firm-Controlled to Consumer-Contributed: Consumer Co-Production of Personal Media Marketing Communication. *Journal of Interactive Marketing*, *28*(2), 117–133. doi:10.1016/j.intmar.2013.12.001

Barassi, V., & Treré, E. (2012). Does Web 3.0 come after Web 2.0? Deconstructing theoretical assumptions through practice. *New Media & Society*, *14*(8), 1269–1285. doi:10.1177/1461444812445878

Bimber, O., Encarnacao, L. M., & Schmalstieg, D. (2003). The Virtual Showcase as a new Platform for Augmented Reality Digital Storytelling. Proceedings of *Eurographics Workshop on Virtual Environments*. doi:10.1145/769953.769964

Bourdaa, M. (2012). Transmedia: between augmented storytelling and immersive practices. *Ina Global. The review of creative industries and media*.

Brake, D. R. (2014). Are We All Online Content Creators Now? Web 2.0 and Digital Divides. *Journal of Computer-Mediated Communication*, *19*(3), 591–609. doi:10.1111/jcc4.12042

Carbone, F., Contreras, J., Hernandez, J. Z., & Gomez-Perez, J. M. (2012). Open innovation in an Enterprise 3.0 framework: Three case studies. *Expert Systems with Applications*, *39*(10), 8929–8939. doi:10.1016/j.eswa.2012.02.015

Cova, B. (1995). Community and consumption: towards a definition of the "linking value" of products and services. *Proceedings of the European marketing Academy Conference ESSEC*. Paris.

Cova, B. & Cova, V. (2002). Tribal marketing: The tribalisation of society and its impact on the conduct of marketing. *European Journal of Marketing, 36* (5), 595, 620.

Dena, C. (2009). *Transmedia practice: theorising the practice of expressing a fictional world across distinct media and environments*. PhD Thesis. Sydney: University of Sydney.

Eftekhari, M. H., & Zeynab, B. (2008). *Web 1.0 to Web 3.0 Evolution and Its Impact on Tourism Business Development*. Working paper.

Erragcha, N. (2014). Social networks as marketing tools. *British Journal of Marketing Studies, 2*(1), 79–88.

Escalas, J. E. (2004). Narrative Processing: Building Consumer Connections to Brands. *Journal of Consumer Psychology, 14*(1&2), 168–180. doi:10.1207/s15327663jcp1401&2_19

Ferrari, S. (2006). *Modelli gestionali per il turismo come esperienza. Emozioni e polisensorialità nel marketing delle imprese turistiche*. Padova: Cedam.

Ferrari, S. (2012). *Marketing del turismo. Consumatori, imprese e destinazioni nel nuovo millennio*. Padova: Cedam.

Gabriel, Y. (2000). *Storytelling in organizations: facts, fictions, and fantasies*. Oxford: Oxford University Press. doi:10.1093/acprof:oso/9780198290957.001.0001

Garrigos-Simon, F. J., Lapiedra Alcami, R., & Barbera Ribera, T. (2012). Social networks and Web 3.0: Their impact on the management and marketing of organizations. *Management Decision, 50*(10), 1880–1890. doi:10.1108/00251741211279657

Gummesson, E. (2004). From one-to-one to many-to-many marketing. In Atverksekonomins Marknadsföring: Attse Marknadsföringen Genom Nätverksglasögon. Malmö: Liber ekonomi.

Hagel, J. III, & Armstrong, A. G. (1997). *Net Gain: Expanding Markets Through Virtual Communities*. Harvard, MA: Harvard Business School Press.

Hirschman, E. C., & Holbrook, M. B. (1982). Hedonic consumption: emerging concepts, methods and propositions, *Journal of Marketing, 46*, 92-101.

Holbrook, M. B., & Hirschman, E. C. (1982). The experiential aspects of consumption: Consumer fantasies, feelings, and fun. *The Journal of Consumer Research, 9*, 132–140.

Jansson, A. (2002). Spatial Phantasmagoria. *European Journal of Communication, 17*(4), 429–443. doi:10.1177/02673231020170040201

Jenkins, H. (2003, November). Why the matrix matters. *Technology Review, 6*.

Jensen, R. (1999). *Dream Society: How the Coming Shift from Information to Imagination Will Transform Your Business*. New York: McGraw-Hill.

Keller, K. L. (1993). Conceptualizing, measuring, and managing customer-based brand equity. *Journal of Marketing, 57*(1), 1–22. doi:10.2307/1252054

Kotler, P., Kartajaya, H., & Setiawan, I. (2010). *Marketing 3.0. From Products to Consumers to the Human Spirit*. Hoboken, NJ: John Wiley & Sons, Inc. doi:10.1002/9781118257883

Maffesoli, M. (1996). *The time of the tribes*. London, GB: Sage.

McGonigal, J. (2007). *Why I Love Bees: A Case Study in Collective Intelligence Gaming*. Paper.

Mistilis, N. (2012). Challenges and potential of the Semantic Web for tourism. *E-Review of Tourism Research, 10*(2), 51–55.

Mödinger, W. (Ed.). (2011). *Marketing 3.0 – New Issues in Marketing: From Integrated Marketing Communication to the Marketing of Sustainable Leaders*. Stuttgart: Stuttgart Media University.

Morgan, M., Lugosi, P., & Ritchie, J. R. (Eds.). (2010). *The tourism and leisure experience* (pp. 117–136). Bristol, GB: Channel View Publications.

Mossberg, L. (2008). Extraordinary Experiences through Storytelling. *Scandinavian Journal of Hospitality and Tourism, 8*(3), 195–210. doi:10.1080/15022250802532443

O'Sullivan, E. L., & Spangler, K. J. (1998). *Experience marketing. Strategies for the new millennium*. State College: Venture Publishing.

Pavlik, J. V., & Bridges, F. (2013). The Emergence of Augmented Reality (AR) as a Storytelling Medium in Journalism. *Journalism & Communication Monographs, 15*(1), 4–59.

Picard, D., & Robinson, M. (Eds.). (2012). *Emotion in Motion. Tourism, Affect and Transformation*. Farnham: Ashgate.

Pine, B., & Gilmore, J. (1999). The experience economy: work is theatre & every business a stage. Boston, Harvard: Harvard Business School Press.

Prahalad, C. K., & Krishnan, M. S. (2008). *The New Age of Innovation: Driving Co-created Value through Global Networks*. New York, NY: Mc Graw-Hill.

Rincón, J. (2012). *XML y Web semántica: Bases de datos en el contexto de la Web semántica*. Universitat Oberta de Catalunya, 1-63.

Rose, F. (2011). *The Art of Immersion: How the Digital Generation Is Remaking Hollywood, Madison Avenue, and the Way We Tell Stories*. New York: W.W. Norton & Co.

Rosen, E. (2000). *The anatomy of buzz: how to create word-of-mouth marketing*. New York: Doubleday.

Salmon, C. (2008). *Storytelling. La fabbrica delle storie*. Roma: Fazi Editore.

Sassoon, J. (2012). *Web Storytelling. Costruire storie di marca nei social media*. Milano: Franco Angeli.

Schmitt, B. (1999). *Experiential Marketing*. New York: The Free Press.

Schmitt, B. (2003). *Customer Experience Management. New Jersey*. Hoboken: John Wiley & Sons.

Schmitt, B., & Simonson, A. (1997). *Marketing aesthetics. The strategic management of brands, identity, and image*. New York: The Free Press.

Scolari, A. (2009). Transmedia Storytelling: Implicit Consumers, Narrative Worlds, and Branding in Contemporary Media Production. *International Journal of Communication, 3*, 586–606.

Sole, D., & Gray-Wilson, D. (1999). *Storytelling in Organizations: The power and traps of using stories to share knowledge in organizations. LILA*. Harvard University.

Stamboulis, Y., & Skayannis, P. (2003). Innovation strategies and technology for experience-based tourism. *Tourism Management, 24*(1), 35–43. doi:10.1016/S0261-5177(02)00047-X

Stavrakantonakis, I., Gagiu, A., Toma, I., & Fensel, D. (2013). Towards Online Engagement via the Social Web (pp. 26-31). Proceedings of *WEB 2013: The First International Conference on Building and Exploring Web Based Environments.*

Sujan, M., Bettam, J., & Baumgartner, H. (1993). Influencing judgments using autobiographical memories: A self-referencing perspective. *JMR, Journal of Marketing Research, 30*(4), 422–436. doi:10.2307/3172688

Tussyadiah, I. P., & Fesenmaier, D. R. (2009). Mediating tourist experiences. Access to places via shared videos. *Annals of Tourism Research, 36*(1), 24–40. doi:10.1016/j.annals.2008.10.001

Zhou, Z., Cheok, A. D., Pan, J. H., & Li, Y. (2004, June). Magic Story Cube: An Interactive Tangible Interface for Storytelling. *ACE*, 3–5.

KEY TERMS AND DEFINITIONS

Alternate Reality Game (ARG): Is a game that links the web to the real word through transmedia storytelling. The players can change the story, normally a mysterious story, with their actions, interacting directly with the game characters. The alternate reality game uses different media, such as emails, blogs and telephone, but the centrality is that of the Internet. Normally it has a promotional scope.

Augmented Reality (AR): Is a virtual reality that represents a real-world environment augmented by means of computer-generated sensory elements such as sound, video, graphics or GPS data. The aim is to create a virtual environment with no difference with respect to the real world.

Digital Storytelling: Is a way of telling a story through the web (not only on companies' websites, but also on social media) with an active participation of Internet users.

Experiential Marketing: Is a marketing strategy that tries to immerse the customer in the product and to provide emotions and unforgettable experiences. It includes companies' marketing activities based on providing sensory experiences, with the aim of meeting hedonistic needs.

Multisensory Marketing: Are marketing activities based on providing multisensory experiences, which aim to meet hedonistic needs.

Social Media: Are digital entities that allow web users to create their own content, disseminate it, and receive in virtual communities and networks information of non-commercial nature about products / services, companies, brands. They are blogs, social networks, forums, newsgroups and communities, which represent independent information networks.

Transmedia Storytelling: Is a form of storytelling that uses multiple channels to spread the several components of a story. These parts have to be adapted to the specificity of the various media used and all together create a more complete and fascinating story.

User Generated Content: Is a digital content created by web users; they can share it online with great ease and without the need for specific technical skills.

Virtual Reality (VR): Is a simulated reality, a virtual simulation created through the use of the computer.

Web 2.0: Is an evolution of the Word Wide Web in which the communication becomes two-way and users can generate their own contents to put them on the Web. It represents the birth of an interactive platform, in which you can share information and feedbacks. It is not a technological evolution but a new way to make and use web content.

Web 3.0: It is also called *Semantic Web*. Its main characteristic is that the interaction is between computers and the aim is to process large quantities of data and information to obtain targeted knowledge. It has three main characteristics: to be ubiquitous, individualized, and efficient. The ubiquity is due to the possibility of being connected anywhere and in anytime. The individualized character refers to the information that is segmented and adapted to varied people and situations. The Web 3.0 is more an attitude than a technological evolution.

Chapter 2
Bare Nothingness:
Situated Subjects in Embodied Artists' Systems

Eleanor Dare
University of Derby, UK

Elena Papadaki
University of Greenwich, UK

ABSTRACT

This chapter examines the current state of digital artworks, arguing that they have not yet made a ground-breaking impact on the cultural landscape of the early 21st century and suggesting that a reason for this lack of notoriety is the obsolete model of agency deployed by many digital artists. As an alternative to what is framed as out-of-date forms of interactivity, the chapter highlights evolving research into interactive systems, artists' tools, applications, and techniques that will provide readers with an insightful and up-to-date examination of emerging multimedia technology trends. In particular, the chapter looks at situated computing and embodied systems, in which context-aware models of human subjects can be combined with sensor technology to expand the agencies at play in interactive works. The chapter connects these technologies to Big Data, Crowdsourcing and other techniques from artificial intelligence that expand our understanding of interaction and participation.

INTRODUCTION

The philosopher Alfred Whitehead wrote that "apart from the experiences of subjects there is, nothing, nothing, nothing, bare nothingness" (Whitehead, 1929, pp. 252-254). The present chapter will look at innovative interactive multimedia systems that integrate new conceptions of the subject into creative digital practice. Drawing on specific case studies and art historical framing the chapter will argue that digital artworks have not yet made a ground-breaking impact on the cultural landscape of the early twenty-first century, one main reason for this being the obsolete model of agency deployed by many artists who use computation as an artistic medium.

DOI: 10.4018/978-1-4666-8659-5.ch002

This chapter presents the argument that a great number of the most current and high profile digital art works have not yet made a significant use of the core technological innovations that have occurred in the last 10 years, and that they are largely out of sync with advances in Computer Science and Web application development, in particular with the framing of subjects and agency.

As an alternative to what is contextualised here as out-of-date forms of interactivity, it will highlight evolving research in interactive systems, artists' tools, applications, and techniques that will provide readers with an insightful and up-to-date examination of emerging multimedia technology trends. More precisely, it will look at situated computing and embodied systems, in which context-aware models of human subjects can be combined with sensor technology to expand the agencies at play in interactive works. The chapter will connect these technologies to Big Data, Crowdsourcing and other techniques from artificial intelligence that expand our understanding of interaction and participation.

The case studies presented here will elucidate the specific technical and design strategies used in real world projects, clearly explaining the mathematical and conceptual processes and procedures at play. Basic code examples are provided, in order to allow readers to hack into and play with the concepts outlined.

The first half of the chapter will look at the emergence of new media art and put it in historical and theoretical context. The second part of the chapter will present a typology of interaction modes and propose a radical vision for digital art, one that deploys a far more sophisticated notion of agency within the participant/creator dyad than the one currently used; it will look at the formation of temporally specific contextualised relationships between subjects and digital works. The final part of the chapter will suggest solutions by examining case studies, describing how a range of more recent artworks (including two by the co-author, Eleanor Dare) present multi-linear, situated and embodied forms of *intra-activity* as an alternative to more linear forms of interaction deployed by most contemporary, high profile, digital art works.

SETTING THE STAGE

The late 1960s and early 1970s signalled the arrival of a new era for exhibition practices as well as the birth of what was later to be called 'media art'. It is appropriate to briefly examine the events of this period, since it laid the foundations for the inclusion of digital works as an acceptable art practice and various issues around display strategies (in relation to new media and technological innovation) that occupied curators, historians and critics at the time and which still prevail today[1].

At the beginning of the decade (1960), the art critic Clement Greenberg wrote "Modernist Painting". The essay came to typify the Modernist critical position on the visual arts and acted as an inspiration for the 'white cube' as the ideal exhibition space. According to Greenberg, the "advanced" or "ambitious" Art was an art that could "test society's capacity for high art"; those called "purists", who defended abstract art as the only defence against kitsch and the decline in culture, were also those who valued art the most. Modernism had to establish itself in the social arena, by demonstrating that the kind of experience it provided was valuable "in its own right and not to be obtained by any other kind of activity" (Greenberg, 1992, p. 775)[3]. The area of competence of each art would lie in the uniqueness of the nature of its medium. Thus, the shared elements between the artistic disciplines should be eliminated in order for each art to reach a culmination with the absolute purity of its particular form. Greenberg's account of artistic standards - and particularly of the ways in which art's separateness as a social practice is secured - called into question his hope that art could become a provider of value in its own right.

The form of Modernism was that of an art "whose object is nothing but itself", constantly discovering that "the self is pure as only pure negativity can be" and offering its audience the assertion that nothing tirelessly and "adequately made over into form" (Clark, 1985, p. 60). Greenberg believed that in High Modernism, the aesthetic experience of a painting can only be understood by other kind of experience in relation to other paintings; there was no point in looking to political or historical meanings because opticality alone guaranteed art.

At the time, the formulation of 'art for art's sake' found its ultimate champion in MoMA and its display tactics. Visitors were to engage in exercises in aesthetic contemplation by following a set path through gallery spaces with white walls and a sparse hang that transcended the pervasiveness of the outside world; nothing distracted from the encounter with the artwork. Numerous artists based their creations - and still do - on this very premise: the whiteness of the walls, the vast space where their work could be shown. The above premise was, however, challenged by the arrival of screen-based works, where time was disrupted and the visitor no longer viewed but 'watched' art. The moving image functioned in the same way that the 19th century heavy frame did: it isolated the surrounding scenery. A new dynamic of exhibits' juxtaposition was created that gave birth to new challenges in curatorial choices of display.

Around the same time, notably through the publication of Jack Burnham's *Beyond Modern Sculpture* (1968) and Gene Youngblood's *Expanded Cinema* (1970), the convergence of art, technology and cybernetics began to be critically evaluated. Youngblood's account praised pioneering video, cinema and computer art practices, whereas Burnham's analysis of modern and contemporary sculpture introduced the crucial distinction between sculpture as 'object' and sculpture as 'system'. According to Burnham, an object "occupies a specific space: it has *place*, remaining inert and stationary" (Burnham, 1968, p. 12). A system, however, is

[...] an aggregate of components; first, its parts are mutually dependent; and second, it may manifest some of the fundamental characteristics natural to life: self-organisation, growth, internal or external mobility, irritability or sensitivity, input and output, kinetically sustained equilibrium and eventual death. (Burnham, 1968, p. 12)

In this context, sculpture could prolong its survival through a "transition from the object to the system" (Burnham, 1968, p. 13).

The distinction between Modernist art and the 'theatricality' of other forms of art practice was integrated intensely by Michael Fried's "Art and Objecthood" (1967). Fried distinguished the opticality of a work of art from the experience of viewing it (which he called 'theatricality') in a text that attacked Minimalism. He was against art appreciation being conditioned by cultural, historical or sociological factors, which, as he claimed, prevented the work from being seen as an independent entity. Minimalist art, he stated, is a "largely ideological [...] enterprise" (Fried, 1967, p. 1). As a "new genre of theatre", it became the negation of art (Fried, 1967, p. 3). Objecthood, in this light, is precicely this context of the "condition of non-art" (ibid.). Drawing on Greenberg, he traced a clear difference between "modernist painting's self-imposed imperative that it defeat or suspend its own obejcthood through the medium of shape" and the literalist "espousal" of objecthood as "an art in its own right" (Fried, 1967, p. 6). In "Art and Objecthood", Fried defined clearly the differentiation between Modernist art and the arts that dealt mostly with space or time. In the case of screen-based works, both of the latter notions usually form a central part in their essence and presentation. If one opens up the argument even further, it could be suggested that contemporary art production "is a proposal to live in a shared world, giving rise to other relations, and so on and so forth, ad infinitum" (Bourriaud, 2002, p. 22). The aesthetic experience here is closer to the notion of social exchanges than artistic appreciation. He found that this new genre, "inasmuch as it compelled a durational viewing experience akin to theatre, undermined both the medium specificity and the presumed instantaneousness of modernism" (Mondloch, 2010, p. 1). Cinema, on the other hand, was never in danger of theatricality, as the screen was not experienced as an object functioning in a specific physical relation to us (Fried, 1967).

Kate Mondloch, in her extensive analysis on viewing media installation art, suggests that the divide suggested by Fried between Minimalism and the cinema gradually shrank with the expanded field of art and media practices in the 1960s and 1970s and the consequent overlapping of boundaries between the sculptural and the cinematic (Mondloch, 2010, p. 1). In 1965, with the release of the first portable video recorder, Portapak, by Sony, the video apparatus became an easy-to-use device for recording the moving image, one that started being used by artists as a means of artistic expression. In the same year, Andy Warhol showed his first recordings with a Norelco slant-track video recorder at a party in New York, and Nam June Paik presented his work *Electronic Video Recorder* in the New York Café *Au Go Go*, created using a Portapak. "Just as collage technic [sic] replaced oil paint, so the cathode ray tube will replace the canvas", he wrote on the flyer that was distributed on the first public showing of the video, a sentence that has come to be referenced innumerable times ever since (Marin & Grosevick, 2006, p. 10, see also Rush, 1999, p. 82) [4]. His footage of the Papal visit (allegedly shot from a cab whilst the Pope and his entourage made their way down 5th Avenue) is considered to be the birth of video art (Rush, 1999, Knight, 1996).

In the same period, and contrary to the Modernist tradition and the praise of optical form alone, the Fluxus movement attempted to break down the barriers separating different forms of art and merge music, theatre, visuals arts and most importantly, the artists and their audience; art and life was seen as one inseparable mode of existence. In 1967, a video installation by Bruce Nauman entered the realm of the museum in *American Sculptures of the Sixties* in the Los Angeles County Museum of Art and the Howard Wise Gallery in New York presented *TV as a Creative Medium*. At the time, the use of the moving image by artists questioned the role of the arts in a technologically driven society, reacted against television and promoted a critical dialogue with conceptual art. Stan Vanderbeek exhibited with Robert Whitman and Dan Graham *(The Projected* Image, ICA Boston, 1967) and Les Levine with Hans Haacke, Douglas Huebler *(Software, Information Technology: Its New Meaning* for Art, Jewish Museum New York, 1970)[5].

In *Electronic Culture: technology and visual representation* (1996), Timothy Druckrey argues that there are "shifting means of reproducibility" to be noted, "particularly the emergence of the screen as the central point of the communicative and aesthetic experience" (Druckrey, 1996, p. 12). The edited volume gathers a series of examinations of forms of visualisation from diverse fields, in order to map the digital revolution that has been taking place since the late 20th century and to contextualise it whilst "reasoning with history" (Druckrey, 1996, p. 21). What is crucial here is the understanding that, even though electronic culture is a phenomenon to be explored, its re-definition of the very concept of representation is largely due to its historical context.

The two trajectories regarding modernist narratives and "machine art" and towards "systems and information technology" (Sutton, 2004, p. 2) that emerged in the late 1960s, still prevail today. Lev Manovich, commenting on "the art establishment's lack of engagement with new technology" attributes the situation to the "division between 'Turing land' (inhabited by the computer arts) and 'Duchamp land' (inhabited by postmodern conceptual art)" (Muller, Edmonds & Connell, 2006, p. 3). Edward A. Shanken suggests that there is a hybrid discourse between mainstream art and new media, since their paths have become increasingly divergent (Shanken, 2011, p. 1). Mainstream art employs the vocabulary of digital culture (such as 'interactivity', 'participation', 'programming', and 'networks'), and which we will examine later in the chapter, while dismissing new media art due to its form or immateriality. In "Exhibiting New Media Art", Gloria Sutton suggests that "the practical and theoretical issues of exhibiting new media art within a traditional museum context" discussed at present employ a "critical syntax [...that] echoes the conversations of the late 1960s and 1970s" (Sutton, 2004, p. 1); indeed, since moving away from the static object to accommodating a broader range of practices that fall into the category of the 'dynamic arts', judgements of quality have yet to find a way to correspond to the situation. In contemporary art criticism, "political, moral and ethical judgements have come to fill the vacuum of aesthetic judgement in a way that was unthinkable forty years ago" (Bishop, 2004, p. 77). Bishop traces this situation back to Postmodernism which "attacked the very notion of aesthetic judgement" and to contemporary art's "solicit[ing] the viewer's literal interaction in ever more elaborate ways" (Bishop, 2004, pp. 77-78).

Shanken argues that even though both mainstream and new media art can learn from the other, the latter deserves a more prominent position in contemporary art history (Shanken 2011, p. 7). In addition, he has analysed Jack Burnham's early writings (for example "The House that Jack built"), to reposition the former. He does note, however, that in the same way that photography was shunned and then endorsed by the mainstream art market (with auction highs of 3,3 million dollars in the period 1994-2008) video reached a 700,000 dollars peak for a Bill Viola (whose piece *The Stopping Mind* [1990] is examined later in the chapter) work in 2000 (Shanken 2011, pp. 15-16). In this light, and while keeping in mind that the auction prime is still reserved for painted canvases, if the post-medium condition really prevailed, "the exclusionary prejudice against the use of technological media in and as art would not exist" (Shanken 2011, p. 18). However, curators, critics and historians do make the distinction between media and the direct or indirect use of technology. In this arena, the "lofty, theoretical ideal" is usually elevated at the expense of the "quotidian, practical tool" (Shanken, 2011, p. 18).

Digital Art and Viewing Regimes

In 1972, the Tate Gallery acquired Carl Andre's *Equivalent VIII*. A sculpture made of 120 bricks placed in a rectangular formation, it became a major representative of Minimalist work. Four years later, *The Times* published an article on the Tate's recent acquisitions that featured a picture of the work. When the latter was put back on display in 1976, *The Daily Mirror* exclaimed on its front page: "What a Load of Rubbish". Archival material from that time shows the public moving around the work and commenting upon the fact that it is indeed a pile of bricks[6]. The anecdote serves to exemplify Fried's conceptualisation of Minimalist art as occupying space rather than focusing on opticality alone, but also to demonstrate the changing viewing regimes of the public over the years.

In the context of digital and interactive art, the more we operate with screen technologies, the more our behaviour around them evolves and changes. This would perhaps be stating the obvious, but the public witnessing of Nam June Paik's sculptural screen installations during the first years of video art would not have generated the same reaction as the public visiting an exhibition dedicated to early video art today, having already been exposed to a plethora of screen media on a daily basis.

In this framework, it is often suggested that, with the current impact of new media technologies on art production, curators have reached a point where they create content instead of a context (Cook, 2003). In order to examine the complexities of curating new media artworks, it is crucial to overview the activities that precede their exhibition. These are:

- The curatorial judgements of quality in order to select and classify new media works
- The creation of a "context" for the work
- The placement of the work in a given space/environment

Curatorial Judgements of Quality

In theories concerning judgements of quality for a work of art (as, for example, in Kant, 1978, Hegel, 1993, Bourdieu, 1979, Greenberg, 1993, Benjamin, 2002, Buck-Morss, 1989) the object of study was to be found in stable and static forms. Moreover, the work of art was considered to be something already made and present for contemplation. There is indeed an awkward, uneasy approach when the communicative character, the mediality and the duration of a work of art come into play. However, the curators of a mixed-media museum focus less on art production and more on art's reception; thus, they "engag[e] in research in order to issue judgements of quality" (Cook, 2003, p. 170).

In "Toward a Theory of the Practice of Curating New Media Art," Sarah Cook examines the "curatorial role of creating context" (Cook, 2003, p. 169) via the examination of theories about curating and the description of the aesthetic characteristics of new media art that challenge that traditional framework.

In this context, a work of art is seen as either a definitive expression by an artist (in which case the methodology used is a reference to his/her biography or to the current context) or a blank screen onto which can be projected any number of art historical interpretations (in which case the work of art needs to be placed either within a specialised body of knowledge around it or within a historical trajectory) (Cook, 2003, p. 171). Even though the 1960s gave birth to an artistic expression that favoured experience to interpretation, the methodologies based on aesthetic theory evolve around the static object, thus limiting and giving a 'closed reading' of a dynamic work of art. When experiencing a constantly mediated reality, these theories might appear obsolete and out of context. In this light, if one placed Leonardo Da Vinci's *Mona Lisa* (circa 1503 – 1506) in the Louvre, on an easel in an artist's studio or hung it in their garage, it could be suggested that the work of art by itself would have remained unaltered in its essence. However, Nam June Paik's multi-screen installations or Tony Oursler's screen-assisted sculptures (to mention two representative examples illustrating this point) become very different works when the exhibiting conditions change (lighting, space, movement of the visitors in space), thus they are experienced in a varied way from one location to another. The aesthetics of projects that present a screen as - or within - their end product can be variable, interactive and experimental. In some cases, the viewers might just watch; in some others they might have to touch buttons, interact, speak, move. This immersion *within* the work excludes them from the disinterested position of the viewer/judge and puts them in a position of co-co-authoring the work. Also, even in 'old' media art - and taking as a hypothesis that most visitors do not watch all moving image works from beginning to end -, one visitor does not see the same 'version' as the other. When time is concerned, the "discursive becomes spatial and the visual becomes discursive" (Rodowick, 2001, p. 39, quoted in Cook, 2003, p. 173).

A great number of screen-based works cannot be seen as self-contained unities: they might refer to other cultural products, ask for the visitor's participation, integrate performances or collaborate with other networks to mention but a few. In this respect, the curators can no longer distance themselves from the work, basing their judgement on its static representation. In order to create a context for the work and subsequently issue judgements, the curators have to research the contexts/environments that the work refers to (for example performance and the software industry or public art and open source coding) in order to form a discourse around it. In the dynamic arts, there is a third dimension (or 'third space', according to Cook [2003]) that needs to be investigated and it is precisely through the knowledge of this dimension that judgements of quality can be accurately made.

Context or Content?

We have seen that one of the main roles of the curator of contemporary art is to create a context for the work to be exhibited. Also, with the deprofessionalisation of the curator and the abundance of curating courses teaching the practical aspects of the role rather than art history or museology, the curator has come to be responsible for the process that leads to an exhibition and not for the knowledge surrounding the exhibits themselves[8].

An important part of this process is the understanding of peripheral requirements - usually of a technical nature - for the presentation of a work. The curators need to be aware of the medium that the artists use as much as they need to know about the work itself; they need to know how the technology of the work behaves and what this means for the work in question. The rule applies equally to works that employ new technology (such as a 360-degree stereoscopic immersive interactive visualisation system, installed at ZKM) or dated media (such as a video tape with its limited life span)[9]. As Christiane Paul has argued, "the history of technology and media sciences plays an equally important role [as art history] in this art's formation and reception", continuing that "new media art requires media literacy" (Paul, 2008, p. 5).

In this context, however, is there not a danger for curators to "get caught up in *only* [sic] the work's medium and not the wider context for the technology as it is used in the artwork?" (Cook, 2003, p. 175). If this indeed happens, will it not it be explicit in the presentation of the work? Especially in exhibitions where screens constitute the main medium of presentation, it is easy for the audience to be directed in examining the screen itself and its inherent meaning rather than the meaning/content of the actual work. It is interesting to examine how exhibitions of this kind handle the above difficulty and how they get across to their visitors (see for example, *Software: Information Technology – Its New Meaning for Art,* Jewish Museum New York [1970], *Spellbound,* Hayward Gallery London [1996], *Art and Money* Online, Tate Britain London [2001], *Videographies – The Early Decades*, The Factory - Hellenic National Museum of Contemporary Art [2005], *China Power Station: Part I*, Battersea Power Station London - Serpentine Gallery, Red Mansion Foundation & Astrup Fearnley Museum of Modern Art [2006]).

As the curator has gradually moved from a strict museology environment to a more process-based practice that focuses chiefly on "temporary exhibitions" and "the specific context of their audiences" (Cook, 2008, p. 29, Greenberg, Ferguson & Nairne, 1996), it is suggested that the context itself sometimes becomes the content (O'Doherty, 1999, pp. 65-86). In the foreword of *Rethinking Curating* (2010), Steve Dietz remembers that around the time he had founded the new media art program at the Walker Art Center (1996), the then Museum Director commented that she did not find net art visually compelling. The example serves for Dietz to illustrate that new media art is not merely about *viewing* but also about processes, interactivity and *networks* (Graham & Cook, 2010, p. xiii).

It then becomes imperative to start thinking in terms of behaviours when the inclusion of screens and interaction are concerned rather than of a specific medium and the way in which this operates. Dietz suggests that the above concept, formulated by Graham and Cook when asked to define the term 'new media', could be useful in order to understand much of contemporary art. He pursues the argument historically, arguing that photography was the 'new medium' that introduced a new way of looking at suspended time, one which challenged the aesthetic understanding of painting, thereby video in turn challenged the aesthetic understanding of film whilst, with television, they were the 'new media' that introduced the idea of real time and, finally, new media[10] challenged the understanding of the behaviour of contemporary art by including in the art equation the elements of interactivity and participation. The conclusion of his positioning is that "art is different after new media because of new media" and this change takes place "not because new media is 'next', but because its behaviours are the behaviours of our technological times" (Graham & Cook, 2010, p. xiv). In short, one could suggest that new media art, and by extension all types of screen-based works, present characteristics that distinguish it from static art and thus create new types of environments where they can be exhibited. As such, the technology used constitutes a context around which the work is developed and serves as a vehicle for the communication of an idea; it is not to constitute the content of the work or to comment about questions surrounding technology.

INTERACTION AND AGENCY IN DIGITAL ARTWORKS

The first half of this chapter looked at the historical and theoretical context of digital artworks, exposing a complex range of conceptual and aesthetic traditions that impact upon our understanding, presentation and reception of digital pieces. This part of the chapter will now look at alternative philosophical approaches to digital artworks and examine a range of technical processes that might alter the conceptual focus of such works, presenting a more contemporary framing of digital technology and its relationship to art in the 21st century. A typology of interaction types will also be presented so that readers might better understand the technical characteristics of common interaction forms encountered in digital art. This section will look in detail at alternative interaction modes and the specific ways in which they have been used by artists. When seeking to define interactivity, it is necessary to also define its inter-dependent elements such as agency, subjectivity and embodiment.

CORE FRAMES OF REFERENCE

In order to support a detailed examination of the types of interaction typically deployed by digital artworks it is helpful to clarify some core terms and outline the frames of reference used, starting with the digital computer itself. While the following explanations may appear to be rudimentary, it is important to recognise that these are for example, binary systems that do not use zeros and ones, as well as historical computers that are not digital, for example analogue computers such as slide rules and human computers. There are also distributed systems that do not deploy a CPU. What is referred to here comprises the current mainstream of computing hardware and computing systems.

A digital computer typically consists of four (sometimes described as 3) parts as follows (Table 1).

Table 1. Four-part structure of a Von Neumann computer model

Input-Output devices: such as keyboards and screens
Main Memory: stores data, such as programs.
ALU: an Arithmetic-Logic Unit performs mathematical-logical operations.
CU: a Control Unit communicates and directs operations performed by the ALU.
The Control Unit: (CU) and the **Arithmetic-Logic Unit** (ALU) together comprise the Central Processing Unit or CPU. Multi-processor computers have more than one CPU. The Control Unit in a digital computer communicates between the memory and the ALU, and directs operations performed by the ALU.
The ALU performs logical and mathematical operations on binary data and typically, though not exclusively, on 0s and 1s.

This four-part architecture is based on the Von Neumann model of computing in which the computer memory stores programs and data. The control unit gets its instructions from the memory and the processing unit performs mathematical operations. Then, the control unit fetches further instructions from the memory. In this system everything is reduced to a binary representation in which there are only two possibilities: either an electrical signal represented by a 1, or no signal represented by a 0.

This is therefore, first and foremost, a system of symbolic representation. There is no "direct experience", no "intuition" and certainly no possibility for non-mathematical engagement with any of the input such a system receives. This point is emphasised now because the later part of this chapter will explore how the body, including its non-symbolic experiences, might be represented within a typical Von Neumann model and its wider systems.

It is important to understand that there is a difference between a computer – the aforementioned four-part entity, and a computer system. A computer system draws in a far wider set of actors and concepts, which we will now aim to define. These include interaction, agents and agency, subjects, situations and embodiment.

Defining Interactivity and Interaction

Interaction is defined by Noble as "the exchange of information between two or more active participants" (Noble, 2012, p. 3) but, unless the concept of an active participant is defined, how far does this definition help to clarify the meaning of interaction? Noble arguably acknowledges this complexity by then pointing out a further complicating concept, that of the feedback loop:

The feedback loop is a process of an entity communicating with itself while checking with either an internal or external regulatory system (2012, p.3).

The notion of the feedback loop is a reminder that when considering interactivity it is also necessary to identify the origins, form and flow of logic that is applied to user input, whether this is linear or non-linear, pre-determined or random, non-determined but not random, human, adaptive or some other form of machine-learning operation. These terms are outlined in Table 2.

Interactivity is further defined by Downes and McMillan (2000) as operating within six formal dimensions:

Table 2. Clarification of terms such as "Linear" and "Pre-determination"

Linear: might also be called "uni-linear". It implies sequential operations and a one-way flow of agency. In contrast, the term "non-linear" implies branching possibilities and choices.   **Multi-linear:** describes many possible choices and directions of agency. The term "multi-linear" might, as Aarseth implies, represent a challenge to the polarity of linear/non-linear agencies (Aarseth, 1997, p.44)   **Pre-determination:** implies an *a priori*, fixed system. The operations of such a system are known beforehand.   **Random:** the specific outcome is not known by the system, but the system is not learning or adapting. For instance, in the case of throwing a virtual dice.   **Non-determined but not random:** implies an adaptive system that may use machine learning, genetic algorithms or some other intelligent operation to change its behaviour as it sees fit. The outcome will not be wholly known by the designer/programmer but will, instead, emerge. It may imply a high degree of autonomy within the system.

- *Direction of communication.*
- *Time flexibility.*
- *Sense of place.*
- *Level of control.*
- *Responsiveness.*
- *Perceived purpose of communication. (Downes & McMillan, 2000, pp. 157-179)*

Downes et al. recognise that many definitions of interactivity are contradictory and sometimes meaningless, a point that has also been made by Manovich (2001) among others. There is however, unanimous agreement that, regardless of the mode of interaction, software is a representational medium, but the representational nature of digital computers should not inhibit the conceptual and practical evolution of interaction modes. Dourish (2001) implores us to conceive of:

a more nuanced understanding of the role that those representations play, how they are subject to a variety of interpretations and actions, and how they figure as part of a larger body of practice. The opportunity is to break the link between an inevitably representationalist stance toward software and a much more questionable stance toward action and interaction (Dourish, 2001, p. 208).

Others, such as Trifonova (2008) have also elucidated useful framings of the interactive, but, when attempting to grasp precisely these more nuanced understandings that Dourish and others encourage, it is useful to go back to the key term Noble (2012) used in defining interaction – 'active participants'. What is meant by the concept of an 'active participant' and how does this help in extending interactivity?

Agents and Agency

Within intelligent software systems, an active participant is an 'agent' and the power an agent wields is called 'agency'. A human agent makes things happen in the world. A software agent is similarly able, within its own world, to effect changes. Agency therefore influences events and processes while acting within a wider environment; however, it is important to dispense with the notion that agency is a 'thing' or a linear force, or that it is restricted solely to human agents.

In their classic text on artificial intelligence Russell and Norvig assert that an agent "is just something that acts" (Russell & Norvig, 2002, p. 4), but they also point out that:

Computer agents are expected to have other attributes that distinguish them from mere 'programs', such as operating under autonomous control, perceiving their environment, persisting over a prolonged time period, adapting to change, and being capable of taking on another's goals. A rational agent is one that acts so as to achieve the best outcome or, when there is uncertainty, the best expected outcome (Russell and Norvig, 2002, p. 4).

Despite this clear-cut description, the conceptual boundaries of agency itself are not so obvious. A significant number of theorists, including Barad (2007), Slack and Wise (2005), Adam (1998), Hayles (1999), Suchman, (2007) and Haraway (1991), agree that the meaning of agency is neither neutral nor implicit. Slack and Wise are at pains to distinguish agency from causality, which they characterise as being restricted and one-dimensional:

The causal approach has a certain universal undertone to it, meaning that its purported causal effects are assumed to be the same under any-and-every-circumstance. The causal approach cannot adequately grasp the particularities of situations (Slack & Wise, 2005, p. 116).

Instead of considering agency as a possession or a thing, agency can be seen as a process and a form of relationship, one that "does not require human intention, which means that technologies can be involved in relations of agency" (Slack et al, 2005, p. 117). In considering software agents, Maes (1997) has stated that the term implies non-passive, proactive, personal helpers. Her description of agent technology evokes a high level, idealised scenario of personalised and proactive helper software agents, while Wooldridge's (2002) requirements for an intelligent agent are precisely that 'he' or 'it' should be as follows:

- *Situated – 'he' is embedded in an environment.*
- *Goal directed – 'he' has goals that 'he' tries to achieve.*
- *Reactive – 'he' reacts to changes in 'his' environment.*
- *Social – 'he' can communicate with other agents (including humans). (Wooldridge, 2002, p. 23)*

Multi-agent systems are built from networks of agents that can act autonomously, often across distributed environments. Multi-agent systems can solve problems that are too complex for individual agents, human or otherwise, to solve. Agents in such systems do not require a global view of any system, in fact they are more likely to have only a 'local view'. A common analogy is to members of a swarm, such as ants or bees; the individual entities of swarms are decentralised, with no single controlling agent. Such agents are often embedded or situated in an environment, making them context-aware via sensors or other types of input.

But what exactly do these terms, particularly 'situated' and 'embedded' imply? The next section will examine the significance of context-aware, 'situated' software agents.

Situated Cognition

In the context of artificial intelligence, situated agents are embedded in an environment. In Haraway's terms (1988), situatedness also constitutes an ethical recognition of the partiality and locatedness of knowledge, as opposed to an idealised notion of objective and placeless universality. The anthropologist Lucy Suchman (1987, 2007) presents the case for a radical re-framing of computer-human interaction; her interaction model is defined by the degree of pre-existent representation needed for computer systems to work satisfactorily. Suchman proposes a new conception of interactivity in which contingent plans work in tandem with situated, context-aware programs; in other words, programs that operate within physical environments.

Embedded in the notion of situatedness is a clear challenge to the conventional idea of a subject, or what Suchman identifies as the "unitary cogniser" (Suchman, 2007), also known as the 'Cartesian cogito', named after the 17th century philosopher René Descartes. The Cartesian cogito is a rational thinker, in classically cognitivist terms his thought processes are almost inseparable from those of a computer; his disembodied models of interaction are characterised by information-processing paradigms, in which symbolic representations are rationally evaluated. These paradigms are predicated on notions of environmental stimulus and behavioural response:

The first premise of cognitive science, therefore, is that people (or 'cognizers' of any sort) act on the basis of symbolic representations: a kind of cognitive code, instantiated physically in the brain, on which operations are performed to produce mental states such as 'the belief that p', which in turn produce behaviour consistent with those states. (Suchman, 2007, p. 37)

The classical emphasis on symbolic representation is significant here, since it posits a mind-body split in which the body has minimal agency. The alternative model is one in which the body is a significantly active agent. The emphasis on embodiment in interaction and cognitive science has been advanced by the writings of Maturana and Varela (1987), Thompson and Rosch (1991), and more recently by Gallagher (2005), Damasio (2005), Alva Noë (2004) and Kiverstein (2010), among many others. In order to look at the significance of embodiment for digital interaction in detail, it is appropriate to explore the idea that all human experience is both situated and embodied, a principle that can also be referred to as 'enactivism'.

Embodiment and Enactivism

In contrast to the mind-body split of the rational cogito as a model for how humans operate within the world, an enactivist approach is a theory of cognition that is inseparable from action and is therefore implicitly embodied. Varela et al proposed the radical notion that experience, knowledge and cognition always emanate from both the body and the mind:

knower and known, mind and world, stand in relation to each other through mutual specification or dependent coorigination (Varela et al., 1991, p. 150).

It is important to also note their emphasis on the situatedness of human actions, that they take place within a non-symbolic, physical world. This, as Dennett explains, is a radical move away from pre-given notions of "internal" and "external" realms, of separate subjects operating on separate objects:

Cognitive scientists standardly assume a division between independently existing ('pregiven') 'external' objects, properties and events on the one hand and their 'internal' representations in symbolic media in the mind/brain on the other. Varela et al. propose to replace this with an 'enactive' account (Dennett, 1993, p. 121).

The idea that there is an emergent world of separate subjects and objects, rather than an implicit, *a priori* set of independent entities, has also been proposed by the physicist Karen Barad (2007), who deploys the term 'intra-action' as an alternative to interaction. In Barad's terms, intra-action does not presuppose "the prior existence of independent entities of relata" (Barad, 2007, p. 139). It does not take for granted atomistic or Cartesian separations between subject and object, instead Barad sees specific situations and actions as allowing phenomenological relata to emerge as specific causal intra-actions. This, in tandem with enactivism, is a very radical alternative to the types of interaction modelled on the classical cognitivist hypothesis.

Barad's challenge is to question the power placed in symbolic representation as tantamount to reality, as the main agent in human knowing and experiencing of the world. Barad calls her intra-active approach "agential realism" (Barad, 2007), in which knowing and knowledge generation are rooted in actions and relationships. The case studies presented towards the end of the chapter will look at how these ideas might work in practice, exploring a range of artworks that have deployed radical alternatives to conventional interaction modes, which, as the next section will evidence, are often characterised by pre-determined systems and pre-given distinctions between subjects and objects. The next section will therefore move away from the high-level, theoretical discussion of interactivity to the specific examination of twenty-five high-profile digital artworks. It will also outline the types of input and logic such works deploy and look at alternative approaches.

A TYPOLOGY OF INTERACTION MODES

A typology involves the analysis and classification of types. Constructing a typology aids researchers in identifying clusters, such as grouped patterns of behaviour, formal properties or attitudes. In the typology constructed for this chapter, a range of interaction types have been examined, while their use (or non use) by a number of high profile digital artworks has also been assessed. A Multiple Correspondence Analysis (MCA) of the typology then enabled the exploration of a range of interactive artworks and their formal interactive and logical structures. The MCA was performed in order to identify patterns and correlations embedded in the data. This process was triangulated by a cluster analysis, providing further evidence for the presence of identifiable classes of artwork.

Before undertaking the typology, a range of input types were identified, which were then condensed into eight identifiable modes and arranged within a contingency table (a table of data relating to two or more categorical variables). The analysis was undertaken with the statistical and machine learning language "R". The types of input identified as well as the process and its outcomes are now described.

Input Devices

The types of input devices used by digital systems help us to identify the forms of agency used by external actors within an interaction process. Contemporary digital computer systems use input devices such as keyboards, mice, touch screens, microphones, and various sensors to acquire the data they will operate upon. They might also acquire data through networks. There are also, of course, many output devices used by contemporary computer systems, for example screens, audio speakers, printers and physical actuators such as motors and pistons.

The simplest definition of an input device is a mechanism that sends data to a computer; the data may take the form of mouse movements, keys on a keyboard being pressed, mouse clicks, and also combinations of inputs, such as a click and a keyboard press, for example the common "ctrl+click" combination.

The typology presented here, though not exhaustive (new input devices will almost certainly be invented at the time of writing), represents all of the most commonly found input devices as well as some very specialist forms of input mechanism, such as medical imaging and head tilt sensors for severely disabled computer users (Table 3).

These devices may be subdivided into the following categories (Table 4).

It should be noted here that Preece et al wisely question the term 'natural' embedded within the acronym 'NUI' (Natural User Interfaces) and ask whether learning a particular gesture to open a file in a NUI is any more natural than using a menu-based GUI for the same job (Preece et al, 2011, p. 215).

Table 3. Table of input devices

Mouse
Keyboard/virtual or physical
Joysticks
Microphone
Microphone and speech recognition systems
Yokes: such as an aircraft simulation pulling or pushing device
Composite game controller: with combinations of buttons and accelerometers, steering wheels, paddle etc.
Touch screen
Graphics tablet/stylus
Midi keyboard/drum and other midi input devices
Digital cameras, Webcams, other visual input
Buttons, switches, potentiometers
Remote control
Breath detection
Head movement detector
Eye tracker
Nouse (detects breath from nose)
Body sensor: such as heart rate, EEG, galvanic skin response, breath etc.
Biometrics: such as finger print and iris scanners
Other medical sensing/imaging technology
Motion and proximity sensors: including the Kinect sensor
Environmental sensors: these detect environmental data such as temperature, pollution, light levels
Scanners
Barcode readers
Card readers
Magnetic-Ink Character Recognition (MICR)
Optical Mark Reader (OMR)
Punched card input
Light pens
Handwriting recognition

CAVEs: computer-assisted virtual environments
VR helmet and gloves
3D Gloves
Haptic Gloves
Electronic Whiteboard: this has been counted as a type of Standard screen input, albeit often collaborative
Networked: input might come automatically via WIFI

Table 4. Categories of input device

Standard: keyboard, mouse, joystick, touch-screen, microphone, Webcam, remote control, whiteboard light pen
MIDI devices
Environmental sensors: temperature, pollution and light sensors etc.
Internal Embodied: sensing internal bodily attributes such as heart rate, brain waves, breath

Biometric: also embodied but usually engaged with surface features, for example iris, finger print and facial patterns.
Embodied: close to the concept of "natural" interactions used by NUIs or "Natural User Interfaces", such as stroking, picking up objects, walking, gesturing, speaking etc. CAVES may also be included in this category, includes handwriting recognition systems.
Readers: card readers, bar code scanners, punched card input, OMR.

Some devices cross categories, such as sound input, which could be classified as embodied as well as environmental, or even as a 'standard' form of computer input. It is important to acknowledge that the construction of a typology is an approximate and in many ways subjective process; another set of researchers might very well come up with a different set of results; this is a point that Aarseth (1997) made very clear when constructing his innovative typology of interactive texts.

When considering interactivity in artworks, the logic that is applied to user input was also identified, whether it was random, pre-determined, non-determined but not random (such as machine learning) human, adaptive or some other form of learning system.

A Multiple Correspondence Analysis (MCA) is a statistical technique that enables the identification of patterns in more than two categorical variables; in this case, seventeen interaction and logic forms and twenty-five artworks. The MCA examined relative frequencies in terms of the mathematical distances between individual rows and columns. The topic of distance metrics will be returned to when the chapter looks at a working example of an "interest matching" or collaborative filtering algorithm. The resulting data evidences statistically significant variations which are then interpreted "as representing a distinct pattern of usage" (Glynn, 2012, p. 134).

Each artwork was evaluated as TRUE or FALSE for the following variables:

The two-dimensional Euclidean cloud of data that resulted enabled the identification of non-random, systematic correlations between variables, graphically represented in the chart below:

The data space represented 25×17×2 or 850 variable positions and 850! (factorial) possible combinations, from which five loose and two major classes of digital artwork emerged. These were also confirmed by the hierarchical cluster dendrogram generated by a cluster analysis in R. The graphical representation of that cluster analysis is illustrated below. The dendrogram arranges clusters hierarchically, indicating which types of data they contain and their sub-groups. In this example the values were binary.

Eigenvalues represent the distinctness of the patterns identified by the MCA analysis. The major patterns of artwork interaction and logic types were identified as follows (Table 8).

The patterns were characterised by the following qualities (Table 9).

The group defined by Pattern 5 represented a very dense cluster of deterministic, disembodied works, while Pattern 3 arguably represents the avant-garde of digital artworks, with notable outliers such as Stelarc's *Parasite*. However, as Pattern 3 was a less densely defined cluster, it was spread across a number of variables and included artworks with some, but not all, aspects of the more contemporary interaction models outlined in this chapter.

The typology of interaction modes and MCA demonstrates that, despite the growing withdrawal from the classical cognitivist approach to human-computer interaction, many major digital artworks are still embedded with the literal construal of the classical cognitivist hypothesis (Varela et al, 1991, p. 43). Interaction researchers such as Dourish (2001), among others, have encouraged a move away from linear, disembodied models of interaction and agency, but, perhaps surprisingly, this is still the dominant model of interaction for many digital artworks. If, as Dourish states, embodiment is "the property of our engagement with the world that allows us to make it meaningful" (Dourish, 2001, p. 126) then it is important to ask how digital artworks can expect to innovate and develop in the future, while operating within an outmoded paradigm.

It is also important to point out that embedded action and engagement with the world does not imply gesture or movement alone; there are, as Dourish states, other types of embedded action, such as social action, "firmly rooted in the setting in which it arises, where that setting is not just material circumstances, but social, cultural, and historical ones as well" (Dourish, 2001, p. 96). And yet many of the works looked at here appear to operate within a cultural, social and physical vacuum. It is thus safe to conclude that digital artworks have not caught up with major paradigm shifts in computer science.

The domain of computer science has arguably recovered from the failure of many AI projects of the 1980s and early 1990s, in particular the grand and unimaginably expensive folly of 5th generation computing that resulted in the 'AI winter' (in which vast, rule-based systems were abandoned and funding

Table 5. Artists and artworks included in the typology

Artist	Artwork
1. Grey World	The Source
2. Julian Opie	Bruce Walking
3. Golan Levin	Eyecode
4. Mark Napier	Shredder
5. Corey Arcangel & Michael Frumin	Pizza Party
6. Bill Viola	The Stopping Mind
7. Camille Utterback	Shifting Times
8. Lozano-Hemmer	Under Scan
9. Nam June Paik	Jacobs Ladder
10. Stelarc	Parasite
11. Jeffrey Shaw	Legible City
12. William Latham	Mutator C
13. Laurie Anderson	The Waters Reglitterized
14. James Faure-Walker	Dark Filament
15. Marius Watz	Arcs (Rockheim)
16. Harold Cohen	Aaron
17. Josh On	They Rule
18. Blast Theory	My Neck of The woods
19. Casey Reas	TI
20. Miguel Chevalier	Sur-Natures
21. Karsten Schmidt	Unstable Energy
22. Daniel Rozin	Weave Mirror
23. Troika	Digital Zoetrope
24. Frost & Koblin	House of Cards
25. John Maeda	Nature

Table 6. Variables applied to the typology of artworks

Not interactive Standard Midi Environment Internal-embodied Biometric Embodied Reader Network Linear Multi-linear Non-linear Determined Random Non-determined Adaptive Context-aware

Figure 1. Artworks represented in two-dimensional space according to patterns of interaction and logic detected by the Multiple Correspondence Analysis

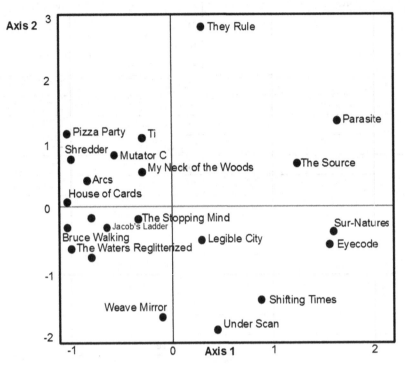

Figure 2. . Modes of interaction and logic represented in two-dimensional space according to patterns of interaction and logic detected by the Multiple Correspondence Analysis

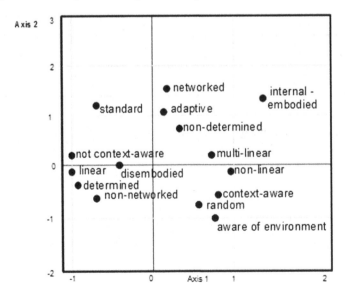

Figure 3. Dendrogram and heat map of clusters, or patterns of interactivity and logic in twenty-five digital artworks

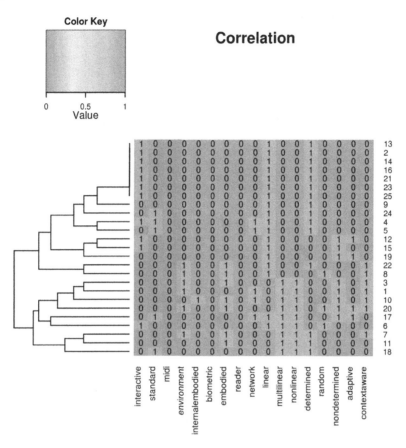

Table 7. Eigenvalues and variances obtained from the Multiple Correspondence Analysis

Number	Eigenvalue	Percentage of Variance	Cumulative Percentage of Variance
1.	0.42332127	16.017561	16.01756
2.	0.22942201	8.680833	24.69839
3.	0.20643118	7.810909	32.50930
4.	0.15796309	5.976982	38.48629
5.	0.14013277	5.302321	43.78861

for AI projects was widely curtailed). Cognitive computing, robotics and machine learning are areas that now pursue more mature notions of agency and intelligence. Contemporary approaches to intelligent systems have, on the whole, less grandiloquent goals than exactly modelling human intelligence or building a 'brain in a vat'. They are often connected to data mining and pattern recognition tasks as well as industrial/military robotics with predominantly pragmatic goals, other researchers, such as Deliyannis (2013) focus on new, intelligent, methodologies for sustainability in multi-media applications.

Table 8. The five patterns of interaction and logic types identified by the typology (provided by the MCA analysis)

Pattern 1:
Arcs
Mutator C
Ti
They Rule
Pattern 2:
House of Cards
Pizza Party
Shredder
Pattern 3:
The Source
Parasite
Sur-Natures
Eyecode
Shifting Times
Legible City, (overlaps with 4)
Weave Mirror
Under Scan
Pattern 4:
Legible City
The Stopping Mind
My Neck of The Woods
Pattern 5:
Jacob's Ladder
Bruce Walking
Nature
The Waters Reglitterized
Aaron
Dark Filament
Unstable Energy

Table 9. Attributes of the five patterns of interaction and logic

Pattern 1:
Networked
Adaptive
Non-Determined
Pattern 2:
Standard
Networked
Pattern 3:
Aware of environment
Non-determined
Random
Embodied
Context-aware
Internal embodied

Pattern 4:
Multi-linear
Non-linear
Pattern 5:
Not context-aware
Linear
Determined
Non-networked
Disembodied

Torrance and Forese (2011) have identified a revived interest in many areas of artificial intelligence and interaction inspired by an enactivist approach, including adaptivity and autonomy, enactive framings of agency and social inter-relationships, as well as enactivism's implications for cognitive science. These ideas are investigated by, among others, Di Paolo (2005, 2009), Thompson (2005, 2007), Barandiaran et al (2008, 2009) and Menary (2010). And yet, despite this significant shift in theoretical emphasis, only a fraction of the major artworks analysed here could claim to have adopted embodied or situated approaches. One reason for this conceptual inertia may relate to a lack of technical or conceptual insight into alternative models. However, there are a number artists who do engage with innovative and embodied approaches, often working outside of the mainstream of the art world. There now follows a brief evaluation of four artworks that have significantly reconceptualised interaction and its associated agencies and contexts.

CASE STUDIES

Sur-Natures, Miguel Chevalier, 2012

Miguel Chevalier's *Sur-Natures* was a virtual reality installation exhibited at the Paris Charles de Gaulle airport in 2012. The installation was both generative and interactive, involving the growth of a virtual garden, comprised initially of eighteen autonomous virtual 'seeds' featuring what the artist describes as "multiple colors, luminescent, scalar plants - herbaceous, red and purple cacti and long yellow flowers with turquoise stems" (Chevalier, 2014). In addition, the system involved situated virtual organisms in which "translucent plants grow and change because of motion detectors which register passing pedestrians" (Lieser, 2009, p.181).

The typology and MCA conducted for the present chapter places *Sur-Natures* as an outlier within the data set of twenty-five digital artworks representing, along with Stelarc's *Parasite*, an extreme and, arguably, innovative form of interactive artwork. Chevalier's virtual flowers are not an attempt to replicate nature. They are strikingly artificial-looking, clearly framed within the materiality of the digital medium; they are also "translucent and fragile, and they refer to the underlying digital structure" (Lieser, 2009, p.181).

The virtual flowers that 'grew' in the installation reacted to the passage of people within the airport via sensor technologies, enabling plants to bend and move according to the visitor's physical orientation, creating a kind of plant ballet. Miguel Chevalier compares this work to Monet's time series, but the former also constitutes an adaptive system, deploying a combination of random elements as well as biologically inspired 'morphogenetic code', in which plants evolve according to the specific conditions in the airport.

To paraphrase Chevalier, the plants grew non-determinedly, blooming and dying according to the evolutionary model of the software; they "grow every day in real time and evolve to infinity" (Chevalier, 2014). But Chevalier's plants also grew in reaction to the specific environmental and embodied actions of people walking through the airport. With its non-determined set of outcomes, *Sur-Natures* exemplifies (whether consciously or not) an *intra-enactive* framing of specific actions and agencies. It represents an isolated minority of mainstream artworks that have integrated new conceptions of the active participant within creative digital practice.

Burning Down Memory, Eleanor Dare, 2014

Burning Down Memory by Eleanor Dare (exhibited at the Slade Research Centre, London, May 2014) was the documentation of a sensor-based performance in which the author attempted to articulate sub-symbolic experiences, i.e. experiences and types of knowledge that cannot be expressed in language or any other types of symbolic system.

The author was attached to a Galvanic Skin Response sensor (sometimes known as a "lie detector" or GSR) as well as an EEG headset (an Electroencephalograph which measures fluctuations in voltage emanating from the scalp). When the GSR unit detected a significant drop in resistance, indicative of anxiety, the author was given an electric shock, which in turn sent signals through the EEG headset. If the EEG signals were beyond a certain threshold of emotional arousal the signals triggered the permanent removal of pixels from an image of a wartime bomb site in South London, via a series of virtual "fires" in the software.

Burning Down Memory destabilised the idea of an originary event, questioning and inverting the status of documentation and the conventional notion that an event precedes and authorises its documentation; an order that is often taken for granted, as Auslander (2006) articulates. At the same time, the vulnerability of bio-sensor technology (even medical grade EEG sensors) to environmental noise and false readings adds another element of ontological doubt to the technologies of representation at play, arguably blurring the boundaries between subjects, objects and the causal flow of documentation.

In *Burning Down Memory*, the body and the computer system became mediums for an investigation into agency and knowledge representation. But, although the EEG headset was positioned around a face, the project was not about "the face as an interface" as Blackman expresses it (2008), but about the frequencies that emanate from the face and the brain, from hands, epidermis and sweat. In this project, bodily fluids are framed as cultural as well as physical agents; the body in this configuration was not "an inert mass in the service of a superior mind" (Blackman, 2008, p. 30) but a co-agent in a dynamic system of meaning-making.

Figure 4. The artist Eleanor Dare is electrocuted; this results in the destructive removal of pixels from an image of a bomb site in South London

Microphone, EunJoo Shin and Alex McLean, 2010

Microphone by McLean and Shin (2010) was exhibited at the *Unleashed Devices* group show, Watermans Gallery, London. The interactive sculpture enabled participants to communicate with each other by speaking into two large funnel-shaped wooden structures. The mouth grimaces that participants made, rather than the actual sounds they produced, were captured by a digital camera.

Using computer vision and machine learning techniques, the software written by the artists then produced vowel sounds. In this way, the physical gestures of users were emphasised, "bringing focus on the role of movement in communication. It evokes a feeling that is literally visceral, of vocal organ encoding patterns of movement into sound, and being perceived as movements" (McLean, 2011, p. 41).

Microphone deploys context-aware models of human subjects and, combined with sensor technology, it expands the agencies at play in interactive works and represents a model of interaction that is far more in keeping with a contemporary framing of agency and embodiment than almost all of the high-profile works examined in the typology.

VAINS, Eleanor Dare and Lee Weinberg, 2011

VAINS is a physical computation system that deploys EEG to sense the electronic brainwave frequencies of individuals while they are interacting with online art sites. The system works by analysing electroencephalographic signals and matching them to suitable artworks based on a collaborative filtering algorithm. On the initial phase of the *VAINS* project, the developers solicited approximately 200 users to establish a database of responses to digital artworks online.

The EEG system calibrates itself uniquely to each individual by observing the flow of their brainwave activity, then allowing for a period of further observation before forwarding users to artworks that might correlate to their alpha, beta and gamma wave patterns and those of previous users. In this way, participants experience an autonomic process of interaction with online artworks. The project is overtly influenced by an enactive and situated methodology that privileges action over *a priori* goals; "it seeks an emergent, fluid and constantly changing set of navigational pathways" (Dare & Weinberg, 2011, p. 20).

The deployment of collaborative filtering within the *VAINS* platform is presented as both a cultural medium and an instrumental agent within the work. The very process of constructing recommendations is exposed and interrogated. The work provocatively channels users to sites that are stereotypically "interest-matched", such as pink Web pages for teenage girls and sombre grey pages for middle-aged men. The extremity of selections challenges users to resist the naturalisation of such processes.

This chapter proposes that the deployment of collaborative filtering and other forms of collective intelligence, while subject to much media hype, is also a fertile ground for the investigation of agency in digital artworks. This is not to revert to an idealised notion of interactivity or 'death of the author' discourse (Barthes, 1967), but an opportunity to recognise and critique an increasingly prevalent cultural and technological form. The next section will outline aspects of the specific algorithm used by the *VAINS* project for collaborative filtering.

Collaborative Filtering

Collaborative filtering is an increasingly significant technique deployed by Web applications. When a site suggests "other products you might like" it is probably using a recommendation algorithm, in which

Figure 5. The VAINS system, an EEG headset identifies brainwaves in individual users and matches them to artworks via similarity metrics. The metrics evolve and change as more people use the system (Dare & Weinberg, 2011)

Figure 6. The online collaborative filtering interface for VAINS, used in the initial phase of data collection (Dare & Weinberg, 2011)

recommendations are generated through a process of collaborative filtering, either explicitly or implicitly invoked. Implicit collaborative filtering might involve surveillance of user choices and patterns of preference, as for example, when making a purchase or clicking on a link. Explicit collaborative filtering asks users directly to choose a preference – to rate a film, book or holiday and so on.

Euclidean Distance

A range of equations can be used to quantify the similarity of preferences or correlation between data sets, such as the Pearson correlation coefficient or Euclidean distance. These yield scores of how strongly (or

Box 1.

$$d(x,y) = \sqrt{(x2 - x1)^2 + (y2 - y1)^2}\ {}_{(1)}$$

not) an individual's preferences are matched or how likely there is to be a correlation between values. In the example provided here, the range for such values will be normalised to between 0 and 1. The formula provided is known as "Euclidean distance" or the "Euclidean metric" algorithm. In the example of VAINS (see the case study section above), Euclidean distance enabled the automatic evaluation of similarities between different individuals and their appreciation for digital artworks online. The Euclidean distance between two sets of points is calculated as shown in Box 1.

The Euclidean metric establishes the distance between these two points in space and calculates how similar two sets of preferences are. A version of the algorithm is provided here in Processing and in the client-side language JavaScript, embedded in html (Algorithm 1.).

The JavaScript code, below, can be saved as 'anything.html' and opened in a browser locally (by double-clicking on the anything.html file) or uploaded to a server (Algorithm 2).

The code above generates similarity scores for our online gallery visitors "Alice" and "Henry". In order to progress into making a more complex recommendation engine, the VAINS project used the Pearson correlation algorithm, i,e. a lengthier formula than Euclidean distance but one that is more robust

Algorithm 1. The Euclidean metric in processing

```
/*processing example, to be run in the Processing IDE available at:
http://www.processing.org/*/
void setup(){
  println(dist(3.0, 1.0, 3.0, 1.0));/* built in distance method*/
  println("inverted:   " +1/(1+dist(3.0, 1.0, 3.0, 1.0)));
  println("our own method:");
  println(euclid_Distance(3.0, 1.0, 3.0, 1.0));
//invert and normalise:
  float a = (euclid_Distance(3.0, 1.0, 3.0, 1.0));
/* for readability we multiplicatively invert the result, so low scores are
high and vice versa: */
    println("inverted and normalised: "+ 1/(1+a));
}
float euclid_Distance(float x1, float y1, float x2, float y2) {
  float dx = x1 - x2;
  float dy = y1 - y2;
  float dis = sqrt(dx*dx + dy*dy);
    return dis;
}
//end
```

Algorithm 2. The Euclidean metric in JavaScript

```html
<!DOCTYPE html>
<html>
<body>
<h1>Euclidean Distance</h1>
<p>Simple Euclidean distance algorithm in JavaScript.</p>
<p id="euclid_demo"></p>
<script>
/*imaginary preference scores for two artworks by two gallery visitors, out of
5, experiment with other values*/

Henry1 = 3.0;
Henry2 = 1.0;
Alice1 = 3.0;
Alice2 = 1.0;
   function euclid_Distance(x1, y1, x2, y2) {
     dx = x1 - x2;
     dy = y1 - y2;
     dis = Math.sqrt(dx*dx + dy*dy);
        return dis;
}
//write the non-normalised result to the document:
document.write("Raw distance metric for Henry and Alice: " +
euclid_Distance(Henry1, Henry2, Alice1, Alice2));

/* With the calculation above the result will be smaller for people who are
more similar, but you can 'flip' (multiplicatively invert) the result to make
it more human-understandable, with a high score for similarity and a low score
for dis-similarity. It will be multiplicatively inverted and normalised to
values from 0 to 1. A division by zero error is also avoided by adding a 1 to
the equation.
The reciprocal of x is 1/x. All numbers have a reciprocal except zero, hence
the addition of 1 below)
*/
   var eucTemp = euclid_Distance(Henry1, Henry2, Alice1, Alice2)
   var euc1 = 1/(1+eucTemp);
/* write the normalised result to the document to two decimal places */
     document.write("<br>Inverted similarity score for Henry and Alice: "
+euc1.toFixed(2));
</script>
</body>
</html>
```

in the presence of non-normalised data, or data with an extreme set of variations. The use of Pearson correlation for collaborative filtering is very clearly described by Toby Segaran in *Programming Collective Intelligence* (2007).

Solutions and Recommendations

Machine learning algorithms increasingly draw upon the millions of terabytes of data that proliferate year on year. This is also known as 'Big Data'. Vendors such as Amazon and Netflix routinely deploy Big Data and machine learning, often to target customers with offers of products that they may be interested in. Such data might originate from sensors, video and audio input, networks, log files, transactional applications, Web, and social media, often in 'real time' and on a very large scale. But, despite the prevalence and increasing cultural significance of these techniques, they are rarely explored, or critiqued by artists; this is despite the growing ease of access to datasets, analytic technology and distributed computing frameworks such as Hadoop.

This chapter proposes that machine learning techniques, in tandem with embodied forms of interaction, offer an alternative configuration of agency to that used by the majority of high-profile digital artworks. This alternative emphasises adaptive software processes in which systems can learn from subjects and situations, resulting in outcomes that are not solely pre-determined. In these systems, agency is multi-linear; this is not to imply a symmetrical form of agency or idealised notions of user empowerment, such as those that emerged in the 1990s (see, for example, Bolter et al (1991)), but something closer to Dourish's (2001) notion of nuanced interaction discussed earlier in the chapter.

In this light, and as proposed in the opening section, galleries and curators need to think of the medium in terms of *context* instead of *content* of the work (Graham and Cook, 2010). The understanding of the peripheral (technical) requirements that frame or support the work is equally crucial for assessing a piece and subsequently making curatorial judgements.

The core recommendations this chapter proposes for developing innovative interactive digital artworks are as follows:

1. Meaning (or intelligibility) in a situated system cannot reside in an *a priori* model of the user (or their possible interactions), but rather in a relation between more generalised plans and specific circumstances.

2. Likewise, subjective representation is problematic; it is more useful to examine dynamic and situated differences.

3. Dominant modes of interaction, such as those based solely on propositional logic, statistics and *a priori* representations of cause and effect (exemplified in rule-based systems) are fixed and reactive and as such are not ideal for generating new ideas or new artistic forms.

4. Open-ended methods are preferable within a system designed to encourage divergent forms of artwork and divergent subjectivities.

5. The artworks in such a system, like the subjects who interact with it, will be multiple, situated and multi-linear.

6. Enactive systems deploy knowledge generated through embodied processes, not only sight, but also smell, touch, taste, sound, social and cultural relations.

From these core findings, an encapsulation of this chapter's theoretical and practical rationale can be condensed into the following two statements:

1. Interaction is a contingent process of shared and collaborative, *ad hoc* understandings within the framework of generalised or more abstracted *a priori* intentions.
2. Difference and specificity are key resources in interactive systems working with subjects – human or virtual.

FUTURE RESEARCH DIRECTIONS

While it is important to acknowledge that Big Data and machine learning, like many other emergent technologies, are subject to an exaggerated form of "hype curve" (Veryard, 2005, p. 1), they are still significant cultural artefacts and are worthy of investigation by contemporary artists. In conjunction with embodied and situated technologies, as well as adaptive programming techniques, the time is ripe for a significant paradigm shift in the framing of agencies and interactivity models in digital artworks. It is proposed that in the future innovative digital artworks might fruitfully deploy the following combinations of technologies and techniques:

- Machine Learning can support systems that learn from "users" and situations as an alternative to *a priori* configurations.
- Collaborative filtering and Crowdsourcing, of the type currently used by many Citizen Science projects, might extend the agencies at play in digital artworks.
- Adaptive systems such as genetic algorithms, artificial immune systems and artificial neural networks can also generate emergent, non-determined outcomes.
- Embodied systems that work via a range of sensors can react to actions and environmental data, enabling a dynamic range of outputs.
- Situated systems, which are socially as well as physically and bodily located in specific environments, expand the field of interaction to a set of relational phenomena in keeping with an enactivist framing of action, agency and perception.

None of these techniques or processes are proposed as offering isolated solutions; rather, they are presented here as parts of dynamic, multi-linear systems, incorporating an enactive approach to human experience that is embodied, situated and emergent, involving multiple forms of agency.

CONCLUSION

The historical background and typology presented in this chapter identified a distinct pattern of high-profile artworks in which disembodied image-objects (or 'spectacles') were deployed. The majority of works identified were, on the whole, also found to be operating on deprecated models of human computer interaction, predicated on classically cognitivist divisions between agents and their environments. The chapter outlined alternatives to these approaches; in particular it highlighted the concept of enactivism.

As Alva Noë has observed (2004), enactivism has evolved significantly since Varela et al first outlined it. It now offers a nuanced and potentially non-polarising alternative to orthodox views of human-computer interaction. Noë (2004), like Barad (2007) and Suchman (2007), offers a view of agency in which agents are entangled with each other in a process of co-origination. Whatever term is applied to this co-constitution of agencies, whether it is called *interactivity*, *intra-activity* or *intra-enactivity*, it is one that will necessitate the integration of radically new conceptions of action and participation within creative digital practice.

Throughout this chapter, innovative research in interactive systems has been highlighted, including artists' tools, applications, and techniques that aggregate to offer a critical engagement with emerging multimedia trends. In particular, the chapter has looked at situated computing and embodied systems, in which context-aware models of human subjects are combined with sensor technology to expand the agencies at play in interactive works. The chapter has connected enactive principals to technologies such as Big Data, Crowdsourcing and other techniques from artificial intelligence that develop the conception of interaction and participation.

The case studies presented here have elucidated some of the specific technical and design strategies used in real world projects. The chapter has critiqued the reduction of mainstream digital art to 'spectacles', and instead highlighted more nuanced works. These works offer forms of interaction that are in keeping with current cognitive and computer scientific understandings of both human and machine agencies. In detail, this chapter has advanced the work of Noë (2004), Maturana and Varela (1987), Suchman (2007), Barad (2007) and Dourish (2001), who all contribute to providing significantly new models for human computer interaction within artistic practice.

REFERENCES

Aarseth, E. (1997). *Cybertext, Perspectives on Ergodic Literature*. Baltimore, MD: John Hopkins University Press.

Adam, A. (1998). *Artificial Knowing, Gender and the Thinking Machine*. London, New York: First Routledge.

Auslander, P. (2006). The Performativity of Performance Documents. *PAJ a Journal of Performance and Art*, *28*(3), 1–10. doi:10.1162/pajj.2006.28.3.1

Barad, K. (2007). *Meeting the Universe Halfway, Quantum Physics and the Entanglement of Matter and Meaning*. Durham, N.C: Duke University Press. doi:10.1215/9780822388128

Barandiaran, X., Di Paolo, E. A., & Rohde, M. (2009). Defining agency: Individuality, normativity, asymmetry, and spatio-temporality in action. *Adaptive Behavior*, *17*(5), 367–386. doi:10.1177/1059712309343819

Barandiaran, X., & Ruiz-Mirazo, K. (Eds.). (2008). BioSystems Journal - Modeling Autonomy [Special Issue], 91(2).

Barthes, R. (1977). *'From Work to Text' and 'The Death of the Author (1967),' from Image-Music-Text*. London: Fontana Press.

Bishop, C. (2004) 'Antagonism and Relational Aesthetics', from *October,* Fall 2004.

Blackman, L. (2008). *The Body*. Oxford, New York: Berg.

Bolter, J. D. (1991). *Writing Space, the Computer, Hypertext, and the History of Writing*. New Jersey: Lawrence Erlbaum Associates.

Bourriaud, N. (2002). *Relational Aesthetics*. Dijon: Les presses du reel.

Burnham, J. (1968). *Beyond Modern Sculpture: The Effects of Science and Technology on the Sculpture of this Century*. New York: George Braziller.

Chevalier, M. (2014). Miguel Chevalier. Retrieved from http://www.miguel-chevalier.com/en/index.html

Clark, T. J. (1985). 'Clement Greenberg's theory of art'. In F. Frascina (Ed). Pollock and After: The Critical Debate. London: P. Chapman.

Cook, S. (2003). Towards a Theory of the Practice of Curating New Media Art. In M. Townsend (Ed). Beyond the Box – Diverging Curatorial Practices. Banff: Banff Centre press.

Damasio, A. (2005). *Descartes' Error: Emotion, Reason, and the Human Brain* [Revised Penguin edition]. New York: Putnam.

Dare, E., & Weinberg, L. (2011). Encountering the Body in Art. Proceedings for the ISEA 2011, *17th International Symposium on Electronic Art*. Retrieved from http://isea2011.sabanciuniv.edu/paper/encountering-body-art-online-vains-visual-art-interrogation-and-navigation-system-abjection-ap

Deliyannis, I. (2013). Sensor Recycling and Reuse. *International Journal of Sensor and Related Networks*, 1(1).

Dennett, D. (1993). Review of F. Varela, E. Thompson, & E. Rosch, The Embodied Mind. *The American Journal of Psychology*, *106*, 121–126. doi:10.2307/1422869

Descartes, R. (2000). *Discourse on Method and Related Writings*. London: Penguin Classics.

Di Paolo, E. A. (2005). Autopoiesis, adaptivity, teleology, agency. *Phenomenology and the Cognitive Sciences*, *4*(4), 429–452. doi:10.1007/s11097-005-9002-y

Di Paolo, E. A. (Ed.). (2009). *Phenomenology and the Cognitive Sciences* [Special issue on "The Social and Enactive Mind], *8*(4).

Dourish, P. (2001). *Where the Action Is: The Foundations of Embodied Interaction*. Cambridge: MIT Press.

Downes, E. J., & McMillan, S. J. (2000). Defining Interactivity. *New Media & Society*, *2*(2), 157–179. doi:10.1177/14614440022225751

Druckrey, (ed) (1996). *Electronic Culture*. Romford: Aperture.

Fried, M. (1967) "Art and Objecthood". Retrieved from http://atc.berkeley.edu/201/readings/FriedObjcthd.pdf

Gallagher, S. (2005). *How the Body Shapes the Mind*. New York: Oxford University Press. doi:10.1093/0199271941.001.0001

Glynn, D. (2012). Correspondence Analysis: Exploring data and identifying patterns. A*cademia.edu*, Retrieved from http://www.academia.edu/926945/Correspondence_Analysis

Graham, B., & Cook, S. (2010). *Rethinking Curating – Art after New Media*. Cambridge Mass. and London: MIT press.

Greenberg, C. (1960). Modernist Painting. In C. Harrison, & P. Wood (Eds), Art in Theory 1900-1990. Oxford: Blackwell.

Haraway, D. (1991). *Situated Knowledges, from, Simians Cyborgs and Women: The Reinvention of Nature*. New York: Routledge.

Hayles, K. N. (1999). *How We Became Post Human*. Chicago, London: The University of Chicago Press. doi:10.7208/chicago/9780226321394.001.0001

Kiverstein, J. (2010). Out of our Heads: Why You Are Not Your Brain, and Other Lessons from the Biology of Consciousness. *Journal of Consciousness Studies, 17*(5-6), 243–248.

Knight, J. (Ed.). (1996). *Diverse Practices: A Critical Reader on British Video Art*. Luton: University of Luton press.

Lieser, W. (2009). *Digital Art*. Königswinter (Germany): h.f. ullmann / Tandem.

Maes, P. (1997). On Software Agents: Humanizing the Global Computer. *IEEE Internet Computing, 1*(4), 10–19. doi:10.1109/MIC.1997.612209

Manovich, L. (2001). *The Language of New Media*. Cambridge: MIT Press.

Martin, S., & Grosenick, U. (Eds.). (2006). *Video Art*. London: Taschen.

Maturana, H. R., & Varela, F. J. (1987). *The Tree of Knowledge: The Biological Roots of Human Understanding*. Boston: Shambhala Publications.

McLean, A. (2011). *Artist-Programmers and Programming Languages for the Arts* [Unpublished PhD Thesis]. University of London, United Kingdom.

Menary, R. (Ed.). (2010). Special issue on 4E Cognition: Embodied, Embedded, Enacted, Extended. *Phenomenology and the Cognitive Sciences, 9*(4).

Mondloch, K. (2010). *Screens – Viewing Media Installation Art*. Minneapolis: University of Minnesota press.

Muller, L., Edmonds, E. and Connell, M. (2006, December 4). Living Laboratories for Interactive Art. *CoDesign, 2*, 195-207.

Noble, J. (2012). *Programming Interactivity*. Sebastopol, CA: O'Reilly Media.

Noë, A. (2004). *Action in Perception*. Cambridge, MA: MIT Press.

Paul, C. (2008). *New Media in the White Cube and Beyond*. London, Berkeley, Los Angeles: University of California press.

Preece, J., Rogers, Y., & Sharp, H. (2011). *Interaction Design: Beyond. Human-Computer Interaction* (3rd ed.). Hoboken, NJ: John Wiley & Sons.

Rodowick, D. N. (2001). *Reading the Figural, or Philosophy After the New Media*. London: Duke University press. doi:10.1215/9780822380764

Rush, M. (1999). *New Media in Late 20th- century Art*. London: Thames & Hudson.

Russell, S., & Norvig, P. (2002). Artificial Intelligence: A Modern Approach (2nd ed.). London: Prentice Hall Series in Artificial Intelligence.

Segaran, T. (2007). *Programming Collective Intelligence: Building Smart Web 2.0 Applications*. Sebastopol, CA: O'Reilly Media.

Shanken, E. A. (2011). *Contemporary Art and New Media: Toward a Hybrid Discourse?* Retrieved from: http://hybridge.files.wordpress.com/2011/02/hybrid-discourses-overview-4.pdf

Slack, J. D., & Wise, J. M. (2005). Culture and Technology. A Primer. New York: Peter Lang.

Suchman, L. (1987). *Plans and Situated Actions: The Problem of Human-machine Communication*. New York: Cambridge University Press.

Suchman, L. (2007). *Human-Machine Reconfigurations: Plans and Situated Actions*. New York: Cambridge University Press.

Sutton, G. (2004). Exhibiting New Media Art. Retrieved from: http://kris.constantvzw.org/?p=20

Thompson, E. (2005). Sensorimotor subjectivity and the enactive approach to experience. *Phenomenology and the Cognitive Sciences*, *4*(4), 407–427. doi:10.1007/s11097-005-9003-x

Thompson, E. (2007). *Mind in Life: Biology, Phenomenology, and the Sciences of Mind*. Cambridge, MA: Harvard University Press.

Torrance, S., & Froese, T. (2001). An Inter-Enactive Approach to Agency: Participatory Sense-Making, Dynamics, and Sociality. *Humana. Mente*, *15*, 21–53.

Trifonova, A., Jaccheri, L., & Bergaust, K. (2008). *Software engineering issues in interactive installation art. International Journal of Arts and Technology* (Vol. 1, p. 1). IJART.

Varela, F. J., Thompson, E., & Rosch, E. (1991). *The Embodied Mind: Cognitive Science and Human Experience*. Cambridge, MA: MIT Press.

Veryard, R. (2005). Technology Hype Curve [blog post]. Retrieved from http://demandingchange.blogspot.co.uk/2005/09/technology-hype-curve.html

Whitehead, A. N. (1929). *Process and Reality*. New York: The Macmillan Company.

Wooldridge, M. (2009). *An Introduction to MultiAgent Systems*. New York: John Wiley and Sons.

Youngblood, G. (1970). *Expanded Cinema*. New York: Dutton.

ADDITIONAL READING

Papadaki, E. (2015). Interactive Video Installations in Public Spaces: Rafael Lozano-Hemmer's Under Scan (pp. 197-212). In V. Crisp, & G. Menotti Gonring (Eds), Besides the Screen: Moving Images through Distribution, Promotion and Curation. London: Palgrave Macmillan. doi:10.1057/9781137471024.0018

KEY TERMS AND DEFINITIONS

Agency: Agency influences events and processes and therefore acts within the world. It is important in the context of interaction models to dispense with the notion that agency is a 'thing' or a linear force, or that it is restricted to human agents only.

Crowdsourcing: The collective acquisition, explicit or implicit, of data as well as actions and resources, this is often undertaken by "lay" people, for example, in the case of Citizen Science projects for classifying galaxy types. The term is also often used to refer to what is really a form of crowd funding.

Enactivism: In contrast to the mind-body split of the Cartesian Cogito as a model for human cognition an enactivist approach posits "the enactment of a world and a mind on the basis of a history of the variety of actions that a being in the world performs" (Varela, Thompson & Rosch, 1991, p. 9). It is a theory of cognition that is inseparable from action and is therefore implicitly embodied.

Inter/Intra: The word "inter" mean "between" or "among" while the word "intra" means "within" The terms therefore imply quite different patterns of agency and action. *Intra* may also imply a degree of containment, in which agency does not extend beyond the variables within a particular configuration, in keeping with an enactive framing of contingent, situated agencies.

Interactivity: Interactivity refers to the linear relations between computers and humans. The dominant mode of interactivity describes a linear process of inputs and outputs, as opposed to the relational causality of intra-activity outlined by Karen Barad (2007).

Intra-Activity: According to Karen Barad (2007), intra-action, unlike interaction, does not presuppose "the prior existence of independent entities of relata" (Barad, 2007, p. 139). Barad does not take for granted atomistic or Cartesian separations between subject and object; instead she sees specific situations and actions as allowing phenomenological relata to emerge as specific causal intra- actions.

Machine Learning: involves computational and statistical processes of learning from data, often deploying adaptive programs. Machine learning systems are therefore not explicitly determined, for example, they may involve self-modifying programs in which rules and procedures will adapt according to the data and specific situations.

Situated/Situatedness: In the context of computer programs situated agents are embedded in an environment. In Haraway's terms (1991) situatedness is also an ethical recognition of the partiality and locatedness of knowledge, as opposed to an idealised notion of objective universality and placeless, disembodied, non-partiality.

ENDNOTES

[1]   See; Sutton, G. (2004). *Exhibiting New Media Art*; Bishop, C. (2011). *Installation Art*; Meijers, D. J. (1996). *The Museum and the 'Ahistorical' Exhibition.*

[3]   Reprinted with significant revisions in 1965, from where we reference.

[4]   See also http://www.medienkunstnetz.de/source-text/35/ The text was originally written for the New School of Social Research in New York, in collaboration with Bill Bryson.

[5]   For a chronological account of time-based media art see; Cubitt, S. (1993). *Videography – Video Media as Art and Culture.* In Grosenick, Martin & Uta (Eds.) (2006). *Video Art.*

[6]   Journeys: Tate History, Retrieved from http://www2.tate.org.uk/archivejourneys/historyhtml/people_public.htm The full title of *The Daily Mirror* front page: "Whichever way you look at Britain's latest work of art… WHAT A LOAD OF RUBBISH - How the Tate dropped 120 bricks", 16 February 1976. Archival material from the reaction of the audience when viewing *Equivalent VIII* is included in Alan Yentob's "How to Get On in the Art World", *BBC ONE*, 20 November 2007.

[8]   The point is also raised at various times in the published discussions of the BALTIC series, as well as in the CRUMB forum (http://www.crumbweb.org/searchsite.php?search=discussion%20list&focus=Discussion&searchDisc=&ts=1224503832) [last accessed: 2 July 2014].

[9]   At the workshop "Digital Audiovisual Preservation in Communities of Practice" (Presto Centre and Institut National de l'Audiovisuel, Paris, 4 December 2013), Pip Laurenson (Head of Collection Care Research, Tate) presented the challenges that arose when copying obsolete technologies (such as a Sony ½ inch tape) onto new formats, in order to preserve the work and enable its future exhibiting. The preservation of digital data is a fertile subject of research, even though it expands beyond the scope of the present chapter. However, it demonstrates that there is a history behind technology-bound pieces that needs be known and acknowledged by curators.

[10]   Again, the term is being used as a solution to accommodate the "varied nomenclature" amassed around the idea of new media art, such as "art & technology, art/sci, computer art, electronic media, variable media, locative media, immersive art, interactive art, and Things That You Plug In" (Graham & Cook, 2010, p. 4). Graham and Cook (2010) note that the CRUMB discussion list frequently focused on issues of terminology and categories; some years back (2004) they concluded that these names often described, apart from the media used in the artwork, the genre, content, theme, and everything in between.

Chapter 3
Families and Multimedia Exhibits:
The Example of an Exhibition about Greek Mathematics

Panagiota Stellaki
Independent Researcher, Greece

ABSTRACT

The purpose of the current article is to present the results of a survey conducted in 2010 in an exhibition at "Hellenic Cosmos", the Cultural Centre of the Foundation of the Hellenic World in Athens, Greece. The title of the exhibition was "Is There an Answer to Everything? A journey to the world of Greek mathematics". The survey was a part of the writer's dissertation at Panteion University at the MA Program "Cultural Management", Department of Communication, Media and Culture. The survey focuses only in families and it gives insight about important aspects regarding exhibition spaces such as the use of multimedia before entering the exhibition space, the relation of visitors towards multimedia exhibits and the role of the museum as an alternative place for learning, especially with the use of innovative interactive multimedia.

INTRODUCTION

Museums[1] nowadays are very different, in relation to their approach towards visitors, than 2 or 3 decades back. Many surveys have been conducted (and still are) in respect of the visitors' relationship to museums, the reasons why some people are frequent museum visitors and some never go there, even if learning could be accomplished in a museum's environment. Visiting a museum is considered (Falk & Dierking, 2000) a characteristic social activity, chosen by the visitor on his free time, to spend it together with other people. Whilst families have been a target group for many surveys in countries like the US and the UK (since they represent a large part of the museum audience there), in Greece there has not been such an extensive research especially in relation to exhibitions that are using new media, like multimedia exhibits.

DOI: 10.4018/978-1-4666-8659-5.ch003

Resent research worldwide deals with the experience of the user in relation to multimedia applications like virtual reality for cultural heritage interpretation (Economou & Pujol Tost, 2011) and interactive new media exhibits (Meyer, 2013) especially in relation to children (Rhee & Kim, 2013). Those researches aim at showing how a museum visit could become memorable and appeal to the entire user's senses. From the simplest to the most complex application, technology has become a part of many exhibitions today, mainly with the form of complementary exhibits. The discussion is whether new media is required for the experience or lower tech technologies could be used, even if interactivity requires new media or just hands- on exhibits.

The present chapter's goal is to contribute to the general discussion considering a varied audience, constituted of different ages, different levels of knowledge, whose members are connected with relational and emotional bonds: families. They are a significant percentage in museums worldwide, between 50-60% of the total of visitors. There is a strong belief that the future of museums relies on the impact museum have on families today; from the families would come the future museum visitors (Wood[2] 1996). And in order to attract such a unique audience, like children, multimedia play a crucial role; it could create a friendly environment for them, an environment close to their everyday life.

METHODOLOGY

The methodological approach followed on the survey was the qualitative[3]. This specific approach was chosen for two reasons. The main one was that qualitative research gives the opportunity to examine a wide range of subjects, which relate to families and new technologies, like how they described their experience, how they compare the exhibitions with virtual reality, if parents think that multimedia facilitate learning or even if multimedia could be a part of school education etc.

The grounded theory was used as a base for the present research, which relies on creating codes for comparison and grouping the data. The approach of the theory was based on Glaser (1992), who thinks that first we should start from the research and the forming of a hypothesis and then continue to the collection of the data. On this specific theory there is a triangular connection between the collection of data, the codification and the notes, where the collection of data and the analysis integrate during the research in combination with the theoretical background. The process begins deductively, to go to the second phase, the inductive, where the initial hypothesis is part of a typological form. This theory includes examination of the data been collected, creation of meanings and connecting them one to the other, additional collection of data and their codification.

For this purpose the method of naturalistic observation[4] on the exhibition environment was used, with the visitors' verbal agreement. All the members of the family were part of the observation, from the exhibition entrance, till the exhibition exit. A non- participant observation was preferred, as well as a discreet presence of the researcher. It was not to the knowledge of the visitor that the researcher (and writer of this chapter) worked as a museum educator at Hellenic Cosmos. An important goal was to prevent the visitors from asking questions about the exhibits and solving their queries, because, by doing that, it was not going to be clear which parts of the exhibition were most difficult to them, or if the exhibits were visitor- friendly and understandable by them.

Combining the observation with the interviews, especially on the part where the visitors described their experience, reduced the danger of the possible subjectivity of relying only in the observation. During the visit in the exhibition the notes were kept handwriting. Observations like, which exhibits attract the visitors most (based on how much time they spend dealing with them), what is the visitors behavior towards multimedia in relation to their age etc, were written down. Details such as: reaction, moves, route in the exhibition area, day, time and duration of visit, as well as general information were also written down.

The interviews were based on a semi- structured questionnaire which was formed based on the goals of the research; in many occasions, the flow of the conversation was followed and the visitors expanded as they liked in some subjects, limiting by that, other subjects. By following this method, the subjects that interested the participants more were highlighted. During the research some questions were added, others were changed, giving a better image on the desired data to process. The visitors' thoughts, emotions and opinions were recorded, since it seemed like many times the visitors "were thinking out loud". For recording during the interview, a digital voice recorder was used. The duration of the conversation was determined mostly by the visitors, since in most cases their time was limited[5], either due to watching other programmes at the museum, or due to other obligations after the museum visit. Most of the questions were addressed to the parents, although children expressed their opinion at the end, if they wanted to. After the interview, a pencil with the museum's logo was offered to each child, as thanks for their time.

For processing the data, the stages of analysis mentioned by Schmidt (2004) were used. From all the interviews specific subjects were chosen and codified. Those codes were dynamic and the ideas were produced from the primary data. If a category was not seen very often, it could be discarded and the codification could be remodeled. By doing that, a comparative table of the results was created and a typical, codified presentation of the data was formed. The codes used on our observation helped contrasting the observation in the exhibition and the interviews. On the next stage similarities or even differences between the interviews were gathered, which were the material for our conclusions. On the last stage particular cases were analyzed making an effort to interpret them. The study of the particular cases allowed us to describe a "typical family", from the information gathered by all the families.

A complete record of the description of the exhibition visit and transcript of the interviews in Greek were included in the appendix of the original Master's thesis (Stellaki, 2010), with numbering of the lines on the texts. Every interview had the code (S) and a number; every exhibition observation the code (E) and the same number with the one on the interview (which means that every family who visited the exhibition had the same number both on the visit and the interview). In the present chapter only the number of the interview is written, and not the number of the exact lines.

Research Sample

The research was conducted from February till April 2010 at Hellenic Cosmos, the Cultural Centre of the Foundation of the Hellenic World[6] in Athens, Greece. The survey's sample (22 interviews) was families, which came with their own initiative in the museum and was divided into three categories. The first one (the main part of the research) were families which visited one or more exhibitions (16 interviews). The route and the pace on the exhibitions were determined by the visitors themselves and each family was observed only in one exhibition. The second group was parents who brought their children to Sunday Educational Programmes, in which parents did not participate (3 interviews). The third category was families who chose to watch virtual reality programmes, but not visit any exhibition (3 interviews). From the second and third category a few interviews were gathered; those data were used auxiliary, to confirm or reject the hypotheses made initially about families in exhibitions.

In our research, from those who visited the exhibition, in total participated 24 adults, from whom 11 were men and 13 women. The adults' ages were in the group 30-44 years, apart from an exception (E21) and all of them had the Greek nationality. The adults accompanied 35 children, from whom 19 were boys and 16 girls. The children were from 4 to 14 years old, with an average age of 9 years. We should also mention that the average age "drops" because the families usually bring to museums also younger children than the exhibition addresses to, because they cannot leave them at home (Black, 2009, pp. 67-73). Something that shows us that when designing an exhibition also this parameter should be taken in notice, so that activities could be designed or there should be a place to play also for young children. From the 16 families we observed in the exhibition, five came from a provincial town of Greece and one from Cyprus. It is also important to note that from the 16 cases we observed in the exhibition only in 5 cases both parents were in the exhibition, while in 17 cases there was only one parent (in 6 cases the father, while in 11 the mother).

The majority of parents had a University degree, as indicated in Figure 1. The upper education level of museum visitors is noted in many previous researches, like Merriman (2000) and Bicknell & Farnello (1993). Some held also a master's degree or a PhD (those specific titles were not included in the research, because the parents were not asked about them, many times they mentioned them after the end of the interview).

All the families were the so- called "nuclear families", no matter if the children came with one or two parents. In all 22 families been interviewed, there were always parents and in no case grandparents. This was impressive, if we consider that Moussouri (2003) in her research mentions representation of this group (over 65) in the museums of UK accompanying children. In our case of course, not having seniors could be justified partly by the fact of the museum's location, which is not very close to the centre

Figure 1. Parents' education level

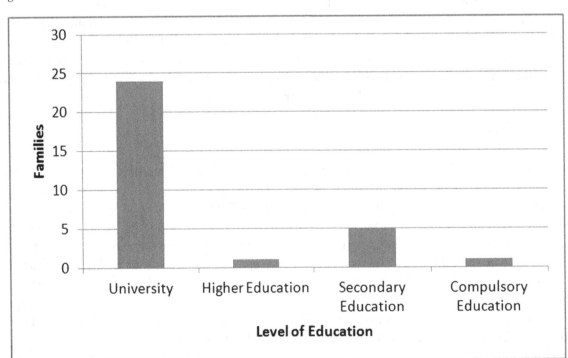

Figure 2. Family activities

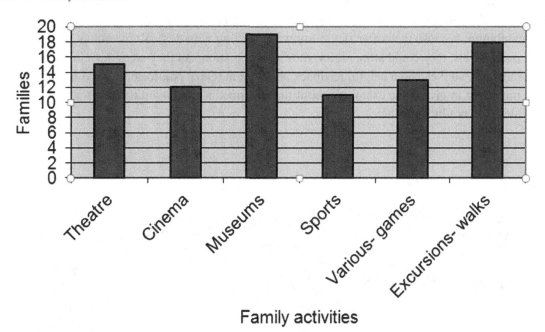

of Athens, with relatively difficult access by Public Transport. Another reason could be that Hellenic Cosmos is considered a "modern" museum, not usually selected by seniors, at least when it has to do with interactive exhibitions.

The general family activities were also noted down in order to have an idea about how they spend their free time. From Figure 2 it is obvious that the activities look balanced and they include both the body's and the mind's exercise, as well as many cultural activities.

EXHIBITION INFORMATION

The interactive exhibition of Hellenic Cosmos "Is There an Answer to Everything? A journey to the world of Greek Mathematics" was chosen for the research. It was the main exhibition of the museum during the years 2003- 2013. The exhibition dealt with the development of mathematics and mathematical thought on the ancient Greek world[7]. The exhibition museologists mentioned even from the beginning that "we want the exhibition to attract mostly families, as well as other mixed groups of adults- children" (Moussouri, Nikiforidou, & Gazi, 2004). In order to achieve that goal, the museologists' team conducted front-end and formative evaluation. A large part of the formative evaluation was focused on the multimedia exhibits. Models of interactive exhibits were used, in order to see if they were effective in communicating mathematical concepts, the meaning visitors would give to those concepts and possible ergonomical problems. The majority of the visitors were able to use the exhibits. The visitors' comments led to modification of some exhibits (Moussouri, Nikiforidou, & Gazi, 2003).

In the exhibition new technologies were used, such as video, digital interactive applications, virtual reality exhibits[8]. As the museologists stated, they chose new technologies and especially interactive means for the exhibition, because they offer flexibility when dealing with difficult meanings, they are accessible in many levels, they could attract the visitor's participation and they were designed with the help of the evaluation, so they had a helpful feedback about them (Gazi, Nikiforidou, & Moussouri, 2004).

It is important to give some examples about the multimedia exhibits in each of the seven stations-stops (videos are not included here):

Figure 3. Thales' Pyramid ©2003 FHW. Used with permission

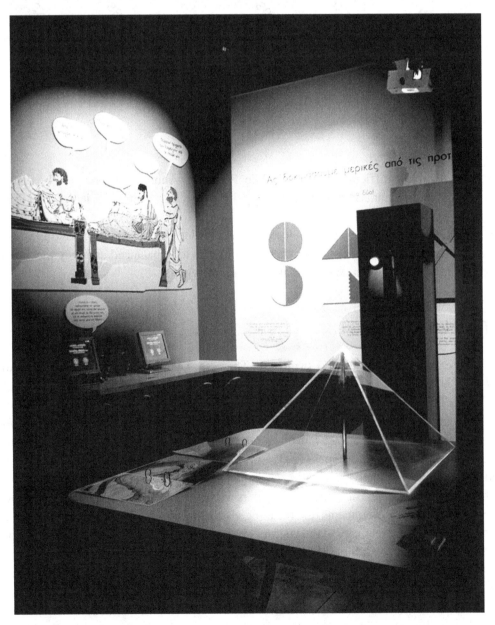

Section 1: Apart from the introduction outside the exhibition, there were multimedia exhibits involving a problem of division in Egypt.

Section 2: Digital exhibits presented a problem solved by Thales, Pythagorean meanings and a game that had to do with figurate numbers. Part of this section is shown in Figure 3.

Section 3: A digital exhibit that explained the proof of the Pythagorean's theorem step by step, as it is shown in Figure 4.

Section 4: Two digital exhibits that showed the method of exhaustion and the area of the parabolic shape, which are shown in Figure 5. In addition, a digital exhibit, where visitors could find the prime numbers.

Section 5: A digital exhibit about two astronomical models of antiquity.

Section 6: A digital exhibit about Heron's Dioptra.

Added to that, there were the recreational areas, where the visitors could find books, children toys and digital exhibits about music in connection with mathematics. Section 7 included only texts.

Figure 4. Digital Exhibits next to the mechanical about the theorem of Pythagoras. ©2003 FHW. Used with permission

Figure 5. Digital Exhibits next to mechanical in Stop 4. ©2003 FHW. Used with permission

THE VISIT AT HELLENIC COSMOS

Multimedia in Exhibition's Introduction

Exactly on the right side of the exhibition entrance there were two computers, as it shown in Figure 6. By using them, visitors could "create" their own course in the exhibition according to his interests. That was a navigational exhibit, an interactive, user-friendly digital device and database of the subjects of the exhibition and the exhibits themselves. This exhibit gave the visitor the opportunity to formulate a personal tour, tailored to his or her particular interests; the visitor could then print it and use it in the exhibition. Visitors could type for example the name of Pythagoras and see the exhibits that referred to him. They could also add e.g. Thales and at the end print a map of their chosen path. Those computers were left unnoticed by the visitors.

At first someone could think that the visitors are not very familiar with those types of multimedia exhibits. The interesting thing though, is that also the written information on the wall on the left side of the exhibition's entrance was left unobserved (information like: the general plan of the room, the numbers and titles of each stations, a summary of what it includes, how visitors can visit the exhibition e.g. parents

Figure 6. Exhibition entrance- Digital exhibits together with written information. ©2003 FHW. Used with permission

with children, what to do if they have a little time, how they are going to recognize the more difficult exhibits, as well as what course they can follow and what that means). There was also a leaflet- map of the exhibition, with noted the quickest route the museologists suggested; this was left unnoticed as well.

Perhaps we can guess that museum visitors (in Greece?) are not yet "trained" to follow directions and use those kinds of auxiliary material and that it was not a problem that had to do with the multimedia outside of the entrance. But to come to a conclusion like that, further research in other museums in Greece is needed. Another possible reason for not using the information is that perhaps the marking of the information (either the multimedia or the written) was not so clear, as the spot of the introduction was not very well lightened most of the times.

The result of not using this specific material available was that the visitors seem to ignore basic information about the exhibition's function. Preschool and primary school children were choosing multimedia exhibits with a content that addressed middle and high school children, without taking in notice (neither the children nor their parents) the symbol- sticker that was next to the exhibit, about the level of difficulty of the specific exhibit. This resulted that the children lost valuable time trying to understand some of the multimedia exhibits that were not designed for their age and educational level. They also lost time finding the right exhibit for them after having trying them all. It also meant that in some cases, not knowing that the exhibition had multiple levels according to the difficulty of the digital exhibits, led the visitors believe that the exhibition was not "suitable for their children's age". This families' practice, not to use the directions accompanying the exhibits, has being noticed from researches also in other countries (Diamond, 1986; Dierking & Falk 1994).

Favourite Exhibits

To what exhibits families seem to focus? Did those exhibits attracted equally parents and children? Figure 7 summarizes what children mention (we must note that we have categorized individually the digital exhibits, because all the rest are mechanical). There were also mentioned (even though they are not included on Figure 7, because there were only mentioned once) the exhibit about doubling the square, the folding shapes of Thales, the theorem of Pythagoras in the Babyloneans, the magnets with the Egyptian numbers (all mechanic exhibits).

There were obvious differences (noticed during the time of the exhibition observation), between the exhibits chosen by the parents and those chosen by the children. The adults seem to favour the written texts, whereas children the games, the multimedia and the mechanic exhibits, something they state almost exclusively on the interview. This tendency of the families has being observed in past researches (a summary of the researches in Dierking & Falk, 1994), where it seems that children function following their curiosity, touching and trying interactive exhibits, generally being attracted by the new, which does not always have the same impact on adults.

Parents mentioned that the interests of the adults were different from those of the children, in relation to the media they used:

And I guess for the children... it was more... tempting, so to say, the computer image, the computer was more attractive to them than .... The grownups we read a bit of a text, the children I saw they mostly went to the computers and everything that was a game, mostly (S10).

Figure 7. Children's favourite exhibits (information taken from the interviews)

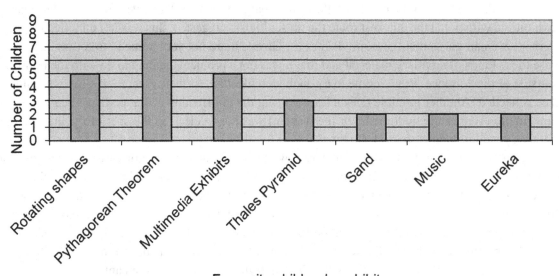

Favourite children's exhibits

Mostly the children enjoyed dealing with the programmes on the computers and with the exercises on the computers; the texts didn't interest them so much, as they were interested in playing and watching on the computer (S4).

It seems a predictable behavior from the children's part, because nowadays they are so much acquainted with new technologies (computers, tablets, electronic games etc.), whereas their parents perhaps are not feeling so comfortable with that, or it does not interest them so much to play, but to learn new things.

Something we observed from our whole research in relation to multimedia exhibits is that, although children seem to deal more time with multimedia exhibits in the exhibition, on the interview they mostly mention the mechanical, as something they liked from everything they saw. Children mentioning how they acted and their focus on mechanical interactive exhibits and not so much on multimedia, can also be seen on similar researches (Moussouri, 1997, 2003). This is perhaps a part of the general questioning, whether modern museums must be "dominated" by new technology or if new technology should have a complementary role, together with real objects (Caulton, 1998, pp.134-140).

In general, the interactivity of the exhibits (digital and mechanical) seemed to help children- parents interaction, because sometimes they had to work together to solve a problem, than just looking at an exhibit. The importance of interaction and dialogue between parents and children in comparison to the interaction between children of the same age or lack of interaction is noted from Crowley's and his partners' research (Crowley et al, 2001).The dialogue and the cooperation in non- school environments could be the base for a scientific way of thinking and this kind of interaction has being noted[9] that it enhances learning (Moussouri, 2003; Ash 2004). A good idea for working in groups could be for example multimedia exhibits operated by multiple users, something missing in the mathematics exhibition.

Multimedia Exhibits: Visitors' Opinion

Table 1 shows the amount of time families spent in the exhibition and particularly dealing with multimedia exhibits.

Something noted during the observation (and is also seen in the parents' comments) is that the time spent for the multimedia exhibits was almost exclusively from the children's part. Another thing that came as a result from the observation, was that when parents "guided" their children, they spent less time in multimedia exhibits, than children who chose on their own where they wanted to go. It is important though to see the general opinion about the multimedia exhibits from some of their comments on the interview:

Nice, very nice (the multimedia exhibits). I think they give a very good supervision of the object they deal with, they were very useful (S8).

It is also remarkable how a mother justifies her children's attraction towards computers:

Is is that it is more of a game to them (the computer) and that game attracts always the most. I mean if you put a person explaining and next a computer, children would again turn to the computer, because it has the form of a game. And it has the form of a slave also, it obeys, while the person would guide you. You would tell it to go somewhere and it would go. I don't know, the computer is at the same time a game and a subordinate. And children perhaps choose it for that reason. I don't know if in that age they know," let's go to the computer to explain it better than my mom or the guide or texts". Certainly, from

Table 1. Duration of exhibition visit and time children dealt with digital exhibits

	Adults Accompanying	Children' Ages	Time in Exhibition (in Minutes)	Time Children Dealt with Digital Exhibits (in Minutes)
S1- E1	Father	Girl- 10 yrs	42 min.	6 min.
S2	Mother	Boy- 6 yrs Girl- 3,5 yrs	-	-
S3	Mother	Boy- 11 yrs Girl- 3 yrs	-	-
S4- E4	Mother	Boy- 11 yrs Girl- 11 yrs	70 min.	20 min.
S5	Mother	Boy- 13 yrs Boy- 8 yrs Girl- 6 yrs	-	-
S6- E6+E7	Both parents (E6)+ family E7	Boy- 6 yrs Girl- 4 yrs	27 min.	6 min.
S7- E7	Mother	Boy- 6 yrs	126 min.	22 min.
S8- E8	Father	Girl- 14 yrs Boy- 10 yrs	72 min.	24 min.
S9- E9	Father	Boy- 8 yrs	32 min.	12 min.
S10- E10	Both parents	Girl- 11 yrs Boy- 9 yrs Girl- 4 yrs (friend)- 11 yrs	80 min.	35 min.
S11- E11	Both parents	Girl- 9 yrs Boy- 9 yrs	40 min.	14 min.
S12- E12	2 families Only mothers	Boy- 13 yrs Girl- 10 yrs Boy- 10 yrs Girl- 7 yrs	45 min.	11 min.
S13	Both parents	Boy- 13 yrs Boy- 10 yrs	-	-
S14- E14	Father	Girl- 7 yrs (niece- 5,5 yrs)	21 min.	0 min.
S15- E15	Both parents	Girl- 10 yrs Girl- 10 yrs Boy- 8 yrs	48 min.	27 min.
S16- E16	Mother	Boy- 13 yrs Girl- 13 yrs	110 min.	30 min.
S17- E17	2 families Only mothers	Boy- 10 yrs Boy- 10 yrs Girl- 10 yrs (friend- 10 yrs)	54 min.	12 min.
S18- E18	Both parents (father in virtual reality- mother in exhibition)	Boy 11 yrs (exhibition) Boy 15 yrs (virtual reality)	34 min.	8 min.
S19	Mother	Girl- 8,5 yrs	-	-
S20	Mother	Boy- 6,5 yrs Girl- 4,5 yrs	-	-
S21- E21	2 families Father in 1st Both parents in 2nd	Boy- 10 yrs Boy- 10 yrs Boy- 10 yrs	28 min.	8 min.
S22- E22	Father	Boy- 6 yrs	46 min.	3 min.

texts in that age, probably the computer says it better, because I don't think children have the patience to sit and read the texts, but they are in the mood of pressing next and watching images. Yes, so there you win, there it wins them (S10).

But what children have to say about digital exhibits? Do they remember some of them specifically or do they mention multimedia in general?

Eh, (I liked) computers and that you... you could do various things. That they (the computers) explained it to me somehow better, because it was a little complicated on the... written texts (girl 11, S10).

what I liked the most is that we solved some problems on the computers and that we were finding something (boy 11, S4).

I liked that in every room there was a computer so we could learn things best (boy 10, S17).

We can spot here the importance of the museum experience, which could be helped through technology, sort- termed at least, because in a long- term basis research has not yet come to a conclusion. In addition, new media can enhance the visitor's experience against more conventional, as we can note from the above quotes (Gazi & Nikiforidou, 2008).

In one and only case the visitors mentioned a problem connected with having or not museum personnel in the exhibition helping with the use of new technologies:

and I think that especially the gentleman or the lady who should had being here and explain, it proved the lack of it mainly to what it has to do with the computer. I mean you saw the children playing with a mouse and trying to understand. In everything else there were suggestions... related so with a mom or dad next (to the children), problem solved; I mean if there was ...someone to guide and give directions ... one in every stand .... while we had two children each and we couldn't gather them both ... in order to explain to them ...Or at least in five main spots to have someone, it would be better entertainment (S17).

Those visitors' mention brings us back to the problematic if visitors could be guided on their own in an interactive exhibition and if there must be expert personnel to "show the way" in particular exhibits or communicate knowledge. Moreover, it brings us back to the potential problems which could occur from the use of modern technology by people who are not acquainted with it. Of course, the fact that no other family that visited the mathematics exhibition mentions a lack of personnel, shows perhaps that probably parents did not have a specific problem with their tour in the exhibition without a guide.

Combination of Different Types of Exhibits

In relation to the variety of types of exhibits, the exhibition museologists' mention *"the interpretive media used include more traditional means, objects/ special constructions, images and texts and new media, like mechanic exhibits, multimedia interactive exhibits, video and virtual reality exhibits. It is interesting that the results from evaluation survey in museums of western Europe and north America agree generally that the ideal interpetive model in an exhibition is that which combines interactive with traditional- static- exhibits"* (Gazi et al, 2004).

But was the combination model of exhibits successful, according to the visitors' opinion?

We liked it because we were able to see in action some things that are not easily seen in books. Always when someone is using his hands, I mean when the mind combines with the hands it is always better than to read a book and imagine how a thing... works. Only when it has a game as a part of it teaching could be pleasant (S1).

because it helps children more ...because if it had only texts ... it would be boring for children, they would not stay ... perhaps they would not understand many things. While by that I guess something will be kept in mind, with the game (S11).

Another comment show using various means for the same subject can enhance learning or even seem more appealing:

Eratosthenes' sieve, for example, was something they have already done by hand, but it very interesting and they wanted to do it anyhow with the computer or with the checkers (S16).

About the interactive exhibits' role in museums a lot has been written, indicative here a reference to Adams & Moussouri (2002), who come to conclusions such as that contact with interactive exhibits is helpful in relation to museum experience, the multi- sense experiences in general contribute to dialogue, discovery, better understanding and reinforcement of the visitors' self belief, since they can try using their own power. They are also "family friendly" (Moussouri, 2003), something we saw for ourselves, since 9 out of 10 families asked about the combination of exhibits answered that it was positive.

In just one case the father was not so sure about the positive results of that combination:

Interesting (the combination), but in some moments a little ... too many choices ... from one hand of course children have choices and you can say it is better, on the other hand we got a little lost (S22).

Video

The exhibition videos gave information about the historical events and important people (mathematicians, astronomers, philosophers) of every period that the exhibition dealt with. They were enhanced with the use of 3D graphics, to explain for example theories being mentioned in each exhibition stop.

But it was the visitors' approach towards them that was remarkable:

With the videos we didn't deal a lot; time was pressing us too, but neither the previous time ... (S8)

Videos were the only interpretative means of the exhibition, which almost none of the visitors' group turned to in our research. This has a great deal of importance in relation to the museologists' opinion about videos in the mathematics exhibition: "*videos are an integral part of the exhibition's structure since they support one of their key messages- that the development of science is also determined by the cultural context of each historical period*" (Gazi et al, 2004, p.82).

But how the visitors justified their choice not to watch the videos?

Of course we could not watch the videos most of the times because we lost our coherence let's say, I mean it started somewhere in the middle ... (S16).

From the visitor's comment above, it becomes clear how important it is to state the exact duration of the videos (which were short, but the visitor did not have the opportunity to know that kind of information).

the worst (moment) was that I couldn't sit and listen what was in the... (video) you cannot see and listen at the same time (S18).

The last observation shows the need of the video to be in a more isolated space, so that the visitors could concentrate. This was also clear in a case, when the children of a family were forced to stop playing music, because another visitor made them a remark, since he could not watch the video (E7). The videos did not seem to work when it came to the families, of course perhaps that relates to the videos content, which addressed, according to the writer's personal opinion, children from the age of 9 or 10, who have dealt with those specific historic periods at school.

In one case indeed, there was a misunderstanding from the visitor's part (S21), because he thought that the videos were available only in English (English speaking visitors watched the video before him and had changed the language), something that shows the need for a better marking about how to switch the language when such an opportunity is available.

Exhibition Presentation: Multimedia Use in Education

Children are those who primarily mentioned that they would like a similar presentation at school, as in the exhibition:

and school like that. If it uses means more entertaining, perhaps the will for education, for learning would get bigger. The school tries with interactive tables, with various means, computers, with those means it can make it better. We personally don't have, in many schools though there are, in some there are not (boy 13, S13).

In two cases children mention that their preference to the way the exhibition is presented comparing it to a lesson at school:

I like it more this way, than a school lesson // me too....it doesn't show it only in text, it has it so you can try, it combines it with thing // yes, and the fact that you make your own conclusions, it is not written I mean, you understand it on your own (girl 14 and boy 10, S8).

The exhibition personally to me refreshed some knowledge with a more pleasant way, I believe I understood it better than in school. Moreover, I was able to learn the history of mathematics, how it all started, how it formed during time and by that I understood better some things, some rules (boy 13, S12).

Their desire for those kinds of applications in school environments is also expressed by parents:

seeing the mathematics in this exhibition area and practicing with the computers, having I mean the chance to play with mathematics, they (the children) realize that it is something more approachable, simpler, more interesting, it is something that should take place in every school, basically all schools must have a room like that and the pupils should experiment, sometimes they listen to the theory but they do not understand it, while when they can experiment, then they comprehend it more easily (S13).

New media like here can have a positive influence, I mean children could understand a lot better; today they use the internet to gather information from many sources, they compare, they deduct, they choose (S12).

As it is shown above, visitors need various kinds of presentation in educational environments nowadays; museums seem to be able to play a crucial role in that. More interesting facts are shown in Ellenbogen's research (2002), in relation to the ability to develop those kinds of informal education.

From the visitors' comments it is clear how important it is for their children the practical part in relation to understanding. This is an observation even from the time of John Dewey and it has a great influence in museums. It is something which, as it looks like, parents seem to take under consideration and for that reason they choose museums as alternative places of learning[10].

What People Need to Find in an Exhibition?

Not having the ability to play could prevent a family from visiting a museum exhibition, something that was mentioned by a parent that chose to watch only a virtual reality programme:

I believe that in that age exhibitions are a little difficult...he (my son) would get bored...I believe that a normal exhibition, ok, it is something usual...it just... intrigues more the senses, I mean when you have also an audio stimulus apart from the visual or in other exhibitions ... now the exhibitions are a little, ok, distant, you go there and it says "don't touch, don't grab", look, somehow it keeps you in a distance generally. It is different if you experience something (S13).

This specific family was the only one from the sample of the 6 families that made the choice of not visiting any exhibition deliberately (the others was either due to lack of time or because they had already visited the exhibitions). The reasons for that choice are explained by the parents, but also the older son:

I basically, my parents also said it, it must have more, visual effects I mean... I believe it would make it more interesting. That... but I don't like an exhibition so much, I prefer something like, something more live (boy 13, S13).

In addition to that, the mother mentioned that she had previously visited as a kindergarten teacher a modern art exhibition and she "got bored", because there were only paintings the visitors was not allowed to touch. So, she prevented her children from visiting another exhibition, believing that they were equally going to get bored. Those examples show us how determinant an experience could be for the future visitors' attitude about museums.

Other visitors mentioned that in order to visit an exhibition they would like to be interested in the subject themselves and the children and it should include action:

Action, something interactive certainly. I mean in the Planetarium (Eugenides Foundation) we have visited, everything that you had to press buttons, to do things, there, it caught their attention (S5).

But what is the exhibition visitors' opinion? What did they want to find in addition? Their needs were mostly at the same track, of adding and not changing or reducing material from the exhibition:

in relation to the title of the exhibition, more mechanical exhibits, but always for older ages... for our children's age something totally different... more playful (S6).

perhaps there should be a workshop with games, mathematic games for the children to solve, to work in groups (S12).

Even though there were a variety of interactive exhibits, mechanical and digital in the exhibition, as we can see, some parents mentioned that they would want more exhibits and activities for children. This visitors' wish for as many things as possible for children to do, to play, to touch, has been recorded in surveys in England, as Hooper-Greenhill (1994, pp.102-103) and Black (2005, pp. 24-26, 66-74) mention.

Problems of Understanding

Were there any problems or difficulties visitors encountered during their tour? A problem for the parents' part was when children found the exhibits difficult and did not understand them:

the worst (moment) is when the children don't know some things and can't continue, I mean when we talk about Pythagorean theorems and stuff ...and they dawdle all around (S11).

This specific comment shows that perhaps visitors evaluate the exhibits and they want their children to earn specific things from the exhibitions that have to do with knowledge and not just have fun (Moussouri 2003). Of course some parents, have realized that this specific visit, will contribute later also to the cognitive part, even if the time that the family is in the exhibition, children do not seem to be interested on what they listen.

Another difficulty was when the parents themselves had problems comprehending the exhibits:

the worst (moment) when we were stuck too and we had to read and explain (S17).

Apart from the difficulty of comprehension, also the lack of interest from the children is mentioned (the lack of comprehension and the lack of interest are probably connected, but it needs further research to be sure if the children were bored because they did not understand the exhibits). But all those mentions are very few in the total of the interviews and especially in this specific exhibition subject which is considered by a family "difficult" (S21), it is possible that the combination of the exhibits helped comprehension.

How Do the Visitors Characterize the Exhibition in General?

It is important to continue with some of the visitors' opinions, which will reveal to us how the visitors saw the mathematics exhibition. It should be noted that visitors were not asked especially about that, those opinions were expressed spontaneously during the talk- interview:

anyway it is a very interesting exhibition and with a lot … a lot of positive elements for information and education of the people visiting it (S21).

it was extremely interesting… an organized exhibition…it leaves you with the idea that it is well designed (S14).

admiration about all this relation of technology and knowledge that we can see here, only here in the Foundation (S18).

Positive comments were expressed almost by the total of the visitors:

I personally didn't know there was also a mathematics exhibition, but, it was a pleasant surprise, because it was something different, a plus, an advantage anyway in everything we saw today (S12).

This mention by the mother brings us back to the conversation about the visitors having many times biased opinions before visiting an exhibition, that perhaps exhibitions are not so interesting.

Comparing Exhibition and Virtual Reality

Apart from very few exceptions, families we spoke to had also watched virtual reality programmes and had an overall view of what virtual reality offered to them in comparison to the exhibition (although the theme of the virtual reality programme was not related to the one of the exhibition, at least directly; the visitors watched programmes that represented ancient Greek cities). A discount ticket was available from the museum, which included two exhibitions and two virtual reality programmes, so it is not certain if the families chose to visit the mathematics exhibition because they really wanted to or because it was already included to their ticket. Only in four cases (S4, S7, S8, S12, S17) the visitors knew about the exhibition and came specifically to see it, without that excluding their participation the same day to other programmes (like virtual reality programmes).

Most of the parents mentioned advantages of the exhibition against virtual reality (which was mostly characterized as impressive):

I believe that in the virtual reality that it simply has an image, of course it is very impressive, but it does not have something to touch, an object to come in relation with it, whereas the exhibition has activities and you can also participate to those… it is different to see than to try (S8).

you cannot compare the exhibition with the virtual reality, they are different. In the exhibition you participate and it is very important. Something you do not do in the virtual reality (S1).

in the virtual reality children see and understand how some things were. In the exhibition they also have the opportunity to experiment (S12).

the virtual reality was very good, because it was really like you were inside…but I don't know if I would enjoy so much the exhibition if it were virtual reality, I mean I liked it (the exhibition) how it was, because there were things to do, it was interactive (S16).

in the virtual reality you don't do anything, you see and hear, while in the exhibition you have to read, to think, to participate (S21).

Those families' comments bring into discussion whether the impressive image is something preferable by the visitors or if they favor something with more participation, since the interactivity in virtual reality is minimum (cf. Roussou, 2008). Most of the families had exactly understood what the virtual reality and the exhibition offered to them and their children.

On the other side, some families have a different opinion:

I believe that virtual reality impresses the children more and it intrigues their interest and … they devote themselves more, whereas a plain exhibition, ok it would not …I mean the interactive they do in the virtual reality with the questions helps you remember more things (S13).

Perhaps the exhibition would interest them, but the virtual reality seems to them more real, more impressive (S3).

I personally found the exhibition more interesting; for children I find virtual reality more interesting, because you seem to participate more; they are too young for the exhibition, they cannot even read well (S14).

In this specific case, from the three families that mentioned the suitability of virtual reality for their children, two (S3 and S13) did not visit the mathematics exhibition and the other family consisted of young children (5,5 and 7 years old) and the father focused on the lack of knowledge from the children's part.

From the visitors' comments we can conclude, that perhaps the ideal would be to combine a virtual reality programme (as it was originally designed, see endnote 8) with the same subject (Greek mathematics) with the exhibition, so that visitors would have a complete idea of the exhibits presented.

CONCLUSION

The present chapter was focused in families, a dynamic museum audience, with a lot of particularities in relation to other visitors and different needs. The conclusions reached, characterize the "typical" family and it is the common ground in most of the families of the present research. Certainly there are differentiations and there have being analyzed to the main part of our research.

From our research we can conclude that, even the families who haven't originally came to the museum knowing about the specific exhibition, were receptive to visiting that with their children and in the majority of the parents were next to their children, helping them when needed and explaining to them the most difficult parts. Most of the families were not using the helpful information given by the exhibition and followed their own course in it, not by a chronological order but according to the exhibits they enjoyed the most. They expressed themselves positively about the variety of media; in addition, parents and children behaved differently to the multimedia exhibits. Parents sometimes seemed to prefer the exhibition against virtual reality, due to the interaction the first included.

Another interesting fact was that parents "gave space" to their children to show their preferences, to choose exhibits and experiment with those as much time as they wanted. In a very few cases there was an organized guided tour by parents; on the contrary, there was flexibility from the parents' part and adaptability when their children seemed to get tired or lose their interest. The present research confirmed Moussouri's findings (2003), about a "child- oriented" family museum visit. The majority of the parents spoke positively about the mathematics exhibition and children seemed to have a nice time in the exhibition, mainly because they played with the exhibits, mechanical and digital.

Parents on the interviews showed that they do not rest in the school's role, they desire to enhance it and offer various experiences to their children from those offered by formal education. Parents are generally informed about the advantages of new technologies and give a great importance to the children's entertainment parallel to their education.

In relation to learning, most of the parents (at least those of an older age), considered that learning is accomplished, mainly because museum finds interesting ways to motivate the children's interest and present with a pleasant way what they have heard in school. The results of learning, especially in exhibitions designed based on constructivist theories are confirmed (Hein 1998) and the present survey comes to complement the research till now.

It would be also interesting to study the characteristics of families that do not visit museums and analyze the reasons of their choice. A hint has given from some families that did not visit the exhibition and preferred the virtual reality (that they consider exhibitions boring), but this is just a hypothesis.

Closing, it is important to mention what parents wanted from the museum, in order to be pleased from their visit. We could say that parents asked for interactive exhibitions, were positive in using new technologies in museums because they believed their children responded with a greater mood in everything new. Moreover, since children (mostly) are positive in using new technologies, it would be nice to design applications that could demand multiple users, so that the social aspect of the visit is not neglected. Our desire is, to expand researching about families in other museum and meet more and more interactive exhibitions in Greece and, of course, more and more families in museums.

ACKNOWLEDGMENT

The author would like to thank the Administration and the Museum Educators of Hellenic Cosmos, for their help (practical and moral) during the research and Costis Dallas, Panteion University, supervisor of the Master's thesis, for his advice and guidelines. Thanks also to all the families that participated, for being so generous about their time and thoughts. Special thanks to my parents, my husband Dimitris Christopoulos and my two sons for being so patient and supportive.

REFERENCES

Adams, M., & Moussouri, T. (2002, May). *The interactive experience: linking research and practice.* Paper presented at the Victoria & Albert Museum International Conference about Interactive Learning in Museums of Art and Design, London. UK.

Ash, D. (2004). Reflective scientific sense-making dialogue in two languages: The science in the dialogue and the dialogue in the science. *Science Education, 88*(6), 855–884. doi:10.1002/sce.20002

Bicknell, S., & Farnello, G. (Eds.) (1993). *Museum Visitor Studies in the 90s.* London, UK: Science Museum.

Black, G. (2005). *The Engaging Museum: Developing Museums for Visitor Involvement.* New York, USA: Routledge.

Caulton, T. (1998). *Hands-on Exhibitions- Managing Interactive Museums and Science Centre.* London, New York: Routledge.

Crowley, K., Callanan, M. A., Jipson, J. L., Galco, J., Topping, K., & Shrager, J. (2001). Shared scientific thinking in everyday parent-child activity. *Science Education, 85*(6), 712–732. doi:10.1002/sce.1035

Csikszentmihalyui, M., & Hermanson, K. (1999). Intrinsic motivation in museums: why does one want to learn? In E. Hooper-Greenhill (Ed.), The Educational Role of the Museum (pp. 146- 160). London; New York, Routledge.

Diamond, J. (1986). The behavior of family groups in science museums. *Curator, 29*(2), 139–154. doi:10.1111/j.2151-6952.1986.tb01434.x

Dierking, L., & Falk, J. (1994). Family behavior and learning in informal science settings: A review of the research. *Science Education, 78*(1), 57–72. doi:10.1002/sce.3730780104

Economou, M., & Pujol Tost, L. (2011). Evaluating the use of virtual reality and multimedia applications for presenting the past. In G. Styliaras, D. Koukopoulos, & F. Lazarinis (Eds.), Handbook of Research on Technologies and Cultural Heritage: Applications and Environments (pp. 223–239). Hershey, PA: IGI Global. doi:10.4018/978-1-60960-044-0.ch011

Ellenbogen, K. M. (2002). Museums in family life: An ethnographic case study. In G. Leinhardt, K. Crowley, & K. Knutson (Eds.), *Learning conversations in museums* (pp. 81–101). Mahwah, NJ: Lawrence Erlbaum Associates.

Falk, J., & Dierking, L. (2000). *Learning from Museums: Visitors Experiences and the Making of Meaning.* USA: Altamira Press.

Flick, U., von Kardoff, E., & Steinke, I. (Eds.). (2004). *A Companion to Qualitative Research. Free University Berlin.* Germany: Sage Publications.

Foundation of the Hellenic World & Hellenic Cosmos Official Website. (n. d.). Retrieved from http://www.fhw.gr/fhw/index.php?lg=2&state=pages&id=82

Gazi, A., & Nikiforidou, A. (2008). Η χρήση των *νέων τεχνολογιών* στις εκθέσεις μουσείων: *ένα μέσον ερμηνείας.* In Α. Μπούνια, Νικονάνου Ν. & Οικονόμου Μ. (Ed.) Η τεχνολογία στην υπηρεσία της πολιτισμικής κληρονομιάς (pp. 373-384). Αθήνα: Καλειδοσκόπιο.

Gazi, A., Nikiforidou, A., Kamara, A., & Paschalidis, G. (Eds.). (2003). Is There an Answer to Everything? A journey to the world of Greek mathematics. Athens: Foundation of the Hellenic World.

Gazi, A., Nikiforidou, A., & Moussouri, T. (2004). Μια έκθεση για τα αρχαία ελληνικά μαθηματικά: Πλαίσιο ανάπτυξης και μουσειολογικός σχεδιασμός. *Museology, 1.* Retrieved from http://museology.ct.aegean.gr/articles/2007127115655.pdf

Given, L. (Ed.). (2008). *The SAGE Encyclopedia of Qualitative Research Methods.Charles Sturt University.* Australia: SAGE Publications Inc. doi:10.4135/9781412963909

Glaser, B. G. (1992). *Basics of grounded theory analysis.* Mill Valley, CA: Sociology Press.

Hein, G. (1998). *Learning in the Museum.* London, New York: Routledge.

Hooper-Greenhill, E. (1994). *Museum and their Vistitors.* London, New York: Routledge.

Merriman, N. (2000). *Beyond the Glass Case: The Past, the Heritage and the Public.* London, UK: Institute of Archaeology.

Meyer, B. (2013). Transporting and Preserving Interactive New Media Exhibits through Time. *Exhibitionist-. National Association for Museum Exhibition, 32*(2), 46–53.

Moussouri, T. (1997). Family Agendas and the Museum Experience. In G. T. Denford (Ed.), *Museums for the 21*st *century* (pp. 20-30). Liverpool: Society of Museum Archaeologists.

Moussouri, T. (2003). Negotiated Agendas: Families in Science and Technology Museums. *International Journal of Technology Management, 25*(5), 477–489. doi:10.1504/IJTM.2003.003114

Moussouri, T., Nikiforidou, A., & Gazi, A. (2003). Front- end and formative evaluation of an exhibition on Greek Mathematics. American Association of Museums, 42-47.

Moussouri, T., Nikiforidou, A. & Gazi, A. (2004). What Can Museums Learn from their Visitors: the Role of Evaluation in Exhibition Development. *IMEros 4*(2), FHW, 192-206.

Rhee, B. T., & Kim, D. J. (2013). Summative evaluation of children's creative engagement through interactive exhibits: a case study on the participatory exhibition of masterpieces in South Korea. *International Journal of Advanced Science and Technology, 59*, 1–12. doi:10.14257/ijast.2013.59.01

Roussou, M. (2006). Οι τάσεις στο χώρο των *νέων τεχνολογιών* για την έρευνα και την ανάδειξη της πολιτιστικής κληρονομιάς. *Tetradia Mouseiologias, 3*, 56–61.

Schmidt, C. (2004). The Analysis of Semi- structured Interviews. In Flick et al. (Eds.), *A Companion to Qualitative Research* (pp. 253–258). Australia: Sage Publications.

Serrell, B., & Adams, R. (1998). *Paying Attention: Visitors and Museum Exhibitions.* Washington, D.C., USA: American Association of Museums.

Silverman, D. (2005). *Doing qualitative research.* London, UK: Sage Publications Ltd.

Stellaki, P. (2010) *Οικογένειες και μάθηση στο χώρο του μουσείου: μελέτη περίπτωσης για τον "Ελληνικό Κόσμο", πολιτιστικό κέντρο του Ιδρύματος Μείζονος Ελληνισμού.* [Unpublished master's thesis]. Panteion University, Athens, Greece.

Wood, R. (1996). Families. In G. Durbin (Ed.), *Developing Museum Exhibitions for Lifelong Learning* (pp. 77–82). London: The Stationery Office.

KEY TERMS AND DEFINITIONS

Child-Oriented: In relation to a museum visit, it means that the children are the ones that define the course of the visit, for example where to stop, what exhibits to see, how much time to stay in an exhibition etc.

Formative Evaluation: Evaluation during exhibition design, mainly to test interactive exhibit elements, how ergonomic they are, if they attract the visitors (e.g. their graphics) and whether visitors could comprehend them.

Front-End Evaluation: Evaluation that takes place before or during the planning of an exhibition, in order to find out what the visitors know about the topic of the exhibition designed.

Greek Mathematics: The history of Greek mathematics includes the period of about 1000 years, from the 6th century BC till the 4th century AD.

Interactivity: The ability to have a dialogue, e.g. with a computer machine, that responds to a person's actions.

Naturalistic Observation: A method, where the researcher observes the sample on its setting.

Non-Participant Observation: A method, where data is collected by observing behavior without interacting with the participants.

Qualitative Method: A method, mainly used in Social Sciences, which aims in better understanding of human behavior though in- depth studying of small groups of people.

Virtual Reality: (here) the term refers to a dome-shaped Virtual Reality "Theatre", named "Tholos", which hosts digital collections. In the "Tholos", interactive programmes like representations of ancient cities are presented (where visitors could answer questions, e.g. which specific direction you want to follow etc.), as well as three- dimensional films. The term also refers to another smaller system, called "Cave®".

ENDNOTES

[1]   The term museum in this text is used more broadly and includes various educational foundations, archaeological sites, botanical- zoological places, planetariums, national forests etc.

[2]   On the same text it is mentioned that a survey in the United States showed that 60% of the regular visitors stated that their interest about museums was formed as families' members and only 3% as members of school groups.

[3]   For detailed information about qualitative research and theoretical data about methodological and practical issues about research see Silverman, 2005; Flick, von Kardoff, Steinke (Ed.), 2004; Given (Ed.), 2008.

[4]   Results of visitors' studies especially through observation of visitors in exhibitions in Serrell & Adams, (1998).

[5]   That was the reason why, two of all the families we addressed to, refused to participate to our survey.

[6]   The FHW, which was envisioned, founded and funded by the family of Lazaros Efraimoglou, is a privately funded, not-for-profit cultural institution based in Athens. Its foundation was ratified in 1993 by unanimous vote of the Hellenic Parliament. FHW's mission is the preservation of Hellenic history and tradition, the creation of an awareness of the universal dimension of Hellenism and the promotion of its contribution to cultural evolution. Hellenic Cosmos, FHW's Cultural Centre, was inaugurated in 1998 and is located at 254 Pireos Street. It is a multifunctional cultural area that has hosted various events, from exhibitions and educational programmes, Virtual Reality programmes, documentaries produced by the FHW, conferences and seminars etc. (information taken from the official website of the FHW).

[7]   Detailed information about the context of the exhibition, see the exhibition's catalogue (Gazi, Nikiforidou, Kamara, & Paschalidis, 2003), as well as Gazi, Nikiforidou, & Moussouri (2004).

[8]   The virtual reality exhibits that completed the exhibition visit were usually open only for schools or other group of 10 people approximately. They dealt with a specific exhibition stop and visualized the inventions of Archimedes.

[9]   A synopsis of older surveys in Dierking & Falk (1994).

[10]   In relation to interaction with the environment and its contribution to learning in the museum, see Csikszentmihalyui & Hermanson (1999, pp. 146-160)

Chapter 4
Developing Augmented Reality Applications Using Branded Authoring Environments

Ioannis Deliyannis
Interactive Arts Research Lab, Greece

Dalila Honorato
Interactive Arts Research Lab, Greece

ABSTRACT

In this chapter, we present the main interaction design issues that arise during the development of edutainment scenarios through the use of branded augmented reality (AR) authoring environments. Most proprietary AR systems offer limited interaction features within their entry-level version, while licensing unlocks the desired advanced features. In order to overcome this problem we employ experimental multimedia development methods for the design of content for those platforms, enabling the development of fully featured case studies where interaction is implemented both physically and virtually. The introduction and literature research sections are complemented by selected experimental case studies that explore the interaction capabilities. It is shown how these may be implemented using limited AR resources. The chapter concludes with the presentation of the social software perspective of the communication process, as the application areas and the content domain presented in this work feature clear collaborative potential that needs to be addressed by system design.

INTRODUCTION

The interest for the development of augmented reality (AR) applications has increased in the last few years, mainly due to the replacement of earlier QR-code technologies (Rowles, 2013) with natural visual tracking recognition (Kerdvibulvech). This feature clearly offers multiple potential uses as it removes the need for visible markers: images, drawings, items and physical spaces can be used as markers that initiate the augmentation. In addition, the wide availability of handheld multimedia-enabled mobile devices (mobile phones, PDA's), combined with their increasing processing power and Internet con-

DOI: 10.4018/978-1-4666-8659-5.ch004

nectivity offer a developmental platform featuring all the technological characteristics that may support augmentation. The most interesting characteristic of augmented reality applications using visual tracking technologies is the fact that everything around the user may potentially be used as an information trigger (Van Krevelen & Poelman, 2010). Furthermore, multiple users may be presented with different types of content, within the same information space, as marker-to-content-mapping is identified uniquely under each AR system. Typical application areas range from advertising campaigns (Stoyanova, Gonçalves, Brito, & Coelho, 2013) and product catalogues (Patil, Balar, Malviya, & Prasad) to art-based applications (T. Song & Jiashan, 2013), museums (Ramirez et al., 2013), tourism (Casella & Coelho, 2013) and educational systems (Cheah, Quah, Wong, & Zainon). An important feature of this technology is its potential connectivity and interoperability with different platforms. Clearly, the development of wearable technologies that include Google Glasses, Microsoft HoloLens and other competing systems that are bound to complement or replace mobile phones and tablets is the targeted technology. These offer a number of features which renders them ideal for navigation in real-life spaces as they provide a new platform for development, permitting the display of augmented content (Paszkiel, 2014).

However the majority of AR platforms used to recognise, retrieve and deliver the content are bound by limitations in various forefronts (Kerdvibulvech). These include poor system performance in varying hardware specifications, reduced artifact recognition in variable lighting conditions, various user-positioning issues as they can only recognise a specific perspective and poor support for the development of systems featuring complex game-like interaction. In this work we particularly focus on the final issue of interaction as it poses a significant limiting factor evident in the majority of AR systems. In order to study and overcome the limitations introduced for each scenario, we developed with our student teams a number of case studies using freely available branded AR authoring environments as experimentation platforms. Various design issues of the systems developed are presented and discussed in this work where we particularly focus on interaction capabilities and the methods developed in order to overcome and implement the end-system.

From the software development perspective, augmented reality multiplexes the processes of creation, integration, encoding, transmission identification and presentation of content containing various media types. Interaction with multimedia content often introduces simultaneous interaction of multiple content types across multiple users in systems referred as "dynamic" (Nardelli, 2010; Trifonova, Ahmed, & Jaccheri, 2009; Trifonova, Jaccheri, & Bergaust, 2008). As interactive multimedia enable the development of customized computer systems and applications, we can safely assume that within a few years this research-field will continue to play a key role at the forefront of developments. In Greece this major shift impacts the sector of new-media arts and more particularly interactive multimedia art. Artists combine multimedia technologies and push sensing systems to the limit in their attempts to discover new possibilities of creation and dissemination of content to their audiences (Deliyannis, 2012; Ioannis Deliyannis, 2013; I. Deliyannis, 2013; Deliyannis, 2014, 2015; Deliyannis, Giannakoulopoulos, & Oikonomidou, 2013; Deliyannis & Papaioannou, 2014). Experimental multimedia technologies excite the imagination of developers and supports their creativity demands, as they offer a palette of new tools for creativity and user-content interaction, while they allow digital delivery of their content over the Internet (Deliyannis, 2012). Devices such as radio, television, computers and sensors are often used as tools to create and present innovative works of art. During this process, various experiments have resulted in challenging the boundaries of art and technology. Typical areas of application of experimental multimedia technology are not only limited to interactive-art performances, happenings and installations that enjoy growing interest and popularity, but they also extend to everyday applications and services

(Strapatsakis, 2008). Many digital applications are developed to support artistic creation in areas that include painting, sculpture, photography, cinema and music. Developers utilize commonly available hardware and software platforms in order to algorithmically extend the capabilities of existing services and applications (Apostolopoulos et al., 2012; Cesar & Chorianopoulos, 2009; Deliyannis et al., 2013; Deliyannis & Kanellopoulos, 2008; Poulos, Deliyannis, & Floros, 2012, 2013). New forms of art are displayed as computer-art, internet-art, multimedia-art, animation and virtual-reality, which alone or in combination with other techniques have already made their presence felt in the field of artistic creation. Artwork in major museums, galleries and journals is a result of state-of-the-art developments on the multifaceted issue of interactive multimedia art. Although the use of new media offers great expressive flexibility to developers, it also introduces new physical limitations, inherited from the physical limitations of technologies employed. Many developers that utilise interactive multimedia technologies to create innovative projects, often face technical problems and have to limit their expectations, or rely on external aid to complete the project. Now more than ever before it is evident that the digital divide influences content experts, as they do not possess the necessary knowledge that will allow them to exploit the expanded opportunities afforded by the technologies of the Information Society.

This research focuses on the development of augmented reality applications, an area that lies within the field of experimental multimedia. Emphasis is given on the qualitative parameters that are important for correct content representation. Today, this is a principal requirement, particularly for rich-media applications that include interactive television systems, mobile phone applications and new media Arts installations. We aim to provide the necessary theoretical background in order to allow readers to verify content quality on every stage of the multimedia development process. For the development of such applications no special computer skills are required as the underlying technologies and standards used for the development and deployment of such systems allow non-experts to build fully-featured applications without programming skills.

AUGMENTED REALITY CASE STUDIES USING BRANDED END-TO-END PLATFORMS

For the development of AR systems we evaluated the capabilities of branded authoring environments as they tend to offer frequent updates, do not require programming and ensure that their browsing application functions within a large number of operating systems and hardware platforms. These include Alive app, Augment, Aurasma, Daqri, Fingo, PendAR, GiftAR, Google Goggles, Junaio, Layar, LZRTAG, Nokia City Lens, RevEye, Right on Target Media, VYZAR, Wikitude, XARMEX, Zappar and ARPA. A number of related testing criteria were selected for each case study in order to reflect the implementation's intended use. The following sections describe the issues that arose during our investigation. Typical issues that needed to be tested before development include system performance in open and enclosed spaces, variable lighting conditions, marker-recognition and content retrieval performance and support for media-types required for the presentation that may include anything between 3D models, animation, video, text, images, hypermedia, panoramas, interactive audio and dynamic interactive links (Weedon, Miller, Franco, Moorhead, & Pearce, 2014). For the purpose of this chapter we use the following conventions: we call "*trigger content*" the representation of the scene or item that the system is called to identify in order to deliver the content. Upon successful recognition, the trigger image is linked to one or more media items termed "*target media*", which are used to augment the user's media space.

Augmented Reality Marker Recognition in Open Spaces

Accurate and fast marker-identification is one of the most important issues that developers need to resolve, as it is clearly a prerequisite for successful AR system implementation. Within most AR platforms, the visual recognition algorithm evaluates trigger content using different algorithms and settings. This introduces varying results that may range anywhere between easy and immediate recognition to difficult or impossible identification. In most cases the content stored as a trigger-image on the system is often decomposed and dealt differently across various authoring environments, hence it is important for the developer to capture digitally and experiment with different platforms in order to identify the most appropriate for the task in hand.

The methodology employed for the development of the educational interactive-games in open spaces is described below. During the initial stage, student teams were introduced to the proposed archeological and architectural units, within the historical center of the city of Corfu at an informal meeting with multiple objectives: the recognition of narrative possibilities connected to a building, the understanding of user-movement, distance and physical effort in real space gameplay and the listing of strategies to capture and maintain the visitor's attention. Ultimately, each team was asked to identify the target-audience, describe the information domain and select the game-development space.

The second stage was fieldwork, carried out by individual teams. Their objectives include the identification of candidate spaces and markers (items) of interest, which can be incorporated in the game script. Important factors for the selection were the distance among those and their visibility during the day. Notes were collected as well as drawing and photography, which were used as recording methods for the scenario storyboard.

The third stage carried out by each team involved historical research, concerning the space and the selected markers. Bibliographical research was completed by interviews and discussions with employees and visitors of the selected spaces. At the end of this stage each team was asked to select the target group and the game genre, documented in a report that combines historical research and the rest of the collected information

The fourth stage included creative writing and each group had to deliver the game script accompanied by its flowchart, floor plan, media choice and storyboard. The script was discussed within class concerning content (information and emotion), having in consideration edutainment theories such as activity, constructivism, flow, motivation and situated learning, and the importance of transition clues was underlined.

The fifth stage involved the development of the projects and testing. Platform selection commenced only when student groups possess the entire scenario, which was completed by a report containing content presentation requirements. In this, students describe technical information about each information node, a process that can clearly reveal the possible technological limitations.

The "Old Asylum of Corfu" edutainment case study was a challenge to create an alternative reality game in real place. The project was initially designed for application in a closed space but was later adapted to open space. The gameplay was developed in the courtyard, instead of the treatment building, in the Old Asylum of Corfu, maintaining this way its initial connection to real place. The target group was targeting users aged 18 and over. The Old Asylum of Corfu opened in 1838 and it was the first mental hospital in Greece. The psychiatric services have been transferred to other location in Corfu and, presently, in its neoclassical buildings, are located three departments of the Ionian University. The narrative takes place in 1941; it is constructed as a detective story where the gamer has to find the author of the murderer of Anthony Nikolouzou, who was found dead in the South courtyard of the Asylum in 1940. During the investigation, the gamers in the role of the detective have to uncover the truth behind a series of multiple murders and investigate the life of six employees of the Asylum and find connections with several metaphysical clues.

The "Old Fortress of Corfu" edutainment case study is designed as system that offers at each point variable exploration options for fortress visitors, while the user is allowed to interactively choose their visiting path through the fortress. Users who select to use the AR application, are prompted to choose between three different systems: a general guide of the fortress that presents information while the user scans the area from specific points; an edutainment tour for children who have to discover information about the fortress in order to complete their mission; and a master system designed for archaeologists and historians which presents links to all the digitised information available today, enabling direct on-site access to the historical content. Each system supports different routes within the same information space that shares the same points of interest (Figure 1). It becomes clear that this kind of application param-eterisation covers multiple presentation and interaction requirements, all supported through the same platform and technologies. In addition, users employ their own devices and mobile networks, a fact that reduces greatly the cost to support and maintain the system. However, in order to develop professional-level service and Quality of Service, we propose the use of a dedicated wireless network and the use of a number of pre-determined devices that have been appropriately tested in various conditions, ensuring the consistency of the user experience.

As all three implementation scenarios use the same information points, it is important to ensure that the buildings will be identified efficiently, regardless of the variation of lighting and weather conditions. Our experimentation with various AR platforms revealed that the trigger image was identified faster by most systems when its pixel-density was reduced significantly (below 800x600 pixels). Despite the increased recognition performance achieved with the reduction of trigger-image resolution, the recogni-tion rate still varied greatly with different lighting conditions: early morning and late night recognition was more difficult than mid-day. Our testing process revealed that the time-based change of the shadow behind the columns of figure 2 affected the recognition process. One way to resolve the issue was to use time-lapse images as triggers, enabling the system to visually identify many instances at different times during the day. This approach introduces system delays and inaccuracy, as multiple images may be identified simultaneously by the underlying AR platform, resulting in a constant reappearance of the displayed information. The issue was resolved when we digitally masked out the front face side of the building, enabling the system to identify the item without the shadow. This may be attributed to the fact that the reduction of the resolution is followed by reduction of contrast, permitting the system to identify images, which contain reduced colour information.

Augmented Reality Marker Recognition and Scalable Navigation in Closed Spaces

The case of the Greek National Gallery, Corfu branch may be considered as a characteristic instance of a closed space implementation. Here, two student teams were asked to design and develop edutainment systems enabling user-groups with specific characteristics and interests to explore the works of art.

The methodology for the development of the educational interactive-games in closed spaces was altered at certain points, in order to suit the task in hand. First, students were introduced to the collec-tion of the Greek National Gallery in Corfu during an informal meeting with the director of the branch.

Figure 1. The real-life map of the fortress with the information points

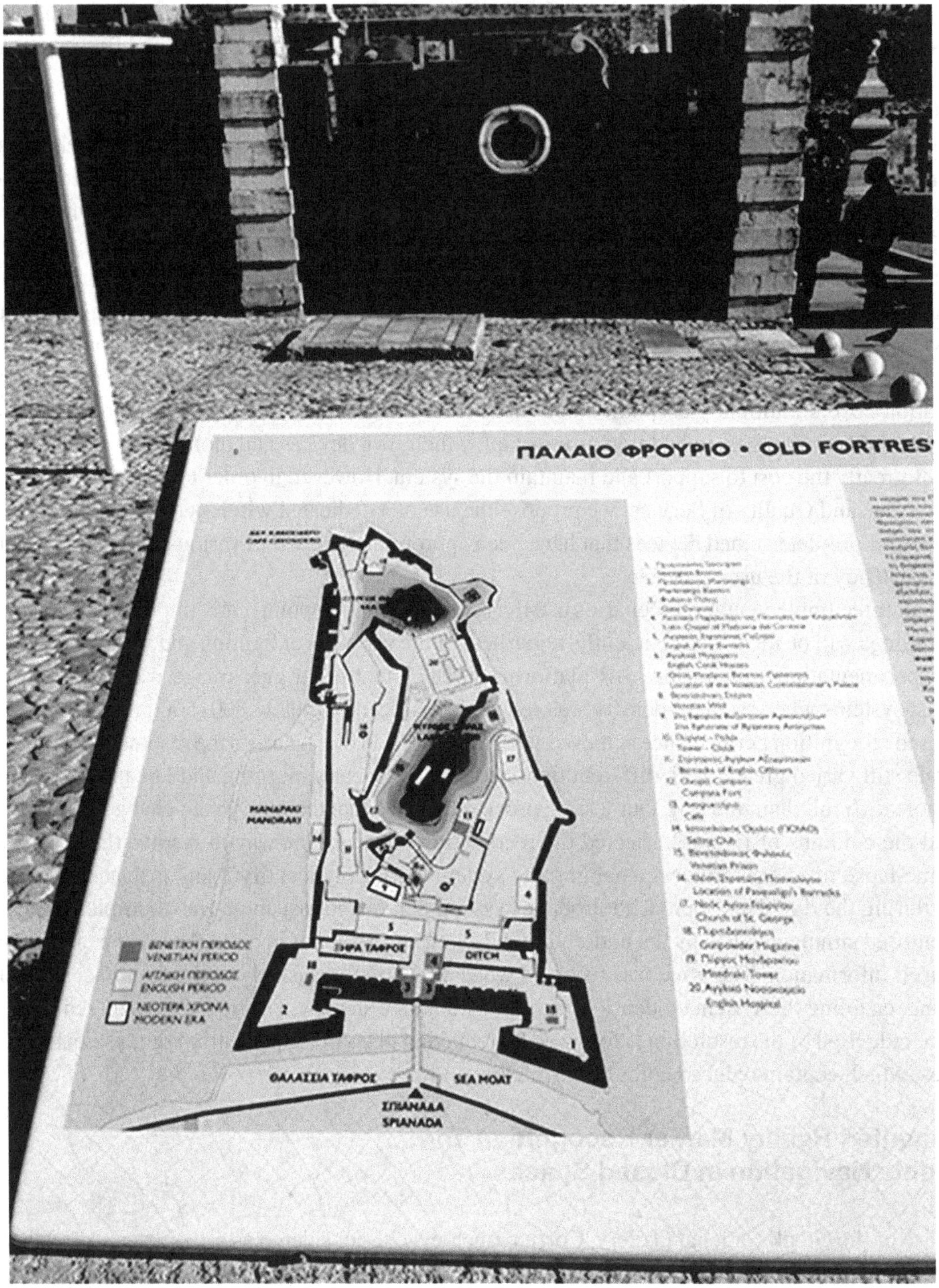

Figure 2. The St. George temple trigger image used to identify a common point of interest used by three distinct AR implementations

During this stage, student groups were introduced to a complete description of the collections and their topology, the main target groups that commonly visit the museum (elementary and high-school students) and the visitor information that is available to visitors from museum guides, the museum website and the curators. Students were able to ask the director of the gallery questions concerning safety issues and typical technical and space limitations. Figure 3 presents the physical interaction of the user with the collection within the ground museum floor.

The second stage involved fieldwork at the Greek National Gallery, after visiting hours. The objective of this stage is to recognise the space architecturally, explore alternative visit trajectories and selecting potential paintings to integrate within the storytelling process. During this visit students collected data, mostly notes with random keywords based on their reaction to the paintings, but also topics such as the localisation of favorite art works (based on intuitive appreciation, such as immediacy and duration) and ergonomic measures (concerning individual and group mobility in the exposition spaces) were addressed, using both drawing and photography.

The third stage included creative writing and was mostly based in brainstorming having as source the keywords and the categorization of favored art works, previously localised and placed on the floor plan, both collected during the previous stage. The first challenge during the creative writing process was to identify common patterns within the paintings, starting by the individual identification of the thematic narrative and visual art technique, in order to avoid the simplistic chronological approach of

Figure 3. The floor diagram presenting the proposed visiting route. Note here that grouped items are represented using a single red line (7,8) while separate adjacent items using two (1,3)

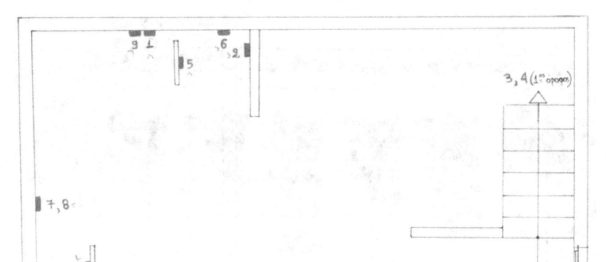

the game script. The results of this challenge were the automatic rejection of items that did not seem to fit into some category and the identification of each teams' thematic based essentially on: a. themes depicted or b. depiction techniques and materials. The second challenge within the same process was to create radical forms of flow, in order to invert the common visit trajectory set by the organization and display of the art works at the Greek National Gallery, by proposing design strategies to influence visitors' spatial behavior, such as the use of arrows or colored lines placed on the floor. Based on the results of these two challenges the teams had to develop a first draft game script, that had to include the paintings organization and transition clues, keywords, based on the theme depicted or the visual elements presented, and a coherent narrative structure and style.

The fourth stage includes three parts. The first part includes research for information concerning the artist, art movement and theme depicted for each painting selected to be a part of the game. The second part involves reviewing and adapting the first draft of the game script in order to include information in the narrative and the selection of the medium for the delivery of the educative experience (text, sound narration, photography, video and mixed-media) according to the narrative style. The third part involved drawing of the storyboards.

Finally the fifth stage was the development of the projects and testing where selection of the appropriate branded AR authoring platform was performed.

The projects developed by each team were quite different concerning narrative content. Their case studies are described below. They have been practically been presented to the public as a demonstration of narrative capabilities that support interactive storytelling.

First team: The project, based in traditional oral storytelling, is a narrated educational interactive-game, based in a selected series of ten paintings, from the end of the 19th century and the beginning of the 20th century, depicting scenes of the private sphere (such as a lady and her dog, a family meal, a boy rehearsing trumpet or a girl walking in a garden), describe how one hundred years ago, the community of Corfu would spend the 1st of May. The team decided to include a floor sticker in the entrance of the Greek National Gallery with the character of a dog present in the first painting. This sticker can be scanned and this way the starting point was easily defined. The story develops as a multiple narrative of the two characters depicted in the first painting, Mrs. Chara and her dog. The dog was chosen by the team as the narrator responsible for the transition clues (mostly objects, faces and colors), while Mrs. Chara tells, in flashback, her memories as a child in Corfu. The story being narrated is not connected with the historical references of each painting. Instead the team chose a more ethnographic approach for the content while the medium chosen was video, with details of the painting, the narration of the two characters and different sounds connected with the theme depicted. The educative experience focus on issues such as emigration, growing older, friendship, nature, family and tradition. At the end of the story the participants in the game are incited to draw their own images of the 1st of May, which in Greece is celebrated with picnics in the countryside and kite flying.

The team proposed to develop a historical novel for 6-12 year old children, delivered through handheld devices and AR technologies. Scanning the paintings in a particular order activates narration. The story is designed to teach children about the selected paintings and reconstruct through narration how life used to be during that era. In addition, each point contains additional information and clues while users are instructed to find the next painting in order to continue on the story. However, this is not always an easy task, particularly at a national gallery setting where only a small sub-set of items is used for this particular scenario. The wide number of paintings, sculptures and new-media-art items offer the opportunity to experiment with trigger-image recognition performance and user-navigation within the exhibits. The availability of constant lighting conditions is advantageous as it may aid the image-recognition process for single trigger-images while developers may employ it in order to group together multiple images, which may be recognised as a single information unit. By using this technique, developers may implement a scalable presentation environment able to adjust the displayed information according to the user's distance from the exhibits.

Figure 4. The paintings represented by 7 and 8 are shown with their frames removed, ready to be inserted to the AR environment in order to be recognised as a combined marker used by users that scan the room for information from further distances

Second team: The project is based on a series of 14 selected paintings organized chronologically according to the art movement and visual technique. This project intends to work as an interactive catalog dedicated to Art History in Modern Greece, providing complementary information about some of the most valuable works available to the public at the Greek National Gallery. The narrative is directly connected with the historical references of each painting. The medium chosen was mostly video with narration, except for two works where the team preferred to include animation and dialogue. The transition clues concerned mostly the themes depicted (characters) and, in some cases, the visual elements presented in the painting (colors and forms). The educative experience focuses on: details concerning the life and creations of an artist and main characteristics of a specific art movement. Although the initial project was the approach of fine art painting techniques and materials, this idea was eventually rejected, by the team, during the fourth stage. The game script can be considered as a direct narrative, integrating description, using expressions and questions adapted to the standard verbal communication of the target group, in order to maintain the young visitors' attention. The main objective of the team was promoting the identification with the artwork and channeling the visit to an art exhibition space as a positive experience.

Third team: The project is based on a series of 8 paintings, selected and organized according to the thematic History of Modern Greece, depicting scenes dating from the 19th century. The team chose as narrator the historical figure of Ioannis Kapodistrias who was minister of the Septinsular Republic (1800-1807) and an extremely important character in the development of the island of Corfu and Greece as an independent state. The objective was the acquaintance with a real personality, one of the more respected ones in modern Greek history, with which name and depiction the visitors were already familiar. Because Kapodistrias is not physically present in any of the paintings, the team decided to include him together with basic instructions concerning the development of game play in a wall sticker at the entrance of the Greek National Gallery. The game script included narration, with the description of the depicted theme and historical data, followed by a more contemporaneous look of the theme in the form of: a) architectural and scenic photographs accompanied by environmental sounds or b) video with animated characters accompanied by dialogues containing social commentaries. The transition clues given were not verbalized, instead the team decided to provide the image of the following painting, directing this way their searching strategy towards observation based on visual identification of an item in digital form and real space. The educative experience focus on issues such as time differences concerning past and present, the understanding of action-consequence and the interconnection of social, political and economic factors in culture and environment.

IMPLEMENTING GAME-LIKE INTERACTIVITY

Implementing game-like interactive systems using AR platforms that offer basic interaction and simple mapping between *"trigger content"* to *"target media"*, is clearly a challenge that requires alternative implementation approaches (Kirner & Kirner, 2013). First we discuss the case where serial and dynamic content routes are multiplexed in one system, enabling the user to interactively navigate through content that supports both serial and user-defined routes (Schianchi). Then we discuss different approaches that allow developers to create score-based games that may be used by one or many players simultaneously (Nilsen, Linton, & Looser, 2004).

From Serial To User-Defined Content Access

For many case studies it is imperative for an AR system to allow or even encourage free user-navigation through content (Leiva, Guevara, Rossi, & Aguayo, 2014). The direct analogy of this process is introduced at the WWW level where users create their own investigative paths by interactively accessing hypermedia. The Old Corfu Fortress information nodes identified within the physical space (Figure 1) describe a natural navigation system, which multiplexes linear and non-linear content access. A serial narrative structure (first four points when the visitor enters the Spianada square) is followed by the selection between two candidate routes that the visitor may choose to follow (middle left or right), that both lead to the lighthouse (top-center). For the first four points, the content at each node is designed to relate to its adjacent point, enabling the user to view again the presentation when exiting the fortress from the opposite perspective (facing the exit). Interactive routes offer generalised content while directional information is ignored, allowing the users to navigate themselves towards the next point of interest. This implies that the scenario for each point is specifically designed to allow navigational freedom, by taking into consideration varying user paths.

Ambiguity within the AR scenario design is particularly desirable as the users often multiplex different routes. The fact that it is not possible to predict user behavior at all presentation nodes, or the possibility of an erroneous user choice should therefore be viewed as another interaction opportunity. It is proposed therefore that the scenario should be written in a way that enriches the user experience with the freedom to explore the physical space and offer a rewarding experience.

A second National Gallery edutainment case study also employs this approach in its attempt to allow primary school students to explore information about the content and the artists who created the artwork (Figure 5). As this is a scenario implemented in a closed space with all the information visible to user, a different content-access strategy was introduced which involved the introduction of a unique card-based printed symbol under each painting. The content access scenario allows full interaction and the user is prompted to explore the paintings and identify common features and information. When visitors want to match and compare two or more paintings, they have to pick-up the symbols, join them together and scan them with the AR application. Correct matching reveals information about the selected paintings. Also in cases with the same thematic theme, for example two paintings of the collection that depict specific locations in the city of Corfu, the user experience is enhanced as target media consist of a composite video specifically designed to combine the painting and contemporary video taken from the same location that the artist selected to draw the artwork, a feature that acts as a link from the past to the future.

Interactive Single Player or Multiplayer AR Games

Typically AR-based games (Fekolkin, 2013) introduce two elements: response correctness for single player while speed of response is important during multiplayer mode. Both these characteristics may be implemented using linear AR technologies within treasure-hunt games or hidden-object scenarios. In the case of a single player game, within the "Old Fortress of Corfu" edutainment scenario we implemented a set of historical sites that users have to visit, scan with their devices and trigger the "*target media*" visual marker, presenting questions. Answering the questions often requires the user to explore the space and locate appropriate information (for example specific dates engraved onto cannons). The responses can then be either filled in at specific web-based forms through the browser, or in our case filled in at a card by filling the appropriate box-area with a coloured pen. When scanning the card with

Figure 5. The paintings used in the second National Gallery edutainment case study

all the questions correctly answered the users are presented with the final video, which congratulates and instructs them to visit the bar of the old fortress and by handing in their correctly filled-in card they can receive complementary refreshments. With little modification at the scenario level, multiple players or teams of players may be introduced to these types of games where the team or player that posts the fastest response wins the competition.

EXTENDING SYSTEM SOFTWARE TO MEET THE CONTENT REQUIREMENTS

In the previous sections we presented how experimental multimedia systems and augmented reality applications developed today can actively cover varying content presentation and interaction requirements within a wide spectrum of educational forefronts. Clearly the majority of system and framework examples traced in the literature cover the requirements of specific application areas. However, they offer limited reusability capabilities due to the lack of generalisation in their design. In order to enhance learning, the traditional content-user interaction has to adapt to the capabilities of the new medium. In this section we furnish the software of a traditional tablet with a number of digital extensions. Essentially we develop an open-ended interactive platform featuring varying modes of content presentation and interaction. On the practical forefront an interactive multimedia prototype is actively employed as an enhanced reading tool, in order to demonstrate the generalised applicability of the model and discover future uses. It is shown that the proposed system offers a new way to interact with content while the requirements of educational models strategies are fulfilled. In this section we propose a new developmental approach designed to furnish existing media with new features while it preserves their existing functionality. In other words it introduces a development approach designed to augment existing media, a process that offers advantages both to developers and users. Developers are presented with a specific platform over which they may develop their own content-enhancement methods and tools. Users on the other hand may instantly use an end-system that requires them to avoid the learning curve, and subsequently explore its capabilities. This learning approach based on Activity Theory is actively supported by the proposed implementation (Bertelsen & Bødker, 2003; Deliyannis, 2007, 2012; Deliyannis & Kanellopoulos, 2008; Pino & Di Salvo, 2011; Polaine, 2005; Stromer-Galley, 2004; Sundar, 2004).

Information Technology (IT) provides today an adaptable platform through which the Information Society (IS) reality is shaped and transformed. The digital divide is one of the most important problems of IS today (Jorge Reina, 2001; Lindgren, 2012; Lynette & Eileen, 2002; Milton & Jorge Reina, 2001; Mossberger, Tolbert, & Stansbury, 2003; Neogi & Brocca, 2012; Nick, 2003; Richard Taylor, 2001; Servon, 2002; Strover, 2003). Interacting with new technologies is confusing for many new users, and the problem's origin is in most cases traced in the lack of suitable user-interface design that fails to appropriately represent the interaction metaphor (Hurst, Jackson, & Glencross, 2012; Rautaray & Agrawal, 2012). This is clearly evident in systems designed for technological and social convergence, experimental (Deliyannis, 2012) and art-based systems (Belluci, Malizia, & Aedo, 2012; Castro, Velho, & Kosminsky, 2012; Hurst et al., 2012; Ko et al., 2011; Mather, 2011; Nardelli, 2010; Paramythis, Weibelzahl, & Masthoff, 2010; Schraffenberger & Heide, 2012; Silva & Barbosa, 2012; Tahir, 2012).

The development of new devices from existing ones is an area of research that has already started to produce working examples in various forefronts (I. Deliyannis, 2013). Under this project, books were selected as the platform for experimentation. However, the approach followed may be employed in various other analogue platforms, including television and radio that offer room for enhancement, or even devices that offer augmented functionality to the user, one example being pens that detect and inform users about their spelling mistakes. It involves three main design stages: assessment of the system that will be augmented, an analytic account of its features according to content requirements and finally emulation of its functionality using a new technological system capable to offer additional functionality. This process requires close cooperation between developers, content experts and users. The availability of a representative group of users is particularly important as it provides feedback during both design and evaluation stages, by assessing the end-user experience.

The transition from analogue to digital books introduces a number of design and development complexities that need to be considered during design time. On the hardware forefront, it is evident that not all devices are suitable for all content types, due to a number of reasons, one of which includes the device's display size. The book format may be identified as the analogue analogy, as in the printing industry various book sizes are commonly employed for different uses. Therefore we may safely assume that this is a primary consideration that will certainly impact the capabilities of future implementation. In terms of resolution quality, the introduction of displays featuring an increased number of dots per inch (DPI) clearly classifies certain devices as more appropriate choices for development, as it relates directly to the visual comfort offered to the user. Of course the printed analogy may be contrasted here when a publication is printed using low-resolution printing. Similarly, the book-reading experience is closer to LCD-based systems like the Kindle e-reader by Amazon, which require an external light source in order to be used. However, most multimedia-enabled systems offering adequate processing power today, feature backlit and glossy displays, a characteristic that needs to be considered when developing content to be used in varying lighting conditions.

From the software perspective, various issues need to be addressed. The capabilities of the authoring environment, affect the functionality of the end-system. Our approach utilises the Adobe Director authoring environment that produces shockwave-based systems that may be published in a variety of operating systems and web-based platforms. Other authoring environments and languages such as HTML-5, offering higher-order functionality, scalability, adaptability and delivery in a wider platform-base, can substitute this developmental platform.

Information Access: Functional Level

Books are considered as information access systems. The content and the use scenario determine the system purpose and functions. For example within an educational setting, printed books that contain course information may be used as learning tools, encyclopaedias and manuals as reference tools. The equivalent use of an electronic realisation does not necessarily require multiple electronic books to be used, as the device may be designed to allow the flexibility to access and present the appropriate content and encapsulate the tools that will furnish the system with the necessary functionality needed for this particular use. In our case study we use the traditional book as an example. A digital model of the traditional book containing the information used within the augmented reality tour is constructed using interactive multimedia authoring environments as a base. A number of augmented features are subsequently added, furnishing the specific content type with additional functionality. This approach demonstrates a number of content and medium-oriented advantages: users with little or no experience with technology can instantly start using the digitised version. Younger users who are not able to read can also use the book as it reads itself, using a simple text selection action.

The application emulates the functionality of a book, in a digital context. Pages can be changed using gesture-based interaction, while buttons controlling the flow are also provided. The initial book cover screen opens to reveal the first page, the user may scan through the pages, read the text manually or when a sentence is selected the application reads out the pre-recorded text and then stops. Visuals follow the flow of interaction while background audio is used to enrich the experience.

RE-ENGINEERING THE COMMUNICATION PROCESS: THE SOCIAL SOFTWARE PERSPECTIVE

The section discusses cultural and social issues relating to the use of communication software, from the perspective of the end-user. The rise of social software is then compared with other technological developments including the introduction of radio and television broadcast networks, where we contrast present-day adoption process and public reactions. The "Digital Divide" phenomenon is approached from various perspectives, one being "non-use non-adoption". As this type of human reaction is commonly observed with new and complex technologies, we suggest that the problem may arise from poor human-computer interaction design choices, issues and practices that need to be addressed in future systems. The wide availability of technology and the reduction of cost are two factors which allow users to use state-of-the-art social software, equipping them with advanced communication, work, research, learning, creativity and recreation capabilities. We focus particularly in the area of learning, and how technological advances affect this. The presentation of adaptive networked learning technologies is followed by real-life examples of the use of social software in the learning process at a university setting. As these technologies provide true and direct interaction capabilities, we examine the implications of social software, by examining the creative aspects in one of the most demanding application areas, that of interactive multimedia for the arts.

Finally the chapter concludes by presenting a new interactive multimedia communications framework and model, covering the advanced needs for direct interaction. The framework is capable to cover mixed user-developer roles. The model specifies true interactive and multi-mode communication where the objective extends beyond data-transmission, to the transportation of meaning between the communication parties. The chapter commences with a discussion on cultural and social issues relating to the use of communication software, from the perspective of the end-user. The rise of social software is then compared with other technological developments including the introduction of radio and television broadcast networks, where we contrast present-day adoption process and public reactions.

The need for communication combined with the wide availability of information-access hardware, multimedia-enabled applications and the reduction of cost are factors that promote the use of social software, equipping it with advanced work, research, learning, creativity, recreation and communication capabilities. This work addresses the issue technological convergence in education. In that respect the learning process is examined under real-life educational settings, targeting the investigation of creative-learning and communication practices. The social software phenomenon is contrasted to other technological developments that revolutionise the area of information acquirement through their multimedia capabilities. The case study presented addresses the demanding application area of interactive multimedia for the arts, revealing specific observations that may be used to extend social-software usability. Finally, an interactive multimedia communications framework and a model are described, furnishing the increasing need for direct interaction, when social software systems are utilised in both research and creative/artistic applications.

Social Software

The introduction of the term "Social Software" signifies the increasing importance of social-networking tools in modern society, allowing single users and community ontologies to publish views, ideas, share content and interact directly or indirectly in virtual spaces. The power of communication, in that sense, relies on the ability to interchange information and collaborate across time and space. In an attempt to design more efficient tools and systems, researchers analyse a plethora of social software attributes (Kietzmann, Hermkens, McCarthy, & Silvestre, 2011) that include both social (Skeels & Grudin, 2009) and technological aspects (Bijker, Hughes, Pinch, & Douglas, 2012), serious or informal system-use (Madge, Meek, Wellens, & Hooley, 2009), the speed of information exchange (McLoughlin & Lee, 2007), the level of user hiding behind the system (Braun, 2013), acceptance of social software (Hemsley & Mason, 2013), use-trends (Autio, Dahlander, & Frederiksen, 2013) and the multi-mode communication and learning capabilities (Du, Fu, Zhao, Liu, & Liu, 2013). The difficulty concerning the agreement on a common definition of the term "Social Software" may be compared to that of "Multimedia" and the long discussion concerning the difficulty on the description of the term "Multimedia", as it is identified by its multiple forms and applications, hence it is perceived differently by single-users and groups.

Technological Evolution and Social Software

The foundation of social software is traced back to the 1960's with the rise of the information-processing sector (Solée et al., 2013) and the human perspective of technology (Partridge, 2007). During the next decade, the evolution of information technology created the need for skilled labour (Haigh, 2013). In the US, Marshall McLuhan predicted economical growth, electronic democracy without centralised control and creativity without copyright complications, while Europeans were more skeptic and cautious (Lash, 2002). In fact, Information Society developments may be compared to biological ecosystem evolution (van Dijck, 2013). Disparate computing centers of the 1960's, were interconnected during the next decade through the use of the TCP/IP protocol and the availability of personal computers provided basic processing power and connectivity to enthusiasts who engaged in virtual forms of social interaction. During the 1980's the information sector became increasingly important, featuring new evolving networked applications, while the active professionals and hobbyists in the information-technology sector increased, a development that also triggered the "digital divide" phenomenon. In the 1990's technology started becoming mobile and more accessible and at the turn of the century the information-ecosystem was already fully developed and interconnected.

Today, users depend on technology for many of their everyday social communication and work activities (Stephanidis, 2001, 2003). Information society develops synchronously in both the technological and the social domains (Arno Scharl, 2007). The introduction of affordable computer technologies and low-cost, fast, reliable wired and wireless networking allows the establishment of innovative applications, increases the number of users and triggers the improvement and reduces the cost of existing communication infrastructures. As a result, handheld communication devices remain constantly connected, enabling social software applications to practically follow the user and provide immediate multimedia-based feedback. The extended bandwidth availability and the social-sharing nature of the developed applications allows users to share information such audio and video playlists, permits video-based chat and conferencing and has transformed traditional broadcasting media that now utilise the Internet in order to reach their audience. In the media sector, many web-cast radio and television stations have evolved, offering beyond streaming various other services including interactive content access (Deliyannis, Antoniou, & Pandis, 2009; Prata, 2009; Prata, Chambel, & Guimarães, 2012; S. Song, Moustafa, & Afifi, 2012; Viel et al., 2012), while the availability of high-speed networks and powerful personal computers, contribute greatly to the enlargement of virtual communities, accessible from the privacy of one's home (Hanson, 2004; Richards & Hanson, 2004). As far as the commercial-software competition front is concerned, established companies include various networking facilities such as video conferencing and instant messaging clients to their operating systems. At the same time software developers introduce new platforms integrating additional multimedia-based options and services such as voice-over-IP (VOIP) telephony, in turn generating new products and customer-bases, which revolutionise the industry.

Communication Providers, Social Software, and Users

Communication providers are being reshaped into information providers, a development that follows the digitisation of their products and services that include telecommunications and multimedia. This places them in a position where they have to compete with smaller businesses that offer inexpensive digital products and services with minimal operational costs and significant profits. Clearly, entrepreneurs play a significant role in social software development, by providing software-based solutions that storm the market; as a result, many software companies change their attitude towards free software and openly provide software versions with limited functionality in an attempt to increase their user-base. Take for example the free application "Viber" that allows users to communicate through their smartphones using VOIP technology and short text messaging via the use of Wifi, 3G or 4G data linking, a chatacteristic that can swiftly transform the communications market. Other key players in the field offer "pre-loaded" software applications that the users will adopt by default and utilise social software techniques that aims to increase their user base. The advantage that smaller companies in the field possess is that they can attract various community ontologies by customising and distributing their products flexibly over the Internet, directly covering advanced user-needs, as opposed to corporate software products that evolve at a slower pace.

Understanding user habits can certainly aid in the design of intelligent and efficient systems, offering advanced human-computer interaction capabilities. To achieve this, one has to understand the user perspective in order to develop usable and efficient social software. Advanced software capabilities and features can attract more users into virtual communities, helping reduce the digital-divide by creating more attractive and increasingly customisable learning and research methods, tools and systems. Usability design is an interactive process. From the computer-science perspective, under most software-specification models, the developer is separated from the user in the design procedure. Nevertheless, most of the state-of-the-art social software applications and systems are designed, implemented and supported by enthusiastic users themselves. The suggested framework presented at the end of the chapter addresses particularly this case, defining the mixed role of the developer, user and content-expert.

Community Ontologies and Social Software Use

The number of users that sign-in to such technologies serves as an indication of the increased need for social interaction software and advanced communication. Social software technologies have evolved and utilise social networking techniques in order to increase their customer-base. Most systems, including "Hi5" and "Facebook" request users to share their communication contact list from other services such as e-mail providers and instant messaging services. As a result, the application retrieves all user-contacts and automatically sends out personalised invitations to selected members of the user list, inviting them to meet their friends who have already joined the service. Other web-based applications such as "http://last.fm" use personal music playlists as a basis that records and analyse musical habits of individuals, in an attempt to recognise listening patterns. Users who type a song or artist's name are presented with songs that other users have included in their playlists. While listening to a music piece, they can rate it, refining further the sophistication of the on-line database.

Concerning more advanced multimedia examples, several network applications may be mentioned which are designed to expand both medium and social capabilities of technology. Internet television broadcasting has been available via multicast networks for many years. With the introduction (Deliyannis et al., 2009; Prata, 2009; Prata et al., 2012; S. Song et al., 2012; Viel et al., 2012)of "Joost", an on-demand video broadcasting application based on peer to peer (P2P) transmission networks, the limits of broadcasting and social software were pushed further. Various advanced features are included such as chat-feature for those watching the same channel and control of medium-content availability: when the last user erases the stream from his playlist, the content is no longer available to other users of the network.

Information, Communication, and Learning

When considering user-interaction through social software systems, the information exchange process extends beyond the transportation of bits and bytes, to the transfer of meaning between the communicating parties, rendering mutual understanding as possibly the most important aspect of the process. Here, the term "information" is defined as "the meaning of the representation of data" for the receiver. In this sense, information may originate from various sources; it can be transferred using different media; and used by one or many persons. Hence, content delivery is defined as the understanding of the true meaning of a message that is delivered from A to B. It should be noted here that both A and B represent most user-system arrangements. To demonstrate this notion, imagine that a Greek sentence is broadcasted from user A to user B who does not recognise the language. Although the message has been successfully encoded and transferred, the receiver is unable to understand its meaning, a fact that results in lack of communication. It is particularly important to focus on the user perspective and on the truly interactive nature of communication under various scenarios, including intrapersonal, exploratory learning, research and artistic creation.

The same phenomenon applies to mass media. Viewers with specific social backgrounds or cultural characteristics may be offended by certain content such as satire and jokes involving their personal values and beliefs. As (Wolton, 1997) underlines: "What is complicated about communication is neither the message nor the technology, but the receptor".

Education in the Information Society, Expanding the Boundaries

The notion of communication is particularly important in the area of learning. Paradigms such as "just in time learning", "student-centered learning", "constructivism" and "collaborative approaches" are commonly utilised in conjunction with technologies used in the information society, to describe how new learning processes may enable a person to gain knowledge and expertise. The majority of pedagogical theories state that the classroom experience is not limited to the curriculum material, but it extends to the social interactions inside and outside the class. Most contemporary e-learning systems provide virtual meeting places enabling students to chat informally, to exchange notes, views or opinions and to interact socially. In that respect the implications of social software in a realistic university-level setting are examined, where students actively use these technologies to expand their expertise, knowledge and aesthetics in the field of interactive multimedia for the arts. Certain existing teaching methods considered obsolete in the light of new and developing technological capabilities, are still employed in various educational practices and institutions worldwide. Yet, the question remains: which are the evolving learning processes, supporting pedagogies and applications in the digital age that can enhance, transform and possibly replace existing methodologies employed today in our existing educational arena, particularly when technological advances are rapidly changing system-capabilities?

Information technology offers new learning possibilities that cannot necessarily be directly perceived in the short term. A principal aim of this work is to introduce a fresh perspective into the user needs. To achieve this it is suggested that any researcher has to address the problem independently from technological capabilities and limitations. As television was once considered a simple "Radio with a Screen" and was later used for educational purposes, hence, interactive Internet broadcasting has been reduced to Internet TV, ignoring all new social and educational aspects that interactivity and novel communication technologies have to offer. Interactive television, video and computer-based exploratory content and interaction technologies have already been applied to various fields including educational, commercial and research applications, with the same content used to cover multiple user-requirements (Deliyannis, 2002).

Understanding of the mechanisms that enable social software to be used as an educational tool requires research beyond the fields of software technologies and system design. As new communication and multimedia capabilities shape a new type of on-line user-behaviour, it is imperative to examine how users are affected socially. To complicate matters further, we argue that the level of user-expertise in information technologies may affect how users perceive social software. The more competent the users, the more immersive their experiences may be, as they are able to perform more complicated actions, customise further their systems and hence extend the level of communication. Other factors that need to be addressed are the user ages, the availability of assistance from local experts, the level of connectivity and networking, their economical level and the time and hardware available to them to experiment. All these factors and possibly many others that need to be identified, most certainly affect the way users perceive and utilise technology.

Another application area of social software is that of investigative e-education that does not necessarily target a specific learning area, instead it is design to aid the users in finding their preferred area of interest. If we examine a computer lab in a public school, with uniform processing and networking capabilities used by a certain phenomenally uniform group of students, it is observed that each student may: consider technology and its uses from different perspectives; become more proficient in different areas; and demonstrate varying levels of understanding. Their background, abilities and personal interests may affect their development, resulting in uneven and unpredicted progress. In the near future the development of customised student-assisting systems that identifies students' personal needs, abilities and talents, will be able to interactively broaden their research horizons or even assist them in using their free time more constructively and productively.

A combined socio-technical approach may be used, when application of knowledge to the society is the primary aim. Various technologies including Social Software may aid in this direction. In that respect the needs and abilities of individuals or social groups should be first taken into account and, on this basis, one may decide on the strategies that need to be followed. In other words, information processing requirements and learning demands are recorded first, followed by strategic approach selection. It is important for a software developer to examine Information Society and educational developments from multiple perspectives, sometimes moving away from traditional methods and practices.

The proposed Educational Social Software Framework (ESSF) describes the interactive relationship between three roles, involved in the construction and use of social software systems. These include users, developers and content-experts. One may utilise an overlapping set-diagram representation for the three parties, to describe the relationships between the various groups. Arrows may indicate group-interaction across the system. Framework-areas may be coloured, to indicate individual and overlapping party-roles. Set unions indicate higher-order interaction say between groups in construction-mode. Such a system is an implied product of the developer's domain.

Various modes of interaction may be described using the above model. Area-exclusive paradigms cover limited interaction scenarios between users, developers and content-experts. Requirements are described individually from each group, according to their individual needs, constraints and understanding of the target-functionality. A common agreement across groups specifies the resulting social software system. From the individual perspective of each group, this is achieved without a detailed understanding of the mechanics of other groups. Line-diagrams may be used to specify relationships, in detail, between these clearly defined groups.

A second setting describes the opposite case, the instance where only the union of all three parties is coloured. Here, the development group possesses knowledge that transcends all three groups. This would encompass the single-developer instance: where one has understanding of MM-development, expertise on the subject matter and appreciates audience expectations.

In passing to a third interaction setting is where users/field-experts assume an active role in development and commute between roles as user/audience. This accurately describes the development scenario of Social Software developed by users with real needs. The same system is used by all users to exchange information, ideas and experiences.

Bi-directional relationships may be indicated by double-arrow (often omitted). In this manner, interaction between the parties involved may be described in a highly informative manner. Other particular to the case studies framework-instances may freely indicated, to cover particular system-needs. To interpret (Carter, 2000) "…developers must understand the intended meaning of the data from the information providers, in order to evaluate its quality". This is a particularly pertinent issue when considering learning-content. One notes that the developer may not always be able to perform this task, commonly due to a lack of expertise, particularly when the syllabus involves practical experience gained in time, which is not easily documented or recorded.

Clearly, one may observe a variation of scenarios emerging under this framework. For example, the users may be musicians, striving to advance the boundaries of their technique. Yet, under the same scenario, one may describe a system that is developed by a user sub-group, via interaction with musicians. Here, a novice (student) may develop the system with the aid of a proficient musician and with courseware firmly in mind say, produce additional facilities that slow-down the video of the performance in order to aid students understand the technique. At a higher level-of-abstraction, other frameworks may be emulated.

The Educational Social Software Model (ESSM)

The proposed model addresses the issue of interactive learning. It is designed to acknowledge that both content and context is either delivered successfully as it was intended from A to B; partially-delivered where more information needs to be provided; or not delivered at all. In that sense, delivery implies transportation of meaning, not simply transfer of data. To achieve that, both parties involved have to be able to exchange information through multiple channels and media forms.

Knowledge Representation

Knowledge domains are composed of entities. Each entity encapsulates all the content, queries and user-response evaluation procedures. An entity consists of a set of valid answers and the appropriate evaluation methods. When an entity is transferred from A to B, the receiving system projects the data to the user and collects responses through all available sensors. From this stage system B is presented with a number of possibilities. If the responses cover all valid correct-answer conditions, according to the evaluation procedure that was sent from A to B, then a response is sent back to A informing that the data has been successfully transferred. If the validity of conditions is partially covered, then B informs A that there is partial lack of understanding or disagreement and A is forced to evaluate the answer appropriately. Under that case A has the choice to re-send the content using different conditions, use another approach on the same subject, change the subject altogether or end the conversation. In the case that all feedback is wrong then the answer has not been answered.

Decision Making

In the last example a decision making problem is presented. An erroneous answer may be caused by various reasons that need to be analysed at runtime. The decision making process has to answer whether the user does not understand the question, or does not possess the necessary knowledge. Answer to this question may be found using various methods, one being the communication progress between A and B. For example if the erroneously answered question is the very first addressed to the user that may occur due to the fact that the information is presented in the wrong language. Under this case the solution is to provide assistance and customisation facilities to correctly adjust system and language settings. Alternatively, the user may not be able to realise how to use the system and provide feedback. That is different to the case where the user has answered correctly the majority questions as in this case an erroneous response may indicate a gap in the user-knowledge. This that can be addressed by expressing the entity differently or lower system-expectations and project lower-level entities to investigate the level of user-understanding of the subject.

In order to make the model more flexible, processing of data may occur in either end, depending on the processing power of each end. For some responses heavy on multimedia data, and when B provides sufficient processing power, evaluation may automatically take place remotely, allowing the result to be communicated back to A in order to progress to the next iteration. This approach can speed-up the process, particularly for systems with limited feedback connectivity.

Case Studies

Note here that bidirectional communication does not necessarily require backward transfer of information from B to A on every case. When content is transferred from A to B, the issue here is for B to realise at least one acknowledgment has to be sent back from B to A in order for A to receive and evaluate the result. Multimedia and multi-channel communication technologies are commonly utilised to transfer multi-sensory information and feedback. At this point it is important to present a few characteristic cases where the model may be utilised, to allow interested parties to map their personal requirements to these examples. Communication becomes an interactive content-context transfer issue as it is shown from the following cases.

Knowledge Multiple-Choice Test

First the case of a multiple-choice test is considered. The test is used to prove the level of user understanding for the knowledge that has already been transferred to the user. The entities are represented in the form of questions perceived as instances taken from the domain of knowledge mentioned above. System A transfers to B the first question and the valid answer. The user may answer the question verbally, by pressing the appropriate keyboard selection, through on-screen selection using the mouse or using gestures via a video camera. In the first question the user responds incorrectly, then B communicates the result to A which in turn instructs B to present the following question, alongside a help screen instructing the user to change language if necessary. If the user changes the language or system attributes, then the score is zeroed and the first question appears again in the correct language. Alternatively the first question is considered wrong and the system progresses further.

Multiple-Choice Test

These tests demonstrate increased complexity, as they are used to assess a user's profile according to psychological theories. The questions are indirect and interconnected, enabling psychologists to evaluate the results, which may not necessarily be bound by "right" or "wrong" answers. They may simply indicate user-preference. In this increasingly complex case, a user may select to randomly answer the questions, resulting in erroneous outcome. Timing here may be essential, while ordering of questions could be randomly selected to avoid user-memorisation of answers.

Conversation

The conversation case involves a truly interactive scenario where opinion is formed through conversation. This may be visualised as two knowledge-domains who are able to update their content constantly by enriching or altering existing entities. This is achieved through conversation between A and B, where both send and receive questions and answers. At each complete iteration stage, both parties may have updated their knowledge-base, forcing internal entities to update accordingly if necessary. The feedback between the two parties involved in this information exchange may be multi-sensory, as facial expressions, hand gestures, sounds and any other feedback or combination that indicates agreement or disagreement may be used as an answer.

Lecture

The lecture example involves the case where A possesses knowledge and experience, which is being offered to B. This particular example involves the dynamics of the "Conversation" example above, but here clearly A has a teaching plan, followed by examples and other hierarchically organised material that may be represented as entities.

Disagreement

The most complex case described here is that of communication. It is an example of "Conversation" where both A and B do not agree, yet each attempts to change the other's opinion.

Conclusion

Therefore it is important to view technology from a fresh viewpoint, particularly for those social software systems that can expand the user's learning and collaboration capabilities. Investigation in the area of education and most particularly the field of learning and creativity through social software has revealed new questions, challenges and use-patterrns that need to be defined and analysed. New methodologies are required through an interdisciplinary perspective, in order to advance existing systems with novel and desired features. Both computer and social scientists can analyse particular task-based needs in an attempt to provide integrated solutions for demanding educational challenges presented in the new era.

The area of interactive arts is a particularly interesting starting point for this type of research. An artist is always trying to expand the boundaries of technology, while pushing social restraints further. Creating novel educational technologies and methodologies in the field of artistic creation may be one of the most difficult tasks that learning technologies can face, as the artistic behaviour is not bounded by easily recognisable patterns. The learning process is characterised by freedom of thought, while it encourages freedom of expression that in most cases it is limited by the artist's personal restraints towards technology. The user who is able to recognise which are the limits of technology, is the user who may help technology expand and extend further.

CONCLUSION

The proposed approaches enable developers to overcome the limitations of typical proprietary augmented reality systems. They permit the implementation of prototype systems featuring advanced exploratory capabilities combining fully featured user-interaction with real-life artifacts, spaces and content. In that sense complex scenarios can be realised within the same information domain where specific user groups can be presented with customised experiences. The support of advanced interactive scenarios is clearly a tool that permits the user to be actively involved in the content exploration process, in both open and closed spaces. Developers are invited to use the proposed approach in order to evaluate the performance of competing available platforms through the development and testing of realistic scenarios. Ultimately they can produce a fully working prototype system that enables users and content experts to practically experience augmenter reality, evaluate its use and extend it through experimentation.

ACKNOWLEDGMENT

We would like to thank the following students of the Department of Audio and Visual Arts, Ionian University, Greece for their contribution in this work: George Dimakidis, final-year student for the Old Fortress case study; the students Myrto Papagiannidou, Athanasia - Semeli Bardaka, Georgia Karagi-annopoulou and Spyridoula Vasilaki for the first National Gallery case study and Nadia Zerva, Elina

Athanasiou, Alexis Sidiropoulos, Magdalena Honsova and Alexandros Panagopoulos Hassound for the second, Marios Tsaousis and Stefanos Farantopoulos for their contribution in the research presented within chapter 4.

REFERENCES

Apostolopoulos, J. G., Chou, P. A., Culbertson, B., Kalker, T., Trott, M. D., & Wee, S. (2012). The Road to Immersive Communication. *Proceedings of the IEEE, 100*(4), 974–990. doi:10.1109/JPROC.2011.2182069

Arno Scharl, K. T. E. (2007). *The Geospatial Web, How Geobrowsers, Social Software and the Web 2.0 are Shaping the Network Society*. London: Springer.

Autio, E., Dahlander, L., & Frederiksen, L. (2013). Information exposure, opportunity evaluation and entrepreneurial action: an empirical investigation of an online user community. *Academy of Management Journal, 56*(5), 1348–1371. doi:10.5465/amj.2010.0328

Belluci, A., Malizia, A., & Aedo, I. (2012). *Towards a framework for the rapid prototyping of physical interaction*. Paper presented at the Fourth International Workshop on Physicality, BCS HCI 2012 Conference. University of Birmingham, UK.

Bertelsen, O. W., & Bødker, S. (2003). Activity theory. *HCI models, theories, and frameworks: Toward a multidisciplinary science*, 291-324.

Bijker, W. E., Hughes, T. P., Pinch, T., & Douglas, D. G. (2012). *The Social Construction of Technological Systems: New Directions in the Sociology and History of Technology*. Mit Press.

Braun, M. T. (2013). Obstacles to social networking website use among older adults. *Computers in Human Behavior, 29*(3), 673–680. doi:10.1016/j.chb.2012.12.004

Carter, J. (2000). *Developments in Web Research and Practice*. Paper presented at the Motivating Multimedia. San Diego, California, US.

Casella, G., & Coelho, M. (2013). *Augmented heritage: situating augmented reality mobile apps in cultural heritage communication*. Paper presented at the Proceedings of the 2013 International Conference on Information Systems and Design of Communication. doi:10.1145/2503859.2503883

Castro, B. P., Velho, L., & Kosminsky, D. (2012). *INTEGRARTE: digital art using body interaction*. Paper presented at the Proceedings of the Eighth Annual Symposium on Computational Aesthetics in Graphics, Visualization, and Imaging, Annecy, France.

Cesar, P., & Chorianopoulos, K. (2009). The Evolution of TV Systems, Content, and Users Toward Interactivity. *Found. Trends Hum.-. Comput. Interact., 2*(4), 373–395. doi:10.1561/1100000008

Cheah, M. S., Quah, Y. P., Wong, P. E., & Zainon, W. M. N. W. (2014). Augmented Reality: A Review on Its Issues and Application in Teaching and Learning. *International Journal of Computer and Information Technology, 3*(2), 269–274.

Deliyannis, I. (2002). *Interactive Multimedia Systems for Science and Rheology*. (Ph.D), Ph.D Thesis, University of Wales, Swansea.

Deliyannis, I. (2007). *Exploratory Learning using Social Software*. Paper presented at the Cognition and Exploratory Learning in the Digital Age (CELDA), Algarve, Portugal.

Deliyannis, I. (2012). From Interactive to Experimental Multimedia. In I. Deliyannis (Ed.), *Interactive Multimedia* (pp. 3–12). Rijeka, Croatia: Intech. doi:10.5772/38341

Deliyannis, I. (2013). Adapting Interactive TV to Meet Multimedia Content Presentation Requirements. [IJMT]. *International Journal of Multimedia Technology*, *3*(3), 83–89.

Deliyannis, I. (2013). Sensor Recycling and Reuse. *International Journal of Sensor and Related Networks*, *1*(1), 8–19.

Deliyannis, I. (2014). Converging multimedia content presentation requirements for interactive television. Lugmayr, A., Dal Zotto, C., & Ferrell Lowe, G. (Eds.), Convergent Divergence? Springer-Verlag Handbook.

Deliyannis, I. (2015). Interactive multimedia installation art development using recycled input and sensing devices [in Press]. *International Journal of Arts and Technology*.

Deliyannis, I., Antoniou, A., & Pandis, P. (2009). *Design and Development of an Experimental Low-Cost Internet-Based Interactive TV Station*. Paper presented at the 4th Mediterranean Conference on Information Systems (MCIS). Athens.

Deliyannis, I., Giannakoulopoulos, A., & Oikonomidou, R. (2013). *Engineering and design issues in urban-oriented edutainment systems*. Paper presented at the Hybrid City II: Subtle rEvolutions. Athens, Greece.

Deliyannis, I., & Kanellopoulos, N. (2008). *Interactive Communication Methodology for Social Software and Multimedia Applications*. Paper presented at the IADIS International Conference IADIS e-Society. Algarve, Portugal.

Deliyannis, I., & Papaioannou, G. (2014). Augmented reality for archaeological environments on mobile devices: a novel open framework. *Mediterranean Archaeology and Archaeometry*, *14*(4), 1–10.

Du, Z., Fu, X., Zhao, C., Liu, Q., & Liu, T. (2013). Interactive and Collaborative E-Learning Platform with Integrated Social Software and Learning Management System. In W. Lu, G. Cai, W. Liu & W. Xing (Eds.), *Proceedings of the 2012 International Conference on Information Technology and Software Engineering* (Vol. 212, pp. 11-18): Springer Berlin Heidelberg doi:10.1007/978-3-642-34531-9_2

Fekolkin, R. (2013). Analysis of Augmented Reality Games on Android platform.

Haigh, T. (2013). Five lessons from really good history. *Communications of the ACM*, *56*(1), 37–40. doi:10.1145/2398356.2398369

Hanson, V. L. (2004). *The user experience: designs and adaptations*. New York City, New York: ACM Press. doi:10.1145/990657.990659

Hemsley, J., & Mason, R. M. (2013). Knowledge and knowledge management in the social media age. *Journal of Organizational Computing and Electronic Commerce*.

Hurst, M., Jackson, T. W., & Glencross, M. (2012, September 7-8). *Emotion recognition &-Theory or practicality.* Paper presented at the Automation and Computing (ICAC), 2012 18th International Conference.

Jorge Reina, S. (2001). Of gaps by which democracy we measure The digital divide: facing a crisis or creating a myth? (pp. 303-307). MIT Press.

Kerdvibulvech, C. (2013). *Augmented reality applications using visual tracking.* KMTL Information Technology Journal.

Kietzmann, J. H., Hermkens, K., McCarthy, I. P., & Silvestre, B. S. (2011). Social media? Get serious! Understanding the functional building blocks of social media. *Business Horizons, 54*(3), 241–251. doi:10.1016/j.bushor.2011.01.005

Kirner, C., & Kirner, T. (2013). Development of online educational games with augmented reality. *Proceedings of EDULEARN13*, 1950-1959.

Ko, A. J., Abraham, R., Beckwith, L., Blackwell, A., Burnett, M., & Erwig, M. et al. (2011). The state of the art in end-user software engineering. *ACM Computing Surveys, 43*(3), 1–44. doi:10.1145/1922649.1922658

Lash, S. (2002). *Critique on Information.* London: Sage Publications.

Leiva, J., Guevara, A., Rossi, C., & Aguayo, A. (2014). Augmented reality and recommendation systems for groups. A new perspective on tourist destinations systems. *Estudios y Perspectivas en Turismo, 23*(1), 40–59.

Lindgren, S. (2012). The Sociology of Media and Information Technologies. In G. C. Aakvaag, M. Hviid Jacobsen, & T. Johansson (Eds.), *Introduction to Sociology: Scandinavian Sensibilities.* London: Pearson.

Lynette, K., & Eileen, M. T. (2002). *The Digital Divide at Work and Home: The Discourse about Power and Underrepresented Groups in the Information Society*: Kluwer, B.V.

Madge, C., Meek, J., Wellens, J., & Hooley, T. (2009). Facebook, social integration and informal learning at university: 'It is more for socialising and talking to friends about work than for actually doing work'. *Learning, Media and Technology, 34*(2), 141–155. doi:10.1080/17439880902923606

Mather, G. (2011). *Sensation and Perception.* Taylor & Francis.

McLoughlin, C., & Lee, M. J. (2007). *Social software and participatory learning: Pedagogical choices with technology affordances in the Web 2.0 era.* Paper presented at the ICT: Providing choices for learners and learning. Proceedings ascilite Singapore 2007.

Milton, L. M., & Jorge Reina, S. (2001). Universal service from the bottom up: a study of telephone penetration in Camden, New Jersey The digital divide: facing a crisis or creating a myth? (pp. 119-146). MIT Press

Mossberger, K., Tolbert, C. J., & Stansbury, M. (2003). *Virtual Inequality: Beyond the Digital divide.* Washington, DC: Georgetown University Press.

Nardelli, E. (2010). *A classification framework for interactive digital artworks.* Paper presented at the International ICST Conference on User Centric Media. Palma, Mallorca.

Neogi, P., & Brocca, J. (2012). Broadband Adoption and Use in Canada and the US: Is the Digital Divide Closing? Nick, C. (2003). Digital divide or discursive design? On the emerging ethics of information space. *Ethics and Information Technology*, 5(2), 89–97.

Nilsen, T., Linton, S., & Looser, J. (2004). Motivations for augmented reality gaming. *Proceedings of FUSE*, 4, 86–93.

Paramythis, A., Weibelzahl, S., & Masthoff, J. (2010). Layered evaluation of interactive adaptive systems: Framework and formative methods. *User Modeling and User-Adapted Interaction*, 20(5), 383–453. doi:10.1007/s11257-010-9082-4

Partridge, H. L. (2007). Establishing the human perspective of the information society.

Paszkiel, S. (2014). Augmented Reality of Technological Environment in Correlation with Brain Computer Interfaces for Control Processes. Recent Advances in Automation, Robotics and Measuring Techniques (pp. 197-203). Springer.

Patil, S., Balar, A., Malviya, N., & Prasad, S. (2013, December). Innovation in Shopping Experience using augmented reality and integration with social networking. *International Journal of Scientific & Engineering Research*, 4(12), 2154–2156.

Pino, C., & Di Salvo, R. (2011). *A survey of semantic multimedia retrieval systems*.

Polaine, A. (2005). *The flow principle in interactivity*. Paper presented at the Proceedings of the second Australasian conference on Interactive entertainment, Sydney, Australia.

Poulos, M., Deliyannis, I., & Floros, A. (2012). Audio Fingerprint Extraction using an Adapted Computational Geometry Algorithm. *Computer and Information Science*, 5(6), 88–97. doi:10.5539/cis.v5n6p88

Poulos, M., Deliyannis, I., & Floros, A. (2013). Efficient Audio Fingerprint Application Verification Using the Adapted Computational Geometry Algorithm. *Computer and Information Science*, 6(1), 70–82. doi:10.5539/cis.v6n1p70

Prata, A. (2009). Interactive Television Evolution. In M. Pagani (Ed.), Encyclopedia of Multimedia Technology and Networking (2nd ed., pp. 757-762). Hershey, PA: IGI Global doi:10.4018/978-1-60566-014-1.ch102

Prata, A., Chambel, T., & Guimarães, N. (2012). Personalized Content Access in Interactive TV-Based Cross Media Environments. In Y. Kompatsiaris, B. Merialdo, & S. Lian (Eds.), *TV content analysis: techniques and applications*. Taylor & Francis.

Ramirez, M., Ramos, E., Cruz, O., Hernandez, J., Perez-Cordoba, E., & Garcia, M. (2013). *Design of interactive museographic exhibits using Augmented reality*. Paper presented at the Electronics, Communications and Computing (CONIELECOMP), 2013 International Conference. doi:10.1109/CONIELECOMP.2013.6525747

Rautaray, S., & Agrawal, A. (2012). Vision based hand gesture recognition for human computer interaction: A survey. *Artificial Intelligence Review*, 1–54. doi:10.1007/s10462-012-9356-9

Richard Taylor, M. J. (2001). *Asian Technology Parks: Lessons For The "Digital Divide"*. Pacific Telecommunications Council.

Richards, J. T., & Hanson, V. L. (2004). *Web accessibility: a broader view*. New York, NY, USA: ACM Press. doi:10.1145/988672.988683

Rowles, D. (2013). *Mobile Marketing: How Mobile Technology is Revolutionizing Marketing, Communications and Advertising*. Kogan Page Publishers.

Schianchi, A. (2013). Location-based virtual interventions. *Leonardo Electronic Almanac, 19*(2), 112–135.

Schraffenberger, H., & Heide, E. (2012). Interaction Models for Audience-Artwork Interaction: Current State and Future Directions. In A. Brooks (Ed.), *Arts and Technology* (Vol. 101, pp. 127–135). Springer Berlin Heidelberg. doi:10.1007/978-3-642-33329-3_15

Servon, L. J. (2002). *Bridging the Digital Divide: Technology, community and Public Policy*. Oxford: Blackwell Publishing. doi:10.1002/9780470773529

Silva, B. S. d., & Barbosa, S. D. J. (2012). *A conceptual model for HCI design cases*. Paper presented at the Proceedings of the 11th Brazilian Symposium on Human Factors in Computing Systems. Cuiaba, Brazil.

Skeels, M. M., & Grudin, J. (2009). *When social networks cross boundaries: a case study of workplace use of facebook and linkedin*. Paper presented at the Proceedings of the ACM 2009 international conference on Supporting group work, Sanibel Island, Florida, USA. doi:10.1145/1531674.1531689

Solée, R. V., Valverde, S., Casals, M. R., Kauffman, S. A., Farmer, D., & Eldredge, N. (2013). The evolutionary ecology of technological innovations. *Complexity*. doi: 10.1002/cplx.21436

Song, S., Moustafa, H., & Afifi, H. (2012). A Survey on Personalized TV and NGN Services through Context-Awareness. *ACM Computing Surveys, 44*(1), 1–18. doi:10.1145/2071389.2071393

Song, T., & Jiashan, L. (2013). *Application Research of Augmented Reality Technology in Jingju Art Dissemination*. Paper presented at the Proceedings of the 2013 International Conference on Business Computing and Global Informatization.

Stephanidis, C. (2001). Adaptive Techniques for Universal Access. *User Modeling and User-Adapted Interaction, 11*(1-2), 159–179. doi:10.1023/A:1011144232235

Stephanidis, C. (2003, February). Towards Universal Access in the Disappearing Computer Environment. *UPGRADE, IV*, 53–59.

Stoyanova, J., Gonçalves, R., Brito, P. Q., & Coelho, A. (2013). Real-time Augmented Reality Pemo Platform for Exploring Consumer Emotional Responses with Shopping Applications. *International Journal of Online Engineering*.

Strapatsakis, M. (2008, November). Invisible Places - Immense White [Sensor-Based Interactive Video Installation]. Strasbourg.

Stromer-Galley, J. (2004). Interactivity-as-Product and Interactivity-as-Process. *The Information Society Journal, 20*(5), 391–394. doi:10.1080/01972240490508081

Strover, S. (2003). Remapping the Digital Divide. *The Information Society Journal, 19*(4), 275–277. doi:10.1080/01972240309481

Sundar, S. S. (2004). Theorizing Interactivity's Effects. *The Information Society Journal, 20*(5), 385–389. doi:10.1080/01972240490508072

Tahir, M. (2012). *Reality Technologies and Tangible Interaction: A brief guide to tangible user interfaces, augmented reality and related technologies.* LAP Lambert Academic Publishing.

Trifonova, A., Ahmed, S. U., & Jaccheri, L. (2009). In C. Barry, M. Lang, W. Wojtkowski, K. Conboy, & G. Wojtkowski (Eds.), *SArt: Towards Innovation at the Intersection of Software Engineering and Art Information Systems Development* (pp. 809–827). Springer, US.

Trifonova, A., Jaccheri, L., & Bergaust, K. (2008). Software engineering issues in interactive installation art. *Int. J. Arts and Technology, 1*(1), 43–65. doi:10.1504/IJART.2008.019882

van Dijck, J. (2013). *The Culture of Connectivity: A Critical History of Social Media.* OUP USA. doi:10.1093/acprof:oso/9780199970773.001.0001

Van Krevelen, D., & Poelman, R. (2010). A survey of augmented reality technologies, applications and limitations. *International Journal of Virtual Reality, 9*(2), 1.

Viel, C. C., Melo, E. L., Godoy, A. P., Dias, D. R. C., Trevelin, L. C., & Teixeira, C. A. C. (2012). *Multimedia presentation integrating interactive media produced in real time with high performance processing.* Paper presented at the Proceedings of the 18th Brazilian symposium on Multimedia and the web. São Paulo, Brazil. doi:10.1145/2382636.2382664

Weedon, A., Miller, D., Franco, C. P., Moorhead, D., & Pearce, S. (2014). Crossing media boundaries: Adaptations and new media forms of the book. *Convergence (London)*, 1354856513515968.

Wolton, D. (1997). *Penser la communication.* Paris: Flammarion.

Chapter 5
Information Retrieval Technologies and the "Realities" of Music Information Seeking

Charilaos Lavranos
Ionian University, Greece

Petros Kostagiolas
Ionian University, Greece

Joseph Papadatos
Ionian University, Greece

ABSTRACT

Music information seeking incorporates the human activities that are carried out for the search and retrieval of music information. In recent years, the evolution of music technology holds a central role affecting the nature of music information seeking behavior. The research area that deals with the accessibility and the retrievability process of music information is known as Music Information Retrieval (MIR). This chapter focuses on the presentation of MIR technologies which has a direct impact in the way that individuals, as well as different music communities such as composers, performers, listeners, musicologists, etc., handle and utilize music information. The aim of this chapter is to investigate the way different music communities interact with MIR systems. Our approach is based on a selected literature review regarding the MIR systems and the information seeking behavior of the musicians.

INTRODUCTION

In the current digital era, information technology has become more and more influential in society as well as in humans' everyday life. It mediates in human's private and public communication, interaction, and transaction. Also, forms the infrastructure for critical, social and institutional functions such as education, research, utilities, commerce, entertainment, etc. (Hadjileontiadou, Nikolaidou, & Hadjileontiadis, 2007). More specifically, the design and advances of multimedia technologies are based

DOI: 10.4018/978-1-4666-8659-5.ch005

on user experiences and users' behavioral aspects (National Research Council [NRC], 2003). The development of digital information systems is comprised by value added services (e.g., digital libraries, e-platforms, etc.) and enforce individuals' information seeking behavior addressing their information searching needs (Papachristopoulos, Tsakonas, & Papatheodorou, 2008). The study of the way these information technologies interact with individuals in order to support their creative activities define a multidisciplinary area with applications in many areas of the creative industry, arts, music, theater, etc. Information technology advances and Internet lead to the development of specific information retrieval and information management practices (Liem et al., 2012). In particular as regards to music information, information technology and the various digital representations of the musical material has deeply affected the way people interact with music. Nowadays, musicians can potentially handle music information through various digital music formats, and access a massive quantity of diverse music information through a plethora of music platforms, databases, directories and other information resources on the Internet (Dittmar, Cano, Abesser, & Grollmisch, 2012). Indeed, the utilization of digital multimedia, including audio, music video and images, has changed musicians' way of thinking and creating (Heo, Suzuki, Ito, & Makino, 2006).

Information technology systems and services aim to address their users' information needs in a way that be as much as possible precise and effective (Papatheodorou, Kapidakis, Sfakakis, & Vassiliou, 2003). The function of an information technology search engine is based on an issued keyword query that describes an information need and receives a list of results that relate to the information sought (Stamou & Christodoulakis, 2005). Many of these services use information retrieval and filtering techniques in order to personalize and customize their content to the users' interests and preferences (Papatheodorou et al., 2003). More specifically, music information services and systems influence the accessibility and retrievability of music information (Yang, Chen, & Wang, 2010; Liem et al., 2012) including among others audio, video, music, animation, images and pictures etc. To the same extent as the online digital music information collections expand, the necessity for efficient seeking and retrieval of music material become apparent (Wang, Deng, Yan, & Wang, 2008). Therefore, a new set of digital information literacy skills is required by musicians; while at the same time the musicians' information behavior perspective is becoming an important matter (Raimond & Sandler, 2008). Moreover, in order for musicians to navigate within the abundance of multimedia information contents, novel and friendly information retrieval systems are required (Downie, 2003). According to the same author, the research area dealing with the accessibility and the retrievability process of digital music information referred to as Music Information Retrieval (MIR). This phrase originates as a sub discipline of computer science with applications in information sciences (Orio, 2006). In the music studies, the MIR is alternatively described as Music Information Research (MIR) retaining however the same acronym (Downie, 2003; Goto, 2012). In recent years, MIR has attracted more and more attention and gradually becomes an important research area with an explosive expansion of the relevant literature (Yang et al., 2010). MIR technologies certainly affect the way that the different music communities such as composers, performers, listeners, musicologists, etc., handle and utilize music information (Liem et al., 2012).

This book chapter aims at the investigation of the relationship between the existing MIR systems with the information seeking behavior of different music communities. Therefore, MIR systems and technologies are identified and their relation with individuals' music information seeking behavior is analyzed and discussed. The analysis is based on a selected literature review for MIR systems and their usage. Moreover, it is attempted to investigate the impact of MIR employment by the musicians in musical creativity. To this end, the music information seeking behavior is explained in the next section, the interaction of musicians with music information technologies is reviewed in the third section and thereafter a conceptual model for MIR is proposed. The findings are discussed and conclusions with recommendations for future research are presented.

MUSIC INFORMATION SEEKING BEHAVIOR

Music information constitutes an important element for the creation, execution and analysis of music, as well as for the scholarly work in the music domain (Laplante & Downie, 2011). Music information includes musical material or material for music, which include bibliographic data, genre issues, media files, etc., in various media formats (e.g., music scores, textual biographical material, oral history collections, recordings, etc.), and through various dissemination channels and information services (Byrd & Crawford, 2002; Laplante & Downie, 2006). According to Rubenstein (1987), music information is considered as an interesting data management domain. The management of music information may include several different musical facets such as bibliographic information, graphical information, sound information, meta-musical information, and conceptual representations of music. Therefore, music information management imposes additional difficulties due to the variety of musical data, including text, graphics, sound, and conceptual abstractions (Rubenstein, 1987). According to Liem, Müller, Eck, Tzanetakis and Hanjalic (2011), music information can be represented in three different main forms: a. the notated - graphemic, b. the physical - acoustic, and c. the auditory form, which correspond to score, performance and listening (Figure 1). Hence, the flow of music information is taking place in three different levels (Liem et al., 2011): a. the music creator captures his thinking and his knowledge in a musical structure, b. the performer converts the written score into sounds, and c. the listener receives the sound as a result of this specific process. Different dimensions characterize the information conveyed by a musical work. Harmony, rhythm, melody, and structure are the dimensions that are carried by the written score. In the case of a musical performance there are other dimensions of music information such as timbre, articulation, and timing, that may be all or in part of interest for the listener (Melucci & Orio, 1999).

The investigation of the information seeking behavior in specialized contexts is multidisciplinary in nature (Futrelle & Downie, 2002; Wilson, 2006). The specialized context of music information seeking includes a wide spectrum of behavioral issues such as music information needs, preferred information resources, barriers/obstacles when seeking information, information literacy skills of musicians, etc., (Futrelle & Downie, 2002; Kostagiolas, Lavranos, Korfiatis, Papadatos & Papavlasopoulos, 2015). Music information seeking aims to satisfy musicians' information needs through the employment of specific online and offline information resources. Furthermore, information seeking includes the techniques and methods for organizing, searching and retrieving music information (Orio, 2006). Information seeking increases the ability to address a need, to resolve a problem by changing the current state of individual's music knowledge (Savolainen, 1995).

Music information seeking is changing the way that individuals understand the very content of music, and process collections of music material for access, research, and preservation (Futrelle & Downie, 2002). Therefore, information availability is important for all those which are engaged with music and relate to all their roles such as composers, performers, educators, students, listeners, etc. Overall studying the information seeking behavior perspective is important for understanding the way musicians seek and utilize information. While several studies in the literature have examined music information seeking in the context of hedonic motives, music information can also be used for utilitarian purposes. Indeed, the

Figure 1. Three forms of music information representation, including the transformation between them
Modified from: Liem et al., 2011

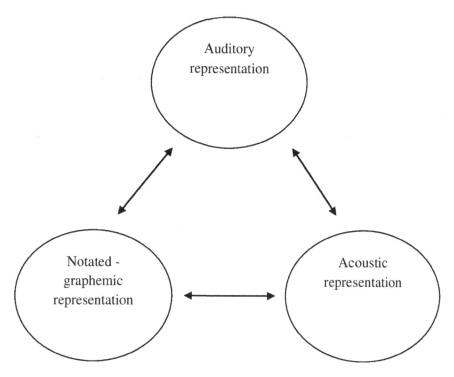

outcomes of music information seeking in everyday life may be of hedonic nature or may be directed to utilitarian purposes (Laplante & Downie, 2011). According to this, the individuals' everyday life usages of music information has both utilitarian (e.g., acquisition of music and information about music by increasing knowledge and enriching listening analysis, acquisition of music scores, acquisition of information about music pieces, etc.) and hedonic (e.g., entertainment, enjoyment reasons, recreational listening, etc.) outcomes.

In recent years, due to the increasing volume and the demand for music information, there has been created a need for the investigation of the information seeking behavior of various musical communities (Dougan, 2012). These consist of non experts, amateur musicians, music lovers, etc., and range up to professional musicians such as composers, musicologists, theorists, performers, etc., who need constant information updating in order to improve their music work and develop specific skills. All of the above play specific roles in the context of their musical avocation and work (e.g., music teachers, students, etc.), their musical expression and creativity (e.g., composers, performers, listeners, etc.) or of the conscious or not integration into groups with similar music interests (e.g., listening classical, pop, rock music, etc.) (Kostagiolas et al., 2015). These roles generate motives and needs in order to seek and use music information from a variety of information resources. However, the effective and efficient use of the available resources of music information require rise above personal or wider barriers/obstacles faced when seeking information (Kostagiolas et al., 2015). In particular, the search for music information is carried out within a specific socioeconomic environment which may (or may not) actually make available modern music information systems and information services and thus presenting a barrier to musicians' seeking information (Weigl & Guastavino, 2011).

MUSICIANS AND MUSIC INFORMATION TECHNOLOGIES

The creation of the Musical Instrument Digital Interface (MIDI) in 1983 is considered to be a technological milestone. MIDI is an interface employed to transmit information between electronic instruments and computers (Gresham-Lancaster, 1998) and converts music to a language recognizable to a computer. This specific digital interface allows the musicians to play their MIDI capable instrument and have their music recognized by the computer as a MIDI file. Once MIDI file is up and running, instruments of all kinds are created to use for various purposes this specific interface. For instance, there are keyboards for pianists, electric string instruments, wind controllers for wind players, xylophones and electronic drum sets for percussionists, which all of them are capable with the MIDI (Gresham-Lancaster, 1998).

As it is shown in Figure 2, the work of Gresham- Lancaster (1998) provides a graphic depiction of the data flow and MIDI channel assignments. According to this depiction, each potential user is assigned a MIDI port (one input and one output) numbered 2 through 7. If the potential user on port 7 wants to communicate with the user on port 2, the only thing he has to do is to send a MIDI channel-type message on MIDI channel 2. The potential user on port 2 receives the identical MIDI channel message rechannelized on MIDI channel 7 and encoded with the identity of the sender. In this way, the music information production has been based on a concept of a network for making music.

Figure 2. A graphic depiction of the data flow and MIDI channel assignments
Modified from: Gresham-Lancaster, 1998

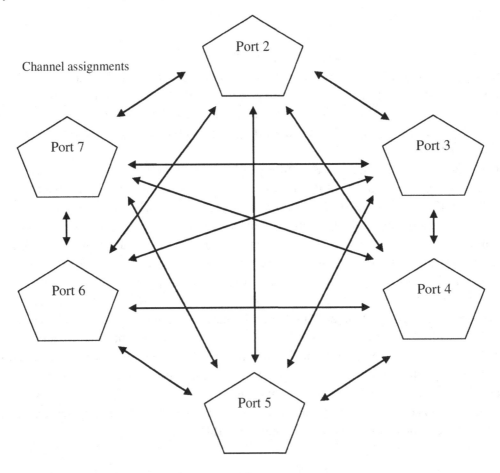

Sequencer is a programmable electronic device for storing sequences of musical notes, chords, or rhythms and transmitting them when required to an electronic musical instrument, and is the software followed the creation of MIDI (Arar & Kapur, 2013). Sequencers give the opportunity to network devices together and use hardware controllers to trigger software audio samples. In this way, a musical performance could not only be recorded but could be notated in actual music notation as well. Sequencers have been around since the early part of recording technology in some form or another but became more accessible to musicians the early 2000s (Arar & Kapur, 2013). It is very much like having a private recording studio where the musician gets to record in real time, following and keeping a steady beat played by the software. Sequencers are different than MIDI because they record actual sound. The terms which are familiar to the most of the people are the four, eight, and sixteen track recorder. In the case of the four track recorder, four different instruments or tracks are recorded. For example, in a typical brass quintet, the trumpets can be on one track while the horn, trombone and tuba can each be on another track. As mentioned above, sequencers began as software applications following the creation of MIDI. However, the technological capabilities were limited and couldn't handle the memory strain of the recorded sound, as well as sound files take up much more space than text files (Arar & Kapur, 2013). However, hardware developments in recent years made sequencers available and now are used quite frequently both by professional and amateur musicians. Indeed, what used to be the exclusive technology of recording engineers is now readily available to the average person in the form of inexpensive or even free, open-source software (Duignan, Biddle, & Noble, 2005). Both MIDI and sequencing applications have changed the musicians' everyday life by creating accessibility to music information that did not exist to the average person. Both have changed the possibilities for musical creative activities such as composition, performance, listening and analysis and opened the door for much wider access to music information.

In the decades between the 1980s and early 2000s all the above methods for pitch detection, music transcription, and sound separation were still in very preliminary stages (Dittmar et al., 2012). As said in this chapter, now these have become powerful and everyday tools for musicians that give instructions and feedback in terms of rhythm, pitch, intonation, expression, and other musical aspects. Overall, the development of online systems and multimedia applications expanded the availability of music information through different media (e.g., television, radio broadcasting, etc.), digital storage devices such as Compact Discs (CDs), as well as on the Internet (e.g. web based online reference services, databases, music related web sites and applications, etc.) (Fu, Lu, Ting, & Zhang, 2011). The value of such technologies and applications in musicians' everyday activities has been extensively appreciated. Advanced digital recording technologies and interactive web pages, CD-ROMs (Compact Disc Read-Only Memory), MP3 (MPEG-1 Audio Layer 3) and WAVE (Waveform Audio File Format) files, are placed next to MIDI and sequencers as powerful novel tools for searching, learning, creating and understanding music (Arar & Kapur, 2013). The development of these technologies increased the amount of music which is being produced by individuals having with formal and/or informal music education. CD-ROMS are packaged multimedia encyclopedias containing information about any aspect of music, as well as MP3 files are CD quality WAVE files that take up much less space on a computer hard drive (Egidi & Furini, 2005). Most of the sequencing programs can convert the music information to WAVE and MP3 files for easy accessibility and sharing. Furthermore, digital recording technology allows live music to be captured directly to a computer for processing and burning to CDs. All of these applications consists human everyday life possibilities for musical creativity that can and should be exploited in the individuals' music information seeking behavior.

Interactive applications with a more formal approach to music information research have been created. These applications include web-based information services, software tools, file compression services, or handheld music devices (Nanopoulos, Rafailidis, Ruxanda, & Manolopoulos, 2009). All of these guide individuals through different musical creative activities like music listening, music performance, or musical composition. The use of these technologies has changed the way of music's distribution and consumption as well as never before individuals had access to such global scale, vast amount of musical resources (Nanopoulos et al., 2009). For example, the recent developments in portable devices like smart phones and tablets resulted in more powerful audio processing features and more appealing visuals. As a result, the app market has had an immense growth and everyday more music information related applications are becoming available (Egidi & Furini, 2005). Also by increasing the demand for music there are created novel opportunities for the music industry. Therefore, several commercial systems have been developed with varying objectives, e.g., online purchasing of tracks, albums, or music recommender systems (Dittmar et al., 2012).

The usage of music information technologies in musicians' everyday life is significant and is considered as a continuous process. On the one hand it is based on the achievements of the scientific community, and on the other hand it is a process that requires changes in a community where many procedures and techniques still remain very traditional (Nanopoulos et al., 2009). Therefore, the development of music information technologies and musical information environment of the 21st century offer opportunities but at the same time cause many challenges such as: a. their continuous and effective distribution to the final user, b. the bridging of the gap between music information and music technology communities, and c. the design of friendly information systems capable of developing real musical skills (Dittmar et al., 2012). Also, the use of information technologies in the music field enables meaningful and constructionist interaction in collaborative music environments. It allows to multiple users in different locations to collaborate in their musical creative activities such as composition, performance, etc., (Nikolaidou, Hadjileontiadou, & Hadjileontiadis, 2004). The need for effective use of music information technologies is important for musicians of all levels and can support their composition activities, their performance, musicologist studies, listening, etc. Due to the variety of musicians' information behavior, as well as the different types of music information needs, their information behavior perspective is important for developing specialized information technology features (Lee, Downie, & Jones, 2007). Therefore, a contextual examination of music information technologies and their uses, gives the opportunity to understand individuals' music information seeking behavior which is directly connected with creative activities such as composition, performance, listening and analysis (Brown, 2002).

A CONCEPTUAL APPROACH ON MUSIC INFORMATION RETRIEVAL (MIR)

The amount of multimedia and audio data available from different information resources has increased significantly over the last decades and has become more accessible to the public (Kirthika & Chattamvelli, 2012). This large amount of music information accessible to the general public created the need for developing tools to effectively retrieve and manage the provided music information by the end users (Nanopoulos et al., 2009). Music Information Retrieval (MIR) is based on the traditions, methodologies, and techniques of a wide range of disciplines including the acoustics, psychoacoustics, signal processing, computer science, musicology, library science, informatics, machine learning, etc., (Futrelle & Downie, 2002; Fu et al., 2011). The main objective of MIR research is the provision of the access to the huge volume of the existing music information on a level equal to, or exceeding, that currently being afforded by the search engines (Downie, 2004). Music information is contained from acoustic, rhythmic, harmonic, structural, and cultural characteristics (Laplante & Downie, 2006). The MIR field is focused on extracting information from music itself and using this information to solve a wide range of problems including automatic music transcription, artist recognition, beat detection, genre classification and music recommendation (Lamere, 2008). MIR is based on the development of retrieval systems which have to do with the music information, whether it be in represented in text (e.g., bibliographic information, lyrics, etc.), auditory (e.g., MP3s, WAVE, etc.) or symbolic (e.g., MIDI, score, etc.) formats is the principal mechanism by which users interact with the systems (Karydis, Nanopoulos, Papadopoulos, & Manolopoulos, 2005).

Characteristics and Architecture of Music Information Retrieval (MIR) Systems

Information retrieval research is expanded through the increase of information systems and resources, and develops additional sets of information services in accordance with the specific needs of the users (Tsakonas & Papatheodorou, 2006). An important issue in achieving efficient and precisely information retrieval is the development of search mechanisms to ensure delivery of qualitative data in response to the users' search requests (Stamou, Kozanidis, Tzekou, & Zotos, 2008). More specifically, MIR research aims to develop systems that allow users to search music content through properly defined queries. The MIR systems are distinguished on the base of strategies and techniques used to retrieve music information (Downie, 2004; Goto, 2012). The successful MIR applications and systems must be capable of analyzing and manipulating the musical contents efficiently (Trohidis & Hadjileontiadis, 2011). According to the literature, there are found four main strategies for MIR systems: a. query by text, b. query by notation, c. query by example, and d. query by humming (Orio, 2006). A query by text system (e.g., bibliographic information, lyrics, etc.) uses conceptual metadata and enables user searches based on textual data. In a query by notation system user placing notes on a musical staff to form the query, and in a query by example system (e.g., submitting a known MP3 to find similar pieces, etc.) user can search a music recording using a sample of the original piece. Furthermore, a query by humming system uses only a sung or hummed melody in order to retrieve the music information (Antonelli, Rizzi, & Del Vescovo, 2010). As it shown in Figure 3, the main components of a typical MIR system may include: a. the query formation, b. the description extraction, c. the matching, and d. the retrieval of music information (Casey et al., 2008). The scope of an MIR system can be situated on a scale of specificity for which the query type and choice of exact or approximate matching define the characteristic specificity of the system (Lippincott, 2002; Typke, Wiering, & Veltkamp, 2005; Casey et al., 2008). The specificity of a retrieval task relates to how much acoustic and musical material a retrieved result must share with a query to be considered relevant. Also, the specificity relates to how many documents in total could be considered relevant retrieval results MIR systems are characterized by certain features that are common between them (Casey et al., 2008).

Some of the existing MIR systems conduct searches through music metadata for artists' biography, music reviews, new releases, concert dates, etc., as well as other systems search for lyrics. There are MIR systems that search by track or artist for music browsing. Also, there exist some systems where users make queries by humming. Media management and track identification are some of the functionalities of the MIR systems. Furthermore, some of these systems have the functionalities for artists and truck recommendations and automatic generation of playlists based on user preferences

Figure 3. Flowchart of a typical content-based MIR query system
Modified from: Casey et al., 2008

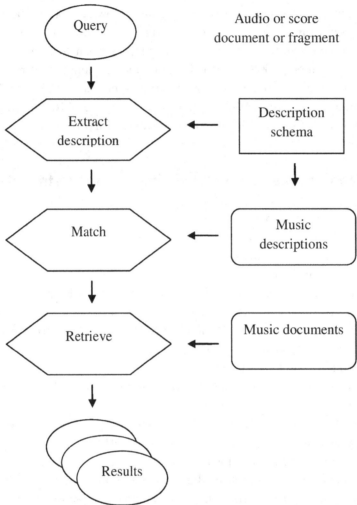

(Downie, 2004; Typke et al., 2005). Another challenge for MIR is the representation of musical information through a set of its features. The feature selection can be distinguished in two stages: a. the symbolic representation (e.g., MIDI format), and b. the acoustic representation (e.g., audio format, WAVE, MP3, etc.) (Karydis et al., 2005). According to this, the types of input that are provided in the MIR systems can be broadly grouped in two categories: a. the textual input, and b. the audio input. Textual input in regard to textual information, like metadata, lyrics, or high-level textual features like smart word (Knees, Pohle, Schedl, & Widmer, 2007) or tags (Levy & Sandler, 2009), as well as other textual features representing high level concepts, like mood or genre (Pampalk & Goto, 2006). Audio input can be a track or other low level features extracted from a track in order to be used for querying by example. Some MIR systems allow users to input an existing track either from a catalog or to upload one while others allow users to generate audio by recording or humming (Lippincott, 2002).

As it shown Figure 4, the architecture of a typical MIR system may include five stages (Melucci & Orio, 1999): a. a Web browser based user interface which would be Java enabled to permit the processing of MIDI objects, b. the segmentation transforming MIDI files into segmented textual files to be indexed by the indexing component, c. the indexing component which generates inverted files to be used as indexes at retrieval time, d. the search engines which retrieve musical documents matching the query of the user, and e. the digital object server, such as database server manages digitized manuscripts, scores and performances at different levels of quality. The flow of the interaction in a typical MIR system is described in Figure 4.

Figure 4. Architecture of a potential MIR system
Modified from: Melucci & Orio, 1999

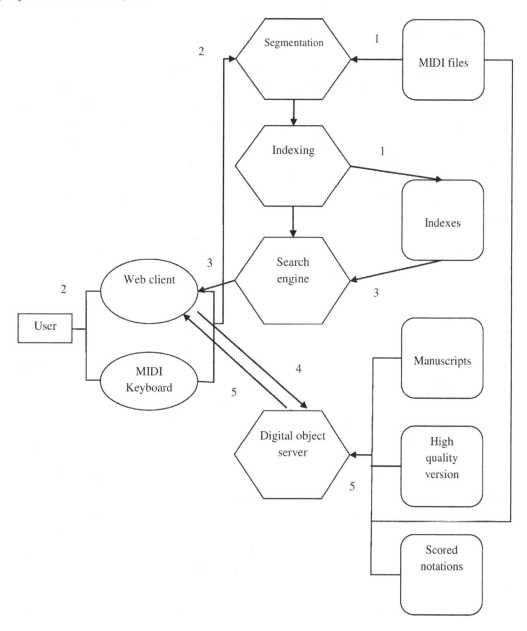

In stage 1 the MIDI files are converted into a form that can be indexed. Stage 2, includes the user queries based on specific information need through a musical graphical (Web form) or a MIDI keyboard interface in which the queries being converted and segmented into a form that can be indexed. In stage 3 is produced a list of digitized versions of the retrieved documents. In stage 4 the user selects one of the retrieved documents and asks the system to retrieve one of the digitized objects. Different types of objects may exist such as manuscripts, performances, scored notations, and MIDI files. Finally, in stage 5 the users access the digitized database and retrieve the selected one (Melucci & Orio, 1999).

The work of Typke et al., (2005) provides an overview of 17 content-based Music Information Retrieval systems, both for audio and for symbolic music notation. More specifically, they provide an overview of the characteristics (e.g., input, matching, features, Indexing, and collection size) of these MIR systems. A detailed list of the abovementioned 17 MIR systems can be found on the Appendix.

Music Information Retrieval (MIR) and Music Information Seeking Behavior

Advances in information technology services and systems (e.g., digital libraries, e-portals, etc.) support information retrieval research. Enforce individuals' information seeking behavior, retrieval and use, and form the way they interact with such information systems (Tsakonas & Papatheodorou, 2006). Information seeking behavior is driven by information needs which are identified by the information research queries. Intend the accomplishment of specific tasks are determined by the information motives that induce the information queries (Kirtsis & Stamou, 2011). More specifically, MIR research includes the investigation of searching, organizing, processing, and accessing the music information in a digital environment (Hsu & Huang, 2014). As mentioned in this chapter, MIR aims to identify various words and properties contained within musical selections within a musical database through a query mechanism in order a user to retrieve the required music information (Wang, Kim, Hong, & Youn, 2009). All of the abovementioned topics constitute part of the music information seeking behavior.

In regards to general information access and retrieval, researchers have developed several information seeking behavior models which include Krikelas' (1983) model, Bates' (1989) berry picking model of information seeking, Kuhlthau's (1991) model of Information search process, Dervin's (1992) sense making model, Ingwersen's (1992) cognitive model, Savolainen's (1995) everyday life information seeking model, Leckie, Pettigrew and Sylvain model (1996), Saracevic's model of stratified interaction (1996),Wilson's (1999) model of information seeking behavior (Lee, 2010). More specifically, the work of Baeza-Yates & Ribeiro Neto (1999) provides a model of the standard information access process. As it shown in Figure 5, this process starts with information needs, continues with the selection of a system and the collections to search on. After that formulates a query, sends the query to the system, and receive the results in the form of information items. Then evaluate the results, and if the process is done, stops. If is not done, then reformulates the query and goes back to send the query again. This model assumes an interaction cycle repeating the process until a perfect result is found. Most of the models mentioned above are concentrated on describing the general process of information seeking from a broad perspective, providing limited information about the information seeking behavior in specific contexts such as music information seeking and retrieval.

Research towards music information seeking and retrieval has been conducted during the last decades in response to the growing interest of digital music collections and a number of different aspects of music information behavior have been investigated (Weigl & Guastavino, 2011). At the same time the MIR systems have become a part of peoples' everyday lives through music listening, purchasing and research

Figure 5. A simplified diagram of the standard model of the information access process
Modified from: Baeza-Yates & Ribeiro Neto, 1999

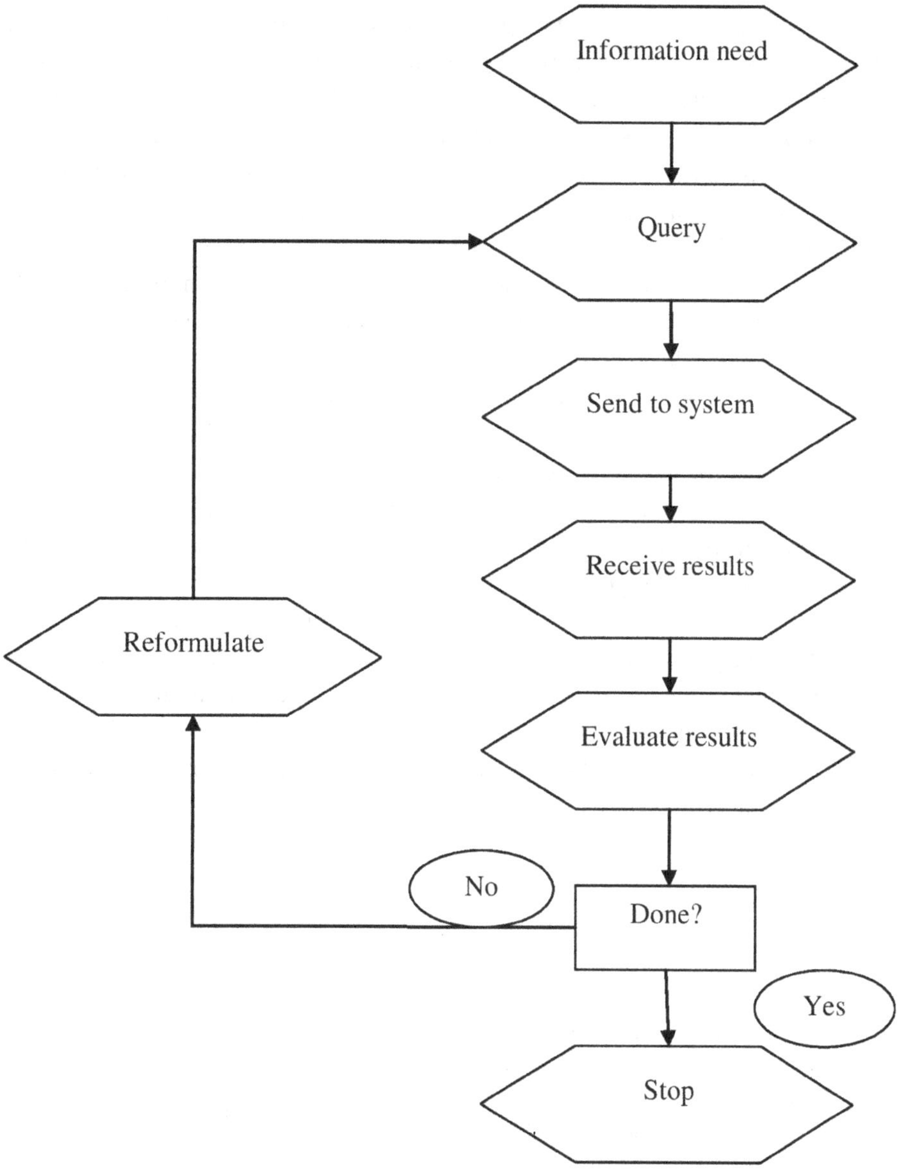

(Laplante & Downie, 2011). Therefore, the use and the development of MIR systems have an effect on a wide range of groups and disciplines which are directly related with music information seeking and retrieval. Specifically, two general categories of people are identified who are dealing with MIR systems: a. the users (e.g., musicians, composers, performers, listeners, etc.) and b. the developers (e.g., music and audio engineers, computer scientists, etc.) of the MIR systems (Downie, 2003). The largest portion of the first category has to do with the general population. Individuals within this category include the amateur listeners who use MIR systems in order to retrieve music for recreational listening. On the other hand, music researchers, theorists, composers, performers, and musicologists, also use MIR systems for the retrieval of music but on a professional level for knowledge and learning acquisition (Orio, 2006).

The second category of people who are dealing with MIR systems includes groups which play a significant role in the development of MIR systems. The first group consists of the audio engineers who develop the technology which enables the connection between text based searching and sound based searching (Downie, 2003). Computer scientists constitute another group of people who are dealing with MIR systems. Computer scientists work together with the audio engineers in order to develop computer systems that will conform to contemporary audio technology and MIR system interfaces (Downie, 2003). Also, another scientific group that of indexing professionals and librarians work with MIR system interfaces to provide bibliographic and cataloging skills in order to organize the textual metadata associated with different musical works, as well as musicologists provide assistance to indexing professionals by pulling metadata from musical works. All of these professional groups play important roles in MIR system development and each one contributes to a different part of the overall complex system (Downie, 2003).

The last decades, despite a lot of research has been conducted on music information seeking and retrieval, only a few researchers focus on user behavior in real life settings (Laplante & Downie, 2011). Such of researches are interested in information seeking behaviors that can be supported in a MIR system. Also, such of researches are focused on the everyday life behaviors of people that are dealing with music that they personally enjoy, as well as the behaviors of music professionals. For this reason, a variety of techniques is used in order to gain as rich a picture as possible of individuals' music information seeking behaviors. Some of these techniques constitute the personalized interviews (e.g., recording of what people do with publicly accessible music collections in conventional music information resources), the participant observations (e.g., finding out how people organize their personal music collections), the query analyses (e.g., music queries posted to Web services), etc., (Cunningham and Nichols, 2009). All of the above mentioned techniques constitute rich examples of music information behaviors, giving valuable information to the researchers about individuals' everyday music information seeking behaviors and their relationship with MIR systems (Cunningham and Nichols, 2009).

DISCUSSION

Thanks to the advances in digital signal processing technologies capable of data storage and transmission of music information material (Liem et al., 2012), various audio formats, coupled with media players, software, and channels have changed the way people interact with music (Tsai & Wang, 2005). Furthermore, with the development of digital media technology, people are exposed to music in everyday life environments like in their work, at home, at restaurants, theaters, etc. The advances of information and communication technologies affected every aspect of individuals' music information seeking behavior (McLean, Oliver, & Wainwright, 2010). Music information technology provides a robust, reliable, and secure information technology infrastructure in order to support both direct and indirect the services that support musicians (Nanopoulos et al., 2009). Nowadays, users can have access to a large amount of music information through digital libraries and the Internet. Therefore, a variety of musical communities professional and not (e.g., composers, performers, listeners, musicologists, etc.) are creatively benefited (NRC, 2003).

Overall the above technologies promote musical creativity, critical thinking and independent understanding. However, at the same time a need is developed for giving users the ability to use these systems and retrieve music data effectively. The conventional keyword based queries retrieval just attaches a set of keywords to the music objects in order to aid information retrieval but at the same time information within the music object is omitted (Orio, 2006). For this reason, content based MIR is developed in order to allow searching music information more directly and accurately. In the context of meeting the information needs of musicians there are developed various information systems to support them in locating music such as music databases, music recommender systems, etc. (Cunningham, Bainbridge, & McKay, 2007). The requirement for MIR systems arises from the very fact that large amount of music data has been made available on the Internet and those interests need an efficient way to navigate in the music information universe. As far as MIR is concerned, the music melody is the most appropriate representation of the music content. Thus, it is very helpful to provide both the keyword based retrieval and the melody based retrieval in a MIR system (Jin & Huang, 2004).

MIR includes searching music information databases, note extraction, melody and rhythm tracking, harmonic structure analysis, timbre and instrument identification, etc. (Wieczorkowska & Ras, 2003). This field focuses on retrieving information from large, online repositories of music content, using various forms of query based approaches. MIR techniques can be applied in a wide variety of contexts, ranging from searches in music libraries, to vast online digital environments (Orio, 2006). In MIR research, strategies are developed for enabling automatic access to music collections. Content based MIR is focused on: a. extracting features from musical pieces, and b. using these features in combination with machine learning techniques, with the purpose of their automatically classification (Roos & Manaris, 2007). Furthermore, MIR systems enable the music industry, music professionals and individual users to search large quantities of musical audio or encoded scores (Casey et al., 2008). Three main components can be discerned in such systems: a. the user interface, b. the database, and c. the similarity measure. The work of the last is to compare the user's query to the items in the database and to return a ranked list of the search results (Wiering, 2006). Therefore, considering the contemporary environment of music digital libraries which include millions of music pieces, MIR approaches that utilize models of human aesthetics are of great importance (Roos & Manaris, 2007).

Music information technologies have increased the accessibility and retrievability of music information within large online repositories (Liem et al., 2012). These technologies have reshaped the music industry in terms of promotion and distribution strategies. According to Liem et al. (2012), the modern music industry has been form by these technological advances. Also, many music information researchers have reworked their strategies based on information technology advances. Some strategic changes are also related to the development of MIR systems through new technologies. Much of these changes have brought about practical applications in response to the information behavior of individuals (Reed, 2004). Furthermore, the obstacles musicians face when seeking information online are gradually reduced (McLean et al., 2010). Therefore, new and more direct link between music and society is gradually established due to the advances of music information technologies (Kostagiolas et al., 2015).

CONCLUSION

This work focuses on the investigation of the technologies and the "realities" of musicians' information seeking behavior. Some of the main technological advances which have led to a new "reality" for processing, organizing and retrieving music information have been presented. The introduction of these novel information technologies affects individuals' music information seeking behavior and overall the way people interact with music itself. The outcomes of this brief review of the literature established a theoretical connection of music information technologies to musicians' information seeking behavior patterns. The way individuals enjoy and relate to music has influenced due to the flexibility given by digital music formats, the huge quantity of available information, the many platforms for searching, sharing, recommending music, and the tools for mixing and editing audio. The technological advances in music have opened new creative capabilities for musical expression and increasing the accessibility and retrievability of music within large data repositories. Hopefully, this work provides the basis for further discourse and research on the topics related to the associations of music information technologies and musicians' information seeking behavior. Certainly, further qualitative and quantitative research is required for the interrelation between music information seeking and retrieval systems as well as musicians' information seeking behavior. Empirical surveys can in the near future further investigate of the theoretical hypotheses presented in the current study.

REFERENCES

Antonelli, M., Rizzi, A., & Del Vescovo, G. (2010). A query by humming system for music information retrieval. *Proceedings of the 10th International Conference on Intelligent Systems Design and Applications (ISDA'10)*. Cairo, Egypt. IEEE. doi:10.1109/ISDA.2010.5687200

Arar, R., & Kapur, A. (2013). A history of sequencers: Interfaces for organized pattern-based music. *Proceedings of the Sound and Music Computing Conference 2013 (SMC'13)*. Stockholm, Sweden. SMC.

Baeza-Yates, R., & Ribeiro-Neto, B. (1999). *Modern information retrieval*. Boston, MA, USA: Addison-Wesley Longman Publishing.

Brown, C. D. (2002). Straddling the humanities and social sciences: The research process of music scholars. *Library & Information Science Research*, *24*(1), 73–94. doi:10.1016/S0740-8188(01)00105-0

Byrd, D., & Crawford, T. (2002). Problems of music information retrieval in the real world. *Information Processing & Management*, *38*(2), 249–272. doi:10.1016/S0306-4573(01)00033-4

Casey, M. A., Veltkamp, R., Goto, M., Leman, M., Rhodes, C., & Slaney, M. (2008). Content-based music information retrieval: Current directions and future challenges. *Proceedings of the IEEE*, *96*(4), 668–696. doi:10.1109/JPROC.2008.916370

Cunningham, S. J., Bainbridge, D., & McKay, D. (2007). Finding new music: A diary study of everyday encounter with novel songs. *Proceedings of the 8th International Society for Music Information Retrieval Conference (ISMIR'07)*. Vienna, Austria. ISMIR.

Cunningham, S. J., & Nichols, D. M. (2009). Exploring social music behaviour: An investigation of music selection at parties. *Proceedings of the 10th International Conference of the Society for Music Information Retrieval (ISMIR 2009)*. Kobe, Japan. ISMIR.

Dittmar, C., Cano, E., Abesser, J., & Grollmisch, S. (2012). Music information retrieval meets music education. In M. Müller, M. Goto, & M. Schedl (Eds.), *Multimodal Music Processing, Dagstuhl Follow-Ups* (Vol. 3, pp. 95–119). Dagstuhl, Germany: Schloss Dagstuhl-Leibniz-Zentrum für Informatik.

Dougan, K. (2012). Information seeking behaviors of music students. *RSR. Reference Services Review*, *40*(4), 558–573. doi:10.1108/00907321211277369

Downie, J. S. (2003). Music information retrieval. In B. Cronin (Ed.), *Annual Review of Information Science and Technology 37* (pp. 295–340). Medford, New Jersey, USA: Information Today.

Downie, J. S. (2004). A sample of music information retrieval approaches. *Journal of the American Society for Information Science and Technology*, *55*(12), 1033–1036. doi:10.1002/asi.20054

Duignan, M., Biddle, R., & Noble, J. (2005). A taxonomy of sequencer user-interfaces. In *Proceedings of the International Computer Music Conference (ICMC'05)*. Barcelona, Spain. ICMC.

Egidi, L., & Furini, M. (2005). Bringing multimedia contents into MP3 files. *IEEE Communications Magazine*, *43*(5), 90–97. doi:10.1109/MCOM.2005.1453428

Fu, Z., Lu, G., Ting, K. M., & Zhang, D. (2011). A Survey of audio-based music classification and annotation. *IEEE Transactions on Multimedia*, *13*(2), 303–319. doi:10.1109/TMM.2010.2098858

Futrelle, J., & Downie, J. S. (2002). Interdisciplinary communities and research issues in music information retrieval. In *Proceedings of the 3rd International Conference of the Society for Music Information Retrieval (ISMIR'02)*. Paris, France. ISMIR.

Goto, M. (2012). Grand challenges in music information research. In M. Müller, M. Goto, & M. Schedl (Eds.), *Multimodal Music Processing, Dagstuhl Follow-Ups* (Vol. 3, pp. 217–226). Dagstuhl, Germany: Schloss Dagstuhl-Leibniz-Zentrum für Informatik.

Gresham-Lancaster, S. (1998). The aesthetics and history of the hub: The effects of changing technology on network computer music. *Leonardo Music Journal*, *8*, 39–44. doi:10.2307/1513398

Hadjileontiadou, S. J., Nikolaidou, G. N., & Hadjileontiadis, L. J. (2007). Action-Research for the design and development of alternative learning environment using ICT: Case studies in environmental education and music lesson. In E. M. Botsari (Ed.), *Themes on Introductory Training for Newly Appointed Teachers* (pp. 104–117). Athens, Greece: Pedagogical Institute.

Heo, S. P., Suzuki, M., Ito, A., & Makino, S. (2006). An effective music information retrieval method using three-dimensional continuous DP. *IEEE Transactions on Multimedia*, *8*(3), 633–639. doi:10.1109/TMM.2006.870717

Hsu, J. L., & Huang, C. C. (2014). Designing a graph-based framework to support a multi-modal approach for music information retrieval. *Multimedia Tools and Applications*, *68*(3), 1–27.

Jin, Y., & Huang, M. (2004). Melody-based retrieval of music. *The Electronic Library*, *22*(3), 269–273. doi:10.1108/02640470410541679

Karydis, I., Nanopoulos, A., Papadopoulos, A. N., & Manolopoulos, Y. (2005). Audio indexing for efficient music information retrieval. *Proceedings of the 11th International Multimedia Modeling Conference (MMM'05)*. Melbourne, Victoria, Australia: IEEE. doi:10.1109/MMMC.2005.22

Kirthika, P., & Chattamvelli, R. (2012). A review of raga based music classification and music information retrieval (MIR). *2012 IEEE International Conference on Engineering Education: Innovative Practices and Future Trends (AICERA'12)*. Kottayam, India. IEEE. doi:10.1109/AICERA.2012.6306752

Kirtsis, N., & Stamou, S. (2011). Query Reformulation for Task-Oriented Web Searches. *Proceedings of the 2011 IEEE/WIC/ACM International Conference on Web Intelligence and Intelligent Agent Technology (WI-IAT'11)*. Lyon, France: IEEE. doi:10.1109/WI-IAT.2011.20

Knees, P., Pohle, T., Schedl, M., & Widmer, G. (2007). A music search engine built upon audio-based and web-based similarity measures. *Proceedings of the 10th annual international ACM SIGIR Conference on Research and Development in Information Retrieval (SIGIR'07)*. Amsterdam, Netherlands. ACM Press. doi:10.1145/1277741.1277818

Kostagiolas, P., Lavranos, Ch., Korfiatis, N., Papadatos, J., & Papavlasopoulos, S. (2015). Music, musicians and information seeking behaviour: A case study on a community concert band. *The Journal of Documentation, 71*(1), 3–24. doi:10.1108/JD-07-2013-0083

Lamere, P. (2008). Social tagging and music information retrieval. *Journal of New Music Research, 37*(2), 101–114. doi:10.1080/09298210802479284

Laplante, A., & Downie, J. S. (2006). Everyday life music information seeking behaviour of young adults. *Proceedings of the 7th International Conference of the Society for Music Information Retrieval (ISMIR'06)*. Victoria, British Columbia, Canada. ISMIR.

Laplante, A., & Downie, J. S. (2011). The utilitarian and hedonic outcomes of music information seeking in everyday life. *Library & Information Science Research, 33*(3), 202–210. doi:10.1016/j.lisr.2010.11.002

Lee, J. H. (2010). Analysis of user needs and information features in natural language queries seeking music information. *Journal of the American Society for Information Science and Technology, 61*(5), 1025–1045. doi:10.1002/asi.21302

Lee, J. H., Downie, J. S., & Jones, M. C. (2007). Preliminary analyses of information features provided by users for identifying music. *Proceedings of the 8th International Conference of the Society for Music Information Retrieval (ISMIR'07)*. Vienna, Austria. ISMIR.

Levy, M., & Sandler, M. (2009). Music information retrieval using social tags and audio. *IEEE Transactions on Multimedia, 11*(3), 383–395. doi:10.1109/TMM.2009.2012913

Liem, C. C. S., Müller, M., Eck, D., Tzanetakis, G., & Hanjalic, A. (2011). The need for music information retrieval with user-centered and multimodal strategies. *Proceedings of the 1st International ACM Workshop on Music Information Retrieval with User-Centered and Multimodal Strategies (MIRUM'11)*. Scottsdale, Arizona, USA. ACM Press. doi:10.1145/2072529.2072531

Liem, C. C. S., Rauber, A., Lidy, T., Lewis, R., Raphael, C., & Reiss, J. D. et al. (2012). Music information technology and professional stakeholder audiences: Mind the adoption gap. In M. Müller, M. Goto, & M. Schedl (Eds.), *Multimodal Music Processing, Dagstuhl Follow-Ups* (Vol. 3, pp. 227–246). Dagstuhl, Germany: Schloss Dagstuhl-Leibniz-Zentrum für Informatik.

Lippincott, A. (2002). Issues in content-based music information retrieval. *Journal of Information Science, 28*(2), 137–142. doi:10.1177/016555150202800205

McLean, R., Oliver, P. G., & Wainwright, D. W. (2010). The myths of empowerment through information communication technologies: An exploration of the music industries and fan bases. *Management Decision, 48*(9), 1365–1377. doi:10.1108/00251741011082116

Melucci, M., & Orio, N. (1999). Musical information retrieval using melodic surface. *Proceedings of the 4th ACM conference on Digital libraries (DL'99)*. San Francisco, California, USA. ACM Press. doi:10.1145/313238.313293

Nanopoulos, A., Rafailidis, D., Ruxanda, M. M., & Manolopoulos, Y. (2009). Music search engines: Specifications and challenges. *Information Processing & Management*, 45(3), 392–396. doi:10.1016/j.ipm.2009.02.002

National Research Council. (2003). Information technology, productivity, and creativity. In W. J. Mitchell, A. S. Inouye, & M. S. Blumenthal (Eds.), *Beyond Productivity: Information, Technology, Innovation, and Creativity* (pp. 15–29). Washington, District of Columbia, USA: The National Academies Press.

Nikolaidou, G. N., Hadjileontiadou, S. J., & Hadjileontiadis, L. J. (2004). On modeling children's non-verbal interactions during computer mediated music composition: A case study in primary school peers. Proceedings of the *4th IEEE International Conference on Advanced Learning Technologies (ICALT'04)* (pp. 756-758). Joensuu, Finland. IEEE. doi:10.1109/ICALT.2004.1357647

Orio, N. (2006). Music retrieval: A tutorial and review. *Foundations and Trends in Information Retrieval*, 1(1), 1–90. doi:10.1561/1500000002

Papachristopoulos, L., Tsakonas, G., & Papatheodorou, C. (2008). Enforcement of information seeking behaviour through digital library services. *Proceedings of the Libraries in the Digital Age Conference (LIDA'08)*. Dubrovnik and Mljet, Croatia. E-LIS.

Papatheodorou, C., Kapidakis, S., Sfakakis, M., & Vassiliou, A. (2003). Mining User Communities in Digital Libraries. *Information Technology and Libraries*, 22(4), 152–157.

Petrantonakis, P. C., & Hadjileontiadis, L. J. (2012). Adaptive Emotional Information Retrieval from EEG Signals in the Time-Frequency Domain. *IEEE Transactions on Signal Processing*, 60(5), 2604–2616. doi:10.1109/TSP.2012.2187647

Raimond, Y., & Sandler, M. (2008). A web of musical information. *Proceedings of the 9th International Conference of the Society for Music Information Retrieval (ISMIR'08)*. Philadelphia, Pennsylvania, USA. ISMIR.

Reed, C. (2004). *Internet Law: Text and Materials*. Cambridge: Cambridge University Press. doi:10.1017/CBO9780511808791

Roos, P., & Manaris, B. (2007). A music information retrieval approach based on power laws. *Proceedings of the 19th IEEE International Conference on Tools with Artificial Intelligence (ICTAI'07)*. Patras, Greece. IEEE. doi:10.1109/ICTAI.2007.170

Rubenstein, W. B. (1987). A database design for musical information. *Proceedings of the 1987 ACM SIGMOD International Conference on Management of Data (SIGMOD'87)*. San Francisco, California, USA. ACM Press. doi:10.1145/38713.38762

Savolainen, R. (1995). Everyday life information seeking: Approaching information seeking in the context of "way of life". *Library & Information Science Research*, 17(3), 259–294. doi:10.1016/0740-8188(95)90048-9

Stamou, S., & Christodoulakis, D. (2005). Retrieval Efficiency of Normalized Query Expansion. *Proceedings of the 6th International Conference on Computational Linguistics and Intelligent Text Processing (CICLing'05)*. Mexico City, Mexico. Springer-Verlag. doi:10.1007/978-3-540-30586-6_64

Stamou, S., Kozanidis, L., Tzekou, P., & Zotos, N. (2008). A Recommendation Model based on Site Semantics and Usage Mining. *International Journal of Digital Information Management, 6*(3), 244–256.

Tsai, W. H., & Wang, H. M. (2005). On the extraction of vocal-related information to facilitate the management of popular music collections. *Proceedings of the 5th ACM/IEEE-CS Joint Conference on Digital Libraries (JCDL'05)*. Denver, Colorado, USA. IEEE. doi:10.1145/1065385.1065432

Tsakonas, G., & Papatheodorou, C. (2006). Analyzing and Evaluating Usefulness and Usability in Electronic Information Services. *Journal of Information Science, 32*(5), 400–419. doi:10.1177/0165551506065934

Typke, R., Wiering, F., & Veltkamp, R. C. (2005). A Survey of music information retrieval systems. *Proceedings of the 6th International Conference of the Society for Music Information Retrieval (ISMIR'05)*. London, United Kingdom. ISMIR.

Wang, J., Deng, H., Yan, Q., & Wang, J. (2008). A collaborative model of low-level and high-level descriptors for semantics-based music information retrieval. *Proceedings of the 2008 IEEE/WIC/ACM International Conference on Web Intelligence and Intelligent Agent Technology (WI-IAT'08)*. Sydney, New South Wales, Australia. IEEE. doi:10.1109/WIIAT.2008.27

Wang, T., Kim, D. J., Hong, K. S., & Youn, J. S. (2009). Music information retrieval system using lyrics and melody information. *Proceedings of the 2009 Asia-Pacific Conference on Information Processing (APCIP'09)*. Shenzhen, China. IEEE. doi:10.1109/APCIP.2009.283

Weigl, D. M., & Guastavino, C. (2011). User studies in the music information retrieval literature. *Proceedings of the 12th International Conference of the Society for Music Information Retrieval (ISMIR'11)*. Miami, Florida, USA. ISMIR.

Wieczorkowska, A. A., & Ras, Z. W. (2003). Editorial-Music information retrieval. *Journal of Intelligent Information Systems, 21*(1), 5–8. doi:10.1023/A:1023543016136

Wiering, F. (2006). Can humans benefit from music information retrieval? *Proceedings of the 4th international conference on Adaptive multimedia retrieval: user, context, and feedback (AMR'06)*. Geneva, Switzerland. Springer-Verlag.

Wilson, T. D. (2006). Revisiting user studies and information needs. *The Journal of Documentation, 62*(6), 680–684. doi:10.1108/00220410610714912

Yang, X. H., Chen, Q. C., & Wang, X. L. (2010). Dictionary based inverted index for music information retrieval. *Proceedings of the 2010 International Conference on Machine Learning and Cybernetics (ICMLC'10)*. Qingdao, China. IEEE. doi:10.1109/ICMLC.2010.5580673

APPENDIX

List of the content-based Music Information Retrieval systems provided in the work of Typke et al., (2005)

- audentify!
- C-Brahms
- CubyHum
- Cuidado Music Browser
- GUIDO/MIR
- Meldex/Greenstone
- Musipedia
- notify! Whistle
- Orpheus
- Probabilistic "Name That Song"
- PROMS
- Cornell's "Query by Humming"
- Shazam
- SOMeJB - The SOM-enhanced JukeBox
- SoundCompass
- Super MBox
- Themefinder

Chapter 6
Affective Audio Synthesis for Sound Experience Enhancement

Konstantinos Drossos
Ionian University, Greece

Maximos Kaliakatsos-Papakostas
Aristotle University of Thessaloniki, Greece

Andreas Floros
Ionian University, Greece

ABSTRACT

With the advances of technology, multimedia tend to be a recurring and prominent component in almost all forms of communication. Although their content spans in various categories, there are two protuber-ant channels that are used for information conveyance, i.e. audio and visual. The former can transfer numerous content, ranging from low-level characteristics (e.g. spatial location of source and type of sound producing mechanism) to high and contextual (e.g. emotion). Additionally, recent results of published works depict the possibility for **automated synthesis** *of sounds, e.g. music and* **sound events**. *Based on the above, in this chapter the authors propose the integration of* **emotion recognition from sound** *with* **automated synthesis** *techniques. Such a task will enhance, on one hand, the process of computer driven creation of sound content by adding an anthropocentric factor (i.e. emotion) and, on the other, the experience of the multimedia user by offering an extra constituent that will intensify the immersion and the overall user experience level.*

INTRODUCTION

Modern communication and multimedia technologies are based on two prominent and vital elements: sound and image/video. Both are employed to transfer information, create virtual realms and enhance the immersion of the user. The latter is an important aspect that clearly enhances usage experience and is in general greatly aided by the elicitation of proper affective states to the user (Law, Roto, Hassenzahl, Vermeeren, & Kort, 2009). Emotion conveyance can be achieved from visual and auditory channels

DOI: 10.4018/978-1-4666-8659-5.ch006

(Chen, Tao, Huang, Miyasato, & Nakatsu, 1998). Focusing particularly on sound, one of its organized forms (music) was evolved as a means to enhance expressed emotions from another audio content type (speech) (Juslin & Laukka, 2003). But both aforementioned types are only a fraction of what actually occupies this perception channel (Drossos, Kotsakis, Kalliris, & Floros, 2013). There are non-musical and non-linguistic audio stimuli that originate from all possible sound sources, construct our audio environment, carry valuable information like the relation of their source and their receiver (e.g. movement of a source towards the receiver) and ultimately affect the listener's actions, reactions and emotions. These generalized audio stimuli are termed Sound Events (SEs) or general sounds (Drossos, Floros, & Kanellopoulos, 2012). They are apparent in all everyday life communication and multimedia applications, for example as sound effects or components of a virtual world depicting the results of user's actions (e.g. sound of a door opening or user's selection indication) (Drossos et al., 2012).

There are two main disciplines that examine the conveyance of emotion through music, namely the Music Emotion Recognition (MER) and Music Information Retrieval (MIR). Results presented from existing studies in these fields show **emotion recognition accuracy from musical data** of approximately 85% (Lu, Liu, & Zhang, 2006). Based on findings from MER and MIR there are some published works that are concerned with the synthesis of music that can elicit specific affective conditions to the listener (Casacuberta, 2004). But since music can be considered as an organized form of sound, the question if such practices can be applied to SEs was raised. Towards exploring this scientific area, recently, an ongoing evolution was initiated of a research field that focuses on **emotion recognition from SEs**. Although published works in that field are rather scarce (Weninger, Eyben, Schuller, Mortillaro, & Scherer, 2013), it has been shown by previous research conducted by the authors that **emotion recognition from SEs** is feasible with an accuracy reaching up to 88% regarding listener's arousal (Drossos et al., 2013). In addition, the authors have proposed and presented several aspects regarding systematic approaches to **automatic music composition** (Kaliakatsos-Papakostas, Floros, & Vrahatis, 2012c) and sound synthesis (Kaliakatsos-Papakostas, Epitropakis, Floros, & Vrahatis, 2012a), focusing on the generation of music and sound that adapts to certain specified characteristics (see also (Kaliakatsos-Papakostas, Floros, & Vrahatis, 2013c) for a review on such methodologies).

Thus, combining the aforementioned **automatic synthesis** methodologies with the findings from **SEs emotion recognition**, one can potentially synthesize SEs capable to elicit specific affective conditions to the listener. In this chapter proposal we intend to present novel findings and methodologies for affective enhanced SEs synthesis. According to authors' knowledge, there is no other similar published work. Such audio material can be used to enhance the immersion and the audio experience of users in multimedia by inflating the emotional conveyance from the application to the user. The rest of this chapter proposal is as follows. In the second section a brief overview is presented that concerns the state-of-the-art in **audio emotion recognition**, particularly focused on **emotion recognition from SEs**. The **automated music and sound synthesis** counterpart of the proposal is discussed in the third section whereas in the fourth section are some possible and proposed applications.

AUDIO EMOTION RECOGNITION

In general, **audio emotion recognition** can be considered as a Machine Learning task (Drossos et al., 2013). It consists of two stages, i.e: i) Training, and ii) Testing. In the former, a classification algorithm is fed with the emotional annotations of the sounds and a group of extracted features and produces a categorization model. The accuracy of the model, and thus of the whole process, is evaluated at the latter stage. This process is illustrated in Figure 1.

As can be seen in Figure 1, for both stages there is a set of components that are essential for the accomplishment of this task (Drossos, Floros, & Giannakoulopoulos, 2014) and these are:

1. **Emotionally annotated audio dataset**, which provide the training and testing data and their emotion annotations
2. Extracted features, resulting from the feature extraction process
3. Classification algorithm, employed in the machine learning phase
4. Classification model, resulting from the machine learning process

The determination of all the above components is relied on basic concepts of the **audio emotion recognition** process. The employed annotated dataset is determined by the emotions model that will be used in the recognition process and the extracted features are likely to focus on specific attributes of the audio signals. In addition, different algorithms exhibit various accuracy results in the process and some perform better when combined with specific models, features and emotions. Regarding the affective synthesis concept presented in this chapter, extracted features and classification algorithms are likely to have an impact both on the synthesis part (i.e. which features of signals will be processed) and to the classification of the produced sounds. In other words, in order to synthesize an **affective sound** the ef-

Figure 1. Illustration of the audio emotion recognition process. With dotted line is the training and with solid the testing stage

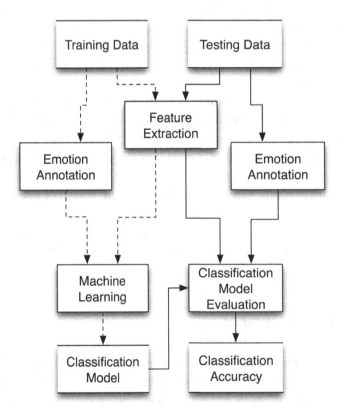

fect of specific features to the elicited emotion must be know and the resulting sound from the synthesis process should be evaluated in terms of the emotion that communicates to the listener.

In the following subsections will be presented the currently used emotional models along, a brief overview of annotation methods, the results and methods of the state-of-the-art in **emotion recognition from music** and **sound events** and the most common features used in such processes.

EMOTIONAL MODELS AND ANNOTATION METHODS

The emotional models can be discriminated in two abstract categories; one using verbal description for referring to emotions (e.g. "Happiness", "Sadness") and another modeling emotion as a resultant of affective states. The former are referred to as discrete models whereas the latter as dimensional models.

Discrete models emerge from the basic emotions model, which is dated back to the Darwing era and based on William James' theory of emotions (Cornelius, 2000). It consists of 4 emotions, termed as basic ("Happiness", "Sadness", "Fear" and "Anger"), and states that all other emotions can emerge from those. This model was questioned thoroughly in (Ortony & Turner, 1990) regarding the claim that a set of emotions can be used as a starting palette for all others. Probably due to immediate connection with human body components and functions, this model is used in modern published researches in the field of neuroscience (Drossos et al., 2012; Koelsch, 2010; Adolphs, 2002). Another frequently used discrete emotional model is the list of adjectives that contains several groups of synonym words (adjectives) (Hevner, 1936; Wieczorkowska, Synak, Lewis, & Ra, 2005). Originally consisted of 8 adjectives groups with each one group corresponding to specific emotional states (Hevner, 1936). An illustration of this model can be seen in Figure 2.

Some enhancements have been proposed to the adjectives list model, mostly regarding the increase of the adjectives groups, e.g. in (Li & Ogihara, 2003) there have been proposed 13 groups instead of the original 8. Although that this model can be considered as discrete (Drossos et al., 2012), the arrangement of the adjectives groups follows the concept of a 2D dimensional model, where each group is placed according to the increment in the affective states. For example, moving from group 8 to group 4 reflect the increase of the listener's arousal, whereas groups 6 and 2 exhibit opposite valence.

Dimensional emotional models represent emotion as a resultant of a set of components and emerged from the Circumplex model of affect (Russell, 1980). The latter render affective states, typically those of arousal and valence, in order to represent emotions. Thus, according to the employed affective states the model can be two-dimensional, three-dimensional etc. Every affective state is regarded as a component to the resulting space (2D, 3D etc.) and the final emotion is the resultant on that space. On a later stage, different verbal descriptions can be assigned to clusters of values in the aforementioned space and thus leading to the mapping of values to emotions (Drossos et al., 2014). Although that there are published works which portray such mapping, this is purely qualitatively since there is not a quantitative association of the values with verbal description of emotions. Typically, there are two dimensions utilized in dimensional models and these are 2: i) Arousal, and ii) Valence. There are proposals for the employment of extra dimensions, e.g. Dominance, but this is likely to result in an increased complexity of the model (Drossos et al., 2014).

The proposal and adoption of dimensional models also reduced a complication that existed regarding the cross-evaluation of emotional research. When a discrete model is utilized, the annotations of the data are performed by directly capturing the elicited emotion, most probably with a "question and answer"

Figure 2. Illustration of the List of Adjectives. (Adapted from Hevner, 1936; Wieczorkowska et al.2005)

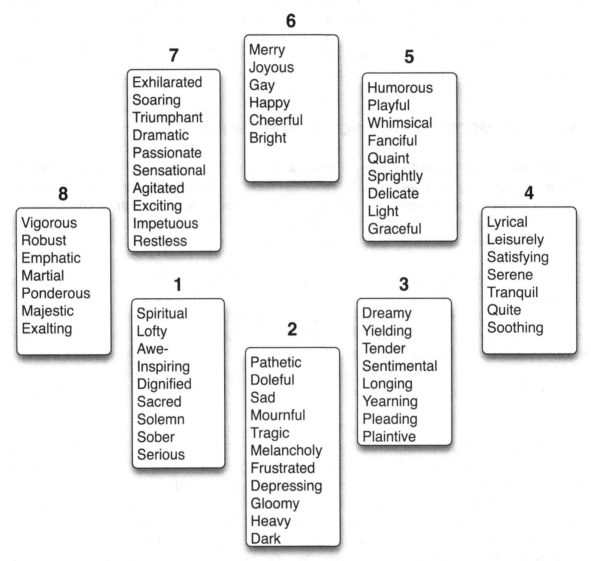

scheme. Thus, the participants in the annotation process have to choose the specific verbal description of emotion that reflects their affective condition in order to perform an annotation. Their choices are limited to the used words by the conductors of the process, which words are also the emotions incorporated in the model being utilized. Although that some verbal descriptions are quite straightforward and most probably used to represent the exactly same emotion (e.g. "Anger" or "Fear"), there are employed words that is not clear what emotional condition represent, for example, "Joy" and "Enjoyment" or "Cheerful" and "Happiness" (Juslin & Laukka, 2003). This uncertainty obscures the cross-evaluation and usage of results between and among different works when discrete emotional models are employed (Juslin & Laukka, 2003).

Contradictory, when dimensional models are utilized the annotation is performed by the depiction of the emotional states employed in the model. Even if there are some published works where the annotation was performed by the direct outline of the resultant in the model's area (Yang, Lin, Cheng, & Chen, 2008), there is an annotation method which allows the representation of 3 emotional states and offers the capability for immediate association with a corresponding emotional model. This is the Self Assessment Manikin (SAM) and was presented in (Bradley & Lang, 1994). With the SAM, the participants in the annotation process choose a figure from a set of images. The chosen image directly reflects the value for the corresponding dimension in the model. An illustration of the available set of figures in SAM is in Figure 3. In Figure 3a are presented the SAM figures for arousal in descending sorting, i.e. from left to right the manikin figures portray a decrease to arousal. In a same arrangement are the SAM figures for valence in Figure 3b, where from left to right the valence is decreasing. In Figure 3c are the SAM figures for Dominance in an ascending fashion, i.e. from left to right the dominance is increasing.

The utilization of an emotional model in the affective synthesis can and will have an impact on the targeted emotions. A discrete one will likely uncomplicate the process of recognition and evaluation, since the targeted state of the listener will be incorporated in a single verbal description. But, this single word is likely to cluster a set of verbal description either not presented in the annotation and evaluation process or perceived from the participants (in both aforementioned stages) as synonyms to the employed emotion verbal description. A dimensional model although that can allow a more elaborate targeting

Figure 3a. SAM figure for arousal

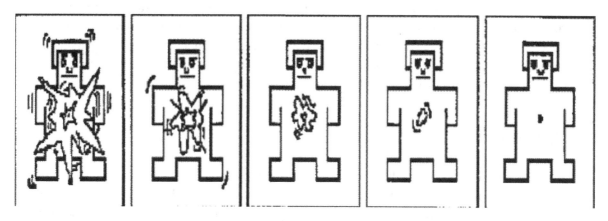

Figure 3b. SAM figure for valence

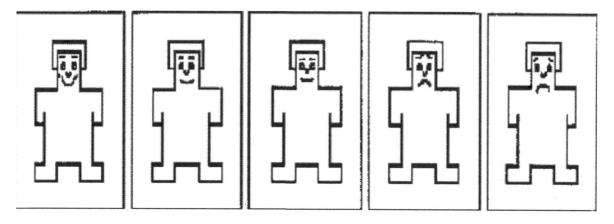

Figure 3c. SAM figure for dominance

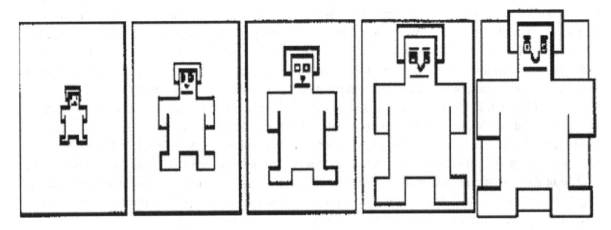

of emotions, by not referring to verbal description but to affective states, will cluster values in the used space (e.g. arousal and valence) almost arbitrary due to the lack of exact quantitavely association of values with verbal descriptions of emotions. On the other hand, a dimensional model offers a more focused approach to the affective states, regardless of what words are used to describe possible combinations.

Taking into account possible applications of **automated synthesis**, e.g. **automated synthesis** of **emotional enhanced sound effects** for video games, the approach of a dimensional model seems to be more appropriate. This is due to the fact that in such artistic and/or application environments the main aim is to target the alteration of an affective state of the spectator/listener, e.g. to elicit more or reduce the arousal or pleasure than to actually induce a specific emotion.

EMOTION RECOGNITION FROM MUSIC

The extraction of emotional information from music falls in the Music Information Retrieval discipline. One of the primary aims is the enhancement of music categorization by adding a content oriented parameter (emotion/mood) in addition to or instead of the legend "Artist / Year / Album" scheme (Zhang, Tian, Jiang, Huang, & Gao, 2008). The process is according to the one illustrated in Figure 1 and typical accuracy values can reach up to 89% (Xiao, Dellandrea, Dou, & Chen, 2008; Schmidt, Turnbull, & Kim, 2010).

In particular, as employed dataset are used annotated excerpts or complete musical pieces. The used emotional models vary. Both discrete and dimensional are employed but it seems that in recent works the latter are preferred (Kim et al., 2010). Typical extracted features are from various categories, i.e. timbre, dynamics, pitch and rhythm, e.g. attack time and slope, Mel-Frequency cepstral coefficients (MFCCs), spectral contrast, RMS energy, tempo, beat spectrum and histogram (Li & Ogihara, 2003; Kim et al., 2010; Yeh, Lin, & Chang, 2009). Usually their extraction is based on a short time scheme, e.g. consequent time frames of the musical information, in order also to evaluate the evolution of features as the musical stimuli develops through time (Schmidt et al., 2010; Lu et al., 2006). The categorization is performed with simple and meta-learning algorithms. Amongst the most used are Support Vector Machines, Tree-Based algorithms (e.g. C4.5), Gaussian Mixture Models and AdaBoost (Kim et al., 2010).

Results indicate that the correct classification of music regarding the elicited emotion is feasible, as indicated earlier in this section. But the question of whether the aforementioned results can be employed in a synthesis process is at interest in this chapter. According to the latter task, the employed classification algorithms seem to have an important role. For example, if a set of features, e.g. F_i, where F is the features set and *i* is each feature's index, there is the need for knowledge of the exact value that each *i* must have in order the synthesized audio material to elicit a specific emotional state or emotion. Thus, in an **automatic synthesis** procedure the results of the classification algorithms must be utilized in order to, one hand, evaluate the produced audio material and, on the other, to define criterions for the technical features' values that the synthesized sounds must have. For a most straightforward approach, Tree-Based algorithms seem to have an advantage, due to an uncomplicated interpretation of the features' values thresholds that determine the final categorization.

There are published works focused on the **affective music** synthesis task (Kejun & Shouqian, 2010). To authors' knowledge, most published works employ a dimensional model for emotions. Also, in order to produce a musical material that elicits specified emotional reactions to listeners, Genetic Algorithms (GAs) are utilized which evolve the material in order to obtained the needed results. For example, in (Zhu, S. Wang, & Z. Wang 2008) an approach for synthesizing **affective music** is presented by employing interactive GAs. The GAs control the performance parameters, based on the KTH rule system (Friberg, Bresin, & Sundberg, 2006), and the user interactively indicates his emotion. User's feedback is further employed in order to alter the performance and achieve the targeted emotion. Also, in (Sugimoto et al., 2008) is presented a work which deals with the design of emotional music through GAs by also employing an interaction from the Autonomic Nervous System (ANS) of human. In it, the final music material induces the targeted emotion by evolving musical characteristics according to the readings from the ANS and the utilization of GAs. The results show that the targeted emotions can be elicited to the listeners. Finally, in (Kejun & Shouqian, 2010) is presented a framework for emotional music design with GAs, which includes a proposed flow that will control the musical material's features alteration in order to perform the induction of the targeted emotion. The work concludes that there is the need for better GAs that will focus on the **automated music synthesis** targeting specific emotion elicitation. This aspect is covered in the **automated synthesis** part of this chapter.

EMOTION RECOGNITION FROM SOUND EVENTS

The recognition of emotion from general sounds (i.e. **sound events**) is a rather new field with sparse published works (Weninger et al., 2013). The recognition process is also conforms to the one outlined in Figure 1 but, and in contrast to the **emotion recognition from music**, there are few public available datasets with emotion annotations (Drossos et al., 2014). These are: a) IADS dataset, consisted of 167 monophonic sounds events with annotations for arousal, valence and dominance (Bradley & Lang, 2007), b) the Emotional Sound Database (ESD), with 360 **emotionally annotated sound events**, retrieved from the findallmusic[1] web page, and annotated by 4 subjects and utilizing the evaluator weighter estimator (Schuller et al., 2012; Grimm, Kroschel, Mower, & Narayanan, 2007), and c) BEADS dataset, consisting of 32 binaural sounds, allocated at 0, 45, 90, 135 and 180 degrees and annotated for arousal and valence (Drossos et al., 2014). According to the published works in the mentioned field, the acoustic cues extracted are similar to the **emotion recognition from music** process (mentioned previously).

Due to the inherent connection of the **sound events** with the acoustic environment and hence to the acoustic ecology, in (Drossos et al., 2012) was proposed the enhancement of this concept. More specifically, it was proposed the **Affective Acoustic Ecology** where the emotional dimension is also regarded in the legend Acoustic Ecology concept. The primary component of the proposed framework is the **sound event** that is defined as a structure having discrete characteristics that can affect the elicited emotions. These characteristics are:

- A sound waveform
- Manifestation of source's instantaneous spatial position, relative to the receiver
- Duration (time)
- Indication of the sound's creation procedure/how the sound was created, e.g. impact, friction etc.
- Evidence of vibrating objects' nature state (i.e. solid, liquid, gas)
- Semantic content

Apart from the last component, i.e. the semantic content, the remaining could be used in the emotion recognition process. Although that there was proposed a framework for the nature of sound which also includes the elements of the creation procedure (impact, friction, etc.) and the nature of the vibrating object, until the time that this work is prepared only the first two elements have been used in emotion recognition from **sound events**.

Regarding the waveform, there are few published works that are concerned with extracted technical features and emotion recognition. In (Drossos et al., 2013) there is a work that evaluates the legacy concept that rhythm has an effect on the arousal. Several acoustic cues, all related to rhythm characteristics, have been utilized and the recognition process was performed using Artificial Neural Networks (ANN), Logistic Regression and K-th Nearest Neighbors. The presented accuracy results reached up to 88%. Also, in (Weninger et al., 2013) was attempted the emotion recognition from the ESD and a investigation on whether there are common features than can be used for **emotion recognition in speech, music and general sounds**. Results indicated that such a task is difficult but there are acoustic cues that are functioning in an opposite manner for these fields, i.e. some features have the opposite effect in speech, music and general sounds.

Summarizing the above, there are a variety of technical cues used for emotion recognition which covers seemingly all attributes of an audio signal as described in the **Affective Acoustic Ecology** concept. The employed models can reveal that there is an association of the affective states with the technical features. Although that there is not an analytic and quantitavely association of the features values with values in the dimensional model, there is a qualitatively connection. In addition, there is also an observed variation of the employed algorithms for the machine learning stage. From the aforementioned algorithms there are some that can be considered as more suitable for **automatic synthesis**, i.e. Tree based. Hence and combining all the above, the creation of a framework for **automatic synthesis** of **affective sounds** is feasible by integrating current findings in the field of audio emotion recognition and **automatic synthesis** techniques. In the next sections these techniques will be presented and discussed.

AUTOMATIC SYNTHESIS

The task discussed in the proposed book chapter concerns the **automated music and sound synthesis** based on the guidelines that are provided by targeted audio-emotional features. To this end, the utilization of adaptable music and sound synthesis techniques will be discussed regarding their potential to compose music and **sound events** that adhere to specific audio and music features that convey emotional information. The systematic approaches that perform the desired task pertain to the category of the supervised synthesis techniques, as analysed in (Kaliakatsos-Papakostas et al., 2013b). Therein, the **intelligent music composition** systems have been categorized in three main groups:

1. Unsupervised **intelligent composition**: the algorithmic composition intelligence is expressed through simple rules that produce complex, unpredictable but yet structured output, a behavior that of- ten resembles natural phenomena.
2. Supervised **intelligent composition**: intelligent algorithms are utilized to modify the **automatic composition** system's parameters so that it may be able to compose music that meets some pre-defined criteria, not necessarily in real-time.
3. Interactive **intelligent composition**: the system is acknowledging the human preference in real-time and becomes adapted to it, by utilizing intelligent algorithms. Human preference is expressed either by a selection-rating scheme, or by performing tasks (like playing an instrument or adjusting target parameters in real-time).

According to the aforementioned categorization, supervised synthesis discusses the automated generation of music and audio according to the "supervision" provided by values describing a targeted output, e.g. by audio and music features. It is therefore studied whether the utilisation of audio and music features that can accurately describe the emotional content of SEs (as discussed in the second section), can indeed provide accurate compositional guidelines to supervised synthesis methodologies.

Supervised music and audio synthesis is performed effectively by evolutionary techniques, which allow the generation of output that adapts to better solutions towards solving a problem. The effectiveness of these algorithms derives from the immense force of population dynamics, which com- bines exploration and exploitation of the solutions' space, based on the sophisticated evolution of the large numbers of possible solutions. Several evolutionary approaches have been examined for the supervised generation of music and sound. Examples of such methodologies that have been employed for tasks related to the problem at hand are genetic programming (GP) (Koza, 1992) for block-based sound synthesis (Garcia, 2001a), genetic algorithms (GAs) (Holland, 1992) for the evolution of rhythms (Kaliakatsos-Papakostas, Floros, Vrahatis, & Kanellopoulos, 2012b) and differential evolution (DE) (Storn & Price, 1997) for the evolution of tones (Kaliakatsos-Papakostas, Epitropakis, Floros, & Vrahatis, 2013a). Thereby, this section of the chapter will describe the development of hybrid evolutionary systems that compose audio material – from the level of sound to the level of music. These systems could encompass specific emotional meaning, potentially harnessing multimedia systems with emotionally–driven content generation capabilities.

Supervised Intelligent Music Composition Systems

The systems that pertain to the category of supervised **intelligent music composition** utilize intelligent algorithms to achieve music composition under some qualitative guidelines, which are often called "target features", or simply "features". The underlying model that these systems utilize to produce music, is either tuned or created from scratch with the utilization of intelligent algorithms, towards the directions dictated by the features that the music output has to satisfy. An advantage of the supervised IMC systems is their ability to produce music with certain aesthetic and stylistic orientation (Manaris et al., 2007), in contrast to unsupervised composition systems. The hypothesis in this chapter, is that these systems could be driven not only by features with aesthetic meaning, but also by features that convey emotional information, proving the composed music and sound an emotionally as well as aesthetically oriented texture. Therefore, the formulation of these systems incorporates the following challenges: a) apply an intelligent algorithm to optimally traverse search spaces, producing numerical output, b) create an interpretation of this output to musical entities and c) select a proper set of features that describe the desired aesthetic and emotional music characteristics.

The selection of proper features is of vital importance for the supervised systems' performance not only in terms of aesthetic quality, but also for accurate emotional orientation. However, while these features provide landmarks for the system to compose music with certain characteristics, it is also important that the algorithm should allow the introduction of a considerable amount of novelty to the composed music. The selection of proper features is thus crucial: on the one hand they should capture the aesthetic and emotional essence of the music to be composed and on the other hand they should not over-determine the compositions, a fact that would lead to "replicate" compositions, depriving form the system the ability to introduce novelty. Research on supervised **intelligent composition** mainly addresses the establishment of effective intelligent methodologies that tune the composition models, restraining from the fact that the quality of the targeted features that describe music, are equally important.

Feature-Driven Composition Systems with Genetic Algorithms

The music composition algorithm may incorporate a set of parameters that define its compositional style and capabilities. It is thus crucial that a proper combination of these parameters is defined for the automatic creation of music, so that it may exhibit certain characteristics and aesthetic value of high quality. The utilization of Genetic algorithms (GA) provides proper values for these parameters, given a set of features that describe how the produced music should sound like. Thus, not only the formulation of a proper parametric model is required, but also, equally importantly, to the formalization of measures that accurately describe the target music texture. Regarding the perspective of this chapter, music texture is not only deteriorated in stylistic constraints, but it extents to the emotions conveyed by the audio/music output.

The Genetic Algorithms (GA) is a class of algorithms inspired by natural evolution, which iteratively produce better solutions to a problem. These algorithms belong to the wider class of "heuristics", meaning that they initially "guess" a set of random solutions and produce new ones grouped in generations, by utilizing information only from their current generation and their product candidate solutions. Specifically, the candidate solutions within a generation in a GA scheme are evolved using operators resembling natural genetic phenomena (like crossover and mutation) and a selection procedure that propagates the consecution of generations towards better solutions. A better solution means that the set of the model's parameters that this solution describes, gives a more satisfactory result in regards with a qualitative measurement that is called "fitness function". Among the most popular genetic operators are the crossover and mutation. Crossover incorporates the combination of the parameter between two "parent" solutions for the creation of two "children" solutions, while mutation is the random reassignment of certain parameter values of a "parent" solution to produce a new "children solution". The progression from one generation of "parent" solutions to the next, is finally accomplished with a selection process that allows the "better" fitted solutions among parents and children to form the new generation.

The key-notion in the GA is the precise and informative description of what a "better" solution is. In the case of supervised IMC, precise denotes the correct demarcation of the target musical attributes that the automatically composed music should encompass. The term informative expresses the necessity to model the target musical attributes in an as "continuous" manner as possible, abstaining the hazard to create non-smooth and discretized error surfaces that abound in local optima.

Among the first works for supervised composition using "objective" musical criteria for the assignment of fitness evaluations, was the work of Papadopoulos and Wiggins (1998). In this work a system was presented which was composing jazz solos over a given chord progression. The solutions to the problem were the melodies themselves, specifically pitch-duration pairs, and after a random initialization, GA with some special genetic operators with "musical meaning" was applied, fostering new generations of possible solutions-melodies. The evaluation process of each candidate solution-melody was based on eight evaluation indicators, borrowed by music theory. The results were reported to be promising, however a thorougher statistical examination of the results was not realized, according also to the authors' opinion in the concluding section of their work. A similar system was introduced in (Ozcan & Eral, 2008), also providing a downloadable application called AMUSE. In this work a set of ten music features were used for fitness evaluation. Furthermore, experimental results of a questionary-based research on a group of 20 participants, indicated that these features are linked to human preference, at some extent. The utilization of a fitness function based on music theoretic criteria was also utilized for the creation of four-part melodies from scratch (Donnelly & Sheppard, 2011).

On the other hand, features not related to music theory have also been utilized. These features are related to informatics and statistics, measuring aspects of melodic information capacity either through compressibility, or through various characteristics of music that can be translated into discrete probabilities. In (Alfonseca, Cebrian, & Ortega, 2007) the Normalized Compression Distance (NCD) is used to allow a GA compose music pieces that resemble the pieces of a certain style. The sum of NCDs between each possible solution-melody and a set of target pieces in a certain style is computed, and a solution-melody with a better fitness is the one for which a smaller sum of NCDs is obtained. Systems that genetically evolve Cellular Automata (CA) (Lo, 2012) and FL-systems (Kaliakatsos-Papakostas et al., 2012b) for music and rhythm composition have also been presented, where again fitness is calculated with the utilization of probability measures like n-Grams (Markov transition tables), Shannon Information Entropy and Compression Rate among others.

Feature-Driven Composition Genetic Programming

Genetic Programming (GP) works under the same evolutionary principle with the GA, that is evolving initially random possible solutions to new ones that are better fitted to the problem at hand. The difference between GP and GA is the problem's formulation. In GA, the optimization process targets at the model's parameters, while the utilization of GP allows the optimization of the model per se, since the populations of possible solutions incorporate entire programs that actually form the model. These programs are constituted of short sub-program segments, hierarchically structured in a tree-like representation. The genetic operators are similar to the ones used by the GA; however, they act on tree branches instead of string-like or numeric chromosomes. The crossover operator for example, exchanges sub-trees of the parents' trees, creating children that comprise of combined sub-program parts of their parents. Through a similar selection process as in the GA, new populations of possible solutions-programs are created which are better or equally fitted to the problem at hand.

Sound Synthesis

Among the first works that examined **automated sound synthesis** through systems evolved with GP was the one presented in (Putnam, 1994). Therein, the author reports on some initial results yielded by a system that evolves simple mathematical functions through GP, with interactive fitness evaluation (i.e. evaluation provided by the user). These functions were producing values that constructed a waveform. Main aim of the system was to lead generations of such functions to ones that produced more pleasant sonic waveforms, since the evaluations incorporated the pleasantness itself, as perceived by the users of the system. However, as the author of the report (Putnam, 1994) notices, not all the noises that were produced by the system sounded either pleasant or interesting.

Although the methodology described in the previously discussed report did not yield the expected results, it is the first document that reveals some of the principles for evolution of sounds up to date. Two of the most important, among others, are:

1. Sound modeling plays an essential role in GP design. Thus, the power of GP is limited to the extent that the modeling methodology demarcates, i.e. very meticulous selection of non–terminal nodes is required.
2. In interactive evolution, it is important that the first few generations encompass interesting and non–disturbing individuals, since if the users lose focus in the first generations, then they are hardly able to drive evolution to a specific area of desired solutions.

The phenomenon discussed in point 2 above is widely known as user fatigue and is a matter of serious concern for all interactive evolutionary systems, not only the ones that produce artistic material. However, when evolution concerns artistic material there can hardly be a subjective target. This fact can intuitively be described as a process of wandering optimizer, since an indecisive user would force the algorithm to wander the space of possible artistic creations without preference to certain regions – further amplifying the fatigue on the user's side.

A different philosophy of GP algorithms for sound synthesis concerns the generation of sounds towards matching a targeted sound. Therefore, the evaluation of the produced output is not the subjective choices of users, but the objective similarity between a produced and the target sound. The distance that defines this similarity is computed through comparing some audio features extracted from both signals (generated and target). A general overview for such systems has been given in (Garcia, 2000) where the sound generation module includes some advanced signal processing units, instead of simple functions. These processing units can either be used as terminal nodes (e.g. sound generating oscillators) or as non–terminal nodes (e.g. with additive or frequency modulation or by combining/splitting signals). Additionally, this primitive work that expanded in subsequent publications discussed in the next paragraphs, introduces an interesting fitness evaluation scheme that concerns the distance computation between the produced and the target sound not only by comparing their features, but also by having human judgment on the similarity. This aspect is interesting, since the similarity in audio features does not necessarily impose perceptual similarity, and vice versa. However, the paper under discussion does not provide any experimental evaluation on neither fitness estimation approach.

The approach discussed in the previous paragraph was materialized in two publications, (Garcia, 2001b) and (Garcia, 2001a), that focused on the generation of sounds according to targeted sounds provided by an acoustic instrument. The sound generating modules that were combined with GP included units categorized in three classes according to the input and output they were receiving and sending:

1. Source: 1 output (e.g. a float number indicating frequency or amplitude).
2. Render: 1 input (e.g. the block where an audio output device will be plugged).
3. Type A: 2 inputs and 1 output (e.g. signal addition and multiplication).
4. Type B: 1 input and 2 outputs (e.g. an oscillator or a filter).

Such blocks can be combined with GP and produce sounds with a great variety of characteristics. Since there is no human evaluation evolved, there are also no requirements for constraints during the initial steps of evolution. Therefore this approach takes advantage of the full potential of evolutionary processes, which lays in combining great numbers of randomly combined and altered individuals. The work presented in (Garcia, 2001a) describes a prototype system that implements the above-described methodology, named automatic generation of sound synthesizers (AGeSS). However, there are no indications about the accuracy of the produced results, except from images of spectrograms for target and produced sounds. Another approach that was inspired by the previously described work was presented in (Donahue, 2013). Therein, a similar formalization of sound producing–altering blocks was followed, but under a more sophisticated evolutionary scheme. These blocks can be divided in three categories, according to the number of children they are allowed to incorporate in the tree representation of the programs. These blocks and their parameters are evolved towards constructing synthesizers that "mimic" target sounds. The currently described thesis provides some very interesting insights about what audio similarity may concern regarding human perception; however for the purposes of the book at hand the focus remains on the evolutionary aspects of the work under discussion.

A considerable amount of work in the field of music acoustics has focused on the formulation of physical models for acoustic musical instruments (Smith, 2010). On the one hand, such an approach allows for further examination and understanding of the underlying dynamics that describe the vibrating parts of an instrument. On the other hand, the model's output potentially leads to the implementation of hardware and/or software sound generators, which produce sounds that are similar to the ones reproduced by the modeled instrument. The question addressed in the paper (Wilson, 2002) is the following: given a recorded note of a musical instrument, can the parameters of its physical model be adjusted so that the model produces a similar note event? The research in (Wilson, 2002) examined the case of the physical model of a violin, which descriptively encompasses some basic parameters that describe not only the frequency of the reproduced note, but also expressional characteristics like the bow velocity or bow force.

To approach the problem of physical modeling, a deep understanding of signal processing is required and therefore a detailed explanation of processes in the work under discussion is beyond the scope of this book chapter. A general description of the methodology concerns the construction of functions by combining simple mathematical expressions with GP. These functions receive audio features as input and produce output that is fed to the parameters of the violin physical model. Therefore, the fitness evaluation is based on the differences between the model output and the target concerning magnitude frequency spectrum among others. The evaluation of the model was based on three different target samples: two recorded violin notes from Bach's solo partitas for violin and a third note recorded by the physical model itself. The presented results are depictions of target and produced sound spectrograms, while the author comment that the system's performance was not satisfactory. The author also proposes that a possible step towards improving the model's performance is to embody an additional model for room reverberation, since the frequencies introduced by room acoustics are not considered by the violin physical model.

Symbolic Music Composition

Automated music composition is a special field of study, since a great portion of the evaluating process also address the factor of subjectivity in what sounds pleasant, or even musical. Systems that incorporate evolutionary mechanisms, as GP-based methodologies, are called to perform fitness evaluation either by interactive means, requiring from the user to provide fitness evaluation through rating simulations, or by developing fitness functions that effectively quantify qualitative characteristics of music. Both approaches have strong and weak points. Interactive evolution "models" the human preference directly, by letting the user decide for the pleasantness of the generated output. However, the implications of user fatigue do not allow a great number of evaluations, imposing restrictions to the number of individuals and generations of the evolutionary scheme, in addition to the potential misleading ratings from the user within the rating simulations – since user fatigue also affects the judgment of the user. The development of qualitative fitness functions solves the problems addressed in interactive evolution, however such functions are doubtfully effective since human subjectivity and creativity are yet imperfectly computationally modeled. The examined GP approaches are therefore presented in two categories. In the first category, advanced machine learning techniques are utilized to "learn" the aesthetic value of music pieces by themselves – thus considering no ground–truth aesthetic measures. The second category discusses interactive GP approaches. The discussion on works that examine aesthetic fitness criteria for evolutionary systems is addressed in the next section of this chapter.

The first documented approach to **automated music composition** using GP was reported in (Spector & Alpern, 1994). Music generation was based on already existing pieces, which are called "case bases". The core concept of this approach was to combine short "atom" programs (or music functions) that receive a melodic part comprising some note events, then alter these events and return as output the resulting melodic part. For example, the program named as REP takes a melody and returns another one that consists of four replications of the first melodies first bar. Another example is the INVERT program, which receives a melody and returns again a new one, which has the inverted intervals of the first. There are 13 such musical programs–functions that are utilized in the work under discussion. The altered melodies were evolved with fitness values provided by musical criteria inspired by the work presented in (Baker, 1988), which descriptively involve five indications of music and rhythmic novelty and balance. The results of this pioneering GP approach were produced by applying the system on a solo part of Charlie Parker. The authors commented on the results that although the fitness evaluation was found to be a good choice, the resulting music did not actually sound pleasant, a fact that indicates the importance and difficulty of describing aesthetic criteria for music.

The immense difficulty to extract music features that encompass aesthetically meaningful information is a thorough matter of discussion that is partly extended in the second section. The first approach in GP methodologies to tackle the problem of aesthetic definitions in music was performed by avoiding such definitions, through utilizing an artificial neural network (ANN) as an automatic fitness rater, an approach that has proven very popular to some GP techniques that followed. The first work to introduce ANN automatic fitness raters was presented in (Spector & Alpern, 1995), which continues the work discussed in the previous paragraph and also utilizes the GP programs–functions that were previously discussed. Therein, only 4 bar melodies are considered, with each bar including 48 equally spaced positions of potential note placements, i.e. each melody comprised 192 possible note values. The integer value of each of the 192 cells indicated the pitch height of the note, while the zero value indicating no note event. These 192 values were given as input to the ANN, which had two outputs, one indicating whether the presented melody is pleasant and one for the contrary case.

The ANN was trained using four sets of melodies, the first of which included the pleasant paradigms (Charlie Parker solos) and the remaining three included randomly altered versions of the pieces in the first category (constituting the non–pleasant paradigms for the ANN). The trained ANN exhibited the ability to recognize some sense of "musicality" since it judged as good music some Charlie Parker solos (not all of the presented ones) and also a solo by Jimi Hendrix, while it gave negative scores to some almost random sequences. The GP individuals were evolved according to the fitness indication provided by the output of the trained ANN, according to their pleasantness. The reported results were again poor generating "bizarre" rhythmic groupings, as described by the authors, and long interval jumps. According to the authors, this is primarily due to the small number of training samples for the ANN. The results were improved slightly by introducing additional explicit rules in the fitness evaluation scheme, which did penalized melodies which had a good ANN fitness but some obviously unpleasing characteristics. The interested reader is also referred to (Spector, Klein, & Harrington, 2005) for more elaborative comments of the systems described in (Spector & Alpern, 1994) and (Spector & Alpern, 1995).

Another approach to fitness evaluation through an "artificial expert" has been proposed in (Phon-Amnuaisuk, Law, & Kuan, 2007) where instead of an ANN, a self organizing map (SOM) (Kohonen, Schroeder, & Huang, 2001) is utilized as an automatic fitness rater. The GP framework is similar to the ones described hitherto in this section, where simple musical programs act as non–terminal nodes (e.g. which modulate the pitch of all notes in an input melody segment or alter its durations of notes). A typical evolutionary scheme is utilized, where monophonic melodies are represented in MIDI format. The melodies are transformed to pitch class and duration vectors and are imported to a trained SOM. The SOM is trained on a target melody, capturing some of its basic pitch and duration characteristics. Thereafter, each GP individual is mapped onto the trained SOM, thus providing fitness evaluations. The presented results concern evaluations with SOMs trained on small size melodies, while the statistical comments and the small score segments that are provided do not allow a deep understanding of the system's capabilities. For further study on artificial critics without aesthetic background, the interested reader is also referred to (Reddin, McDermott, & O'Neill, 2009) and (McDermott & O'Reilly, 2011).

POSSIBLE AND PROPOSED APPLICATIONS

Automatic synthesis can be integrated in all aspects of a multimedia application. Although that is not a necessary supposition, a context connection between audio and other multimedia communication chan-

Figure 4. An abstract illustration of the audio and multimedia content connection in the automated synthesis driven by emotion process

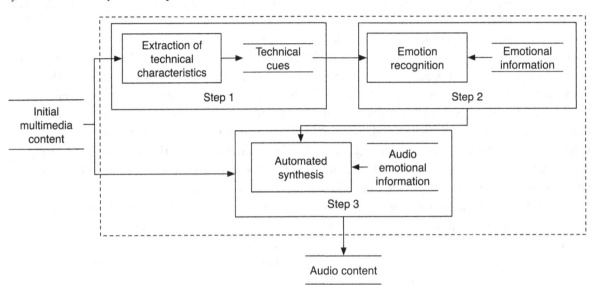

nels will definitely increase the perceived, by the user, value of the presented information. Thus, in the follow proposed and possible applications the **automated synthesis** process is driven by a prior extraction of information by the actual and non-audio content. A general and abstract illustration of the latter process is in Figure 4. In this Figure, the illustrated process can be organized in three steps:

1. Extraction of technical characteristics from the non-audio multimedia content that serves as the main communication interface to the user. The nature of these cues is application and content specific. For example, if an audio track for news is to be generated then the extracted information will be the descriptors for emotion analysis from text (Calix, Mallepudi, Chen, & Knapp, 2010; Wu & Ren, 2010; Wu, Chuang, & Lin, 2006; KalaiSelvi, Kavitha, & Shunmuganathan, 2014)
2. Emotion recognition from the obtained technical cues by Step 1. According to each application, the extracted cues from previous step will be employed as input to an emotion recognition process that will generate the appropriate emotion description for the content
3. Having all the above information, the last step is the **automated synthesis**. Employing the description of the recognized emotions and the previous knowledge of what and how the technical features of audio can affect the conveyed emotion, the algorithms of **automated synthesis** will generate the final audio content for the multimedia application, as described in the previous sections of this chapter.

The choice of the proposed applications serves a two fold cause; a) the following approaches are believed that cover a wide range of everyday utilization of multimedia, and b) the employment of the proposed integration of **automated synthesis** techniques and emotion recognition will allow the faster creation of proper audio content for areas that, by empirical observation and evidence, provide a swift creation of new constituents. Thus, in the following first sub-section is presented a possible application for the automated generation of soundtrack for movies and videos that will serve as a tool for directors and movie producers. In the second sub-section is proposed the automated generation of audio content for video games that will allow a real-time interaction between the player and the game machine. The latter will be capable to produce a user and story specific sound track according to the actions and choices that the player made in his game course. Finally, in the third sub-section is proposed an enhancement of the text-based information. The reader of news will be capable to hear an accompanied music or soundscape that will be based on the text native emotion, either recognized by automated procedures or indicated by the news writer.

Audio Track for Videos and Movies

As written in this chapter, audio is one prominent element of multimedia applications. The other is video. Thus, as a first and possible application for **emotionally enhanced automated synthesis** is the creation of soundtracks for videos and movies. Although that the cinema is a vast industry, in nowadays video making is also possible in a home environment. The advances in digital image processing, embedded systems and electronic sensors have allowed the utilization of high quality hand-held video recorders. Internet platforms, e.g. the well-known youtube[2], exist that host videos from enthusiasts and professionals.

Even in semi-professional situations, a music composer is not always in the video creation team. In addition, pre-recorded musical creations of artists are not always fit in the emotional content of the movie. Thus with the proposed **emotionally enhanced automated synthesis**, a video creator could add musical content to his artistic creations in an automated fashion.

According to Figure 4, such an application would accept as input the video material and possible emotional annotations. The latter could be combined with recognized emotion, by the utilization of existing techniques for video emotion recognition, and serve as input to Step 3. Finally, the proper audio would be created and used as an audio track to the video material. The aforementioned process could be employed to various video contents and applications, e.g. video casts.

Computer Game Audio Track

The application of **automated synthesis** of **emotionally enhanced music** could be beneficial for computer video games. The current, and most common, status of sound reproduction in video games is the playback of pre-recorded, pre-stored and pre-associated sounds with actions and key-points in the game. Although that these audio clips are connected with the story, plot, scenario and user actions and emotional experience, they are static. Thus, with the adaptation of the aforementioned automatic creation of audio clips, a video game could render in real time a proper audio content based on the user's actions and game's elements.

User's actions and game choices will serve as the technical cues that must be extracted from the multimedia content, according to Figure 4. Story, plot and other scenario based elements of the game and the affective pursuits of the user's progress will be the emotional information which, altogether with the technical cues, will result to the description of player's targeted emotion(s). Again, as the final Step, the **emotional enhanced automated synthesis** will produce the proper audio material in order to reflect the needs of respective situations. Such employment of the proposed framework is believed that will also intensify the immersion of the players by providing a personal and tailor made experience based on their individual game style.

Enhancement of Text-Based Information

Internet and offline applications for providing text-based news are a common element in the pursuit for briefing of political, cultural, sport and other kind of news in modern culture. Although those applications do offer thoroughly detailed information, they are static and utilize only the visual channel for communication. By employing the proposed framework, an audio content with appropriate emotional matching could be also offered to the readers and thus enhance their overall experience. In an extent, the same application could also be utilized in educational content by providing means for emotional interaction and feedback in the process.

The textual information would serve as the technical cues, regarding Step 1 in Figure 4, and the targeted emotion according to the reader as the emotional information for Step 2. Finally, in Step 3, the proposed integration of **automated synthesis** and **emotion recognition** would provide the proper audio material in order to, on one hand, comply with the targeted emotions by the writer/journalist and, on the other hand, escalate user's involvement and experience.

CONCLUSION

In this chapter was attempted a proposal for the enhancement of **automated sound and music synthesis** with an affective dimension. As can be seen, the existing level of technology and research in **automated synthesis** can provide a feature driven composition of audio material. In addition, the latter task can also be driven with an interactive scheme by employing GAs and having as targeted state an audio material that will present particular values for specific technical features. The exact values emerging from the audio emotion recognition process, which will also provide the association of those with the targeted listener's emotions.

Thus, a combination of the presented technologies, methods and results can lead to the implementation of an **automated affective sound synthesis**. Such audio material could be employed in various tasks, as depicted from the proposed applications, in order to enhance user experience by adding content or task-oriented dimension, i.e. the emotion.

REFERENCES

Adolphs, R. (2002). Neural systems for recognizing emotion. *Current Opinion in Neurobiology, 12*(2), 169–177. doi:10.1016/S0959-4388(02)00301-X PMID:12015233

Alfonseca, M., Cebrian, M., & Ortega, A. (2007). A simple genetic algorithm for music generation by means of algorithmic information theory. *Proceedings of IEEE Congress on Evolutionary Computation (CEC 2007)*. Singapore. IEEE doi:10.1109/CEC.2007.4424858

Baker, D. (1988). *David Baker's Jazz Improvisation: A Comprehensive Method for All Musicians*. U.S.A.: Alfred Music Publishing.

Bradley, M. M., & Lang, P. J. (1994). Measuring emotion: The self-assessment manikin and the semantic differential. *Journal of Behavior Therapy and Experimental Psychiatry, 25*(1), 49–59. doi:10.1016/0005-7916(94)90063-9 PMID:7962581

Bradley, M. M., & Lang, P. J. (2007). *The international affective digitized sounds (2nd edition; iads-2): Affective ratings of sounds and instruction manual* [Technical Report B–3]. Gainesville, Fl: NIMH Center for the Study of Emotion and Attention.

Calix, R., Mallepudi, S., Chen, B., & Knapp, G. (2010). Emotion recognition in text for 3-d facial expression rendering. *IEEE Transactions on Multimedia, 12*(6), 544–551. doi:10.1109/TMM.2010.2052026

Casacuberta, D. (2004). Dj el nino: Expressing synthetic emotions with music. *AI & Society, 18*(3), 257–263. doi:10.1007/s00146-003-0290-x

Chen, L., Tao, H., Huang, T., Miyasato, T., & Nakatsu, R. (1998). Emotion recognition from audiovisual information. *Proceedings of IEEE Second Workshop on Multimedia Signal Processing*. Redondo Beach, California, U.S.A. IEEE.

Cornelius, R. R. (2000). Theoretical approaches to emotion. In *Proceedings of International Speech Communication Association (ISCA) Tutorial and Research Workshop (ITRW) on Speech and Emotion*. Newcastle, N. Ireland, U.K: ISCA.

Donahue, C. (2013). *Applications of genetic programming to digital audio synthesis.* [Doctoral dissertation]. University of Texas at Austin, Texas, USA.

Donnelly, P., & Sheppard, J. (2011). Evolving four-part harmony using genetic algorithms. *Proceedings of the 2011 international conference on Applications of evolutionary computation - Volume Part II, EvoApplications'11*. Berlin, Heidelberg. Springer-Verlag.

Drossos, K., Floros, A., & Giannakoulopoulos, A. (2014). Beads: A dataset of binaural emotionally annotated digital sounds. *Proceedings of 5th International Conference on Information, Intelligence, Systems and Applications (IISA 2014)*. Chania, Crete, Greece. IEEE. doi:10.1109/IISA.2014.6878749

Drossos, K., Floros, A., & Kanellopoulos, N. G. (2012). Affective acoustic ecology: Towards emotionally enhanced sound events. *Proceedings of the 7th Audio Mostly Conference: A Conference on Interaction with Sound*. Corfu, Greece. ACM. doi:10.1145/2371456.2371474

Drossos, K., Kotsakis, R., Kalliris, G., & Floros, A. (2013). Sound events and emotions: Investigating the relation of rhythmic characteristics and arousal. *Proceedings of Fourth International Conference on Information, Intelligence, Systems and Applications (IISA 2013)*. Piraeus, Greece. IEEE. doi:10.1109/IISA.2013.6623709

Friberg, A., Bresin, R., & Sundberg, J. (2006). Overview of the kth rule system for music performance. *Advances in Cognitive Psychology, 2*(2), 145–161. doi:10.2478/v10053-008-0052-x

Garcia, R. A. (2000). Towards the automatic generation of sound synthesis techniques: Preparatory steps. *Proceedings of AES 109th Convention*. Los Angeles. AES.

Garcia, R. A. (2001a). Automating the design of sound syntheses techniques using evolutionary methods. *Proceedings of the COST G-6 Conference on Digital Audio Effects (DAFX- 01)*. Limerick, Ireland.

Garcia, R. A. (2001b). Growing sound synthesizers using evolutionary methods. In *Proceedings of European Conference in Artificial Life 2001 (ECAL2001) special workshop in Artificial Life Models for Musical Applications*. Prague, Chez Republic. Springer.

Grimm, M., Kroschel, K., Mower, E., & Narayanan, S. (2007). Primitives-based evaluation and estimation of emotions in speech. *Speech Communication*, *49*(10-11), 787–800. doi:10.1016/j.specom.2007.01.010

Hevner, K. (1936). Experimental studies of the elements of expression in music. *The American Journal of Psychology*, *48*(2), 246–268. doi:10.2307/1415746

Holland, J. H. (1992). *Adaptation in natural and artificial systems*. Cambridge, MA, USA: MIT Press.

Juslin, P. N., & Laukka, P. (2003). Communication of emotions in vocal expression and music performance: Different channels, same code? *Psychological Bulletin*, *120*(5), 770–814. doi:10.1037/0033-2909.129.5.770 PMID:12956543

KalaiSelvi., R., Kavitha, P., & Shunmuganathan, K. (2014). Automatic emotion recognition in video. *Proceedings of International Conference on Green Computing Communication and Electrical Engineering (ICGC- CEE)*. Coimbatore, India. IEEE

Kaliakatsos-Papakostas, M. A., Epitropakis, M. G., Floros, A., & Vrahatis, M. N. (2012a). Controlling interactive evolution of 8-bit melodies with genetic programming. *Soft Computing*, *16*(12), 1997–2008. doi:10.1007/s00500-012-0872-y

Kaliakatsos-Papakostas, M. A., Epitropakis, M. G., Floros, A., & Vrahatis, M. N. (2013a). Chaos and music: From time series analysis to evolutionary composition. *International Journal of Bifurcation and Chaos (IJBC)*. 23, 1350181–1–1350181–19.

Kaliakatsos-Papakostas, M. A., Floros, A., & Vrahatis, M. N. (2012d). Intelligent real-time music accompaniment for constraint-free improvisation. In Proceedings of *24th IEEE International Conference on Tools with Artificial Intelligence (ICTAI 2012)*. Piraeus, Athens, Greece: IEEE. doi:10.1109/ICTAI.2012.67

Kaliakatsos-Papakostas, M. A., Floros, A., & Vrahatis, M. N. (2013b). Intelligent music composition. In X. S. Yang, Z. Cui, R. Xiao, A. H. Gandomi, & M. Karamanoglu (Eds.), *Swarm Intelligence and Bioinspired Computation* (pp. 239–256). Amsterdam, The Netherlands: Elsevier. doi:10.1016/B978-0-12-405163-8.00010-7

Kaliakatsos-Papakostas, M. A., Floros, A., Vrahatis, M. N., & Kanellopoulos, N. (2012b). Genetic evolution of L and FL–systems for the production of rhythmic sequences. *In Proceedings of 21st International Conference on Genetic Algorithms and the 17th Annual Genetic Programming Conference (GP) (GECCO 2012), 2nd Workshop in Evolutionary Music*. Philadelphia, USA. ACM.

Kejun, Z., & Shouqian, S. (2010). Music emotional design by evolutionary algorithms. *Proceedings of IEEE 11th International Conference on Computer-Aided Industrial Design Conceptual Design (CAIDCD)*. Yiwu, China. IEEE.

Kim, Y. E., Schmidt, E. M., Migneco, R., Morton, B. G., Richardson, P., & Scott, J., … Turnbull, D. (2010). Music emotion recognition: A state of the art review. Proceedings of 11th International Society for Music Information Retrieval Conference (ISMIR 2010). Utrecht, Netherlands.

Koelsch, S. (2010). Towards a neural basis of music-evoked emotions. *Trends in Cognitive Sciences*, *14*(3), 131–137. doi:10.1016/j.tics.2010.01.002 PMID:20153242

Kohonen, T., Schroeder, M. R., & Huang, T. S. (Eds.). (2001). *Self-Organizing Maps* (3rd ed.). Secaucus, NJ, USA: Springer-Verlag New York, Inc. doi:10.1007/978-3-642-56927-2

Koza, J. R. (1992). *Genetic Programming: On the Programming of Computers by Means of Natural Selection*. Cambridge, MA, USA: The MIT Press.

Law, E. L. C., Roto, V., Hassenzahl, M., Vermeeren, A. P., & Kort, J. (2009). Understanding, scoping and defining user experience: A survey approach. In *Proceedings of the SIGCHI Conference on Human Factors in Computing Systems, CHI '09*. Boston, USA. ACM. doi:10.1145/1518701.1518813

Li, T., & Ogihara, M. (2003). Detecting emotion in music. In *Proceedings of 4th International Symposium on Music Information Retrieval*. U.S.A.

Lo, M. Y. (2012). Evolving Cellular Automata for Music Composition with Trainable Fitness Functions [Doctoral dissertation]. University of Essex, Essex.

Lu, L., Liu, D., & Zhang, H.-J. (2006). Automatic mood detection and tracking of music audio signals. *IEEE Transactions on Audio, Speech, and Language Processing*, *14*(1), 5–18. doi:10.1109/TSA.2005.860344

Manaris, B., Roos, P., Machado, P., Krehbiel, D., Pellicoro, L., & Romero, J. (2007). A corpus-based hybrid approach to music analysis and composition. *Proceedings of 22nd International conference on Artificial intelligence*. Vancouver, British Columbia, Canada. AAAI Press.

McDermott, J., & O'Reilly, U.-M. (2011). An executable graph representation for evolutionary generative music. *Proceedings of the 13th Annual Conference on Genetic and Evolutionary Computation, GECCO '11*. Dublin, Ireland. ACM. doi:10.1145/2001576.2001632

Ortony, A., & Turner, T. J. (1990). What's basic about basic emotions? *Psychological Review*, *97*(3), 315–331. doi:10.1037/0033-295X.97.3.315 PMID:1669960

Ozcan, E., & Eral, T. (2008). A genetic algorithm for generating improvised music (pp. 266–277). In Monmarch, N., Talbi, E.-G., Collet, P., Schoenauer, M., & Lutton, E. (Eds.). Artificial Evolution, volume 4926 of Lecture Notes in Computer Science. Berlin/Heidelberg: Springer.

Papadopoulos, G., & Wiggins, G. (1998). A Genetic Algorithm for the Generation of Jazz Melodies. *Proceedings of Finnish Conference on Artificial Intelligence (STeP)*. Jyväskylä.

Phon-Amnuaisuk, S., Law, E., & Kuan, H. (2007). Evolving music generation with som-fitness genetic programming. In M. Giacobini (Ed.), Lecture Notes in Computer Science: Vol. 4448. *Applications of Evolutionary Computing* (pp. 557–566). Berlin, Germany: Springer. doi:10.1007/978-3-540-71805-5_61

Putnam, J. B. (1994). Genetic programming of music. Retrieved from ftp://ftp.cs.bham.ac.uk/pub/tech-reports/1997/CSRP-97-07.ps.gz

Reddin, J., McDermott, J., & O'Neill, M. (2009). Elevated pitch: Automated grammatical evolution of short compositions. In M. Giacobini, I. De Falco, & M. Ebner (Eds.), *Applications of Evolutionary Computing, EvoWorkshops2009* (Vol. 5484, pp. 579–584). Tubingen, Germany. Springer Verlag. doi:10.1007/978-3-642-01129-0_65

Russell, J. A. (1980). A circumplex model of affect. *Journal of Personality and Social Psychology*, *39*(6), 1161–1178. doi:10.1037/h0077714

Schmidt, E. M., Turnbull, D., & Kim, Y. E. (2010). Feature selection for content-based, time-varying musical emotion regression. *Proceedings of International Conference on Multimedia Information Retrieval, MIR '10*. Philadelphia, PA, USA. ACM. doi:10.1145/1743384.1743431

Schuller, B., Hantke, S., Weninger, F., Han, W., Zhang, Z., & Narayanan, S. (2012). Automatic recognition of emotion evoked by general sound events. *Proceedings of IEEE International Conference on Acoustics, Speech and Signal Processing (ICASSP)*. Kyoto, Japan. IEEE doi:10.1109/ICASSP.2012.6287886

Smith, J. O. (2010). *Physical audio signal processing: for virtual musical instruments and audio effects*. Stanford: W3K Publishing.

Spector, L., & Alpern, A. (1994). Criticism, culture, and the automatic generation of artworks. In *Proceedings of the twelfth national conference on Artificial intelligence (*vol. 1*), AAAI '94*. Seattle, Washington, USA. American Association for Artificial Intelligence.

Spector, L., & Alpern, A. (1995). Induction and recapitulation of deep musical structure. *Proceedings of the IFCAI-95 Workshop on Artificial Intelligence and Music*. Montreal, Quebec, Canada.

Spector, L., Klein, J., & Harrington, K. (2005). Selection songs: Evolutionary music computation. *YLEM Journal*, *25*(6 & 8), 24–26.

Storn, R., & Price, K. (1997). Differential evolution – a simple and efficient adaptive scheme for global optimization over continuous spaces. *Journal of Global Optimization*, *11*(4), 341–359. doi:10.1023/A:1008202821328

Sugimoto, T., Legaspi, R., Ota, A., Moriyama, K., Kurihara, S., & Numao, M. (2008). Modeling affective-based music compositional intelligence with the aid of ANS analyses. *Knowledge-Based Systems*, *21*(3), 200–208. doi:10.1016/j.knosys.2007.11.010

Weninger, F., Eyben, F., Schuller, B. W., Mortillaro, M., & Scherer, K. R. (2013). On the acoustics of emotion in audio: What speech, music and sound have in common. *Frontiers in Psychology*, 4. PMID:23750144

Wieczorkowska, A., Synak, P., Lewis, R., & Ra, W. Z. (2005). Extracting emotions from music data. In Hacid, M.-S., Murray, N., Ra, Z., & Tsumoto, S. (Eds.), Foundations of Intelligent Systems (LNCS) (Vol. 3488, pp. 456–465). Berlin Heidelberg: Springer.

Wilson, R. S. (2002). First steps towards violin performance extraction using genetic programming. In J. R. Koza (Ed.), *Genetic Algorithms and Genetic Programming at Stanford 2002*. Stanford, California, USA: Stanford Bookstore.

Wu, C.-H., Chuang, Z.-J., & Lin, Y.-C. (2006). Emotion recognition from text using semantic labels and separable mixture models. [TALIP]. *ACM Transactions on Asian Language Information Processing*, *5*(2), 165–183. doi:10.1145/1165255.1165259

Wu, Y., & Ren, F. (2010). Improving emotion recognition from text with fractionation training. *Proceedings of International Conference on Natural Language Processing and Knowledge Engineering (NLP-KE)*. Beijing, China. IEEE. doi:10.1109/NLPKE.2010.5587800

Xiao, Z., Dellandrea, E., Dou, W., & Chen, L. (2008). What is the best segment duration for music mood analysis? *Proceedings of* International Workshop on *Content-Based Multimedia Indexing (CBMI 2008)*. London, U.K. IEEE.

Yang, Y. H., Lin, Y. C., Cheng, H. T., & Chen, H. H. (2008). Mr. emo: music retrieval in the emotion plane. *Proceedings of 16th ACM international conference on Multimedia*. Vancouver, Canada: ACM. doi:10.1145/1459359.1459550

Yeh, C. H., Lin, H. H., & Chang, H. T. (2009). An efficient emotion detection scheme for popular music. *Proceedings of IEEE International Symposium on Circuits and Systems (ISCAS 2009)*. Taipei, Taiwan. IEEE. doi:10.1109/ISCAS.2009.5118126

Zhang, S., Tian, Q., Jiang, S., Huang, Q., & Gao, W. (2008). Affective mtv analysis based on arousal and valence features. *Proceedings of IEEE International Conference on Multimedia and Expo (ICME 2008)*. Hanover, Germany. IEEE. doi:10.1109/ICME.2008.4607698

Zhu, H., Wang, S., & Wang, Z. (2008). Emotional music generation using interactive genetic algorithm. *Proceedings of International Conference on Computer Science and Software Engineering* (volume 1). Wuhan, Hubei, China. IEEE. doi:10.1109/CSSE.2008.1203

KEY TERMS AND DEFINITIONS

Affective Acoustic Ecology: An enhanced concept of the Acoustic Ecology that contains also the emotional interaction between the listeners and the audio environment.

Affective Sound/Music: Sound or music that is capable to elicit emotions to listener.

Automated Music Synthesis/Composition: The automated synthesis/composition of music by utilizing proper algorithms.

Emotion Recognition From Sound/Music/Audio/Sound Events: The process of automatically identifying the emotion that the listeners of a sound, music sound event or in general audio stimulus will feel.

Emotionally Annotated: Something that also contains emotion annotations (labels) for it.

Emotionally Enhanced: Something that is created or altered in order to elicit specific emotion(s) to its recipients/receivers.

Intelligent Music/Sound Synthesis: The automated synthesis of music/sound that also automatically adapts to specific pre-requisites.

Sound Event (SE): A generalized audio stimulus, non-linguistic and non-musical.

ENDNOTES

[1]   http://www.findsounds.com
[2]   http://www.youtube.com

Chapter 7
Euterpe:
An Experimental Multimedia Database System Designed to Dynamically Support Music Teaching Scenarios

May Kokkidou
University of Western Macedonia, Greece

Zoe Dionyssiou
Ionian University, Greece

ABSTRACT

This work focuses on the application of experimental multimedia in the field of music education. The end-system produced is a multimedia service designed to support music teachers who wish to generate and implement teaching scenarios, during their singing teaching session, as this progresses and evolves dynamically. The system allows them to adjust on the fly their educational content, in order to cover their classroom needs that evolve continuously during practice. The end-system combines a fully searchable multimedia database complemented by an access process designed to serve constantly changing content requirements. Most importantly, the system is designed to provide meaningful teaching-learning scenarios with the appropriate content on demand, through the implementation of a task-specific system-as-a-service access method. This chapter provides a walk through the most important characteristics of the process from the content expert perspective. This information was actively employed by developers enabling the system parameterization to cover the functional requirements of the teaching-learning process.

INTRODUCTION

The *2012 International ISME-Gibson Award* was granted to the Greek Society for Music Education (G.S.M.E.) and the Music Library of Greece "Lilian Voudouri" (MLG), supporting the development of *Euterpe: Digital Music Anthology*. The project was designed having in mind the ISME-Gibson Award call "to reach out through, and in, music to people who are at the margins of society, at risk of social exclusion and for whom involvement in music will make a positive and enriching difference to their

DOI: 10.4018/978-1-4666-8659-5.ch007

lives" (ISME, 2012). In the technological forefront the project involves the design, development, and delivery of a digital song database supporting the task in hand through dynamic and adaptive content delivery. The song database consists of Greek and non-Greek songs suitable for use in school music lessons at all educational levels. The *Euterpe* project began its life in 2012. On behalf of the Greek Society for Music Education a scientific team undertook the task to develop the parameters and criteria for appropriate material selection and presentation. The team of the Greek Society for Music Education (GSME) consists of Zoe Dionyssiou, May Kokkidou, Nikos Theodoridis, and Sofia Aggelidou. A second team, organized by the Music Library of Greece "Lillian Voudouri" with Stephania Merakou, Vera Kriezi, George Mpoumpous, and Valia Vraka, undertook the technical support of the project. Finally the database was transferred in the repositories of the National Documentation Centre, using the SaaS Repository Service. During the project development, a group of content experts and system designers were involved in order to manage the data and to organize their presentation. The content experts through comprehensive procedures defined and agreed on their goals, and planned the way they would perform the tasks. They were engaged in a fruitful dialogue about how they could organize the instructional material and what type of information they had to collect and present for each database item (song).

Euterpe was not meant to be a digital music curriculum. Instead it may be viewed as a new ICT tool for music teaching-learning. It encapsulates complementary material, which can be used by teachers to enrich their teaching methodologies and song repertoire as to help their students learn new songs in challenging and enjoyable ways. It is a set of guidelines, practical classroom activities, ideas, and suggestions about how to educate children through music (social-emotional skills, critical thinking, creativity, self-esteem, etc.), for music (musical skills, musical thinking, aesthetic appreciation and experience), and about music (e.g., music as art, music history, musical genres, music and society). *Euterpe* is designed to appeal to both specialized music educators and to general teachers as well. By the very beginning of the project we specified a set of axioms. These are listed below:

- All children have the potential to express themselves through music.
- Students have to "experience" music (to sing, to play in classroom instruments, to dance), before being introduced to music theory. Performance is at the heart of the music classroom.
- The teaching-learning of music ought to emphasize the true understanding of concepts and avoid the traditional process of information transmission.
- When teaching-learning is experiential-centered, students can make sense of more complex content.
- In music lessons students ought to be provided with opportunities that allow them to become able to recognize their own music preferences, values, and interests, and accept/respect those of others.

Euterpe's design axioms are complemented with task-specific and focused aims. These target to offer music teachers and general school teachers music material for educational use, and specialized help including music scores, instructional ideas and recommendations for classroom music teaching. In other words, the system is designed to help teachers present the content in a way that engages and activates students. This process will be implemented via the use of a multimedia end-system featuring a song database of a rich digital anthology of Greek songs and songs from other music cultures for educational use. This system is designed in order to enrich the school music repertoire with new songs and provide free access to material and guidelines to everyone who wants to expand his/her view for music teaching-learning. In addition the end-system is designed to support and promote modern and innovative music teaching methods. It also includes cross-disciplinary links and connections with other school subjects, following the open information access movement.

TECHNOLOGY AS AN AID FOR MUSIC TEACHERS

One of the missions of education in the 21th century is to help educators share ideas, strategies, and resources within every field (Koong & Wu, 2011; Lee, Messom, & Yau, 2013; Lindgren, 2012; Oliver, 2011; Xia, 2011). Educational material and resources have already been made available and easily accessible through the use of technology. In many cases the mode of delivery is also extended using interdisciplinary technologies, such as smart user interfaces, computer games and game-like interfaces (Karydis, Deliyannis, & Floros, 2011). Edutainment is clearly the way of the future, as it integrates useful and attractive learning methods with meaningful content (Deliyannis, Giannakoulopoulos, & Oikonomidou, 2013; Deliyannis, Giannakoulopoulos, & Varlamis, 2011; Green & McNeese, 2007).

Euterpe is run on Dspace, an open source software package created by MIT and used for digital collections. The project is hosted on Apache Tomcat web server and the digital items are stored in PostgreSQL database and it may be accessed directly via the www. Once the description fields were specified, the Dublin Core metadata scheme was configured as to respond to the requirements for the description of the songs, which would be entered on the database. In April 2014, the first records were uploaded together with the relevant digitized documents, in order for trials to be carried out as the proper running of the database would be ensured. The interface of *Euterpe*'s web application was fully customized according to the needs of the project (including browse and search indices) in February 2015 (Figure 01). The first presentation of the database took place at the National Documentation Centre, Athens, in one Day Conference entitled "Euterpe: A digital music anthology for songs in school" (27/2/2015), which is available via the web broadcasting service of the organisation.

In this figure the user is able to view the information and sample of the content. Songs are categorized according to the composer/creator (left column) and the age-level of the students (right-column). A pilot study was completed during the early stages of project development for the corpus of the system's initial design. Music teachers featuring diverse professional expertise and teaching perspectives were involved in this process. They were asked to use, review and comment on the initial design of the system. This process provided critical information, which were used to improve the end-system. One important outcome, which was brought out by this process, was that several songs were transcribed to a different tonality as to fit to the singing abilities of children of a given age.

SONG SELECTION IN *EUTERPI*

There is an ongoing debate in the music education community over which songs should be taught at school and which should not, over how singing should be taught, and what is the most appropriate teaching singing method. Regarding the criteria for the selection of songs, certain questions were raised: Which songs are appropriate for school use? Which songs ought to be selected in order to enhance students' musical learning? Is it wise to use songs that amuse and excite students even if their musical, aesthetic, and cultural values are in question? Should the songs be acknowledged only for their own sake? How could we help students use the songs in meaningful ways, in multiple situations? How could we promote

Figure 1a. Euterpe's main user interface screen

Figure 1b. Euterpe's main user interface screen

ethical values while teaching singing? How could we avoid students' passivity and indifference in singing activities and encourage their willingness to learn new songs? What is the way as to facilitate connections between school songs and students' personal preferences? What kind of activities must be included in order to force students take a critical stance, investigate, and address broader societal and ethical issues?

The songs included in the database were derived from the following sources: a) Historical sources and rare Greek music anthologies from the 19th century and the first half of the 20th century, b) Greek and non-Greek traditional/folk songs, c) Well known children's songs, and d) Songs composed by contemporary Greek and non-Greek composers, and music educators. The repertoire consists of traditional Greek songs, traditional songs from other music cultures, children's songs, nursery songs, religious songs, patriotic/national songs, educational songs, game songs, popular songs, choral songs, lullabies, ritual songs, and contemporary songs.

Regarding the selected contemporary songs, composers and lyricists were contacted by mail or e-mail. They were informed about the project, its purpose and scope, and they were kindly asked to give their permission to have their specific song included in the database. All the creators responded positively to our request. At the same time we contacted and asked composers who belong to the Greek Composers Union and to the Greek Society for Music Education to offer suitable songs for the purposes of the project. The process of settling the intellectual property rights of the creators had been a major concern of the "Music Library" team and had taken a lot of effort.

THE CENTRAL ROLE OF SINGING IN MUSIC EDUCATION

Signing is one of the most important activities in school music education. Songs are considered as "the most powerful, personal, pleasurable, and above all, permanent tool in our pedagogical arsenal to establish an educational concept" (Balkin, 2009:1). Songs are not simply a music product. They have power; they provide a valuable form of communication and an avenue for emotional expression; they instill an intrinsic motivation in students to learn; they invite individuals to become acquainted with their cultural heritage; they call to action as many songs deal with important societal issues (biases, stereotypes, alienation, racism etc); they create strong bounds to the members of a group, they turn individualism to togetherness (O'Neill, 2012; Welch, 2005; Acker, 2010; Nichols & Honig, 1997; Katsch & Merle-Fishman, 1985).

Singing is a widespread music activity (Campbell, 1998). All over the world all cultures engage in singing for a number of reasons: friendship, joy, comfort, knowledge, religion and love (Levitin, 2008). Custodero and Chen-Hafteck (2008: 4) note that "the role played by singing in socialization is significant and has been used for centuries to transmit cultural values, to teach language, and to establish qualities of rhythmic energy that typify a way of being". There is also evidence that the more we sing, the more we strengthen the inter-connections between the two sides of the brain (Pascale, 2005).

O'Neill (2012) had described singing activity as "transformative music engagement". The vast majority of school music curricula are singing-centered (Kokkidou, 2009). However, restricting the singing experience to learning to read music and to stage performances for public school events is not enough. Singing is an activity that should be always kept spontaneous and alive. Songs are often regarded as mere entertainment, but the use of songs as a pedagogical tool is much more complex and broad (Foley 2006). There is evidence that singing is important for the cognitive, social, emotional, and language development of children (O'Neill, 2012; Vuckovic, 2006; Welch, 2005; Pascale, 2005; Nyland, Ferris

& Deans, 2010; Campbell, 1998; Murphy, 1992). Thurman and Welch (2000) have introduced the term "bodymind and voice" implying that singing involves both intellectual skills and physical skills.

Young children are very responsive to singing; they enjoy singing, they make fun inventing their own songs (Campbell, 1998). In school music education teachers can enhance the joy of singing for its own sake and as well support children developing musical skills, musical knowledge, and skills in domains other than music. In addition, singing in participatory ways, as well as performing in instruments and dancing, gives students a sense of community and collectivity (Welch, 2005), alongside the development of coordination skills (keeping together in time, synchronizing our breathing).

The database includes the music scores of the songs in *Finale* or *Musescore* musical-notation software format (in .mus, or .mcsz, .xml and .pdf files). It also provides guidelines for teaching students aged 4 to 18, in the following categories: 4-8, 8-12, 12-18, Music Schools (School choirs and bands). All information is organized in building blocks as units. Each of the unit gives a detailed and practical picture for the instruction of the song. Teachers are free to follow their own pace and to find their own order when exploring the multimedia song database. They may start by looking for song titles, song theme or for key words; they can search for songs by creator, by genre, by age group, by musical aims, by pedagogical aims, and so on.

Each song unit encapsulates the following information: song title, contextual-factual information (date of composition/first release, region/country of origin, composer, lyricist/poet, other contributors, original language of the lyrics), sources (title of the music album, title of songbook), first words of the song, key words, teaching-learning suggestions (outlining method, musical terms, cognitive tasks), musical goals, non-music learning goals (pedagogical features: social, emotional, moral, cultural goals), cross-disciplinary concepts, cross-disciplinary links with other school subjects, musicological information (song genre, vocal range, tonality, meter, number of voices), targeted age groups, and suggestions for use in school life (i.e., special events, school celebrations). There are neither benchmarks nor performance standards: teachers are those who will determine the level of mastery expected of students for each topic, according to their background.

The proposed teaching methodology is supported by current evidence and trends from music educational and music psychology research. The methodological practices include: student-centered, experiential, reflective, authentic, holistic, collaborative, challenging. Many teaching units are designed and built around a central concept, either musical (i.e., dynamics, form, expressive musical elements) and/or cross-disciplinary concepts (i.e., communication, tradition, time, space, antithesis, symbolism).

The proposed activities create chances for children to sing each song a number of times, productively, creatively, and enjoyably, enriching the music instruction routines. Each time a song is practiced, a different task can be set: sound exploration, listening, performing, composing, improvisation, movement/dance, drama, drawing/painting, writing, discussing, and narrating. Furthermore, students are encouraged to extend the song in multiple ways based on their musical ideas, to build a new case for each song, to make every song their own through creative manipulation of its elements. By this, students will be able to see the intrinsic value in learning music, to find and learn how to use their singing voices, to develop awareness of the basic musical elements, to apply their learning in meaningful new contexts, and to explore the relationships between music and other ways of expression and communication.

Though the educational activities offered were found to work well together in our pilot stage of implementation, teachers may find out that an activity does not work well for their particular educational setting. Consequently, they can try content changes and adaptation; they can modify the song, refine it, or abandon it. In general, teachers are those who will make the ultimate decision about the use of the material: they will take into account students' background, they will match the level of the content and the pace at which it will be presented according to the students' prior knowledge, they will keep the workload to a level that allows students to be challenged and to maintain their interest, they could design additional age-appropriate activities, and they could look for other ways in order to capture students' attention.

INSTRUCTIONAL GUIDELINES IN *EUTERPE*

In *Euterpe* each song can be used to enhance the understanding of musical concepts. Moreover, through rich integrated thematic units students can deal with broader conceptual ideas and investigate issues, pose questions, examine, visualize, and synthesize informations in meaningful ways.

There are whole-class, group, peer, and individual activities. There is also teacher-centered lesson time, where students are introduced to new songs and participate in more structured and instruction-based singing experiences and in guided listening and singing. However, this must not be limited to a procedure where the teacher sings the melody of the song and asks students to imitate her/him or to join in through repetitions phrase-by-phrase. It is important for teachers to find a variety of modes for the song presentation, to reinforce the messages of the songs, and to surprise their students through new, motivating, and interesting ways. As for general teachers, if they do not feel confident about their singing skills (see Heyning, 2011), they can use pre-recorded versions of the songs.

The majority of the proposed activities are "learning by doing", project-based and interdisciplinary actions, a process followed in various learning application areas (Fleischmann & Hutchison, 2012; Kay, 2011; Oliver, 2011). This model for classroom activities shifts away from the isolated teacher-centered classroom practices, and emphasizes learning activities that are student-centered, and integrated with real world issues (Lindgren, 2012; Prata, 2009). The "learning by doing" activities are consistent to "practice-before-theory" approach and give students opportunities to demonstrate and apply their new learning. The project-based learning situations can clearly be supported by experimental multimedia (Deliyannis, 2012). The multimedia component gives students opportunities to use technology effectively as tool in their planning, data investigation, or presentation of their projects. It also give teachers the freedom to act based on their intuition and experience, and to design flexible teaching scenarios as they are based in various and easily accessible sources.

The interdisciplinary concepts are means for content extension. These concepts provide pathways for applying new information to other subject areas and experiences, they enhance comprehension, they link classroom experiences to real-world situations, and they integrate topics in order to broaden and deepen students' connections to new information (Burnaford, Aprill, & Weiss, 2001; Hargreaves & Moore, 2000; Erickson, 1998; Beane, 1997). According to Janet Barrett (2001:27) deep understanding depends upon the intersections and interactions of the disciplines. Interdisciplinary connections, therefore, open up new windows for comprehensive study while preserving the integrity and validity of musical experience.

The suggested activities are also intended to promote collaboration among students, and between students and the teacher as well (Fleischmann & Hutchison, 2012; Lindgren, 2012). It is important to give students opportunities to develop collaborative skills, such as group decision-making, relying on the work of peers, and working with others as researchers (Cohen, 2006; Elliott, 1995; Gardner, 1993). In collaborative activities, students can express their opinions, present their arguments, seek answers to certain music questions and problems, brainstorm ideas, solve music quiz, consider multiple perspectives and points of view, discuss their views and their music ideas, compose, and prepare their performances.

Moreover, following the principles of informal music learning, they can co-operate in order to explore several songs of a specific genre, to play songs by ear, to analyze it (riffs, patterns, structure, melodic layers), and to improvise. It is also documented that small-group instruction helps teachers to use classroom time effectively (Green 2008; Green, 2014).

There are activities that will take no more than a few minutes of class time, and projects that may occupy students for several weeks. The project-oriented activities embrace language, visual arts, history, geography, physical education, civics, and other school subjects. The presentations of the projects can be combinations of music performances, lectures, and videos, just to name a few possibilities. There are a lot of chances for conversation cycles where students and teachers can discuss in detail, can focus on open-ended questions, can have self-reflective discussions about particular songs, and can share their views apart from conventional limits.

The instructional suggestions emphasize opportunities for teachers to build relationships with their students while being coaches, facilitators, and co-learners (Steele 2009). There are a lot of chances for conversation cycles where students and teachers can discuss in detail, can focus on open-ended questions, can have self-reflective discussions about particular song, and can share their views apart from conventional limits (Eisner 2002). Students are encouraged to focus and reflect on what they listen to, by noticing details, by comparing new information with what they have listened before, by thinking about how a song is alike and different from other songs (Bowman, 2002; Elliott, 1995).

Question-type activities embrace new possibilities for the music classroom (Eisner, 2002). In the educational suggestions of *Euterpe* an inquiry-based teaching is embraced. This is linked naturally to problem solving or to decision-making questions (Willingham 2009). It is easy for teachers, after studying the educational suggestions, to formulate questions that give life to the proposed activities such as: What is the song about? What issues and ideas are presented? In your opinion, what does the song mean? Are there any symbolic meanings in the song? Why do you like /you do not like this song?

Teaching-learning activities also include feedback as to help students reflect on their learning and to make thoughtful evaluation and revisions, if needed (Ferm-Thorgersen, 2011; Elliott, 1995). In *Euterpe*, assessment is considered as an ongoing process, including group assessment, peer assessment, self-assessment, and reflection. The assessment of students' performances is based mainly on recording: when students listen to the recorded version of their performance they are provided with clarity about how they performed and they have the opportunity to revise it in the light of their own remarks. In the second trial they can improve their synchronization, tonal accuracy, rhythmic accuracy and so on. By doing all these, they learn to better control their voice while their confidence in singing can be increased.

In sum, in Euterpe project it was made clear that creative school music teaching can start from song singing and flow into a lot of other activities, such as music listening, instrument playing, moving, dancing, improvising, composing and understanding. The ultimate goal of music education is to foster students' enjoyment of music making.

EUTERPE FOR INTERNATIONAL USERS

Digital communication can be effectively used for educational exchanges. Technology has many advantages in this case: it has no cost, it is environmental-friendly, it fosters cultural exchange, and it allows users to reach a material which otherwise could not be included in their repertoire. *Euterpe* allows users to build the knowledge base for the teaching and learning of new songs and to broaden their perspectives regarding singing by drawing data from educational systems from all over the world.

Technology enables music educators from other countries to have access to new material and get the scores and the information they want. It is broadly accepted that when children are provided with opportunities to sing songs from other cultures they develop an interest in these cultures, they understand the significance of cultural diversity, and they are able to re-examine the value of their own cultural heritage (Nichols & Honig, 1997; Acker, 2010). Moreover, singing in a foreign language offers opportunities for children to appreciate and participate in diverse cultural activities that expand their world view (Kramer, 2001).

Since the 1980s there was a recognition that the songs of other cultures were to be sung in their original language (Campbell, 2004; Campbell, Williamson, & Perron, 1996; Lundquist & Szego, 1998). In this vein, we created a corpus of songs, a representative set of both Greek traditional and contemporary songs, which can serve as a resource of authentic material, and may bring teachers from other countries closer to Greek music. The inclusion of Greek songs in the school repertoire allows teachers and students to recognize the rich cultural diversity and to expose children to the Greek culture in engaging ways. Yet given no precedent for the preparation of this set of material for the use of a non-Greek teacher, we faced the problem of renderings in English.

The Greek songs were translated into English and transliterated as to offer the foreign users a clear picture of their original language. Yet, literal translations of song lyrics from one language to another cannot adequately project critical meanings (Krupat, 1992). Therefore, the process of lyrics translation was a challenging task; it was difficult to find equivalent English words for cultural perspectives not shared by English speakers, words and expressions that could capture in English the nature, sense, and essence of Greek thinking. So, we had to be creative, to translate more freely, and to find out words that could convey the inner ideas of the songs. Finally, the fields with the instructional guidelines and the metadata have all been translated in English for the presentation of the English template.

CONCLUSION

This work demonstrates how an experimental multimedia system was designed to provide direct and meaningful access to an array of courseware information based on digital libraries. Familiarization with a new digital singing content is not as simple as attending a workshop or reading a chapter in a book. Multimedia content access needs to evolve from static to dynamic in order for the learning process to advance and remain interesting and rewarding. The *Euterpe project* was designed to cover a number of particular requirements, which are unique in this subject area. It ensures the adequacy of material (sufficient data, enough detail and depth) and its efficiency (fast processing pace, material that corresponds to a large variety of classroom situations). Users can find what they need at this site relatively quickly, while they can download the music scores in order to distribute the information in other media and for practicing purposes. In addition the end-system displays information in a user-friendly format characterized by direct access to rich multimedia content. Furthermore it offers the option to automatically provide context-specific suggestions in authentic classroom settings, enabling its applicability, a characteristic that is viewed by many as a novel and highly important functionality as it provides a wide range of generic and context-specific data, and pathways for cross-curriculum topics.

Euterpe is an ongoing project, which is best evaluated through practice. Therefore the factors that determine the success of this project include music teachers' reception of the project and response to it, and the extent to which teachers believe that the material provided in *Euterpe* is useful in music classroom. For this reason the support is continuous; appropriate communication methods are available on the project's website for teachers to provide feedback and help tweak the end-system. Professional teaching communities are key to any such efforts. It would be also important to receive feedback from the music teachers regarding the usability of the database. In the future, we expect music teachers to help developing further the database. In all, both individuals and communities have a powerful role to play in the future of the *Euterpe*.

ACKNOWLEDGMENT

We would like to thank Dr. Ioannis Deliyannis for his valuable comments and advice on the preparation of the manuscript.

REFERENCES

Acker, A. (2010). Early childhood, music and diversity: exploring the potential of music for three and four year olds. *Proceedings of the CDIME Conference 2010* (pp. 6-14). Sydney, Australia: Sydney Conservatorium of Music.

Balkin, A. (2009). *Tune up to literacy: Original songs and activities for kids*. Chicago: American Library Association.

Barrett, J. R. (2001). Interdisciplinary work and musical integrity. *Music Educators Journal, 87*(5), 27–31. doi:10.2307/3399705

Beane, J. A. (1997). *Curriculum integration: Designing the core of democratic education*. New York: Teachers College Press.

Bowman, W. D. (2002). Educating musically. In R. Colwell, & C. Richardson (Eds.), The new handbook of research on music teaching and learning: A project of the music educators national conference (pp. 63-84). New York, NY: Oxford University Press.

Burnaford, G., Aprill, A., & Weiss, C. (2001). *Renaissance in the classroom: Arts integration and meaningful learning*. Mahwah, NJ: Lawrence Erlbaum.

Campbell, P. S. (1998). *Songs in their heads: Music and its meaning in children's lives*. New York, NY: Oxford University Press.

Campbell, P. S. (2004). *Teaching Music Globally*. New York: Oxford University Press.

Campbell, P. S., Williamson, S., & Perron, P. (1996). *Traditional songs of singing cultures: A world sampler*. Alfred Music Publishing.

Cohen, J. (2006). Social, emotional, ethical, and academic education: Creating a climate for learning, participation in democracy, and well-being. *Harvard Educational Review, 76*(2), 201–237. doi:10.17763/haer.76.2.j44854x1524644vn

Custodero, L. A., & Chen-Hafteck, L. (2008). Harmonizing research, practice, and policy in early childhood music: A chorus of international voices (Part 2). *Arts Education Policy Review, 109*(3), 3–8. doi:10.3200/AEPR.109.3.3-8

Deliyannis, I. (2012). From Interactive to Experimental Multimedia. In I. Deliyannis (Ed.), *Interactive Multimedia* (pp. 3–12). Rijeka, Croatia: Intech. doi:10.5772/38341

Deliyannis, I., Giannakoulopoulos, A., & Oikonomidou, R. (2013). Engineering and design issues in urban-oriented edutainment systems. Paper presented at the *Hybrid City II: Subtle rEvolutions.* Athens, Greece.

Deliyannis, I., Giannakoulopoulos, A., & Varlamis, I. (2011). Utilising an Educational Framework for the Development of Edutainment Scenarios. Paper presented at the *5th European Conference on Games Based Learning*, ECGBL 2011.

Du, Z., Fu, X., Zhao, C., Liu, Q., & Liu, T. (2013). Interactive and Collaborative E-Learning Platform with Integrated Social Software and Learning Management System. In W. Lu, G. Cai, W. Liu & W. Xing (Eds.), *Proceedings of the 2012 International Conference on Information Technology and Software Engineering* (Vol. 212, pp. 11-18). Springer Berlin Heidelberg. doi:10.1007/978-3-642-34531-9_2

Eisner, E. (2002). *The Arts and the Creation of Mind.* New Haven, London: Yale University Press.

Elliott, D. J. (1995). *Music Matters: A New Philosophy of Music Education.* New York: Oxford University Press.

Erickson, H. L. (1998). *Concept-based curriculum and instruction: Teaching beyond the facts.* Thousand Oaks, CA: Corwin Press.

Ferm-Thorgersen, C. (2011). Assessment of musical knowledge from a life-world-phenomenological perspective. *Hellenic Journal of Music, Education, and Culture, 2*, 37–45.

Fleischmann, K., & Hutchison, C. (2012). Creative exchange: An evolving model of multidisciplinary collaboration. *Journal of Learning Design, 5*(1), 23–31. doi:10.5204/jld.v5i1.92

Foley, M. B. (2006). The music, movement and learning connection: A review. *Childhood Education, 82*(3), 175–176. doi:10.1080/00094056.2006.10521372

Gardner, H. (1993). *Multiply Intelligences: The Theory into Practice.* New York: Basic Books.

Green, L. (2008). *Music, Informal Learning and the School: A New Classroom Pedagogy.* Aldershot: Ashgate Press.

Green, L. (2014). *Hear, Listen, Play! How to Free Your Students' Aural, Improvisation, and Performance Skills.* Oxford: Oxford University Press.

Green, M., & McNeese, M. N. (2007). Using Edutainment Software to Enhance Online Learning. *International Journal on E-Learning, 6*(1), 5–16.

Hargreaves, A., & Moore, S. (2000). Curriculum integration and classroom relevance: A study of teachers' practice. *Journal of Curriculum and Supervision, 15*, 89–112.

Heyning, L. (2011). "I can't sing!" The concept of teacher confidence in singing and the use within their classroom. *International Journal of Education & the Arts*, 12(13). Retrieved from http://www.ijea.org/v12n13

ISME. (2012). ISME-Gibson International Award Winners 2012. Retrieved from http://www.isme.org/awards/39-isme-g/155-isme-gibson-international-award-winners-2012

Karydis, I., Deliyannis, I., & Floros, A. (2011). Augmenting virtual-reality environments with social-signal based music content. Paper presented at the *17th International Conference on Digital Signal Processing* (DSP), 2011. doi:10.1109/ICDSP.2011.6004944

Katsch, S., & Merle-Fishman, C. (1985). *The Music within You*. New York: Simon and Schuster.

Kay, R. (2011). Evaluating learning, design, and engagement in web-based learning tools (WBLTs): The WBLT Evaluation Scale. *Computers in Human Behavior, 27*(5), 1849–1856. doi:10.1016/j.chb.2011.04.007

Kokkidou, M. (2009). European Music Curriculum: philosophical orientations, trends, and comparative validation (bilingual edition). Thessaloniki: Greek Society for Music Education (G.S.M.E.).

Koong, C. S., & Wu, C. Y. (2011). The applicability of interactive item templates in varied knowledge types. *Computers & Education, 56*(3), 781–801. doi:10.1016/j.compedu.2010.10.021

Kramer, D. J. (2001). A blueprint for teaching foreign languages and cultures through music in the classroom and on the Web. *ADFL Bulletin, 33*(1), 29–35. doi:10.1632/adfl.33.1.29

Krupat, A. (1992). On the Translation of Native American Song and Story: A Theorized History. In B. Swann (Ed.), *On the Translation of Native American Literature* (pp. 3–32). Washington, D.C.: Smithsonian Institution Press.

Lee, H. J. J., Messom, C., & Yau, K. L. A. (2013). Can an electronic textbooks be part of K-12 Education? *The Turkish Online Journal of Educational Technology, 12*(1), 32–44.

Levitin, D. (2008). *The world in six songs*. New York, NY: Plume Publishers Group.

Lindgren, S. (2012). The Sociology of Media and Information Technologies. In G. C. Aakvaag, M. H. Jacobsen, & T. Johansson (Eds.), *Introduction to Sociology: Scandinavian Sensibilities*. London: Pearson.

Lundquist, B., & Szego, C. K. (Eds.), (1998). Musics of the world's cultures. Perth, Australia: Callaway.

Manovich, L. (2011). Trending: The Promises and the Challenges of Big Social Data. In M. K. Gold (Ed.), *Debates in the Digital Humanities*. Minneapolis, MN: The University of Minnesota Press.

Marsh, K. (2002). Children's song acquisition: an ethnomusicological perspective. In C. Stephens, D. Burnham, G. McPherson, E. Schubert & J. Renwick (Eds.) Proceedings of the 7th International Conference of Music Perception and Cognition (pp. 256-268). Adelaide: Causal Productions.

Murphy, T. (1992). *Music and Song*. Oxford: Oxford University Press.

Nichols, B., & Honig, A. (1997). Music Teaches Children about Themselves and Others. *Early Child-hood Education Journal, 24*(4), 213–216. doi:10.1007/BF02354834

Nyland, B., Ferris, J., & Deans, J. (2010). Young children and music: Constructing meaning through a performance. *Australian Journal of Music Education, 10*(1), 5–17.

O'Neill, S. A. (2012). Becoming a music learner: Towards a theory of transformative music engagement. In G. E. McPherson & G. Welch (Eds.), *The Oxford handbook of music education* (Vol. 1, pp. 163–186). New York, NY: Oxford University Press.

Oliver, J. (2011). Multimedia systems: Tools for learning. Proceedings of INTED 2011 (pp. 4633-4635).

Pascale, L. (2005). The power of simply singing together in the classroom. *Music Education Research, 9*(1), 1–15.

Prata, A. (2009). Interactive Television Evolution. In M. Pagani (Ed.), Encyclopedia of Multimedia Technology and Networking (2nd ed., pp. 757–762). Hershey, PA: IGI Global. doi:10.4018/978-1-60566-014-1.ch102

Snelgrove, W. X., & Baecker, R. M. (2010). A system for the collaborative reading of digital books with the partially sighted: project proposal. Paper presented at the *Proceedings of the third workshop on Research advances in large digital book repositories and complementary media*. Toronto, ON, Canada. doi:10.1145/1871854.1871870

Steele, C. F. (2009). *Inspired Teacher*. Alexandria, VA: ASCD.

Thurman, L., & Welch, G. (Eds.). (2000). *Bodymind and Voice: foundations of voice education* (revised Edition). Iowa City, Iowa: National Center for Voice and Speech.

Vuckovic, A. (2006). *Singing the tunes of the world: preschool children responses to songs in diverse languages* [Unpublished master thesis]. LaTrobe University, Bundoora, Victoria, Australia.

Welch, G. F. (2005). Singing as Communication. In D. Miell, R. Mac- Donald, & D. Hargreaves (Eds.), Musical Communication (pp. 239-259). New York: Oxford University Press. doi:10.1093/acprof:oso/9780198529361.003.0011

Willingham, D. T. (2009). *Why don't students like school?* San Francisco: Jossey-Bass.

Xia, S. (2011). Interactive Design Research of Multimedia Courseware in Teaching. *Advanced Materials Research, 271*, 1472–1477. doi:10.4028/www.scientific.net/AMR.271-273.1472

KEY TERMS AND DEFINITIONS

Digital Song Anthology: A collection of songs and educational metadata offered in a multimedia database.

Euterpe: The muse of lyric poetry and music in Greek Mythology.

Music Notation Software: Software programs for the presentation of music scores (in music conventional notation), in which the user can listen to the music, print the score, make interventions to the score, such as different arrangements of the melodies/harmonies, and instrumentations for particular musical instruments and their combinations. Some notation software programs are: MuseScore, Finale, Sibelius, etc.

Music Teaching Scenarios: The many aspects of music teaching that may arise through using different methodologies, teaching styles, classroom activities, class arrangements, etc.

Music Teaching-Learning: The contemporary approach to teaching and learning of music, seen as a unity in a dynamic dialogue.

Singing-Centered Music Education: Singing being the core in music education that flows in various activities.

Songs for Educational Use: Appropriate songs selected for school use in all levels of education.

Chapter 8

Dealing with the Uncertainty of Satisfaction Surveys in Organizations That Employ Interactive Multimedia:
An Analysis of False Answers Statistical Models through a Digital Music Library Case Study

Stelios Zimeras
University of the Aegean, Greece

Petros Kostagiolas
Ionian University, Greece

Charilaos Lavranos
Ionian University, Greece

ABSTRACT

The meaning of customer satisfaction has introduced many research analyses in many scientific fields during the recent years. Customer satisfaction represents a modern approach for evaluating quality in any kind of organizations. Customer satisfaction provides a useful and objective feedback about preferences and expectations. This can be particularly important for the design of services based on multimedia and interactive technologies, which are novel to most users. During the evaluation process, surveys analysis must be applied with main task to understand customer satisfaction. For that reason questionnaires have been proposed to reflect the previous analysis. Many times in that process, individuals that participate in the interviewing process misunderstand the pose questions leading to false answers and error results, without evaluating all recourses during the interview. The aim of this chapter is to analyze a statistical modeling of that false answers considering categorical data analysis through a digital music library case study. This chapter focuses on a proposed method which is based on the probabilities of the positive or negative TRUE and FALSE answers, with main task to reduce the variability of the errors during the survey.

DOI: 10.4018/978-1-4666-8659-5.ch008

INTRODUCTION

Both public and private sectors have given much attention to the concept of customer satisfaction in the past couple of decades. In today's competitive world high quality service is the key for improving any organization under competition. Customer satisfaction does have a positive effect on an organization's value generation, outcome and impact. Depending on the type of organization, satisfied customers, users or visitors form the foundation of any successful operation because satisfaction leads to repeat purchases, usage, visitation, brand loyalty, and positive word of mouth. Many researchers point out the fact that satisfied customers share their experiences with other people with main purpose to effect small groups of them. On the contrary, dissatisfied customers are more likely to communicate with a large amount of people chairing their own experiences.

Measuring customer satisfaction can be done by simply asking a series of questions. In particular each questions measure the degree of satisfaction or dissatisfaction for the customer under consideration. Satisfaction is best measured on a continuous scale, but for obvious reasons we cannot use an unlimited scale. The scale should be such that it allows the customer enough flexibility to express his opinion and yet be limited. Evaluation is a very complex task; it is referred to psychological and cognitive needs and wants, affecting personal behaviors and activity (Pearce, 1982). Under this evaluation approach survey analysis is the key point to measure that degree of satisfaction or expectation. Many times misleading results could appear based on errors during the questionnaires procedure. Loch (1999) has introduced some of them, reflecting the errors that probably maybe introduced in the analysis. To overcome this problem of errors under uncertain conditions statistical models must be introduced and analysis would take place based on these models.

The goal of the proposed modeling is to reduce the false negative answers during the evaluation process of multimedia and interactive technologies. This can be important to the design of services employing multimedia and interactive technologies. Feedback from the customer/user provides an understanding on the relationship between multimedia technology and the usability of the related web-based applications. Moreover, satisfaction surveys provide researchers and practitioners important information for the quality of multimedia technology services. Moreover, the employment of interactive multimedia systems in non conventional context increases the inherited uncertainty and imposes additional difficulties. Often, developers are still experimenting and exploring the interaction of humans with augmenting reality technologies, and other innovative multimedia systems. Services based on content presentation and interaction is including a wide variety of organizations and domains that include art, publishing, library science, museums, etc. This chapter presents the uncertainty of satisfaction surveys in organizations that employ interactive multimedia through a digital music library case study. More specifically, this chapter examines one of the few studies which have dealt with the usability and user satisfaction of two digital music library projects of Indiana University named VARIATIONS and VARIATIONS2.

MODELS FOR CUSTOMER/USER/VISITOR SATISFACTION

Over the last few decades several studies on satisfaction have been published and an evaluation of customer satisfaction methods has been attempted using various theories. Some researchers have looked at comparison of standards used in service quality and satisfaction and provided different measures (Liljander, 2005). Many researchers began to investigate customer satisfaction models in order to measure

Figure 1. Traditional macro-model of customer satisfaction
Modified from: Woodruff & Gardial, 1996

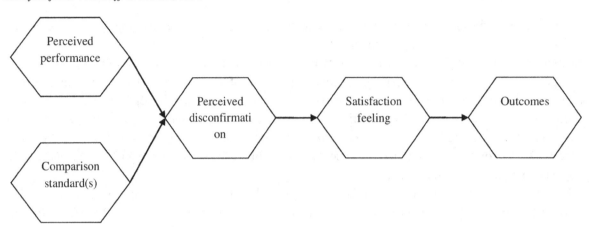

expectations and performance. Customer satisfaction has becomes a typical process for overall evaluation of the effectiveness of service quality (Johnson and Gustafsson, 2000).

Organizations the employ interactive multimedia systems that try to analyze preferences and expectations should begin with an understanding of various customer/user/visitor satisfaction models. Knowledge of satisfaction must be a basic parameter to evaluate the performance of products and services (Noe and Uysal, 1997; Churchill and Surprenant, 1982). Oliver (1997) suggests that "Satisfaction is the consumer's fulfillment response. It is a judgment that a product or service feature, or the product of service itself, provided (or is providing) a pleasurable level of consumption-related fulfillment, including levels of under-or over-fulfillment...". From a literature review, there are many factors that affect customer satisfaction. Such factors include friendly, courteous, knowledgeable and helpful employees, accuracy of billing, billing timeliness, competitive pricing, service quality, and good value, billing clarity and service promptness (Hokanson, 1995). From many studies carried out in many countries, factors like: service quality, and perceived value, are the key components affecting the customer's satisfaction for any services. Studies also point out that customer satisfaction results include trust, price tolerance, and customer loyalty. Factors like: customer satisfaction, service quality, customer perception, customer loyalty, are the main concerns of the any kind of service companies, which improves organization's performance.

In general satisfaction is a feeling where the attitude is changing according to various circumstances. It is part of the user's mind and is different from observable behaviors such as product choice, complaining, and repurchase. The macro-model of customer satisfaction based on the Woodruff & Gardial (1996) suggestions is provided in Figure 1. Later research has introduced an alternative model shown in Figure 2. This model highlights the concept of value as a leading force in product choice and satisfaction's relationship proposing values chain (or "hierarchy").

Oliver (1999) proposes another version of this model, which appears in Figure 3. An important point about customer value models is the use of gross benefit-cost judgments by consumers.

Some models differentiate between technical service quality and perceived service [quality]. Figure 4 shows one such model and how satisfaction results from a comparison between expected service and perceived service (Bateson, 1991). This model is explicit about the cyclical, feedback loop that affects

Figure 2. Model of linkage of customer value chain to customer satisfaction
Modified from: Woodruff & Gardial, 1996

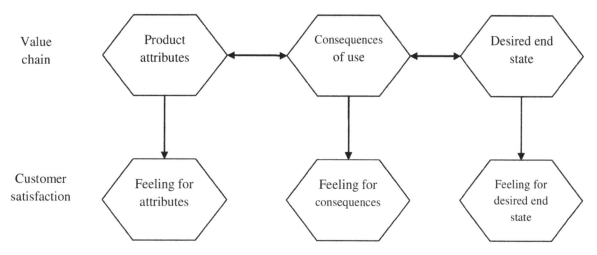

satisfaction. A consumer's prior experience joins "other data inputs" to shape current satisfaction with a service.

For more details on Customer Satisfaction, see e.g. Siskos et al. 1998, Cassel, 2000, Lundström, 2005). The American Customer Satisfaction Index (ACSI) is the national indicator of customer evaluations of the quality of goods and services available to U.S. residents since 1994 (Fornell et al, 1996; Anderson and Fornell, 2000). It is the only uniform, cross-industry and government measure of customer satisfaction. The Customer Satisfaction Index is a weighted average of three questions. The questions are answered on a 1-10 scale and converted to a 0-100 scale for reporting purposes. The three questions

Figure 3. Model of link between satisfaction and value
Modified from: Oliver, 1999

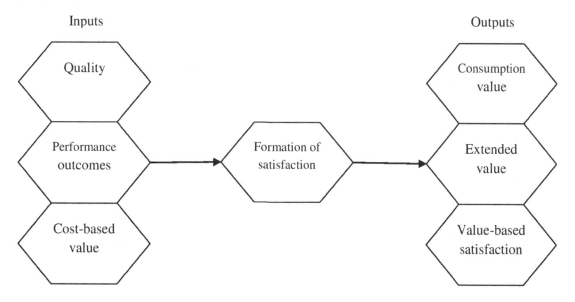

Figure 4. Model of sources of customer satisfaction
Modified from: Bateson, 1991

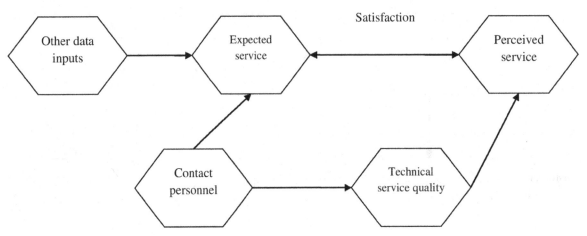

measure: Overall satisfaction, Satisfaction compared to expectations, and Satisfaction compared to an 'ideal' organization (Figure 5).

Accordingly, ACSI uses a multiple indicator approach to measure overall customer satisfaction as a latent variable" (Fornell et al., 1996). Generally, the nature of the choices is categorical, and for that reason categorical data analysis must consider for the statistical evaluation using binary analysis techniques (Cox, 1970; Franses and Paap, 2001; Train, 2003). All the above models are equally applicable to the wide range of organizations that employ interactive multimedia and augmented reality systems.

Figure 5. American Customer Satisfaction Index model
Modified from: Fornell et al., 1996

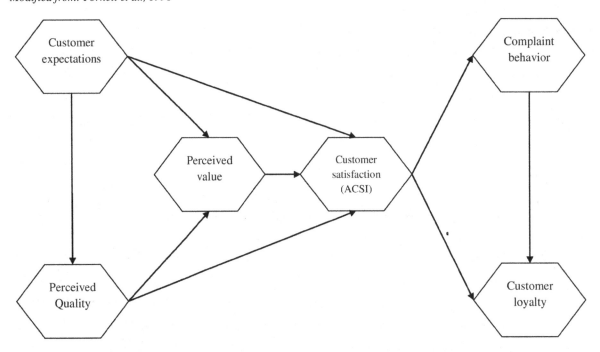

POTENTIAL ERRORS IS SURVEY INTERVIEW PROCESS

Any customer satisfaction procedure includes survey analysis based on specific questionnaires. Based on the results of these questionnaires useful information may be achieved concerning the behaviors of the people who taking place in the survey. Most surveys rely on self-reports to collect data explaining their behaviors. Self-report is, therefore, a major step to estimate the opinion of the people who take place in the analysis. Important part of the self-report analysis based on the survey literature, is the concern of the ways to measure the errors which maybe take place via the questions: question wording and question order (Schuman and Presser, 1981; Schwarz et al., 1985; Tourangeau et al., 2000), misunderstanding of survey concepts (Schober and Conrad, 1999; Schober and Conrad, 1997; 1998), inappropriate use of estimation strategies (Conrad et al., 1998), deliberate misreporting (Tourangeau and Smith, 1998), and the effects of the interview mode (Tourangeau and Smith, 1998). However, the size and direction of these errors associated with self-report behavior are often unknown.

Many studies suggest that the presence of an interviewer sometimes reflects negative feelings considering both ways: the person who takes place into the interview and the person who gives the interview (Tourangeau et al., 2000). Especially for social surveys, like customer satisfaction analysis, where the answers of the persons who taking the interview reflect the general feelings of the population, when the sample is large and representative. Lohr (1999) suggests eight possible errors during the survey interview process:

- People sometimes do not tell the truth
- Misunderstanding the questions
- People forget
- Answers are varies during different interviews
- People misleading the person who contact the interview
- Incorrect reading from the interviewer
- The meaning of the word is different for some people
- The kind of the questions sometimes leading to depressing feelings

Based on the Lohr (1999) proposed possible errors during the survey analysis, many times it is difficult to extract reliable results, with ways which leading the analysis to uncertain conditions under the difficulty of the questions (Figure 6). This uncertainty gives us many times false or unreliable results. Under those uncertain conditions, the main goal is to reduce false negative rate relative to the interviews. For that reason statistical models could be introduced to overcome the error process under uncertain conditions, reducing the variability of false negative answers into the questionnaires.

STATISTICAL MODELS BASED ON FALSE ANSWERS

Due to the evaluation of any models satisfaction, questionnaires must be proposed and based on their answers useful results could be achieved. Many times, the answers are based on misunderstandings during the questionnaires process, and false results could be represented based on these answers (especially in interviews procedures) leading us to error analysis. In that case, the survey procedure must be

Figure 6. Relations between multiple difficulty index goals
Modified from: Lohr, 1999

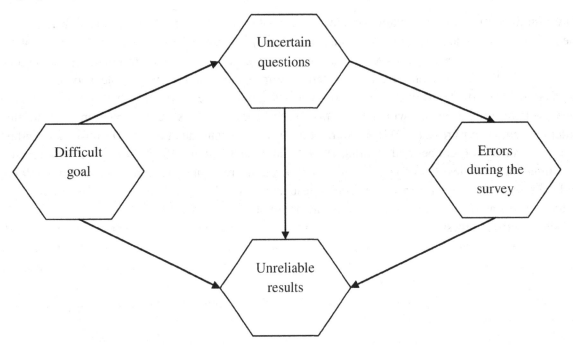

Table 1. Two-ways categorical data analysis (frequencies)

	Y_1	Y_2	**Total**
X_1	n_{11}	n_{12}	$n_{1.}$
X_2	n_{21}	n_{22}	$n_{2.}$
Total	$n_{.1}$	$n_{.2}$	$N=n_{..}$

reviewed and the new results maybe compared with the old one. Let us consider a two way analysis of the available categorical data with dichotomous variables X and Y which are put in the form of Table 1.

In Table 1, nij, for i,j=1,2 denotes the frequencies for every cell, n.j denotes the sum of j-columns, ni. denotes the sum of i-rows and N=n.. the total summation. The two ways table illustrates the possible combination outcome between initial interviews and the reinterviews. The index of inconsistency (I) is used many times as a reliability measure for continuous and scale variables. It is defined by Biemer, and Trewin (1997) and Biemer et. al. (2001) as:

$$I = \frac{g}{p_1 q_1 + p_2 q_2}$$

Table 2. Two-ways categorical data analysis (probabilities)

	$Y_1=0$	$Y_2=1$	Total
$X_1=0$	π_{00}	π_{01}	$\pi_{0.}$
$X_2=1$	π_{10}	π_{11}	$\pi_{1.}$
Total	$\pi_{.0}$	$\pi_{.1}$	$\pi_{..}=1$

where $g = \dfrac{n_{12}+n_{21}}{n_{..}}$ is the amount of agreement, $p_1 = \dfrac{n_{11}+n_{22}}{n_{..}}$ is the proportion of the positive answers

in the initial interview and $p_2 = \dfrac{n_{11}+n_{12}}{n_{..}}$ is the proportion of the positive answers in the reinterview.

Also, $q_i = 1 - p_i$ with i=1,2 are the proportions of negative answers during the interview and the rein-terview. The expected value of the I-measure is given by the form (Pritzker and Hanson, 1962):

$$E(I) = \frac{\sigma_R^2}{\sigma_T^2}$$

where σ_R^2 is half the average squared difference between the variables X and Y responses across the individuals in the population, and σ_T^2 is the average total variance of potential responses across the population for both X and Y.

Considering the probabilities of Table 1 we can develop Table 2 as follows.

The symbol π_{00} represents the proportion in the population of those who answer correct (TRUE/TRUE) in first and the second interviews; π_{01} represents the proportion of the population who answer correct (TRUE) in the first interview, but would report false answer (FALSE) in the second interview; π_{10} represents the proportion of persons in the population who answer false (FALSE) the first interview, but not in the second interview (TRUE); and π_{11} represents the proportion of the population who answer false (FALSE/FALSE) in both the first and second interviews.

If θ and φ are the probabilities for one false negative and one false positive answers then the probabilities for every cell considering the Table 2 design given by Bross (1954):

$$\pi_{00} = \pi\theta^2 + (1-\pi)(1-\varphi)^2$$

$$\pi_{01} = \pi\theta(1-\theta) + (1-\pi)\varphi(1-\varphi)$$

$$\pi_{10} = \pi\theta(1-\theta) + (1-\pi)\varphi(1-\varphi)$$

$$\pi_{11} = \pi(1-\theta)^2 + (1-\pi)\varphi^2$$

For example, the probability π_{11} includes two factors: the first explains the case where the probability (π) that a person gives a positive answers (YES) in both situations interview and reinterview. The probability $(1-\theta)^2$ implies that there is none false negative answer in both cases. The combination is the joint probability $\pi(1-\theta)^2$. The second factor explains the case where the probability a person to answer false in both situations is $(1-\pi)$, with false positive answers (φ^2). The combination is the joint probability $(1-\pi)\varphi^2$.

The calculations of the final probabilities could be achieved by applying Latent Class Analysis (LCA). The standard latent class analysis measures one or more unobserved (latent) categorical variables through a set of observed one. The basic idea of LCA is that the associations between the observed indicators can be explained by the latent variable(s). The relationship between the indicators is achieved by distribution of indicators across different classes of the latent variable. (Lazarsfeld and Henry, 1968). In the case of 2x2 categorical table, the marginal probabilities π_{ij} where $i,j \in \{0,1\}$ are given by the multinomial distribution

$$p\left(n_{ij}, i, j \in \{0,1\}\right) = \frac{n!}{n_{00}! \, n_{01}! \, n_{10}! \, n_{11}!} \pi_{00}^{n_{00}} \pi_{01}^{n_{01}} \pi_{10}^{n_{10}} \pi_{11}^{n_{11}}$$

In case of estimation, a maximum likelihood approach could be suggested for the estimation of the parameters π, θ and φ.

Considering the general formulation of the false answers analysis using multinomial distribution, let S denotes the random sample n-values and i a specific index for S. Suppose X_i is the value for index i with A_i and B_i the corresponding measures (for example A_i could be the answer of one particular question in the interview and B_i the answer of this corresponding question in the reinterview. The variables X, A, and B are taking values 1 for positive answer and 0 for negative answer. If π_Z is defined as the probability of Z, then π_a is p(A=a), π_{xa} is p(X=x, A=a) and $\pi_{x|a}$ is p(X=x|A=a).

Also it could be defined as $\pi_{a=1|x=0}$ as the false positive probability and $\pi_{a=0|x=1}$ as the false negative probability for A. For B the above probabilities becomes as $\pi_{b=1|x=0}$ and $\pi_{b=0|x=1}$ respectively. So for the reinterviewing process the hypothesis for the calculation of the previous probabilities are given by:

1. $\pi_{a|x} = \pi_{b|x}$
2. $\pi_{ab|x} = \pi_{a|x} \, \pi_{b|x}$

$\pi_{ab|x}$ is given by p(A=a, B=b|X=x) based on the hypothesis of local independence (McCutcheon, 1987).

USABILITY AND SATISFACTION ISSUES IN DIGITAL MUSIC LIBRARIES

Digital libraries have been developed the last decades evolving increasingly with the technological advances and the growth of the Internet (Brogan, 2003). The technological advances in recent years have opened up new horizons across a broad array of issues related to design, implementation, development and evaluation of digital libraries (Bawden & Rowlands, 1999). According to the Digital Library Federation, digital libraries are defined as *"organizations that provide the resources, including the specialized staff, to select, structure, offer intellectual access to, interpret, distribute, preserve the integrity of, and ensure the persistence over time of collections of digital works so that they are readily available for use by a defined community or set of communities"* (Council on Library and Information Resources [CLIR], 1998). This definition involves three key components, which constitute the theoretical framework underlying digital libraries. These are: a. people, b. information resources, and c. technology. Digital libraries consist of electronic resources as well as associated technical capabilities for creating, searching and using information (Brogan, 2003). In that context, they represent the enhancement of information storage and retrieval systems supporting the analysis information process. Digital libraries content includes data and metadata (Jones, Cunningham, McNab, & Boddie, 2000). The metadata may consist of links whether internal or external to the digital library, describing at the same time various aspects of the data (e.g. representation, owner, copyright issues, etc.) (Jones et al., 2000). Digital libraries' functional capabilities are organized in order to support the information needs and uses of several user communities. In that context, digital libraries constitute the extension of a variety of information institutions where resources are selected, collected, organized, preserved and accessed in support of a user community (Bawden & Rowlands, 1999).

In recent years, music production has created a vast collection of music resources, which lie interspersed in different media applications (Margounakis & Politis, 2010). The advances of new technologies and the digital format of musical material have led to the necessity of creating digital music libraries in the Internet, which provide the user with great possibilities of acquiring and listening to music and giving to the music community new perspectives and capabilities (Bainbridge, Nevill-Manning, Witten, Smith, & McNab, 1999). A digital music library is a digital library for music content (Blandford & Stelmaszewska, 2002). This definition involves four key components, which constitute the theoretical framework underlying digital music libraries. These are: a. the digitized materials are delivered over a network, b. the use of technology to allow easy access to the musical material, c. the contents are stored as a standalone collection, and d. they allow retrieval of information in multiple formats (e.g., audio, visual, textual) (Blandford & Stelmaszewska, 2002). Digital music libraries require addressing issues of description, representation, organization, and use of music information and have capabilities such as classification, filing and sharing of music, music information retrieval, etc. Apart from the format and presentation of the digital content, special interfaces are designed to achieve the goals of digital music libraries. Furthermore, a crucial issue on the design of a digital music library constitutes the interaction with the user and factors that are bound together with the successful interaction with the user are: a. search, b. personalization, c. usability and d. user's satisfaction (Blandford & Stelmaszewska, 2002).

VARIATIONS and VARIATIONS2: A Digital Music Library System Research and Development

The recent advances in multimedia technologies and the Internet, as well as the variety of information formats used by musicians, give a great opportunity for the development of digital music library systems and services (Margounakis & Politis, 2010). The VARIATIONS project was developed in 1996 at Indiana University. This is a digital music library providing online access to music recordings, scores and other formats in the Indiana University Music Library (Dunn & Mayer, 1999). The name VARIATIONS was intended to promote the idea that musical information by its nature is presented in many different formats (e.g., notation, sound, time based information, text, video, etc.) and the access to all of these formats is a unique goal for a digital music library system. According to Notess (2004) the collection available in VARIATIONS encompasses a fairly large number of scores and sound recording titles (over than 8.000 pieces), representing a broad range of musical material reflecting the curriculum of the Indiana University School of Music. The recordings are digitized at CD quality and stored as both WAVE format file and MPEG files for delivery to the users. Users are able to locate sound recordings either by browsing reserve lists, or by searching Indiana University's online library catalog system. Sound files are streamed to users via an IBM Video Charger server and a customized player application.

In 2003, there was developed at Indiana University the VARIATIONS2 project, a completely new digital music library system (Notess, 2004). This project focuses on three individual areas of research and development: a. system architecture, b. component based application architecture, and c. network services. The following technical environment supports VARIATIONS2 (VARIATIONS2, 2003):

- Client and server developed in Java
- Java RMI used for client-server communication
- Windows and Mac OS X client platforms, AIX and Linux servers
- Database: IBM DB2, DB2 Net Search Extender
- Audio streaming: Apple Quicktime for Java, Apple Darwin Streaming Server
- Audio compression: MPEG1 layer 3 (MP3) and MPEG4 AAC
- Image compression: DjVu from AT&T Labs and Lizardtech

The VARIATIONS2 digital music library also offers an audio player window, as well as a score viewer and search window. These applications along with additional functionality such as bookmarking make VARIATIONS2 a far more capable system than the original VARIATIONS.

VARIATIONS and VARIATIONS2 User's Satisfaction

In recent years, collections of music are becoming more and more available through web based digital libraries (Cunningham, Jones, & Jones, 2004). These music collections are stored in various formats and can be accessed by various mechanisms from a wide variety of users, over an international platform, with differing levels of musical and information retrieval expertise (Cunningham et al., 2004). In that context, the broad outlines of the types of problems facing digital music libraries development focus on usability of these systems. The design and development of digital music libraries must take into account that there are many different categories of users who may be potential users of a digital music library system (e.g., professional musicians and not, students, researchers, librarians, etc.) (Blandford & Stelmaszewska, 2002). One of the few studies which have dealt with the usability of a digital music library is conducted by Notess (2004) about the projects VARIATIONS and VARIATIONS2. This study has followed an empirical technique considering the usability of these systems. Moreover, this study has involved testing systems with users and focused on general usability issues and user satisfaction, rather than issues that are particular to digital music libraries.

The work of Notess (2004) describes the user satisfaction ratings after user tests with ratings obtained following actual use of a digital music library software. The software in question is successive versions of digital music library software used by music students in the Indiana University Music Library (VARIATONS and VARIATIONS2). There have been used two questionnaire based studies of actual use. The first study aimed at the usage of VARIATIONS project and the second study aimed at the usage of VARIATIONS2 during a pilot deployment. Both studies used a user satisfaction questionnaire which contained a section for collecting demographic information, presented 11 subjective satisfaction ratings on 7 point Likert scale, and invited respondents to offer additional comments. Table 3 gives a summary of the user satisfaction survey findings from the first (VARIATIONS) as well as from the second study (VARIATIONS2) of Notess (2004). The topics that this summary presents have to do with the answers that the respondents gave about the "Frequency of VARIATIONS/VARIATIONS2 use", "Purpose for using VARIATIONS/VARIATIONS2", "Satisfaction ratings", "Positive comments", "Negative comments", and "Recommendations". As it is shown in Table 3, comparing the user satisfaction ratings from the first (VARIATIONS) with the ratings from the second study (VARIATIONS2), the overall mean rating is lower for the VARIATIONS2 project (5.38) than the overall mean rating of the VARIATIONS project (5.56). As a result from this comparison of the two studies is that the difference in user satisfaction with the two versions of the VARIATIONS project may result from the familiar being more satisfactory (Notess & Swan, 2003).

Table 3. VARIATIONS/VARIATIONS2 satisfaction survey findings summary

	VARIATIONS	VARIATIONS2
Topic	**Findings (n=30)**	**Findings (n=12)**
Frequency of use	- 26 use VARIATIONS at least once a week - 7 of these use it more than 5 times per week - 14 had first use VARIATIONS more than 2 years ago	- All use VARIATIONS twice per week or more - 3 use it five times a week or more
Purpose for using	- 17 were studying an exam or completing an assignment for class - 5 were doing personal listening	- Class assignments, listening to course reserves, or exam preparation (11) - Performance or voice lesson preparation (11) - personal listening or pleasure (4) - research (1)
Satisfaction ratings	- Overall mean: 5.56 (1-7) scale - All items averaged above 5 except for "slow...fast" for which the average was 4.77	- Overall mean: 5.38 (1-7) scale - All items averaged above 5 except for "numbers of screens/windows confusing... very clear" for which the average was 4.86
Positive comments	- "Very useful" (2) - "Simply tremendous to use...a veritable heaven for all musicians here"	- Five students specifically praised the easy availability of the scores and song texts, saying that it saves time and improves the overall experience: "my listening was accelerated greatly because I could reference the translations at any time", "great to have the translations and text handy, saves time as well---great program", "I love that I can look at a score and the text while listening to a song! That saves me so much time & my experience is 10x better because of it. Thanks." - Other positive comments mentioned the speed improvement over VARIATIONS (2)
Negative comments	- Waiting to retrieve recordings and the inability to launch multiple retrievals simultaneously (7) - Difficulty in moving to a specific point in a recording and the delay in hearing the music (2) - Sound skipping of cutting off (2)	- Students offered disparate complaints - The only issue mentioned by more than one student was the difficulty of handling the many windows (2) - Most respondents offered just one critique although one respondent offered 5 thoughtful, well described user interface issues
Recommendations	- Provide more detailed information (liner notes, track times, etc.) (3) - More music or types of music (2) - Improved search (2)	- Two students mentioned that they would like to have a "repeat" option (VARIATION does this but VARIATIONS2 does not)

Source: Notess, 2004

CONCLUSION

User/visitor/customer satisfaction becomes an important factor for any organization evaluation, and more specifically for a digital music library. Based on the results of this evaluation, improvements of the structure of the organization maybe propose and useful results for the perceptions and expectations must be achieved. Many models for customer satisfactions have been proposed including the Macro-Model of Customer Satisfaction (Woodruff & Gardial, 1996), the modified chain customer model (Woodruff & Gardial, 1996), the linking model between Satisfaction and Value (Oliver, 1999) and the circular customer satisfaction model (Bateson, 1991).

The indicative analysis and discussion provided above are rather omnibus and as such can be applied in many settings. Under any type of statistical model, the evaluation procedure would take place based on survey analysis. In the survey analysis, a various questions are proposed with main purpose to measure the general feelings of the people who take place in the survey. Many times due to this process, misunderstandings could be achieved, based on the Lohr (1999) errors, leading the procedure to false results. To reduce the false negative results, models based on categorical analysis have been introduced, with task to reduce the variability of the errors, so the illustrated results include more reasonable answers. Future research can provide additional guidance in relation to the indicatively proposed methods and specifically towards satisfaction surveys contexts related to organizations such as museums, libraries etc. which can include augmented reality services.

REFERENCES

Anderson, E. W., & Fornell, C. (2000). Foundations of the American customer satisfaction index. *Total Quality Management*, *11*(7), 869–882. doi:10.1080/09544120050135425

Bainbridge, D., Nevill-Manning, C. G., Witten, I. H., Smith, L. A., & McNab, R. J. (1999) Towards a Digital Library of Popular Music. In *Proceedings of the 4th ACM Conference on Digital Libraries (DL'99)*. Berkeley, California: ACM Press. doi:10.1145/313238.313295

Bateson, J. E. G. (1991). Understanding Services Consumer Behavior. In C. A. Congram (Ed.), The AMA Handbook of Marketing for the Service Industries (pp. 135-150). New York: American Management Association.

Bawden, D., & Rowlands, I. (1999). Digital Libraries: Assumptions and Concepts. *Libri*, *49*(4), 181–191. doi:10.1515/libr.1999.49.4.181

Biemer, P., Herget, D., Morton, J., & Willis, G. (2001), The Feasibility of Monitoring Field Interviewer Performance Using Computer Audio Recorded Interviewing (CARI). *Proceedings of the Section on Survey Research Methods, American Statistical Association.*

Biemer, P., & Trewin, D. (1997). A Review of Measurement Error Effects on the Analysis of Survey Data. In L. Lyberg, P. Biemer, M. Collins, E. De Leeuw, C. Dippo, N. Schwarz, & D. Trewin (Eds.), Survey Measurement and Process Quality (pp. 603-632). New York: Wiley. doi:10.1002/9781118490013.ch27

Blandford, A., & Stelmaszewska, H. (2002). Usability of Musical Digital Libraries: a Multimodal Analysis. *Proceedings of the 3rd International Society for Music Information Retrieval Conference (ISMIR'02)*. Paris, France. ISMIR.

Brogan, M. L. (2003). *A survey of digital library aggregation services*. Washington, District of Columbia: The Digital Library Federation, Council on Library and Information Resources.

Bross, I. (1954). Misclassification in 2x2 tables. *Biometrics, 10*(4), 478–486. doi:10.2307/3001619

Cassel, C. M. (2000). Measuring customer satisfaction on a national level using a super population approach. *Total Quality Management, 11*(7), 909–915. doi:10.1080/09544120050135452

Churchill, G. A. Jr, & Surprenant, C. (1982). An investigation into the determinants of customer satisfaction. *JMR, Journal of Marketing Research, 19*(4), 491–504. doi:10.2307/3151722

Conrad, F. G., & Schober, M. F. (1998). A conversational approach to computer-administered questionnaires. *Proceedings of the American Statistical Association, Section on Survey Methods Research.* Alexandria, VA. American Statistical Association.

Council on Library and Information Resources [CLIR]. (1998). Retrieved from http://www.clir.org/pubs/issues/issues04.html#dlf

Cox, D. R. (1970). *Analysis of binary data*. London: Methuen.

Cunningham, S. J., Jones, M., & Jones, S. (2004). Organizing digital music for use: An examination of personal music collections. In *Proceedings of the 5th International Society for Music Information Retrieval Conference (ISMIR'04)*. Barcelona, Spain. ISMIR.

Dunn, J. W., & Mayer, C. A. (1999). VARIATIONS: A digital music library system at Indiana University. *Proceedings of the 4th ACM Conference on Digital Libraries (DL'99)*. Berkeley, California: ACM Press. doi:10.1145/313238.313242

Fornell, C., Johnson, M. D., Anderson, E. W., Cha, J., & Bryant, B. E. (1996). The American customer satisfaction index: Nature, purpose, and findings. *Journal of Marketing, 60*(4), 7–18. doi:10.2307/1251898

Franses, P. H., & Paap, R. (2001). *Quantitative Models in Marketing Research*. Cambridge, UK: Cambridge University Press. doi:10.1017/CBO9780511753794

Hayes, B. E. (1998). *Measuring Customer Satisfaction: Survey Design, Use, and Statistical Analysis Methods* (2nd ed.). Milwaukee, Wisconsin. ASQ Quality Press.

Johnson, M. D., & Gustafsson, A. (2000). *Improving Customer Satisfaction, Loyalty and Profit. San-Fransico*. Jossey-Bass.

Jones, S., Cunningham, S. J., McNab, R., & Boddie, S. (2000). A transaction log analysis of a digital library. *International Journal on Digital Libraries, 3*(2), 152–169. doi:10.1007/s007999900022

Koch, G. G., Landis, J. R., Freeman, J. L., Freman, D. H., & Lehnen, R. G. (1977). A general methodology for the analysis of experiments with repeated measurements of categorical data. *Biometrics, 33*(1), 133–158. doi:10.2307/2529309 PMID:843570

Lazarsfeld, P. F., & Henry, N. W. (1968). *Latent Structure Analysis*. Boston: Houghton Mifflin.

Liljander, V. (1994). Modeling perceived service quality using different comparison standard. *Journal of Consumer Satisfaction and Dissatisfaction, 7*, 126–142.

Lohr, S. L. (1999). *Sampling: Design and Analysis. California, CA: Duxbury Press*. Pacific Grove: Brooks/Cole Thomson Learning.

Lundström, S., & Särndal, C. E. (2005). *Estimation in Surveys with No response*. John Wiley and Sons, Ltd.

Margounakis, D., & Politis, D. (2010). Implementation and Interaction Issues in Digital Music Libraries, *WSEAS Transactions on Systems, 9*(2), 146-155.

McCutcheon, A. L. (1987). Latent class analysis. Quantitative Applications in the Social Sciences Series No. 64. California: Thousand Oaks.

Noe, F. P., & Uysal, M. (1997). Evaluation of outdoor recreational settings. A problem of measuring user satisfaction. *Journal of Retailing and Consumer Services, 4*(4), 223–230. doi:10.1016/S0969-6989(96)00030-6

Notess, M. (2004). Three looks at users: a comparison of methods for studying digital library use. *Information Research, 9*(3). Retrieved from http://www.informationr.net/ir/9-3/paper177.html

Notess, M., & Swan, M. B. (2003). Predicting user satisfaction from subject satisfaction. In *Proceedings of the CHI 2003 Conference on Human Factors in Computing Systems (CHI'03)*. Fort Lauderdale, Florida. ACM Press.

Oliver, R. (1999). Value as Excellence in the Consumption Experience. In M. Holbrook (Ed.), Consumer Value: A Framework for Analysis and Research (pp. 43-62). New York: Routledge. doi:10.4324/9780203010679.ch2

Oliver, R. L. (1997). *Satisfaction: A Behavioral Perspective on the Consumer*. New York: Irwin/McGraw-Hill.

Pearce, P. L. (1982). *The Social Psychology of Tourist Behavior*. Oxford: Pergamon Press.

Pritzker, L., & Hanson, R. (1962). Measurement Errors in the 1960 Census of Population. *Proceedings of the Section on Survey Research Methods. American Statistical Association*.

Schober, M. F., & Conrad, F. G. (1997). Does Conversational Interviewing Reduce Survey Measurement Error? *Public Opinion Quarterly, 61*(4), 576–602. doi:10.1086/297818

Schober, M. F., & Conrad, F. G. (1998). Response Accuracy When Interviewers Stray from Standardization. *Proceedings of the American Statistical Association, Section on Survey Methods Research*. Alexandria, VA. American Statistical Association.

Schober, M. F., Conrad, F. G., & Fricker, S. S. (1999). Further explorations of conversational interviewing. How gradations of flexibility affect cost. *Paper presented at the 54th Annual Conference of the American Association for Public Opinion Research*. St. Petersburg, FL.

Schuman, H., & Presser, S. (1981). *Questions and Answers in Attitude Surveys: Experiments on Question Form, Wording, and Context.* San Diego, California: Academic Press.

Schwarz, N., Hippler, H., Deutsch, B., & Strack, F. (1985). Response Order Effects of Category Range on Reported Behavior and Comparative Judgments. *Public Opinion Quarterly, 49*(3), 388–395. doi:10.1086/268936

Siskos, Y., Grigoroudis, E., Zopounidis, C., & Saurais, O. (1998). Measuring Customer Satisfaction Using a Collective Preference Disaggregation Model. *Journal of Global Optimization, 12*(2), 175–195. doi:10.1023/A:1008262411587

Tourangeau, R., Rips, L., & Rasinski, K. (2000). *The Psychology of Survey Response.* Cambridge, UK: Cambridge University Press. doi:10.1017/CBO9780511819322

Tourangeau, R., & Smith, T. W. (1998). Collecting Sensitive Information with Different Modes of Data Collection. In M. P. Couper, R. P. Baker, J. Bethlehem, C. Z. F. Clark, J. Martin, W. L. Nicholls II, and J. M. O'Reilly (Eds.), Computer Assisted Survey Information Collection (pp. 431-453). New York: Wiley

Train, K. E. (2003). *Discrete Choice Methods with Simulation.* Cambridge, UK: Cambridge University Press. doi:10.1017/CBO9780511753930

VARIATIONS2. (2003). VARIATIONS2: the Indiana University Digital Music Library Project. Retrieved from http://variations2.indiana.edu/research/

Woodruff, R. B., & Gardial, S. F. (1996). *Know Your Customer: New Approaches to Understanding Customer Value and Satisfaction.* Cambridge, Massachusetts: Blackwell.

Chapter 9
From Illustration to Gamification of the Book:
Re-Developing Aesthetics in Publishing, Re-Inventing Taste in the Digital Era

Christina Banou
Ionian University, Greece

ABSTRACT

The chapter focuses on the aesthetic-artistic identity of the book nowadays with the aim to discuss patterns of publishing, and more specifically of the aesthetics in publishing. The chapter takes as key elements that A. the values and strategies of our age are in use for centuries, and B. the aesthetic identity of the book is still essential in its production, promotion and marketing. After a short overview of the publishing industry nowadays, the past of the publishing activity since Renaissance is studied so as to provide, through common features and values, a theoretical background and explanation of publishing strategies. Thereafter, patterns of illustration of the printed book and of gamification / use of multimedia in publishing are provided; the illustration chain is proposed as part of the publishing one. Conclusions regarding the proposed methodological framework and the opportunities of the publishing industry may enlighten issues and challenges of our era and offer to the publishing studies a specific point of view.

1. INTRODUCTION

In a changing world, innovation, globalization and convergence seem to be among the bedrocks of the publishing industry; even though, these have to be recognized as old values of publishing, going hand in hand with the publishers' aim to widen the reading audience and augment sales as well as to improve the book both as content and as physical object. In that context, the past of the publishing activity since Renaissance ought to be studied in order to provide, through common features and values, a theoretical background. The chapter focuses on the transformations (mainly due to information technologies) of the book in the digital, [even better hybrid era due to co-existence of printed with electronic/virtual material], with the aim to discuss and exhibit patterns of publishing, and more specifically issues re-

DOI: 10.4018/978-1-4666-8659-5.ch009

garding the aesthetic identity of the book in its evolution. The field of publishing studies is obviously interdisciplinary, a "marvelous blend of theories" according to Greco et al (2013), thus in the chapter publishing studies, history of the book, art history and media communication offer to the provision of the methodological framework and historic background so as to explain the current trends.

Initially a short overview of the publishing industry nowadays is provided. Thereafter, challenges and values are discussed and studied since the invention of printing in Renaissance; the chapter takes as key elements that A. values of our age -such as globalization, convergence, democratization, access to information, innovation, discoverability- are in use since the invention of printing, and B. the aesthetics of the book are essential in the development, promotion and marketing of the titles as well as in the cultivation of taste. It is obvious that we cannot always refer to the book as physical object, since its materiality is constantly changing and lost when reading on ebooks, tablets, iphones etc (Phillips, 2014). Thus, its aesthetic identity, being always of significance, is in turn re-created or re-invented by new means.

Thereafter, the chapter focuses on the role and function of book illustration and of the artistic identity of the book from Renaissance till nowadays investigating issues of gamification (the use of games in publishing for achieving the engagement of the reader) and of the use of new media technologies that alter the book as it was known redefining at the same time patterns of reading, writing, thinking, communicating. In that context the illustration chain of Renaissance and the Baroque as part of the publishing chain is re-developed for the publishing activity nowadays taking into consideration the new impact of new technologies. Gamification and the use of new media technologies, considered as successful ways to reach readers, are related with A. the use of pictures/images in the text having both aesthetic and utilitarian impact, B. promotion and marketing of the book, C. participation of the reader. In that framework, certain questions are raised regarding not only their impact on the aesthetic identity of the book but also on the tools for their description, explanation and discussion. The provision of a methodological framework for the aesthetics of the book can also be recognized among the aims of this chapter.

2. THE PUBLISHING INDUSTRY IN A CHANGING ERA

Mergers and acquisitions of publishing houses have definitely changed issues of the publishing activity during the last decades leading not only to the dominance of large publishing companies and conglomerations but also to the essential role of bestsellers' methods and innovative promotion strategies in a rather hard competitive framework. Even though, competition and innovation have always gone hand in hand in the publishing activity. At the same time, new information and communication technologies are constantly transforming the publishing activity and the book itself as it was known for centuries, altering thus the publishing value chain by re-defining the roles of the publisher, editor, agent, bookseller (Thompson, 2010; Clark & Phillips, 2014; Smith 2013; Greco et al, 2013; Miller, 2007; Kist, 2008). It seems that "new" aspects of value are added to the publishing chain (Tian and Martin, 2013; Breede, 2008). As self-publishing and the open access movement emerged, the role of the publisher was and is under question; even though, publishers are extremely adaptable exploiting in every era the opportunities provided by technology and often managing to turn problems into challenges – and this seems to be the case nowadays.

Additionally, electronic bookstores are developing new consuming and reading cultures exploiting at the same time strategies and tactics of the past, such as pre-orders (Miller, 2007). Online sales have introduced features such as "personalized" recommendations, customer reviews, ease of access to old titles, broader information, breath of range (Laing and Royle, 2013). In that context, Amazon and other major bookstores try to further establish their power not only as retailer but as tastemakers as well. Meanwhile, chain bookstores are facing problems (e.g. bankruptcy of Borders) that alter their catalytic role whereas other retail points, such as mass merchants, superstores, terminals etc., seem to take a leading role (Greco et al, 2013); in that framework the independent bookstores, the brick and mortar sales, after their decline, try to get a step forward while experts point out their influential role.

One of the recognized opportunities and challenges for the publishing industry nowadays is the direct communication with the reader-customer as well as direct sales. "Word of mouth" has been through the centuries the key element in promotion and marketing. Information and communication technologies provide new tools and opportunities for the promotion of titles and for building communities of readers (Clark & Phillips, 2014; Thompson, 2010): newsletters, emails, websites, electronic catalogues are some of the –already traditional- ways. Social media (e.g. bookblogs) build communities of readers taking reader participation a step forward. But in a world of abundance where "variety is not enough" (Anderson, 2006), according to the current trends, the reader-customer should be further encouraged to participate in such a way so as to go beyond information and communication – that next step is engagement of the reader obtained by multimedia or by gamification regarding certain kind of texts and age groups.

We must though bear in mind that publishing has always been a business and the book a product, although unique consisting of intangible (intellectual capital) and tangible assets. In a hybrid era of co-existence of the printed, digital and electronic material, when the tangible features of the book are gradually in some forms lost (when reading on computer, ebook, tablet, iphone etc.), the unique features of the book and the creative character of the publishing industry are still based not only on the content – intellectual capital, but also on its aesthetic-artistic identity.

3. THE GLOBALIZED WORLD OF RENAISSANCE: COMMON VALUES AND CHALLENGES

In an era when information is the main product, among the key values of the publishing activity, the following take the leading role: globalization, convergence, access, innovation. Phillips (2014) identifies also disintermediation and discoverability as two of the "big themes" of nowadays. The question raised is whether these are really "new" values and patterns or they just repeat and/or continue a tradition of common values and strategies since Renaissance.

The invention of printing has been called the "printing revolution" (Eisenstein, 1983; Johns, 2000) due to the changes brought about in cultural, social, political, religious, artistic and economic reality. The printed book since its appearance was a democratic information medium that gradually revolutionized all forms of learning and developed taste in augmented audiences. Access to information and knowledge changed rapidly and deeply since a new, more economic, friendly and accessible medium than the manuscript was produced. In an era of great changes, such as the Renaissance, the new medium satisfied the needs and the expectations of the readers re-developing them at the same time, while education, scholarly communication and research were altering leading gradually to the Scientific Revolution in the middle of 16th century. Scholars recognized a new medium for knowledge dissemination, dialogue, collaboration, educational progress (Richardson, 1999; Lowry, 1979); at the same time the religious and political power used the printed book as a symbol of fame, power, wealth, and as a medium for propaganda.

3.1 Defining and Widening the Reading Audience

The reading audience of the first printed books was naturally the same with that of the manuscript, thus reduced mainly to humanist scholars, students, noblemen (Richardson, 1999); printers-publishers of the era aimed to satisfy the needs and meet the expectations of an established reading audience by adopting used and thus successful methods. But, due to a number of reasons, typography included, new reading groups had raised for whom the printed book had different meaning, function, typology, value and aesthetics (Chartier, 1994). The publishers adopted the techniques and the technology provided for the production, promotion, advertising and sales of their titles, aiming at those "new" readers, who may read with difficulty (used to extensive and not intensive reading). This audience was not always homogenous though common features can be found. It is though noteworthy that the book both as content (in vernacular) and as object was developing for that audience: breviaries, religious texts, almanacs, chapbooks, romances, educational books, even courtesy books or manuals of polite behaviour were among these "new kinds of books", according to Richardson (1999, p. 139-145).

3.2 Globalization, Bestsellers, and Multicultural-Multilingual Book Markets

The first reading audience of scholars, students and noblemen expected the edition of classic texts, both in Latin and ancient Greek; at the same time the Latin was the lingua franca of scholarly communication. Thus, the first printers-publishers aspired to a rather globalized reading audience not easily defined in terms of place. Aldus Manutius, for example, intended to reach and satisfy a wide audience, not only in Venice but throughout Europe. His editions were of such success, that the printers in Lyon imitated, copied and reproduced them in pirate books (Lowry, 1979). Other publishers-printers, such as Christoph Plantin in Antwerp, systemized book production and distribution for a wide reading audience, spread across Europe. Furthermore, political, economic and cultural changes enforced a kind of globalization even through restrictions and of the attempt to prohibit and encourage common, authorized, often homogenous features [for example, the Index Librorum Prohibitorum tried to provide the framework of how and what to publish (Infelise, 2013)]. Actually, multicultural and multilingual - polyglot book markets could be found in Renaissance Venice, and afterwards in Amsterdam and Antwerp; London took the leading role during the Industrial Revolution due to a number of reasons, colonization included (Briggs and Burke, 2005, p. 47-50). From this point of view, the book production often intended to reach not only the local but the European market.

Moreover, bestsellers for a globalized market constituted a central feature of the publishing activity. Briggs and Burke talk about "global consciousness" (2005, p. 33) in which successful books, such as romances, created the bestselling phenomenon that explains and develops patterns of production and promotion. "Word of mouth" and fame of the author or of the plot seemed to be the most important factors for the success of a title and for augmented sales (and translations as well) even in forbidden works. Darnton (1996) identifies in the forbidden best-sellers of pre-revolutionaty France an agent of change not only in the production, distribution and promotion of books but also in reading, communicating and understanding the current political environment creating the conscious of class through novels in which sex and metaphysics went hand in hand.

3.3 Libri Portatiles

The portable, economic, friendly, easily accessible book is a goal tried to be achieved in every era according to the opportunities provided by technology (Howard, 2009) as well as by economic, artistic and social factors. Technology nowadays aspires to reduce cost, weight, time. MacWilliam (2013, p. 3) states that "A third generation of device saw ebook readers become *smaller in size, lighter in weight, [and] providing readability, navigation and features.* Perhaps most important of all, books became more portable. This generation also strengthened the book metaphor and offered the user a degree of familiarity." The same could also be said for the printed book during Renaissance and the Baroque era. It is interesting to study the words used and the values defined: A. Smaller in size, portable, lighter in weight are obviously "libri portatiles", easily to be carried, in small formats (octavo preferably), printed by Aldus Manutius (Lowry, 1979). Actually, the aim for easily readable books has also been common. In that framework, typographic characters, headings, subheadings, pagination, illustration, ornamentation were developed so as to improve reading by helping readers to navigate in the text.

3.4. Combination of Media-Convergence

Convergence between printed and manuscript book, between hand illumination and woodcut illustration at the first decades of printing, between oral and printed text (Rak, 2003) and between different types of reading can certainly be found since the beginning of the printing activity. Briggs and Burke talk about "interactions between media" regarding previous centuries (2005, p. 36-40), while Phillips (2014) writes that there is nowadays convergence of people's tastes around the latest cross-media franchise. This convergence of taste is very well pointed out at the first decades of printing concerning not only the illustration and ornamentation of printed books, but also the luxury unique copies with special binding and hand illumination from miniaturists, printed sometimes on parchment or on paper of better quality and/or of different colour. Printed dedications to these texts are studied as symbols of power, wealth and fame exhibiting issues of the book as object and as a work of art; meanwhile issues regarding –among others- patronage and propaganda are further examined (Richardson, 1999). Thus, the hybrid environment of cross-media and of co-existence of printed with digital/electronic material nowadays reproduces patterns of the continuity between old and new means. It is noteworthy that innovation has actually been a steady feature of the publishing activity. Howard states (2009), the opportunities provided by technology were always exploited by publishers and booksellers for the production, promotion and distribution of books.

3.5 Knowledge Dissemination and Access to Information

Access to knowledge has always been desirable and improved from Renaissance due to bibliographies, printed catalogues, dictionaries, maps, thesauri, atlases, mirrors, encyclopedias, theaters, digests, compendia (Rhodes and Sadway, 2000, p. 9; Briggs and Burke, 2005, p. 15). Bibliographies since Conrad Gesner, the first bibliographer, changed access to information and offered an effective tool for scholars, students and librarians. Successful ways to organize and have access to information are thus recognized even from the invention of printing. Even in the book itself, headings, subheadings, contents, indexes, footnotes, tables, illustration were developed so as to help the reader as to navigate in the text. The term "renaissance computer" is used by Sadway and Rhodes (2000) so as to give light to methods and practices for the organization and access to printed information.

The systematization in the dissemination of information and knowledge was a value obtained during Renaissance and further enforced during the Enlightenment and the Industrial Revolution when the reading audience was really widened with new dynamic reading groups: women, children, working class (Cavallo-Chartier, 1999). It was after the French Revolution and the movement to the industrial cities that women and workers gained and established their identity of sex, age and/or class. For them, the book was the powerful medium for education, improvement, success, struggle, as well as of self-development and entertainment.

3.6 Short Forms

Another crucial feature for the future of the publishing activity and of reading is that short forms thrive nowadays due not only to technological developments (Phillips, 2014) but rather to competition from other media and to the developed reading behaviour. Thus, the medium defines not only what we read but also how we read it providing the experience as well as the motivation that we can finish the text (for example on the tablet) shortly. As experiences of reading are constantly changing, we must bear in mind that short forms were popular in vernacular printed texts (tales, lives of saints, prays, almanacs etc.) for the wide reading audience sold often outside the main distribution channels, for example in fairs: apart from being cheap and familiar, the target group included readers who could barely read or could read with difficulty. Illustration played a central role by explaining the text, helping reading and offering an aesthetic experience through familiar iconographic types. In that context, we should interpret the impact of short forms in terms of continuity in a long tradition of reading experiences and produced publications in accordance with economic and social factors.

3.7 Discoverability

Discoverability has always been one of the peak-points served by promotion strategies and advertisement in publishing. "Marketing in the roots" express the methods used by printers-publishers in order to promote and advertise books, to inform readers and communicate with them in a truly competitive environment. Backlist, apart from forming the intellectual capital and creating the fame (symbolic capital) of the publishing company, provided the longsellers that reached certain audiences. In that context, publishing models and methods such as subscriptions - pre-orders have their precedents centuries ago developed by publishers so as to provide readers with tools that would help them to identity and consume titles.

3.8 Finally, Globalized Worlds of Publishing Business

The almost immediate access to information of our era influences the typology of the book according to the kind of text and to the readers. But we are not yet able to estimate and understand the dimensions and the extent of these opportunities and features. The speed is though impressive but we have to consider that people's behaviour and customs tend sometimes and for certain activities to change gradually and slowly. Reading may be obviously one of these activities due to its importance and complexity. That may explain the survival and the continuous use, even the flourishing in some cases and in certain markets, of the printed book. Meanwhile, part of the reading audience is adjusted to new methods and mediums. From this point of view, widening the reading audience is connected not only with technological but mainly with cultural changes and aesthetic patterns.

4. THE AESTHETIC IDENTITY OF THE BOOK

Publishers usually aspire to propose, develop and use innovative strategies in a publishing continuity. It must though be pointed out that innovation stands not only in the technique itself but also in its use and conception. "The tool in our hands demands to be used and to demonstrate to us its creative power – today no less than many centuries ago", wrote Gombrich (2006, p. 224). Regarding gamification and the use of new media technologies in publishing, as boundaries between reading, being informed and playing are constantly redefined, "different", even heterogeneous aspects take the leading role and redefine reading experience as well as the aesthetic identity of the book. Illustration continues (sometimes in experimental forms) at the printed book which in certain kinds of text still thrives; on the other hand, multimedia and games offer innovative, experimental opportunities and experiences. And as the book becomes digital and loses its physical entity, the aesthetic identity of the book has to be further discussed and explained in its historical context.

4.1. Illustrating Text in Renaissance and the Baroque

First printed books naturally resembled the manuscript which was the only known and used book. But as the printed book was a different product implying different organization and structure for its production, promotion and sales, it started to gain its specific physical identity from the beginning. For example, the title-page is one of the main features of the printed book having practical, aesthetic, advertising and information impact and value; its evolution from the blank page may serve to an extent for explaining patterns of the evolution of the printed book itself (Smith, 2001; Baldacchini, 2004).

Illustration and ornamentation of the printed books reveal issues of book production, consumption, promotion, publishing policy and taste. Woodcuts were initially used (Johns, 2000) so as to illustrate text bringing about a "revolution" in the development of taste; the democratization that typography brought about referred not only to the text but also to the aesthetic identity of the book. Typography provided a democratic -easy to use, economic to acquire, friendly – product for the information, education, entertainment as well as for the development of taste to large and non homogenous communities of readers, although it is often difficult for data to be found; that is connected with the opportunity that typography provided for acquiring and owning books (Richardson, 1999), thus of owning -apart from the content and the information medium- an object of aesthetic value. Popularization of book illustration was achieved through the use of pictures in popular even bestselling titles, in which familiar iconographic types and thematic objectives were reproduced.

Certainly, illustration and ornamentation always explored and exploited all the opportunities provided by technology and techniques of the era so as to develop the quality of the book, to augment sales and establish fame of the publisher. Parameters that strongly influenced and developed the physical appearance of the book include:

- The influence from the manuscript during the first decades of printing,
- The iconographic and typographic-publishing tradition of special texts (e.g. religious texts),
- The working methods of printers – publishers who often imitated successful illustrations and reproduced them using material from their stock,
- The art of the period,
- The available printing techniques (printing in red, for example),

- Illustration techniques,
- The publishing policy of the printing shop (goals, aims, values),
- The guidelines of the author,
- The needs and expectations of the reading audience (existed and to be),
- Competition,
- Market's orientation
- The artist
- Patronage

Obviously, the above, having either hedonic or utilitarian function, must be studied taking into consideration the social, economic, political, cultural and religious factors.

In that framework, illustration may A. be explanatory to the text (with straight or looser relationship with it), B. have artistic-aesthetic value, C. advertise and promote the title, D. protect the first pages of the book, especially when regarding the development of the title page (Smith, 2001; Baldacchini, 2004), E. remind the topics to the readers, F. divide the text into sections, G. offer information, I. offer enjoyment.

Illustration in popular texts and in bestsellers was used so as to explain the text taking into consideration that part of the readers could bear read. Some of them were semi-illiterate who tried to learn reading and to understand the text; for them pictures narrated the story, explained the plot and helped not only to understand but also to read or to learn others to read. Richardson wrote regarding Renaissance Italy that "[these editions] were typically of quarto or smaller formats; they were no longer than about two hundred pages; they had many small illustrations (these would have had the functions of dividing up the text into sections and of providing landmarks, thus helping readers to find their way around and to remember the topic)" (1999, p. 142). While Rak (2003) identifies the interrelation between image and text, and the impact of printed illustration in Baroque Naples on the creation of oral tradition, exhibiting as well issues of reading, communication, understanding and taste. In that framework, it is also noteworthy that extensive reading was the rule for the wide reading audience; they were reading the same, few texts, owned by them or by a wider community again and again (Ginzburg, 2009); although the printing technology provided economic and friendly copies, really intensive reading became the rule truly during the industrial revolution (Cavallo & Chartier, 1999). Popular reading audience during Renaissance and the Baroque needed and expected from illustration to help them understand, read, navigate in the text.

Thus, the relation between text and picture had been flexible and usually under question; in most printed books, illustrations often did not match the text as they were repeated from previous publications. Publishers tended to use their stock so as to save time and reduce the cost for new illustrations and ornaments. We must bear in mind that publishing has always been a market oriented business, and publishers tried to improve their product, to reduce the time and expense for its production. Thus, the artistic-aesthetic value of their books must be studied in that framework as a tool and vehicle not only for illustrating and ornamenting but also for promoting, advertising, competing, selling, reaching audiences. Undoubtedly, "marketing" of the era used the book to a great extent as object (title page, illustration, ornamentation, quality of paper, size, pagination). As Bornstein (2006, p. 6) writes: "…the literary texts consist not only of words (its linguistic code) but also of the semantic features of its material instantiations (its bibliographic code)" relating these material features to Walter Benjamin's concept of the "aura".

Apart from publishers-printers who (occasionally or not) innovated or ordered new pictures, the majority of them reproduced the already known, successful iconographic and decorative types and used certain illustrations and ornaments, sometimes till they were completely destroyed or wore out.

Most publishers followed and imitated the already successful typology of decoration and illustration or acquired the stock of other printers/publishers continuing their tradition or even better their habits in other ways, certainly not always innovative but indicative of the working and publishing conditions of the era. These illustrations did not match the text but the extent to which they were used may lead to conclusions for the publishing policies and the development of taste to the wide audience. It seems that apart from the protagonists "leaders" who innovated, the majority of printers-publishers tended to work rather modestly adopting the publishing and iconographic tradition of the kind of text conservatively. On the other hand, the protagonists developed a specific policy for the book as physical object implementing illustration, ornamentation, typographic characters, title-page, cover (later on) that influenced the other printers. Illustration thus added value to the text and to the publishing chain making the content more desirable and accessible.

It must though be recognized that illustration and ornamentation has a straight relationship with the art of the era. Furthermore, well known editions not for the wide audience are famous for their illustration creating often a tradition. The illustration and the publication of the still enigmatic *Hypnerotomachia Poliphili* by Francesco Colonna? (Aldus Manutius, Venice 1499) is an illustrious example that has offered a privileged dialogue between art historians and historians of the book (Szepe, 1997).

4.2 Gamifying Text

"Gamification is the use of game-play mechanics for non game applications. Any application, task, process or context can theoretically be gamified. Gamification's main goal is to rise the engagement of users by using game-like techniques…", according to Muntean (2011, p. 323). In other words, "gamification is the integration of game mechanics into non-game material to increase user engagement" (Johnson, 2011). The term "gamification" was coined in 2002 by Nick Pelling, but it was not widely used until 2010 (Hagglund, 2012); nowadays it is used extensively by management and marketing as a strategy for companies so as to be more competitive and promote successfully their products (Zickermann & Linder, 2013). It must be noted that in a number of books published during the last couple of years the words "revolution" or "revolutionize" are used so as to describe and express the aims and the opportunities of gamification. Certainly, one could wonder if these words exaggerate.

For explaining the impact of games on publishing we may bear in mind what Marshall McLuhan wrote: "Games are dramatic models of our psychological lives providing release of particular tensions. They are collective and popular art forms with strict conventions… Art, like games, became a mimetic echo of, and relief from, the old magic of total involvement…Like our vernacular tongues, all games are media of interpersonal communication, and they could have neither existence nor meaning except as extensions of our immediate inner lives" (1997, p. 237-238). In that explanatory context, the attempt to integrate reading and playing through participating is among the "new" methods used by the publishers so as to meet the expectations of specific reading audience widening at the same time the boundaries of the book itself and reading experience. Questions raised inevitably include the relationship and the boundaries between playing and reading, the future and the quality of reading and communicating, the disadvantages of gamification such as pointification, and naturally the influence on consumer behaviour, marketing strategies, book policy and reading habits. As nowadays the spread of games to a wider population due to mobiles, computers and tablets is a feature of our era, issues of limitations and opportunities provided are under discussion.

Engagement of the reader seems to be one of the key elements in the publishing industry, bringing about communication with sales. Zichermann and Linder (2014, p. xi-xii) write for gamification concerning companies, non profits and governments in general: "They are engaging customers as never before, aligning employees, and driving information that seemed virtually impossible only a decade ago. They've realized that their strength is in marshaling the intelligence, motivation, and –most critically- engagement of their communities to drive their business objectives". According to them, gamification implements "design concepts from games, loyalty programs, and behavioral economics to drive used engagement". Emphasis is given on psychological rewards such as self-efficacy or social approval (Muntean, 2011); recognized as a motivation strategy, gamification is used so as to reach target reading groups influencing their consumer and reading behavior. Aiming at the reader's engagement transforms at the same time the book and the publishing chain. Through gamification, the reader participates, even better takes an active role in the publishing chain, not only by becoming a member of a reading community (e.g. like book clubs, bookblogs) but also by interfering in the creation of the book.

It would though be rather better to use the term "gamification in publishing" and not "of publishing" since gamification is a method used for certain kind of books (in their typology and content) and for certain audiences; it is not the publishing process that is gamified but specific titles. We have also to recognize the three steps of gamification extending from the publishers' promotion strategy till sales and social media identifying thus the value chain of gamification from information to sales and success of the books through engagement of the reader and direct communication with the publisher.

The roots, remote or not, of gamification can be identified in the printed book, and more specifically in children's books and manuals. The former do not have always the typology of the book as largely known; size and cover may differ; puzzles, quizzes, toys, pop ups are used which are considered to further encourage reading and learning. Apart from paper, other material was and is often proposed for games and other activities; whereas concerning the context, questions, exercises and activities lead often to the reward of the child who has managed to complete the tasks.

Furthermore, in manuals and practical books (e.g. cookbooks) new media offer a much more explanatory impact obtaining the desirable scope. As the picture has an explanatory and crucial function in these kinds of text, gamification and multimedia may expand the traditional limits and opportunities of illustration through the use of pictures, videos, music, photographs. Gombrich in "Pictorial Instructions" wrote that "the image had been used for instruction even before the development of sequential narrative" (2006: 231), recognizing Leonardo as the pioneer "here too" who "in his scientific drawings usually inserted a letter key to which he referred in his explanatory texts" (2006: 232).

In a world where "variety is not enough", gamified content tries to enrich the aesthetic identity of the new forms of the book going beyond illustration and decoration as known for centuries. Creativity, empathy, individuality, emotional satisfaction, communication and certainly engagement can be counted among the features and the aims of gamified texts, although experiences of participation are not as new as believed. The digital revolution brings about the transformation of the book. For example, augmented reality tries to widen the boundaries of the book furthermore. "In Augmented Reality, a digital overlay allows content creators to add extra multi-media content to the printed page. Readers download an app and scan the pages with a smart phone or tablet, and extra content pops up, including video, audio, online and social media links, and more" (Rosen, 2014). Links to social media and webpages as well as comments on the text may lead to "atomized" copies for specific readers or groups of readers.

Changes in the materiality of the book thus mean new ways of reading, writing, thinking and publishing. Even though we should bear in mind that "are these technologies for reading and publishing experiences are progressing faster than market demands" (Danet, 2014, p. 276). Barron (2009) in his work has pointed out that readers and writers are seeking for a "better pencil" outlining the co-existence co-existence of the new tools with the traditional ones discussing at the same time the impact of the digital revolution on writing and communication technologies. Bolter (2001) had exhibited changes brought about in the printed text that changed the traditional patterns of publishing, reading and writing as well as the relationship between stakeholders; the dynamic role of the reader is also pointed out. Gamification and the use of new media technologies (multimedia, augmented multimedia) seem to be at a rather experimental phase, but they endorse new ways, methods and attitudes that go hand in hand with the demand for innovation and with long tail theories (Anderson, 2006) as well as with new business models in publishing changing gradually the value chain.

4.3 The Illustration Chain as Part of the Publishing Chain: Changes and Trends

A publication is a work of many. Nowadays, old roles (such as the agent's) are becoming more significant and emerging in the publishing chain called also value chain (Thompson, 2012:). But even from Renaissance, we could recognize a "smaller" chain, part of the publishing one, for the illustration and decoration of the book (not for the art of the book which is more general and includes typographic characters, the title-page, binding etc) in which collaborations were developed at a rather experimental stage of the publishing activity defining rules and roles.

The author, through the press copy decided to a certain extent the type of illustration; the point is that press copies are rarely found, been considered thus the holy grail of book history. The editor and the publisher-printer decided or co-decided on illustration and decoration in patterns not only aesthetic but -often and mostly- of promotion taking into consideration the parameters referred above. Questions and research topics that depend on the case, time and place include the role of the artist / designer, the extension of his innovation, the instructions/guidelines that probably were provided, the role of the patrons, as well as the artist's collaboration with the publisher / author / editor.

During the first decades of printing, the work of miniaturists is exhibited. As recognized, the artist-designer was usually a different person from the woodcutter. Szepe (1997, p. 43) writes: "although sometimes the professions of miniaturist and painter overlapped, there are no documents indicating a painter drew woodblock designs for books until the sixteenth century. Only later in the book production from the 1530s to the late 1550s ... do we find painters designated as figureri documented as working on woodcuts for books". It is indicative what Francesco Gonzaga wrote to the Duke of Milan in 1480: "I received the design you sent and urged Andrea Mantegna to turn it into a finished form. He says it is more a book illuminator's job than his, because he is not used to painting little figures" (Baxandall, 1972: 12). The editor had obviously the eye on the edition and on the preparation of the publication together with the author, if alive. The publisher/printer, not only by his publishing policy but by the economics of his company, was the other protagonist.

Thus, the publishing chain for the illustration of the book during Renaissance and the Baroque era could be as in figure 1:

This "illustration chain" has to be examined from the publisher's – printer's (and patron's) point of view (policy, collaborations, list building, market expand, aspects, tradition, background, catalogue-backlist etc.) into a larger, more expanded framework (consisting of the economic, political, social, reli-

Figure 1. The publishing chain for the illustration of the book during Renaissance and the Baroque era

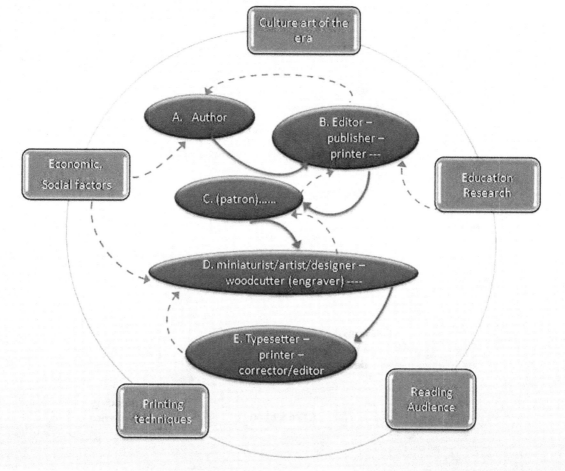

gious, educational, cultural factors; competition; reading audience etc). For example, the patron, when existed, could set the rules usually not directly to the printer or editor but through his power. Patronage and issues of authority in book production (Bromilow, 2013) may enlighten patterns of book production and consumption, including the book as object and the influence on taste of the period. Even though, patronage and authority in the book should be investigated in accordance with the issues in the art and culture of the period (Haskell, 1980).

Certain aspects of the book have today to be reconsidered into a methodological framework that cannot ignore the past of the publishing activity, and more specifically of the used strategies, as well as diachronic values, aims and roles; history of the book and art history meet in the illustration and decoration of the book providing a rather privileged dialogue and keys for describing, interpreting, explaining, analyzing the book as object.

Figure 2. The publishing chain for the artistic identity of the book nowadays

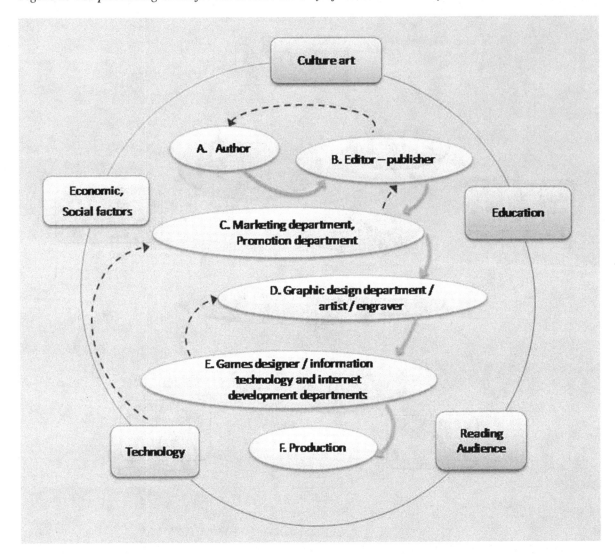

Technology and art of the era certainly influence the book in its artistic identity. Regarding multimedia and gamification, questions that are raised and issues that must be taken under consideration, as mentioned thereafter, include the extent and the rules of the collaboration between game designers and publishers and more specifically the role of promotion and marketing departments of the publishing company, the interrelation between text and image, the professional development of those involved in the publishing chain. For example, iphoneography, a new term used for describing and interpreting iphone photography in which "apps" have been introduced, has been characterized as "an emergent art world" (Halpern & Humphreys, 2014) since aesthetic capabilities have attracted artists in using these opportunities. Halpern & Humphreys (2014) have distinguished the aesthetics of iphoneography into three categories. Thus, technologies change the traditional book illustration chain that includes marketing and promotion as well.

5. DISCUSSION - CONCLUSION

It is noteworthy that the words "revolution" and "new" are used widely regarding the publishing activity both of Renaissance and of the digital age. Meanwhile, as the paces of technology are accelerating, the need for new publishing models and for the exploitation of challenges is stronger than ever. In that framework, the most successful ebook is the "vanilla ebook" (Phillips, 2014) that imitates the printed one since now it is taken for granted that "ebooks should be of the same aesthetic and ergonomic quality as traditional printed books" (Danet, 2014: 279). Undeniably, emotional attachment and familiarity to the printed book, as well as aesthetic, psychological and consumer patterns may be recognized among the factors of its influence and use. "Familiarity with contents is also important. This is the reason why, despite the technological progressions, there is a continued emphasis on re-creating the book metaphor on an electronic platform. An emphatic 83% strongly agreed or agreed that the physical properties of the book were important to them" (MacWilliam, 2013, p. 9). According to the same author, "Only 11% of respondents were positive when asked whether fiction books are improved on an electronic platform, although the majority (44%) were neutral in their opinion" (8). Danet writes that (2014, p. 276), "the proportion of the US population who has read an ebook in 2013 increased from 17% to 28& just three years later. In the UK…one out of four consumer titles bought in 2013 was an ebook, up from one out of five a year earlier". The above should though be taken into consideration according to the kind of text. For instance, "art ebooks, when one stops to think about it, aren't *meant* to be read on a smartphone, or really even on a tablet" (Wilkolaski & DiCamillo, 2014).

The extent of the use of new media technologies in the book is still rather limited, although percentages are getting higher. The kindle makes its way around and "battles" or even wars of power and market control are taking place (for example between Google and libraries, between Amazon and publishers such as Hachette etc.). As the influence of the printed book has been inevitable and as factors such as the cover are still included among the important parameters that define consumer behaviour and selection of titles, the "new" aesthetic identity of the texts/books without materiality takes a significant role regarding not only the book per se but also and mainly (from the publishers' view point) the promotion and marketing of the title. Generally, the adding value that multimedia and gamification have on the aesthetics of the book should be further studied, not only theoretically, but through empirical surveys and data collected.

Undeniably, the development and re-invention of old strategies concerning the aesthetic value of the book in new forms (such as tablets, mobiles, etc.) marks initially for questions but for answers. Questions and research issues include: extent of the use of gamification; boundaries between reading and playing; collaboration between game designers and editors – specific publishing departments, such as marketing, promotion, etc; professional development of game designers; role of augmented reality; role of the front matter of the book; aesthetic value; informational value; the influence form the printed book; the influence from video art; disadvantages of gamification (pointification, for example); kind of rewards and their relationship with promotion of other titles of the author/ publishing house (discounts, offers); relationship and interaction with social media; relationship with educational platforms; the kind of text; interaction and relationship with the author; publishing policy; book policy; reader development; cultivation of taste; innovation; user interaction with the image and text. Another question regards the tools of describing, explaining and interpreting these new media on the book.

In a world of multiplication and metamorphosis of the publishing activity, it is though more than obvious that the aesthetics of the book still count. No matter that the materiality of the book changes, the goal of the artistic identity remains the same with centuries ago. The value of the aesthetic identity of the book as adding value to the product should be studied as part of the publishing activity and chain. Meanwhile, this identity per se ought to be described, identified, analyzed and studied in terms defined from the printed book taking into consideration the features of the new technologies. Meanwhile, participation and engagement of the reader become more active; the role of the reader will certainly be more significant in deciding on the aesthetic matters and one of the challenges will probably be to insert in the book personalized material, whether image (such as doodles) or text (annotations, for example). In that context, common values and goals as described above create the background, define the rules and lead to decisions, categorizations and strategic planning. As taste is the mirror of the society and the book a constant agent of change, new forms of the transmission of knowledge and new kinds of books are competing by re-using old strategies in a technological and economic framework.

Meanwhile, as the book is transformed, cultural and literary life changes together with reading behavior and the understanding of text; "the electronic representations of printed texts have as much capacity to change the users as they have of changing the text... We are in the infancy of a textual revolution comparable with the one initiated by the invention of printing..." (Schillinburg, 2006, p. 4). These textual changes are interrelated with the visual, artistic ones. It is though noteworthy that in a world of deep changes, innovation and experiment, the printed book is still a privileged medium related to the taste of readers connected not only with aesthetic value but with the impact of personal memory. It is characteristic that "even those publishers that have started with e-book only strategies are adopting Printing On Demand to meet the continuous demand for print copies of titles from consumers" (Gallagher, 2014, p. 246).

In a changing era, publishers re-develop their role, by reconstructing policies and exploring challenges. In a world of open access, self-publishing and new publishing models, the question set is if publishers are still gatekeepers of knowledge; obviously, their power consists in their decisions, innovations and the risk they are taking by proposing, re-developing strategies and re-inventing taste. Publishers as tastemakers, according to their aims and values, express on the one hand the market orientation and the needs of the reading audience and on the other propose and innovate in a specific economic, political and cultural background. Their protagonist role has been though redefined as social media provide the opportunity of building communities of readers who discuss, propose and judge. Although publishers have taken advantage of social media (by blogs of their authors, for example), they cannot predict their influence on readers. Furthermore, their role in the development of the book as object is more than crucial.

The word "tastemaker" has also to be redefined. It is interesting to note that when marketing experts refer to taste, we usually read of tastemakers, (Amazon, Google, social media etc.) under the consideration that readers are deeply and mass influenced by them (Anderson, 2006, p. 98-124); the word focuses more on sales and consumption but to taste and certainly, as used, it does not derive from art history but from marketing methods. But as taste is more complex than this, its development has to be studied and defined in accordance with the cultural, economic, educational, social conditions in which the precise and often flexible role of stakeholders (publishers, editors, authors, scholars, critics, special departments of publishing companies, etc.) is determined.

In that framework, interdisciplinary methodology has to be used so as to describe and study the aesthetic value and transformations of the book. What Baxandall (1985, p.1) stated, for works of art, that "we do not describe pictures but remarks about pictures", seems to be crucial too on the description of books of our era. Bibliography's aim is mainly to describe the books in a rather objective, according to the rules, way providing thus to researchers and readers a tool, a precise description that will guide them to the identity of the book both as content and object; rather rarely we do find in bibliographies an evaluation for the illustration and ornamentation [but, for example, when we read that the ornaments or the title page are repeated or are imitations, this is a feature leading to the evaluation of the book as object; the same happens for illustrated books by well known artists]. We must also bear in mind that familiarity with specific iconographic or decorative types create the framework or the convention for understanding and for interrelating text and picture, word and image. Readers tend to evaluate pictures according to the type of the text, the guidelines created by the tradition, their educational background, sex and age. In the digital era, the familiarity of specific reading groups (confined by age, education, access to information) with particular, multiple iconographic types of diverse origins create and different cultures create often a poly-prismatic framework or even better mirror of our time. In that context, the past provides tools and the experts propose. "Reflections on changing, *postmodern* conceptions of space, real and virtual, commonly refer to baroque aesthetics", identify Ciavolella and Coleman (2005, p. 3).

But when coming to describing, explaining, studying the aesthetic identity of the ebook developed by multimedia and gamification, the methodological interdisciplinary framework with specific methods (qualitative and quantitative) and theories may be set based on history of the book, publishing studies, art history as well as on the nature of technological impact. In that context, regarding description, "remarks about pictures" seems to take the leading role depending on the specific point of view varying accordingly. Describing pictures, photographs, videos, music, reproductions and their interrelation with the text may lead to interesting and challenging conclusions but simultaneously and certainly to debates and dilemmas according to the tools and the theories used.

Halsall (2008, p. 8) writes: "the notion of aesthetic judgment helps to understand how standards of truth and value, now understood in terms of validity, can be maintained despite their contextual nature… Validity claims, in general, must be recognized as phenomena that, like artworks, evoke multiple interpretations, not universal, once-and-for all explanations. They are not based on abstract, extra worldly principles, but are features of the complex, everyday disciplines and practices we use to understand and explain them. Thus, aesthetic judgments show how we expect discourse to function in general – not in a neutral and absolute way but as interlocutory, argumentative and open to debate". Thus, integrated research methods would describe, identify the origins and the influences, categorize and discuss the aesthetic identity of the book nowadays certainly from specific point of view each time.

The publishing industry nowadays, apart from the problems, being certainly at crossroads, has though these key words: challenges, great opportunities, innovation, vitality, ability to explore and develop new forms - new strategies - new talents. In a world of constant change but also of great gaps technological (info-rich and info-poor), economic (rich and poor) and certainly gaps of taste, reading and writing have to compete with their present and explore their past. Ebooks try to look like the printed books. Readers still ask for the aesthetic identity as developed and established through the centuries; at the same time, although the "revolutionary" methods seem experimental to certain audiences, they have started to thrive to specific groups. While kindle offers the opportunity of obtaining, reading and carrying thousands of titles with ease at a low cost, as Amazon sells and promotes books through new tactics, the printed book is still a privileged medium for certain audiences.

Aesthetic identity of the books and publications define the way we read, write, communicate, understand and act; every change in the material forms of information and knowledge transmission has brought about certain changes. Nowadays, the book through its continuity is a mirror of our era expressing the values, redefining the strategies and reinventing taste in complex environments where the competition with other media is hard and technologies are faster than needs and desires of people. Questions that call for answers set the scene while interactivity and engagement of the reader may lead the book beyond the used, familiar concepts of interrelation between text and picture. But as in the past, the book, being a powerful and adaptable medium, explores and exhibits the boundaries of time, especially the personal time of memories and re-discoveries.

REFERENCES

Anderson, C. (2006). *The Long Tail. Why the Future of Business is Selling Less of More*. New York: Hyperion.

Baldacchini, L. (2004). *Aspettando il frontespizio. Pagine bianche, occhietti a colophon nel libro antico*. Milano: Edizioni Sylvestre Bonnard.

Barron, D. (2009). *A Better Pencil. Readers, Writers and the Digital Revolution*. Oxford: Oxford University Press.

Baxandall, M. (1985). *Patterns of Intention. On the Historic Explanation of Pictures*. New Haven, London: Yale University Press.

Baxandall, M. (1988). *Painting and Experience in 15th Century Italy. A Primer in the Social History of the Pictorial Style* (Original edition 1972). Oxford: Oxford University Press.

Bolter, J.-D. (2001). *Writing Space. Computers, Hypertext, and the Remediation of Print*. New Jersey: Lawrence Erlbaum Associates.

Bornstein, G. (2006). *Material Modernism. The Politics of the Page*. Cambridge: Cambridge University Press.

Breede, M. (2008). *The Brave New World of Publishing: the Symbiotic Relationship between Printing and Book Publishing*. Oxford: Chandos Publishing. doi:10.1533/9781780632186

Bromilow, P. (Ed.). (2013). *Authority in European Book Culture 1400-1600*. Surrey: Ashgate.

Cavallo, G., & Chartier, R. (Eds.). (1999). *Storia della lettura nel mondo occidentale*. Roma, Bari: Edizioni Laterza.

Chartier, R. (1994). *The Order of Books. Readers, Authors and Libraries in Europe between the Fourteenth and Eighteenth Centuries* (L. Cochrane, Trans.). Cambridge: Polity Press.

Ciavolella, M. & Coleman, P ed. (2005). *Culture and Authority in the Baroque*. Toronto: Toronto University Press.

Clark, G., & Phillips, A. (2014). *Inside Book Publishing* (5th ed.). London, New York: Routledge.

Danet, P. (2014). The Future of Book Publishing: Seven Technology Trends and Three Industry Goals, *Publishing. Research Quarterly, 30*(3), 275–281.

Eisenstein, E. (1983). *The Printing Revolution in Early modern Europe*. Cambridge: Cambridge University Press.

Gallagher, K. (2014). Print-On Demand: New Models and Value Creation, *Publishing. Research Quarterly, 30*, 244–248.

Ginzburg, C. (2009). Il formaggio e i vermi. Il cosmo di un mugnaio del '500 (Original Edition 1976). Torino: Einaudi.

Gombrich E. (2006). *The Uses of Images. Studies in the Social Function of Art and Visual Communication.* (Original edition 1999). Phaidon.

Greco, A. – Milliot, J. – Wharton, R. (2013) The Book Publishing Industry, third edition New York & London: Routledge.

Hagglund, P. (2012), *Taking gamification to the Next Level. A detailed overview of the past, the present and a possible future of gamification* [thesis]. Umea Universitet.

Halpern, M., & Humphreys, L. (2014). Iphoneography as an Emergent Art World. *New Media and Society.* Retrieved from http://nms.sagepub.com/content/early/2014/06/05/1461444814538632, doi:10.1177/1461444814538632

Halsall, F., Jansen, J., & O'Connor, T. (Eds.) (2008). Rediscovering Aesthetics: Transdisciplinary Voices from Art History, Philosophy, and Art Practices. Stanford University Press.

Haskell, F. (1980). *Patrons and Painters: A Study in the Relations between Italian Art and the Society in the Age of the Baroque* (2nd ed.). New Haven, London: Yale University Press.

Howard, N. (2009). *The Book. The Life Story of a Technology.* Baltimore: The Hopkins University Press.

Infelise, M. (2013). *I libri proibiti da Gutenberg all' Encyclopedie* (Original Edition 1999). Roma-Bari: Laterza.

Johns, A. (2000). *The Nature of the Book. Print and Knowledge in the Making.* Chicago: University of Chicago Press.

Kist, J. (2008). *New Thinking for 21st Century Publishers. Emerging Patterns and Evolving Stratagems.* Oxford: Chandos Publishing. doi:10.1533/9781780632179

Laing, A., Royle, J. (2013). Bookselling Online: An Examination of Consume Behavioural Patterns, *Publishing. Research Quarterly, 29*(2), 110–129.

Lowry, M. (1979). *The world of Aldus Manutius. Business and Scholarship in Renaissance Venice.* Cornell University Press.

MacLuhan, M. (1997). *Understanding Media. The Extensions of Man, fifth printing.* Cambridge Massachusetts – London: MIT Press.

MacWilliam, A. (2013). The engaged reader. A human centred evaluation of ebook user experience. *Publishing Research Quarterly, 29*(1), 1–11. doi:10.1007/s12109-013-9305-8

Miller, L. J. (2007). *Reluctant Capitalists. Bookselling and the Culture of Consumption.* Chicago, London: The University of Chicago Press.

Muntean, C. I. (2011). Raising engagement in e-learning through gamification, *Proceedings of the 6th International Conference on Virtual Learning* (pp. 323-329). Bucharest.

Rak, M. (2003). *Immagine e scrittura. Sei studi sulla teoria e la storia dell' imagine nella cultura del barocco a Napoli.* Napoli: Liguori.

Rhodes, N., & Sadway, J. (Eds.). (2000). *The Renaissance Computer. Knowledge Technology in the First Age of Print*. London, New York: Routledge.

Richardson, B. (1999). *Typography, Writers and Readers in Renaissance Italy*. Cambridge: Cambridge University Press.

Rosen, L. (2014). Augmented Reality and the Future of Publishing, *Publishing Perspectives*. Retrieved from http://publishingperspectives.com/2014/08/augmented-reality-and-the-future-of-publishing/

Shillingsburg, P. (2006). *From Gutenberg to Google: Electronic Representations of Literary Texts*. Cambridge: Cambridge University Press. doi:10.1017/CBO9780511617942

Smith, K. (2012). *The Publishing Business. From pbooks to ebooks*. Lausanne: Ava Publishing.

Smith, M. (2000). *The Title-Page. Its Early Development. 1460-1510*. London – Newcastle Delaware: Oak Knoll Press.

Szepe, H. (1997). Artistic Identity in the Poliphilo. *Papers of the Bibliographical Society of Canada.*, *35*(1), 39–73.

Thompson, J. B. (2010). *Merchants of Culture. The Publishing Business in the Twenty-First Century*. Cambridge: Polity Press.

Tian, X., & Martin, B. (2013). Value Chain Adjustments in Educational Publishing, *Publishing. Research Quarterly*, *29*(1), 12–25.

Wilkolaski, S., & DiCamillo, K. (2014). Publishing Picasso in the Infinite Real Estate of Digital. *Publishing Perspectives*. Retrieved from http://publishingperspectives.com/2014/07/publishing-picasso-in-the-infinite-real-estate-of-digital/

Zichermann, G., & Linder, J. (2013). The Gamification Revolution: How Leaders Leverage Game Mechanics to Crush the Competition. McGraw Hill.

Chapter 10
What Is A Book By Any Other Name?

Roxana Theodorou
Hellenic American University, Greece

ABSTRACT

For quite a while now there is an ongoing and fueled debate about the future of the book, the implications of the eBook, the act of reading and reading habits and so on and so forth. An eBook is primarily a piece of software, an application. And with that said, a huge world of possibilities opens up. The question that we should try to answer then, is, what exactly is the purpose of an eBook, what should it do, how should it be designed, used or consumed. Integration of multimedia, in a meaningful and practical way, gamefication, non-linearity, design and usability are a few of the concepts that are explored in relation to the eBook and how they can add value to a medium that has been significantly underexploited.

INTRODUCTION

There was a time when things were pretty simple. There were books. Books contained written or printed words that one could read, and sometimes, there could also be pictures and illustrations. In order to use a book, you only needed to know how to turn pages, to know how to trace the text with your finger and follow the lines and thus read. If you read one book, you knew how to read them all, essentially. But that was a long time ago.

The future of the Book is one of the favorite discussions or our time – and our profession. Everyone, from publishers, to printers, to authors, to booksellers, to readers seem really upset about what future lies ahead. Because the book is no longer one thing. It evolves, it changes shapes and flavors, it shifts and transforms. Although publishing is a huge industry that remained essentially unchanged through centuries, now, for the first time since the invention of the moving type, everything seems to be uncertain.

When the Internet conquered communications, everything changed. All disruptive technologies do that, one way or another. But, Internet is not just another invention, which brought up some changes in our lives. Internet changed the way people work, do business, communicate, think, act, react, teach and learn, spend their free time, their perception of property, personal space, the definition of friendship etc. Reading couldn't be left unaffected, after all.

DOI: 10.4018/978-1-4666-8659-5.ch010

And, it should come as a surprise that books remained virtually unaffected for as long as they did. On a large part this was due to the fact that publishers refused to release electronic versions of their books online. On the other hand eBook readers were, until recently, hard to use, bulky and unattractive. And reading a pdf file on a desktop computer can hardly be considered comfortable and relaxing.

But things has progressed a lot and eBooks have changed, evolved and now eBooks account for 30% of all book sales in the US (Bercovici, 2014). Of course, the vast majority of these sales belong to Amazon and go through the Kindle store, which actually means that their readers use the Kindle app, if not a Kindle device as well.

The domination of one seller in a debatable point, and it is very easy to point out all the disadvantages that this may bring upon the publishing industry, the readers and the authors alike, but for the time being, the dispersion of the eBook is in by large the result of the pricing policies of Amazon, that made the eBook much cheaper that it print equivalent, and thus much more attainable by readers.

Subsequently, a very heated discussion has arisen, although this discussion is not in fact new, or unexpected, that debates the value of the eBooks, its pros and its cons, and how it can (from one perspective) reinvent the books and (form another perspective) destroy it all together.

The eBook adversaries have a multitude of arguments against it. Print books do not need a power source; they can function anywhere and anytime. That makes them extremely portable and safe to use by anyone. They have increased readability; the majority of eReaders cannot be used in direct sunlight. Also, the print book's contrast level is the best for easy, restful reading. This is especially important for the readers that enjoy reading for a long time.

Print books are tangible; you can smell, touch and feel a book, and thus have a more enriched and bonding experience. They can also be stored in a (physical) library and are more easily browsed and admired. Also, more than one can be used at the same time, by the same person. Finally, the tangible object brings a more intense sense of accomplishment when read, because of it visible length.

Print books can be used by anyone even if s/he is not computer literate. Although computers are a common good nowadays, this is only true for the western society and still 5 out of the 7 billion people on earth have never used the Internet, at least according to the CIA Factbook (2014). On the other hand the literacy rate is 85% worldwide. This means that books are still much more useful than eBooks.

Ownership of eBooks is permanent, under normal conditions. When someone buys the book, s/he owns it for good and the seller or the publisher have no power over the right of ownership. Whereas, with eBooks, the seller, at least in theory, has the ability to delete the eBook from the buyers Library and make it impossible to use. Another aspect of complete ownership is the ability to give away, share or resell the book to other people. On the other hand eBooks cannot be shared, unless the owner is willing to share the device upon which the eBook runs, as well.

Finally, print book trade supports the local markets and the small bookstores, while eBook trade can help eliminate the competition and gather the majority of the market share in the hands of huge multinational corporations.

On the other hand, the defenders of eBooks have a lot counterarguments to offer: eBooks take up a very small storage space and allow for bigger collections. It is true that and eBooks demands no physical space at all, and even the digital equivalent is not of great significance, most of the time, as eBook files are relatively small. As a result eBooks have high portability and the reader can carry with him/her a large collection of books any time, any place. This can be extremely useful to students and researchers, which usually need access to several resources simultaneously, but is also very comfortable for vacationers and travelers.

eBooks readers have evolved a lot, and maybe they cannot be used in direct sunlight, (although there are some that can cope with that as well) but they can be used in the dark, without the need of any other lighting source. That makes them easier and more comfortable to use. eBooks can be a lot more environmentally friendly, as no trees need to be cut down in order to make the paper needed for millions of perfect copies.

On the other hand, the time between buying an eBook and starting reading is usually mere seconds, eliminating any delivery times that the tangible book would require in order to reach the buyer. This of course makes sense when we are talking about online or telephone purchases but given that Amazon is the largest book retail store worldwide, this means that a very large proportion of readers use online stores to buy books.

eBooks are, at least for the time being, a lot less expensive than the print books. Of course, Amazon played a huge role to that end (Lynn, 2012), as it has been accused of price fixing, and thus creating unrealistic expectations to the public as to the retail pricing of eBooks. Still, however, eBooks are much more affordable and inexpensive to the average reader.

Finally, eBook can offer a richer reading experience, with mixed media, sound and music, games and any other medium of information delivery. This cannot only make the eBook more fun to use, but also in certain cases, increase the informational value of the medium.

The truth is that this constant exchange of arguments could go on for a long time, but is also true that it is a little bit misguided as well. Both sides tend to treat the book and the eBooks as enemies to each other, as opponents to a death match. That could only be valid, though, if the eBook was essentially, a book in another format. But, it is not. The eBook is not a Book. It is something else entirely.

As the German Gestalt psychologist Wolfgang Köhler suggested, the words convey symbolic ideas beyond their meaning (Alter A., 2013). Words, that is, carry hidden – or not so hidden- baggage that may play at least some role in shaping thought. So, by naming the eBook as such, we instantly considered it a book by nature, something born by it, related, fathered and maybe something which, in order to inherit its ancestor, it has to kill it first. But eBooks are not books in the sense that live Jazz performances are not music CDs. Or as theatrical plays are not films. Maybe you can turn a theatrical play into a movie, but it will be something else. Not something more, or something less, just something different of its own merit.

Now, of course, books and eBooks can both be read. They contain words and pictures. And that is all they have in common. So do websites, however, and no one suggested that books and websites are a threat to one another. We, as readers, as users, instinctively understand their different nature and purpose.

SO WHAT IS AN EBOOK IF NOT A BOOK?

eBooks are software (Bacon, 2013). According to Britannica (2014) Software is a set of instructions that tell a computer what to do. Software comprises the entire set of programs, procedures and routines associated with the operation of a computer system. The term was coined to differentiate these instructions from hardware – the physical, that is, components of a computer system. More specifically, eBooks are application software (much like a word processor or a database, a computer game or music player), and that essentially means that it directs the computer to execute commands given by the user (on the opposite hand, there is system software, that controls a computer's internal functioning, chiefly through an operating system, and which also controls and peripherals, such as monitors, printers, and storage devices).

Given that's, it is relatively easy to see why an eBook would be considered a piece of software. It is, practically, a program that reacts to user commands (even if they are pretty basic, like turning pages, making notes, setting placeholders etc) and need hardware in order to function. Sometimes the hardware used to read eBooks is also referred to as eBook, but in fact they are eBook readers, if we are actually talking about dedicated devices, like Kindle Fire, or Nook or anything else.

It is true that the first application of what we now call the eBook, consisted of an almost accurate reproduction of the image of the printing word against white paper. Of course, reading on the screens of the first eReaders was much more tiresome than reading on paper. Also, eReaders could (and still can) only reproduce black and white text and images. That, of course, applies a lot more restrictions to the final product when compared to an actual print book.

But eBooks are not meant to be used solely by eReaders. There is absolutely no reason why they should be used on dedicated devices (although some of them have become very comfortable to use). eBooks can take many forms and shapes, exactly because they are not tangible. They can perform a lot of different functions and serve as a multifaceted means of communication. Obviously this can lead to great diversity as well. There is not a single one right manifestation for the eBook.

This is obvious to at least some authors (or better, in this case, creators) and publishers, and now there are eBooks that apart from being used with the help of a dedicated eBooks reader, there are many applications that sit on other operating systems and allow the user to read eBooks (like the Kindle app, or Calibre) or even, in some cases, eBooks can be standalone pieces of software, totally independent of anything, but the operating system of the computer.

And, in that sense, an eBook may contain text, solely, or text and images, moving images, image and sound, interactive content, games for entertaining and testing features for reader evaluation. All these, and even more can be combined to create a form of communication, unprecedented.

There are various examples of how, at least some of, the potential of this medium can be exploited, with wonderful results. The first eBook app that created a big buzz, and actually presented a new way of reading, viewing, or using an eBook, not in a theoretical way, but rather in a very successful, tasteful and meaningful implementation was, in my view, Alice for iPad. To make Alice for iPad, the designers found an incredibly old copy of Alice in Wonderland and scanned the illustrations (Stevens, 2010), cleaned them up in Photoshop, redrew the scenes and characters and added new illustrated objects that could move around the screen. Then they added virtual gravity and physics to the characters and objects. It was the first time this kind of technology was applied this way and the result was to top-gross the children's books in the iPad store.

"The Monster at the End of this Book", by Sesame Street, is an app that essentially recreates the print book balancing narration (or reading) with interaction, while totally respecting the essence of the original book. The child gets to act on what was previously just described in the print version of the book: untie knots, knock down brick walls, etc.

"A story before Bed" is another app for children that essentially, narrates bed time stories. The advantage of this particular eBook, is that allows the parents to record their voices reading the book, so the child can listen to them, instead of some professional narrator. At first glance that may seem easy and unimportant but, in a sense, the parents/narrators become artists themselves, diving into the text, making it their own, interpreting and enacting it in a personal and unique way.

"The Castle" is an "actionbook". The reader gets to wonder inside a village from the Middle ages, and while playing with the interface, exploring the streets, the castles and the houses, the app produces historical and educational information. Apart from visually appealing, the app is also enhanced with sounds and music, making the user experience more rich and engaging.

Finally, "Anne Frank" published by Penguin Books, is another, interactive iPad take on Anne Frank's famous diary. "Anne Frank" has three main components – the diary, Story trails and Timeline. The diary itself is exactly as we know it, except it includes a series of links to illustrative content, such as photos, videos, maps and additional background information. For example, the reader can see a full 3D model of Anne Frank's home in Amsterdam, which helps to bring the story to life. The Story Trails section lets her/him delve into key aspects of the story, linking directly to excerpts of the diary with additional notes and narration on the highlighted segments. Similarly, Timeline takes the reader through an easy-to-follow calendar of key events in the Anne Frank story. There are actually dual timelines, featuring family images from Anne's life before the war, as well as historic wartime images from international archives accompanied by commentary on key events (Sawers, 2013).

A somehow related genre to children's books are comic books. Nowadays, of course, comic books are no more intended just for kids. On the contrary, they are extremely popular to readers well in their 20s and 30s, and at least a quarter of overall comic book readers are over 65 (Simba Information, 2010). Comic books (or graphic novels, if you prefer) have a very distinct form and means of presenting information. This combination, this unconstrained blend of text and illustration, that sometimes feel all too static in the print environment, can be elevated, perfected in the digital environment. Of course, many applications have been created dedicated to comic book reading, (Comics by Comixology, Marvel Comics, IDW Comics, The Carrier, iVerse Comics, Verm etc), but most of them do not really add anything to the genre. In fact, the majority of them are dedicated apps to a certain publisher. However, some of them stand out.

Madefire, for example, is an application that turns comic books into Motion Books (as the creator of the app call them). The book is transformed into an interactive application, which runs dynamically in mobile devises (mainly iPad and iPhone). Apart from motion, music and sounds can be added to create a more evocative environment. The end result however, does not resemble an animated movie, but remains true to the comic "book" feeling. Each panel is animated and projected subtly and individually, without interfering with the next, and this way the reader is allowed to duel on the illustration longer, being able to focus on the details, without losing the coherence of storytelling.

Certainly, not all eBook apps are dedicated for younger users, or playful content; and this is proof that the medium is truly transforming itself. One particular eBook application that I think is especially interesting is Papercut. Papercut is still at its experimental stages and comes with three pre-installed short stories by world famous authors. As the reader moves along the text, the application tries to transform simple reading into an interactive experience, automatically triggering relevant video, animation, image sequences, and sound content. All these "additions" to the text, however, are subtle enough so that do not become a nuisance or a distraction to the reader, but powerful enough to add emotion and depth to the narration. The goal of the team that designed the specific application was to create a publishing platform for eBooks. But since the online, digital environment is paperless, they focused on the concept of what would happen to the books if the pages disappeared (Bryant, 2011). The answer in this case, according to them, was that it becomes something different, however the content does not disappear, and it merely is communicated in a different way.

The case of the eBooks is a first class embodiment of the famous McLuhan phrase *"The medium is the message"* (McLuhan, 1964). And he continues "it is only too typical that the "content" of any medium blinds us to the character of the medium." And it is the character of the medium that is its potency or effect - its message. In other words, "This is merely to say that the personal and social consequences of any medium - that is, of any extension of ourselves - result from the new scale that is introduced into our affairs by each extension of ourselves, or by any new technology."

McLuhan also offers his own definition of medium. In Understanding Media, he refers to the medium as "any extension of ourselves." Classically, he suggests that a hammer extends our arm and that the wheel extends our legs and feet. Each enables us to do more than our bodies could do on their own. Similarly, the medium of language extends our thoughts from within our mind out to others. Indeed, since our thoughts are the result of our individual sensory experience, speech is an "outering" of our senses - we could consider it as a form of reversing senses - whereas usually our senses bring the world into our minds, speech takes our sensorially-shaped minds out to the world (Federman, 2004). And, although, the book has always in some way been an extension of one's self, even in the sense that expands the minds and horizons of the reader, the eBook is an even more elaborate expression of that notion.

The examples already presented illustrate the potential of the eBook, at least as far as multimedia are concerned. But limiting the eBook to the parallel use of several media would be like scratching the surface. After all, multimedia can be used for a lot more, than simply adding beauty to the experience of reading. eBooks can turn out to be a great reading alternative to the visually impaired, for example. The opportunities designers have nowadays, are limitless and can now actually create eBooks that can be used by anyone. Until recently, the visually impaired had very limited choices when it came to reading; it was only Braille books or talking books. However, production of those could be really expensive, and given the relatively limited audience either the publishers did not produce them at all, or they were really expensive to buy. And in any case, they were hard to buy as mainstream bookstores did not (and still do not) carry significant collections of them.

Now, Amazon for example has a very vast collection of audio books, covering almost all possible genres, from biographies, to romantic novels, to children's books, and science. It should also be noted that in most cases the kindle editions of the audio books are less expensive than the audio CD, where available. Of course, a kindle book can be used by anyone, not just the visually impaired (assuming the readers are willing to share a kindle device or app, since eBooks are usually under DRM lock and key). Also, the reader can significantly adjust the font size of the text that is being read. This can make the eBooks text appear significantly bigger than the text in a physical large print book. A computer screen can always be adjusted for contrast and brightness to help those in need to see better. Finally, the eBooks allows the user to both read and listen at the same time, using one resource.

Usability design has evolved a lot in the recent years as well. The stories about toddlers using iPads more efficiently than their parents have been circulating amongst awed users since the release of the 1st generation iPad. Although the first eBook readers well very bulky and uncomfortable to use, todays devices (either dedicated to the purpose of reading, or tablets that use certain apps) are so much more comfortable and easy to read that makes the comparison between them totally unfair. This is a very important step in the evolution of the eBook as most of the people would refuse to spend a lot of time learning to use a machine that allows them to do the same thing as a print book, an art that most people mastered when they were six years old. Ease of use, though, is only one side of the coin. Fun can be the other one. UI designers have tried very hard to develop interfaces that not only are obvious in their use, but also enjoyable. Certainly, Apple, Steve Jobs, and the iPad played an important role to that, but, fortunately, the story did not end there, and now, almost all new electronic devices and interfaces try on some level to incorporate beauty, ease, and fun into the overall user experience.

Enjoyable reading and interacting with the eBook may prove to be a critical characteristic, especially for the educational genre. For example, such eBooks can use gamification to increase their value and approach teaching and studying in a more advanced and effective way. Gamification is, in essence, the use of game thinking and game mechanics in non-game contexts to engage users in solving problems.

(Zichermann & Cunningham, 2011) (Huotari & Hamari, 2012). Gamification is not a new concept and has been utilized in several different environments and with several different purposes (i.e. to engage the user, to teach, to entertain, to measure and to improve the perceived ease of use of information systems (Herzig, 2014).

Gamification places the user in the center of the application's attention, thus making his/her motivations and interests an integral part of the design and evolution of the experience. In a more narrow sense, gamification is used in a non-game context, in order, not to create a game, but to create a playful experience. Gamification taps into the need of people to gain status and accomplish achievements.

Though this concept can undoubtedly find many applications, the most obvious one would be through textbooks and teaching materials. Teaching and studying could become a lot more interactive and possible a lot more fun, if the eBooks used for that purpose, took advantage of the new technology and it possibilities, creating an education environment that is more user friendly on one hand, but on the other helps students absorb information and knowledge more easily and seamlessly. For example, a physics formula could be more easily understood, if alongside it there was a video portraying its application. Or, in the case of chemistry, for example, students could have the chance to create chemical reactions, not simply by writing down the elements, but by using visual representation of actual materials that would create reactions like explosions, boiling, melting etc. Engaging the attention of students to studying, would, ultimately, increase the effectiveness of the teaching process.

Another aspect of the digital text, that has been hugely unexplored, is non-linearity. Books are basically manufactured in ordered to be read from cover to cover (with the notable exception of Reference works, like dictionaries and encyclopedias), forcing the reader to follow a specific and predetermined path. We have become so much accustomed to this, that, in fact, most of reading or studying is performed in a linear way, so to speak. But the human mind does not necessarily follow linear paths in order to learn or construct new knowledge. The act of thinking is highly associative and thus non-linear, creating connections between seemingly unconnected notions, or at least unconnected according to the point of view of another thinker. Each mind works in its own way. Taking this into account, certain kinds of eBooks could incorporate the notion of non-linearity allowing each to user to essentially create their own reading process and experience.

In "Chopsticks" (Alter A., 2012) for example, a novel that was realized both in print and as an iPad app, reader can select "shuffle read" which reorders the pages of the book creating a different reading path. The app, apart from some very basic text, includes family photos, letters, documents, instant messages and YouTube videos. The creation of this app proved to be very difficult, not only from a technical point of view, so that every made sense, and were tied together in a meaningful yet loose way, so that the reader can rearrange the reading sequence, but also from a financial point of you, as the project involved the rights' management of several different resources from several different right holders. In any case, however, this was an interesting approach to the eBook, as it tried to create an alternative experience, not necessarily one limited to reading, or linearity for that matter, but rather, continuity.

It is possible, that several questions will be raised as to whether the extended used of multimedia will trivialize the book and diminish reading to something different and "easier" all together. There are many opposing the eBook concept for this reason exactly; because they believe that eBooks do not educate readers to the art of reading and committing to the written word as readers of the print book have to do. They do not create or encourage the devoted reader, but rather nourish the more lazy instincts of the user.

First of all, not all eBooks have to adopt multimedia, non-linearity or gamification. There are, and should be, simple text books, that present their matter with the sole use of words. On the other hand there could also be a different category of eBook, more content rich, which address different needs and desires. After all, not all content would benefit from a conversion from text to something entirely (or even slightly) different. It is going to take a lot of experimenting and a lot of user feedback to actually determine what would be the best combination for each kind of book.

And, certainly, the existence of one, perfectly good medium of publication, should not be an inhibitive factor to the creation of something different entirely. Because, the final point is this; Books and eBooks are, or at least can be, completely different tools. One does not exclude the other, and every tool is made to serve a specific purpose. As a final note, it would be important to clarify, however, that all these new potential of the medium makes sense only when it used appropriately, enhancing the used of the eBook, without distracting and making the user lose focus of the content.

The debate on the eBook has just started but it seems that we, as users, authors, publishers and handlers have not exactly decided what we want to do with this new and shiny thing. There are a few people, the instant haters and the instant lovers of eBooks, that seem to have a very clear opinion on the subject, but the majority, all those left in-between, in truth, feel that they have not yet explored the full potential or even the best practices as to how we could fully take advantage of this form of publication. More and more applications, fortunately, explore this subject and in the time to come the eBook will find its place. The print book, after all, cannot be threatened as long as there people that want to use it, and the truth is, that it will take a long time for people to completely abolish their dependence on paper. But even so, even if paper, at some point, becomes obsolete, that does not mean that novels, poetry, essays, and any other kind of narrative will disappear as well. eBook is not a threat to the creativity or to reading. It is simply another way of exploring creativity.

REFERENCES

Alter, A. (2012, January 20). Blowing up the book. *The Wall Street Journal.* Retrieved from http://online.wsj.com/news/articles/SB10001424052970204468004577169001135659954

Alter, A. (2013, May 29). The power of names. *New Yorker.* Retrieved from www.newyorker.com/tech/elements/the-power-of-names

Anne Frank App Launches for Holocaust Memorial Day. (2013, January 24). Anne Frank Fonds. Retrieved from http://www.annefrank.ch/news-view/items/anne-frank-app-launches-for-holocaust-memorial-day.html

Alice for iPad. (2010). Atomic Antelope. Retrieved from Atomic Antelope: http://www.atomicantelope.com/alice

Bacon, B. (2013, March 18). *Ebooks are actually not books - schools among first to realize.* Retrieved from www.digitalbookworld.com/2013/ebooks-are-actually-not-books-schools-among-first-to-realize/

Bercovici, J. (2014, February 10). Amazon vs. Book Publishers, By the Numbers. *Forbes.* Retrieved from www.forbes.com/sites/jeffbercovici/2014/02/10/amazon-vs-book-publishers-by-the-numbers/

Bryant, M. (2011, September 15). *Papercut for iPad turns ebooks into multimedia experiences with audio, video and animations.* Retrieved from The Next Web: http://thenextweb.com/apps/2011/09/15/papercut-for-ipad-turns-ebooks-into-multimedia-experiences-with-audio-video-and-animations/

Federman, M. (2004). *What is the Meaning of the Medium is the Message?* Retrieved from http://individual.utoronto.ca/markfederman/MeaningTheMediumistheMessage.pdf

Herzig, P. (2014). Gamification as a service [Ph.D.].

Huotari, K., & Hamari, J. (2012). Defining Gamification - A Servce Marketin Perspective. *Proceedings of the 16th International Academic MindTrek Conference 2012.* Tampere, Finland.

Jackson Fish Market. (2012). *A story before bed.* Retrieved from A story before bed: http://www.astorybeforebed.com/

Lynn, B. C. (2012, 04). The real bad guy in the e-Book price fixing case: Amazon's continued domination of the publishing industry will hurt the book market. *Slate.* Retrieved from www.slate.com/articles/technology/future_tense/2012/04/e_book_price_fixing_amazon_is_the_real_bad_guy_.html

McLuhan, M. (1964). *Undersstanding Media: The Extentions of Man.* New York: McGraw Hill.

Sawers, P. (2013, January 28). Anne Frank for iPad and Nook reimagines The Diary of a Young Girl for the digital age. *TheNextWeb.* Retrieved from http://thenextweb.com/apps/2013/01/28/anne-franks-diary-for-ipad/

Sesame Street. (2011). *The Monster at the End of This Book...starring Grover!* Retrieved from https://itunes.apple.com/us/app/monster-at-end-this-book...starring/id409467802?mt=8

Overview of the U.S. Comic Book & Graphic Novel Market 2010-2011. (2010). Simba Information. Retrieved from http://www.simbainformation.com/Overview-Comic-Book-2523144/

Stevens, C. (2010, April 10). *Making Alice for the iPad.* Retrieved from The Literary Platform: http://www.theliteraryplatform.com/2010/04/making-the-alice-for-the-ipad/

Zichermann, G., & Cunningham, C. (2011). Introduction. In G. Zichermann, & C. Cunningham (Eds.), Gamification by Design: Implementing Game Mechanics in Web and Mobile Apps (p. xiv). Sebastopol, CA: O'Reily Media, Inc.

The Castle. (2010). *Zuuka!* Retrieved from http://download.cnet.com/The-Castle/3000-20412_4-75304654.html

Chapter 11

Learning by Playing:
Development of an Interactive Biology Lab Simulation Platform for Educational Purposes

Vasilis Zafeiropoulos
Hellenic Open University, Greece

Dimitris Kalles
Hellenic Open University, Greece

Argyro Sgourou
Hellenic Open University, Greece

ABSTRACT

The practical training of students and employees in laboratories containing scientific instruments constitutes an educational challenge. Laboratory equipment is by definition sensitive, costly and requires specific safety rules for its use. Therefore, students do not have the opportunity to make improper use of the equipment and get trained by "trial-and-error". The educational process becomes even trickier when students are many and training takes place simultaneously within the same laboratory; damages to instrumentation and accidents are possible and as a consequence, the effectiveness of learning is greatly limited. For such purposes, an adventure-style computer game -Onlabs- has been developed to provide an interactive simulation environment of a biology laboratory where students may experiment and make several harmless mistakes and where no time or space restrictions are imposed on them. This chapter describes how Onlabs was developed to serve a real need for a remote tool for familiarization and safe experimentation within the laboratory space.

INTRODUCTION

Experimenting in wet laboratories can be interesting, exciting, and rewarding; however, it can also involve risks for both participants and the laboratory equipment. A typical day, during a practical

DOI: 10.4018/978-1-4666-8659-5.ch011

workshop in a teaching laboratory, tends to be densely populated with large numbers of individuals with limited experience in the hazards of a science laboratory, including hazardous organisms (for example, microbes and pathogens) which much be properly handled. Numerous common procedures conducted in a teaching laboratory may include aerosols' creation when preparing liquid buffers and mixing chemical solutions, sources of contamination coming from improper sterilization of microbiological resources or spills, use of centrifugation and micro-centrifugation techniques, use of bead beaters or shearing blenders, pipetting, handling of contaminated animal bedding or culturing and manipulating human cancer cells and tissues and/or analysis of several biological fluids. Each of the mentioned procedures involves various risks and requires specific precautions (Miller, Witherow & Carson, 2011; *Molecular Biology*, 2010).

Personal alert and proper safety precautions should be taken at all times when the trainees are actively conducting and observing experiments in the lab. Unsafe practices may endanger other trainees and the expensive lab equipment as well. The responsibility for maintaining an enjoyable, instructional, and safe environment in the biology laboratory requires extensive training and familiarization with all safety rules governing practical workshops that cover various and complex experimental methods (Furr, 2000; Committee on Anticipating Biosecurity Challenges of the Global Expansion of High-Containment Biological Laboratories, 2011).

Laboratory instructors put their efforts to offer careful counseling to increase student awareness of potential biosafety risks and educate students in good laboratory practice to minimize any possible risk factors. Workshops' initial courses always consist of learning the laboratory safety rules and of guided tours through the premises and the procedures to be performed. The purpose is to smoothly familiarize the trainees with the expensive and sensitive laboratory equipment and the consolidation of the rules to be respected for their personal safety, before they switch to the hands-on experience.

Distance education, where trainees lack the ability of a constant contact with the laboratories, apparently requires additional training to improve understanding of the rigorous experimental methods and of how better address the educational outcomes. There is an emerging need to explore innovative educational practices for newly introduced trainees for both distance laboratory education and special courses comprised with the use of very expensive and precise modern lab technology. A common issue that is raised is to gain laboratory experience, to assimilate with the technology to be used by (potentially distantly) interacting with the experimental apparatuses and to operate safely and consistently in the laboratory environment. Such preliminary lab education could reduce the amount of time actually required of trainees to be present in laboratory areas and the costs of failed experimental efforts, and might increase familiarity with safety rules, providing a more mature and constructive use of laboratory equipment.

To obtain the potential benefits and educational outcomes of how to make appropriate use of the laboratory equipment and how to conduct successful experiments, we have developed and applied an interactive virtual game representing the biology laboratory at the Hellenic Open University, namely Onlabs. The newly introduced trainees to the lab environment, using Onlabs from the convenience of their own premises, may explore the laboratory area, interact with the instruments in many permitted ways and unlimitedly experiment and visualize their results with various combinations of the laboratory instruments. As the current generation of students and junior employees are familiar with online games since childhood, one expects that such game-like learning platforms would be, in principle, a good bet.

BACKGROUND

Simulations and games are powerful tools for addressing many goals and mechanisms for learning science: the motivation to learn science, the conceptual understanding, science process skills, as well as the extensive scientific discourse and argumentation.

A prominent application for teaching physics has been Interactive Physics, developed by Design Simulation Technologies. Interactive Physics provide students with a simulation environment upon which they are able to visualize and learn abstract concepts of physics; moreover, they are able to change the values of its properties and view the changes in it. Among the tasks that a user can accomplish are reproducing physical experiments, measuring physical quantities like velocity, force and momentum, hearing and measuring sound frequencies and Doppler effects and creating linear actuators and rotational motors (*Interactive Physics*, n.d.).

Yet, there are also commercial games which simulate laws of physics and offer the player the chance to get acquainted with them. One of the most famous games of this kind is Angry Birds by Rovio Entertainment. Although Angry Birds are designed for entertainment purposes and don't provide the user with a direct learning interface, they do offer the user the chance to familiarize themselves with Newtonian laws of gravitation and physical procedures such as shooting and crash (Allen, 2010).

Another commercial game with educational prospect is Minecraft, originally developed by Mojan which later on was bought by Microsoft. Among other tasks, Minecraft offers the players the opportunity to build various constructions by combining blocks of several particular materials like dirt, stone, ores and tree trunk. (Ashdown, 2010). For that reason, Minecraft has been suggested as a useful rendering tool for people to get a good idea of the functionality of particular constructions such as houses and parks (Spillman, 2011).

Within the same domain of game applications which simulate and reproduce laws of physics are flight and drive simulators. Two characteristic games of this kind are Microsoft Flight Simulator and Playseat Redbull Racing F1; the former, which, as its name suggests, simulates a real airplane flight, offers the user the ability to interact conventionally through their computer, by using the keyboard and mouse (*Microsoft Flight Simulator*, n.d.), whereas the latter, simulating the driving of a F1 car offers a full set of driving seat, stirring wheels and pedals as an interface (*Playseat Redbull Racing F1*, n.d.).

Moving from the field of physics to the one of biology and medicine, one meets the use of Second Life platform for virtually recreating medical procedures, in which the users are being trained in providing healthcare and medical services. Imperial College's Virtual Hospital and Polyclinic and University of California's Virtual Pharmacy consist of some of Second Life's most characteristic medical worlds Lee & Berge, 2011).

Recently, Labster an online laboratory simulator, has been created and allows students or teachers to perform various experiments (Kotey, 2013). Experimenting is based on some real-life scenarios on modern topics as the investigation of a murder based on DNA fingerprints, organic meat analysis or environmental contamination issues.

Several applications including 3D types of visualization or educational video games have been applied and tested among high school students to induce their interest in science lessons. Presentation of complex scientific issues with interactive 3D animations or 3D animations compared to static illustrations increased in general students' (13-14 years old) learning capacity (Korakakis, Pavlatou, Palyvos & Spyrellis, 2009). However, this study also concludes that there is an inverse proportional relationship between the duration of narrations and students' focusing, due to a cognitive overload. Thus, to obtain advantages by the use of interactive 3D animations, cognitive load needs to be respected. Another attempt to achieve high levels of scientific knowledge consolidation for college prep students has been the design of a virtual world under the name of Multiplayer Educational Gaming Application (MEGA). Rather aimed to enhance the acquisition of some critical "twenty-first century skills" than simply educate people about science, students who played MEGA performed laboratory experimentation, observations and interacted via communication channels. Eventually, 94% of the participating students successfully implemented their newly acquired scientific skills to solve a CSI-like murder case (thus, understanding about DNA inheritance, creating family pedigrees, blood types and DNA fingerprinting). Also, all but three students succeeded to complete positively the game within a 90-minute class (Annetta, Cheng & Holmes, 2010).

Upon the same motivation, a computer-based simulation of animal models (transgenics) used in molecular biology techniques, was evaluated on high school biology students (17-18 years old). Researchers of this study claimed that the simulation teaching strategy provides significant academic influence and advanced educational outcomes (Shegog et al., 2012).

Nevertheless, the assessment of the learning outcomes of simulations and games and their potential to both motivate and support students' science learning is still a vibrant area where further developments remain to be demonstrated.

VIRTUAL LABORATORY

Actively interacting through virtual classes is widely admitted to be more efficient than attending lectures or reading books. A necessary prerequisite when studying sciences is to attend laboratory practical lessons, which by its nature requires active involvement with experimental procedures in laboratory areas. Such practical training is impossible to be effected only by reading laboratory manuals and experimental protocols. While reading reportedly helps a student to assimilate a subject by 10% and lectures by an even lower rate, the respective percentage for practicing (in which interacting through a virtual world is included) is set at 75% (De Freitas, 2008). Practical laboratory experience at a distance (at least to some extent) is a particularly difficult challenge for educational institutions.

Taking these parameters into consideration, we took the initiative to implement a virtual biology laboratory environment for the Hellenic Open University students to be trained in. The initiative is named *Onlabs* and is mainly targeted at students who need laboratory experience in studying physical sciences.

Conceptual Design

The environment of the virtual laboratory is **discrete**; the objects in it can be perceived separately from one another. In this environment, an agent acts and represents the human user. Each time, the agent can be in a finite number of distinct states while the way it interacts with the environment is through a finite set of actions. Moreover, the environment is **deterministic**; that is, when the agent is in a specific initial state and performs a specific action, the new state it gets to is uniquely determined by these two (initial state and action) and therefore always the same (Russell & Norvig, 2007).

Those properties are common in adventure games (Amir & Doyle, 2002); the latter's environment comply with the philosophy of being discrete and deterministic and renders themselves an ideal, yet realistic, field for an agent to act and learn through focusing on the necessary procedures. Such an en-

Figure 1. View of the lab's bench with several instruments.

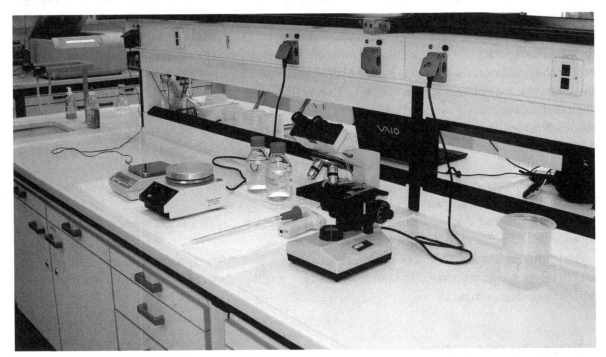

vironment, apart from being discrete and deterministic as described above, is also "noise-free", meaning that the agent receives neither spurious nor extraneous information of what it perceives (so, "noise cancellation" is not required).

Within the real biology lab environment, there are several **objects** like the microscope, the magnetic stirrer, the electric scale, the pipette, the beaker, the pen, the alcohol bottle, the xylene bottle etc. A typical view of the lab's bench with many of the afore-mentioned instruments on it is given in Figure 1.

In the virtual lab, the lab objects being simulated along with the **human agent** (user), or, in gaming terms, a character directly controlled by the human player, consist of the game's **entities**.

One or more kindred entities belong to a **class**. Conversely, each particular entity is an **instance** of its respective class. For example, the pipette in the virtual lab is an instance of the *pipette* class, the name assigned to it being *pipette_1* (in case of a second pipette, that would be called *pipette_2*). The alcohol and the xylene bottles are both instances of the *vessel* class, namely *alcohol_bottle* and *xylene_bottle*. Finally, the human agent is represented by the *trainee* instance of the *ego* class which in turn represents all potentially-implemented user characters (as would be required in a –planned- multi-player context).

It should be mentioned that some entities are *organically connected* with several other "smaller" ones. Such an organic connection is obvious in the case of the microscope. Although there is a class of entities called *microscope*, this refers to the main body of a microscope; the latter also comprises the stage, the stage-base, the coarse focus knob, the fine focus knob, the light switch, the light intensity knob, the lamp, the revolving nosepiece with the objective lenses, the oculars, the condenser, the condenser knob, the knob configuring the iris diaphragm and the knobs for the adjustment of the x and y co-ordinates of the concoction placed on the stage, all consisting of separate entities, yet providing and receiving feedback to that microscope and each other. For example, the coarse focus knob of a microscope affects the height of the microscope's stage-base.

Each class of entities (excluding the *ego* one) has some actions that can be performed on it by the user. Those actions are mainly the following four; *look, rotate, singularly_use* and *jointly_use*; all but the second one are common in many modern adventure games.

The *look* action returns a description of the instance that it is being performed on. For example, a *pipette* instance full of alcohol which contains nothing inside, when looked at by the user, returns the following message: "An empty pipette". On the other hand, if the *pipette* instance contains distilled water, the user-friendly message becomes: "A pipette filled with water". In other words, the *look* action helps the user get some info for a particular entity that may not be easy to grasp immediately.

The *rotate* action is only valid on knobs, like the coarse and fine focus knobs and the light intensity knob of a microscope. The *rotate* action always comes together with an offset, the sign of which defining the direction of the rotation; positive and negative offsets determine clockwise and counter-clockwise rotations respectively. A *rotate* action taken each time by the user, independent of its direction, is defined to be *elementary*, that is, take place for a minimum amount of degrees, defined separately for each knob class; nevertheless, one or more successive elementary rotations of the same direction consist of a *composite* rotation. In most cases, a knob's rotation affects other entities as well; for example, the rotation of the coarse focus knob of a microscope changes the height of the latter's stage-base, as mentioned before.

The *singularly_use* action's result depends on the entity being performed on. In case of a collectable object, it results in its placement in the user's inventory, that is, as in conventional adventure games, the personal repository of the user in which they can store the object the gather from their environment; for example, the singular use of a pipette lying in the lab results in its being picked up and stored in the inventory. However, in case of a switch, like the AC switch of a microscope or the power button of a magnetic stirrer, the *singularly_use* action produce as an outcome that those things are being turned on or off. Of course, there are cases that the *singularly_use* action is not valid at all, like an unplugged socket or even a pipette, when already picked up in the inventory.

Lastly, the *jointly_use* action refers to the combination of two separate entities together. For example, the user may combine a *pipette* instance with a *vessel* one; as long as the first one is empty, this combination results in the former's being filled with the content of the latter. Though not all combinations between classes are possible, we will defer such discussion until the internal structure of classes has been illustrated.

Each class of entities in the environment has several, yet specific, **features**. Each of the features can be either numeric of alphanumeric depending on the type of *values* they can take. For example, the feature *content* of a *pipette* instance is alphanumeric as it may have the value of *nothing* (in case it's empty) or *distilled_water* (in case it contains distilled water) while the feature *height* of a *stage_base* instance which has already been mentioned twice is numeric, taking real arithmetic values within a specific range, e.g. 0.1170-0.1366.

A feature that is common to all classes is the *place* one. This "keeps" the place that each instance lies; *lab*, in case the instance lies in the lab; *inventory,* in case it's stored in the user's inventory; or even another instance, in case the former instance is "contained" in the latter, a case to be discussed later on. For now, let us assume that all objects (instances) lie either in the lab or the inventory.

In case of alphanumeric features, the following abstraction is made: a value that the feature takes is a **state** and the action to be made in order for a state to change into another one is a **transition**. For the purpose of illustration, let us focus on the paper class, representing the tiny pieces of paper which get a

Figure 2. Paper's condition feature's STD.

PAPER

- Condition

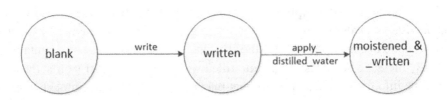

letter "E" written on them with a pen and then moistened with water from a pipette, in order to be used as a test specimen to be microscoped. Each *paper* instance has a feature called *condition,* representing the condition it is at any time; the values that the *condition* feature of an instance, e.g. *paper_1*, can take are considered as the various states that *paper1* can be at in terms of this specific feature. It is assumed that these states are *blank, written* and *moistened_&_written.* Starting from the *blank* state, the *written* state is reached through the *write* transition and from this state to *moistened_&_written* through the *apply_distilled_water* one.

In order for those concepts to be clear as well as easily-manipulated, we have liberally employed the notation of **State-Transition Diagrams** (STDs) for their representation. Generally, STDs consist of a useful abstraction for representing state changes in time-critical systems as well as time-independent ones (Yourdon, 1989). We have opted to use the STD term instead of the (equally valid) **State Diagrams** (SDs) mainly because we want to stress the importance of actions in our world; secondarily, STDs are particularly good at also conveying domain models to domain experts who are not computing scientists. For the afore-mentioned case of the *condition* feature of a *paper* instance, the respective STD will be as depicted in figure 2.

As derived from this one and as applied to all STDs in our design, the states are depicted by *circles* while the transitions are represented by *arrows;* the state a transition arrow starts from and the one leading to are the *initial* and *final* states for this transition, respectively.

A transition from a state of an entity's feature to another one is most of the time triggered by an *action* performed by the user on this entity; nevertheless, there are cases of transitions which are triggered *externally* or *automatically,* that is to say not by any action of the user on them.

In the *paper's* case, the *write* transition is achieved when the *paper* instance is jointly used with a *pen* instance, as the latter's class is provided with a *function* feature with the *write* value. It should be noted here that if there was another class, e.g. a *pencil* one, having the same *function* feature with the same *write* value, the result would be the same, that is, the transition would be accomplished, too. That way, the level of abstraction is raised, we the focus lies on the properties of the objects and not the objects themselves. Similarly, the *apply_distilled_water* transition is achieved when the *paper* instance is jointly used with a *pipette* instance, provided the latter's content is *distilled_water,* or, in our technical language, the *content* feature of it has the value of *distilled_water.*

Having just mentioned the *content* feature of *pipette,* the latter's STD is depicted in figure 3.

Figure 3. Pipette's content feature's STD.

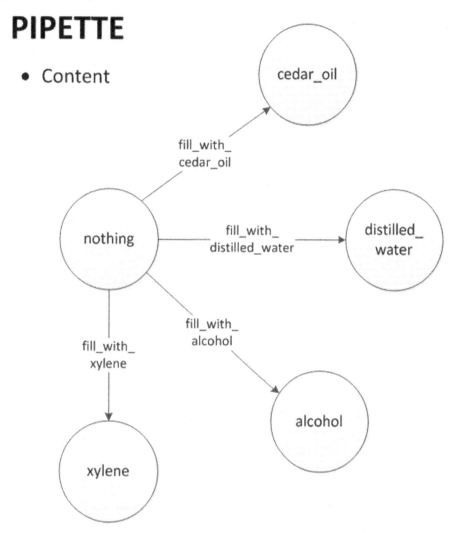

Starting from the *nothing* state, the *content* feature can "move" to the *cedar_oil*, *distilled_water*, *alcohol* or *xylene* state, depending on the *content* feature's value of the *vessel* instance that is jointly used with the *pipette* one; for example, if the *content* of the vessel has the value of *distilled_water*, the same becomes the value of the pipette's *content* as well.

A more sophisticated STD is the one of the *tidiness* feature of the *concoction* class, which represents the concoctions being placed on a microscope's stage to be microscoped (in our case created by combining a nosepiece, a written and moistened piece of paper that was mentioned before and a cover glass), and is depicted in figure 4.

In this, one notices three different "types" of transitions, two of which having also been illustrated in figures 2 and 3. Firstly, the *apply_cedar_oil* transition is triggered with by the joint use of the particular *concoction* instance and the *vessel* instance of *cedar_oil_bottle*. Secondly, the *clear* transition is triggered by the joint use of the *concoction* instance and a *cleaning_wipe* instance provided the latter's *function* feature' value is *clear*, which is the default one; similarly, the *clean* transition needs for the

Figure 4. Concoction's tidiness feature's STD.

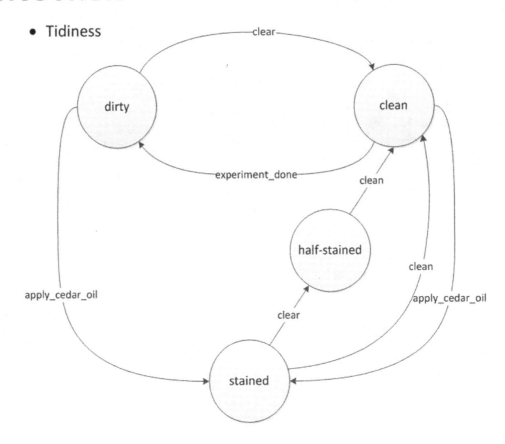

CONCOCTION

- Tidiness

function feature of the *cleaning_wipe* instance to be *clean*, and in order for it to be clean, it must have already been jointly used with a pipette filled with alcohol or xylene, or, in technical language, a *pipette* instance with its *content* feature having the value of *alcohol* or *xylene*. And thirdly, a type of transition never encountered before in our design, the *experiment_done* one, is triggered automatically (that is to say, internally by the game, not externally, by the user) as soon as the experiment procedure is completed, so the concoction will need to be wiped over again.

As most classes have several features, there can be STDs for more than one of them. Such is the case of the *stage* class, representing any microscope stage which the concoction to be microscoped is placed on; its STD is depicted in Figure 5.

While *stage*'s *tidiness* feature's STDs is similar to *concoction*'s one of the same name, albeit less complicated, its *concoction* feature's STD presents a concept briefly mentioned before, that of an object "contained" by another one. In fact, the *concoction* feature of a *stage* instance keeps track of the particular concoction instance placed on it; for example, if *stage_1* (organic part of *microscope_1*) has *concoction_2* on it, then its *concoction* feature has the value of *concoction_2*; if, on the other hand, there is no *concoction* instance on *stage_1*, the *concoction* feature of it takes the value of *nothing*. The *concoction_N* state of *concoction*'s STD has darker font, which is conventionally assigned the mean-

Figure 5. Stage's tidiness and concoction features' STDs.

STAGE

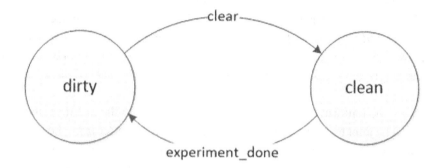

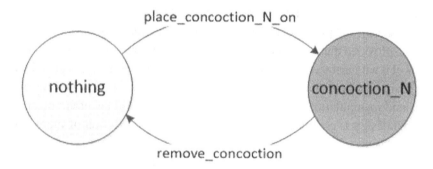

ing that the *concoction* feature has the value of another stand-alone instance (object), *concoction_2* in our example, instead of an abstract property like *dirty*, *clean* etc. or non-stand-alone entities like *distilled_water*, *alcohol* etc. Considering the transitions from *nothing* to *concoction_N* (concoction_2) and vice versa, those are achieved through the joint use of *stage_1* and *concoction_2* and the singular use of the latter, respectively. In the first transition, however, apart from the change of *stage1*'s *concoction* feature to *concoction_2*, the latter's *place* feature is changed from lab or *inventory* (depending where it had been before) into *stage_1*, and that illustrates the case of one entity "contained" in another, which had briefly been mentioned before.

Having mentioned several joint uses (combinations) between classes, it's time to discuss the "order" in which those and the rest of classes are jointly used. For this purpose, a little more focus must be set on the STD of *paper*'s class in Figure 1. In this, the *apply_distilled_water* transition from *written* state to *moistened_&_written* one is achieved through the *jointly_use* action on *paper* and *pipette* instances provided the latter's *content* feature has the value of *distilled_water*. One might assume that instead of a *pipette* instance, any instance of a class for storing fluids, like *vessel* or *wash_bottle*, would accomplish the same result as long as its *content* is *distilled_water*, too. Nevertheless, as the disposition of water from a large vessel or wash bottle on a small piece of paper, our design forbid the joint use of *paper* and *vessel* classes as well as this of *paper* and *wash_bottle* ones. The joint uses that our design permits are depicted by arrows in Figure 6.

In this, the direction of an arrow of a joint use distinguishes between the main class and the secondary one within this particular use. By the term *main class* of a joint use we refer to that class whose one of the features undergoes the sole – or the most important – change; the one to remains renders itself this use's *secondary class*. For example, as the joint use of *pen* and *paper* instances changes the *condition* feature of the latter and none of the former, we define the main class as *paper* and the secondary one as *pen*. The arrow direction is drawn from the secondary class to the main one, as it's like one uses the former "on" the latter; in our case, the *pen* on the *paper*, where the state of *paper* is changed while this of *pen* doesn't.

Yet, apart from the uniform arrows representing joint uses like the one described above, one sees a few dashed ones. The joint uses represented by the dashed arrows differ from the uses represented by the uniform ones in that the former have the particularity that *place* feature of the instance of the secondary class changes and the new value assigned to it is the instance of the main class itself; in other words, the joint uses with dashed arrows are actions in which the instance of the secondary class is placed on (or in) the instance of the main class. For example, when the user places a cover glass, e.g. *cover_glass_1* instance, on a nosepiece, e.g. *nosepiece_1* instance, *cover_glass_1*'s *place* becomes *nosepiece_1*.

In figure 6, one finally notices a dotted arrow directed from *nosepiece* class to *concoction* one. This arrows doesn't represent any joint use; it rather deals with the *transformation* of a *nosepiece* instance into a *concoction* one, provided that on the latter the appropriate actions have been performed (which consists of the joint uses of it with instances of *paper* and *cover_glass* successively, depicted with dashed arrows).

So far, our design has been *low level*, meaning that it has referred to the various objects in the lab and their attributes and manipulation. Complying with the hierarchical agent architecture (Poole & Mackworth, 2010), the design is complemented by a higher level description of more general tasks carried out by the human agent.

Assume that *trainee* (our *ego* instance representing the human agent) agent has the aim to get acquainted with the microscope and its function. This target consists of the following:

1. Connecting the microscope in the socket
2. Turning the light switch on
3. Configuring the light intensity at 2/3 of the maximum intensity
4. Lifting the condenser to the highest position
5. Setting the 4X objective lens to be the active one
6. Testing the coarse focus knob
7. Testing the fine focus knob

Those 7 steps are "encoded" in a STD for *ego* class's *state* feature, representing the state in terms of task accomplished that the user character is in each time. The STD is depicted in Figure 7.

In this, one sees eight (8) different states; *beginning* is the starting state while all other states describe the situations having come up after the afore-mentioned steps from 1 to 7 were made successfully and in that specific order. Furthermore, the uniform arrows represent the transitions from one state to another

Figure 6. The permitted pairs of joint uses of classes.

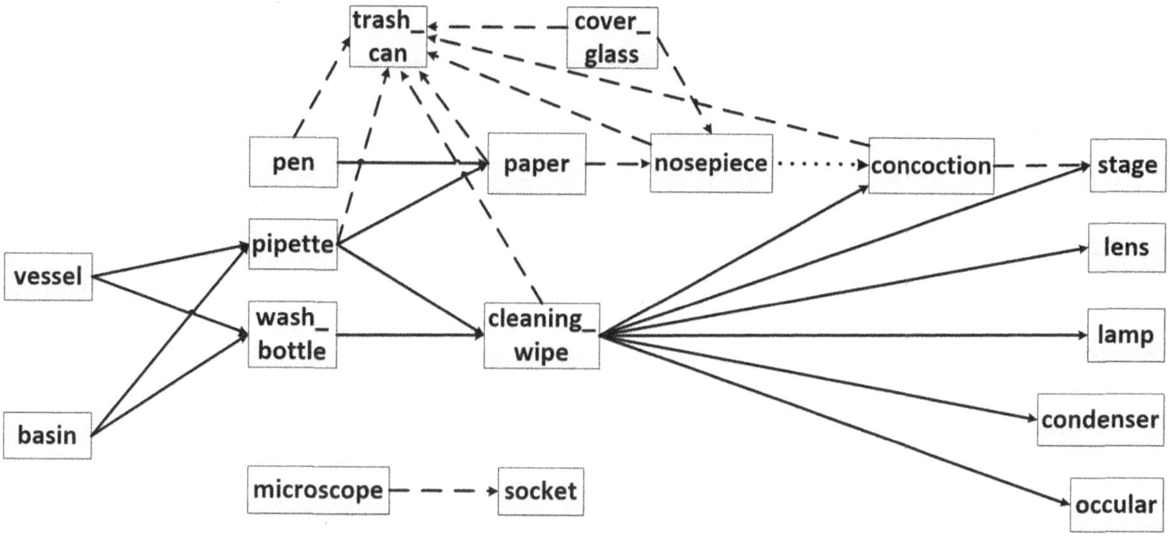

each one of which coincide with those steps while the lighter dashed arrows represents the transitions which get the user one step back.

As one easily notices, Figure 6's STD is *high level* compared to the STDs encountered before. Although the states are named after the most crucial actions that lead to them, they take the state of more than one features of more than one entities into consideration; for example, considering the *condenser_lifted* state, not only has it got the *condenser* instance's *height* feature set to its maximum value but it also "remembers" the values of all other instances' features that were assigned through the previous transitions, like the *microscope*'s instance *connected_to* feature having the value of the *socket* instance to which it was plugged in through the *connect_microscope_to_socket* transition.

Another thing that needs to be taken into account is that despite the first two transitions, *connect_microscope_to_socket* and *turn_on_light,* require one single use action each in order to be accomplished (joint use of *microscope* and *socket* instances and singular use of *light_switch* instance respectively), the rest of transitions require more than one user actions; for example, *configure_voltage* requires several elementary rotation of the corresponding *light_intensitiy_knob* instance until the right voltage is achieved while *test_coarse_focus_knob* (similarly *test_fine_focus_knob*) requires at least one singular left rotation and one right of the corresponding *coarse_focus_knob* instance (respectively *fine_focus_knob*).

Implementation

Onlabs was implemented using two approaches. The first implementation was made using the Prolog programming language (so it was text-based), for testing purposes, in which the user acted by typing their commands in the language's listener, while the second one was using the Hive3D game engine and consisted of a 3D realistic adventure game, in which the agents interacts with their environment in a game-like fashion by using the keyboard and the mouse.

Figure 7. Ego class's state feature's STD.

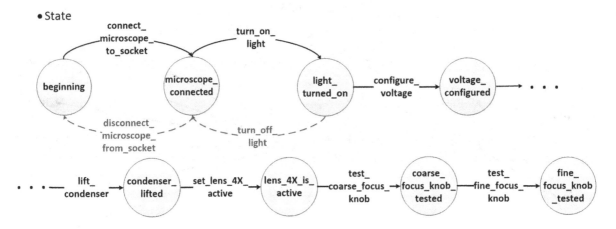

Text-Based Kernel

Unlike the imperative programming languages like C++ and Java, Prolog is a declarative one, meaning that the programmer has to type *facts* and *rules* instead of explicit commands and call them each time through *queries* in the listener ("?-"), and previous work suggested it was suitable for simulating the design of our virtual lab (Zafeiropoulos, 2008). The Prolog version employed for our application was SWI-Prolog, but it was also extended in an object-oriented fashion with the use of the "Object-Oriented Programming" extension[1].

In the Prolog environment, the user performs their actions in form of queries in the listener like *?-use(pen_1).*, *?-look(stage).*, etc., and in return they get informed in form of text messages about the outcome of their actions in terms of state changes concerning the features of the various entities (including themselves as the *trainee* instance).

In our Prolog implementation, features are represented by facts while actions are simulated by rules. For example, the fact *tidiness(dirty)* for an instance of concoction class represents that its tidiness feature is at dirty state while the *look(microscope_1)* rule represents the *look* action on *microscope_1* instance of *microscope* class. Furthermore, an (Initial State, Action, Final State) triplet is simply represented by a three-argument predicate containing each one of those in that specific order, e.g. the predicate *tidiness_order(dirty,clear,clean)* corresponds to the 'dirty-clear-clean' transition of the tidiness feature of any instance of *concoction* class.

Each change taking place in any object's feature provides the ego instance with feedback which in turn may cause the ego instance change its state feature, too.

Apparently, such an ontological design unleashes its full potential when implemented as a 3D graphics-based game under a high-end 3D Game Engine.

3D Game Application

The Onlabs 3D game was deployed and implemented under Hive3D game engine; Hive3D is a high-end 3D game engine developed by Eyelead[2].

Figure 8. Graphical design of the biology laboratory at the Hellenic Open University.

Figure 9. Graphical design of the biology laboratory's microscope and equipment at the Hellenic Open University.

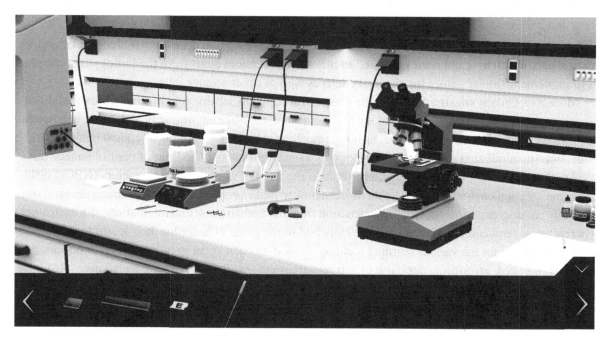

The game resembles a modern 3D Adventure Game in which the user navigates using the arrow keys and performs on the various objects all the permitted actions discussed before (*look*, *rotate*, *singularly_use* and *jointly_use*) by using the mouse.

Figures 8 and 9 illustrate two descriptive screenshots of the game.

Evaluation

The 3D Game Application was initially evaluated during August, 2013 by 19 biology students, aged from 35 to 50; all of them consisted of the same class, that is, they were all conducting their activities in the lab, both simultaneously and in private.

We adopted a qualitative research approach for our evaluation. The qualitative approach in regard of the data collection and the elaboration of the results were considered to be the most appropriate as it focuses on the attitudes and the beliefs of the research subject themselves (Yin, 2011). For the collection of the qualitative research data, the focus groups technique was selected (Vanderstoep & Johnston, 2008).

The evaluation as well as the discussion that followed revolved around a set of questions-statements, in which the participants were supposed to state their view or their answer. The questions for this purpose were picked out from System Usability Questionnaire (SUS) for systems engineering (Brooke, 1996).

The results of the evaluation process were positive; all students found the application easy to use and were acquainted with it immediately while two of them managed to carry out the required tasks to complete the game before they were even suggested how to do that; those who had already read the laboratory manual did not face any difficulty at all in playing the game but those who had not read it, only a few minutes of illustration were necessary in order for them to handle the application successfully; all students concluded that the game is a helpful tool for learning how to use the biology lab equipment and four of them asked if there was a website to download it from in order to use it at home as well.

FUTURE RESEARCH DIRECTIONS

In future research terms, Onlabs 3D game is first of all going to expand in order to include all laboratory instruments which have not been simulated in this current version; apart from the biology lab, our plan is to implement similar games for chemistry labs as well as other science labs.

Moreover, Onlabs's design principles are generalizable for any lab domain; in other words, Onlabs can be adjusted to simulate any procedure taking place in a laboratory-like environment and therefore be useful for various purposes such as vocational training (machinery handling, cooking, etc.) and manufacturing education (manipulation of industrial components, configuration and handling of control panels, etc.).

Another goal is to introduce computer agents in the form of non-playable characters (NPCs) inside the game's virtual environment and let them learn how to make proper use of the lab equipment and successfully conduct experiments, both by instruction from the human agent and interaction with each other. Thereafter, several computer agents will be launched in the game in order for their learning interaction to be studied and for the various learning techniques used by each agent to be compared to one another in terms of speed, error-proneness, use of lab resources etc., while the learning agents may also have to compete against one another for resources. This will also allow us to study more complex situations, since multiple agents will each time occupy a specific place in the lab conducting experiments thereby not allowing other agents to come close and, thus, compromising the initial assumption of the ability to have a full observation of the environment.

CONCLUSION

Our work so far has been two-fold; the conceptual design of the virtual lab and the implementation of it in a text-based kernel under Prolog and in a 3D Game under Hive3D.

Considering the design, we have complied with the discrete and deterministic nature of the laboratory environment and upon that, we have used ontologies to describe the various entities in it and their features as well as State-Transition Diagrams for the representation of the changes in the latter's states.

Considering the implementation, we have used Prolog for the text-based kernel, as its declarative programming nature perfectly suits the discrete environment and our design approach, while the 3D graphics-based game application has been developed under Hive3D Game Engine. The latter was evaluated by a class of 19 biology students as a user-friendly and very helpful learning tool.

A demo version of Onlabs can be downloaded from its site[3] and installed on a computer with minimum suggested requirements being Windows Vista (and subsequent editions) and 1GB RAM.

REFERENCES

Allen, R. (2010, August 10). *The Physics of Angry Birds*. WIRED. Retrieved from: http://www.wired.com/2010/10/physics-of-angry-birds/

Amir, E., & Doyle, P. (2002). *Adventure Games: A Challenge for Cognitive Robotics (Publication)*. American Association for Artificial Intelligence.

Annetta, L. A., Cheng, M., & Holmes, S. (2010). Assessing twenty-first century skills through a teacher created video game for high school biology students. *Research in Science & Technological Education, 28*(2), 101–114. doi:10.1080/02635141003748358

Ashdown, J. (2010, November 11). *This is Minecraft*. IGN. Retrieved from: http://www.ign.com/articles/2010/11/11/this-is-minecraft

Brooke, J. (1996). SUS: a "quick and dirty" usability scale. In *P. W. Jordan, B. Thomas, B. A. Weerdmeester, & A. L. McClelland (Eds.), Usability Evaluation in Industry*. London, UK: Taylor and Francis.

Carson, S., Miller, H., & Witherow, D. S. (2012). *Molecular Biology Techniques: A Classroom Laboratory Manual*. San Diego, CA: Elsevier Science.

Biosecurity Challenges of the Global Expansion of High-Containment Biological Laboratories. (2011). Committee on Anticipating Biosecurity Challenges of the Global Expansion of High-Containment Biological Laboratories. Washington, DC: National Academies Press (US).

De Freitas, S. (2008). *Serious Virtual Worlds – A scoping study*. JISC.

Furr, A. K. (2000). *CRC Handbook of Laboratory Safety* (5th ed.). Boca Raton, FL: CRC Press. doi:10.1201/9781420038460

Interactive Physics (n. d.). Retrieved from: http://www.design-simulation.com/IP/

Korakakis, G., Pavlatou, E. A., Palyvos, J. A., & Spyrellis, N. (2009). *3D visualization types in multimedia applications for science learning: A case for 8th grade students in Greece* (Publication). *Computers & Education*. doi:10.1016/j.compedu.2008.09.011

Kotey, S. (2013). *Launching Science Laboratories into the 21st Century: Labster* (2013). AvatarGeneration. Retrieved from: http://www.avatargeneration.com/2013/10/launching-science-laboratories-into-the-21st-century-labster/

Lee, A., & Berge, Z. L. (2011). *Second Life in Healthcare Education: Virtual Environment's Potential to Improve Patient Safety* (Publication). Knowledge Management & E-Learning. *International Journal (Toronto, Ont.)*, *3*(1).

Microsoft Flight Simulator (n. d.). Retrieved from: http://www.microsoft.com/Products/Games/FSInsider/

Miller, H., Witherow, D. S., & Carson, S. (2011). *Oxford Handbook of Clinical and Laboratory Investigation* (3rd ed.). New York, NY: Oxford University Press (USA).

Playseat Redbull Racing F1 (n. d.). Retrieved from: http://www.playseat.com/en/playseat-rbr-1-seat

Poole, D. L., & Mackworth, A. K. (2010). *Artificial Intelligence - Foundations of Computational Agents*. New York, NY: Cambridge University Press. doi:10.1017/CBO9780511794797

Russell, S., & Norvig, P. (2007). *Artificial Intelligence - A modern Approach* (2nd ed.). Upper Saddle River, NJ: Prentice Hall.

Shegog, R., Lazarus, M., M., Murray, N., G., Diamond, P., M., Sessions, N., & Zsigmond, E. (2011). *Virtual Transgenics: Using a Molecular Biology Simulation to Impact Student Academic Achievment and Attitudes*. Springer Science+Business Media.

Spillman, R. (2011, December 6). *Inside the geeky, revolutionary world of "Minecraft"*. SALON. Retrieved from: http://www.salon.com/2011/12/06/inside_the_geeky_revolutionary_world_of_minecraft/

Vanderstoep, S., & Johnston, D. (2008). *Research Methods for Everyday Life: Blending Qualitative and Quantitative Approaches*. San Francisco, CA: John Wiley & Sons.

Yin, R. (2011). *Qualitative research from start to finish*. New York, NY: The Guilford Press.

Yourdon, E. (1989). *Modern Structured Analysis*. Upper Saddle River, NJ: Yourdon Press.

Zafeiropoulos, V. (2008). *Adventure Game Implementation under the Prolog Programming Language*. Master Thesis. Mälardalen University.

KEY TERMS AND DEFINITIONS

Adventure Game: A computer game in which the player assumes the role of protagonist in an interactive story driven by exploration and puzzle-solving.

Biology Laboratory: A place equipped to conduct biological experiments, tests, investigations.

Distance Education: A mode of delivering education and instruction, often on an individual basis, to students who are not physically present in a traditional setting such as a classroom.

Game Programming: The software development of video games. It is a subset of game development.

Logic Programming: A kind of programming based on formal logic.

Ontology: A form of representation knowledge within a domain. It provides a common vocabulary to denote the types, properties and interrelationships of concepts in a domain.

Serious Game: A game designed for a primary purpose other than pure entertainment.

State-Transition Diagram: A diagram used to describe the behavior of a system in terms of all its possible states and the transitions between them.

Virtual World: A 3D computer environment in which users interact through avatars in real time with other users.

ENDNOTES

[1]   Developed by Mario Di Nuzzo.
[2]   Computer Games Company in Athens, Greece.
[3]   Onlabs @ Hellenic Open University: https://sites.google.com/site/onlabseap/

Chapter 12
Visualization of Neuro–Fuzzy Networks Training Algorithms:
The Backpropagation Algorithm Approach

Antonia Plerou
Ionian University, Greece

Elena Vlamou
Democritus University of Thrace, Greece

Basil Papadopoulos
Democritus University of Thrace, Greece

ABSTRACT

The fusion of Artificial Neural Networks and Fuzzy Logic Systems allows researchers to model real world problems through the development of intelligent and adaptive systems. Artificial Neural networks are able to adapt and learn by adjusting the interconnections between layers while fuzzy logic inference systems provide a computing framework based on the concept of fuzzy set theory, fuzzy if-then rules, and fuzzy reasoning. The combined use of those adaptive structures is known as "Neuro-Fuzzy" systems. In this chapter, the basic elements of both approaches are analyzed while neuro-fuzzy networks learning algorithms are presented. Here, we combine the use of neuro-fuzzy algorithms with multimedia-based signals for training. Ultimately this process may be employed for automatic identification of patterns introduced in medical applications and more specifically for analysis of content produced by brain imaging processes.

INTRODUCTION

This chapter focuses on artificial and fuzzy artificial networks structures and applications. Several structures of artificial neural networks are evaluated as well as methods in which those system and fuzzy logic techniques could be combined in order to enhance pattern recognition efficiency. This study focuses on the power of visualization and efficiency of several training algorithms in order to minimize the typi-

DOI: 10.4018/978-1-4666-8659-5.ch012

cal network performance errors and enhance the network's efficiency. We focus on the performance of generalized Multi-Layer Perception architectures trained with the Backpropagation algorithm using various different activation functions for the neurons of hidden and output layers. For the visualization of neuro-fuzzy networks performance, different variants of sigmoid activations functions such as Bi-polar and Uni-polar sigmoid were simulated using Matlab within the frame of fuzzy logic. Simulation outcomes demonstrate the efficiency of neuro-fuzzy networks, the importance of visualization and the wide applicability of experimental multimedia methods in the process that enables interactive features such as action-response events (Tsiridou, Zannos, & Strapatsakis, 2011) (Timmerer, Waltl, Rainer, & Hellwagner, 2012) (Weyns, Malek, & Andersson, 2012) (Deliyannis, 2013) that can help enhance further the simulation process.

Cognitive Science and Biological Neural Networks

The structural differences between the human brain and the computer do not prevent the attempt to substitute some cognitive functions of the brain by a computer system. Under this perspective the branch of computer science which deals with the design and the implementation of systems that simulate human intelligence, logical thinking and behavior known as artificial intelligence may be employed for the task in hand (O'Regan & Noë, 2001). Interdisciplinary issues that are addressed within this research include the representation of knowledge and the adaptation of semantic descriptions.

The idea that the human mind is a computer whose operation is perceived via a process of reverse engineer returned to the forefront of cognitive science a number of issues that relate with evolutionary theory and natural evolution of the mind. According to the evolutionary theory, living species does not remain unaffected over time (Matthen & Stephens, 2007). Brain functions have changed over time under a series of adaptive changes. Several psychologists and cognitive scientists suggest that this approach renders the reverse approach as a strong candidate, allowing to study the human brain structure (Ivancevic & Ivancevic, 2007). Computer simulation may be employed to examine the cognitive function processes. Cognitive processes simulation is related to the perception and the analysis of brain process under mental or cognitive function. The simulation program uses a computational model that consists of a series mathematical equations or algorithms. Such systems are inspired by the biological neural networks are the artificial neural networks (Kowaliw, Bredeche, Chevallier, & Doursat, 2014). Artificial neural networks provide an alternative model, which is inspired, by biological models. Here, calculations are conducted massively and in parallel. A neuron is the smallest part of the brain that processes information and is identified as the basic difference between animals and plants (plants do not have neurons). There are approximately 10 billion neurons and 60 trillion connections in the cortex of the brain. A biological neuron consists of three main sections, which is the body, the axis, and dendrites. The dendrites, receive signals from neighboring neurons. These signals are electrical pulses that spread between the axis of the neuron transmitter and receiver dendrites of the neuron with the help of chemical processes. The point of a chemical process where the axis of a neuron transmits a signal to the dendrites of the next is called the conclusion. Then the body accumulates incoming signals where several brands have been sending the processed signal to adjacent neurons through the shaft. Thus, each neuron receives many signals as input and after processing only one spreading all the neurons with which it is linked (Levine et al., 2014).

Figure 1. Biological and Artificial Network Simulation

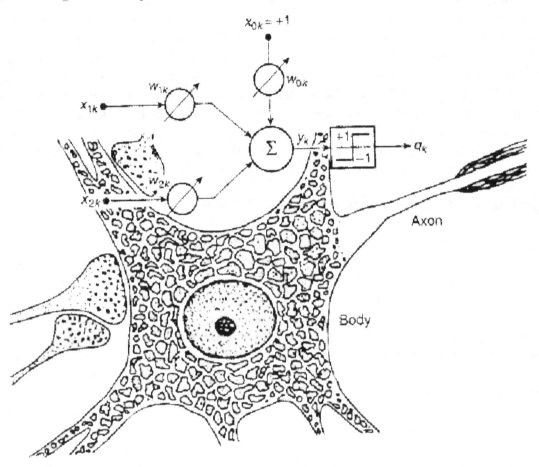

Artificial Neural Networks

Artificial neural networks approach the function of the human brain and perform calculations on a massively parallel way (Kalogirou, 2001). The artificial neural network is a computing model inspired by the way that the biological nervous systems process information functions. Artificial neural networks are comprised of a large number of associated processing units called neurons (PUs) which are linked and activated simultaneously while they are structured in layers. All PUs are composed by several input gates, but there is only one output gate which in turn provide the signal as a new input gate to other PUs. The PUs synapse significance varies and is related with the weight designated for each PU connection. The response of each neuron is specified according to activation function which controls the neural networks output result in relation to the inputs and the weight factor (Yegnarayana, 1994).

McCulloch and Pits described the first Neural Network model and Rosenblatt (Perceptron) and Widrow (Adaline) developed the first training algorithm. The main characteristic of neural networks is that they can learn with the use of examples (training vectors, input and output samples of the system). The neural network modifies its internal structure and the weights of the connections between neurons by adjusting the error in relevance to the expected output (Vieira, Dias, & Mota, 2004).

Figure 2. The model of an Artificial Neuron

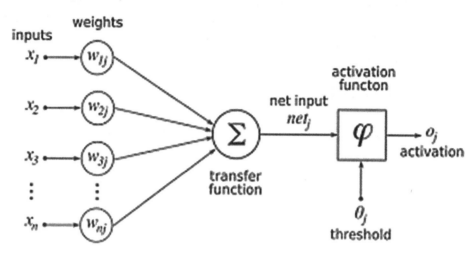

In order to use a network, a training process is a prerequisite. The learning procedure includes changes in synaptic links (weights) contained between neurons. A specific part of education is the process of determining the appropriate weight factor which is achieved with the use of appropriate training algorithms. After this procedure, the artificial neural network has acquired empirical knowledge and is capable to perform further calculations. The role of learning factors can be interpreted as a store of knowledge, providing the system with the help of examples of this is true in biological neural networks (Plerou, 2012). In this way, the neural networks learn from their environment, or, in other words, the physical model that provides the data. In summary, we conclude the following definition in accordance with Aleksander and Morton (1990) (Patan, 2008). Artificial neural networks resemble the brain in two aspects:

1. The knowledge is obtained through a training process.
2. The knowledge storage is acquired through neuron synaptic changes (Jansen, 2002).

Artificial Neuron Network Model

A neuron is the fundamental unit of information processing of a neural network.

The main features neural network model is:

1. A set of synapses characterized of adaptive weights. Specifically, a signal x_j considered as an input and is multiplied with the synaptic weight w_{kj}. The first refers to the neuron and, therefore, the second entry in the award where the weight. The weight w_{kj} is positive if the conclusion is a stimulant that induces neurons to respond to stimulation and negative if the conclusion is that prohibition prevents ton neuron to produce a response.
2. A summing node where input signals multiplied with their weights is added. Such a system is known as the adaptive linear combiner u_k.

3. An activation function φ to fire the neuron and provide the output. The model includes an externally applied bias or else threshold th_k, which effects on decreasing the applied input activation function below. Instead, the input of the network can be increased by using a bias term, which is opposed by the polarization (Yegnarayana, 1994).

In mathematical terms, a *k* neuron is described by the following equations:

$$u_k = \sum_{j=1}^{p} w_{kj} \, x_j$$

and

$$y_k = Æ(u_k - ,_k)$$

where:

x_j: Input signals
w_{kj}: Synaptic weights
u_k: Linear output
k: Polarization
φ: Neuron activation function
y_k: Neuron output (Jansen, 2002).

Artificial Neural Networks Architectures

The way in which neurons are structured in an Artificial Neural Networks is closely related to the algorithm used for training the network. Generally there are four different classes of network architectures.

Single Layer Feedforward Networks

The most simplified neural network is the single layer neural network. In this case, the network consists of an input layer with nodes displayed in a layer of output neurons. This network is strictly a forward fed system and consists of a single layer of output nodes; the inputs are fed directly to the outputs via a series of weights(State, Cocianu, Stefanescu, & Vlamos, 2004). The sum of the products of the weights and the inputs is calculated in each node, and if the computed value is above some threshold (typically 0) the neuron fires and takes the activated value (typically 1); otherwise it takes the deactivated value (typically -1).This perceptron is activated under the step activation function (Sanger, 1989).

Multilayer Feedforward Networks

A multilayer feed-forward network differs from a single layer feed-forward network because it structured by one or more hidden layers, whose neurons are called hidden neurons. The role of hidden neurons is

Figure 3. Multilayered Feedforward Network

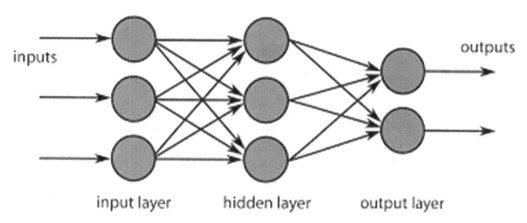

to receive and transfer input signals to the next layer. By adding the signal of one or more layers, the neural network is ready to approximate more complex functions. The output signals of neurons of the second layer are used as input signals to the third layer and so on (Hornik, 1991). Each neuron in the hidden layer is connected to a local set of input nodes that are close to him. This set is called the local Receptive field of the neuron. Similarly, each neuron in the output layer is connected with a local set of neurons in the hidden layer. A multilayer Feedforward network with hidden layers is presented in Figure 3.

In figure 4 a multilayer feed-forward network with a hidden layer is presented. This network mode is mentioned as 10-4-2 because the network has 10 inputs, 4 neurons in the hidden layer and 2 neurons in output layer. Generally a system with p input nodes, h_1 neurons in first hidden layer, h_2 neurons in the second hidden layer, etc. h_n neurons in the n-th hidden layer and q neurons in the output layer is referred as a p-h_1 - h_2 - ... - h_n - q network.

The above presented neural network is fully connected, in the sense that each node in each layer of the network is connected to each node of the next layer of the network. In any other case, the network is partially connected (Hornik, Stinchcombe, & White, 1990).

Recurrent Neural Networks

A recursive neural network differs from a Feedforward powered network because it contains at least one feedback loop (Cao & Wang, 2005). This means that at least one neuron's output signal affects the signal that comes again as an input to the neuron as it presented in Figure 5. For example, a recursive neural network may consist of a single layer of neurons where each neuron returns the output as input to all other neurons of the layer. Another mode of recursive neural networks with hidden neurons known as retrospective modes of synapses as shown in Figure 6, starting from both the hidden neurons and the output neurons (Guler, Ubeyli, & Guler, 2005). The use of such loops significantly affect the networks performance.

Figure 4. Multilayer Feedforward Network with a Hidden Layer (10-4-2 topology)

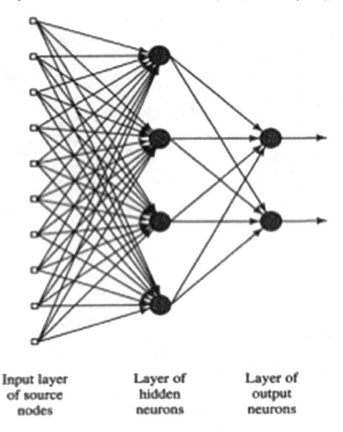

Input layer
of source
nodes

Layer of
hidden
neurons

Layer of
output
neurons

Figure 5. Loop on Recursive Neural Network

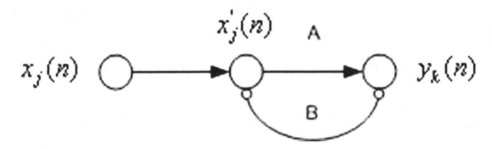

Lattice Structures

This network consists of one, two or multidimensional array of neurons with a corresponding set of input nodes that provide input signals to the table. The dimension of the grid refers to the number of dimensions of space within which the grid. A linear grid with three input nodes is presented in Figure 7. Note that each node entry is connected with each neuron in the grid. Practically, a lattice network is a forward fed network and its neurons are placed in rows and columns (Vaidyanathan & Hoang, 1988).

Figure 6. Hidden Layer of Fully Connected Recurrent Nodes

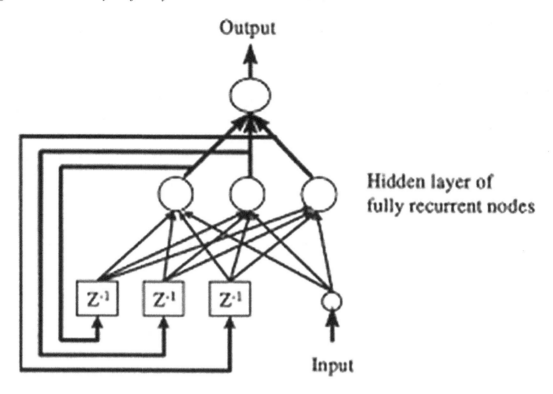

Activation Functions

The most important unit in neural network structure is their net inputs by using a scalar-to-scalar function called "the activation function or threshold function or transfer function", output a result value called the "unit's activation". An activation function for limiting the amplitude of the output of a neuron. The activation functions used in this paper in order control visually artificial network learning algorithms efficiency are Uni-Polar Sigmoid and Bipolar Sigmoid Function. The activation function of Uni-polar sigmoid function is given as follows:

$$y(v_i) = \frac{1}{1 + e^{-v_i}}$$

This function is especially advantageous to use in neural networks trained by Backpropagation algorithms. Because it is easy to distinguish, and this can interestingly minimize the computation capacity for training. The term sigmoid means 'S-shaped', and logistic form of the sigmoid maps.

Figure 7. Multi-dimensional grid

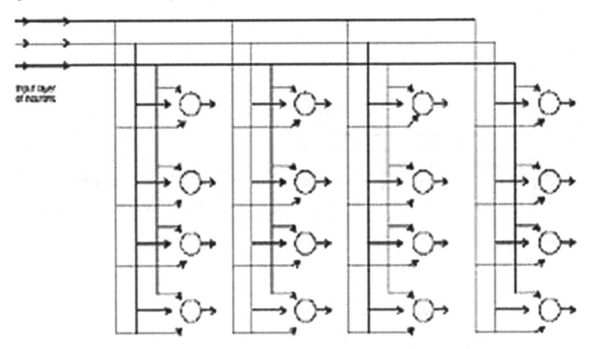

Figure 8. Uni-Polar Sigmoid Function

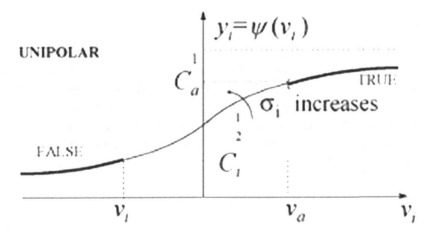

Activation function of Bi-polar sigmoid function is:

$$y(v_i) = \frac{1 + e^{v_i}}{1 + e^{-v_i}}$$

This function is similar to the sigmoid function. For this type of activation function described in the following figure, it goes well for applications that produce output values in the range of [-1, 1] (Karlik & Olgac, 2011).

Figure 9. Bi-Polar Sigmoid Function

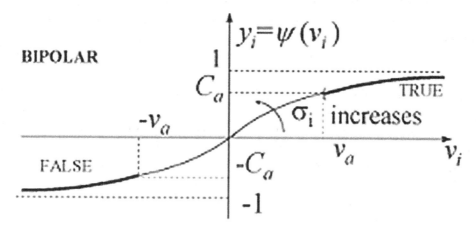

Fuzzy Logic

Fuzzy logic provides an inference morphology that enables approximate human reasoning capabilities to be applied to knowledge-based systems. The theory of fuzzy logic provides a mathematical strength to capture the uncertainties associated with human cognitive processes, such as thinking and reasoning. The conventional approaches to knowledge representation lack the means for representation of fuzzy concepts.

As a consequence, the approaches based on first-order logic and classical probability theory do not provide an appropriate conceptual framework for dealing with the representation of commonsense knowledge, since such knowledge is by its nature both lexically imprecise and non-categorical (Fuller, 2000).

The fuzzy logic is an approach to computing based on "degrees of truth" rather than the usual "true or false" (1 or 0) Boolean logic on which the modern computer is based. The idea of fuzzy logic was first advanced by Dr. Lotfi Zadeh of the University of California at Berkeley in the 1960s. Dr. Zadeh was focused on the problem of computer perceiving of natural language. Natural language is not easily translated into the absolute terms of 0 and 1. Fuzzy logic includes 0 and 1 as extreme cases of truth but also includes the various states of truth in between so that (Sharma & Badri, 2013).

Fuzzy logic seems closer to the way our brains work. We ensemble data and form a number of partial truths which we aggregate further into higher truths which in turn when certain thresholds are exceeded, cause certain further results such as motor reaction. A similar kind of process is used in artificial computer neural networks and expert systems. It may help to perceive fuzzy logic as the way reasoning really works and binary or Boolean logic is simply a special case of it (Vieira et al., 2004).

The fuzzy logic is a form of many-valued logic which deals with reasoning that is approximate rather than fixed and exact. Compared to traditional binary sets (where variables may take on true or false values), fuzzy logic variables may have a truth value that ranges in degree between 0 and 1. Fuzzy logic has been extended to handle the concept of partial truth, where the truth value may range between completely true and completely false (Mahadev & Kulkarni, 2013). Fuzzy systems propose a mathematic calculus to translate the subjective human knowledge of the real processes. The term "fuzzy logic" was introduced with the 1965 proposal of fuzzy set theory by Lotfi A. Zadeh (Dubois, Ostasiewicz, & Prade, 2000). Fuzzy logic has been applied to many fields, from control theory to artificial intelligence. Fuzzy logic had, however, been studied since the 1920s, as infinite-valued logic—notably by Łukasiewicz and Tarski (Ryan, 2014). Namely a fuzzy system advantage are:

1. The capacity to represent inherent uncertainties of the human knowledge with linguistic variables.
2. A simple interaction of the expert of the domain with the engineering designer of the system.
3. An easy interpretation of the results, because of the natural rules representation.
4. An easy extension of the base of knowledge through the addition of new rules;
5. Robustness in a relation of the possible disturbances in the system (Vieira et al., 2004).

A brief overview of fuzzy logic, introducing the concepts of fuzzy sets, fuzzy logic inference, and fuzzy control system is provided.

Fuzzy Sets

A fuzzy set is represented by a membership function defined on the universe of discourse. The universe of discourse is the space where the fuzzy variables are defined. The membership function gives the grade, or degree, of membership within the set, of any element of the universe of discourse (Zhang, 2008). The membership function maps the elements of the universe onto numerical values in the interval [0, 1]. A membership function value of zero implies that the corresponding element is definitely not an element of the fuzzy set, while a value of unity means that the element fully belongs to the set. A grade of membership in between corresponds to the fuzzy membership to set (Baldo & Zorzi, 2008).

The traditional set theory has a crisp concept of membership: an element either belongs to a set or it does not. In Fuzzy Logic, the term crisp is used to indicate variables having exact values, as opposite to the term fuzzy which indicates a qualitative rather than quantitative method of representation. Fuzzy Set Theory differs from traditional set theory in that partial membership is allowed, i.e., an element can belong to a set only to a certain degree. This degree of membership is commonly referred to as the membership value and is represented using a real value in [0; 1], where 0 and 1 correspond to full non-membership and membership, respectively (Baldo & Zorzi, 2008).

Formally, a set S is said to be crisp, if and only if given an element $x \in U$, wherein U is called the universe of discourse, we either have $x \in S$ or x S. For fuzzy logic sets, this no longer true. Every element $x \in U$ belongs to a fuzzy set but only to some degree. A set S becomes fuzzy, if it is paired with a function $\mu S: U \to [0, 1]$ called its membership function that, given an element $x \in U$, defines its membership degree to S. A pair $(x, \mu S(x))$ is called a singleton and so each fuzzy set can be considered as the crisp set defined as the union of all singletons $(x, \mu S(x))$, for all $x \in U$. Note that the definition of fuzzy sets subsumes that of crisp ones as we can always write the membership function of the latter as in (1.1) $\mu S \to \{0, 1\}$ $\mu S(x) = 1$, if $x \in S$ 0, if x S There many example of crisp vs. fuzzy sets in the literature (Zhang, 2008).

Fuzzy Logic Inference

Fuzzy inference systems (FIS) are widely used for process simulation or control. They can be designed either from expert knowledge or from data. For complex systems, FIS based on expert knowledge only may suffer from a loss of accuracy. This is the main incentive for using fuzzy rules inferred from data. Designing a FIS from data can be decomposed into two main phases: automatic rule generation and system optimization. Rule generation leads to a basic system with a given space partitioning and the corresponding set of rules. System optimization can be done at various levels. Variable selection can be an overall selection or it can be managed rule by rule. Rule base optimization aims to select the most useful rules and to optimize rule conclusions. Space partitioning can be improved by adding or removing fuzzy sets and by tuning membership function parameters. Structure optimization is of a major importance: selecting variables, reducing the rule base and optimizing the number of fuzzy sets (Guillaume, 2001).

The fuzzy inference mechanism consists of three stages: in the first stage, the values of the numerical inputs are mapped by a function according to a degree of compatibility of the respective fuzzy sets, this operation can be called fuzzification. In the second stage, the fuzzy system processes the rules in accordance with the firing strengths of the inputs. In the third stage, the resultant fuzzy values are transformed again into numerical values; this operation can be called defuzzification. Essentially, this procedure makes possible the use fuzzy categories in representation of words and abstracts ideas of the human beings in the description of the decision taking procedure (Viharos & Kis, 2014).

- Fuzzifier: Translates crisp inputs into fuzzy values
- Inference engine: Applies reasoning to compute fuzzy outputs
- Defuzzifier: Translates fuzzy outputs into crisp values
- Knowledge base: Defines rules and membership functions

Fuzzification is the process of decomposing a system input and/or output into one or more fuzzy sets. Many types of curves can be used, but triangular or trapezoidal shaped membership functions are the

Figure 10. Fuzzy Inference System

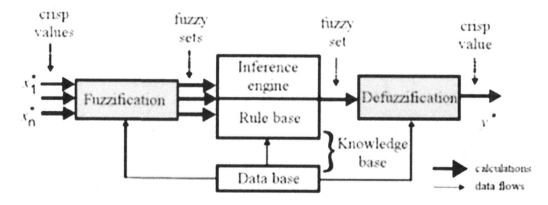

most common because they are easier to represent in embedded controllers. Figure 11 presents a system of fuzzy sets for an input with trapezoidal and triangular membership functions. Each fuzzy set spans a region of input (or output) value graphed with the membership. Any particular input is interpreted from this fuzzy set and a degree of membership is interpreted. The membership functions should overlap to allow smooth mapping of the system. The process of fuzzification allows the system inputs and outputs to be expressed in linguistic terms so that rules can be applied in a simple manner to express a complex system.

Suppose a simplified implementation for an air-conditioning system with a temperature sensor. The temperature might be acquired by a microprocessor which has a fuzzy algorithm to process an output to continuously control the speed of a motor which keeps the room in a "good temperature," it also can direct a vent upward or downward as necessary. The figure illustrates the process of fuzzification of the air temperature. There are five fuzzy sets for temperature: COLD, COOL, NOMINAL, WARM, and HOT.

After fuzzy reasoning, we have a linguistic output variable which needs to be translated into a crisp value. The objective is to derive a single crisp numeric value that best represents the inferred fuzzy values of the linguistic output variable. Defuzzification is such inverse transformation which maps the output from the fuzzy domain back into the crisp domain. Some defuzzification methods tend to produce an integral output considering all the elements of the resulting fuzzy set with the corresponding weights. Other methods take into account just the elements corresponding to the maximum points of the resulting membership functions. The following defuzzification methods are of practical importance / Center-of-Area (C-o-A). The C-o-A method is often referred to as the Center-of-Gravity method because it computes the centroid of the composite area representing the output fuzzy term. Center-of-Maximum

Figure 11. Fuzzy sets defining temperature

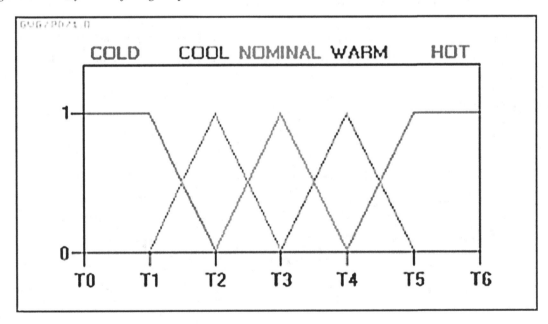

Figure 12. Fuzzy Controller Block Diagram

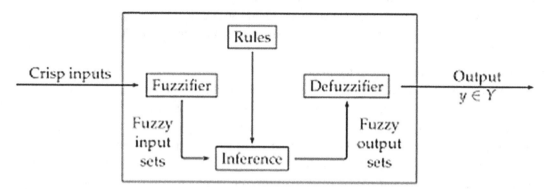

(C-o-M). In the C-o-M method only the peaks of the membership functions is used. The defuzzified crisp compromise value is determined by finding the place where the weights are balanced. Thus, the areas of the membership functions play no role and only the maxima (singleton memberships) are used. The crisp output is computed as a weighted mean of the term membership maxima, weighted by the inference results. Mean-of-Maximum (M-o-M). The M-o-M is used only in some cases where the C-o-M approach does not work. This occurs whenever the maxima of the membership functions are not unique and the question is as to which one of the equal choices one should take (Shaw, 1998).

Fuzzy Controllers

Most commercial fuzzy products are rule-based systems that receive current information in the feedback loop from the device as it operates and control the operation of a mechanical or another device. A fuzzy logic system has four blocks as shown in Figure 12.

Crisp input information from the device is converted into fuzzy values for each input fuzzy set with the fuzzification block. The universe of discourse of the input variables determines the required scaling for correct per-unit operation (Rashmi, Halse, & Teli, 2015).The scaling is very important because the fuzzy system can be retrofitted with other devices or ranges of operation by just changing the scaling of the input and output. The decision-making-logic determines how the fuzzy logic operations are performed (Sup-Min inference), and together with the knowledge base determine the outputs of each fuzzy IF-THEN rules. Those are combined and converted to crispy values with the defuzzification block. The output crisp value can be calculated by the center of gravity or the weighted average (Simões & Farret, 2014).

In order to process the input to get the output reasoning there are six steps involved in the creation of a rule-based fuzzy system:

1. Identify the inputs and their ranges and name them.
2. Identify the outputs and their ranges and name them.
3. Create the degree of fuzzy membership function for each input and output.

4. Construct the rule base that the system will operate under.
5. Decide how the action will be executed by assigning strengths to the rules.
6. Combine the rules and defuzzify the output (Sumathi & Paneerselvam, 2010).

In contrast to conventional control techniques, fuzzy logic control (FLC) is best utilized in complex ill-defined processes that can be controlled by a skilled human operator without much knowledge of their underlying dynamics. The basic idea behind FLC is to incorporate the "expert experience" of a human operator in the design of the controller in controlling a process whose input – output relationship is described by collection of fuzzy control rules (e.g., IF-THEN rules) involving linguistic variables rather than a complicated dynamic model (Roshandeh, Puan, & Joshani, 2009). The utilization of linguistic variables, fuzzy control rules, and approximate reasoning provides a means to incorporate human expert experience in designing the controller.

Neuro-Fuzzy Networks

Since the moment that fuzzy systems become popular in industrial application, the community perceived that the development of a fuzzy system with good performance is not an easy task. The problem of finding membership functions and appropriate rules is frequently a tiring process of attempt and error. This led to the application of learning algorithms to fuzzy systems as well. The neural networks, that have efficient learning algorithms, had been presented as an alternative to automate or to support the development of tuning fuzzy system (E.Alhanafy, Fareed, & Abdou Saad El Din, 2010) .

The first studies of the neuro-fuzzy systems date of the beginning of the 90's decade, with Jang, Lin and Lee in 1991, Berenji in 1992 and Nauck from 1993, etc. The majority of the first applications were in process control. Gradually, its application spread for all the areas of the knowledge like data analysis, data classification, imperfections detection and support to decision-making, etc. Neural networks and fuzzy systems can be combined to join its advantages and to cure its individual illness. Neural networks introduce its computational characteristics of learning in the fuzzy systems and receive from them the interpretation and clarity of systems representation. Thus, the disadvantages of the fuzzy systems are compensated by the capacities of the neural networks. These techniques are complementary, which justifies its use together (Vieira et al., 2004).

Fuzzy Neural Network Description

A fuzzy neural network or neuro-fuzzy system is a learning machine that finds the parameters of a fuzzy system (i.e., fuzzy sets, fuzzy rules) by exploiting approximation techniques from neural networks. Both neural networks and fuzzy systems have some things in common. They can be used for solving a problem (e.g. pattern recognition, regression or density estimation) if there does not exist any mathematical model of the given problem (Hahn, 2013). They solely do have certain disadvantages and advantages which almost completely disappear by combining both concepts. Neural networks can only come into play if the problem is expressed by a sufficient amount of observed examples. These observations are used to train the black box. On the one hand, no prior knowledge about the problem needs to be given. On the other hand, however, it is not straightforward to extract comprehensible rules from the neural network's structure (Kumar, Aruna, & Reddy, 2011).

Figure 13. Fuzzy Neuron models

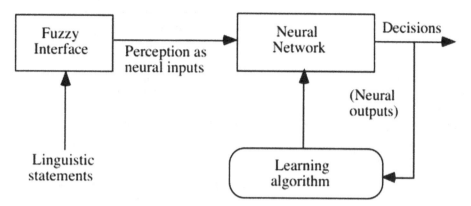

On the contrary, a fuzzy system demands linguistic rules instead of learning examples as prior knowledge. Furthermore, the input and output variables have to be described linguistically. If the knowledge is incomplete, wrong or contradictory, then the fuzzy system must be tuned. Since there is not any formal approach for it, the tuning is performed in a heuristic way. This is usually very time consuming and error-prone (Ping, Teng, Jingsheng, & Weimin, 2011).

Fuzzy Neuron Model

Neural networks are used to tune membership functions of fuzzy systems that are employed as decision-making systems for controlling equipment. Although fuzzy logic can encode expert knowledge directly using rules with linguistic labels, it usually takes a lot of time to design and tune the membership functions which quantitatively define these linguistic labels. Neural network learning techniques can automate this process and substantially reduce development time and cost while improving performance (Fuller, 2013).

Two prospective models of fuzzy neural systems are presented as follows. In response to linguistic statements, the fuzzy interface block provides an input vector to a multi-layer neural network. The neural network can be adapted (trained) to yield desired command outputs or decisions (Fuller, 2013)._

Fuzzy Neuron Structure

In theory, neural networks, and fuzzy systems are equivalent in that they are convertible, yet practically each has its own advantages and disadvantages. For neural networks, the knowledge is automatically acquired by the Backpropagation algorithm, but the learning process is relatively slow and analysis of the trained network is difficult (black box). Neither is it possible to extract structural knowledge (rules) from the trained neural network nor can we integrate special information about the problem into the neural network in order to simplify the learning procedure. Fuzzy systems are more favorable in that their behavior can be explained based on fuzzy rules and thus their performance can be adjusted by tuning the rules. But since, in general, knowledge acquisition is difficult and also the universe of discourse of each input variable needs to be divided into several intervals, applications of fuzzy systems are restricted to

Figure 14. Fuzzy Neuron models

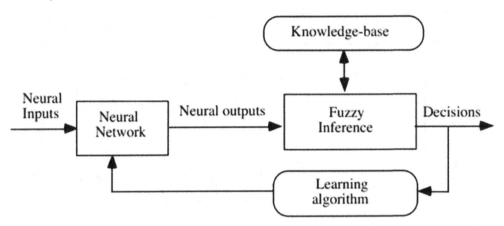

the fields where expert knowledge is available and the number of input variables is small. To overcome the problem of knowledge acquisition, neural networks are extended to automatically extract fuzzy rules from numerical data. Cooperative approaches use neural networks to optimize certain parameters of an ordinary fuzzy system, or to preprocess data and extract fuzzy (control) rules from data. Based upon the computational process involved in a fuzzy-neuro system, one may broadly classify the fuzzy neural structure as feedforward (static) and feedback (dynamic) (Fuller, 2013).

Types of Neuro-Fuzzy Systems

Cooperative Neuro-Fuzzy System

In the case of cooperative neural fuzzy systems, both artificial neural network and fuzzy system work independently from each other. The ANN tries to learn the parameters from the fuzzy system. This can be either performed offline or online while the fuzzy system is applied (Karthekeyan, 2014).

The upper left fuzzy neural network learns fuzzy set from given training data. This is usually performed by fitting membership functions with a neural network. The fuzzy sets are then determined offline. They are then utilized to form the fuzzy system by fuzzy rules that are given as well.

The upper right neuro-fuzzy system determines fuzzy rules from training data by a neural network. Here as well, the neural network learns offline before the fuzzy system is initialized. The rule learning is usually completed by clustering on self-organizing feature maps. It is also possible to apply fuzzy clustering methods to obtain rules.

In the lower left neuro-fuzzy model, the system learns all membership function parameters online, i.e. while the fuzzy system is applied. Thus, initially fuzzy rules and membership functions must be defined beforehand. Moreover, the error has to be measured in order to improve and guide the learning step.

The lower right one determines rule weights for all fuzzy rules by a neural network. This can be done online and offline. A rule weight is interpreted as the influence of a rule. They are multiplied with the rule output. In the authors argue that the semantics of rule weights are not clearly defined. They could be replaced by modified membership functions. However, this could destroy the interpretation of fuzzy sets. Moreover, identical linguistic values might be represented differently in dissimilar rules (Kruse, 2008).

Figure 15. Four different kinds of cooperative fuzzy neural networks

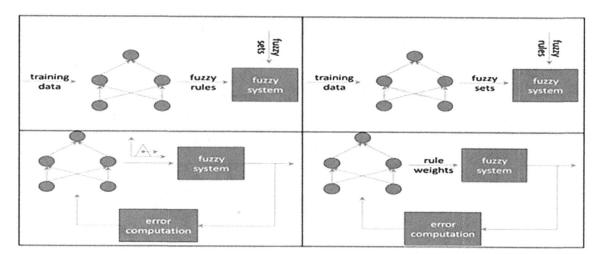

Figure 16. Cooperative Neuro-Fuzzy System Function

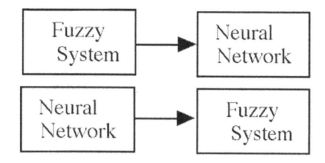

Concurrent Neuro-Fuzzy System

In a cooperative system, the neural networks are only used in an initial phase. In this case, the neural networks determine sub-blocks of the fuzzy system using training data, after this, the neural networks are removed and only the fuzzy system is executed. In the cooperative neuro-fuzzy systems, the structure is not total interpretable what can be considered a disadvantage (Vieira et al., 2004).

Hybrid Neuro-Fuzzy System

Hybrid neuro-fuzzy systems are homogeneous and usually resemble neural networks. Here, the fuzzy system is interpreted as special kind of neural network. The advantage of such hybrid NFS is its architecture since both fuzzy systems and neural network do not have to communicate anymore with each other. They are one fully fused entity. These systems can learn online and offline.

Figure 17. Concurrent Neuro-Fuzzy System

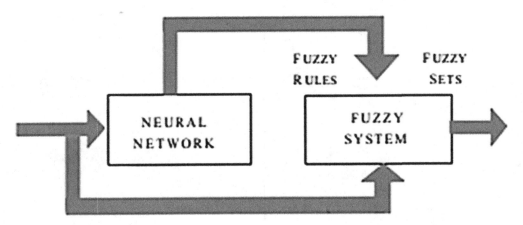

Figure 18. Hybrid Fuzzy Neural Network

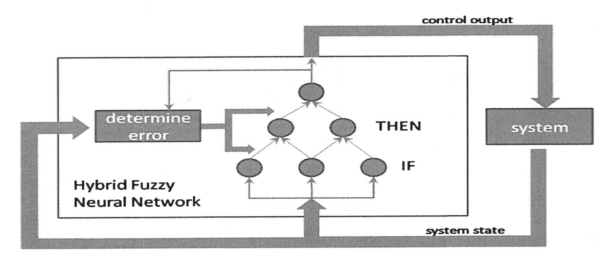

The rule base of a fuzzy system is interpreted as a neural network. Fuzzy sets can be regarded as weights whereas the input and output variables and the rules are modeled as neurons. Neurons can be included or deleted in the learning step. Finally, the neurons of the network represent the fuzzy knowledge base. Obviously, the major drawbacks of both underlying systems are thus overcome (Kruse, 2008).

In order to build a fuzzy controller, membership functions which express the linguistic terms of the inference rules have to be defined. In fuzzy set theory, there is no formal approach to define these functions. Any shape (e.g., triangular, Gaussian) can be considered as membership function with an arbitrary set of parameters. Thus, the optimization of these functions in terms of generalizing the data is very important for fuzzy systems. Neural networks can be used to solve this problem.

By fixing a distinct shape of the membership functions, say triangular, the neural network must optimize their parameters by gradient descent. Thus, aside information about the shape of the membership functions, training data must be available as well (Kruse, 2008).

Another fuzzy logic approach is to group the training data $\{(x_i,y_i)|x_i \in X, y_i \in Y, i=1,2,\ldots,l\}$ into M clusters. Every cluster represents a rule R m where $m=1,2,\ldots,M$. Hence, these rules are not defined linguistically but rather by crisp data points $x=(x_1,x_2,\ldots,x_n)$. Thus a neural network with n input units, hidden layers and M output units might be applied to train on the pre-defined clusters. For testing, an arbitrary pattern x is presented to the trained neural network. Every output unit m will retrn a degree to which extend x may fit the antecedent of rule R m.

To guarantee the characteristics of a fuzzy system, the learning algorithm must enforce the following mandatory constraints:

- Fuzzy sets must stay normal and convex.
- Fuzzy sets must not exchange their relative positions (they must not pass each other).
- Fuzzy sets must always overlap.

Additionally there are some optional constraints like the following:

- Fuzzy sets must stay symmetric.
- The membership degrees must sum up to 1 (Kruse, 2008).

Related Work

The Nauck and Kruse approach employs the fuzzy error of the Backpropagation algorithm. This is a special learning algorithm inspired by the standard BP-procedure for multivariable neural networks. An extended version was rendered able to learn fuzzy if-then rules by reducing the number of nodes in the hidden layer of the network. This network is not trained using use examples but by evaluating a fuzzy error measure. In this case, the algorithm efficiency was not visually evaluated and confirmed (Nauck & Kruse, 1993).

The Nakashima et al approach focuses in a method for generating fuzzy if-then rules from numerical data for pattern classification problems. The performance of a fuzzy classification system with the ability to adjust the membership functions is examined, in this case, where an error-correction learning method for adjusting membership functions is used. Additionally computer simulations on several real-world pattern classification problems with continuous attributes were used in order to check the performance of the proposed method. Although simulation results provided evidence that this method performed well, the performance of the fuzzy classification system using the Backpropagation algorithm approach was also not evaluated (Nozaki, Ishibuchi, & Tanaka, 1996).

The Wang and Mei approximation proposed a new scheme to generate fuzzy membership functions with unsupervised learning using self-organizing feature map. However, the proposed scheme was applied to extract directly the fuzzy membership function during the training and retrieving phases of

SOFM. Simulation results were used in order support the new scheme in relevance to member function estimation while the Backpropagation training algorithm performance evaluation was not included (Wang & Mei, 2010).

In the Raitamaki and Jyvaskyla work, a method of input space partitioning was presented. It used a quadtree structure, B-spline functions as fuzzy basis functions and a multiresolution aspect inspired by the wavelet theory. As the different scales of resolution and the corresponding basic elements are formed, a wavelet transform using those basic functions as scaling functions is applied to a data set. In this case, wavelet coefficients are used to prune the quad tree to find the final partition suitable for the problem while two example problems to evaluate this method. In this case, the evaluation of fuzzy Backpropagation training algorithm efficiency has not been included (Raitamaki, 1998).

According to Shiqian and Meng paper, architectures of dynamic fuzzy neural networks (D-FNN) implementing Takagi-Sugeno-Kang (TSK) fuzzy systems based on extended radial basis function (RBF) neural networks are proposed. Simulation studies and comprehensive comparisons with some other learning algorithms demonstrate that a more compact structure with higher performance can be achieved by the proposed approach, while this evaluation fail to evolve fuzzy Backpropagation learning algorithm performance (Wu & Er, 2000).

Pal's et al., demonstrated a way of formulating neuro-fuzzy approaches for both feature selection and extraction under unsupervised learning. A fuzzy feature evaluation index for a set of features is defined in terms of degree of similarity between two patterns in both the original and transformed feature spaces. A concept of flexible membership function incorporating weighted distance introduced for computing membership values in the transformed space. The network for feature selection results in an optimal order of individual importance of the features. The superiority of the networks trained under unsupervised learning to some related ones is established experimentally, but the case of fuzzy Backpropagation training algorithm was not included (Pal, De, & Basak, 2002).

Fuzzy Algorithms

Training Algorithms

Neuro-Fuzzy networks have 3 main modes of operation – supervised, reinforced and unsupervised learning (Cybenko, 1989). In supervised learning the output from the neuro-fuzzy network is compared with a set of targets, the error signal is used to update the weights in the neural network. Reinforced learning is similar to supervised learning regarding the cumulate reward process. Unsupervised learning updates the weights based on the input data only. The network learns to cluster different input patterns into different classes (Omondi & Ralapakse, 2006).

Training is the means by which the weights and threshold values of a neural network are adjusted to give desirable outputs, thus making the network adjust the response to the value which best fits the training data. Propagation training is a form of supervised training, where the expected output is given to the training algorithm. Propagation training can be a very effective form of training for feed-forward, simple recurrent and other types of neural networks. There are several forms of propagation training (Kotsiantis, 2007).

Backpropagation Learning Algorithm

Backpropagation Learning Algorithm is a supervised learning method, and is an implementation of the Delta rule. As the name itself suggests, the errors are propagated backward from the output nodes to the inner nodes and, therefore, the learning. So back-propagation is used to calculate the gradient of the error of the network with respect to the network's modifiable weights. This gradient is almost always then used in a simple stochastic gradient descent algorithm to find weights that minimize the error. But, the term "Backpropagation" is used in a more general sense and refers to the entire procedure encompassing both the calculation of the gradient and its use in stochastic gradient descent. Backpropagation usually allows quick convergence on satisfactory local minima for error in the kind of networks to which it is suited. But, this also brings out its inherent drawback since it usually converges to the local minima, instead of the global minima (Mehrotra, Mohan, & Ranka, 1996).

There are two passes before the weights are updated. In the first pass (forward pass) the outputs of all neurons are calculated by multiplying the input vector by the weights. The error is calculated for each of the output layer neurons. In the backward pass, the error is passed back through the network layer by layer. The weights are adjusted according to the gradient descent rule, so that the actual output of the MLP moves closer to the desired output. A momentum term could be added which increases the learning rate with stability (Abougarir & Abosdel, 2013).

During the second backward pass, the difference between the target output and the actual output - error is calculated:

$$\textstyle e[k]=T[k] - y[k]$$.

The errors are backpropagated through the layers and the weight changes are made. The formula for adjusting the weights is:

$$\textstyle w[k+1] = w[k]+\mu e[k]x[k].$$

Once the weights are adjusted, the feed-forward process is repeated. The weights are adapted until the error between the target and actual output is low. The approximation of the function improves as the error decreases.

The Backpropagation algorithm can be summarized as follows:

1. Present a training sample to the neural network.
2. Compare the network output to the desired output from that sample. Calculate the error in each output neuron.
3. For each neuron, calculate what the output should have been, and a scaling factor, how much lower or higher the output must be adjusted to match the desired output. This is called the local error.
4. Adjust the weights of each neuron to lower the local error.
5. Assign an inertial value for the local error to neurons at the previous level, giving greater responsibility to neurons connected by stronger weights.
6. Repeat from step 3 on the neurons at the previous level, using each one's inertial value as an error.

Figure 19. Backpropagation Algorithm

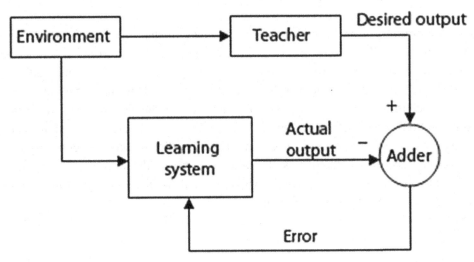

The quality of the fuzzy neural model is tested by calculating the MSE (mean squared error). The MSE gives a good indication of the accuracy of the model. The MSE between the model and the process should be low. A model could have a low MSE but not predict any of the dynamics of the pendulum system. The output from the model and process is plotted to compare the dynamics. Basically, we want to see whether the model predicts the movement of the inverted pendulum. Increasing the number of hidden layer neurons allows for more complex functions to be modeled. During testing, neural networks with a range of hidden layer neurons were simulated. It was expected that as the number of hidden neurons increased the most accurate the model would become (Suzuki, 2011).

Perceiving Matlab Pattern Recognition Plots and Optical Efficiency Control

Backpropagation Algorithm and Matlab Implementation

The Backpropagation algorithm is a supervised learning method for MLP (multi-layer perceptron) networks and Fuzzy neural networks with sigmoid activation units. The goal is to find a good mapping from input data to output data. When a new data record is fed to a network, the network provides a good mapping to the output space by using the intrinsic structure of the training set. This implementation allows the user to use several different training methods. Although the basic training algorithm is slow compared to other methods, it can provide, in some cases, a better representation of the training set (Mehrotra et al., 1996). Some example of commands in the relation of Backpropagation algorithm visualization and the optical estimation of optimization or divergence of learning algorithms with the use of MATLAB software are as follows.

Figure 20. Training of a three-layer (input + hidden + output layer) fuzzy MLP network and the network output plot.

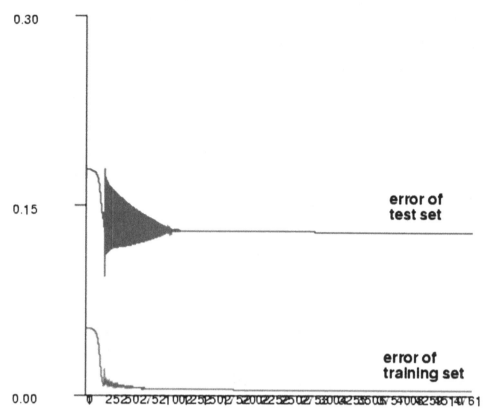

The following command trains a Fuzzy Multi Layer Perceptron (MLP) network using the MATLAB style training algorithm. The method is based on a global learning rate parameter with a momentum term. By default, one neuron for each input is used.

```
NDA> load sin.dat
NDA> select sinx -f sin.x
NDA> select siny -f sin.y
NDA> bp -di sinx -do siny -net 3 1 10 1 -types s s s -em 2000
     -nout wei -ef virhe -bs 0.01
NDA> fbp -d sinx -dout out -win wei
NDA> select output -f sin.x out.0
NDA> save output
```

The following command is used for training a Backpropagation network using an MATLAB style training algorithm. This method is based on a global adaptive learning rate parameter. By default, one neuron for each input is used.

Figure 21. Training of a three-layer (input + hidden + output layer) MLP network with sine data using sigmoid activation functions in neurons. After training, the network output is saved and visualized.

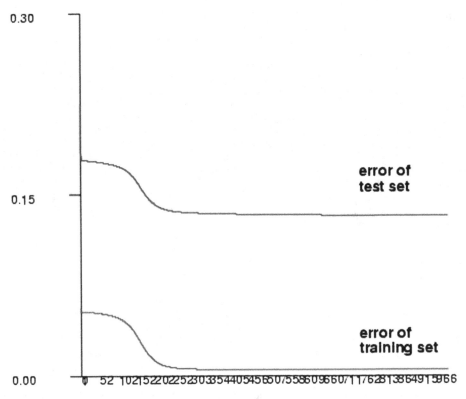

```
NDA> load sin.dat
NDA> select sinx -f sin.x
NDA> select siny -f sin.y
NDA> mbp -di sinx -do siny -net 3 1 10 1 -types s s s -em 1000
      -nout wei -ef virhe -bs 0.2 -mom 0.1
NDA> fbp -d sinx -dout out -win wei
NDA> select output -f sin.x out.0
NDA> save output
```

This command trains a Backpropagation network using the MATLAB style of training algorithm. This method is based on a global adaptive learning rate parameter and a momentum term. By default one neuron for each input is used.

```
NDA> load sin.dat
NDA> select sinx -f sin.x
NDA> select siny -f sin.y
NDA> abp -di sinx -do siny -net 3 1 10 1 -types s s s -em 350
      -nout wei -ef virhe -bs 1.2 -ac 1.04 -mup 1.1 -mdn 0.8
NDA> fbp -d sinx -dout out -win wei
```

Figure 22. Training a three-layer (input + hidden + output layer) fuzzy MLP network with sine data using sigmoid activation functions in the neurons. After training, the network output is presented.

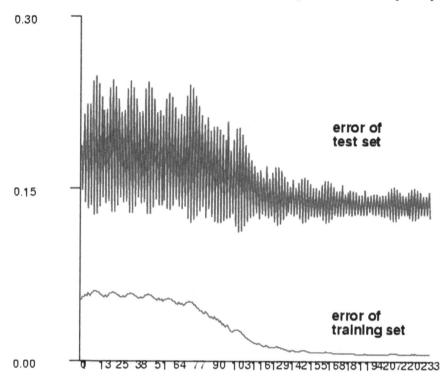

```
NDA> select output -f sin.x out.0
NDA> save output
```

This command is applied in a trained network. One remark of using –layer option: the user should keep in mind that the layer numbers start from zero.

```
NDA> load sint.dat
NDA> load sink.dat
NDA> select sinx -f sink.ox
NDA> select siny -f sink.oy
NDA> select sinox -f sink.ox
NDA> select sintx -f sint.tx
NDA> select sinty -f sint.ty
NDA> lmbp -di sinx -do siny -net 2 3 1 -types s s s -nout wei
        -ef virhe -lamda 1.0 -mup 2.0 -mdn 0.8 -em 40
        -ti sintx -to sinty
NDA> fbp -d sinox -dout out -win wei
NDA> mkgrp xxx
NDA> ldgrv xxx -f virhe.TrainError -co black
```

Figure 23. Training a three-layer (input + hidden + output layer) fuzzy MLP network with sine data using sigmoid activation functions in neurons. After training is complete, the training and testing error graphs is presented.

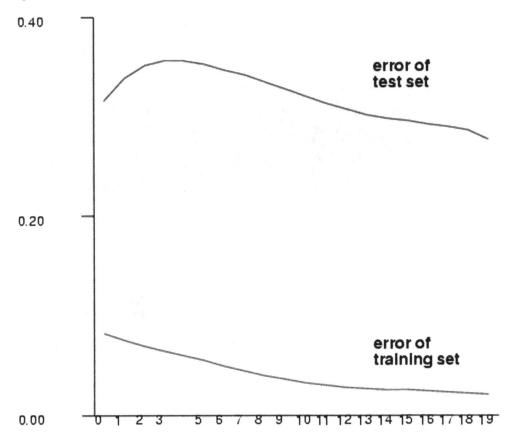

```
NDA> ldgrv xxx -f virhe.TestError -co red
NDA> show xxx
```

This command trains a Backpropagation network using an MATLAB style of the training algorithm. This method is based on a global adaptive learning rate parameter and a momentum term. By default, one neuron for each input is used.

```
NDA> load sin.dat
NDA> select sinx -f sin.x
NDA> select siny -f sin.y
NDA> mlbp -di sinx -do siny -net 3 1 15 1 -types t t t -em 100
      -nout wei -ef virhe -bs 0.1 -ac 1.1 -mup 1.1 -mdn 0.7
      -mom 0.95
NDA> fbp -d sinx -dout out -win wei
NDA> select output -f sin.x out.0
NDA> save output
```

Figure 24. Training of a three-layer (input + hidden + output layer) fuzzy MLP network with sine data using sigmoid activation functions in neurons. After training, this is the visualization of the networks output.

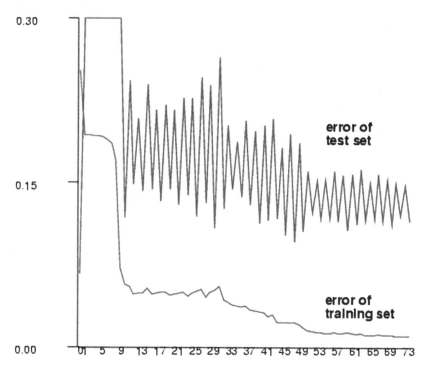

This command trains a Backpropagation network using the RPROP training algorithm. The method is based on adaptive learning rate parameters on each neuron's weight. By default, one neuron for each input is used.

```
NDA> load sin.dat
NDA> select sinx -f sin.x
NDA> select siny -f sin.y
NDA> sabp -di sinx -do siny -net 3 1 10 1 -types s s s -em 100
     -nout wei -ef virhe -bs 1.0 -mup 1.1 -mdm 0.8
NDA> fbp -d sinx -dout out -win wei
NDA> select train -f virhe.TrainError
NDA> select output -f sin.x out.0
NDA> save output
NDA> mkgrp xxx
NDA> ldgrv xxx -f virhe.TrainError -co black
NDA> show xxx
```

This command trains a Backpropagation network using the RPROP training algorithm. The method is based on adaptive learning rate parameters on each neuron's weight. By default, one neuron for each input is used.

Figure 25. Training a three-layer (input + hidden + output layer) Fuzzy MLP network with sine data using sigmoid activation functions in neurons. After training, the network output is presented with a plot a training error graph.

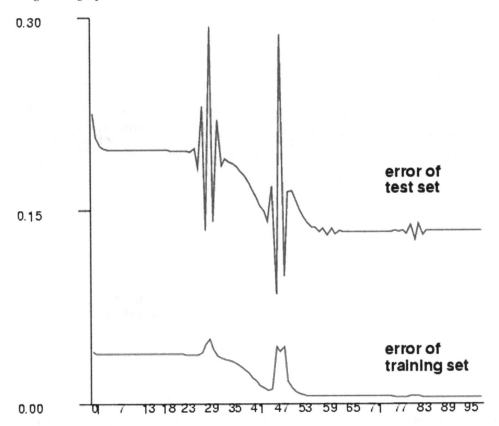

```
NDA> load sink.dat
NDA> load sint.dat
NDA> select sinx -f sink.ox
NDA> select siny -f sink.oy
NDA> select sinox -f sink.ox
NDA> select sintx -f sint.tx
NDA> select sinty -f sint.ty
NDA> rprop -di sinx -do siny -net 3 1 3 1 -types s s s -em 40
     -bs 0.05 -mup 1.1 -mdm  0.8 -nout wei -ti sintx -to sinty
     -ef virhe
NDA> fbp -d sinox -dout out -win wei
NDA> select test -f virhe.TrainError virhe.TestError
NDA> select output -f sink.ox out.0
NDA> save output
NDA> save test
```

Figure 26. Training a three-layer (input + hidden + output layer) Fuzzy MLP network with sine data using sigmoid activation functions in neurons. After training is done the network output and error is presented.

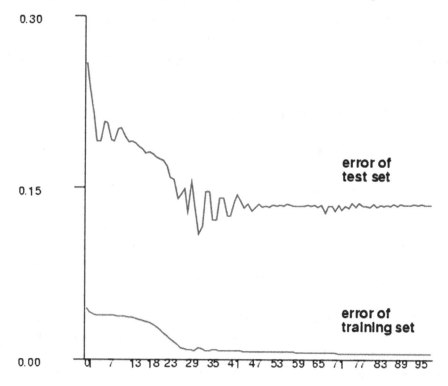

Pattern Recognition

In artificial network supervised learning, we are given a set of example pairs (x, y), $x \in X$, $y \in Y$ and the aim is to find a function $f: X \rightarrow Y$ in the allowed class of functions that matches the examples. In other words, we wish to infer the mapping implied by the data; the cost function is related to the mismatch between our mapping and the data and it implicitly contains prior knowledge about the problem domain (Govindarajan & Chandrasekaran, 2007).

A commonly used cost is the mean-squared error, which tries to minimize the average squared error between the network's output, $f(x)$, and the target value y over all the example pairs. When one tries to minimize this cost using gradient descent for the class of neural networks called multilayer perceptron's, one obtains the common and well-known Backpropagation algorithm for training neural networks. Tasks that fall within the paradigm of supervised learning are pattern recognition (also known as classification) and regression (also known as function approximation). The supervised learning paradigm is also applicable to sequential data (e.g., for speech and gesture recognition). This can be thought of as learning with a "teacher", in the form of a function that provides continuous feedback on the quality of solutions obtained thus far (Baby, Bhuvaneswari, & Sasirekha, 2013).

Among the various traditional approaches of pattern recognition, the statistical approach has been most intensively studied and used in practice. More recently, the addition of artificial neural network techniques theory have been receiving significant attention. The design of a recognition system requires careful attention to the following issues: definition of pattern classes, sensing environment, pattern representation, feature extraction and selection, cluster analysis, classifier design and learning, selection of training and test samples, and performance evaluation. In spite of almost 50 years of research and development in this field, the general problem of recognizing complex patterns with arbitrary orientation, location, and scale remains unsolved. New and emerging applications, such as data mining, web searching, retrieval of multimedia data, face recognition, and cursive handwriting recognition, require robust and efficient pattern recognition techniques (Ayyasamy & Sivanandam, 2010).

Searching for Multi-Layer Perceptron Inputs to match given outputs

This special command allows you to search for such input values for an MLP neural network that correspond to given outputs.

Assume that the studied phenomenon concerns the number of outputs: $y_{i \in} \{y_1, y_2, ..., y_n\}$ and inputs: $x_{j \in} \{x_1\}, x_2, ..., x_m\}$.

Then, an MLP neural network is trained to model this phenomenon. In other words, the network is used to estimate values y_i by values of x_j. Often it is useful to solve the inverse problem; to find out the input values that give us certain output values. The input search command can be used to obtain these input values using an algorithm similar to the Gibbs sampler.

The idea of the algorithm is as follows. A random walk along the estimated MLP surface is conducted by advancing from a random starting point by randomly changing the value of one input parameter at a time. The main goal is to locate the points in the input parameter space, which give the desired output values. The rule of the random walk is to accept always the next point if its goodness is better than the goodness of the previous point, and to accept it with a probability that depends on the difference between points of goodness, if the goodness of the next point is worse. The bigger the difference, the smaller the probability to move to the next point. If the point is rejected, another point is taken. While walking the point whose output values are closest to the desired values is stored. Parameters for the command are: -n specifies the data frame with weights of the trained MLP, -d the data frame with desirable outputs, preprocessed with the same statistics as used for preprocessing of the outputs in the MLP training process, and –dout the name of the data frame with results.

Assume that the MLP has been trained to model a normal bivariate function (see the first figure below). The inputs for the MLP are parameters x_1 and x_2, and the output is y, and the goal is to find those input combinations that give us the output value 0.2. It is obvious that there are many such combinations and they form some kind of curve in the 3-D space. The input search algorithm will find one combination of inputs for each starting point, so a large number of starting points is needed in order to obtain several

Table 1.

Input search	Searching for MLP-inputs
-n *\<mlp\>*	the frame with MLP weights
-d *\<pretarget\>*	the data frame with desirable (preprocessed) outputs
-dout *\<result\>*	the name of the result data frame
[-p *\<points\>*]	the number of starting points (default 1)
[-it *\<iterations\>*]	the number of iterations (default is 1000)
[-fac *\<factor\>*]	the factor's values (default is 0.7)

points from the curve. The number of starting points should in most cases be 100 or more (parameter -p). The second figure below illustrates the results of the input searching for the output values 0.2, 0.3, 0.4 and 0.5, with 200 starting points for each search.

Switch-it specifies the number of iterations or steps the algorithm should accomplish. The higher the number of steps the better the accuracy of the results. However, a large number of steps increases the amount of computing time required. The number of iterations should be 10000, or more.

Switch-fac specifies a value, which influences the length of the steps. By default, the value is 0.7, and it can be adjusted between 0 and 1. In the algorithm, a point, whose goodness is worse than the goodness of the previous point can be accepted with a probability, which depends on the difference between the goodnesses of those points. If the difference is large a longer step is taken from this point in order to move away from the bad region of the surface. In this case, the value specified with the switch-fac controls the size of this step.

DISCUSSION AND FUTURE WORK

This paper summarized and elaborated on the efficiency of artificial networks learning algorithms with the use of visualized methods of pattern recognition. Our goal is to control the artificial neural network learning algorithms error variance using the visualized presentation. Future ideas are related to the use normal EEG database in order to make decisions and diagnosis learning difficulties automatically. The design of a pattern recognition system for EEG analysis essentially involves data acquisition and preprocessing, additional data representation, and diagnosis. This process can clearly be aided by the application of interactive multimedia scenarios where the user will be presented an edutainment scenario and will have to respond to it interactively. This will enable the measurement of response to specific stimuli when the trigger event is known and can be matched to the response.

REFERENCES

Abougarir, A. J., & Abosdel, A. A. M. (2013, September 29). Intelligent Controller for Nonlinear Chemical Process using Artificial Neural Networks. Proceedings of *International Academic Conference on Electrical, Electronics and Computer Engineering*.

Alhanafy, E., Th., Fareed, Z., & Abdou Saad El Din, M. (2010). Neuro Fuzzy Modeling Scheme for the Prediction of Air Pollution. *Journal of American Science, 6*(12).

Ayyasamy, S., & Sivanandam, S. N. (2010). Trust Based Content Distribution for Peer-ToPeer Overlay Networks. *International Journal of Network Security & Its Applications, 2*(2).

Baby, P., Bhuvaneswari, P., & Sasirekha, K. (2013). A Study on Learning Techniques in Artificial Neural Network. *Journal of Environmental Science. Computer Science and Engineering & Technology, 2*(4), 1001–1006.

Baldo, N., & Zorzi, M. (2008). Fuzzy logic for cross-layer optimization in cognitive radio networks. *IEEE Communications Magazine, 46*(4), 64–71. doi:10.1109/MCOM.2008.4481342

Cao, J., & Wang, J. (2005). Global exponential stability and periodicity of recurrent neural networks with time delays. *IEEE Transactions on Circuits and Systems I, 52*(5), 920–931. doi:10.1109/TCSI.2005.846211

Cybenko, G. (1989). Approximation by superpositions of a sigmoidal function. *Mathematics of Control, Signals, and Systems, 2*(4), 303–314. doi:10.1007/BF02551274

Deliyannis, I. (2013). Sensor Recycling and Reuse. *International Journal of Sensor and Related Networks, 1*(1).

Dubois, D., Ostasiewicz, W., & Prade, H. (2000). Fuzzy Sets: History and Basic Notions. *Fundamentals of Fuzzy Sets The Handbooks of Fuzzy Sets Series, 7*, 21–124. doi:10.1007/978-1-4615-4429-6_2

Fuller, R. (2000). *Introduction to Neuro-Fuzzy Systems*. New York: Springer Science & Business Media. doi:10.1007/978-3-7908-1852-9

Fuller, R. (2013). *Introduction to Neuro-Fuzzy Systems*. London: Springer Science & Business Media.

Govindarajan, M., & Chandrasekaran, R. M. (2007). Classifier Based Text Mining for Neural Network. *World Academy of Science, Engineering and Technology International Journal of Computer, Control, Quantum and Information Engineering, 1*(3).

Guillaume, S. (2001). Designing Fuzzy Inference Systems from Data: An Interpretability-Oriented Review. *IEEE Transactions on AFuzzy Systems, 9*(3). http://doi.org/1063–6706/01

Guler, N., Ubeyli, E., & Guler, I. (2005). Recurrent neural networks employing Lyapunov exponents for EEG signals classification. *Expert Systems with Applications, 29*(3), 506–514. doi:10.1016/j.eswa.2005.04.011

Hahn, T. (2013). *Option Pricing Using Artificial Neural Networks : an Australian Perspective.*

Hornik, K. (1991). Approximation capabilities of multilayer feedforward networks. *Neural Networks, 4*(2), 251–257. doi:10.1016/0893-6080(91)90009-T

Hornik, K., Stinchcombe, M., & White, H. (1990). Universal approximation of an unknown mapping and its derivatives using multilayer feedforward networks. *Neural Networks, 3*(5), 551–560. doi:10.1016/0893-6080(90)90005-6

Ivancevic, V. G., & Ivancevic, T. T. (2007). Human and Computational Mind. *Human and Computational Mind. Studies in Computational Intelligence Springer-Verlag Berlin Heidelberg, 60*, 1–269.

Jansen, J. (2002). *Introduction to Artificial Neural Networking. Engineering 315: Control Systems.*

Kalogirou, S. A. (2001). Artificial Intelligence in Renewable Energy Systems Modeling and Prediction. *Science Direct, 5*(4), 373–401.

Karlik, B., & Olgac, V. (2011). Performance Analysis of Various Activation Functions in Generalized MLP Architectures of Neural Networks. [IJAE]. *International Journal of Artificial Intelligence And Expert Systems, 1*(4), 111–122.

Karthekeyan, A. R. (2014). Fuzzy neural network based extreme learning machine technique in credit risk management. *International Journal of Research in Engineering, IT &. Social Sciences, 4*(9).

Kotsiantis, S. B. (2007). Supervised Machine Learning: A Review of Classification Techniques. *Informatica*, *31*, 249–268.

Kowaliw, T., Bredeche, N., Chevallier, S., & Doursat, R. (2014). Artificial Neurogenesis: An Introduction and Selective Review. In T. Kowaliw, S. Chevallier, R. Doursat (Eds.), *Studies in Computational Intellience* (Vol. 557, pp. 1-60). Springer-Verlag Berlin Heidelberg. http://doi.org/<ALIGNMENT.qj></ALIGNMENT>10.1007/978-3-642-55337-0_1

Kruse, R. (2008). Fuzzy neural network. *Scholarpedia*, *3*(11), 6043. doi:10.4249/scholarpedia.6043

Kumar, A. V. Aruna, & Reddy, M. V. (2011). A Fuzzy Neural Network for Speech Recognition. *Journal of Systems and Software, 1*(9), 284–290.

Levine, A. J., Hinckley, C. A., Hilde, K. L., Driscoll, S. P., Poon, T. H., Montgomery, J. M., & Pfaff, S. L. (2014). Identification of a cellular node for motor control pathways. *Nature Neuroscience*, *17*(4), 586–593. doi:10.1038/nn.3675 PMID:24609464

Mahadev, M. M., & Kulkarni, R. (2013). A Review: Role of Fuzzy Expert System for Prediction of Election Results. *Reviews of Literature*, *1*(2). http://doi.org/2347-2723

Matthen, M., & Stephens, C. (2007). *Philosophy of Biology*. Oxford: Elsevier.

Mehrotra, K., Mohan, C. K., & Ranka, S. (1996). *Elements of Artificial Neural Networks*. Chester: Bradford Book CO Inc.

Nauck, D., & Kruse, R. (1993). A fuzzy neural network learning fuzzy control rules and membership functions by fuzzy error backpropagation. Proceedings of *IEEE International Conference on Neural Networks* (pp. 1022–1027). http://doi.org/ doi:10.1109/ICNN.1993.298698

Nozaki, K., Ishibuchi, H., & Tanaka, H. (1996). Adaptive Fuzzy Rule-Based Classification System. *IEEE Transactions on Fuzzy Systems*, *4*(3), 238–250. doi:10.1109/91.531768

O'Regan, J. K., & Noë, A. (2001). A sensorimotor account of vision and visual consciousness. *Behavioral and Brain Sciences*, *24*(05), 939–1031. doi:10.1017/S0140525X01000115 PMID:12239892

Omondi, A. R., & Ralapakse, J. C. (2006). *FPGA Implementations of Neural Networks. Springer*. Dordrecht: Springer. doi:10.1007/0-387-28487-7

Pal, S. K., De, R. K., & Basak, J. (2002). Unsupervised feature evaluation: A neuro-fuzzy approach. *Elsevier. Fuzzy Sets and Systems*, *126*, 277–291. doi:10.1109/TFUZZ.2002.1006431

Patan, K. (2008). *Artificial Neural Networks for the Modelling and Fault Diagnosis of Technical Processes*. Springer; doi:10.1007/978-3-540-79872-9

Ping, Y., Teng, L., Jingsheng, L., & Weimin, H. (2011). Synchronization of Fuzzy High-order Cohen-Grossberg Neural Networks with Reaction-diffusion Term and Time-varying. *Journal of Computer Information Systems*, *7*(11), 4145–4152.

Plerou, A. (2012). Artificial Neural Networks Simulating Human Brain | Antonia Plerou - Academia. edu. *Open Education - The Journal for Open and Distance Education and Educational Technology, 8*(1).

Raitamaki, J. (1998). Improving the performance of fuzzy systems by using local partitioning. Proceedings of *EUROMICRO Conference* (Vol. 2, pp. 745–752). IEEE Comput. Soc. http://doi.org/ doi:10.1109/ EURMIC.1998.708097

Rashmi, N., Halse, S. V., & Teli, D. (2015). Research Article non Linear Load Simulation for Power Quality Control using Fuzzy Controller. *International Journal of Recent Scientific Research Research*, *6*(1), 2608–2612.

Roshandeh, A. M., Puan, O. C., & Joshani, M. (2009). Data Analysis Application for Variable Message Signs Using Fuzzy Logic in Kuala Lumpur. *International Journal of Systems Applications, Engineering & Development*, *3*(1).

Ryan, M. (2014). *The Digital Mind: An Exploration of artificial intelligence*. Michael Ryan.

Sanger, T. D. (1989). Optimal unsupervised learning in a single-layer linear feedforward neural network. *Neural Networks*, *2*(6), 459–473. doi:10.1016/0893-6080(89)90044-0

Sharma, A. kumar, & Badri, V. P. (2013). Fuzzy logic based systems in management and business applications. *International Journal of Innovative Research in Engineering & Science*, *1*(2), 1–6.

Shaw, I. S. (1998). *Fuzzy Control of Industrial Systems*. Boston, MA: Springer US; doi:10.1007/978-1-4757-2813-2

Simões, M. G., & Farret, F. A. (2014). *Modeling and Analysis with Induction Generators* (3rd ed.). Taylor & Francis.

State, L., Cocianu, C., Stefanescu, V., & Vlamos, P. (2004). A Neural Network Framework for Implementing the Bayesian Learning. In *International Conference on Informatics in Control, Automation and Robotics* (pp. 328–331). Setúbal,Portugal.

Sumathi, S., & Paneerselvam, S. (2010). *Computational Intelligence Paradigms: Theory & Applications using MATLAB*. CRC Press.

Suzuki, K. (2011). *Artificial Neural Networks-Methodological Advances and Biomedical Applications*. Rijeka, Croatia: InTech. doi:10.5772/644

Timmerer, C., Waltl, M., Rainer, B., & Hellwagner, H. (2012). Assessing the quality of sensory experience for multimedia presentations. *Signal Processing Image Communication*, *27*(8), 909–916. doi:10.1016/j. image.2012.01.016

Tsiridou, T., Zannos, I., & Strapatsakis, M. (2011). An interactive windscape. *Technoetic Arts: A Journal of Speculative Research*, *9*(2), 153–162.

Vaidyanathan, P. P., & Hoang, P.-Q. (1988). Lattice structures for optimal design and robust implementation of two-channel perfect-reconstruction QMF banks. *IEEE Transactions on Acoustics, Speech, and Signal Processing*, *36*(1), 81–94. doi:10.1109/29.1491

Vieira, J., Dias, F. M., & Mota, A. (2004). Neuro-Fuzzy Systems: A Survey. Proceedings of *International Conference on Neural Networks and Applications*.

Viharos, Z. J., & Kis, K. B. (2014). Fuzzy Systems and their Applications in Technical Diagnostics. Proceedings of *Workshop on Technical Diagnostics Advanced measurement tools in technical diagnostics for systems' reliability and safety*. Warsaw, Poland.

Wang, R., & Mei, K. (2010). Analysis of Fuzzy Membership Function Generation with Unsupervised Learning Using Self-Organizing Feature Map. Proceedings of *2010 International Conference on Computational Intelligence and Security* (pp. 515–518). IEEE. http://doi.org/ doi:10.1109/CIS.2010.118

Weyns, D., Malek, S., & Andersson, J. (2012). FORMS. *ACM Transactions on Autonomous and Adaptive Systems*, *7*(1), 1–61. doi:10.1145/2168260.2168268

Wu, S., & Er, M. J. (2000). Dynamic fuzzy neural networks-a novel approach to function approximation. *IEEE Transactions on Systems, Man, and Cybernetics. Part B, Cybernetics : A Publication of the IEEE Systems. Man, and Cybernetics Society*, *30*(2), 358–364. doi:10.1109/3477.836384

Yegnarayana, B. (1994). Artificial neural networks for pattern recognition. *Scidhanci*, *19*(2), 189–238.

Zhang, P. (2008). *Industrial Control Technology: A Handbook for Engineers and Researchers*. William Andrew.

Chapter 13
Web Healthcare Applications in Poland:
Trends, Standards, Barriers and Possibilities of Implementation and Usage of E–Health Systems

Anna Sołtysik-Piorunkiewicz
University of Economics in Katowice, Poland

Małgorzata Furmankiewicz
University of Economics in Katowice, Poland

Piotr Ziuziański
University of Economics in Katowice, Poland

ABSTRACT

This publication consists three main areas of interest: management of patient information in Polish health care system, novel ideas and recent trends on healthcare Web-based applications in Poland and healthcare information behavior of users of self-diagnosis and self-treatment systems in Poland. The methodology adopted includes a literature review for the utilization of Web-based healthcare applications in Poland as well as the trends of medical information systems and healthcare system in Poland. Furthermore the results of a survey research for the management of patient information in Poland are provided. Respondents have been asked about their interested and experiences on the new Polish information electronic health record system or others information systems dedicated to the management of the healthcare processes in Poland. Also another survey researches are presented. Respondents have been asked which internet tools they use for self-treatment and self-diagnosis and are also asked to rate their credibility.

DOI: 10.4018/978-1-4666-8659-5.ch013

SUMMARY

The chapter presents the development and analysis of the use of ICT tools in e-health in the light of the results of studies conducted in the years 2013 - 2014. The authors described the trends and standards of medical information systems and healthcare system. In this chapter authors characterized the different kind of information system in health care, i.e. Electronic Verification of Beneficiary Entitlements (Polish original name of system is "Elektroniczna Weryfikacja Uprawnień Świadczeniobiorców", abbr. e-WUŚ), Integrated Patient System (Polish original name of system is "Zintegrowany Informator Pacjenta", abbr. ZIP), Health insurance card, Electronic European Health Insurance Card, and the system of electronic prescription e-Prescription. Based on literature review authors proposed the classification of ICT tools used in e-health. The results of a survey research for the management of patient information in Poland were also described in this chapter. Additionally the analysis of the factors determining the behavior of Internet users in the field of medical knowledge sharing via the Internet, communication tools used in e-health and medical diagnostics over the Internet were conducted and described. In the last part of this chapter authors proposed SWOT analyses "Web healthcare applications: Strengths, Weaknesses, Opportunities, and Threats" of determinants influencing the Internet user behavior in health care, taking into account the popularity and credibility of ICT tools in self-diagnosing and self-treatment. In the summary of this chapter authors concluded the e-health readiness in Polish information society.

INTRODUCTION

There is a Virgil quote which says: "The greatest wealth is health", indicating the importance of health to most if not all people. As a result most of us since the dawn of time look for information about healthy lifestyle, preventive healthcare and especially pieces of information connected with diseases and treatment. Nowadays, the majority of those interested in seeking information for healthcare is taking advantage of up-to-date technologies and hence are using the Internet. Although the available healthcare information has been radically increased over the years, the abundance of information impose additional difficulties when seeking trusty and reliable web-based resources as well as the information found in the internet should be evaluated since it could be dangerous. On the other hand, medical service providers see potential opportunities and try to apply modern technologies to enhance the healthcare services and reduce the associated costs. E-health for example provides interesting opportunities relating the modern information technologies with doctors' knowledge. E-health applications can include specialized medical portals, internet expert systems for disease diagnose based on symptoms, doctors' Internet advice, online (video) consultation with doctors, etc. (Furmankiewicz, Sołtysik-Piorunkiewicz, & Ziuziański, 2014; Ziuziański, Furmankiewicz, & Sołtysik-Piorunkiewicz, 2014). Multimedia and Web technologies can help in the specific healthcare applications to grow up the impact of their usability (Sołtysik-Piorunkiewicz, 2009, 2014a, 2014b, 2014c, 2015a, 2015b) and can change the favorable circumstances of user behavioral intention. The favorable circumstance is one of the dimensions of the Venkatesh unified user acceptance of information technology model (Venkatesh, Morris, Davis G., & Davis F.D, 2003). This model is presented in Figure 1. Unified theory of acceptance and use of technology (UTAUT) was proposed by American professor K. Viswanath (Venkatesh, Morris, Davis G., & Davis F.D, 2003) and

Figure 1. UTAUT model.
Source: own study based on: V. Venkatesh, M.G. Morris, G.B. Davis and F.D. Davis, User acceptance of information technol-ogy: Toward a unified view, „MIS Quarterly" 2003, nr 27, pp. 425–478.

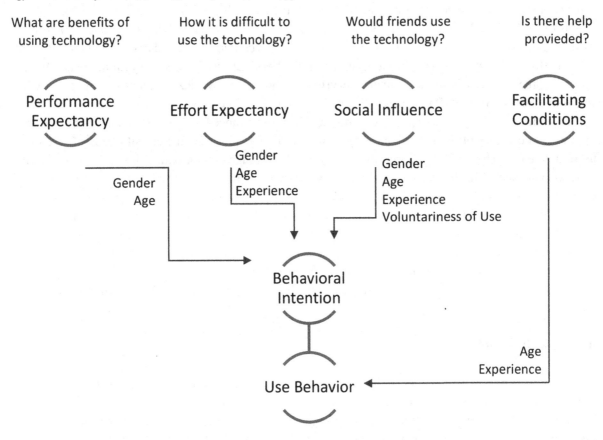

his collaborators at University of Maryland. UTAUT is based on occurrence four factors influencing on intention using given technology: facilitating conditions, social influence, effort expectancy, and performance expectancy.

Nowadays web healthcare applications are enriched by multimedia like texts, sounds, still images, animations, videos. Multimedia plays an increasingly important role in supporting medical diagnosing, treatment and prevention (Przelaskowski, 2011). Authors of blogs, specialized medical portals / websites about health and members of online forums / discussion groups use many kinds of multimedia forms to transfer knowledge. They use forms like photographs videos, text to describe illnesses, symptoms, methods of treatment, share experience.

It is worth mentioning that there are medical encyclopaedias, i.e. MedlinePlus (National Library of Medicine, n.d.), where Internet users, especially medical students and doctors besides definitions can find surgery videos, anatomy videos and interactive tutorials. It could be very helpful for them owing to multi-stream transmission of information. Multimedia play significant role in e-learning. Multimedia forms raise curiosity, interest and it has enormous potential (Opoka, 2008). On the other side multimedia could be used in diagnosing area. One of specific example of multimedia usage in this area is study of medical diagnostics imaging named echocardiography. The transmission of information in this form is a deeply interactive (Przelaskowski, 2011).

Usage of multimedia make possible to online transfer information between patient and doctors during online medical visits. Patients can send i.e. their results, photos of symptoms, radiographs, etc.

Usage of multimedia is clearly noticeable in e-commerce. Online pharmacies use online advertising through i.e. text, logos, animations, videos, photographs, sounds. Drug price comparisons websites consists, i.e. photos and descriptions of products.

BACKGROUND

IT systems, which are used to streamline, improve the functioning of health care, are the area of interest as well in Poland (Kawiorska, 2004; Pankowska, 2004), as in many countries across the world and Europe, e.g. Germany (Deutsche Krankenhausgesellschaft, 2002), Switzerland (Thatcher, 2013), Netherlands (Shekelle, Morton, & Keeler, 2006). The transformation, due to implementation of IT systems, into a uniform, integrated and flexible structure, is undoubtedly beneficial for the safety and comfort of patients and streamlining activities in a health care system (Kaplan & Harris-Salamone, 2009). Benefits from implementing IT systems fulfill the expectations of patients and health services providers, as well as improving the whole process of decision making by participants of the health care system. One of the most important e-health systems is electronic health record (EHR). The research of United States academic medical centers reported generally positive attitudes towards using the electronic health record (EHR) as a structured, distributed documentation systems that differ from paper charts (Han & Lopp, 2013) in the ambulatory setting and significant concerns about the potential impact of the EHR on their ability to conduct the doctor-patient encounter (Rouf, Chumley, & Dobbie, 2008).

However the clinical documentation, an essential process within electronic health records (EHRs), takes a significant amount of clinician time. There is luck of methods to optimize documentation ways to deliver effective health care (Pollard et al., 2013). The results of a large-scale statewide analysis in 2006 in United States showed the adoption of health information technologies in physician's offices (Menachemi & Brooks, 2006; Menachemi, Perkins, van Durme, & Brooks, 2006). They discovered that the use of quality enhancing technologies such as PDAs, use of e-mail with patients and EHR was less common. But the state of adoption of health information technologies in physician's offices is still changing. The American Medical Information Association (AMIA) recommendations are based on research and publication, best practices, advocacy, education, certification, databases and knowledge integration. With the United States joining other countries from Europe, e.g. The Great Britain, in national efforts to reap the many benefits that use of health information technology can bring for health care quality and savings, to minimize complexity and difficulties of implementing even smaller-scale systems (Kaplan & Harris-Salamone, 2009).

The last research about factors affecting physician professional satisfaction and their implications for patient care, health systems, and health policy, based on cooperation between RAND Health, a division of the RAND Corporation and AMA (American Medical Association), was published in 2013 (Friedberg et al, 2013). A major factor limiting efficiency and quality gains from clinical information technologies is the lack of full use by the clinicians (Kralewski et al., 2008).

Projects for implementing IT systems in health care for management of patient information are complex and complicated undertakings. These processes should be carried out in stages. To achieve best effects, individual stages should be implemented efficiently and consistently. Moreover, appropriate legislative changes are required and – importantly – persuading decision makers about necessity of such solutions. Any IT systems implemented in health care must comply with legal standards in force and be adaptable to changes made to the national law. Due to the mass scale of health care, they must also be efficient both for patient and health protection system (Sołtysik-Piorunkiewicz, 2012).

There are many benefits of health information technology that can be bring more health care quality and savings, sobering reports recall the complexity and difficulties of implementing even smaller-scale systems (Kaplan & Harris-Salamone, 2009). The ability of EHRs to improve the quality of care in ambulatory care settings was demonstrated improvements in provider performance when clinical information management and decision support tools were made available within an EHR system (Shekelle, Morton, & Keeler, 2006). The developers, implementers and certifiers of EHRs should focus on increasing the adoption of robust EHR systems and increasing the use of specific features rather than simply aiming to deploy an EHR regardless of functionality to maximize health care quality (Poon et al., 2010). Over the past several years, Sittig and others (2011) have carried out an extensive qualitative research program focusing on the barriers and facilitators to successful adoption and use of advanced, state-of-the-art clinical information systems based on commercially available EHR vendors and the internally developed EHRs. They concluded that if the well-designed commercially-available systems are coupled with the other key socio-technical concepts required for safe and effective EHR implementation and use, and organizations have access to implementable clinical knowledge, the transformation of the healthcare enterprise that so many have predicted, is achievable using commercially-available, state-of-the-art EHRs (Sittig et al., 2011).

Accelerating the adoption of IT health care systems will require greater public-private partnerships, new policies to address the misalignment of financial incentives, and a more robust evidence base regarding IT implementation (Goldzweig, C.L., Towfigh, A., Maglione, M., & Shekelle P.G., 2009). But it seems more and more important the development of Web-based health care system for common usage of patients, doctors and others users in health care system.

One of the more important cases in area of healthcare is National Health Service (NHS) in England which was started in 1948. The NHS has grown to become the world's largest publicly funded health service. In 1998 was launched the "NHS Direct". This service was the one of the largest single e-health services in the world, handling more than half a million calls each month. The NHS Direct service closed in 2014. Now instead, a new non-emergency number 111 was introduced to make it easier for people to access local NHS healthcare services in England (NHS.uk, n.d.).

Another examples of the tools used in e-health care expert systems, namely computer programs whose task is to solve the intellectual-based problems (Mulawka, 1996). Expert systems can also be used as a support for decision making, e.g. by prompting the user potential solutions (Cieciura, 2006). As an illustration of an expert system related to health, the MYCIN system can be used (Buchanann & Shortlife, 1984). Its aim was to diagnose contagious blood diseases, and to recommend the medicaments, as well as to suggest doses, taking into account the following parameters: sex, weight, or blood group (Karnowka, Shafer, & Sularz, n.d.). Also the others expert systems were used in England: INTERNIST (Pople at al., 1975), FUNAGES (Dimitroula, Bassiliades, Vlahavas, & Dimitrakos, 2001), CASNET (Weiss, Kulikowski, & Safir, 1978), PUFF (Kunz at al., 1978).

TRENDS AND STANDARDS OF MEDICAL INFORMATION SYSTEMS AND HEALTHCARE SYSTEM IN POLAND

The directions of implementing IT systems in Polish health care are now concentrated mainly on putting into effect the assumptions of the European Commission concerning e-Health. The main issues presented in the „e-Health Poland" plan which require implementation by 2015 include the following (Directions, 2009):

1. Ensuring citizens easier access to health care information.
2. Improving effectiveness of the health care system with regard to electronic flow of information.
3. Creating procedures and guidelines, gathering and giving access to good practices to improve management of a health care centre thanks to implementing information and communication systems.
4. Modernizing the system of medical information to analyze the demand for provided health services.
5. Practical realization of the development of IT solutions in protection of health in line with the guidelines the European Commission which will allow the Republic of Poland to be included into the area of interpretational Electronic Health Record.

Currently, due to accepting for implementation Programmes financed from structural measures, the following activities are of key importance: implementation of the Programme of Health Protection Informatization and creating the conditions for the development of health protection e-services – especially telemedical systems (teleconsultations, telemonitoring, online patients' registration) e-prescriptions and electronic health records, which will be linked with a new identity card (Sołtysik-Piorunkiewicz, 2012).

There are some lacks of information health care systems in Poland:

- Certain data redundancy – similar data is stored in different registers, kept by two different entities, e.g. Central List of Insured Persons and Central Register of Insured Persons (The National Health;
- Federation and Health Insurance Company;
- Incoherence of data between different registers – the same data in different registers may vary (e.g. change of address is not automatically updated in all registers in which the address appeared);
- Lack of cooperation with reference registers – generally, registers do not refer to base reference registers;
- Lack of cooperation between registers in health protection – registers in health protection do not use source information which already exists in other health protection registers;
- Lack of a uniform data model – registers and databases in health protection do not use a uniform data model;
- Lack of structure and relationships between registers in health protection.

There are systems for pharmacists' shops being implemented, i.e. EuroMedica (Apteka Euromedica, 2012), based on modern Internet technologies. Clinics implement InfoMedica or OSOZ systems. However, it seems necessary to implement such IT systems in health protection for management of patient information in Polish health care system e.g. a Health Patient Information System (System Zdrowotny Informator Pacjenta, 2013) which will ensure (Directions, 2011) creation of information conditions that will allow taking long-term optimal decisions in health policy, irrespective of the adopted organizational model of health protection and principles of financing it; creation of a stable information system in health protection, characterized by a flexible approach to the organization of the system of health protection resources, including a model of financing services from public funds, and resilience to disturbance in data gathering and archiving, caused by system changes in health care; decreasing the information gap in the health protection sector that makes it impossible to build an optimal model of health protection; organizing an existing system for information gathering, processing and analyzing (e.g. in Business Intelligence systems); building a system ensuring electronic communication and possibility of exchanging documents and reports between health protection entities and the proprietary body.

Nowadays two projects are being developed in Poland in accordance with the law on publicly funded health care benefits: Electronic Verification of Beneficiary Entitlements (Polish original name of system is "Elektroniczna Weryfikacja Uprawnień Świadczeniobiorców", abbr. e-WUŚ) and Integrated Patient System (Polish original name of system is "Zintegrowany Informator Pacjenta", abbr. ZIP).

The system Electronic Verification of Beneficiary Entitlements was tested from the 15th of October to the end of 2012 and its aim is to streamline the system for confirming the entitlement to health care. Thanks to the system, doctors will no longer be responsible for checking whether the patient is entitled to health care. The project was the result of the cooperation of the Ministry of Administration and Digitalization with the Ministry of Health, National Health Fund (ZUS), Social Insurance Institution and Agricultural Social Insurance Fund (KRUS), and was consulted with the Chief Inspectorate of Personal Data Protection. From the 1st of January 2013, patients visiting doctors should present their PESEL number and identity card, driving licence or passport in order to confirm their entitlement to publicly funded health care (Korczak, 2014; Ministerstwo Admnistracji i Cyfryzacji, 2012).

Thanks to the information exchange between the Central List of the Insured of the National Health Fund and ZUS and KRUS registers, it will be possible to check online in a hospital or clinic reception whether the patient is insured. There will be no need for the RMUA slip (although it still will be valid, as will be the pensioner identity card and other documents entitling to benefits) (Sidorko, 2012).

If the system doesn't confirm the entitlement to health care (e.g. when the employer has not registered the employee for insurance), the citizen's declaration that he/she is insured will suffice (art. 7 and 8 of the relevant law). The introduction of the e-WUŚ system made the procedure of issuing the European Health Insurance Card (Polish EKUZ) more efficient. The citizen doesn't have to produce the RMUA slip in a National Health Fund institution; instead he/she can show a document proving his/her identity.

Integrated Patient System is a Polish nationwide service providing registered users with historical data about their treatment and financing of treatment, collected since 2008 by the National Health Fund. The Integrated Patient System was implemented at the 1st of July 2013 and is successfully developed, and now has some important functionality, e.g. quick access to information about right to health care for the citizen, knowledge of treatment and benefits granted and the medicines prescribed, and information about the amounts that have been transferred to finance treatment of patient. To have access to information about health care, medical records and financing of the services provided, the citizen first should to read the rules of use of EHR, and then go to the registration page and fill out the included electronic form. After completing the application the citizen should take the ID card to a branch of the National Health Fund in order to access data (user ID and temporary password). After receiving the access, the citizen can start to use the service. Both the registration and use of the site are free for the citizen. Medical information is available in the latest issue and is so-called "sensitive data". So according to the principles of data protection and guidance of the Inspector General, the data are under special protection.

Therefore the personal visit of each citizen to the headquarters of the Fund is required (Zintegrowany Informator Pacjenta, n.d.).

Health Insurance Card

Electronic health insurance card was implemented in the Silesia voivodeship about 10 years ago as part of works connected with informatization of Silesia voivodeship department of National Health Fund. Electronic health insurance card is used to verify insurance status of an authorized card holder in the system of Silesia voivodeship department of National Health Fund. It also provides personal data and is used for authorization of the services provided as part of performing a contract with Silesia voivodeship department of National Health Fund (Narodowy Fundusz Zdrowia, 2013). This card may be issued to an insured person with a Universal Electronic System for Registration of the Population national identification number who can prove his/her residence on the territory of the Silesia voivodeship.

Since 2004, it has been planned in Poland to implement country-wide Health Insurance Card modelled on the Silesian card. To continue the works ordered by Health Minister on February 8, 2005, a Group was set up to draw up a strategy for the development of a medical information system in health protection and prepare a conception of implementing European Health Insurance Card and Health Insurance Card. The tasks of this group included drawing up a strategy for the development of a medical information system in health protection and preparing a conception of implementing European Health Insurance Card and Health Insurance Card. It was decided that representatives of Health Ministry would be involved in the works of a Group for developing a conception and design of electronic Health Insurance Card (e-HIC), electronic Medical Services Register (e-MSR) and programmes of their implementation, set up by order of the President of the National Health Fund No 40/2004 of 25 November 2004 for the purpose of preparing a functional conception, scope of application and design of e-HIC, linked with European Health Insurance Card, and a conception and design of a system for electronic registration and medical services monitoring (e-MSR) and programmes (strategy, plan, schedule) for implementing e-HIC and e-MSR (Reply of the Secretary, 2013). Up to now, the implementation has not been completed.

Another proposal of implementing electronic medical report was using the function of a health insurance card in an electronic identity card as part of the implementation of the programme MSR II. This project was described in a publication on the connection between Health Insurance Card and pl.ID. Its basic aim is to ensure the verification of the parties, place and sequence of a medical transaction (patient and professionals) by means of a cryptographic secret carrier. This project was based on the use of a crypto processor card (Health Insurance Card, Professional's Card) in an environment that was safe for creation of electronic signature. It was also assumed that pl.ID would constitute an electronic document which might be used for verifying a person (including limited identification), creating personal and qualified signatures, and entitles to cross the borders of the countries united by the Schengen Agreement, as well as serves the function of HIC. As a result of a decision by National Council of Ministers of December 2009, the project was linked with pl.ID, in which there was a separate space for HIC. The National Health Fund was developing and handing to the Ministry of the Interior and Administration the document „Technical and functional requirements for Health Insurance Card, HIC application and their environment.

Electronic European Health Insurance Card

One of the elements of a Polish health care system in managing patient information is electronic European Health Insurance Card. It was created as a response to the necessity of verification of a patient in the European Union and in the countries of the Schengen area.

Currently the project of Health Insurance Card for the patient developed in connection with the pl.ID system is suspended in Poland. However, the work on the system of European Health Insurance Card is still underway due to the development of a new conception of the system of patient identification in the countries of European Free Trade Association (Departament Współpracy Międzynarodowej Centrali NFZ, 2012). The most important part of implementation of pl.ID in polish National Registers System is now in the stage of consultation and analysis of future functionalities (Ministerstwo Spraw Wewnętrznych, 2013).

This card may be issued to an insured person with a national identification number Universal Electronic System for Registration of the Population who can prove his/her residence on the territory of the Silesia province. To continue the works ordered by the Health Minister on February 8, 2005, a Group was set up to draw up a strategy for the development of a medical information system in health care, and prepare a conception of implementing European Health Insurance Card and Health Insurance Card. The tasks of this group included drawing up a strategy for the development of a medical information system in health protection and preparing a conception of implementing European Health Insurance Card and Health Insurance Card. The main aim of the implementation of this solution was to (Ujejski, 2011):

- Facilitate the process of registration and confirming the right to health services (effectiveness);
- Improve the reliability of accounting data sent to the National Health Fund (integrity and indisputability);
- Secure access to data (confidentiality);
- Increase the chance of a rescue in emergencies;
- Satisfaction of the entitled, possibility of getting remote access to own data;
- Increase the effectiveness of medical centers (automation of activities);
- Decrease the number of frauds, mainly in the area of accounting for services that have not been provided;
- Improve the quality of data.

Ultimately, health insurance card should be an element of the information system in the health protection system in Poland. However, using such a card entails access to sensitive data, thus one of basic requirements is ensuring security of the information system used in medical services. It should also be able to integrate with the medical services register and medication register. It may also be an instrument for checking insurance as part of processing European Health Insurance Card instead of the National Health Fund slip of the monthly report for the insured person. Electronic medical report should be integrated with the information system for pharmacies and health care centers as well as the electronic system for prescriptions and electronic system for medical appointment referrals (Sołtysik-Piorunkiewicz, 2014c).

The Electronic Verification of Beneficiary Entitlements

At the same time, the Electronic Verification of Beneficiary Entitlements project is being developed in Poland, i.e. Electronic Verification of Beneficiary Entitlements, in compliance with the law on the healthcare services financed from the public funds. From January 1, 2013 patients visiting doctors should present Universal Electronic System for Registration of the Population number and identity card, driving licence or passport, in order to confirm their entitlement to receiving healthcare from public funds [Do lekarza, 2012]. The tests of the system were conducted from October 15 to the end of 2012, and its aim is to introduce orderliness into the system of confirming the entitlement to receive healthcare services. It also takes from doctors the responsibility for checking whether the patient is entitled. The project was created from the cooperation of the Ministry of Administration and Digitalization with the Ministry of Health, National Health Fund (Polish ZUS), Social Insurance Institution and Agricultural Social Insurance Fund, and was consulted with, among other things, the Chief Inspectorate of Personal Data Protection. Thanks to information exchange among the Central List of the Insured of the National Health Fund and Agricultural Social Insurance Fund registers, it will be possible to check online in a hospital or clinic reception whether the patient is insured. There will be no need for the National Health Fund slip of the monthly report for the insured person (although it still will be valid, just like the pensioner identity card and other documents entitling for receiving services).

In the case when the system did not confirm the entitlement to receiving the services (e.g. when the employer did not register the employee for insurance), the statement of the insured person will suffice (art. 7 and 8 of the relevant law).

The introduction of the Electronic Verification of Beneficiary Entitlements system made the procedure of issuing the National Health Fund slip of the monthly report for the insured person more efficient. The citizen doesn't have to produce the monthly report for the insured person slip in the National Health Fund institution, instead he/she can show identity document.

The System of Electronic Prescription E-Prescription

The e-Prescription system is one of the first projects of building a modern IT system in health protection. It is being implemented under the project „Electronic Platform for Gathering, Analysing and Sharing digital resources about medical events", which is part of the country-wide Programme for Health Protection Informatization. The entity responsible for implementing the electronic prescription system is the Centre for Health Information Systems, set up by the Health Minister [Poznaj system e-recepta, 2012]. All the information gathered in the e-Prescription system is protected in accordance with security standards in force. The information in the e-Prescription system is exchanged using encrypted SSL protocol (Secure Sockets Layer), which is a widely used data transmission standard. This allows for the communication in the e-Prescription system to take place only between entitled participants of the prototype and an unauthorized access to data is prevented. Moreover, cryptographic techniques are used to verify and ensure information consistency. The technique of encryption is based on process of transforming plain text or data into cipher data that cannot be read by anyone other than the sender and the intended receiver (Laudon & Laudon, 2011). Usage of encryption is necessary to protect digital information that are stored, transferred, or sent over the Internet. The capability to generate secure session is built into Internet client browser software and servers. SSL is designed to establish a secure connection between both two computers of the client and the server.

The e-Prescription system allows electronic prescription to function parallel with its formal counterpart in the form of a paper prescription. The use of electronic prescription along with a paper prescription does not disturb the existing model of prescriptions circulation which is based only on paper prescriptions. Currently, due to the lack of appropriate regulations regarding the functioning of prescriptions only in an electronic form, an electronic document does not constitute a prescription in the light of law. Writing a prescription in an electronic form takes place by means of a doctor's medical computer program, and in the case when a doctor does not have internal software in his/her surgery, communication with the e-Prescription system occurs through an on-line application.

Pharmacists work with the e-Prescription system directly through their chemist's program, and can also dispense electronic prescriptions through a dedicated on-line application. Patients get access to information about the history of their pharmacotherapy through the e-Prescription Internet Account.

The prototype of the e-Prescription system was launched in mid-March 2011, but the actual processing of prescriptions using this system started on 18 April 2011. The delays were connected with the need to install and launch the system in the entities that signed a cooperation agreement with the Centre for Health Information Systems, and necessity of providing training to medical personnel and pharmacists on how to operate the system.

The e-Prescription system supported 20 facilities, i.e. 2 clinics, 2 doctor's surgeries and 16 chemist's shops. This implementation can be regarded as a pilot implementation across the country in 2012 (Sołtysik-Piorunkiewicz, 2012). However, for the system to be successfully implemented across the whole country, electronic prescription should be regulated by new legal regulations, and in the whole country there should be access to the public database of medicines, patient's insurance card and a tool for doctors authentication.

THE WEB-BASED HEALTHCARE APPLICATIONS IN POLAND FOR SELF-DIAGNOSIS AND SELF-TREATMENT

There is a variety of Internet systems, web pages and portals and other applications connected with healthcare and e-health. This tools, especially used in self-diagnosis and self-treatment has been classified into nine categories:

1. Blogs,
2. Doctors' Internet advices,
3. Drug price comparisons websites,
4. Internet encyclopedias (i.e. Wikipedia),
5. Internet systems indicate disease based on symptoms,
6. Online forums / discussion groups,
7. Online pharmacies,
8. Online video consultation with doctors,
9. Specialized medical portals/ websites about health.

Online pharmacies constitute the next type of the tools used in e-health. The Polish example of an online pharmacy is www.doz.pl, which apart from enabling to order a product, provides a range of information from the "Encyclopedia" concerning a given preparation, e.g. composition, form, effect, dosing, and possible side effects, which accounts for the most of the information placed on the drug information leaflet. The above-mentioned pharmacy also allows asking a "Question to a Pharmacist". Furthermore, it provides a "Related Products" mechanism, which presents a list of products similar to the one already chosen by the user (Doz.pl (n.d.).

The e-health application also includes drug search engines, whose task is to find the equivalent of the refunded drug. An example of a search engine is www.leku.pl, which allows finding a cheaper equivalent of a drug using a name of a preparation or the name of the active substance being an ingredient of the medicament (Leku.pl, n.d.).

Expert systems can also be used as a support for decision making, e.g. INTERNIST in internal medicine (Pople at al., 1975), and others: MYCIN (Buchanann & Shortlife, 1984), FUNAGES (Dimitroula, Bassiliades, Vlahavas, & Dimitrakos, 2001), CASNET (Weiss, Kulikowski, & Safir, 1978), PUFF (Kunz at al., 1978).

Nowadays, the www.dooktor.pl portal operates and provides a free information system. Basing on primary symptoms, the www.dooktor.pl portal allows identification of a particular disease. Therefore, it has the attributes of an expert system (Dooktor.pl (n.d.); Furmankiewicz, Sołtysik-Piorunkiewicz, & Ziuziański, 2014).

The Internet network allows for a round-the-clock contact with a doctor. This is enabled by www.qzdrowiu.pl portal, which provides video-consultations. The user can choose a doctor and make an appointment for a specific date of a video-consultation (Qzdrowiu.pl, n.d.).

The user can also use tools such as comparison shopping engine for comparing the drug prices, Internet forums, and encyclopedias, e.g. www.wikipedia.pl. Comparison shopping engines enable people to find the cheapest product. Additionally, one can share health-related information when using online forums, ask questions, and find alternative treatments. Moreover, the user can write about the progress in a fight against the illness or addiction, and to exchange opinions about doctors or drugs.

Modern technologies, including the Internet, have been widely used in the field of public health, which is reflected in the concept of e-health. To be more specific, the e-health notion can be defined as activities in the spheres such as diagnosis, treatment, control, prevention, and leading a healthy lifestyle with the use of information and communication technologies (Rozpędowska-Matraszek, 2012; Zdrowie publiczne, n.d.).

The Internet plays a key role in the field of health care and treatment, as evidenced by the results of a survey conducted by the ARC Rynek i Opinia company. According to the company's research conducted in 2012, over 60% of the Internet users declare searching the Internet for health information. On the other hand, more than half (52%) of respondents, who search for information on diseases, admitted that they happen to heal themselves or their relatives using methods that have been found via Internet, at the same time resigning from the consultation with a doctor or pharmacist. As many as 91% of respondents claimed that the method found via the Internet roved to be effective (ARC Rynek i Opinia, 2012a). It should also be noted that over 90% of the respondents expressed their willingness to contact a specialist online at the health care unit's official website (e.g. hospital, clinic), if there was such a possibility (ARC Rynek i Opinia, 2012b).

THE RESULTS OF A SURVEY RESEARCH FOR THE MANAGEMENT OF PATIENT INFORMATION IN POLAND

Nowadays usage of artificial intelligent systems such as expert systems, agent systems and others systems for decision support diagnostics support is very interesting topic. This chapter presents results of two kinds of researches: first connected with systems dedicated to the management of the healthcare processes and second on connected with self-diagnosis and self-treatment tool usage.

The main study of usage trends of electronic health care systems was provided in academic year 2013-14 in University of Economics in Katowice. About 200 second year students of master degree were invited to complete a questionnaire after explaining the topic about e-health during one of the course. The authors elicited themes for the questionnaire by asking a focus group of second year students how they use and know the implementation of electronic health care systems for citizens in Poland and in the world and what is the most important functionality of electronic health care system for them as the patients. Three themes emerged: using of EKUZ during vacations and going abroad, access to online resources about medical health care record and personal medical history, and implementation of other IT systems in e-health. The authors added a two theme: using of e-WUŚ for the publicly funded health care and the Integrated Patient System (EHR) for finding the historic data about amount of treatment of patient. The author created a 5-item questionnaire, based on these themes. Each answer had the three possibility to choose in questionnaire: "Yes", "No", and "I don't know". The survey was prepared on web platform Net-ankieta.pl. The authors emailed an electronic survey link to consenting students.

The Polish Information Electronic Health Record System or Others Information Systems Dedicated to the Management of the Healthcare Processes in Poland

In April 2014, the research team conducted a study on the management of information concerning the patient. The study was conducted using an online questionnaire (Computer-Assisted Web Interview method, abbr. CAWI). The questionnaire was completed by 229 respondents. Men accounted for 36% of the survey sample, whereas women constituted 64% of the group.

The respondents gave answers to the question whether they use health services in the Polish health care system based on health insurance in accordance with the data in the e-WUŚ system, a system of electronic verification of patients' rights (Elektroniczna Weryfikacja Uprawnień Świadczeniobiorców, abbr. e-WUŚ). The results are presented in Figure 2.

The e-WUŚ system was implemented January 1, 2013, and is used by health care units cooperating with the National Health Fund (Narodowy Fundusz Zdrowia, abbr. NFZ). Around 57% of respondents using health care benefits acknowledge their right for a free execution of these services via e-WUŚ system. When using health care benefits, 27% of respondents do not know whether they use the e-WUŚ system or not, whereas 16% of the surveyed claimed they do not use e-WUŚ system.

Subsequently, the respondents were asked about the use of health services in the European health care system based on the European Health Insurance Card (abbr. EHIC). The results are presented in Figure 3.

As many as 22% of respondents using health services in the European health care system confirm their rights resulting from EHIC.

Then, respondents were asked whether they are registered in ZIP system, the integrated patient information (Zintegrowany Informator Pacjenta, abbr. ZIP), which, like e-WUŚ was implemented in Poland in 2013. The respondents' answers are presented in Figure 4.

Figure 2. The use of the e-WUŚ by respondents

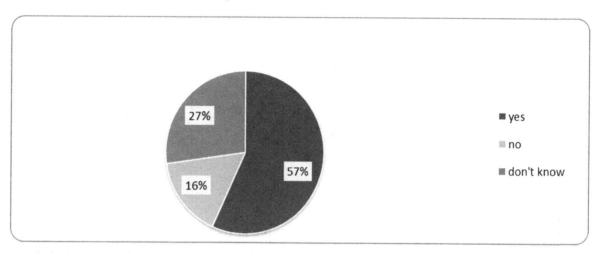

Figure 3. The use of the EHIC by respondents

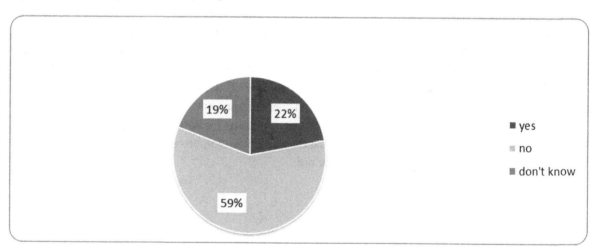

Figure 4. The registration in the ZIP system

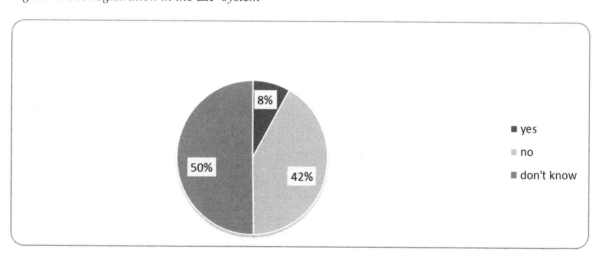

Figure 5. Consistency of data in the ZIP system

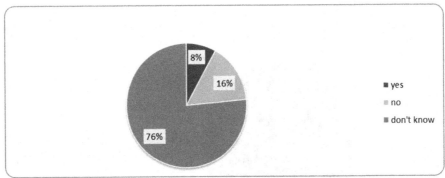

Being registered in the ZIP system was declared by 8% of the people participating in the survey. Around 42% of respondents declared that they are not registered in the ZIP system. However, it is disturbing that a half of the respondents do not know whether they are registered in the system or not. This may result from ignorance concerning the implementation and purpose of the system.

Respondents also answered a question concerning the consistency of the data gathered in the ZIP system with the actual course of the respondent's medical history. The results are presented in Figure 5.

As many as 8% of the respondents, the identical percentage of respondents that declared to be registered in the ZIP, confirmed the consistency of the data stored in the system with the actual state.

The last question to be answered by the surveyed concerned the use of other systems designed to manage the patient information. The respondents' answers are presented in Figure 6.

Only 2% of the respondents claim that they use other systems for patient information management. A huge majority, i.e.75% of the surveyed state that they do not use other systems, and 23% do not know if they use other information technology tools or not.

Figure 6. The use of other systems for patient information management

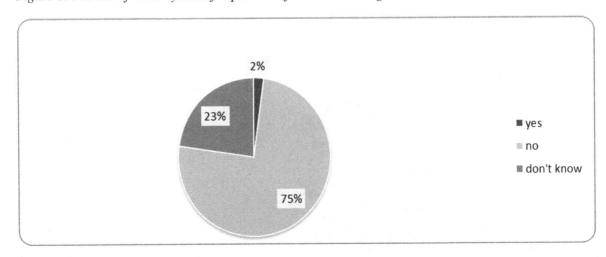

Self-Diagnosis and Self-Treatment Tool Usage Researches

In 2013 research team conducted a study on the evaluation of the use ICT (especially Internet technologies) in the self-treatment and self-diagnosis process. One year later team conducted researches once again. Researches main aim is checking popularity and reliability of these tools and Internet evaluation in the context of traditional sources of information about health and its role that it assumes in modern human life (Furmankiewicz & Ziuziański, 2013). The researches were carried out with the use of an Internet questionnaire (CAWI method). The survey was conducted in late April and early May 2014 and lasted less than a month. Previous study lasted for 10 days in March 2013. The survey in 2013 had a pilot character. It was conducted among 212 respondents. In 2014 research sample was significantly increased to 526 respondents. Gender distributions of these two samples are presented in the Figure 7.

Respondents were asked about their use of self-diagnosis and self-treatment tool. The results are presented in Figure 8.

According to the respondents the most commonly used tools include: online forums / discussion groups, specialized medical portals/ websites about health and internet encyclopedias (i.e. Wikipedia). Least likely respondents use online video consultation with doctors, Internet systems indicate disease based on symptoms and doctors' Internet advices. The results compared to a year earlier survey do not differ too much, which confirms that the most popular tools, the use of which fluctuates around 70% are online forums / discussion groups, specialized medical portals/ websites about health.

Noteworthy respondents evaluation of the reliability of self-diagnosis and self-healing tools. Their task was to evaluate the different tools on a scale from 1 to 5 then calculated the average scores of all respondents. The results are presented in the Figure 9.

The most reliable of these tools became online video consultation with doctors, specialized medical portals/ websites about health and Doctors' Internet advices. According to respondents least credible are blogs, internet systems indicate disease based on symptoms and online forums / discussion groups.

Comparison of test results from the previous year to this year's research suggests only conclude that the assessment of the respondents in the two studies are similar.

Figure 7. Structure of respondents by gender and sample numbers.

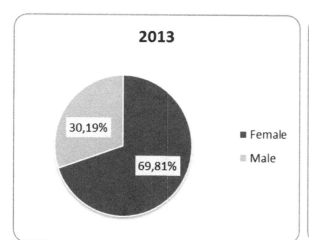
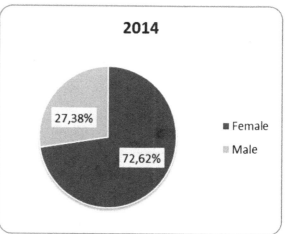

Figure 8. Self-diagnosis and self-treatment tools using by respondents.

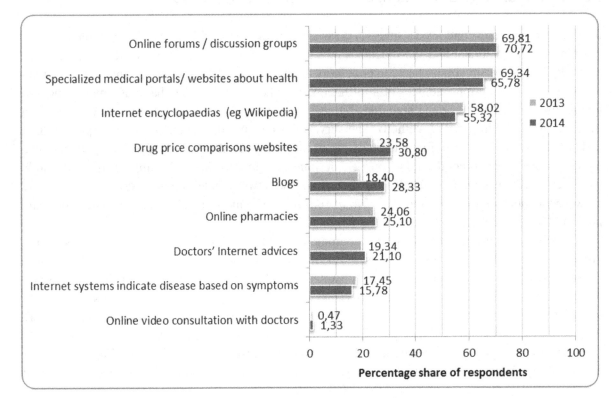

Figure 9. Respondents ratings about the reliability of self-diagnosis and self-healing tools

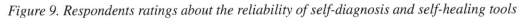

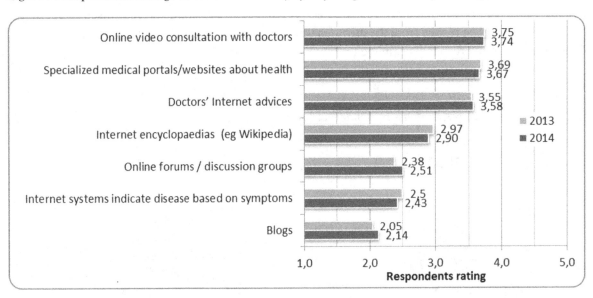

Figure 10. Evaluation of the reliability of source knowledge about health according to respondents

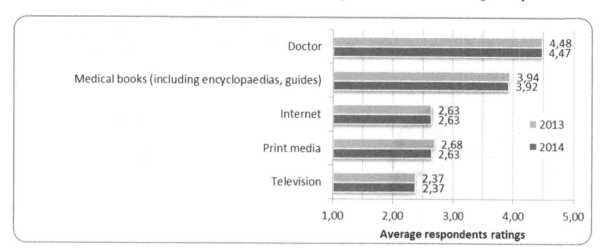

In addition to evaluation of the credibility of the individual tools used for self-diagnosis and self-medication, respondents were asked to evaluate the credibility of various sources of information about health on a scale from 1 to 5. Evaluations have calculated the average. The lowest was rated television, then print media and the internet. The above were evaluated medical books (including encyclopedias, guides) and the highest doctor. The results are presented in the Figure 10.

The results from last year are almost identical to current research findings. It appears that the Internet is perceived better than television and on the same level as the print media in the context of credibility.

Invariably, the most reliable source of health information is a doctor.

A very interesting question in questionnaire was question about the effectiveness of tips obtained on the Internet. As many as 44% of respondents said that the tips are usually effective, 27% of respondents said that it is not looking for advice on the Internet. The results are presented in graph X. Another question about self-diagnosing was a question about failing visiting doctor because of advice obtained on the Internet. Of the 18% of respondents answered that happened to them (previous year: 20.75%). Respondents' answers are presented in the Figure 11.

Failure of medical visits can be interpreted in terms of both positive and negative. Because the Internet has replaced to some extent, e.g. GP or medical specialist queue waiting times can be reduced. You can also avoid a situation in which a patient visits a doctor with trivial reason that he does not endanger the lives and health. On the other hand, disregard the symptoms of disorders of homeostasis or misinterpretation of symptoms can result in serious consequences and lead in extreme cases, even death. It is also alarming that only 13% of respondents using health-related websites verify competencies' advice. One of the questions in questionnaire was dedicated to respondents' level of agreement or disagreement on a Likert scale regarding to statement: *The anonymity on the Internet allows freer discussion of shameful topics about the health.* 84,03% of respondents strongly agreed or agreed with this statement.

Figure 11. Tips obtained on the Internet: effectiveness and risks according to respondents

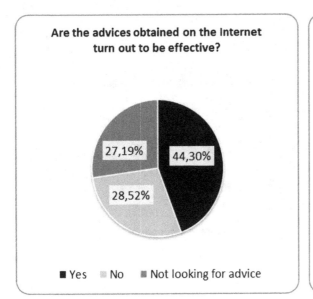
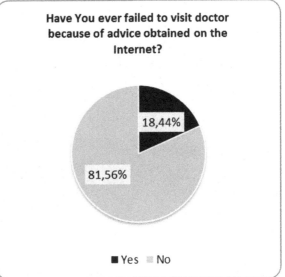

WEB HEALTHCARE APPLICATIONS: STRENGTHS, WEAKNESSES, OPPORTUNITIES, THREATS

The authors of this publication as a form of summary previous considerations chosen SWOT analysis.

Strengths of Web-Based Application

The strengths of Web-based application for e-health are easy way of communication between: patient and health care unit (i.e. arrange visit, obtain medical results), National Health Fund and healthcare providers (i.e. checking if patient is insured), and Government and other stakeholders in Polish healthcare system (i.e. information portals, e-mails). Source of knowledge for patients, doctors, pharmacists and other people are involved into health care. Also power of healthy lifestyle promoting tools is helping to monitor sport activity and food consumed.

Weaknesses of Web-Based Application

There are a few weaknesses of Web-based application. First it is hard to verify truthfulness and original source of knowledge, and second patients without access to Internet cannot take advantage of the benefits of the Web-based application.

Opportunities of Web-Based Application

There are a lot of opportunities of Web-based application: chance to solve not very important Internauts' health problems without medical consultation, and connecting people with the same health problem from all over the world in order to mentally support each other and get knowledge about methods of

Figure 12. Results of SWOT analysis of Web-based application in health care

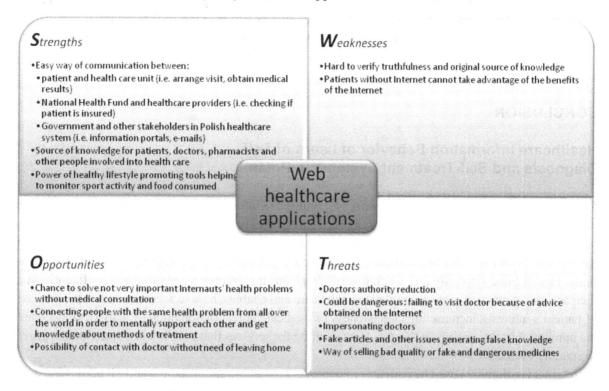

treatment. And one of the most important during self-diagnosis and self-treatment is the possibility of contact with doctor without need of leaving home

Threats of Web-Based Application

We can describe also some threats of Web-based application, e.g. doctor's authority reduction. The Web-based application also could be dangerous because of failing to visit doctor thanks to advice obtained on the Internet, or impersonating doctors, fake articles and other issues generating false knowledge, and it could be the way of selling bad quality or fake and dangerous medicines.

The results of analysis of Web-based application for health care is presented in the Figure 12.

FUTURE RESEARCH DIRECTIONS

EHR implementation is essential to improving patient safety but is still highly heterogeneous across health care systems and providers, and this heterogeneity leads to equally variable implications for patient safety (Sittig & Singh, 2012). As a conclusion of the study about trends of using electronic health care systems by patient, students of University of Economics in Katowice reported some needs of usage of the European Health Insurance Card, but they mostly reported the lack of knowledge about implementation and functionality of information systems in Polish health care. Only part of them was interested in finding the information about health care in EHRs data bases of Integrated Patient System, and only a few of them had the own id and tried to use it on the online platform for e-health services.

The future research should be conducted to discover the reason of this state of knowledge about Polish electronic health care system.

CONCLUSION

Healthcare Information Behavior of users of Self-Diagnosis and Self-Treatment Systems in Poland.

The most important reason of future changes of healthcare information behavior could be to learn the citizens about functionality of implemented electronic systems in health care (usage of courses at the universities to make a progress in that field), facilitate the process of registration and confirmation of the right to health services (effectiveness), improve the reliability of accounting data sent to the National Health Fund (integrity and incontrovertibility), ensure a secure access to data (confidentiality), increase the satisfaction of those entitled to health care and enable a remote access to own data (increase of patient's interest), increase the effectiveness of medical centers (automation of activities), decrease the number of frauds, mainly in the area of accounting for services that have not been provided improve the quality of data.

Internet is a common used by patients or people seeking information about health. It allows freedom especially in the discussion of embarrassing health topics. It should be emphasized that the respondents indicated that the Internet is a more reliable source of information than television and it is at similar level in relation to print media. Conducted researches shows that Polish Internet users mostly use specialized medical portals/websites about health and online forums/discussion groups, while the least likely they use online video consultation with doctors. It is worth noting that video consultation is considered as the most reliable tool, while online forums/discussion groups, internet systems indicate disease based on symptoms and blogs are the least reliable.

The Web-based application in e-health could be a valuable source of knowledge, but it should be rather complement of the knowledge, not a substitute for a medical visit. In order to avoid the dangers arising from the use of the Internet in the area of e-health, patients should use it with caution: trust credible sources, respectively filter pieces of information and consult with specialists. Due to the fact that the respondents showed great confidence in online video consultation with doctors, it can be assumed that maybe there will be a some breakthrough in healthcare and traditional stationary clinic could be replaced by a virtual clinic in a future.

Presented researches in e-health area in Poland should be deepened and extended. Usage of web tools for self-diagnosis and self-treatment and government e-health systems usage by Poles is a very interesting area.

E-Health Readiness in Polish Information Society

The computerisation of the Polish health care are still concentrated mainly on meeting the objectives set by the European Commission concerning e-Health. The main issues presented in the „e-Health Poland" plan which must be implemented by 2015, generally:

1. Creating procedures and guidelines, collecting and sharing good practices to improve the management of a health care centre through the implementation of information and communication Web-based systems .
2. Modernizing the medical information system to ensure the analysis of the demand for health services
3. Practical realization of the development of IT solutions in health protection following the guidelines of the European Commission to allow the Republic of Poland to be included into the area of interoperational Electronic Health Record.

Additionally the Web-based application could ensure citizens an easier access to health care information, improve the effectiveness of the health care system with regard to an electronic flow of information.

REFERENCES

Apteka Euromedica. (2014). Aptekaeuromedica.pl. Retrieved from http://www.aptekaeuromedica.pl

Buchanann, B., & Shortlife, E. (1984). Rule-Based Expert Systems. The Mycin Experiments of the Stanford Heuristic Project. Reading: Addison-Wesley; Retrieved from http://aitopics.org/sites/default/files/classic/Buchanan/Buchanan00.pdf

Cieciura, M. (2006). *Podstawy technologii informacyjnych z przykładami zastosowań.* Warszawa: Wyd. Opolgraf SA.

Departament Współpracy Międzynarodowej Centrali, N. F. Z. (2012). Departament Współpracy Międzynarodowej Centrali NFZ. Retrieved from https://www.ekuz.nfz.gov.pl/

Handbuch zur Kalkulation von Fallkosten. Version 2.0 (2002). Deutsche Krankenhausgesellschaft. Retrieved from http://www.aokgesundheitspartner.de/imperia/md/gpp/bund/krankenhaus/drg_system/kalkulation/kalkulationshandbuch_2_0.pdf

Dimitroula, V., Bassiliades, N., Vlahavas, I., & Dimitrakos, S. (2001). FUNAGES: An expert system for fundus fluorescein angiography. *Health Informatics Journal, 7*(3-4), 214–221. http://lpis.csd.auth.gr/publications/shimr2001.pdf doi:10.1177/146045820100700317

Direction *Directions of development of e-services in health protection in West Pomeranian Voivodeship for the years 2011-2020.* (2011). Szczecin. Retrieved from www.wz.wzp.pl/download/index/biblioteka/7620

Directions of informatisation "e-Health Poland" for the years 2011-2015. (2009). Retrieved from www.csioz.gov.pl/publikacja.php

Dooktor.pl. (n.d.). *Dooktor.pl.* Retrieved from http://www.dooktor.pl/diagnoza.html

Doz.pl. (n.d.). *Dbam o zdrowie.* Retrieved from http://www.doz.pl

Friedberg, M. W., Chen, P. G., Van Busum, K. R., Aunon, F. M., Pham, Ch., Caloyeras, J. P., et al. (2013). *Factors Affecting Physician Professional Satisfaction and Their Implications for Patient Care, Health Systems, and Health Policy,* The RAND Corporation. Retrieved from http://www.rand.org/content/dam/rand/pubs/research_reports/RR400/RR439/RAND_RR439.pdf

Furmankiewicz, M., Sołtysik-Piorunkiewicz, A., & Ziuziański, P. (2014). Artificial Intelligence Systems for Knowledge Management in e-Health: The Study of Intelligent Software Agents. In *Proceedings of the 18th International Conference on Systems* (part of CSCC '14), Santorini, pp. 551-556.

Furmankiewicz, M., & Ziuziański, P. (2013). Ocena wykorzystania technologii teleinformatycznych w procesie autodiagnozy i samoleczenia w świetle badania opinii internautów. H. Sroki & T. Porębska-Miąc (Eds.) Systemy Wspomagania Organizacji SWO 2013, Katowice: Wydawnictwo Uniwersytetu Ekonomicznego w Katowicach.

Goldzweig, C. L., Towfigh, A., Maglione, M., & Shekelle, P. G. (2009). Costs and benefits of health information technology: new trends from the literature. Retrieved from http://www.ncbi.nlm.nih.gov/pubmed/19174390

Han, H., & Lopp, L. (2013). Writing and reading in the electronic health record: an entirely new world. *Medical Education Online*. Retrieved from http://www.ncbi.nlm.nih.gov/pmc/ articles /PMC3566375/

Kaplan, B., & Harris-Salamone, K. (2009). Health IT Success and Failure: Recommendations from Literature and an AMIA Workshop. Retrieved from http://www.ncbi.nlm.nih.gov/pmc/articles/PMC2732244/

Karnowka, A., Shafer, K., & Sularz, B. (n.d.). *System ekspertowy Mycin*. Retrieved from zsi.tech.us.edu. pl/~anowak/index.php?s=file_download&id=21

Kawiorska, D. (2004). *Narodowe Rachunki Zdrowia*. Kraków: Kantor Wydawniczy ZAKAMYCZE.

Korczak, K. (2014). *Internetowe narzędzia wspomagające opiekę zdrowotną*. Warszawa: Wolters Kluwer.

Kralewski, J. E., Dowd, B. E., Cole-Adeniyi, T., Gans, D., Malakar, L., & Elson, B. (2008). Factors influencing physician use of clinical electronic information technologies after adoption by their medical group practices. *Health Care Manage Rev*. Retrieved from http://www.ncbi.nlm.nih.gov/pubmed/18815501

Kunz, J. C., Fallat, R. J., McClung, D. H., Osborne, J. J., Votteri, R. A., & Nii, H. P. ... Feigenbaum, E.A. (1978). A Physiological Rule-based System for Interpreting Pulmonary Function Test Results, Stanford University.

Laudon, K., & Laudon, J. (2011). Essentials of management information systems [9th Edition]. New Jearey: Pearson.

Leku.pl. (n. d.). Retrieved from http://www.leku.pl

Menachemi, N., & Brooks, R. G. (2006). EHR and other IT adoption among physicians: results of a largescale statewide analysis. *J Healthc Inf Manag*. Retrieved from http://www.ncbi.nlm.nih.gov/pubmed/16903665

Menachemi, N., Perkins, R. M., van Durme, D. J., & Brooks, R. G. (2006). Examining the adoption of electronic health records and personal digital assistants by family physicians in Florida. *Inform Prim Care*. Retrieved from http://www.ncbi.nlm.nih.gov/pubmed/16848961

Ministerstwo Administracji i Cyfryzacji. (2012). *Do lekarza z PESELem, czyli e-WUŚ*. Retrieved from http://mac.gov.pl/dzialania/e-administracja/do-lekarza-z-peselem/

Ministerstwo Spraw Wewnętrznych. (2013). *Nowa odsłona projektu pl.ID*. Retrieved from https://msw. gov.pl/pl/aktualnosci/11600,Nowaodslona-projektu-plID.html

Mulawka, J. J. (1996). *Systemy ekspertowe*. Warszawa: Wydawnictwo Naukowo-Techniczne.

Narodowy Fundusz Zdrowia. (2013). Karta Ubezpieczenia Zdrowotnego. Retrieved from http://www. nfzkatowice.

National Library of Medicine. (n.d.). Medline Plus. Retrieved from http://www.nlm.nih.gov/medlineplus

NHS.uk. (n.d.). The NHS in the 1990s. Retrieved from http://www.nhs.uk/NHSEngland/thenhs/nhshistory/Pages/NHShistory1990s.aspx

Opoka, J. (2008). Multimedia w edukacji. *Studia i Materiały Centrum Edukacji Przyrodniczo-Leśnej*, 10, 1[17], p. 120.

Pankowska, M. (2004). Value-driven management in e-healthcare. *Studies in Health Technology and Informatics*, *105*, 3–11. PMID:15718588

Pollard, S. E., Neri, P. M., Wilcox, A. R., Volk, L. A., Williams, D. H., & Schiff, G. D. … Bates, D.W. (2013). How physicians document outpatient visit notes in an electronic health record. Retrieved from http://www.ncbi.nlm.nih.gov/pubmed/22542717

Poon, E. G., Wright, A., Simon, S. R., Jenter, C. A., Kaushal, R., & Volk, L. A. … Bates, D.W. (2010). Relationship between use of electronic health record features and health care quality: results of a statewide survey. *Med Care*. Retrieved from http://www.ncbi.nlm.nih.gov/pubmed/20125047

Pople, H. E. Jr., Myers, R.D., Miller, R.A. (1975). DIALOG: A Model of Diagnostic Logic for Internal Medicine. *International Joint Conferences on Artificial Intelligence* 4.

Poznaj system e-Recepta (2012). *Poznaj system e-recepta*. Retrieved from http://e-recepta.gov.pl/web/ sim/poznaj-system-e-recepta

Przelaskowski, A. (2011). *Techniki multimedialne*. Warszawa: PW OKNO (pp. iii, 3).

Qzdrowiu.pl. (n. d.). Retrieved from http://www.qzdrowiu.pl

Reply of the Secretary. (2013). Reply of the Secretary of State Zbigniew Podraza in Health Ministry – on behalf of the Minister – to the question no 9353 concerning resigning from introducing a medical services register 02.03.2005. Retrieved from http://orka2.sejm.gov.pl/IZ4.nsf/main/7719F1C7

Rouf, E., Chumley, H. S., & Dobbie, A. E. (2008). Electronic health records in outpatient clinics: perspectives of third year medical students, *BMC Med Educ*. Retrieved from http://www.ncbi.nlm.nih.gov/ pubmed/18373880

Rozpędowska-Matraszek, D. (2012). e-Zdrowie w kształtowaniu zatrudnienia w opiece zdrowotnej. In Zieliński Z. (Ed.), Rola informatyki w naukach ekonomicznych i społecznych. Innowacje i implikacje interdyscyplinarne, Tom 1/2012, Kielce: Wydawnictwo Wyższej Szkoły Handlowej w Kielcach.

Rynek i Opinia, A. R. C. (2012a). *Internet leczy skutecznie*. Retrieved from http://www.arc.com.pl/ internet_leczy_skutecznie-40999450-pl.html

Rynek i Opinia, A. R. C. (2012b). *Lekarz online poszukiwany*. Retrieved from http://www.arc.com.pl/lekarz_online_poszukiwany-41999453-pl.html

Shekelle, P. G., Morton, S. C., & Keeler, E. B. (2006). Costs and benefits of health information technology. [Full Rep]. *Evid Rep Technol Assess*, (132): 1–71. Retrieved from http://www.ncbi.nlm.nih.gov/pubmed/17627328 PMID:17627328

Sidorko, A. (2012). *Druk RMUA co miesiąc tylko na wyraźne żądanie pracownika*. Retrieved from http://serwisy.gazetaprawna.pl/praca-i-kariera/artykuly/613096,druk_rmua_co_miesiac_tylko_na_wyrazne_zadanie_pracownika.html

Sittig, D. F., & Singh, H. (2012). *Electronic Health Records and National Patient-Safety Goals*. Retrieved from http://www.ncbi.nlm.nih.gov/pmc/articles/PMC3690003/#!po=50.0000

Sittig, D. F., Wright, A., Meltzer, S., Simonaitis, L., Evans, R. S., & Nichol, W. P. … Middleton B. (2011). Comparison of clinical knowledge management capabilities of commercially-available and leading internally-developed electronic health records. *BMC Med Inform Decis Mak*. Retrieved from http://www.ncbi.nlm.nih.gov/pubmed/21329520

Sołtysik-Piorunkiewicz, A. (2009). Kontroling w organizacji i zarządzaniu. Koncepcja informatyzacji. Sosnowiec: Oficyna Wydawnicza „HUMANITAS", 2009, p. 177.

Sołtysik-Piorunkiewicz, A. (2012). Implementation of IT system in health protection. In R. Knosala (Ed.), *Innovations in management and production engineering* (pp. 568–576). Opole: Oficyna Wydawnicza Polskiego Towarzystwa Zarządzania Produkcją.

Sołtysik-Piorunkiewicz, A. (2014a, June 24). The Telecom Business Strategies: a Comparative Study of Corporate Blogs. *Proceedings of the 2014 Multimedia, Interaction, Design and Innovation International Conference on Multimedia, Interaction, Design and Innovation* (pp. 1-11). ACM. doi:10.1145/2643572.2643592

Sołtysik-Piorunkiewicz, A. (2014b). Technologie mobilne w zarządzaniu organizacją opartą na wiedzy. In R. Knosala (Ed.), *Komputerowo Zintegrowane Zarządzanie. Część VIII. Zarządzanie wiedzą, transfer wiedzy, systemy wspomagania podejmowania decyzji* (pp. 263–274). Opole: Oficyna Wydawnicza Polskiego Towarzystwa Zarządzania Produkcją.

Sołtysik-Piorunkiewicz, A. (2014c). The management of patient information in Polish health care system. International Journal Information Theories and Applications, 21(2).

Sołtysik-Piorunkiewicz, A. (2015a). Knowledge management impact of information technology Web 2.0/3.0. The case study of agent software technology usability in knowledge management system. *AIP Conference Proceedings*, *1644*(1), 219–227. doi:10.1063/1.4907840

Sołtysik-Piorunkiewicz, A. (2015b): The evaluation method of Web 2.0/3.0 usability in e-health knowledge management system. *Online Journal of Applied Knowledge Management*, 3(2), 168-180.

System Zdrowotny Informator Pacjenta. (2013). System: Zdrowotny Informator Pacjenta. Retrieved from https://zip.nfz.poznan.pl/ap-zip-user/

Thatcher, M. (2013). IT Governance in Acute Healthcare: A Critical Review of Current Literature. In C. George, D. Whitehouse, P. Duquenoy (Eds.), *eHealth: Legal, Ethical and Governance Challenges* (pp. 349-370). Retrieved from http://link.springer.com/chapter/10.1007/978-3-642-22474-4_15

Ujejski, M. (2011). Funkcje karty ubezpieczenia zdrowotnego realizowane w elektronicznym dowodzie osobistym. Proceedings of *Materiały konferencyjne "IT w służbie zdrowia GigaCon"*, Warszawa. Retrieved from http://sdcenter.pl/system/lectures/attachment1s/1729/original/Funkcje_KUZ_w_pl.ID_23.03.2011_final_pdf?1301043192

Venkatesh, V., Morris, M. G., Davis, G. B., & Davis, F. D. (2003). User acceptance of information technology: Toward a unified view. *Management Information Systems Quarterly*, *27*, 425–478.

Weiss, S. M., Kulikowski, C. A., & Safir, A. (1978). A Model-Based Consultation System the Long-term Management Glaucoma. *International Joint Conferences on Artificial Intelligence*, *5*.

Zdrowie publiczne (n. d.). Retrieved from http://www.ec.europa.eu/health-eu/care_for_me/e-health/index_pl.htm

Zintegrowany Informator Pacjenta. (n.d.). *Zintegrowany Informator Pacjenta*. Retrieved from https://zip.nfz.gov.pl

Ziuziański, P., Furmankiewicz, M., & Sołtysik-Piorunkiewicz, A. (2014). E-health artificial intelligence system implementation: Case study of knowledge management dashboard of epidemiological data in Poland. *International Journal of Biology and Biomedical Engineering*, *8*, 164–171.

KEY TERMS AND DEFINITIONS

Decision Support Systems (DSS): Information system supporting activities connected with decision-making process.

E-Health: An emerging area in the intersection of public health, medical informatics and business.

Electronic Health Record (EHR): Also named electronic medical record (EMR). A systematic set of electronic health information about population or individual patient.

Expert System: A computer program which perform tasks in many categories using knowledge base.

Information Society: A society where information is a significant activity equal or even more valuable than material goods.

Management of Patient Information System: It is the information management system dedicated for patient and health protection, generally brings satisfaction and their implications for patient care, health systems, and health policy. IT systems in health care is implemented for management of patient information and gives many benefits; the using of information technology can bring for health care more quality and savings, implementing of even smaller-scale systems can minimize complexity and difficulties of health care processes.

Medical Portal: Specially-designed Web page connected with medicine and/or health which is aimed to distribute pieces of information from many sources in homogeneous way.

Online Consultation with Doctors: The form of consultation when patient and doctor are using computer and Internet to communicate using text-messaging, sound and/or view.

Self-Diagnosis or Self-Treatment Tool: A webpage, forum, computer/mobile application (like expert system), etc. using by patients to auto diagnosing or auto heal themselves.

Chapter 14
Evaluation of Mathematical Cognitive Functions with the Use of EEG Brain Imaging

Antonia Plerou
Ionian University, Greece

Panayiotis Vlamos
Ionian University, Greece

ABSTRACT

During the last decades, the interest displayed in neurocognitive and brain science research is relatively high. In this chapter, the cognitive neuroscience field approach focuses in the aspect of the way that cognitive functions are produced by neural circuits in the brain. Within this frame, the effects of impairment to the brain and subsequent changes in the thought processes due to changes in neural circuitry resulting from the ensued damage are analyzed and evaluated. All cognitive functions result from the integration of many simple processing mechanisms, distributed throughout the brain. Brain cortex structures, linked with cognitive disorders, are located in several parts like the frontal, the parietal, the temporal, the occipital lobe and more are analyzed and specified. A critical topic of this chapter in the evaluation of brain operations is mapping regions that control cognitive and mathematical concepts functions. Dyscalculia, in this chapter, is described as a specific disorder of managing and conceiving mathematical concepts. Dyscalculia could be identified by difficulties in visual perception, in spatial number organization, in basic mathematical operations and in mathematical induction logic. Moreover, people who deal with dyscalculia present problems, in Euclidean and Non-Euclidean Geometry concepts perception, in Calculus aspects as well as in solving algorithmic problems where the design, the description and the application of algorithmic steps are required. In order to enhance cognitive brain functions perception, the use of EEG brain imaging is proposed measuring cerebral activity and event-related potentials. The procedure described in this chapter is about the comparison and contrasts EEG brain imaging patterns of healthy volunteers to EEG samples taken of adults considered being at risk of mathematics learning disabilities such as Dyscalculia and algorithmic thinking difficulties. EEG interpretation analysis is to follow where the deviation of a normal and an abnormal range of wave's frequency are defined. Several

DOI: 10.4018/978-1-4666-8659-5.ch014

visualized EEG patterns in relevance with specific abnormalities are presented while several neuro-cognitive generated disorders could be identified with the use of EEG Brain-imaging technique. The electroencephalogram EEG brain imaging procedure, in order to evaluate problems associated with brain function, is to be further analyzed in this chapter as well. The EEG is the depiction of the electrical activity occurring at the surface of the brain. The recorded waveforms reflect the cortical electrical activity and they are generally classified according to their frequency (Delta, Theta, Beta, Alpha, Beta, and Gamma) amplitude, and shape. EEG Implementation with the use of 10/20 system of the standardized position of scalp electrodes placement for a classical EEG recording is described as well. The EEG implementation objective is to identify, classify and evaluate those frequencies and regions in the brain that best characterize brain activity associated with mathematical learning disabilities. Mapping the brain with non-invasive techniques based on trigger and sensing/evaluation experimental multimedia methods similar to those used in computer games and applications are expected to provide relevant results in order to enhance and confirm theoretical cognitive aspects. At that point, a cognitive and mathematical perception evaluation is to follow and specifically the assessment of the relation of difficulties in mathematics with particular parts of the human brain. EEG wave data visualization is contacted with the use of Acknowledge an interactive, intuitive program which provides data analysis instantly. At the end of this chapter EEG computational evaluation with the use of pattern recognition methods as well as the intuition of author's future work in relevance with the use of experimental multimedia technologies to enhance the dynamic recognition and evaluation of user cognitive responses during EEG implementation are noted.

INTRODUCTION

All thought several brain imaging techniques are used in order to evaluate several neurocognitive disorders like Alzheimer disease, dipolar disorder, epilepsy, ADHD and so one, the field concerning learning difficulties with the use of brain imaging techniques is yet to be explored. Especially while dyscalculia has been studied for many years within the frame of an educational field, cognitive neuroscience research on dyscalculia is a recent lighted research field. This paper presents a review of the use of EEG brain imaging for the recognition of mental tasks from on-line spontaneous EEG signals. Within this study the importance of the visualization and evaluation and of the neurological frame related to brain structure and function is presented as well as the use of EEG brain imaging technique in order to the neurological aspects of dyscalculia. In this process, experimental multimedia technologies may be employed in order to identify and compare imaging data. Dyscalculia is difficulty in learning or comprehending arithmetic, such as difficulty in understanding numbers, learning how to manipulate numbers, and learning facts in Mathematics and much more. It is considered to be a specific developmental disorder. With the use electroencephalogram, brain imaging technique abnormalities in the brain waves or electrical activity of the brain are evaluated. Findings of the EEG visualization method implementation and evaluation aim to confirm a potential compensatory mechanism of brain function related with dyscalculia and algorithmic thinking difficulties.

Related Work

According to S. Rotzer research using functional brain imaging (fMRI) applied to adults indicated a number of brain regions involved in the performance of arithmetic tasks. Especially the horizontal segment of the intraparietal sulcus (HIPS) is the region noted to be the most involved with number representation capacities. Additional areas which are related to working memory and visuospatial attention such as frontal and anterior cingulate components were noted to be activated during number processing (Rotzer et al., 2008).

Additionally according Stanescu-Cosson et al. research neuropsychological study revealed that bilateral intraparietal, precentral, dorsolateral and superior prefrontal regions showed greater activation during approximation, while the left inferior prefrontal cortex and the bilateral angular regions were more activated during exact calculation. However, approximation and exact calculation with large numbers in this case study showed higher activation on the left and right parietal cortices, which may encode numbers in a non-verbal quantity format. (Stanescu-Cosson, 2000)

Anja's Ischebeck et al. functional magnetic resonance imaging (fMRI) study is focused in modifications of brain activation patterns of adults while training in two different arithmetic operations, multiplication, and subtraction. Contrasts between untrained and trained operations showed stronger activation of inferior frontal and parietal regions, especially along the banks of the intraparietal sulcus. The reverse contrasts, trained minus untrained operations, yielded significantly higher activation in the left angular gyrus for multiplication but no significantly activated area for subtraction. A basic concussion conducted of this study is that learning appears not only to depend on the method of learning but also on its content. (Ischebeck et al., 2006)

According to Martijn Arns work, the different brain activation patterns in dyslexic children are explored. The research group is evaluated with EEG brain imaging technique in reference to dyslexic children using QEEGQ (Quantitative electroencephalography) and neuropsychological tests in order to investigate the underlying neural processes in dyslexia. In this case study, a group of dyslexic children were compared with a matched control group from the Brain Resource International Database on measures of cognition and brain function. The dyslexic group showed increased slow activity (Delta and Theta) in the frontal and right temporal regions of the brain. Beta-1 was specifically increased at F7. Additionally EEG coherence was increased in the frontal, central and temporal regions for all frequency bands. There was a symmetrical increase in coherence for the lower frequency bands (Delta and Theta) and a specific right temporal-central increase in coherence for the higher frequency bands (Alpha and Beta). (Arns, Peters, Breteler, & Verhoeven, 2007)

Cognitive Neuroscience

Cognitive neuroscience is an academic field concerned with the scientific study of biological substrates underlying cognition, with a specific focus on the neural substrates of mental processes (Gazzaniga, 2011). It addresses the questions of how psychological - cognitive functions are produced by neural circuits in the brain. Cognitive neuroscience is a branch of both psychology and neuroscience, overlapping with disciplines such as physiological psychology, cognitive psychology, and neuropsychology. Cognitive neuroscience relies upon theories in cognitive science coupled with evidence from neuropsychology and computational modeling (Gazzaniga, 2013).

Methods employed in cognitive neuroscience include experimental paradigms from psychophysics and cognitive psychology, functional neuroimaging, electrophysiology, cognitive genomics and behavioral genetics. Studies of patients with cognitive deficits due to brain lesions constitute an important aspect of cognitive neuroscience (Rugg & Yonelinas, 2003). Within the frame of cognitive neuroscience the effects of damage to the brain and subsequent changes in the thought processes due to changes in neural circuitry resulting from the ensued damage are analyzed and evaluated (Robertson, Manly, Andrade, Baddeley, & Yiend, 1997). Additionally, cognitive abilities based on brain development are studied and examined under the subfield of developmental cognitive neuroscience (Munakata, Casey, & Diamond, 2004).

Cognitive neuroscience researchers may use various methods to study and analysis their hypothesis due to its multidisciplinary nature of the scientific field. Methods employed in cognitive neuroscience include experimental paradigms from psychophysics and cognitive psychology, functional neuroimaging, electrophysiology, cognitive genomics and behavioral genetics (Haueis, 2014). Studies of patients with cognitive deficits due to brain lesions constitute a vital aspect of cognitive neuroscience (Nadel & Piattelli-Palmarini, 2002).

Cognitive science has a pre-history traceable back to ancient Greek philosophical texts of Plato's Aristotle's and includes writers such as Descartes, Immanuel Kant, Benedict de Spinoza, and Leibniz. Nevertheless, although these primary writers contributed greatly to the philosophical sighting of mind and this would ultimately lead to the development of psychology, they were working with an entirely different set of tools and core concepts than those of the cognitive scientist (Angus & Libscher, 2010).

The modern culture of cognitive science is drawn to the early cyberneticists in the 1930s and 1940s when Warren McCulloch and Walter Pitts, studied and organized basic principles of the mind. McCulloch and Pitts developed the first artificial neural networks, models of computation inspired by the structure of biological neural networks (Skinner, 2012).

Computational models require a mathematically and logically formal representation of a given problem. Computer models are used in the simulation and experimental corroboration of several specific and general properties of intelligence. Computational modeling supports the perception of the functional organization of a specific cognitive phenomenon. There are two basic approaches to cognitive modeling. Initially is focused on abstract mental functions of an intelligent mind and operates using symbols, and secondary, which follows the neural and associative properties of the human brain, such as neural network models (Buckner, 2011).

Other approaches gaining in popularity include the use of dynamical systems theory and also techniques putting symbolic models and connectionist models into correspondence i.e. neural-symbolic integration and Bayesian models, often drawn from machine learning, are also increasing acceptance (Matthews, 2006).

Brain Cortex and Relative Functions

All cognitive functions result from the integration of many simple processing mechanisms, distributed throughout the brain. Several neuroscientist research suggests that intelligence is related to brain anatomy features like the size of the cortex which is the outer part of the brain and is positively correlated to intelligence (Gazzaniga, 2011). Recent progress in neuroimaging has allowed researchers to visualize the brain, providing vivid pictures of its subcomponents and their associated functions. The outer layer of the forebrain constitutes the familiar wrinkled tissue that is the cerebral cortex or cortex.

The large folds in the cortex are called gyri originated from a Greek word which means 'circle' and the small creases within these folds are called fissures from the Greek which means 'trench'). Each hemisphere of the cortex consists of four lobes, namely the frontal lobe, the parietal, the temporal lobe and the occipital. Brainstem, cerebellum and limbic system (which include the amygdala and hippocampus) are important structures of the brain as well (Kolb, 2009).

Brain associated functions are emotion, language, learning, memory, movement, perception sensation, thinking and several others functions (Ledoux, 1998). Cognitive disorders are correlated to multiple regions in the brain. Structures that are correlated with cognitive disorders are located in several parts due to the fact that genes associated with cognition are expressed throughout the brain. For instance ADHD, Alzheimer's autism, bipolar disorder, depression, and schizophrenia are disorders correlated to brain dysfunctions (LaPierre, 2004).

The frontal lobes are part of the cerebral cortex and are the largest of the brain's structures. It is responsible for the so–called 'higher' cognitive functions. (Stuss & Knight, 2012) The frontal lobes consist of important substructures, including the prefrontal cortex, orbitofrontal cortex, motor and premotor cortices as well as and Broca's area (Allen, 2009). In particular frontal lobes substructures are associated with functions like voluntary behavior such as decision making, planning, problem–solving, and thinking, voluntary motor control, cognition, intelligence, attention, language processing and comprehension, and many others (Feinstein, 2006).

Therefore, frontals lobes have been associated with a number of disorders namely ADHD, schizophrenia, and bipolar disorder which are related to the prefrontal cortex (Baldaçara, Borgio, Lacerda, & Jackowski, 2008). Especially frontal lobes is associated with damage paralysis, loss of spontaneity in social interactions, mood changes, an inability to express language, atypical social skills and personality traits, substructures, prefrontal cortex, orbitofrontal cortex, premotor cortex, motor cortex, Broca's area, frontal eye fields, middle frontal gyrus, inferior frontal gyrus (Stuss & Knight, 2012).

The temporal lobes contain a large number of substructures, whose functions include perception, face recognition, object recognition, memory acquisition, understanding language, and emotional reactions (Lau, Gramfort, Hämäläinen, & Kuperberg, 2013). Damage to the temporal lobes can result in intriguing neurological deficits called agnosia, which is referred to the inability to recognize specific categories like body parts, colors, faces, and music (Cheadle & Zeki, 2014).

Functions that are associated with the temporal lobe are recognition like sensing of a smell, visual and auditory perception, language perception as well as knowledge achievement and memory ability (Clark, Boutros, & Mendez, 2010). Schizophrenia is the most closely aligned to temporal lobe dysfunction in reference to associated cognitive disorders. Several reviews related to neurodevelopmental disorders suggest that schizophrenia is to be considered as a neurodevelopmental abnormality as well (Harrison, 1999). The primary impairment in early Alzheimer's may be traced to the medial temporal lobe, and speech and social dysfunction in autism have been linked to the superior temporal sulcus (Clark et al., 2010). Temporal lobe is associated with damages like difficulties in understanding speech (Wernicke's aphasia), faces (prosopagnosia), and objects (agnosia). Additionally it is related to the inability to attend to sensory input, persistent talking, as well as of long and short term memory loss.

The parietal cortex consists a vital part in integrating data from numerous senses to form a coherent perception of the environment (Shafritz, Gore, & Marois, 2002). Parietal cortex integrates information from the ventral visual pathways (related to what things are) and dorsal visual pathways (related to where things are). This permits the brain to coordinate body movements in response to the objects in our environment. It encloses a number of distinct reference maps of the body like near and distant space, which are continually updated while moving and interacting with the environment (Kravitz, Kadharbatcha, Baker, & Mishkin, 2011) The parietal cortex processes attentional awareness of the environment, is involved in manipulating objects, and representing numbers (Cheadle & Zeki, 2014).

Parietal lobes associated functions are perception and integration of somatosensory information (e.g. touch, pressure, temperature, and pain) visuospatial processing, spatial attention, spatial mapping and number representation (Kravitz et al., 2011). Atrophy in an amount of brain structures, including among others the right temporal–parietal region, could be related to Alzheimer's disease emersion (Soltész, Szucs, Dékány, Márkus, & Csépe, 2007). Researchers provided evidence of right parietal dysfunctions in a subgroup of children suffering from ADHD (Durston et al., 2003). Additionally an association between the inferior parietal lobule and schizophrenia are noted under neuroanatomical studies aimed at schizophrenia localization (Torrey, 2007).

Parietal lobes is also associated with inability to locate and recognize objects events and parts of the body (hemispatial neglect) difficulty in discriminating between sensory, information, disorientation and lack of coordination (Kravitz et al., 2011). Basics parietal lobe substructures are the somatosensory cortex, the inferior parietal lobule, the superior parietal lobule and the precuneus (Wagner, Shannon, Kahn, & Buckner, 2005).

The occipital cortex is the primary visual area of the brain. It receives projections from the retina (via the thalamus) from where different groups of neurons separately encode different visual information such as color, orientation, and motion (Pasternak, Bisley, & Calkins, 2003).

Pathways from the occipital lobes reach the temporal and parietal lobes and are eventually processed consciously. Two important pathways of information originating in the occipital lobes are the dorsal and ventral streams. The dorsal stream projects to the parietal lobes and processes where objects are located. The ventral stream projects to structures in the temporal lobes and processes what objects are (Stiles, Akshoomoff, & Haist, 2013). Because damage to the occipital lobes can cause visual hallucinations, the region has been investigated as a neurobiological correlate of schizophrenia (Uehara, 2011) and also bipolar disorder (Mahona, Burdicka, & Szeszkoa, 2010).

A number of studies have found evidence of overgrowth in the occipital cortex in individuals with autism (Lahiri et al., 2013). Changes in blood flow in the occipital lobes have been correlated with depression (Ishizaki et al., 2008). Optical cortex is related with hallucinations, blindness, inability to perceive color, motion, or perceiving direction and synesthesia (Paulesu et al., 1995).

Dyscalculia

Developmental Dyscalculia or DD is a cognitive disorder "affecting the ability of an otherwise intelligent and healthy child to learn arithmetic". DD appears despite normal intelligence, proper schooling, adequate environment, socioeconomic status and motivation (DSM-IV). Some researchers suggest that the main factor behind DD is the impairment of general cognitive abilities, like attention and executive functioning. Others hypothesize that some types of Developmental Dyscalculia may be related to the dysfunction of specific number processing circuits. (Soltész et al., 2007).During last decades there were various attempts in order to describe the difficulties, some students have in mathematical concepts observing the features those people pose. Dyscalculia is described as a specific disorder of managing and conceiving mathematical concepts. Dyscalculia can be diagnosed even at an early age by difficulties noticed in the direct estimation of quantities, in counting and in the recognition of numerical symbols, as well as in the perception of the spatial concept. When dyscalculia arises it could be identified by difficulties in visual perception, in spatial number organization, in basic mathematical operations and in mathematical problem solving in general (Plerou, 2014). Additionally, people who deal with dyscalculia present problems in mathematical induction logic, in Euclidean and Non-Euclidean Geometry concepts perception, in Algebra and in Calculus, which are to be further analyzed. Moreover, incomplete capabilities in solving an algorithmic problem are observed when these problems require design, description and application of algorithmic steps (Plerou, Vlamos, & Kourouthanasis, 2014). Although dyscalculia's features are classified under specific clusters it would be hard to get a strict and absolute classification of dyscalculia features. This is why there are some common characteristics in each type and dyscalulia's features are somehow interrelated (Plerou et al., 2014).

In spite of the lack of definitional consistency, the prevalence of Developmental Dyscalculia across countries is relatively uniform, ranging from 3–6% in the normal population, which is similar to that of developmental dyslexia and attention deficit hyperactivity disorder (ADHD). Unlike these other learning disabilities, girls and boys seem to be affected by Developmental Dyscalculia equally (Kucian et al., 2006). Furthermore, Developmental Dyscalculia seems to be an enduring specific learning difficulty, persisting into late adolescence. While it is clearly the case that Developmental Dyscalculia is frequently co-morbid with a variety of disorders, like dyslexia, ADHD, poor hand-eye coordination, poor working memory span, epilepsy, fragile X syndrome, Williams syndrome and Turner syndrome, causal relationships between these disorders have not been established. For illustration, about one-quarter of dyscalculics show comorbidity with ADHD and dyslexia. Over the past two decades, sufficient genetic, neurobiological, and epidemiologic evidence has accumulated to indicate that learning disabilities, including DD, are in fact expressions of brain dysfunction (Kucian et al., 2006)

Brain Imaging and Mapping Techniques

New brain mapping technologies allow researchers to investigate experimental strategies of cognitive psychology by observing brain function. Although this is often thought of as a new method (most of the technology is relatively recent), the underlying principle goes back as far as 1878 when blood flow was first associated with brain function. Angelo Mosso, an Italian psychologist of the 19th century, had monitored the pulsations of the adult brain through neurosurgical created bony defects in the skulls of patients. He noted that when the subjects engaged in tasks such as mathematical calculations the pulsations of the brain increased locally. Such observations led Mosso to conclude that blood flow of the brain followed function (Raichle, 2009)

Nowadays PET scan, MRI, fMRI and EEG brain imaging methods are mainly used in order to evaluate brain activity in relevance with human cognitive abilities. Pet scan or Positron Emission Tomography produces a visual display of brain activity and the computer translates signals into a map of the brain. Pet scan enables researchers to see what areas of the brain are most active during certain tasks. Additionally different scans are used for different chemicals such as neurotransmitters, drugs, & oxygen flow. The patients are injected with radioactive tracer while detectors track release of gamma rays around patient's head. During this test, patients may be asked to respond to stimuli or perform simple tasks (Hernandez, Wager, & Jonides, 2014). Multimedia-based technologies can be applied in the above processes in order to interactively record and contrast the collected data with patient responses, as these are linked to external stimuli (Deliyannis, 2013) (Waltl, Rainer, Timmerer, & Hellwagner, 2012). MRI brain imaging technique or Magnetic Resonance Imaging uses magnetic fields and radio waves to make computer-generated images. Within this technique visual "slices" of the brain are produced hence a detailed picture of brain structure is provided and density, as well as the location of brain material, is measured. Patients are secured in a scanner platform and should remain motionless during this procedure (Alač, 2006).

In reference to fMRI brain imaging procedure, elements of MRI and PET scans are combined. Within this technique, the brain structure with info about blood flow in the brain is as well as brain activity during cognitive tasks is displayed. Patients could be asked to respond to stimuli or perform simple tasks while they are secured in scanners platform(Berman, Jonides, & Nee, 2006).

During an EEG or Electroencephalograph brain imaging technique amplified tracings of waves of electrical activity in the brain are produced as well as the electrical activity of the brain is recorded. The patients are lying down while electrodes are placed on their scalp therefore it is additionally used in sleep analysis. EEG brain imaging procedure is to be further analyzed (Carhart-Harris, 2007).

EEG Brain Imaging

Over the last years, evidence has accumulated to show the possibility to recognize a few mental tasks from on-line EEG signals. The electroencephalogram (EEG) is a measure of brain waves or else is the depiction of the electrical activity occurring at the surface of the brain. The electroencephalogram (EEG) is the depiction of the electrical activity occurring at the surface of the brain. This activity appears on the screen of the EEG machine as waveforms of varying frequency and amplitude measured in voltage (specifically micro-voltages). EEG waveforms are generally classified according to their frequency, amplitude, and shape, as well as the sites on the scalp at which they are recorded (Feldman, 2012). It is a readily available test that provides evidence of how the brain functions over time. The EEG is used in the evaluation of brain disorders. Most commonly it is used to show the type and location of the activity in the brain during a seizure. It also is used to evaluate people who are having problems associated with brain function. These problems might include confusion, coma, tumors, long-term difficulties of thinking or memory and weakening of specific parts of the body (such as weakness associated with a stroke) etc. An EEG is also used to determine brain death. It may be used to prove that someone on life-support equipment has no chance of recovery (Popescu, Fazli, Badower, Blankertz, & Müller, 2007).

EGG Method Advantages and Risk

The EEG is used to evaluate several types of brain disorders. When epilepsy is present, seizure activity will appear as rapid spiking waves on the EEG. Patients with lesions of the brain, which can result from tumors or stroke, may have unusually slow EEG waves, depending on the size and the location of the lesion. The test can also be used to diagnose other disorders that influence brain activity, such as Alzheimer's disease, certain psychoses, and a sleep disorder called narcolepsy. The EEG may also be used to determine the overall electrical activity of the brain (for example, to evaluate trauma, drug intoxication, or extent of brain damage in comatose patients). The EEG may also be used to monitor blood flow in the brain during surgical procedures (Lüders & Comair, 2001).

The EEG has been used for many years and is considered a safe procedure. The test causes no discomfort. The electrodes only record activity and do not produce any sensation. In addition, there is no risk of getting an electric shock. In rare instances, an EEG can cause seizures in a person with a seizure disorder due to the flashing lights or the deep breathing that may be involved during the test. If this occurs, a doctor will treat the seizure immediately. There may be other risks depending on your specific medical condition. Be sure to discuss any concerns with your doctor prior to the procedure (Bone, 2007).

EEG is a powerful tool for tracking brain changes during different phases of life. EEG sleep analysis can indicate significant aspects of the timing of brain development, including evaluating adolescent brain maturation. Hardware costs are significantly lower than those of most other techniques. EEG sensors can be used in more places than fMRI, SPECT, PET, MRS, or MEG, as these techniques require bulky and immobile equipment. For example, MEG requires equipment consisting of liquid helium-cooled detectors that can be used only in magnetically shielded rooms, altogether costing upwards of several million dollars; band fMRI requires the use of a 1-ton magnet in, again, a shielded room. EEG is relatively tolerant of subject movement, unlike most other neuroimaging techniques. There even exist methods for minimizing, and even eliminating movement artifacts in EEG data. EEG is silent, which allows for better study of the responses to auditory stimuli. EEG does not aggravate claustrophobia, unlike fMRI, PET, MRS, SPECT, and sometimes MEG. EEG does not involve exposure to high-intensity (>1 Tesla) magnetic fields, as in some of the other techniques, especially MRI and MRS. These can cause a variety of undesirable issues with the data, and also prohibit the use of these techniques with participants that have metal implants in their body, such as metal-containing pacemakers. EEG does not involve exposure to radioligands, unlike positron emission tomography (Thakur, Pawar, & Rajput, 2014).

EEG Brain Waves

The electroencephalogram (EEG) is a recording of the electrical activity of the brain from the scalp. The recorded waveforms reflect the cortical electrical activity which is quite small, measured in microvolts (μV). The main signal frequencies of the human EEG waves are:

- The Delta band has a frequency of 3 Hz or below. It tends to be the highest in amplitude and the slowest waves. It is normal as the dominant rhythm in infants up to one year and in stages 3 and 4 of sleep. It may occur focally with subcortical lesions and in general distribution with diffuse lesions, metabolic encephalopathy hydrocephalus or deep midline lesions. It is usually most prominent frontally in adults (e.g. FIRDA - Frontal Intermittent Rhythmic Delta) and posteriorly in children e.g. OIRDA - Occipital Intermittent Rhythmic Delta).The lowest wave frequencies are Delta (1- 4Hz), and they occur in deep sleep (Fort Grèbol, 2014).
- The Theta band has a frequency of 3.5 to 7.5 Hz and is classified as "slow" activity. It is perfectly normal in children up to 13 years and in sleep but abnormal in awaked adults. It can be seen as a manifestation of focal subcortical lesions; it can also be seen in generalized distribution in diffuse disorders such as metabolic encephalopathy or some instances of hydrocephalus. Theta waves (4-8Hz), on the other hand, are classified as slow waves (low frequencies or low oscillation), and are found to be strong during internal focus and during meditation(Cohen & Sweet, 2011)
- The Alpha band has a frequency between 7.5 and 13 Hz. Is usually best seen in the posterior regions of the head on each side is higher in amplitude on the dominant side. It appears when closing the eyes and relaxing, and disappears when opening the eyes or alerting by any mechanism (thinking, calculating). It is the major rhythm seen in normal relaxed adults. It is present during most of life especially after the thirteenth year. Earlier studies have determined that Alpha (8-13 Hz) waves occur whenever the person is alert, but not actively processing information (Frude, 2006).
- The Beta activity is "fast" activity. It has a frequency of 14 and greater Hz. It is usually seen on both sides in symmetrical distribution and is most evident frontally. It is accentuated by sedative-hypnotic drugs especially the benzodiazepines and the barbiturates. It may be absent or reduced in areas of cortical damage. It is generally regarded as a normal rhythm. It is the dominant rhythm in patients who are alert or anxious or have their eyes open. Beta waves are 14 Hz to 20 Hz waves of lower amplitude than alpha waves associated with a more active mental state.

Figure 1. Basic waves frequency bands.

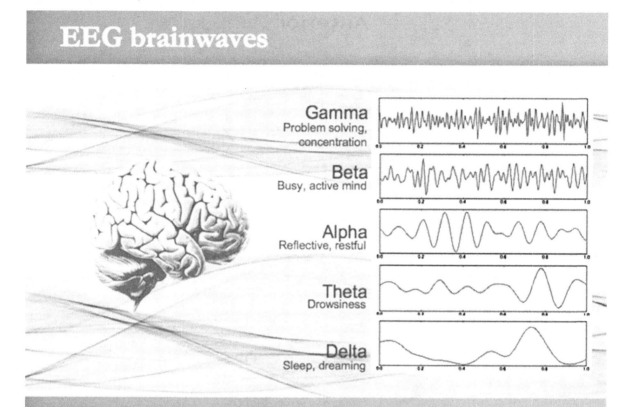

Beta1 activity is defined as 13-20Hz and Beta2 activity as 20-30Hz. (The Beta wave was subdivided in the study to look for possible differences between low Beta and high Beta frequencies.) Beta waves, in general, are considered fast (high frequencies or high oscillation) and are the dominant rhythm in those who are alert and are listening and thinking (processing information), among other activities(Moore & Zouridakis, 2004).

- The Gamma wave is a pattern of neural oscillation in humans with a frequency between 25 and 100 Hz, though 40 Hz is typical. (Niedermeyer & Lopes da Silva, 2004) Gamma waves are located to the somatosensory cortex and displayed during cross-modal sensory processing that is related to the perception that combines two different senses, such as sound and sight) (Kisley & Cornwell, 2006). Also is shown during short-term memory matching of recognized objects, sounds, or tactile sensations. A decrease in gamma-band activity may be associated with cognitive decline, especially when related to the theta band; however, this has not been proven for use as a clinical diagnostic measurement. The figure that follows illustrates the visual representation of the above-mentioned brainwaves frequency bands.

Figure 2. Visualization of the electrode placement according to 10/20 System

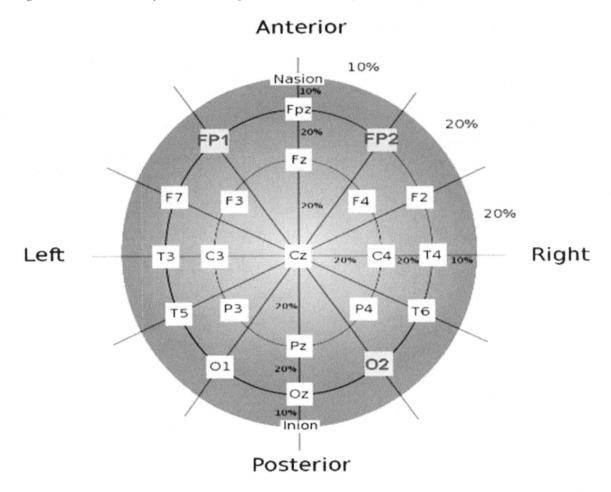

EEG Implementation - 10/20 Electrode Positioning System

During the procedure, electrodes consisting of small metal discs with thin wires are pasted on the scalp. The electrodes detect tiny electrical charges that result from the activity of the brain cells. The charges are amplified and appear as a graph on a computer screen or as a recording that may be printed out on paper. The standardized placement of scalp electrodes for a classical EEG recording has become common since the adoption of the 10/20 system. The essence of this system is the distance in percentages of the 10/20 range between Nasion-Inion and fixed points. These points are marked as the Frontal pole (Fp), Central (C), Parietal (P), occipital (O), and Temporal (T). The midline electrodes are marked with a subscript z, which stands for zero. The odd numbers are used as a subscript for points over the left hemisphere, and even numbers over the right (Admiraal-Behloul et al., 2003). An electroencephalogram (EEG) is a test that measures and records the electrical activity of your brain. Special sensors (electrodes) are attached to your head and hooked by wires to a computer. EEG test results are ready on the same or the next day (Freye & Levy, 2005). In the figures that follow the exact electrodes position during the EEG test implementation are presented.

Figure 3. Visualization of the electrode placement according to 10/20 System

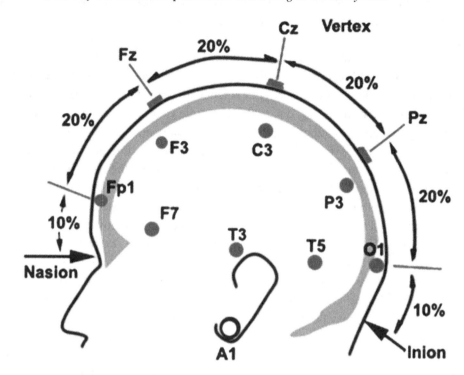

EEG Interpretation Analysis

In order to interpret the record properly, one must have clearly in mind the elements of a normal EEG. This establishes a template, against which all deviations are to be compared. In the case of adults, recall that the normal waking record contains an alpha rhythm, of the maximum amplitude in the posterior quadrants. Beta activity is presented in the front-central area, in greater or lesser amounts. A few theta frequencies are acceptable if not lateralized. Little else is present. The response to hyperventilation may be marked in younger adults. Consistent lateralization is not permitted. A following (driving) response to intermittent photic stimulation is variable, but there should be no activation of epileptic mode activity. The elements of drowsiness and sleep fill out a normal adult profile. One may appreciate a hint of paroxysmal activity or a possible asymmetry of background activity. In any event, such analysis can set the stage for a more rapid analysis of subsequent recording, providing clues on what to look for. Another hint that often pays dividends is to divide reading into vertical and horizontal appraisals.

Horizontal reading appraises and compares channels on the left side of the head with those on the right by scanning the record from left to right, choosing, for example, the left and right temporal leads followed by the left and right paracentral leads. Vertical reading, scanning a particular segment of a second or so from top to bottom, concentrates more on particular waveforms and their distributions. A common problem with the beginner is that he or she becomes enmeshed in the complicated polyrhythmic mode of the EEG by reading only vertically. This results in confusion (Duncan, Spillane, & Morrison, 2014).

Reading horizontally reveals abnormalities that may not be at all evident when reading vertically. In essence, horizontal reading reveals the broad picture presented by the EEG. For example, this is the best way to determine alpha asymmetry. One can easily determine alpha asymmetries, abundance, and irregularities. This is not evident with vertical reading. Unilateral or bilateral slowing also becomes more evident during horizontal reading. Importantly, the appearance of a new, paroxysmal frequency, diagnostic of an electrographic seizure, may not be evident with vertical reading. Many cases of recurrent electrographic seizures have been missed due to this oversight (Rowan & Tolunsky, 2003).

Now, look for pages where the patient is in his or her most alert state. Here is the point to analyze the alpha rhythm. Is it well organized (that is, nicely rhythmic, devoid of admixed slower frequencies), or is it irregular or poor persistent, or variable in frequency? Now, evaluate the beta rhythm. The Beta band offers a few clues to the presence of pathology. If asymmetric, it usually points to pathology on the side of diminished amplitude. If abundant, it may reveal a drug effect. In any case, it is an important aspect of the basic or resting record. The next task is to determine the presence of slow waves in the background.

The slowing may be diffuse – that is, not lateralized and non-focal. Look for both theta and delta frequencies. Is there a small amount of intermittent theta activity? Are there mainly delta waves or a combination of those two? We sometimes look at the broad picture and try to decide if it belongs in the theta box or the delta box. Note that slowing may be more or less continuous, discontinuous, paroxysmal, rhythmic or arrhythmic. There may be variable but inconsistent lateralization (Panayiotopoulos, 2005).

Generally speaking, delta activity does not appear in the normal, waking adult EEG. Perhaps a few random low-voltage delta waves might be acceptable. Note that delta is common in the EEGs of children. Also, in the elderly, delta waves are commonly recorded in the temporal derivations, indicative of some degree of cerebral pathology but not necessarily structural disease demonstrable on an imaging study. Now, describe any consistent focal slowing, theta or delta band that indicates localized cerebral pathology. The focality may be present in a setting of a slow disorganized background, or may stand out against a relatively normal background. Finally, describe any bifrontal delta activity, its symmetry or asymmetry, rhythmicity and amount (Grigg-Damberger et al., 2007).

After determining what the background of the record contains in terms of slowing, evaluate the presence or absence of epileptic mode activity. Describe the type and location of any spikes, sharp waves, spike-wave complexes, or other paroxysmal discharges (e.g. episodic sharp theta or delta frequencies, including FIRDA). A statement concerning discharge abundance should be made. Focal discharges such as spikes may be obvious, or hidden in the ongoing background. Reliance on fairly strict definitions of epileptic form discharges is essential. Sometimes, the record seems to contain sharp potentials everywhere. Careful analysis will reveal that most of these putative sharp waves are simply the result of a polyrhythmic background – superimposition of various frequencies (Rowan & Tolunsky, 2003).

Recording of drowsiness is an essential element in EEG diagnosis. Often, pathological findings occur mainly, or only, during this state. Of particular importance is the precipitation, or exaggeration, of epileptic mode activity (spikes, spike-wave complexes – also sharp waves if a broad definition is accepted). Slow wave abnormalities are frequently exaggerated during drowsiness. Bifrontal rhythmic delta (FIRDA) may become more prominent during this state. In any case, indicate the effect of drowsiness on the major findings (Panayiotopoulos, 2005). After drowsiness, we move to the main phenomena of sleep. Describe the features of Stage II sleep (established sleep spindles, vertex sharp waves, K-complexes, POSTS, and increased diffuse slowing in theta and delta ranges). At first, theta predominates, followed by increasing amounts of delta band. Note that vertex sharp waves are not always sharp. On the other hand, they may be very sharp and resemble spike potentials. In addition, they may be isolated and sporadic, or highly rhythmic (Blum & Rutkove, 2007). The above techniques are summarized in Table 1.

EEG Normal and Abnormal Patterns

With the use of EEG brain-imaging technique, several neurocognitive generated disorders could be identified. We then analyze the EEG by visual inspection to assist in the diagnosis and prognosis of the newborn. Our analysis usually involves locating abnormal EEG in a recording. The normal EEG appears to be a random signal without any obvious pattern. A normal EEG recording is presented to the figure that follows.

The EEG becomes abnormal when certain patterns appear in the EEG and it loses the underlying randomness of a normal recording. In addition to pattern analysis we also analyze more general characteristics of the EEG such as continuity, amplitude, frequency, synchrony and symmetry as well as more clinical features such as maturational characteristics, sleep state differentiation and reactivity (Coben & Evans, 2011). A normal EEG pattern and several abnormal EEG patterns are visualized in the figure that follows.

The excess theta pattern is the most common pattern seen in children with ADHD diagnoses. That means that if excess theta and diminished beta activity are present, there is very likely going to be an ADHD diagnosis. In the learning disabled brain, the appropriate frequencies are not called into use in the right area at the right time. For example, many children with ADHD have an EEG that reveals too much slow frequency activity in the pre-frontal cortex (Coben & Evans, 2011). The following image illustrates the electrical brain activity of a young boy with ADHD.

Table 1.

Normal:	In adults who are awake, the EEG shows mostly alpha waves and beta waves.
	The two sides of the brain show similar patterns of electrical activity.
	There are no abnormal bursts of electrical activity and no slow brain waves on the EEG tracing.
	If flashing lights (photic stimulation) are used during the test, one area of the brain (the occipital region) may have a brief response after each flash of light, but the brain waves are normal.
Abnormal:	The two sides of the brain show different patterns of electrical activity. This may mean a problem in one area or side of the brain is present.
	The EEG shows sudden bursts of electrical activity (spikes) or sudden slowing of brain waves in the brain. These changes may be caused by a brain tumor, infection, injury, stroke, or epilepsy. When a person has epilepsy, the location and exact pattern of the abnormal brain waves may help show what type of epilepsy or seizures the person has. Keep in mind that in many people with epilepsy, the EEG may appear completely normal between seizures. An EEG by itself does not diagnose or rule out epilepsy or a seizure problem.
	The EEG records changes in the brain waves that may not be in just one area of the brain. A problem affecting the entire brain—such as drug intoxication, infections (encephalitis), or metabolic disorders (such as diabetic ketoacidosis) that change the chemical balance in the body, including the brain—may cause these kinds of changes.
	The EEG shows delta waves or too many theta waves in adults who are awake. These results may mean brain injury or a brain illness is present.
	The EEG shows no electrical activity in the brain (a "flat" or "straight-line" EEG). This means that brain function has stopped, which is usually caused by lack of oxygen or blood flow inside the brain. This may happen when a person has been in a coma. In some cases, severe drug-induced sedation can cause a flat EEG.

Figure 4. A normal EEG recording.

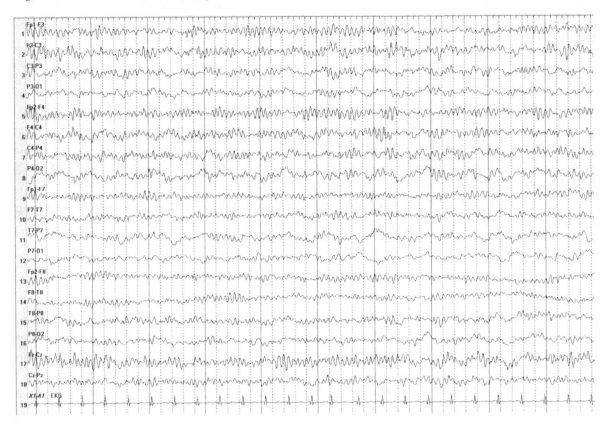

Epileptic activity is visible in the EEG in the form of prolonged discharges accompanying clinical seizures and interictal spikes, short events without clinical accompaniments. In epileptic patients, and particularly in those suffering from medically intractable seizures, it is important to record such events and to find which part of the brain generates them. This information helps classify the type of epilepsy and, therefore, administer optimal medical treatment. When medical treatment fails, it is possible to consider the surgical removal of epileptic brain tissue, provided this tissue can be accurately localized and provided it is not critical for normal brain function (Panayiotopoulos, 2005). The following image depicts the electrical brain activity of an adult on epileptic seizure.

Cognitive and Mathematical Perception Evaluation

Proper databases are needed in order to evaluate impairments in cognitive science. Especially difficulties in mathematics, widely known as dyscalculia are connected with particular parts of human brain. As mentioned before dyscalculia is connected to spatial perception, which is located in the temporal and not the posterior parietal lobe. Additionally a significant role is working and permanent memory which is located mainly in the medial temporal lobe as well as in several lobes. Auditory, comprehension and answering tasks as measured by these four main brain waves activities identify specific involvement of each cerebral hemisphere. Each brain lobe (frontal, temporal, parietal and occipital) is associated with a different human function (Battro, Dehaene, & Singer, 2010).

Figure 5. EEG normal pattern and several abnormal EEG patterns.

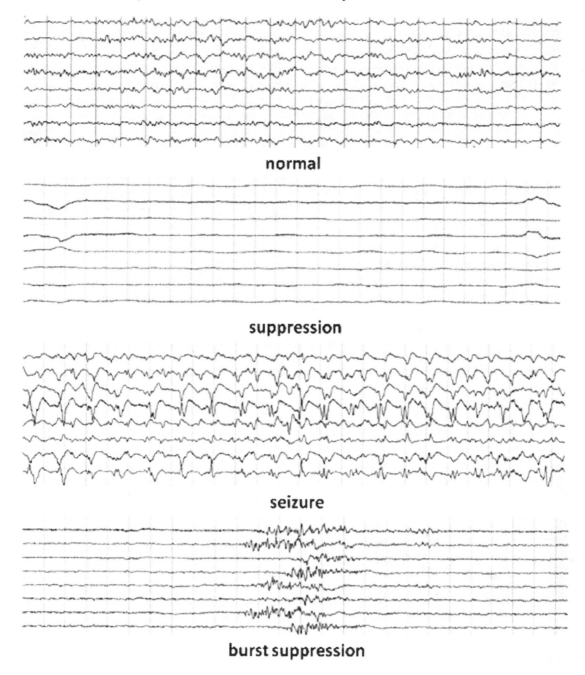

normal

suppression

seizure

burst suppression

In general, the frontal lobe is concerned with reasoning, parts of speech and movement, emotions, and problem-solving; the temporal lobe is concerned with hearing and memory; the parietal lobe is concerned with perception of stimuli such as touch and pain and the occipital lobe is concerned with vision. Therefore, it is important to know the involvement of the two brain hemispheres (left and right) as well as the involvement of each region of the brain during an comprehension test (Battro et al., 2010).

Figure 6. This EEG Wave recording represents a 13 years old boy dealing with ADHD.

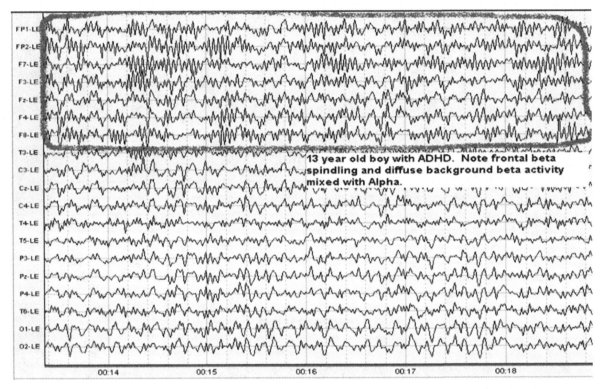

Figure 7. EEG waves imaging the brain of an epileptic adult.

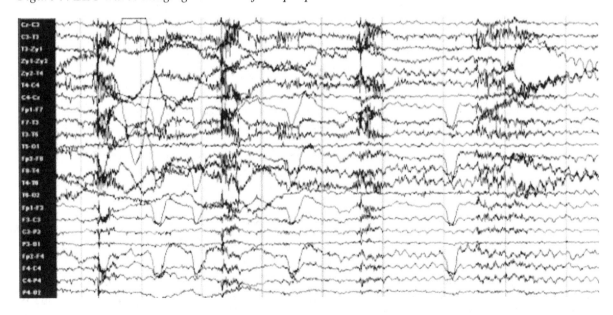

EEG Computational Evaluation Methods

For the EEG wave data visualization is to be contacted with the use of Acknowledge. AcqKnowledge is an interactive, intuitive program that allows the instant observation, measurement, transformation and data analysis. Perform complex data acquisition, stimulation, triggering and analyses using simple pull-down menus and dialogs-no need to learn a programming language or new protocol. AcqKnowledge software runs on both the latest Windows and Mac OS X operating systems to provide an industry leading data acquisition and analysis platform.

For the analysis and the evaluation of EEG visualized results taken several methods could be implied. For instance evaluation with the use of neural networks, pattern recognition i.e. with the use of clustering algorithms, machine learning, fuzzy logic systems and data mining algorithms is suggested. Additionally as pattern recognition software's like Weka, PRTools etc. in the case where for the EEG evaluation no additional software development design is needed (Gacek & Pedrycz, 2012).

DISCUSSION AND FUTURE WORK

In this study the methods of evaluating the neurocognitive frame of difficulties in mathematics within the frame of dyscalculia as a learning difficulty disorder and analyzed. The critical aspect of this study is the visualization of brain waves with the use of EEG brain imaging techniques. The analysis of expected difference of regions of brain activation in all the frequency bands between the left and right hemispheres as well as the evaluation of the changes in the activation of brain regions (frontal, temporal, parietal, central, and occipital) is proposed in order to evaluated EEG samples taken in relevance to a normal EEGs pattern database. Research in dyscalculia is still in its emergent stage, lagging behind other learning disabilities an overall evaluation of dyscalculia features is proposed. Future directions include the development of an interactive multimedia-based screener, in order to deal with dyscalculia's total evaluation, in respect to the proposed feature classification, emphasizing additionally on algorithmic thinking difficulties as well as the connection among their features. This evaluation process can be implemented by the use of experimental multimedia technologies by adapting existing sensor-based edutainment software that can provide stimuli followed by dynamic recognition and evaluation of user responses (Deliyannis, 2013). The use of EEG brain imaging technique is the most suitable method in order to evaluate the connection of the above-mentioned difficulties with cognitive neuroscience aspects. EEG analysis results are about to be useful in order provide educational proposals to enhance the learning procedure in the frame of a recent lighted scientific field known as Neuroeducation. Additional work in relevance to EEG implementation as well as analysis of the proposed classification screening procedure is ongoing.

REFERENCES

Admiraal-Behloul, F., Schmitz, N., van den Heuvel, M. J. D., Olofsen, H., Reiber, J. H. C., & van Buchem, M. A. (2003). Geriatric LUMC brain template. Proceedings of *International Conference on Functional Mapping of the Human Brain*.

Alač, M. (2006, January 1). *How brain images reveal cognition: an ethnographic study of meaning-making in brain mapping practice.*

Allen, J. S. (2009). *The Lives of the Brain. Human Evolution and the Organ of Mind.* Cambridge, Mass: Belknap Press of Harvard University Press. doi:10.4159/9780674053496

Angus, N., & Libscher, M. (2010). Thinking the Unconscious: Nineteenth-Century German Thought. Cambridge: Cambridge University Press.

Arns, M., Peters, S., Breteler, R., & Verhoeven, L. (2007). Different brain activation patterns in dyslexic children: evidence from EEG power and coherence patterns for the double-deficit theory of dyslexia. *Journal of Integrative Neuroscience, 6*(1), 175–190. doi:10.1142/S0219635207001404 PMID:17472228

Baldaçara, L., Borgio, J. G. F., de Lacerda, A. L. T., & Jackowski, A. P. (2008). Cerebellum and psychiatric disorders. *Revista Brasileira de Psiquiatria (Sao Paulo, Brazil), 30*(3), 281–289. doi:10.1590/S1516-44462008000300016 PMID:18833430

Battro, A. M., Dehaene, S., & Singer, W. J. (2010). Human Neuroplasticity and Education. In The Pontifical Academy of Sciences.

Berman, M. G., Jonides, J., & Nee, D. E. (2006). Studying mind and brain with fMRI. *Social Cognitive and Affective Neuroscience, 1*(2), 158–161. doi:10.1093/scan/nsl019 PMID:18985126

Blum, A. S., & Rutkove, S. B. (2007). The Clinical Neurophysiology Primer Th. Totowa, New Jersey 07512: Humana Press Inc. doi:10.1007/978-1-59745-271-7

Bone, G. (2007). *Understanding Neurology a problem-orientated approach.* New York: Manson Publishing.

Buckner, C. (2011). Computational methods for the 21st-century philosopher: recent advances and challenges in cognitive science and metaphilosophy. Proceedings of IACAP. Aarhus.

Carhart-Harris, R. (2007). Waves of the unconscious: the neurophysiology of dreamlike phenomena and its implications for the psychodynamic model of the mind. *Neuro-psychoanalysis, 9*(2), 183–221. doi:10.1080/15294145.2007.10773557

Cheadle, S. W., & Zeki, S. (2014). The role of parietal cortex in the formation of color and motion based concepts. *Frontiers in Human Neuroscience, 8*, 535. doi:10.3389/fnhum.2014.00535 PMID:25120447

Clark, D. L., Boutros, N. N., & Mendez, M. F. (2010). The brain and tha behavior. An introduction to behavior neuroanatomy. Cambridge: Cambridge University Press. doi:10.1017/CBO9780511776915

Coben, R., & Evans, J. R. (2011). *Neurofeedback and Neuromodulation: Analysis Techniques.* San Diego: Academic Press Elsevier.

Cohen, R. A., & Sweet, L. H. (2011). *Brain Imaging in Behavioral Medicine and Clinical Neuroscience.* New York: Springer. doi:10.1007/978-1-4419-6373-4

Deliyannis, I. (2013). Sensor Recycling and Reuse. *International Journal of Sensor and Related Networks, 1*(1).

Duncan, H., Spillane, K., & Morrison, I. (2014). Electroencephalography – An Overview. *Scottish Universities Medical Journal, 3*(1), 47–53.

Durston, S., Tottenham, N. T., Thomas, K. M., Davidson, M. C., Eigsti, I.-M., & Yang, Y. et al. (2003). Differential patterns of striatal activation in young children with and without ADHD. *Biological Psychiatry, 53*(10), 871–878. doi:10.1016/S0006-3223(02)01904-2 PMID:12742674

Feinstein, S. (2006). *The Praeger Handbook of Learning and the Brain*. London: Praeger Publishers.

Feldman, R. S. (2012). *Understanding Psychology*. New York: McGraw-Hill. doi.

Fort Grèbol, P. (2014, December 12). *Symbolic Dynamics applied to Electroencephalographic signals to Predict Response to Noxious Stimulation during Sedation-Analgesia.* Universitat Politècnica de Catalunya.

Freye, E., & Levy, J. V. (2005). Cerebral monitoring in the operating room and the intensive care unit: an introductory for the clinician and a guide for the novice wanting to open a window to the brain. Part I: The electroencephalogram. *Journal of Clinical Monitoring and Computing, 19*(1-2), 1–76. doi:10.1007/s10877-005-0712-z PMID:16167222

Frude, N. (2006). *Understanding Biological Psychology*. Oxford: Blackwell Publishing Ltd.

Gacek, A., & Pedrycz, W. (2012). *ECG Signal Processing, Classification and Interpretation*. London: Springer London. doi:10.1007/978-0-85729-868-3

Gazzaniga, M. S. (2013). *Cognitive Neuroscience: The Biology of the Mind* (4th ed.). New York: W. W. Norton & Company.

Gazzaniga. (2011). *The Cognitive Neurosciences*. Cambridge: The MIT Press.

Grigg-Damberger, M., Gozal, D., Marcus, C. L., Quan, S. F., Rosen, C. L., & Chervin, R. D. et al. (2007). The Visual Scoring of Sleep and Arousal in Infants and Children. *Journal of Clinical Sleep Medicine, 3*(2). PMID:17557427

Harrison, P. J. (1999). The neuropathology of schizophrenia: A critical review of the data and their interpretation. *Brain, 122*(4), 593–624. doi:10.1093/brain/122.4.593 PMID:10219775

Haueis, P. (2014). Meeting the brain on its own terms. *Frontiers in Human Neuroscience, 8*, 815. doi:10.3389/fnhum.2014.00815 PMID:25352801

Hernandez, L., Wager, T., & Jonides, J. (2014). *Introduction to Functional Neuroimaging*. Cambridge: The MIT Press.

Ischebeck, A., Zamarian, L., Siedentopf, C., Koppelstätter, F., Benke, T., Felber, S., & Delazer, M. (2006). How specifically do we learn? Imaging the learning of multiplication and subtraction. *NeuroImage, 30*(4), 1365–1375. doi:10.1016/j.neuroimage.2005.11.016 PMID:16413795

Ishizaki, J., Yamamoto, H., Takahashi, T., Takeda, M., Yano, M., & Mimura, M. (2008). Changes in regional cerebral blood flow following antidepressant treatment in late-life depression. *International Journal of Geriatric Psychiatry, 23*(8), 805–811. doi:10.1002/gps.1980 PMID:18214999

Kisley, M. A., & Cornwell, Z. M. (2006). Gamma and beta neural activity evoked during a sensory gating paradigm: Effects of auditory, somatosensory and cross-modal stimulation. *Clinical Neurophysiology*, *117*(11), 2549–2563. doi:10.1016/j.clinph.2006.08.003 PMID:17008125

Kolb, B. (2009). *Fundamentals of human neuropsychology*. New York: Worth Publishers.

Kravitz, D. J., Kadharbatcha, S., Baker, C. I., & Mishkin, M. (2011). A new neural framework for visuo-spatial processing. *Nature Reviews. Neuroscience*, *12*(4), 217–230. doi:10.1038/nrn3008 PMID:21415848

Kucian, K., Loenneker, T., Dietrich, T., Dosch, M., Martin, E., & von Aster, M. (2006). Impaired neural networks for approximate calculation in dyscalculic children: A functional MRI study. *Behavioral and Brain Functions : BBF*, *2*(1), 31. doi:10.1186/1744-9081-2-31 PMID:16953876

Lahiri, D. K., Sokol, D. K., Erickson, C., Ray, B., Ho, C. Y., & Maloney, B. (2013). Autism as early neurodevelopmental disorder: Evidence for an sAPPα-mediated anabolic pathway. *Frontiers in Cellular Neuroscience*, *7*, 94. doi:10.3389/fncel.2013.00094 PMID:23801940

LaPierre, A. (2004). Body Psychotherapy. *The USA Body Psychotherapy Journal, 3*(2).

Lau, E. F., Gramfort, A., Hämäläinen, M. S., & Kuperberg, G. R. (2013). Automatic semantic facilitation in anterior temporal cortex revealed through multimodal neuroimaging. *The Journal of Neuroscience*, *33*(43), 17174–17181. doi:10.1523/JNEUROSCI.1018-13.2013 PMID:24155321

Ledoux, J. (1998). *The Emotional Brain: The Mysterious Underpinnings of Emotional Life*. Simon & Schuster.

Lüders, H., & Comair, Y. G. (2001). *Epilepsy Surgery*. California: Lippincott Williams & Wilkins.

Mahona, K., Burdicka, K. E., & Szeszkoa, P. R. (2010). A Role for White Matter Abnormalities in the Pathophysiology of Bipolar Disorder. *Neurosci Biobehav*, *34*(4), 533–554. doi:10.1016/j.neubiorev.2009.10.012 PMID:19896972

Matthews, D. (2006). Book Review: How People Learn Brain, Mind, Experience, and School. In J. D. Bransford, A. L. Brown, & R. R. Cocking (Eds.), Learning Committee on Developments in the Science of Learning, Gifted Children: 1(1).

Moore, J., & Zouridakis, G. (2004). *Biomedical Technology and Devices Handbook*. New York: CRC Press.

Munakata, Y., Casey, B. J., & Diamond, A. (2004). Developmental cognitive neuroscience: Progress and potential. *Trends in Cognitive Sciences*, *8*(3), 122–128. doi:10.1016/j.tics.2004.01.005 PMID:15301752

Nadel, L., & Piattelli-Palmarini, M. (2002). What is Cognitive Science? In L. Nadel (Ed.), The Encyclopedia of Cognitive Science. John Wiley & Sons.

Niedermeyer, E., & Lopes da Silva, F. (2004). *Electroencephalography: Basic Principles, Clinical Applications, and Related Fields*. Philadelphia: Lippincott Williams & Wilkins.

Panayiotopoulos, C. (2005). *Optimal Use of the EEG in the Diagnosis and Management of Epilepsies*. Oxfordshire, UK: Bladon Medical Publishing.

Pasternak, T., Bisley, J. W., & Calkins, D. (2003). Visual processing in the primate brain. In B. Weiner (Ed.), Handbook of Psychology (Vol. I). Hoboken, NJ, USA: John Wiley & Sons, Inc.

Paulesu, E., Harrison, J., Baron-Cohen, S., Watson, J. D. G., Goldstein, L., & Heather, J. … Frith, C. D. (1995). The physiology of coloured hearing A PET activation study of colour-word synaesthesia. Brain - Oxford University Press, 118, 661–676.

Plerou, A. (2014). Dealing with Dyscalculia over time. In *International Conference on Information Communication Technologies in Education.*

Plerou, A., Vlamos, P., & Kourouthanasis, P. (2014). Screening Dyscalculia and Algorithmic Thinking Difficulties. In *Difficulties 1st International Conference on New Developments in Science and Technology Education.*

Popescu, F., Fazli, S., Badower, Y., Blankertz, B., & Müller, K.-R. (2007). Single trial classification of motor imagination using 6 dry EEG electrodes. *PLoS ONE, 2*(7), e637. doi:10.1371/journal.pone.0000637 PMID:17653264

Raichle, M. E. (2009). A brief history of human brain mapping. *Trends in Neurosciences, 32*(2), 118–126. doi:10.1016/j.tins.2008.11.001 PMID:19110322

Robertson, I. H., Manly, T., Andrade, J., Baddeley, B. T., & Yiend, J. (1997). `Oops!': Performance correlates of everyday attentional failures in traumatic brain injured and normal subjects. *Neuropsychologia, 35*(6), 747–758. doi:10.1016/S0028-3932(97)00015-8 PMID:9204482

Rotzer, S., Kucian, K., Martin, E., von Aster, M., Klaver, P., & Loenneker, T. (2008). Optimized voxel-based morphometry in children with developmental dyscalculia. *NeuroImage, 39*(1), 417–422. doi:10.1016/j.neuroimage.2007.08.045 PMID:17928237

Rowan, J., & Tolunsky, E. (2003). *Primer of EEG: With A Mini-Atlas. Neuroscience.* Oxford, UK: Butterworth-Heinemann Ltd. doi:.

Rugg, M. D., & Yonelinas, A. P. (2003). Human recognition memory: A cognitive neuroscience perspective. *Trends in Cognitive Sciences, 7*(7), 313–319. doi:10.1016/S1364-6613(03)00131-1 PMID:12860190

Shafritz, K. M., Gore, J. C., & Marois, R. (2002). The role of the parietal cortex in visual feature binding. *Proceedings of the National Academy of Sciences of the United States of America, 99*(16), 10917–10922. doi:10.1073/pnas.152694799 PMID:12149449

Skinner, R. E. (2012). *Building the Second Mind: 1956 and the Origins of Artificial Intelligence Computing.* California: Smashwords.

Soltész, F., Szucs, D., Dékány, J., Márkus, A., & Csépe, V. (2007). A combined event-related potential and neuropsychological investigation of developmental dyscalculia. *Neuroscience Letters, 417*(2), 181–186. doi:10.1016/j.neulet.2007.02.067 PMID:17367929

Stanescu-Cosson, R. (2000). Understanding dissociations in dyscalculia: A brain imaging study of the impact of number size on the cerebral networks for exact and approximate calculation. *Brain, 123*(11), 2240–2255. doi:10.1093/brain/123.11.2240 PMID:11050024

Stiles, J., Akshoomoff, N., & Haist, F. (2013). The Development of Visuospatial Processing. *Comprehensive Developmental Neuroscience: Neural Circuit Development and Function in the Brain, 3*, 271–296.

Stuss, D. T., & Knight, R. T. (2012). *Principles of Frontal Lobe Function*. New York: Oxford University Press.

Thakur, S., Pawar, S., & Rajput, S. (2014). Electroencephalography: A Wide Approach. *International Journal of Innovative Research in Technology, 1*(6).

Torrey, E. F. (2007). Schizophrenia and the inferior parietal lobule. *Schizophrenia Research, 97*(1-3), 215–225. doi:10.1016/j.schres.2007.08.023 PMID:17851044

Uehara, T. (2011). *Psychiatric Disorders – Trends and Developments*. Rijeka: InTech. doi:10.5772/2330

Wagner, A. D., Shannon, B. J., Kahn, I., & Buckner, R. L. (2005). Parietal lobe contributions to episodic memory retrieval. *Trends in Cognitive Sciences, 9*(9), 445–453. doi:10.1016/j.tics.2005.07.001 PMID:16054861

Waltl, M., Rainer, B., Timmerer, C., & Hellwagner, H. (2012). A toolset for the authoring, simulation, and rendering of sensory experiences. Proceedings of ACM international conference on Multimedia - MM '12 (p. 1469). New York, USA. ACM Press. doi:10.1145/2393347.2396522

Chapter 15
Augmented Reality Edutainment Systems for Open–Space Archaeological Environments:
The Case of the Old Fortress, Corfu, Greece

Ioannis Deliyannis
Ionian University, Greece

Georgios Papaioannou
Ionian University, Greece

ABSTRACT

In this chapter we discuss the development of edutainment systems supported by augmented reality applications, in order to enable augmented reality technologies for archaeology within the so-called communication engine for museums and cultural tourism. The task in hand is interdisciplinary and its successful implementation relies heavily on information technology as a detailed analysis of content-user needs and sound interaction design capable to support edutainment scenario is needed. This work identifies the role of each building component, describes their interrelationship within the wider context and adopts a suitably designed framework in order to develop multiple guided-tour types. Real-life case study scenario on a specific case, that of the Old Fortress in the UNESCO-listed Old Town of Corfu, Greece, are used to demonstrate the adaptive nature of content and how the system and developers handle different uses. The proposed approach offers new narration tools for content experts while it may be used to support personalised visitor experiences.

DOI: 10.4018/978-1-4666-8659-5.ch015

INTRODUCTION

Handheld devices and social software influence greatly the area of information science, where the following shift pattern is commonly observed: older information-centered systems featuring single access-points are replaced with new dynamic systems allowing physical navigation and information-exchange in real spaces (Graube, Ziegler, Urbas, & Hladik, 2013; Vlist, Niezen, Rapp, Hu, & Feijs, 2013). The wide availability of handheld multimedia-enabled networked devices (Stobbe, Just, Heng, Kaiser, & Walter, 2006), the rise of networking and social software (Chatti, Jarke, & Frosch-Wilke, 2007; McLoughlin & Lee, 2007), the changing trends in mobile (Kenteris, Gavalas, & Economou, 2009) and urban tourism (Wang, 2013) may be identified as the main drivers of the convergence process introduced in the area of cultural tourism (Smith & Richards, 2013). However, existing content is for most instances not suitable for interactive augmented-reality based navigation within physical spaces (Hable et al., 2012; Ledermann & Schmalstieg, 2005; Takacs et al., 2008; Van Krevelen & Poelman, 2010), as it is designed for access within existing information-organization paradigms (linear, tree-based or graph-based). Take for example a narration designed to cover a specific museum collection using a multimedia kiosk or a mobile headset using headphones. Designers of such systems base the functionality of their end-systems on a specific hierarchical tree of information or a pre-determined visitor route. As a result the user is forced to follow a pre-determined guided route (Abas & Badioze Zaman, 2010; Blanton & Design II, 2011; Garrand, 2010; Lombardo & Damiano, 2012; Ursu et al., 2008), where deviation from this path is either not allowed or it creates inconsistent and loose navigation paths as narration is reduced to the minimum and fails to present content through a rewarding experience. On the other hand, the use of mobile devices enables users to employ event-driven sensing mechanisms for direct content exploration (I. Deliyannis, 2013) and their social software applications (Ioannis Deliyannis & Kanellopoulos, 2008; Ioannis Deliyannis, Karydis, & Anagnostou, 2011) for the identification of user-preferences and even advertising purposes. Users are accustomed to the use of such applications today in a wide array of domains. In those implementations utilize different sensing devices provided by the hardware. Commonly such software is designed to collect various streams that are aveluated in order to produce the appropriate user-content interaction mode (Blanton & Design II, 2011; I. Deliyannis, 2013; Khan, Xiang, Aalsalem, & Arshad, 2012; Timmerer, Waltl, Rainer, & Hellwagner, 2012; Tsiridou, Zannos, & Strapatsakis, 2012; Waltl, Rainer, Timmerer, & Hellwagner, 2012a, 2012b). As a result, a pre-determined navigational route does not always have to bind the system's interaction capabilities, but it may be used as a new and adaptive content access method for interaction with content (Ioannis Deliyannis, 2012a). From the narration point of view, it is necessary to advance beyond the linear or the top-to-bottom hierarchy of content to a local-to-global information organization paradigm that covers multiple user-paths (Abas & Badioze Zaman, 2010; Blanton & Design II, 2011; Garrand, 2010; Lombardo & Damiano, 2012). In short, a single information trigger (user action) may have to be linked to multiple content entities (multiple system reactions), serving various user needs and content presentation requirements (Deliyiannis, Floros, & Webster, 2009). Some view the convergence process as the combination of existing "content" with new "delivery" mechanisms (Flattum, 2011). Although correct in principle, this definition is oversimplified and often underestimates the scope of change introduced with convergence (Ioannis Deliyannis, 2014a). As a result, the need for information re-engineering (Pino & Di Salvo, 2011) supported by the development of adaptive systems, are both significant factors that need to be implemented in order to cover the interactive information access requirements that arise by state of the art experimental multimedia applications (Weyns, Malek, Andersson, & Schmerl, 2012).

Section 2 briefly approaches the current state of archaeological tours and presents the development of such a system. Section 3 deals with edutainment system design for the intended purpose. The generalization of this process is introduced in the form of a framework that permits the development and organization of content in order to cover multivariate presentation requirements, which may be categorized as edutainment systems due to their adaptability. Section 4 describes the development of a working prototype. It shows how the combination of handheld multimedia-enabled networked devices with image-based object recognition may be employed as a tool capable to deliver adaptable content, which covers the demands of different target user-groups. Chapter 5 concludes the work by providing a roadmap that the developer may utilize in order to adapt the design to their particular needs.

FROM PHYSICAL TO VIRTUAL ARCHAEOLOGICAL TOURS

Virtual reality applications are introduced in various modes: Window on World Systems (WoW), Video Mapping, Immersive Systems, Telepresence, Mixed Reality, Semi-Immersive (Nesamalar & Ganesan, 2012). Multimedia-enabled virtual tours within archaeological sites are in most cases developed as highly structured systems. These either allow users to scan through their indexed content in order to access the appropriate information or follow a specific presentation order. Multimedia kiosks employ structured menus and interactive maps allowing users to access information on a geographical area (Blanton & Design II, 2011). As a result, most of those systems feature strict narrative structures and pre-written stories that minimize interactive user capabilities and offer limited narrative intelligibility (Koenitz, Haahr, Ferri, Sezen, & Sezen, 2013). Another way to access content is via the use of interfaces that are either based or resemble Geographical Information Systems (GIS). Information is visualized using appropriate maps that feature layers of information that can be dynamically accessed by the user. Although this mode of content access offers increased interaction flexibility when compared to older systems, it requires increased user attention and it reveals information upon user request, as it requires continuous user-system interaction. This practice is not often practically achievable due to need for shared attention between the real and virtual worlds, often introduced in real-life use scenaria. A third highly popular yet costly and space-restrictive method to implement a virtual archaeological tour is with the use of immersive virtual reality. This method utilises 3D models and suitable Computer Aided Virtual Environments (CAVE) where the user with specialized hardware is immersed in a virtual environment that offers a full multimedia experience. Other examples include the Google Art Project (Proctor, 2011) and the use of robots as museum guides (López, Pérez, Santos, & Cacho, 2013; Nieuwenhuisen & Behnke, 2013). Most implementations are composed and tested via the interaction between three groups of participants: content experts, developers and end-users, following the development of complex interactive systems in the literature (Ioannis Deliyannis, 2012b). Interaction be described using a new diagram for every stage, depicting the expert ontologies, while overlapping areas A, B, C and D are used to describe their expertise exchange process (Figure 1).

In the forefront of interactive multimedia systems, we observe that interaction between physical and virtual worlds has become a reality for many users (Fuchs, 2008; Shea, 2008; Van Krevelen & Poelman, 2010). Users spend a big part of their time communicating their everyday life views, thoughts and feelings with their social circle with the use of social media software (Madge, Meek, Wellens, & Hooley, 2009; Vinciarelli, Pantic, & Bourlar, 2009). This information exchange process goes beyond triggering dialogue between users and reaches the point where they share and exchange socially their experiences

Figure 1. Overlapping diagram describing the interaction between developing parties

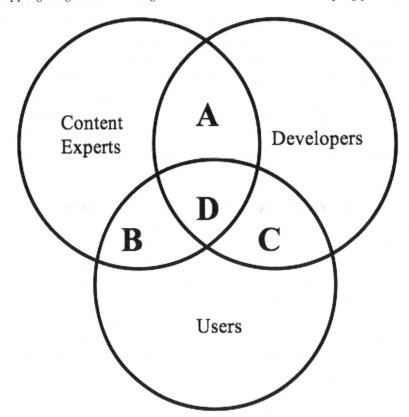

(Hemsley & Mason, 2013; Lindgren, 2012; van Dijck, 2013). In fact this new medium has the capacity to accelerate a global cultural shift where multimedia information is re-broadcasted using an intelligent multicast network (Ioannis Deliyannis, 2014b; Ioannis Deliyannis & Karydis, 2011). Often, information of interest surfaces and becomes a global phenomenon. One may refer to the "Gangnam Style" video clip that set the 1.2 billion viewing record on YouTube, or the "Harlem Shake" clip that triggered the production of more than ten versions built by individuals using a common musical track, a process that introduced further viewing by over 0.5 million users. This trend may be explained from multiple perspectives (Boyd & Crawford, 2011; Harrison & Barthel, 2012; Kietzmann, Hermkens, McCarthy, & Silvestre, 2011; Long, Chei Sian, & Goh, 2012; Madge et al., 2009).

The availability of augmented reality applications for handheld devices that recognize image-based markers instead of QR codes is nowadays a reality. The video-enabled device matches the captured video frames to those stored in a web-based database. When a match is found the image is augmented at real time with additional information: links, interactive labels, video, 3D animation, audio and other multimedia content types. Many have employed those advanced features commercially in order to promote their products and services, by permitting access to special offers and featured content featured by the key players in the field today that include software-based platforms *Aurasma, Blippar, Junaio, Metaio, Vuforia, Wikitude* and hardware-based solutions such as *Vuzix, Google glasses* and *Microsoft HoloLens*.

This allows the developmental flexibility to provide access to virtual content anywhere provided that networking is available. Most importantly, this can be implemented at the user's expense by using their own portable devices: tablets and mobile phones (Ioannis Deliyannis, 2015; Khan et al., 2012). Those devices allow network access, sensing, multimedia processing and delivery capabilities (Ioannis Deliyannis, 2015) and most importantly they do not impose additional system costs as they belong to the users. However, a number of points may be raised regarding the selection of this approach. It is common for users to share their experiences on social media, so this is a point that needs to be considered during development as it can be used by the end-system's marketing strategy. The ability to physically navigate through content provides a powerful system characteristic for the development of various types of virtual tours. One needs to keep in mind that the flexibility of interactive storytelling is often limited by the system, not the user's imagination. It becomes clear that a novel design paradigm is demanded for the development of virtual tours based on augmented reality technologies (Casella & Coelho, 2013; Ioannis Deliyannis & Papaioannou, 2013; Kirner & Kirner, 2013; Leiva, Guevara, Rossi, & Aguayo, 2014; Ramirez et al., 2013; Tahir, 2012). On the content access forefront the user ability to physically navigate requires the freedom to adapt the tour on the point of interest, while logging user progress is a feature that can adjust the presentation content dynamically to suit individual user requirements (Ioannis Deliyannis, Giannakoulopoulos, & Oikonomidou, 2013; Fleischmann & Hutchison, 2012; Hemsley & Mason, 2013; Manovich, 2011). The issue here is not to replace the real-life tour mode with the virtual, but to use technology in order to augment the user experience of the visitor, to inform, educate and deliver customized content that covers visitors' requirements (Ioannis Deliyannis, Giannakoulopoulos, & Varlamis, 2011; Egenfeldt-Nielsen, 2007; Encarnação, 2007; Rice, 2007; Ronchi, 2009; Torrente, Mera, Moreno-Ger, & Fernández-Manjón, 2009). In order to achieve this goal, the system has to present content that adapts dynamically to the user's profile and the path selected, presenting a satisfying experience.

EDUTAINMENT SYSTEM DESIGN FOR ARCHAEOLOGICAL SITES AND MUSEUMS

The development process combines three functional components: *content experts*, *developers* and *users*. We utilize the Augmented Reality Framework for Archaeology Augmented Reality Framework for Archaeology (acronym ARFA) (Ioannis Deliyannis & Papaioannou, 2013) that allows the development of customized interactive storytelling scenaria. It is designed to enable multiple content types to be delivered to multiple users based on a specific decision mechanism through single trigger-image recognition. This feature permits variable user scenaria to be realized, enabling users to access customized information through their personal user profile. Varying user profiles are linked to different content pools enabling the delivery of specific information, while navigation is free and triggers adaptive scenario customization. As system design commences with the identification of user needs, it is informative to view the design process through examples based on real-life scenaria. This enables developers and content experts to identify content breadth and depth and select how information is organized and delivered through the available technological platforms.

Figure 2 displays a selection of information points at which the user interacts with historical content. This image is the actual trigger located at the entrance of the fortress and successful identification of the object by the AR system initiates the presentation. The current case study is described as a system designed to support three user groups simultaneously, combining both linear and dynamic navigation areas for all three navigation routes. The points of information indicated by superimposed dots to the map represent the central navigation points of the end-system.

Figure 2. Map of the Old Venetian Fortress of Corfu featuring AR Information Points.

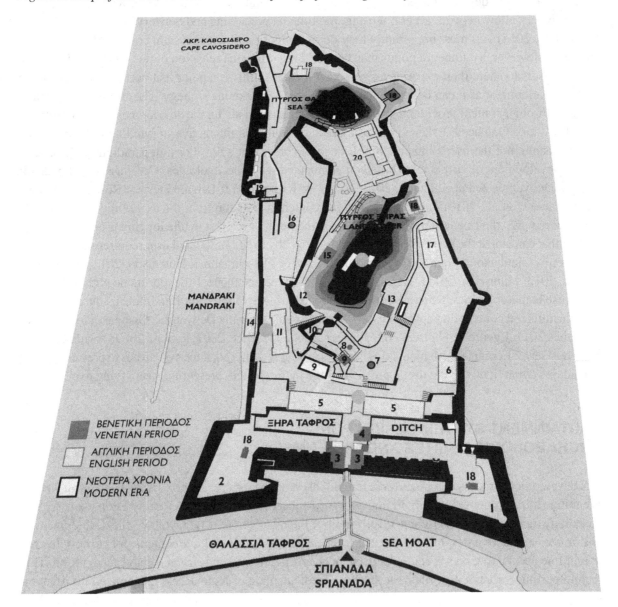

The first four spots are located at the fortress's entrance, from "*Spianada*" to the area after the "*ditch*". This path is linear and the system offers content about each information point. At each location the user is informed on the location of the previous and the next points, while at the fourth point the user is allowed to choose one out of two different routes (right route towards the building 11 or left route towards the building 17), in order to reach the "*Land Tower*", which is the final point of both routes. In section 3.1.2 we provide an example of the presentation features and choices supported at the first information access point. These include text, photos, video, audio-based narration, interactive content access to augmentation and 3D graphics used to enhance the user's reality, connected through contextual linking to the underlying multimedia database which is designed to deal with both internal and external content.

Each user group is served with its own subset of information organized into channels. Users select a specific channel in order to start the presentation tour. For visitors interested in detailed information, information is provided in a manner that enables further investigation via linking to multimedia sources, such as academic papers, documentaries, media collections and electronic sources or physical points of interest. Tourists and mainstream visitors access the standard guided tour, which reduces the content to only the essential facts, combining video-based information and augmented-reality media. For groups with special narration requirements, 9-11 year-old children in our case, a special version of a hidden object game using augmented reality is realized. They receive educational engaging content, enabling them to experience the fortress using a game-based perspective. This content customization functionality offers a highly valuable tool from the edutainment perspective that extends beyond personalized content delivery. Our experiments with augmented reality technologies and real-life trigger-content range from buildings to books and drawings. They reveal that it is possible to create edutainment applications, which are engaging and immersive, enabling the user to discover content via physical exploration.

User Profiles, Content and Technology

When dealing with archaeological and museum-based information system design and development, it is essential to identify first the requirements for the targeted *user-groups* that the system is designed to support. In the current case study these include *visitors interested in detailed information* to whom the system provides full access to the stored information, *mainstream visitor*s that receive specially filtered and adapted content according to their particular needs / interests and a *special target group* where content is adapted in order to suit a particular presentation scenario. The latter user group was chosen to consist of school children between 9-11 years old, able to use a networked tablet device or a mobile phone.

Content Re-Use and Updates

A web-based multimedia database service links a real-life image or an artificial symbol or design to various content instances. Successful recognition of an image triggers a reaction, which downloads, renders and displays the content on the mobile device. As a result, when the device is pointed towards the image and this is recognized, the user is presented with the composite result, which consists of the original image and the augmented content superimposed on that image. Content types supported by the selected augmented-reality application chosen to implement the current case study include text, hypertext links, images, video and 3D graphics. We selected *Aurasma* as the augmented reality platform.

Users are offered three methods of interaction with information: passive, interactive and dynamic-interactive (Nardelli, 2010; Trifonova, Jaccheri, & Bergaust, 2008). The passive access mode is introduced when information is overlaid in order to present information. Displaying the title of a building, triggering a voiceover or a video are three types of characteristic passive content, destined for use by the general visitor of the archaeological site. Due to their size, these media components must be accessed using an appropriate loading strategy, in order to minimize delivery delays and provide a rewarding experience (Ransburg, Timmerer, & WHellwagner, 2008).

Interactive content access involves the use of metadata, accessed in the form of hypertext or hyper-media (Pino & Di Salvo, 2011; Schallauer, Bailer, Troncy, & Kaiser, 2011). These, when chosen by the user, permit access to content stored either within the database or externally on appropriately designed web repositories. The detailed content historical information access scenario employs this form of interactivity, enabling users to access the sources of information directly. Under the current scenario, the breadth of information available was quite dense and for the case study described in this work we only allowed direct user access via hyperlinks.

Dynamic interactive content relates directly to the realization of edutainment-based scenaria (De Paolis, Aloisio, Celentano, Oliva, & Vecchio, 2011; Ioannis Deliyannis et al., 2013; Ioannis Deliyannis, Giannakoulopoulos, et al., 2011; Torrente et al., 2009). Here, the narrative structure of the application relates directly to the user location, the task in hand and the user's response. Within the current case study, the story presented to the user adapts appropriately according to the path selection of the user at the fourth point just after the "ditch" area, Figure 2. There exist two possible routes that the visitor is possible to take, one clockwise and another anti-clockwise. Both lead to the top of the castle, offering different information subsets. The first route scenario encapsulates a hidden object game where the users try to identify historical information of interest, in order to correctly answer the question presented, and allow them to progress to the lighthouse. The right route reveals information about a hidden cannon repair establishment behind the St. George's temple, providing information about the types of cannon found in the area.

All the different guiding options described above can all be accessed via channel switching within a single application-software title. Their delivery is scalable, enabling the deployment of content in a wide variety of devices and operating systems. From the networking perspective, content delivery requires a wireless network to be operational, while users may also employ 4G networks in areas that are not covered by Wi-Fi, a fact that provides continuous quality of service even on remote locations.

In terms of content organization, our development strategy was based on a top-to-bottom approach. First the points of interest were located and photographed. Then the three user target-groups were identified, the content availability was researched and user-scenario was created for each group, following the points of interest, by visiting the site. A number of tests were performed at different times during the day, in order to ensure successful content delivery during varying lighting conditions. Content-development was then completed first for the detailed content, via the creation of a web repository containing all the information, featuring appropriate metadata. Then based on this large dataset, a scenario was compiled for the guided tour. Ultimately, this content was enriched with an appropriate scenario to suit the interests of children within the 9-11 years of age.

Setting the Scene: Interactive Space-Bound Narration

Advanced narrative design techniques are combined for each content domain (Abas & Badioze Zaman, 2010; Berndt & Hartmann, 2008; Egenfeldt-Nielsen, 2005; Garrand, 2010; Lindgren, 2012; Lombardo & Damiano, 2012; McMahon & Ojeda, 2008; Ursu et al., 2008; Waraich, 2004). The case of detailed *content* contains a vast amount of content, yet its accessibility is hierarchically ordered in a manner that resembles access within a GIS-based portal of information or a map-based multimedia kiosk. The physical navigation of the user is then directly mapped to the virtual cross-node navigation introduced in such a system. Therefore, when the user reaches a specific point, various top-level menu options appear on screen, via a simple scan of the surrounding area. It is informative at this point to present an example of the information at the first point of interest.

In terms of user action, users read the operational instructions at the point and they are instructed how to set-up and access the appropriate information through the application on their handheld device. Then they are asked to select the appropriate information channel (A. detailed, B. guided tour, C. edutainment game). The user is then ready to scan the fortress surroundings via their mobile device.

In terms of system content:

- Selection A leads to detailed information for users interested in receiving as much information available as possible. For level of information A, content experts prepared a detailed historical / archaeological account for every spot.
- Selection B leads to a guided tour on the site with informative presentations on every spot. Users wishing additional information can select level A.
- Selection C initiates the edutainment content and relates to informative games on the site and its features. The user is led from spot to post with a mission as part of an overall mission to be achieved. Content experts adapted the task to suit 9-11 year-old children that can use a mobile device. Again, if users want more information, they can choose levels A (detailed content) and/or level B (guided tour).

It is informative at this point to present as an example the information at the first point of interest (entrance to site) in information levels A, B and C.

Point 01, Information Level A (detailed content):

You are at the entrance of the old Venetian fortress of Corfu. The fortress is situated on the eastern edge of the city onto a rocky fortified peninsula with two distinct hills ("koryfes" in Greek, meaning "peaks"). These "koryfes", the "peaks", comprise the origin of the current island's name in Latin languages: "Koryfes", Corfu. The area was fortified in the 6th century AD, when it was mass inhabited by the survivors of the disaster of the ancient city of Kerkyra, which is located further south. It was from the 11th to the 15th century that the whole city was called "Corifo", Corfu, because of these two characteristic and fortified hills. From the 16th century onwards, Corfu city extended outside the fortress and gained more or less its present form. Since then, the area of the fortified rocky peninsula with its two hills turned into a military fort, hence the name Fortress.

The construction of the impressive fortifications lasted for about 15 centuries and can be divided into three distinct historical phases: the Byzantine period, the early Venetian period and later Venetian period. During the Byzantine period, the Eastern hill (the so-called Castello Vecchio) was fortified. It is the second hill, the back one, from where you stand now. During the early Venetian period, the peninsula was converted into an island by the opening of the sea moat and the fortification of the western hill (the so-called Castello Novo). It is the hill in front of you. During the later Venetian period, the fortifications were extended and took their present form, in order to face the new military threat, the cannons. At the same period, the impressive "Spianada Square" was built, in front of the fortress' entrance. It is the big square behind you. To create and flatten the space for this square, all buildings in front of the entrance were demolished.

The enemy never occupied this Fortress. It met many owners, because of the political changes in the last few centuries in Europe. At times, it was owned by the Byzantines, the Venetians, the French, the Russians, the British, the Greeks, the Italians, and the Germans. All of them have left their marks and, by their distinct interventions, shaped the character of the site in front of you, the Old Fortress of Corfu. Let's proceed in meeting them in detail. Take a look at the map built right in front of you and let's walk the bridge.

Here is a list of books and papers on the Old Fortress of Corfu (a list of references and sources follows).
Point 01, Information Level B (guided content):
You are at the entrance of the Old Fortress of Corfu. Right at the entrance and to your left you can see the Tickets Office and then a bridge that crosses the fosse and leads inside the fortress. The Old Fortress of Corfu is a fortified peninsula for the last 1500 years. You can see its two distinctive rock hills in the fortress, on right in front of you and the second one a bit further at the back of the first one. These two hills ("koryfes" in Greek) comprise the origin of the island's name, Corfu, due to the foreign name of the island, Corfu. This fort has a history of political rulers (Byzantines, Venetians, French, Russians, British, Greeks, Italians and German), but none of them conquered it in war. Take a quick look at the map built right in front of you, and then let's enter the Fortress by walking down the bridge.
Point 01, Information Level C (edutainment content):
You're at the Old Fortress of Corfu. Here is your mission. You need to solve a problem you do not know yet. Please focus, 'cause I won't say that again. The Old Fortress of Corfu is an almost 1500 year-old Fortress with 1500 year-old secrets. Make sure you know where you are. You have the Spianada Square behind you. The Fortress entrance if in front of you. There is a built map next to you. Take a look at the map. Locate the moat, the bridge and the Land Tower. Now you need to walk down the bridge over the sea moat. Stop in the middle for further instructions. Hurry up!

At the edutainment-level design strategy, there are certain options that one may decide to employ in order to allow further interactivity in archaeological environments (Ioannis Deliyannis & Papaioannou, 2013). As augmented reality applications can recognize images, one strategy is to create custom puzzles, the items of which can be distributed into physical space, a technique used by many edutainment systems and applications designed to support learning and exploration of content (De Paolis et al., 2011; Egenfeldt-Nielsen, 2005; Göbel, Malkewitz, & Becker, 2006; Sauvé, 2009; Wylin & Desmet, 2005). In our case, users have to find the pieces, which will provide instructions in order to locate other pieces of the same puzzle. The goal here is to find all the pieces and complete the puzzle in order to win the game. By visiting appropriate points they can solve certain riddles, locate pieces and put the puzzle together, where successful recognition of this completed item enables them to finish the game.

During the final stage of the edutainment route (the Land Tower), the user can view a composite panoramic animation that combines the lighthouse surrounding area with a representation of the Turkish sailing fleet invading Corfu from the south in 1816, plotted using 3D graphics (Figure 3). Here, only the view towards the old hospital is depicted, while the user is presented with many more perspectives, simply by rotating the device to the appropriate direction.

FURTHER WORK AND CONCLUSIONS

Additional content may be added at the system at node level within a channel. This is a process that requires the developer to add content to the database link to each node, so that it becomes accessible via insertion of the element to the appropriate position of the trigger-image. The same problem was addressed by previous research in complex visualization systems accessed using similar interactive multimedia systems (Ioannis Deliyannis, 2011). Static content such as images, hypertext, hypermedia and buttons linking to external metadata can be added directly. However, at present, video, audio and replacement of composite content, such as overlaid graphics on images, need to be rendered to a single media element before they are used, as the underlying AR system recognises and links one media file per content chan-

Figure 3. The animated view from the lighthouse

nel and for each scene. Various user-based issues are introduced when there is a close proximity between two points, and elements of one point are visible from the other. This requires careful placement of the information access point in order to avoid such issues. When this is not possible, new points need to be added to an existing system that split existing information domains into subdomains, shared between new and existing nodes. The complexity of this process can be tackled hierarchically. Firstly the existing content links must be removed from individual information points. Then the information domain is split again to the points. The contextual information is refined on the database and will create new contextual links, which are subsequently added to the information point media for each node. A number of experiments have been performed, in order to automate this process for complex media components, such as video and 3D graphics, using dynamic context linking. However, this step requires solid and uniform contextual description at a database level and insertion of generalised tags on the videos.

The web analogy of such a system is the developments of a web-based presentation offering dynamic links which, when selected, instigate a process that filters the content accordingly, in order to present each user with the intended information. The use of interactive storytelling systems featuring such experimental characteristics may lead to customized edutainment-based uses, permitting interaction based on the person's interest and content's intended use, instead of a generalized approach applicable to all user-groups. This is particularly interesting for the development of interactive edutainment scenaria, where the user reality is augmented through their personal mobile devices.

REFERENCES

Abas, H., & Badioze Zaman, H. (2010). *Digital Storytelling Design with Augmented Reality Technology for Remedial Students in Learning Bahasa Melayu.* Paper presented at the Global Learn Asia Pacific 2010, Penang, Malaysia.

Berndt, A., & Hartmann, K. (2008). The Functions of Music in Interactive Media. In U. Spierling & N. Szilas (Eds.), Interactive Storytelling (Vol. 5334, pp. 126-131). Springer Berlin / Heidelberg. doi:10.1007/978-3-540-89454-4_19

Blanton, H. E., & Design II, E. (2011). A Review of Interactive Displays in Museums.

Boyd, D., & Crawford, K. (2011). Six Provocations for Big Data.

Casella, G., & Coelho, M. (2013). *Augmented heritage: situating augmented reality mobile apps in cultural heritage communication.* Paper presented at the Proceedings of the 2013 International Conference on Information Systems and Design of Communication. doi:10.1145/2503859.2503883

Chatti, M. A., Jarke, M., & Frosch-Wilke, D. (2007). The future of e-learning: a shift to knowledge networking and social software. *International journal of knowledge and learning, 3*(4), 404-420.

De Paolis, L. T., Aloisio, G., Celentano, M. G., Oliva, L., & Vecchio, P. (2011, 25-27 April 2011). *A simulation of life in a medieval town for edutainment and touristic promotion.* Paper presented at the Innovations in Information Technology (IIT), 2011 International Conference on.

Deliyannis, I. (2011). *Interactive Multimedia Systems for Science and Rheology: Interactive Interrogation of Complex Rheological Data Using Media-Rich Adaptive Multimedia Technologies.* Germany: VDM Verlag Dr. Muller.

Deliyannis, I. (2012a). From Interactive to Experimental Multimedia. In I. Deliyannis (Ed.), *Interactive Multimedia* (pp. 3–12). Rijeka, Croatia: Intech. doi:10.5772/38341

Deliyannis, I. (Ed.). (2012b). *Interactive Multimedia.* Rijeka, Croatia: InTech. doi:10.5772/2394

Deliyannis, I. (2013). Sensor Recycling and Reuse. *International Journal of Sensor and Related Networks, 1*(1), 8–19.

Deliyannis, I. (2014a). Converging multimedia content presentation requirements for interactive television. In A. Lugmayr, C. Dal Zotto, & G. Ferrell Lowe Lowe (Eds.), *Convergent Divergence? - Cross-Disciplinary Viewpoint on Media Convergence.* Germany: Springer-Verlag.

Deliyannis, I. (2014b). Converging multimedia content presentation requirements for interactive television. In A. Lugmayr, C. Dal Zotto, & G. F. Lowe (Eds.), Convergent Divergence? Springer-Verlag Handbook

Deliyannis, I. (2015). Interactive multimedia installation art development using recycled input and sensing devices (in Press). *International Journal of Arts and Technology.*

Deliyannis, I., Giannakoulopoulos, A., & Oikonomidou, R. (2013). *Engineering and design issues in urban-oriented edutainment systems.* Paper presented at the Hybrid City II: Subtle rEvolutions, Athens, Greece.

Deliyannis, I., Giannakoulopoulos, A., & Varlamis, I. (2011). *Utilising an Educational Framework for the Development of Edutainment Scenarios.* Paper presented at the 5th European Conference on Games Based Learning ECGBL 2011.

Deliyannis, I., & Kanellopoulos, N. (2008). *Interactive Communication Methodology for Social Software and Multimedia Applications.* Paper presented at the IADIS International Conference IADIS e-Society, Algarve, Portugal.

Deliyannis, I., & Karydis, I. (2011). *Producing and broadcasting non-linear art-based content through open source interactive internet-tv.* Paper presented at the Proceedings of the 9th international interactive conference on Interactive television. doi:10.1145/2000119.2000171

Deliyannis, I., Karydis, I., & Anagnostou, K. (2011). *Enabling Social Software-Based Musical Content for Computer Games and Virtual Worlds.* Paper presented at the 4th International Conference on Internet Technologies and Applications (ITA2011), Wrexham, North Wales, UK.

Deliyannis, I., & Papaioannou, G. (2013). *Augmented Reality for Archaeological Environments on mobile devices: a novel open framework.* Paper presented at the 1st International Workshop on Virtual Archaeology, Museums and Cultural Tourism, Delphi, Greece.

Deliyiannis, I., Floros, A., & Webster, M. F. (2009). *An Adaptive Complex Data Investigation Methodology using Interactive Multi-Menus* (pp. 393–402). Springer, US: Metadata and Semantics.

Egenfeldt-Nielsen, S. (2005). *Beyond Edutainment: Exploring the Educational Potential of Computer Games.* University of Kopenhagen, Kopenhgen.

Egenfeldt-Nielsen, S. (2007). Third generation educational use of computer games. *Journal of Educational Multimedia and Hypermedia, 16*(3), 263–281.

Encarnação, J. (2007). Edutainment and Serious Games. In K.-c. Hui, Z. Pan, R. Chung, C. Wang, X. Jin, S. Göbel & E. Li (Eds.), Technologies for E-Learning and Digital Entertainment (Vol. 4469, pp. 2-2). Springer Berlin / Heidelberg

Flattum, J. (2011). Convergence and the entertainment society. Retrieved from http://www.jerryflattum. com/wp-content/uploads/Convergence-and-the-Entertainment-Society1.pdf

Fleischmann, K., & Hutchison, C. (2012). Creative exchange: An evolving model of multidisciplinary collaboration. *Journal of Learning Design, 5*(1), 23–31. doi:10.5204/jld.v5i1.92

Fuchs, C. (2008). The implications of new information and communication technologies for sustainability. *Environment, Development and Sustainability, 10*(3), 291–309. doi:10.1007/s10668-006-9065-0

Garrand, T. (2010). Interactive Multimedia Narrative and Linear Narrative. *Write Your Way Into Animation and Games: Create a Writing Career in Animation and Games.*

Göbel, S., Malkewitz, R., & Becker, F. (2006). Story Pacing in Interactive Storytelling. In Z. Pan, R. Aylett, H. Diener, X. Jin, S. Göbel, & L. Li (Eds.), Technologies for E-Learning and Digital Entertainment (Vol. 3942, pp. 419-428). Springer Berlin / Heidelberg doi:10.1007/11736639_53

Graube, M., Ziegler, J., Urbas, L., & Hladik, J. (2013, 10-13 Sept. 2013). *Linked data as enabler for mobile applications for complex tasks in industrial settings*. Paper presented at the Emerging Technologies & Factory Automation (ETFA), 2013 IEEE 18th Conference on.

Hable, R., Rößler, & Schuller, C. (2012). *evoGuide: implementation of a tour guide support solution with multimedia and augmented-reality content*. Paper presented at the Proceedings of the 11th International Conference on Mobile and Ubiquitous Multimedia, Ulm, Germany. doi:10.1145/2406367.2406403

Harrison, T. M., & Barthel, B. (2012). Wielding new media in Web 2.0: Exploring the history of engagement with the collaborative construction of media products. *New Media & Society, 11*(1-2), 155–178. doi:10.1177/1461444808099580

Hemsley, J., & Mason, R. M. (2013). Knowledge and knowledge management in the social media age. *Journal of Organizational Computing and Electronic Commerce* (just-accepted).

Kenteris, M., Gavalas, D., & Economou, D. (2009). An innovative mobile electronic tourist guide application. *Personal and Ubiquitous Computing, 13*(2), 103–118. doi:10.1007/s00779-007-0191-y

Khan, W., Xiang, Y., Aalsalem, M., & Arshad, Q. (2012). Mobile Phone Sensing Systems: A Survey. *Communications Surveys & Tutorials, IEEE, PP* (99), 1-26.

Kietzmann, J. H., Hermkens, K., McCarthy, I. P., & Silvestre, B. S. (2011). Social media? Get serious! Understanding the functional building blocks of social media. *Business Horizons, 54*(3), 241–251. doi:10.1016/j.bushor.2011.01.005

Kirner, C., & Kirner, T. (2013). Development of online educational games with augmented reality. *Proceedings of EDULEARN13* (pp. 1950-1959).

Koenitz, H., Haahr, M., Ferri, G., Sezen, T., & Sezen, D. (2013). Mapping the Evolving Space of Interactive Digital Narrative - From Artifacts to Categorizations. In H. Koenitz, T. Sezen, G. Ferri, M. Haahr, D. Sezen, & G. [UNKNOWN ENTITY &Cogon;]atak (Eds.), *Interactive Storytelling* (Vol. 8230, pp. 55–60). Springer International Publishing; doi:10.1007/978-3-319-02756-2_6

Ledermann, F., & Schmalstieg, D. (2005, March 12-16). APRIL: a high-level framework for creating augmented reality presentations. Paper presented at the Proceedings of VR 2005 Virtual Reality 2005. IEEE.

Leiva, J., Guevara, A., Rossi, C., & Aguayo, A. (2014). Augmented reality and recommendation systems for groups. A new perspective on tourist destinations systems. *Estudios y Perspectivas en Turismo, 23*(1), 40–59.

Lindgren, S. (2012). The Sociology of Media and Information Technologies. In G. C. Aakvaag, M. Hviid Jacobsen, & T. Johansson (Eds.), *Introduction to Sociology: Scandinavian Sensibilities*. London: Pearson.

Lombardo, V., & Damiano, R. (2012). Semantic annotation of narrative media objects. *Multimedia Tools and Applications, 59*(2), 407–439. doi:10.1007/s11042-011-0813-2

Long, M., Chei Sian, L., & Goh, D. H. L. (2012, April 16-18). *Sharing in Social News Websites: Examining the Influence of News Attributes and News Sharers*. Paper presented at the Ninth International Conference of Information Technology: New Generations (ITNG).

López, J., Pérez, D., Santos, M., & Cacho, M. (2013). GuideBot. A Tour Guide System Based on Mobile Robots. *International Journal of Advanced Robotic Systems*, 10.

Madge, C., Meek, J., Wellens, J., & Hooley, T. (2009). Facebook, social integration and informal learning at university: 'It is more for socialising and talking to friends about work than for actually doing work'. *Learning, Media and Technology*, *34*(2), 141–155. doi:10.1080/17439880902923606

Manovich, L. (2011). Trending: The Promises and the Challenges of Big Social Data. In M. K. Gold (Ed.), *Debates in the Digital Humanities*. Minneapolis, MN: The University of Minnesota Press.

McLoughlin, C., & Lee, M. J. (2007). *Social software and participatory learning: Pedagogical choices with technology affordances in the Web 2.0 era*. Paper presented at the ICT: Providing choices for learners and learning. Proceedings ascilite Singapore.

McMahon, M., & Ojeda, C. (2008). *A Model of Immersion to Guide the Design of Serious Games*. Paper presented at the World Conference on E-Learning in Corporate, Government, Healthcare, and Higher Education, Las Vegas, Nevada, USA.

Nardelli, E. (2010). *A classification framework for interactive digital artworks*. Paper presented at the International ICST Conference on User Centric Media, Palma, Mallorca.

Nesamalar, E. K., & Ganesan, G. (2012). An introduction to virtual reality techniques and its applications. *International Journal of Computing Algorithm*, *1*(2), 59–62.

Nieuwenhuisen, M., & Behnke, S. (2013). Human-like interaction skills for the mobile communication robot Robotinho. *International Journal of Social Robotics*, *5*(4), 549–561. doi:10.1007/s12369-013-0206-y

Pino, C., & Di Salvo, R. (2011). *A survey of semantic multimedia retrieval systems*.

Proctor, N. (2011). The Google Art Project: A New Generation of Museums on the Web? *Curator: The Museum Journal*, *54*(2), 215–221. doi:10.1111/j.2151-6952.2011.00083.x

Ramirez, M., Ramos, E., Cruz, O., Hernandez, J., Perez-Cordoba, E., & Garcia, M. (2013). *Design of interactive museographic exhibits using Augmented reality*. Paper presented at the International Conference Electronics, Communications and Computing (CONIELECOMP). doi:10.1109/CONIELE-COMP.2013.6525747

Ransburg, M., Timmerer, C., & WHellwagner, H. (2008). *Dynamic and Distributed Multimedia Content Adaptation based on the MPEG-21 Multimedia Framework* (Vol. 101/2008). Berlin: Springer.

Rice, J. (2007). Assessing Higher Order Thinking in Video Games. *Journal of Technology and Teacher Education*, *15*(1), 87–100.

Ronchi, A. M. (2009). *Games and Edutainment Applications eCulture* (pp. 375–378). Springer Berlin Heidelberg.

Sauvé, L. (2009). *Design Tools for Online Educational Games: Concept and Application Transactions on Edutainment II* (pp. 187–202). Springer-Verlag.

Schallauer, P., Bailer, W., Troncy, R., & Kaiser, F. (2011). Multimedia Metadata Standards. *Multimedia Semantics*, 129-144.

Shea, G. (2008). *Art, design, education and research in pursuit of interactive experiences.* Paper presented at the Proceedings of the 7th ACM conference on Designing interactive systems, Cape Town, South Africa. doi:10.1145/1394445.1394482

Smith, M., & Richards, G. (2013). *Routledge Handbook of Cultural Tourism.* Routledge.

Stobbe, A., Just, T., Heng, S., Kaiser, S., & Walter, N. (2006). The dawn of technological convergence. *Deutsche Bank. Research in Economics, 56.*

Tahir, M. (2012). *Reality Technologies and Tangible Interaction: A brief guide to tangible user interfaces, augmented reality and related technologies.* LAP Lambert Academic Publishing.

Takacs, G., Chandrasekhar, V., Gelfand, N., Xiong, Y., Chen, W.-C., Bismpigiannis, T., et al. (2008). *Outdoors augmented reality on mobile phone using loxel-based visual feature organization.* Paper presented at the Proceedings of the 1st ACM international conference on Multimedia information retrieval, Vancouver, British Columbia, Canada. doi:10.1145/1460096.1460165

Timmerer, C., Waltl, M., Rainer, B., & Hellwagner, H. (2012). Assessing the quality of sensory experience for multimedia presentations. *Image Commun., 27*(8), 909–916. doi:10.1016/j.image.2012.01.016

Torrente, J., Mera, P. L., Moreno-Ger, P., & Fernández-Manjón, B. (2009). Lecture Notes in Computer Science: Vol. 5660. *The Relationship between Game Genres, Learning Techniques and Learning Styles in Educational Computer Games. Transactions on Edutainment II* (pp. 1–18). Doi:10.1007/978-3-642-03270-7_1

Trifonova, A., Jaccheri, L., & Bergaust, K. (2008). Software engineering issues in interactive installation art. *Int. J. Arts and Technology, 1*(1), 43–65. doi:10.1504/IJART.2008.019882

Tsiridou, T., Zannos, I., & Strapatsakis, M. (2012). An interactive windscape. *Thechnoetic Arts, 9*(2-3), 153–162. doi:10.1386/tear.9.2-3.153_1

Ursu, M. F., Thomas, M., Kegel, I., Williams, D., Tuomola, M., & Lindstedt, I. et al. (2008). Interactive TV narratives: Opportunities, progress, and challenges. *ACM Trans. Multimedia Comput. Commun. Appl., 4*(4), 1–39. doi:10.1145/1412196.1412198

van Dijck, J. (2013). *The Culture of Connectivity: A Critical History of Social Media.* OUP USA. doi:10.1093/acprof:oso/9780199970773.001.0001

Van Krevelen, D., & Poelman, R. (2010). A survey of augmented reality technologies, applications and limitations. *International Journal of Virtual Reality, 9*(2), 1.

Vinciarelli, A., Pantic, M., & Bourlar, H. (2009). Social signal processing: Survey of an emerging domain. *Image and Vision Computing, 27*(12), 1743–1759. doi:10.1016/j.imavis.2008.11.007

Vlist, B., Niezen, G., Rapp, S., Hu, J., & Feijs, L. (2013). Configuring and controlling ubiquitous computing infrastructure with semantic connections: A tangible and an AR approach. *Personal and Ubiquitous Computing, 17*(4), 783–799. doi:10.1007/s00779-012-0627-x

Waltl, M., Rainer, B., Timmerer, C., & Hellwagner, H. (2012a). An end-to-end tool chain for Sensory Experience based on MPEG-V. *Signal Processing Image Communication.* doi:10.1016/j.image.2012.10.009

Waltl, M., Rainer, B., Timmerer, C., & Hellwagner, H. (2012b). *A toolset for the authoring, simulation, and rendering of sensory experiences*. Paper presented at the Proceedings of the 20th ACM international conference on Multimedia, Nara, Japan. doi:10.1145/2393347.2396522

Wang, I. (2013). Globalization and Theater Spectacles in Asia. *CLCWeb: Comparative Literature and Culture, 15*(2), 22.

Waraich, A. (2004). *Using narrative as a motivating device to teach binary arithmetic and logic gates.* Paper presented at the Proceedings of the 9th annual SIGCSE conference on Innovation and technology in computer science education, Leeds, United Kingdom. doi:10.1145/1007996.1008024

Weyns, D., Malek, S., Andersson, J., & Schmerl, B. (2012). Introduction to the special issue on state of the art in engineering self-adaptive systems. *Journal of Systems and Software, 85*(12), 2675–2677. doi:10.1016/j.jss.2012.07.045

Wylin, B., & Desmet, P. (2005). *How to integrate games or game elements in educational multimedia: a typology of educational game use*. Paper presented at the World Conference on Educational Multimedia, Hypermedia and Telecommunications 2005, Montreal, Canada.

Compilation of References

Aaker, D. A. (1991). *Managing brand equity: Capitalizing on the value of a brand name*. New York: The Free Press.

Aarseth, E. (1997). *Cybertext, Perspectives on Ergodic Literature*. Baltimore, MD: John Hopkins University Press.

Abas, H., & Badioze Zaman, H. (2010). *Digital Storytelling Design with Augmented Reality Technology for Remedial Students in Learning Bahasa Melayu*. Paper presented at the Global Learn Asia Pacific 2010, Penang, Malaysia.

Abougarir, A. J., & Abosdel, A. A. M. (2013, September 29). Intelligent Controller for Nonlinear Chemical Process using Artificial Neural Networks. Proceedings of *International Academic Conference on Electrical, Electronics and Computer Engineering*.

Acker, A. (2010). Early childhood, music and diversity: exploring the potential of music for three and four year olds. *Proceedings of the CDIME Conference 2010* (pp. 6-14). Sydney, Australia: Sydney Conservatorium of Music.

Adam, A. (1998). *Artificial Knowing, Gender and the Thinking Machine*. London, New York: First Routledge.

Adams, M., & Moussouri, T. (2002, May). *The interactive experience: linking research and practice*. Paper presented at the Victoria & Albert Museum International Conference about Interactive Learning in Museums of Art and Design, London. UK.

Addis, M., & Holbrook, M. B. (2001). On the conceptual link between mass customisation and experiential consumption: An explosion of subjectivity. *Journal of Consumer Behaviour*, *1*(1), 50–66. doi:10.1002/cb.53

Admiraal-Behloul, F., Schmitz, N., van den Heuvel, M. J. D., Olofsen, H., Reiber, J. H. C., & van Buchem, M. A. (2003). Geriatric LUMC brain template. Proceedings of *International Conference on Functional Mapping of the Human Brain*.

Adolphs, R. (2002). Neural systems for recognizing emotion. *Current Opinion in Neurobiology*, *12*(2), 169–177. doi:10.1016/S0959-4388(02)00301-X PMID:12015233

Agren, M., & Ölund, M. (2007). *Storytelling. A Study of Marketing Communication in the Hospitality Industry* [Master's Thesis]. Jönköping International Business School, Jönköping University.

Alač, M. (2006, January 1). *How brain images reveal cognition: an ethnographic study of meaning-making in brain mapping practice*.

Alexander, B., & Levine, A. (2008). Web 2.0 Storytelling. Emergence of a New Genre. *EDUCAUSE Review*, *43*(6), 41–56.

Alfonseca, M., Cebrian, M., & Ortega, A. (2007). A simple genetic algorithm for music generation by means of algorithmic information theory.*Proceedings of IEEE Congress on Evolutionary Computation (CEC 2007)*. Singapore. IEEE doi:10.1109/CEC.2007.4424858

Alhanafy, E., Th., Fareed, Z., & Abdou Saad El Din, M. (2010). Neuro Fuzzy Modeling Scheme for the Prediction of Air Pollution. *Journal of American Science, 6*(12).

Alice for iPad. (2010). Atomic Antelope. Retrieved from Atomic Antelope: http://www.atomicantelope.com/alice

Allen, R. (2010, August 10). *The Physics of Angry Birds.* WIRED. Retrieved from: http://www.wired.com/2010/10/physics-of-angry-birds/

Allen, J. S. (2009). *The Lives of the Brain. Human Evolution and the Organ of Mind.* Cambridge, Mass: Belknap Press of Harvard University Press. doi:10.4159/9780674053496

Alter, A. (2012, January 20). Blowing up the book. *The Wall Street Journal.* Retrieved from http://online.wsj.com/news/articles/SB10001424052970204468004577169001135659954

Alter, A. (2013, May29). The power of names. *New Yorker.* Retrieved from www.newyorker.com/tech/elements/the-power-of-names

Amir, E., & Doyle, P. (2002). *Adventure Games: A Challenge for Cognitive Robotics (Publication).* American Association for Artificial Intelligence.

Anderson, C. (2006). *The Long Tail. Why the Future of Business is Selling Less of More.* New York: Hyperion.

Anderson, E. W., & Fornell, C. (2000). Foundations of the American customer satisfaction index. *Total Quality Management, 11*(7), 869–882. doi:10.1080/09544120050135425

Angus, N., & Libscher, M. (2010). Thinking the Unconscious: Nineteenth-Century German Thought. Cambridge: Cambridge University Press.

Anne Frank App Launches for Holocaust Memorial Day. (2013, January 24). Anne Frank Fonds. Retrieved from http://www.annefrank.ch/news-view/items/anne-frank-app-launches-for-holocaust-memorial-day.html

Annetta, L. A., Cheng, M., & Holmes, S. (2010). Assessing twenty-first century skills through a teacher created video game for high school biology students. *Research in Science & Technological Education, 28*(2), 101–114. doi:10.1080/02635141003748358

Antonelli, M., Rizzi, A., & Del Vescovo, G. (2010). A query by humming system for music information retrieval.*Proceedings of the 10th International Conference on Intelligent Systems Design and Applications (ISDA'10).* Cairo, Egypt. IEEE. doi:10.1109/ISDA.2010.5687200

Apostolopoulos, J. G., Chou, P. A., Culbertson, B., Kalker, T., Trott, M. D., & Wee, S. (2012). The Road to Immersive Communication. *Proceedings of the IEEE, 100*(4), 974–990. doi:10.1109/JPROC.2011.2182069

Apteka Euromedica . (2014). Aptekaeuromedica.pl. Retrieved from http://www.aptekaeuromedica.pl

Arar, R., & Kapur, A. (2013). A history of sequencers: Interfaces for organized pattern-based music.*Proceedings of the Sound and Music Computing Conference 2013 (SMC'13).* Stockholm, Sweden. SMC.

Arno Scharl, K. T. E. (2007). *The Geospatial Web, How Geobrowsers, Social Software and the Web 2.0 are Shaping the Network Society.* London: Springer.

Arns, M., Peters, S., Breteler, R., & Verhoeven, L. (2007). Different brain activation patterns in dyslexic children: evidence from EEG power and coherence patterns for the double-deficit theory of dyslexia. *Journal of Integrative Neuroscience, 6*(1), 175–190. doi:10.1142/S0219635207001404 PMID:17472228

Ash, D. (2004). Reflective scientific sense- making dialogue in two languages: The science in the dialogue and the dialogue in the science. *Science Education*, *88*(6), 855–884. doi:10.1002/sce.20002

Ashdown, J. (2010, November 11). *This is Minecraft*. IGN. Retrieved from: http://www.ign.com/articles/2010/11/11/this-is-minecraft

Auslander, P. (2006). The Performativity of Performance Documents. *PAJ a Journal of Performance and Art*, *28*(3), 1–10. doi:10.1162/pajj.2006.28.3.1

Autio, E., Dahlander, L., & Frederiksen, L. (2013). Information exposure, opportunity evaluation and entrepreneurial action: an empirical investigation of an online user community. *Academy of Management Journal*, *56*(5), 1348–1371. doi:10.5465/amj.2010.0328

Ayyasamy, S., & Sivanandam, S. N. (2010). Trust Based Content Distribution for Peer-ToPeer Overlay Networks. *International Journal of Network Security & Its Applications*, *2*(2).

Baby, P., Bhuvaneswari, P., & Sasirekha, K. (2013). A Study on Learning Techniques in Artificial Neural Network. *Journal of Environmental Science. Computer Science and Engineering & Technology*, *2*(4), 1001–1006.

Bacile, T. J., Ye, C., & Swilley, E. (2014). From Firm-Controlled to Consumer-Contributed: Consumer Co-Production of Personal Media Marketing Communication. *Journal of Interactive Marketing*, *28*(2), 117–133. doi:10.1016/j.intmar.2013.12.001

Bacon, B. (2013, March 18). *Ebooks are actually not books - schools among first to realize*. Retrieved from www.digitalbookworld.com/2013/ebooks-are-actually-not-books-schools-among-first-to-realize/

Baeza-Yates, R., & Ribeiro-Neto, B. (1999). *Modern information retrieval*. Boston, MA, USA: Addison-Wesley Longman Publishing.

Bainbridge, D., Nevill-Manning, C. G., Witten, I. H., Smith, L. A., & McNab, R. J. (1999) Towards a Digital Library of Popular Music. In *Proceedings of the 4th ACM Conference on Digital Libraries (DL'99)*. Berkeley, California: ACM Press. doi:10.1145/313238.313295

Baker, D. (1988). *David Baker's Jazz Improvisation: A Comprehensive Method for All Musicians*. U.S.A.: Alfred Music Publishing.

Baldaçara, L., Borgio, J. G. F., de Lacerda, A. L. T., & Jackowski, A. P. (2008). Cerebellum and psychiatric disorders. *Revista Brasileira de Psiquiatria (Sao Paulo, Brazil)*, *30*(3), 281–289. doi:10.1590/S1516-44462008000300016 PMID:18833430

Baldacchini, L. (2004). *Aspettando il frontespizio. Pagine bianche, occhietti a colophon nel libro antico*. Milano: Edizioni Sylvestre Bonnard.

Baldo, N., & Zorzi, M. (2008). Fuzzy logic for cross-layer optimization in cognitive radio networks. *IEEE Communications Magazine*, *46*(4), 64–71. doi:10.1109/MCOM.2008.4481342

Balkin, A. (2009). *Tune up to literacy: Original songs and activities for kids*. Chicago: American Library Association.

Barad, K. (2007). *Meeting the Universe Halfway, Quantum Physics and the Entanglement of Matter and Meaning*. Durham, N.C: Duke University Press. doi:10.1215/9780822388128

Barandiaran, X., & Ruiz-Mirazo, K. (Eds.). (2008). BioSystems Journal - Modeling Autonomy [Special Issue], *91*(2).

Barandiaran, X., Di Paolo, E. A., & Rohde, M. (2009). Defining agency: Individuality, normativity, asymmetry, and spatio-temporality in action. *Adaptive Behavior*, *17*(5), 367–386. doi:10.1177/1059712309343819

Barassi, V., & Treré, E. (2012). Does Web 3.0 come after Web 2.0? Deconstructing theoretical assumptions through practice. *New Media & Society, 14*(8), 1269–1285. doi:10.1177/1461444812445878

Barrett, J. R. (2001). Interdisciplinary work and musical integrity. *Music Educators Journal, 87*(5), 27–31. doi:10.2307/3399705

Barron, D. (2009). *A Better Pencil. Readers, Writers and the Digital Revolution.* Oxford: Oxford University Press.

Barthes, R. (1977). *'From Work to Text' and 'The Death of the Author (1967),' from Image-Music-Text.* London: Fontana Press.

Bateson, J. E. G. (1991). Understanding Services Consumer Behavior. In C. A. Congram (Ed.), The AMA Handbook of Marketing for the Service Industries (pp. 135-150). New York: American Management Association.

Battro, A. M., Dehaene, S., & Singer, W. J. (2010). Human Neuroplasticity and Education. In The Pontifical Academy of Sciences.

Bawden, D., & Rowlands, I. (1999). Digital Libraries: Assumptions and Concepts. *Libri, 49*(4), 181–191. doi:10.1515/libr.1999.49.4.181

Baxandall, M. (1988). *Painting and Experience in 15th Century Italy. A Primer in the Social History of the Pictorial Style* (Original edition 1972). Oxford: Oxford University Press.

Baxandall, M. (1985). *Patterns of Intention. On the Historic Explanation of Pictures.* New Haven, London: Yale University Press.

Beane, J. A. (1997). *Curriculum integration: Designing the core of democratic education.* New York: Teachers College Press.

Belluci, A., Malizia, A., & Aedo, I. (2012). *Towards a framework for the rapid prototyping of physical interaction.* Paper presented at the Fourth International Workshop on Physicality, BCS HCI 2012 Conference. University of Birmingham, UK.

Bercovici, J. (2014, February 10). Amazon vs. Book Publishers, By the Numbers. *Forbes.* Retrieved from www.forbes.com/sites/jeffbercovici/2014/02/10/amazon-vs-book-publishers-by-the-numbers/

Berman, M. G., Jonides, J., & Nee, D. E. (2006). Studying mind and brain with fMRI. *Social Cognitive and Affective Neuroscience, 1*(2), 158–161. doi:10.1093/scan/nsl019 PMID:18985126

Berndt, A., & Hartmann, K. (2008). The Functions of Music in Interactive Media. In U. Spierling & N. Szilas (Eds.), Interactive Storytelling (Vol. 5334, pp. 126-131). Springer Berlin / Heidelberg. doi:10.1007/978-3-540-89454-4_19

Bertelsen, O. W., & Bødker, S. (2003). Activity theory. *HCI models, theories, and frameworks: Toward a multidisciplinary science,* 291-324.

Bicknell, S., & Farnello, G. (Eds.) (1993). *Museum Visitor Studies in the 90s.* London, UK: Science Museum.

Biemer, P., & Trewin, D. (1997). A Review of Measurement Error Effects on the Analysis of Survey Data. In L. Lyberg, P. Biemer, M. Collins, E. De Leeuw, C. Dippo, N. Schwarz, & D. Trewin (Eds.), Survey Measurement and Process Quality (pp. 603-632). New York: Wiley. doi:10.1002/9781118490013.ch27

Biemer, P., Herget, D., Morton, J., & Willis, G. (2001), The Feasibility of Monitoring Field Interviewer Performance Using Computer Audio Recorded Interviewing (CARI). *Proceedings of the Section on Survey Research Methods, American Statistical Association.*

Bijker, W. E., Hughes, T. P., Pinch, T., & Douglas, D. G. (2012). *The Social Construction of Technological Systems: New Directions in the Sociology and History of Technology*. Mit Press.

Bimber, O., Encarnacao, L. M., & Schmalstieg, D. (2003). The Virtual Showcase as a new Platform for Augmented Reality Digital Storytelling. Proceedings of *Eurographics Workshop on Virtual Environments*. doi:10.1145/769953.769964

Biosecurity Challenges of the Global Expansion of High-Containment Biological Laboratories. (2011). Committee on Anticipating Biosecurity Challenges of the Global Expansion of High-Containment Biological Laboratories. Washington, DC: National Academies Press (US).

Bishop, C. (2004) 'Antagonism and Relational Aesthetics', from *October,* Fall 2004.

Black, G. (2005). *The Engaging Museum: Developing Museums for Visitor Involvement*. New York, USA: Routledge.

Blackman, L. (2008). *The Body*. Oxford, New York: Berg.

Blandford, A., & Stelmaszewska, H. (2002). Usability of Musical Digital Libraries: a Multimodal Analysis.*Proceedings of the 3rd International Society for Music Information Retrieval Conference (ISMIR'02)*. Paris, France. ISMIR.

Blanton, H. E., & Design II, E. (2011). A Review of Interactive Displays in Museums.

Blum, A. S., & Rutkove, S. B. (2007). The Clinical Neurophysiology Primer Th. Totowa, New Jersey 07512: Humana Press Inc. doi:10.1007/978-1-59745-271-7

Bolter, J. D. (1991). *Writing Space, the Computer, Hypertext, and the History of Writing*. New Jersey: Lawrence Erlbaum Associates.

Bolter, J.-D. (2001). *Writing Space. Computers, Hypertext, and the Remediation of Print*. New Jersey: Lawrence Erlbaum Associates.

Bone, G. (2007). *Understanding Neurology a problem-orientated approach*. New York: Manson Publishing.

Bornstein, G. (2006). *Material Modernism. The Politics of the Page*. Cambridge: Cambridge University Press.

Bourdaa, M. (2012). Transmedia: between augmented storytelling and immersive practices. *Ina Global. The review of creative industries and media*.

Bourriaud, N. (2002). *Relational Aesthetics*. Dijon: Les presses du reel.

Bowman, W. D. (2002). Educating musically. In R. Colwell, & C. Richardson (Eds.), The new handbook of research on music teaching and learning: A project of the music educators national conference (pp. 63-84). New York, NY: Oxford University Press.

Boyd, D., & Crawford, K. (2011). Six Provocations for Big Data.

Bradley, M. M., & Lang, P. J. (2007). *The international affective digitized sounds (2nd edition; iads-2): Affective ratings of sounds and instruction manual* [Technical Report B–3]. Gainesville, Fl: NIMH Center for the Study of Emotion and Attention.

Bradley, M. M., & Lang, P. J. (1994). Measuring emotion: The self-assessment manikin and the semantic differential. *Journal of Behavior Therapy and Experimental Psychiatry*, *25*(1), 49–59. doi:10.1016/0005-7916(94)90063-9 PMID:7962581

Brake, D. R. (2014). Are We All Online Content Creators Now? Web 2.0 and Digital Divides. *Journal of Computer-Mediated Communication*, *19*(3), 591–609. doi:10.1111/jcc4.12042

Braun, M. T. (2013). Obstacles to social networking website use among older adults. *Computers in Human Behavior*, *29*(3), 673–680. doi:10.1016/j.chb.2012.12.004

Breede, M. (2008). *The Brave New World of Publishing: the Symbiotic Relationship between Printing and Book Publishing*. Oxford: Chandos Publishing. doi:10.1533/9781780632186

Brogan, M. L. (2003). *A survey of digital library aggregation services*. Washington, District of Columbia: The Digital Library Federation, Council on Library and Information Resources.

Bromilow, P. (Ed.). (2013). *Authority in European Book Culture 1400-1600*. Surrey: Ashgate.

Brooke, J. (1996). SUS: a "quick and dirty" usability scale. In *P. W. Jordan, B. Thomas, B. A. Weerdmeester, & A. L. McClelland (Eds.), Usability Evaluation in Industry*. London, UK: Taylor and Francis.

Bross, I. (1954). Misclassification in 2x2 tables. *Biometrics*, *10*(4), 478–486. doi:10.2307/3001619

Brown, C. D. (2002). Straddling the humanities and social sciences: The research process of music scholars. *Library & Information Science Research*, *24*(1), 73–94. doi:10.1016/S0740-8188(01)00105-0

Bryant, M. (2011, September 15). *Papercut for iPad turns ebooks into multimedia experiences with audio, video and animations*. Retrieved from The Next Web: http://thenextweb.com/apps/2011/09/15/papercut-for-ipad-turns-ebooks-into-multimedia-experiences-with-audio-video-and-animations/

Buchanann, B., & Shortlife, E. (1984). Rule-Based Expert Systems. The Mycin Experiments of the Stanford Heuristic Project. Reading: Addison-Wesley; Retrieved from http://aitopics.org/sites/default/files/classic/Buchanan/Buchanan00.pdf

Buckner, C. (2011). Computational methods for the 21st-century philosopher: recent advances and challenges in cognitive science and metaphilosophy. Proceedings of IACAP. Aarhus.

Burnaford, G., Aprill, A., & Weiss, C. (2001). *Renaissance in the classroom: Arts integration and meaningful learning*. Mahwah, NJ: Lawrence Erlbaum.

Burnham, J. (1968). *Beyond Modern Sculpture: The Effects of Science and Technology on the Sculpture of this Century*. New York: George Braziller.

Byrd, D., & Crawford, T. (2002). Problems of music information retrieval in the real world. *Information Processing & Management*, *38*(2), 249–272. doi:10.1016/S0306-4573(01)00033-4

Calix, R., Mallepudi, S., Chen, B., & Knapp, G. (2010). Emotion recognition in text for 3-d facial expression rendering. *IEEE Transactions on Multimedia*, *12*(6), 544–551. doi:10.1109/TMM.2010.2052026

Campbell, P. S. (1998). *Songs in their heads: Music and its meaning in children's lives*. New York, NY: Oxford University Press.

Campbell, P. S. (2004). *Teaching Music Globally*. New York: Oxford University Press.

Campbell, P. S., Williamson, S., & Perron, P. (1996). *Traditional songs of singing cultures: A world sampler*. Alfred Music Publishing.

Cao, J., & Wang, J. (2005). Global exponential stability and periodicity of recurrent neural networks with time delays. *IEEE Transactions on Circuits and Systems I*, *52*(5), 920–931. doi:10.1109/TCSI.2005.846211

Carbone, F., Contreras, J., Hernandez, J. Z., & Gomez-Perez, J. M. (2012). Open innovation in an Enterprise 3.0 framework: Three case studies. *Expert Systems with Applications*, *39*(10), 8929–8939. doi:10.1016/j.eswa.2012.02.015

Carhart-Harris, R. (2007). Waves of the unconscious: the neurophysiology of dreamlike phenomena and its implications for the psychodynamic model of the mind. *Neuro-psychoanalysis, 9*(2), 183–221. doi:10.1080/15294145.2007.10773557

Carson, S., Miller, H., & Witherow, D. S. (2012). *Molecular Biology Techniques: A Classroom Laboratory Manual.* San Diego, CA: Elsevier Science.

Carter, J. (2000). *Developments in Web Research and Practice.* Paper presented at the Motivating Multimedia. San Diego, California, US.

Casacuberta, D. (2004). Dj el nino: Expressing synthetic emotions with music. *AI & Society, 18*(3), 257–263. doi:10.1007/s00146-003-0290-x

Casella, G., & Coelho, M. (2013). *Augmented heritage: situating augmented reality mobile apps in cultural heritage communication.* Paper presented at the Proceedings of the 2013 International Conference on Information Systems and Design of Communication. doi:10.1145/2503859.2503883

Casey, M. A., Veltkamp, R., Goto, M., Leman, M., Rhodes, C., & Slaney, M. (2008). Content-based music information retrieval: Current directions and future challenges. *Proceedings of the IEEE, 96*(4), 668–696. doi:10.1109/JPROC.2008.916370

Cassel, C. M. (2000). Measuring customer satisfaction on a national level using a super population approach. *Total Quality Management, 11*(7), 909–915. doi:10.1080/09544120050135452

Castro, B. P., Velho, L., & Kosminsky, D. (2012). *INTEGRARTE: digital art using body interaction.* Paper presented at the Proceedings of the Eighth Annual Symposium on Computational Aesthetics in Graphics, Visualization, and Imaging, Annecy, France.

Caulton, T. (1998). *Hands-on Exhibitions- Managing Interactive Museums and Science Centre.* London, New York: Routledge.

Cavallo, G., & Chartier, R. (Eds.). (1999). *Storia della lettura nel mondo occidentale.* Roma, Bari: Edizioni Laterza.

Cesar, P., & Chorianopoulos, K. (2009). The Evolution of TV Systems, Content, and Users Toward Interactivity. *Found. Trends Hum.-. Comput. Interact., 2*(4), 373–395. doi:10.1561/1100000008

Chartier, R. (1994). *The Order of Books. Readers, Authors and Libraries in Europe between the Fourteenth and Eighteenth Centuries* (L. Cochrane, Trans.). Cambridge: Polity Press.

Chatti, M. A., Jarke, M., & Frosch-Wilke, D. (2007). The future of e-learning: a shift to knowledge networking and social software. *International journal of knowledge and learning, 3*(4), 404-420.

Cheadle, S. W., & Zeki, S. (2014). The role of parietal cortex in the formation of color and motion based concepts. *Frontiers in Human Neuroscience, 8*, 535. doi:10.3389/fnhum.2014.00535 PMID:25120447

Cheah, M. S., Quah, Y. P., Wong, P. E., & Zainon, W. M. N. W. (2014). Augmented Reality: A Review on Its Issues and Application in Teaching and Learning. *International Journal of Computer and Information Technology, 3*(2), 269–274.

Chen, L., Tao, H., Huang, T., Miyasato, T., & Nakatsu, R. (1998). Emotion recognition from audiovisual information. *Proceedings of IEEE Second Workshop on Multimedia Signal Processing.* Redondo Beach, California, U.S.A.IEEE.

Chevalier, M. (2014). Miguel Chevalier. Retrieved from http://www.miguel-chevalier.com/en/index.html

Churchill, G. A. Jr, & Surprenant, C. (1982). An investigation into the determinants of customer satisfaction. *JMR, Journal of Marketing Research, 19*(4), 491–504. doi:10.2307/3151722

Ciavolella, M. & Coleman, P ed. (2005). *Culture and Authority in the Baroque.* Toronto: Toronto University Press.

Cieciura, M. (2006). *Podstawy technologii informacyjnych z przykładami zastosowań.* Warszawa: Wyd. Opolgraf SA.

Clark, D. L., Boutros, N. N., & Mendez, M. F. (2010). The brain and tha behavior. An introduction to behavior neuro-anatomy. Cambridge: Cambridge University Press. doi:10.1017/CBO9780511776915

Clark, T. J. (1985). 'Clement Greenberg's theory of art'. In F. Frascina (Ed). Pollock and After: The Critical Debate. London: P. Chapman.

Clark, G., & Phillips, A. (2014). *Inside Book Publishing* (5th ed.). London, New York: Routledge.

Coben, R., & Evans, J. R. (2011). *Neurofeedback and Neuromodulation: Analysis Techniques.* San Diego: Academic Press Elsevier.

Cohen, J. (2006). Social, emotional, ethical, and academic education: Creating a climate for learning, participation in democracy, and well-being. *Harvard Educational Review, 76*(2), 201–237. doi:10.17763/haer.76.2.j44854x1524644vn

Cohen, R. A., & Sweet, L. H. (2011). *Brain Imaging in Behavioral Medicine and Clinical Neuroscience.* New York: Springer. doi:10.1007/978-1-4419-6373-4

Conrad, F. G., & Schober, M. F. (1998). A conversational approach to computer-administered questionnaires. *Proceedings of the American Statistical Association, Section on Survey Methods Research.* Alexandria, VA. American Statistical Association.

Cook, S. (2003). Towards a Theory of the Practice of Curating New Media Art. In M. Townsend (Ed). Beyond the Box – Diverging Curatorial Practices. Banff: Banff Centre press.

Cornelius, R. R. (2000). Theoretical approaches to emotion. In *Proceedings of International Speech Communication Association (ISCA) Tutorial and Research Workshop (ITRW) on Speech and Emotion.* Newcastle, N. Ireland, U.K: ISCA.

Council on Library and Information Resources [CLIR]. (1998). Retrieved from http://www.clir.org/pubs/issues/issues04.html#dlf

Cova, B. & Cova, V. (2002). Tribal marketing: The tribalisation of society and its impact on the conduct of marketing. *European Journal of Marketing, 36* (5), 595, 620.

Cova, B. (1995). Community and consumption: towards a definition of the "linking value" of products and services. *Proceedings of the European marketing Academy Conference ESSEC.* Paris.

Cox, D. R. (1970). *Analysis of binary data.* London: Methuen.

Crowley, K., Callanan, M. A., Jipson, J. L., Galco, J., Topping, K., & Shrager, J. (2001). Shared scientific thinking in everyday parent-child activity. *Science Education, 85*(6), 712–732. doi:10.1002/sce.1035

Csikszentmihalyui, M., & Hermanson, K. (1999). Intrinsic motivation in museums: why does one want to learn? In E. Hooper-Greenhill (Ed.), The Educational Role of the Museum (pp. 146- 160). London; New York, Routledge.

Cunningham, S. J., Bainbridge, D., & McKay, D. (2007). Finding new music: A diary study of everyday encounter with novel songs.*Proceedings of the 8th International Society for Music Information Retrieval Conference (ISMIR'07).* Vienna, Austria. ISMIR.

Cunningham, S. J., Jones, M., & Jones, S. (2004). Organizing digital music for use: An examination of personal music collections. In *Proceedings of the 5th International Society for Music Information Retrieval Conference (ISMIR'04).* Barcelona, Spain. ISMIR.

Cunningham, S. J., & Nichols, D. M. (2009). Exploring social music behaviour: An investigation of music selection at parties. *Proceedings of the 10th International Conference of the Society for Music Information Retrieval (ISMIR 2009)*. Kobe, Japan. ISMIR.

Custodero, L. A., & Chen-Hafteck, L. (2008). Harmonizing research, practice, and policy in early childhood music: A chorus of international voices (Part 2). *Arts Education Policy Review*, *109*(3), 3–8. doi:10.3200/AEPR.109.3.3-8

Cybenko, G. (1989). Approximation by superpositions of a sigmoidal function. *Mathematics of Control, Signals, and Systems*, *2*(4), 303–314. doi:10.1007/BF02551274

Damasio, A. (2005). *Descartes' Error: Emotion, Reason, and the Human Brain* [Revised Penguin edition]. New York: Putnam.

Danet, P. (2014). The Future of Book Publishing: Seven Technology Trends and Three Industry Goals, *Publishing. Research Quarterly*, *30*(3), 275–281.

Dare, E., & Weinberg, L. (2011). Encountering the Body in Art. Proceedings for the ISEA 2011, *17th International Symposium on Electronic Art*. Retrieved from http://isea2011.sabanciuniv.edu/paper/encountering-body-art-online-vains-visual-art-interrogation-and-navigation-system-abjection-ap

De Freitas, S. (2008). *Serious Virtual Worlds – A scoping study*. JISC.

De Paolis, L. T., Aloisio, G., Celentano, M. G., Oliva, L., & Vecchio, P. (2011, 25-27 April 2011). *A simulation of life in a medieval town for edutainment and touristic promotion.* Paper presented at the Innovations in Information Technology (IIT), 2011 International Conference on.

Deliyannis, I. (2002). *Interactive Multimedia Systems for Science and Rheology.* (Ph.D), Ph.D Thesis, University of Wales, Swansea.

Deliyannis, I. (2007). *Exploratory Learning using Social Software.* Paper presented at the Cognition and Exploratory Learning in the Digital Age (CELDA), Algarve, Portugal.

Deliyannis, I. (2013). Sensor Recycling and Reuse. *International Journal of Sensor and Related Networks*, *1*(1).

Deliyannis, I. (2014). Converging multimedia content presentation requirements for interactive television. Lugmayr, A., Dal Zotto, C., & Ferrell Lowe, G. (Eds.), Convergent Divergence? Springer-Verlag Handbook.

Deliyannis, I. (2014b). Converging multimedia content presentation requirements for interactive television. In A. Lugmayr, C. Dal Zotto, & G. F. Lowe (Eds.), Convergent Divergence? Springer-Verlag Handbook

Deliyannis, I. (2015). Interactive multimedia installation art development using recycled input and sensing devices (in Press). *International Journal of Arts and Technology*.

Deliyannis, I. (2015). Interactive multimedia installation art development using recycled input and sensing devices [in Press]. *International Journal of Arts and Technology*.

Deliyannis, I., & Kanellopoulos, N. (2008). *Interactive Communication Methodology for Social Software and Multimedia Applications.* Paper presented at the IADIS International Conference IADIS e-Society, Algarve, Portugal.

Deliyannis, I., & Kanellopoulos, N. (2008). *Interactive Communication Methodology for Social Software and Multimedia Applications.* Paper presented at the IADIS International Conference IADIS e-Society. Algarve, Portugal.

Deliyannis, I., & Karydis, I. (2011). *Producing and broadcasting non-linear art-based content through open source interactive internet-tv.* Paper presented at the Proceedings of the 9th international interactive conference on Interactive television. doi:10.1145/2000119.2000171

Deliyannis, I., & Papaioannou, G. (2013). *Augmented Reality for Archaeological Environments on mobile devices: a novel open framework.* Paper presented at the 1st International Workshop on Virtual Archaeology, Museums and Cultural Tourism, Delphi, Greece.

Deliyannis, I., Antoniou, A., & Pandis, P. (2009). *Design and Development of an Experimental Low-Cost Internet-Based Interactive TV Station.* Paper presented at the 4th Mediterranean Conference on Information Systems (MCIS). Athens.

Deliyannis, I., Giannakoulopoulos, A., & Oikonomidou, R. (2013). *Engineering and design issues in urban-oriented edutainment systems.* Paper presented at the Hybrid City II: Subtle rEvolutions, Athens, Greece.

Deliyannis, I., Giannakoulopoulos, A., & Oikonomidou, R. (2013). *Engineering and design issues in urban-oriented edutainment systems.* Paper presented at the Hybrid City II: Subtle rEvolutions. Athens, Greece.

Deliyannis, I., Giannakoulopoulos, A., & Varlamis, I. (2011). *Utilising an Educational Framework for the Development of Edutainment Scenarios.* Paper presented at the 5th European Conference on Games Based Learning ECGBL 2011.

Deliyannis, I., Giannakoulopoulos, A., & Varlamis, I. (2011). Utilising an Educational Framework for the Development of Edutainment Scenarios. Paper presented at the *5th European Conference on Games Based Learning*, ECGBL 2011.

Deliyannis, I., Karydis, I., & Anagnostou, K. (2011). *Enabling Social Software-Based Musical Content for Computer Games and Virtual Worlds.* Paper presented at the 4th International Conference on Internet Technologies and Applications (ITA2011), Wrexham, North Wales, UK.

Deliyannis, I. (2011). *Interactive Multimedia Systems for Science and Rheology: Interactive Interrogation of Complex Rheological Data Using Media-Rich Adaptive Multimedia Technologies.* Germany: VDM Verlag Dr. Muller.

Deliyannis, I. (2012). From Interactive to Experimental Multimedia. In I. Deliyannis (Ed.), *Interactive Multimedia* (pp. 3–12). Rijeka, Croatia: Intech. doi:10.5772/38341

Deliyannis, I. (2013). Adapting Interactive TV to Meet Multimedia Content Presentation Requirements.[IJMT]. *International Journal of Multimedia Technology, 3*(3), 83–89.

Deliyannis, I. (2013). Sensor Recycling and Reuse. *International Journal of Sensor and Related Networks, 1*(1), 8–19.

Deliyannis, I. (2014a). Converging multimedia content presentation requirements for interactive television. In A. Lugmayr, C. Dal Zotto, & G. Ferrell Lowe Lowe (Eds.), *Convergent Divergence? - Cross-Disciplinary Viewpoint on Media Convergence.* Germany: Springer-Verlag.

Deliyannis, I. (Ed.). (2012b). *Interactive Multimedia.* Rijeka, Croatia: InTech. doi:10.5772/2394

Deliyannis, I., & Papaioannou, G. (2014). Augmented reality for archaeological environments on mobile devices: a novel open framework. *Mediterranean Archaeology and Archaeometry, 14*(4), 1–10.

Deliyiannis, I., Floros, A., & Webster, M. F. (2009). *An Adaptive Complex Data Investigation Methodology using Interactive Multi-Menus* (pp. 393–402). Springer, US: Metadata and Semantics.

Dena, C. (2009). *Transmedia practice: theorising the practice of expressing a fictional world across distinct media and environments.* PhD Thesis. Sydney: University of Sydney.

Dennett, D. (1993). Review of F. Varela, E. Thompson, & E. Rosch, The Embodied Mind. *The American Journal of Psychology, 106,* 121–126. doi:10.2307/1422869

Departament Współpracy Międzynarodowej Centrali, N. F. Z. (2012). Departament Współpracy Międzynarodowej Centrali NFZ. Retrieved from https://www.ekuz.nfz.gov.pl/

Descartes, R. (2000). *Discourse on Method and Related Writings*. London: Penguin Classics.

Di Paolo, E. A. (2005). Autopoiesis, adaptivity, teleology, agency. *Phenomenology and the Cognitive Sciences*, *4*(4), 429–452. doi:10.1007/s11097-005-9002-y

Di Paolo, E. A. (Ed.). (2009). *Phenomenology and the Cognitive Sciences [* Special issue on "The Social and Enactive Mind], *8*(4).

Diamond, J. (1986). The behavior of family groups in science museums. *Curator*, *29*(2), 139–154. doi:10.1111/j.2151-6952.1986.tb01434.x

Dierking, L., & Falk, J. (1994). Family behavior and learning in informal science settings: A review of the research. *Science Education*, *78*(1), 57–72. doi:10.1002/sce.3730780104

Dimitroula, V., Bassiliades, N., Vlahavas, I., & Dimitrakos, S. (2001). FUNAGES: An expert system for fundus fluorescein angiography. *Health Informatics Journal*, *7*(3-4), 214–221. http://lpis.csd.auth.gr/publications/shimr2001.pdf doi:10.1177/146045820100700317

Direction *Directions of development of e-services in health protection in West Pomeranian Voivodeship for the years 2011-2020*. (2011). Szczecin. Retrieved from www.wz.wzp.pl/download/index/biblioteka/7620

Directions of informatisation "e-Health Poland" for the years 2011-2015. (2009). Retrieved from www.csioz.gov.pl/publikacja.php

Dittmar, C., Cano, E., Abesser, J., & Grollmisch, S. (2012). Music information retrieval meets music education. In M. Müller, M. Goto, & M. Schedl (Eds.), *Multimodal Music Processing, Dagstuhl Follow-Ups* (Vol. 3, pp. 95–119). Dagstuhl, Germany: Schloss Dagstuhl-Leibniz-Zentrum für Informatik.

Donahue, C. (2013). *Applications of genetic programming to digital audio synthesis*. [Doctoral dissertation]. University of Texas at Austin, Texas, USA.

Donnelly, P., & Sheppard, J. (2011). Evolving four-part harmony using genetic algorithms.*Proceedings of the 2011 international conference on Applications of evolutionary computation - Volume Part II, EvoApplications'11*. Berlin, Heidelberg. Springer-Verlag.

Dooktor.pl. (n.d.). *Dooktor.pl*. Retrieved from http://www.dooktor.pl/diagnoza.html

Dougan, K. (2012). Information seeking behaviors of music students. *RSR. Reference Services Review*, *40*(4), 558–573. doi:10.1108/00907321211277369

Dourish, P. (2001). *Where the Action Is: The Foundations of Embodied Interaction*. Cambridge: MIT Press.

Downes, E. J., & McMillan, S. J. (2000). Defining Interactivity. *New Media & Society*, *2*(2), 157–179. doi:10.1177/14614440022225751

Downie, J. S. (2003). Music information retrieval. In B. Cronin (Ed.), *Annual Review of Information Science and Technology 37* (pp. 295–340). Medford, New Jersey, USA: Information Today.

Downie, J. S. (2004). A sample of music information retrieval approaches. *Journal of the American Society for Information Science and Technology*, *55*(12), 1033–1036. doi:10.1002/asi.20054

Doz.pl. (n.d.). *Dbam o zdrowie*. Retrieved from http://www.doz.pl

Drossos, K., Floros, A., & Giannakoulopoulos, A. (2014). Beads: A dataset of binaural emotionally annotated digital sounds.*Proceedings of 5th International Conference on Information, Intelligence, Systems and Applications (IISA 2014).* Chania, Crete, Greece. IEEE. doi:10.1109/IISA.2014.6878749

Drossos, K., Floros, A., & Kanellopoulos, N. G. (2012). Affective acoustic ecology: Towards emotionally enhanced sound events.*Proceedings of the 7th Audio Mostly Conference: A Conference on Interaction with Sound.* Corfu, Greece. ACM. doi:10.1145/2371456.2371474

Drossos, K., Kotsakis, R., Kalliris, G., & Floros, A. (2013). Sound events and emotions: Investigating the relation of rhythmic characteristics and arousal.*Proceedings of Fourth International Conference on Information, Intelligence, Systems and Applications (IISA 2013).* Piraeus, Greece. IEEE. doi:10.1109/IISA.2013.6623709

Druckrey, (ed) (1996). *Electronic Culture.* Romford: Aperture.

Du, Z., Fu, X., Zhao, C., Liu, Q., & Liu, T. (2013). Interactive and Collaborative E-Learning Platform with Integrated Social Software and Learning Management System. In W. Lu, G. Cai, W. Liu & W. Xing (Eds.), *Proceedings of the 2012 International Conference on Information Technology and Software Engineering* (Vol. 212, pp. 11-18): Springer Berlin Heidelberg doi:10.1007/978-3-642-34531-9_2

Dubois, D., Ostasiewicz, W., & Prade, H. (2000). Fuzzy Sets: History and Basic Notions. *Fundamentals of Fuzzy Sets The Handbooks of Fuzzy Sets Series, 7*, 21–124. doi:10.1007/978-1-4615-4429-6_2

Duignan, M., Biddle, R., & Noble, J. (2005). A taxonomy of sequencer user-interfaces. In *Proceedings of the International Computer Music Conference (ICMC'05).* Barcelona, Spain. ICMC.

Duncan, H., Spillane, K., & Morrison, I. (2014). Electroencephalography – An Overview. *Scottish Universities Medical Journal, 3*(1), 47–53.

Dunn, J. W., & Mayer, C. A. (1999). VARIATIONS: A digital music library system at Indiana University.*Proceedings of the 4th ACM Conference on Digital Libraries (DL'99).* Berkeley, California: ACM Press. doi:10.1145/313238.313242

Durston, S., Tottenham, N. T., Thomas, K. M., Davidson, M. C., Eigsti, I.-M., & Yang, Y. et al. (2003). Differential patterns of striatal activation in young children with and without ADHD. *Biological Psychiatry, 53*(10), 871–878. doi:10.1016/S0006-3223(02)01904-2 PMID:12742674

Economou, M., & Pujol Tost, L. (2011). Evaluating the use of virtual reality and multimedia applications for presenting the past. In G. Styliaras, D. Koukopoulos, & F. Lazarinis (Eds.), Handbook of Research on Technologies and Cultural Heritage: Applications and Environments (pp. 223–239). Hershey, PA: IGI Global. doi:10.4018/978-1-60960-044-0.ch011

Eftekhari, M. H., & Zeynab, B. (2008). *Web 1.0 to Web 3.0 Evolution and Its Impact on Tourism Business Development.* Working paper.

Egenfeldt-Nielsen, S. (2005). *Beyond Edutainment: Exploring the Educational Potential of Computer Games.* University of Kopenhagen, Kopenhgen.

Egenfeldt-Nielsen, S. (2007). Third generation educational use of computer games. *Journal of Educational Multimedia and Hypermedia, 16*(3), 263–281.

Egidi, L., & Furini, M. (2005). Bringing multimedia contents into MP3 files. *IEEE Communications Magazine, 43*(5), 90–97. doi:10.1109/MCOM.2005.1453428

Eisenstein, E. (1983). *The Printing Revolution in Early modern Europe.* Cambridge: Cambridge University Press.

Eisner, E. (2002). *The Arts and the Creation of Mind.* New Haven, London: Yale University Press.

Ellenbogen, K. M. (2002). Museums in family life: An ethnographic case study. In G. Leinhardt, K. Crowley, & K. Knutson (Eds.), *Learning conversations in museums* (pp. 81–101). Mahwah, NJ: Lawrence Erlbaum Associates.

Elliott, D. J. (1995). *Music Matters: A New Philosophy of Music Education*. New York: Oxford University Press.

Encarnação, J. (2007). Edutainment and Serious Games. In K.-c. Hui, Z. Pan, R. Chung, C. Wang, X. Jin, S. Göbel & E. Li (Eds.), Technologies for E-Learning and Digital Entertainment (Vol. 4469, pp. 2-2). Springer Berlin / Heidelberg

Erickson, H. L. (1998). *Concept-based curriculum and instruction: Teaching beyond the facts*. Thousand Oaks, CA: Corwin Press.

Erragcha, N. (2014). Social networks as marketing tools. *British Journal of Marketing Studies*, *2*(1), 79–88.

Escalas, J. E. (2004). Narrative Processing: Building Consumer Connections to Brands. *Journal of Consumer Psychology*, *14*(1&2), 168–180. doi:10.1207/s15327663jcp1401&2_19

Falk, J., & Dierking, L. (2000). *Learning from Museums: Visitors Experiences and the Making of Meaning*. USA: Altamira Press.

Federman, M. (2004). *What is the Meaning of the Medium is the Message?* Retrieved from http://individual.utoronto.ca/markfederman/MeaningTheMediumistheMessage.pdf

Feinstein, S. (2006). *The Praeger Handbook of Learning and the Brain*. London: Praeger Publishers.

Fekolkin, R. (2013). Analysis of Augmented Reality Games on Android platform.

Feldman, R. S. (2012). *Understanding Psychology*. New York: McGraw-Hill. doi.

Ferm-Thorgersen, C. (2011). Assessment of musical knowledge from a life-world-phenomenological perspective. *Hellenic Journal of Music, Education, and Culture*, *2*, 37–45.

Ferrari, S. (2006). *Modelli gestionali per il turismo come esperienza. Emozioni e polisensorialità nel marketing delle imprese turistiche*. Padova: Cedam.

Ferrari, S. (2012). *Marketing del turismo. Consumatori, imprese e destinazioni nel nuovo millennio*. Padova: Cedam.

Flattum, J. (2011). Convergence and the entertainment society. Retrieved from http://www.jerryflattum.com/wp-content/uploads/Convergence-and-the-Entertainment-Society1.pdf

Fleischmann, K., & Hutchison, C. (2012). Creative exchange: An evolving model of multidisciplinary collaboration. *Journal of Learning Design*, *5*(1), 23–31. doi:10.5204/jld.v5i1.92

Flick, U., von Kardoff, E., & Steinke, I. (Eds.). (2004). *A Companion to Qualitative Research. Free University Berlin*. Germany: Sage Publications.

Foley, M. B. (2006). The music, movement and learning connection: A review. *Childhood Education*, *82*(3), 175–176. doi:10.1080/00094056.2006.10521372

Fornell, C., Johnson, M. D., Anderson, E. W., Cha, J., & Bryant, B. E. (1996). The American customer satisfaction index: Nature, purpose, and findings. *Journal of Marketing*, *60*(4), 7–18. doi:10.2307/1251898

Fort Grèbol, P. (2014, December 12). *Symbolic Dynamics applied to Electroencephalographic signals to Predict Response to Noxious Stimulation during Sedation-Analgesia*. Universitat Politècnica de Catalunya.

Foundation of the Hellenic World & Hellenic Cosmos Official Website. (n. d.). Retrieved from http://www.fhw.gr/fhw/index.php?lg=2&state=pages&id=82

Franses, P. H., & Paap, R. (2001). *Quantitative Models in Marketing Research*. Cambridge, UK: Cambridge University Press. doi:10.1017/CBO9780511753794

Freye, E., & Levy, J. V. (2005). Cerebral monitoring in the operating room and the intensive care unit: an introductory for the clinician and a guide for the novice wanting to open a window to the brain. Part I: The electroencephalogram. *Journal of Clinical Monitoring and Computing*, *19*(1-2), 1–76. doi:10.1007/s10877-005-0712-z PMID:16167222

Friberg, A., Bresin, R., & Sundberg, J. (2006). Overview of the kth rule system for music performance. *Advances in Cognitive Psychology*, *2*(2), 145–161. doi:10.2478/v10053-008-0052-x

Fried, M. (1967) "Art and Objecthood". Retrieved from http://atc.berkeley.edu/201/readings/FriedObjcthd.pdf

Friedberg, M. W., Chen, P. G., Van Busum, K. R., Aunon, F. M., Pham, Ch., Caloyeras, J. P., et al. (2013). *Factors Affecting Physician Professional Satisfaction and Their Implications for Patient Care, Health Systems, and Health Policy*, The RAND Corporation. Retrieved from http://www.rand.org/content/dam/rand/pubs/research_reports/RR400/RR439/RAND_RR439.pdf

Frude, N. (2006). *Understanding Biological Psychology*. Oxford: Blackwell Publishing Ltd.

Fuchs, C. (2008). The implications of new information and communication technologies for sustainability. *Environment, Development and Sustainability*, *10*(3), 291–309. doi:10.1007/s10668-006-9065-0

Fuller, R. (2000). *Introduction to Neuro-Fuzzy Systems*. New York: Springer Science & Business Media. doi:10.1007/978-3-7908-1852-9

Furmankiewicz, M., & Ziuziański, P. (2013). Ocena wykorzystania technologii teleinformatycznych w procesie autodiagnozy i samoleczenia w świetle badania opinii internautów. H. Sroki & T. Porębska-Miąc (Eds.) Systemy Wspomagania Organizacji SWO 2013, Katowice: Wydawnictwo Uniwersytetu Ekonomicznego w Katowicach.

Furmankiewicz, M., Sołtysik-Piorunkiewicz, A., & Ziuziański, P. (2014). Artificial Intelligence Systems for Knowledge Management in e-Health: The Study of Intelligent Software Agents. In *Proceedings of the 18th International Conference on Systems* (part of CSCC '14), Santorini, pp. 551-556.

Furr, A. K. (2000). *CRC Handbook of Laboratory Safety* (5th ed.). Boca Raton, FL: CRC Press. doi:10.1201/9781420038460

Futrelle, J., & Downie, J. S. (2002). Interdisciplinary communities and research issues in music information retrieval. In *Proceedings of the 3rd International Conference of the Society for Music Information Retrieval (ISMIR'02)*. Paris, France. ISMIR.

Fu, Z., Lu, G., Ting, K. M., & Zhang, D. (2011). A Survey of audio-based music classification and annotation. *IEEE Transactions on Multimedia*, *13*(2), 303–319. doi:10.1109/TMM.2010.2098858

Gabriel, Y. (2000). *Storytelling in organizations: facts, fictions, and fantasies*. Oxford: Oxford University Press. doi:10.1093/acprof:oso/9780198290957.001.0001

Gacek, A., & Pedrycz, W. (2012). *ECG Signal Processing, Classification and Interpretation*. London: Springer London. doi:10.1007/978-0-85729-868-3

Gallagher, K. (2014). Print-On Demand: New Models and Value Creation, *Publishing. Research Quarterly*, *30*, 244–248.

Gallagher, S. (2005). *How the Body Shapes the Mind*. New York: Oxford University Press. doi:10.1093/0199271941.001.0001

Garcia, R. A. (2000). Towards the automatic generation of sound synthesis techniques: Preparatory steps. *Proceedings of AES 109th Convention*. Los Angeles. AES.

Garcia, R. A. (2001b). Growing sound synthesizers using evolutionary methods. In *Proceedings of European Conference in Artificial Life 2001 (ECAL2001) special workshop in Artificial Life Models for Musical Applications*. Prague, Chez Republic. Springer.

Garcia, R. A. (2001a). Automating the design of sound syntheses techniques using evolutionary methods.*Proceedings of the COST G-6 Conference on Digital Audio Effects (DAFX- 01)*. Limerick, Ireland.

Gardner, H. (1993). *Multiply Intelligences: The Theory into Practice*. New York: Basic Books.

Garrand, T. (2010). Interactive Multimedia Narrative and Linear Narrative. *Write Your Way Into Animation and Games: Create a Writing Career in Animation and Games*.

Garrigos-Simon, F. J., Lapiedra Alcami, R., & Barbera Ribera, T. (2012). Social networks and Web 3.0: Their impact on the management and marketing of organizations. *Management Decision, 50*(10), 1880–1890. doi:10.1108/00251741211279657

Gazi, A., & Nikiforidou, A. (2008). Η χρήση των νέων τεχνολογιών στις εκθέσεις μουσείων: ένα μέσον ερμηνείας. In Α. Μπούνια, Νικονάνου Ν. & Οικονόμου Μ. (Ed.) Η τεχνολογία στην υπηρεσία της πολιτισμικής κληρονομιάς (pp. 373-384). Αθήνα: Καλειδοσκόπιο.

Gazi, A., Nikiforidou, A., & Moussouri, T. (2004). Μια έκθεση για τα αρχαία ελληνικά μαθηματικά: Πλαίσιο ανάπτυξης και μουσειολογικός σχεδιασμός. *Museology, 1*. Retrieved from http://museology.ct.aegean.gr/articles/2007127115655.pdf

Gazi, A., Nikiforidou, A., Kamara, A., & Paschalidis, G. (Eds.). (2003). Is There an Answer to Everything? A journey to the world of Greek mathematics. Athens: Foundation of the Hellenic World.

Gazzaniga. (2011). *The Cognitive Neurosciences*. Cambridge: The MIT Press.

Gazzaniga, M. S. (2013). *Cognitive Neuroscience: The Biology of the Mind* (4th ed.). New York: W. W. Norton & Company.

Ginzburg, C. (2009). Il formaggio e i vermi. Il cosmo di un mugnaio del '500 (Original Edition 1976). Torino: Einaudi.

Given, L. (Ed.). (2008). *The SAGE Encyclopedia of Qualitative Research Methods.Charles Sturt University*. Australia: SAGE Publications Inc. doi:10.4135/9781412963909

Glaser, B. G. (1992). *Basics of grounded theory analysis*. Mill Valley, CA: Sociology Press.

Glynn, D. (2012). Correspondence Analysis: Exploring data and identifying patterns. *Academia.edu*, Retrieved from http://www.academia.edu/926945/Correspondence_Analysis

Göbel, S., Malkewitz, R., & Becker, F. (2006). Story Pacing in Interactive Storytelling. In Z. Pan, R. Aylett, H. Diener, X. Jin, S. Göbel, & L. Li (Eds.), Technologies for E-Learning and Digital Entertainment (Vol. 3942, pp. 419-428). Springer Berlin / Heidelberg doi:10.1007/11736639_53

Goldzweig, C. L., Towfigh, A., Maglione, M., & Shekelle, P. G. (2009). Costs and benefits of health information technology: new trends from the literature. Retrieved from http://www.ncbi.nlm.nih.gov/pubmed/19174390

Gombrich E. (2006). *The Uses of Images. Studies in the Social Function of Art and Visual Communication*. (Original edition 1999). Phaidon.

Goto, M. (2012). Grand challenges in music information research. In M. Müller, M. Goto, & M. Schedl (Eds.), *Multimodal Music Processing, Dagstuhl Follow-Ups* (Vol. 3, pp. 217–226). Dagstuhl, Germany: Schloss Dagstuhl-Leibniz-Zentrum für Informatik.

Govindarajan, M., & Chandrasekaran, R. M. (2007). Classifier Based Text Mining for Neural Network. *World Academy of Science, Engineering and Technology International Journal of Computer, Control, Quantum and Information Engineering, 1*(3).

Graham, B., & Cook, S. (2010). *Rethinking Curating – Art after New Media*. Cambridge Mass. and London: MIT press.

Graube, M., Ziegler, J., Urbas, L., & Hladik, J. (2013, 10-13 Sept. 2013). *Linked data as enabler for mobile applications for complex tasks in industrial settings*. Paper presented at the Emerging Technologies & Factory Automation (ETFA), 2013 IEEE 18th Conference on.

Greco, A. – Milliot, J. – Wharton, R. (2013) The Book Publishing Industry, third edition New York & London: Routledge.

Greenberg, C. (1960). Modernist Painting. In C. Harrison, & P. Wood (Eds), Art in Theory 1900-1990. Oxford: Blackwell.

Green, L. (2008). *Music, Informal Learning and the School: A New Classroom Pedagogy*. Aldershot: Ashgate Press.

Green, L. (2014). *Hear, Listen, Play! How to Free Your Students' Aural, Improvisation, and Performance Skills*. Oxford: Oxford University Press.

Green, M., & McNeese, M. N. (2007). Using Edutainment Software to Enhance Online Learning. *International Journal on E-Learning, 6*(1), 5–16.

Gresham-Lancaster, S. (1998). The aesthetics and history of the hub: The effects of changing technology on network computer music. *Leonardo Music Journal, 8*, 39–44. doi:10.2307/1513398

Grigg-Damberger, M., Gozal, D., Marcus, C. L., Quan, S. F., Rosen, C. L., & Chervin, R. D. et al. (2007). The Visual Scoring of Sleep and Arousal in Infants and Children. *Journal of Clinical Sleep Medicine, 3*(2). PMID:17557427

Grimm, M., Kroschel, K., Mower, E., & Narayanan, S. (2007). Primitives-based evaluation and estimation of emotions in speech. *Speech Communication, 49*(10-11), 787–800. doi:10.1016/j.specom.2007.01.010

Guillaume, S. (2001). Designing Fuzzy Inference Systems from Data: An Interpretability-Oriented Review. *IEEE Transactions on A Fuzzy Systems, 9*(3). http://doi.org/1063–6706/01

Guler, N., Ubeyli, E., & Guler, I. (2005). Recurrent neural networks employing Lyapunov exponents for EEG signals classification. *Expert Systems with Applications, 29*(3), 506–514. doi:10.1016/j.eswa.2005.04.011

Gummesson, E. (2004). From one-to-one to many-to-many marketing. In Atverksekonomins Marknadsföring: Attse Marknadsföringen Genom Nätverksglasögon. Malmö: Liber ekonomi.

Hable, R., Rößler, & Schuller, C. (2012). *evoGuide: implementation of a tour guide support solution with multimedia and augmented-reality content*. Paper presented at the Proceedings of the 11th International Conference on Mobile and Ubiquitous Multimedia, Ulm, Germany. doi:10.1145/2406367.2406403

Hadjileontiadou, S. J., Nikolaidou, G. N., & Hadjileontiadis, L. J. (2007). Action-Research for the design and development of alternative learning environment using ICT: Case studies in environmental education and music lesson. In E. M. Botsari (Ed.), *Themes on Introductory Training for Newly Appointed Teachers* (pp. 104–117). Athens, Greece: Pedagogical Institute.

Hagel, J. III, & Armstrong, A. G. (1997). *Net Gain: Expanding Markets Through Virtual Communities*. Harvard, MA: Harvard Business School Press.

Hagglund, P. (2012), *Taking gamification to the Next Level. A detailed overview of the past, the present and a possible future of gamification* [thesis]. Umea Universitet.

Hahn, T. (2013). *Option Pricing Using Artificial Neural Networks : an Australian Perspective.*

Haigh, T. (2013). Five lessons from really good history. *Communications of the ACM, 56*(1), 37–40. doi:10.1145/2398356.2398369

Halpern, M., & Humphreys, L. (2014). Iphoneography as an Emergent Art World. *New Media and Society.* Retrieved from http://nms.sagepub.com/content/early/2014/06/05/1461444814538632, doi:10.1177/1461444814538632

Halsall, F., Jansen, J., & O'Connor, T. (Eds.) (2008). Rediscovering Aesthetics: Transdisciplinary Voices from Art History, Philosophy, and Art Practices. Stanford University Press.

Han, H., & Lopp, L. (2013). Writing and reading in the electronic health record: an entirely new world. *Medical Education Online.* Retrieved from http://www.ncbi.nlm.nih.gov/pmc/ articles /PMC3566375/

Handbuch zur Kalkulation von Fallkosten. Version 2.0 (2002). Deutsche Krankenhausgesellschaft. Retrieved from http://www.aokgesundheitspartner.de/imperia/md/gpp/bund/krankenhaus/drg_system/kalkulation/kalkulationshandbuch_2_0.pdf

Hanson, V. L. (2004). *The user experience: designs and adaptations.* New York City, New York: ACM Press. doi:10.1145/990657.990659

Haraway, D. (1991). *Situated Knowledges, from, Simians Cyborgs and Women: The Reinvention of Nature.* New York: Routledge.

Hargreaves, A., & Moore, S. (2000). Curriculum integration and classroom relevance: A study of teachers' practice. *Journal of Curriculum and Supervision, 15*, 89–112.

Harrison, P. J. (1999). The neuropathology of schizophrenia: A critical review of the data and their interpretation. *Brain, 122*(4), 593–624. doi:10.1093/brain/122.4.593 PMID:10219775

Harrison, T. M., & Barthel, B. (2012). Wielding new media in Web 2.0: Exploring the history of engagement with the collaborative construction of media products. *New Media & Society, 11*(1-2), 155–178. doi:10.1177/1461444808099580

Haskell, F. (1980). *Patrons and Painters: A Study in the Relations between Italian Art and the Society in the Age of the Baroque* (2nd ed.). New Haven, London: Yale University Press.

Haueis, P. (2014). Meeting the brain on its own terms. *Frontiers in Human Neuroscience, 8*, 815. doi:10.3389/fnhum.2014.00815 PMID:25352801

Hayes, B. E. (1998). *Measuring Customer Satisfaction: Survey Design, Use, and Statistical Analysis Methods* (2nd ed.). Milwaukee, Wisconsin. ASQ Quality Press.

Hayles, K. N. (1999). *How We Became Post Human.* Chicago, London: The University of Chicago Press. doi:10.7208/chicago/9780226321394.001.0001

Hein, G. (1998). *Learning in the Museum.* London, New York: Routledge.

Hemsley, J., & Mason, R. M. (2013). Knowledge and knowledge management in the social media age. *Journal of Organizational Computing and Electronic Commerce* (just-accepted).

Hemsley, J., & Mason, R. M. (2013). Knowledge and knowledge management in the social media age. *Journal of Organizational Computing and Electronic Commerce.*

Heo, S. P., Suzuki, M., Ito, A., & Makino, S. (2006). An effective music information retrieval method using three-dimensional continuous DP. *IEEE Transactions on Multimedia, 8*(3), 633–639. doi:10.1109/TMM.2006.870717

Hernandez, L., Wager, T., & Jonides, J. (2014). *Introduction to Functional Neuroimaging*. Cambridge: The MIT Press.

Herzig, P. (2014). Gamification as a service [Ph.D.].

Hevner, K. (1936). Experimental studies of the elements of expression in music. *The American Journal of Psychology*, *48*(2), 246–268. doi:10.2307/1415746

Heyning, L. (2011). "I can't sing!" The concept of teacher confidence in singing and the use within their classroom. *International Journal of Education & the Arts*, 12(13). Retrieved from http://www.ijea.org/v12n13

Hirschman, E. C., & Holbrook, M. B. (1982). Hedonic consumption: emerging concepts, methods and propositions, *Journal of Marketing, 46*, 92-101.

Holbrook, M. B., & Hirschman, E. C. (1982). The experiential aspects of consumption: Consumer fantasies, feelings, and fun. *The Journal of Consumer Research*, *9*, 132–140.

Holland, J. H. (1992). *Adaptation in natural and artificial systems*. Cambridge, MA, USA: MIT Press.

Hooper-Greenhill, E. (1994). *Museum and their Vistitors*. London, New York: Routledge.

Hornik, K. (1991). Approximation capabilities of multilayer feedforward networks. *Neural Networks*, *4*(2), 251–257. doi:10.1016/0893-6080(91)90009-T

Hornik, K., Stinchcombe, M., & White, H. (1990). Universal approximation of an unknown mapping and its derivatives using multilayer feedforward networks. *Neural Networks*, *3*(5), 551–560. doi:10.1016/0893-6080(90)90005-6

Howard, N. (2009). *The Book. The Life Story of a Technology*. Baltimore: The Hopkins University Press.

Hsu, J. L., & Huang, C. C. (2014). Designing a graph-based framework to support a multi-modal approach for music information retrieval. *Multimedia Tools and Applications*, *68*(3), 1–27.

Huotari, K., & Hamari, J. (2012). Defining Gamification - A Servce Marketin Perspective. *Proceedings of the 16th International Academic MindTrek Conference 2012*. Tampere, Finland.

Hurst, M., Jackson, T. W., & Glencross, M. (2012, September 7-8). *Emotion recognition &-Theory or practicality*. Paper presented at the Automation and Computing (ICAC), 2012 18th International Conference.

Infelise, M. (2013). *I libri proibiti da Gutenberg all' Encyclopedie* (Original Edition 1999). Roma-Bari: Laterza.

Interactive Physics (n. d.). Retrieved from: http://www.design-simulation.com/IP/

Ischebeck, A., Zamarian, L., Siedentopf, C., Koppelstätter, F., Benke, T., Felber, S., & Delazer, M. (2006). How specifically do we learn? Imaging the learning of multiplication and subtraction. *NeuroImage*, *30*(4), 1365–1375. doi:10.1016/j.neuroimage.2005.11.016 PMID:16413795

Ishizaki, J., Yamamoto, H., Takahashi, T., Takeda, M., Yano, M., & Mimura, M. (2008). Changes in regional cerebral blood flow following antidepressant treatment in late-life depression. *International Journal of Geriatric Psychiatry*, *23*(8), 805–811. doi:10.1002/gps.1980 PMID:18214999

ISME. (2012). ISME-Gibson International Award Winners 2012. Retrieved from http://www.isme.org/awards/39-isme-g/155-isme-gibson-international-award-winners-2012

Ivancevic, V. G., & Ivancevic, T. T. (2007). Human and Computational Mind. *Human and Computational Mind. Studies in Computational Intelligence Springer-Verlag Berlin Heidelberg*, *60*, 1–269.

Jackson Fish Market. (2012). *A story before bed*. Retrieved from A story before bed: http://www.astorybeforebed.com/

Jansen, J. (2002). *Introduction to Artificial Neural Networking. Engineering 315: Control Systems.*

Jansson, A. (2002). Spatial Phantasmagoria. *European Journal of Communication, 17*(4), 429–443. doi:10.1177/0267 3231020170040201

Jenkins, H. (2003, November). Why the matrix matters. *Technology Review,* 6.

Jensen, R. (1999). *Dream Society: How the Coming Shift from Information to Imagination Will Transform Your Business.* New York: McGraw-Hill.

Jin, Y., & Huang, M. (2004). Melody-based retrieval of music. *The Electronic Library, 22*(3), 269–273. doi:10.1108/02640470410541679

Johns, A. (2000). *The Nature of the Book. Print and Knowledge in the Making.* Chicago: University of Chicago Press.

Johnson, M. D., & Gustafsson, A. (2000). *Improving Customer Satisfaction, Loyalty and Profit.* San-Fransico. Jossey-Bass.

Jones, S., Cunningham, S. J., McNab, R., & Boddie, S. (2000). A transaction log analysis of a digital library. *International Journal on Digital Libraries, 3*(2), 152–169. doi:10.1007/s007999900022

Jorge Reina, S. (2001). Of gaps by which democracy we measure The digital divide: facing a crisis or creating a myth? (pp. 303-307). MIT Press.

Juslin, P. N., & Laukka, P. (2003). Communication of emotions in vocal expression and music performance: Different channels, same code? *Psychological Bulletin, 120*(5), 770–814. doi:10.1037/0033-2909.129.5.770 PMID:12956543

KalaiSelvi., R., Kavitha, P., & Shunmuganathan, K. (2014). Automatic emotion recognition in video. *Proceedings of International Conference on Green Computing Communication and Electrical Engineering (ICGC- CEE).* Coimbatore, India. IEEE

Kaliakatsos-Papakostas, M. A., Epitropakis, M. G., Floros, A., & Vrahatis, M. N. (2013a). Chaos and music: From time series analysis to evolutionary composition. *International Journal of Bifurcation and Chaos (IJBC).* 23, 1350181–1–1350181–19.

Kaliakatsos-Papakostas, M. A., Floros, A., & Vrahatis, M. N. (2012d). Intelligent real-time music accompaniment for constraint-free improvisation. In Proceedings of *24th IEEE International Conference on Tools with Artificial Intelligence (ICTAI 2012).* Piraeus, Athens, Greece: IEEE. doi:10.1109/ICTAI.2012.67

Kaliakatsos-Papakostas, M. A., Floros, A., Vrahatis, M. N., & Kanellopoulos, N. (2012b). Genetic evolution of L and FL–systems for the production of rhythmic sequences. *In Proceedings of 21st International Conference on Genetic Algorithms and the 17th Annual Genetic Programming Conference (GP) (GECCO 2012),2nd Workshop in Evolutionary Music.* Philadelphia, USA. ACM.

Kaliakatsos-Papakostas, M. A., Epitropakis, M. G., Floros, A., & Vrahatis, M. N. (2012a). Controlling interactive evolution of 8-bit melodies with genetic programming. *Soft Computing, 16*(12), 1997–2008. doi:10.1007/s00500-012-0872-y

Kaliakatsos-Papakostas, M. A., Floros, A., & Vrahatis, M. N. (2013b). Intelligent music composition. In X. S. Yang, Z. Cui, R. Xiao, A. H. Gandomi, & M. Karamanoglu (Eds.), *Swarm Intelligence and Bioinspired Computation* (pp. 239–256). Amsterdam, The Netherlands: Elsevier. doi:10.1016/B978-0-12-405163-8.00010-7

Kalogirou, S. A. (2001). Artificial Intelligence in Renewable Energy Systems Modeling and Prediction. *Science Direct, 5*(4), 373–401.

Kaplan, B., & Harris-Salamone, K. (2009). Health IT Success and Failure: Recommendations from Literature and an AMIA Workshop. Retrieved from http://www.ncbi.nlm.nih.gov/pmc/articles/PMC2732244/

Karlik, B., & Olgac, V. (2011). Performance Analysis of Various Activation Functions in Generalized MLP Architectures of Neural Networks.[IJAE]. *International Journal of Artificial Intelligence And Expert Systems, 1*(4), 111–122.

Karnowka, A., Shafer, K., & Sularz, B. (n.d.). *System ekspertowy Mycin*. Retrieved from zsi.tech.us.edu.pl/~anowak/index.php?s=file_download&id=21

Karthekeyan, A. R. (2014). Fuzzy neural network based extreme learning machine technique in credit risk management. *International Journal of Research in Engineering, IT &. Social Sciences, 4*(9).

Karydis, I., Deliyannis, I., & Floros, A. (2011). Augmenting virtual-reality environments with social-signal based music content. Paper presented at the *17*th *International Conference on Digital Signal Processing* (DSP), 2011. doi:10.1109/ICDSP.2011.6004944

Karydis, I., Nanopoulos, A., Papadopoulos, A. N., & Manolopoulos, Y. (2005). Audio indexing for efficient music information retrieval.*Proceedings of the 11th International Multimedia Modeling Conference (MMM'05)*. Melbourne, Victoria, Australia: IEEE. doi:10.1109/MMMC.2005.22

Katsch, S., & Merle-Fishman, C. (1985). *The Music within You*. New York: Simon and Schuster.

Kawiorska, D. (2004). *Narodowe Rachunki Zdrowia*. Kraków: Kantor Wydawniczy ZAKAMYCZE.

Kay, R. (2011). Evaluating learning, design, and engagement in web-based learning tools (WBLTs): The WBLT Evaluation Scale. *Computers in Human Behavior, 27*(5), 1849–1856. doi:10.1016/j.chb.2011.04.007

Kejun, Z., & Shouqian, S. (2010). Music emotional design by evolutionary algorithms.*Proceedings of IEEE 11th International Conference on Computer-Aided Industrial Design Conceptual Design (CAIDCD)*. Yiwu, China. IEEE.

Keller, K. L. (1993). Conceptualizing, measuring, and managing customer-based brand equity. *Journal of Marketing, 57*(1), 1–22. doi:10.2307/1252054

Kenteris, M., Gavalas, D., & Economou, D. (2009). An innovative mobile electronic tourist guide application. *Personal and Ubiquitous Computing, 13*(2), 103–118. doi:10.1007/s00779-007-0191-y

Kerdvibulvech, C. (2013). *Augmented reality applications using visual tracking*. KMTL Information Technology Journal.

Khan, W., Xiang, Y., Aalsalem, M., & Arshad, Q. (2012). Mobile Phone Sensing Systems: A Survey. *Communications Surveys & Tutorials, IEEE, PP* (99), 1-26.

Kietzmann, J. H., Hermkens, K., McCarthy, I. P., & Silvestre, B. S. (2011). Social media? Get serious! Understanding the functional building blocks of social media. *Business Horizons, 54*(3), 241–251. doi:10.1016/j.bushor.2011.01.005

Kim, Y. E., Schmidt, E. M., Migneco, R., Morton, B. G., Richardson, P., & Scott, J., … Turnbull, D. (2010). Music emotion recognition: A state of the art review. Proceedings of 11th International Society for Music Information Retrieval Conference (ISMIR 2010). Utrecht, Netherlands.

Kirner, C., & Kirner, T. (2013). Development of online educational games with augmented reality. *Proceedings of EDULEARN13* (pp. 1950-1959).

Kirner, C., & Kirner, T. (2013). Development of online educational games with augmented reality. *Proceedings of EDULEARN13*, 1950-1959.

Kirthika, P., & Chattamvelli, R. (2012). A review of raga based music classification and music information retrieval (MIR).*2012 IEEE International Conference on Engineering Education: Innovative Practices and Future Trends (AICERA'12)*. Kottayam, India. IEEE. doi:10.1109/AICERA.2012.6306752

Kirtsis, N., & Stamou, S. (2011). Query Reformulation for Task-Oriented Web Searches.*Proceedings of the 2011 IEEE/WIC/ACM International Conference on Web Intelligence and Intelligent Agent Technology (WI-IAT'11)*. Lyon, France: IEEE. doi:10.1109/WI-IAT.2011.20

Kisley, M. A., & Cornwell, Z. M. (2006). Gamma and beta neural activity evoked during a sensory gating paradigm: Effects of auditory, somatosensory and cross-modal stimulation. *Clinical Neurophysiology*, *117*(11), 2549–2563. doi:10.1016/j.clinph.2006.08.003 PMID:17008125

Kist, J. (2008). *New Thinking for 21st Century Publishers. Emerging Patterns and Evolving Stratagems*. Oxford: Chandos Publishing. doi:10.1533/9781780632179

Kiverstein, J. (2010). Out of our Heads: Why You Are Not Your Brain, and Other Lessons from the Biology of Consciousness. *Journal of Consciousness Studies*, *17*(5-6), 243–248.

Knees, P., Pohle, T., Schedl, M., & Widmer, G. (2007). A music search engine built upon audio-based and web-based similarity measures.*Proceedings of the 10th annual international ACM SIGIR Conference on Research and Development in Information Retrieval (SIGIR'07)*. Amsterdam, Netherlands. ACM Press. doi:10.1145/1277741.1277818

Knight, J. (Ed.). (1996). *Diverse Practices: A Critical Reader on British Video Art*. Luton: University of Luton press.

Ko, A. J., Abraham, R., Beckwith, L., Blackwell, A., Burnett, M., & Erwig, M. et al. (2011). The state of the art in end-user software engineering. *ACM Computing Surveys*, *43*(3), 1–44. doi:10.1145/1922649.1922658

Koch, G. G., Landis, J. R., Freeman, J. L., Freman, D. H., & Lehnen, R. G. (1977). A general methodology for the analysis of experiments with repeated measurements of categorical data. *Biometrics*, *33*(1), 133–158. doi:10.2307/2529309 PMID:843570

Koelsch, S. (2010). Towards a neural basis of music-evoked emotions. *Trends in Cognitive Sciences*, *14*(3), 131–137. doi:10.1016/j.tics.2010.01.002 PMID:20153242

Koenitz, H., Haahr, M., Ferri, G., Sezen, T., & Sezen, D. (2013). Mapping the Evolving Space of Interactive Digital Narrative - From Artifacts to Categorizations. In H. Koenitz, T. Sezen, G. Ferri, M. Haahr, D. Sezen, & G. [UNKNOWN ENTITY &Cogon;]atak (Eds.), *Interactive Storytelling* (Vol. 8230, pp. 55–60). Springer International Publishing; doi:10.1007/978-3-319-02756-2_6

Kohonen, T., Schroeder, M. R., & Huang, T. S. (Eds.). (2001). *Self-Organizing Maps* (3rd ed.). Secaucus, NJ, USA: Springer-Verlag New York, Inc. doi:10.1007/978-3-642-56927-2

Kokkidou, M. (2009). European Music Curriculum: philosophical orientations, trends, and comparative validation (bilingual edition). Thessaloniki: Greek Society for Music Education (G.S.M.E.).

Kolb, B. (2009). *Fundamentals of human neuropsychology*. New York: Worth Publishers.

Koong, C. S., & Wu, C. Y. (2011). The applicability of interactive item templates in varied knowledge types. *Computers & Education*, *56*(3), 781–801. doi:10.1016/j.compedu.2010.10.021

Korakakis, G., Pavlatou, E. A., Palyvos, J. A., & Spyrellis, N. (2009). *3D visualization types in multimedia applications for science learning: A case for 8th grade students in Greece* (Publication). *Computers & Education*. doi:10.1016/j.compedu.2008.09.011

Korczak, K. (2014). *Internetowe narzędzia wspomagające opiekę zdrowotną*. Warszawa: Wolters Kluwer.

Kostagiolas, P., Lavranos, Ch., Korfiatis, N., Papadatos, J., & Papavlasopoulos, S. (2015). Music, musicians and information seeking behaviour: A case study on a community concert band. *The Journal of Documentation, 71*(1), 3–24. doi:10.1108/JD-07-2013-0083

Kotey, S. (2013). *Launching Science Laboratories into the 21st Century: Labster* (2013). AvatarGeneration. Retrieved from: http://www.avatargeneration.com/2013/10/launching-science-laboratories-into-the-21st-century-labster/

Kotler, P., Kartajaya, H., & Setiawan, I. (2010). *Marketing 3.0. From Products to Consumers to the Human Spirit.* Hoboken, NJ: John Wiley & Sons, Inc. doi:10.1002/9781118257883

Kotsiantis, S. B. (2007). Supervised Machine Learning: A Review of Classification Techniques. *Informatica, 31,* 249–268.

Kowaliw, T., Bredeche, N., Chevallier, S., & Doursat, R. (2014). Artificial Neurogenesis: An Introduction and Selective Review. In T. Kowaliw, S. Chevallier, R. Doursat (Eds.), *Studies in Computational Intellience* (Vol. 557, pp. 1-60). Springer-Verlag Berlin Heidelberg. http://doi.org/<ALIGNMENT.qj></ALIGNMENT>10.1007/978-3-642-55337-0_1

Koza, J. R. (1992). *Genetic Programming: On the Programming of Computers by Means of Natural Selection.* Cambridge, MA, USA: The MIT Press.

Kralewski, J. E., Dowd, B. E., Cole-Adeniyi, T., Gans, D., Malakar, L., & Elson, B. (2008). Factors influencing physician use of clinical electronic information technologies after adoption by their medical group practices. *Health Care Manage Rev.* Retrieved from http://www.ncbi.nlm.nih.gov/pubmed/18815501

Kramer, D. J. (2001). A blueprint for teaching foreign languages and cultures through music in the classroom and on the Web. *ADFL Bulletin, 33*(1), 29–35. doi:10.1632/adfl.33.1.29

Kravitz, D. J., Kadharbatcha, S., Baker, C. I., & Mishkin, M. (2011). A new neural framework for visuospatial processing. *Nature Reviews. Neuroscience, 12*(4), 217–230. doi:10.1038/nrn3008 PMID:21415848

Krupat, A. (1992). On the Translation of Native American Song and Story: A Theorized History. In B. Swann (Ed.), *On the Translation of Native American Literature* (pp. 3–32). Washington, D.C.: Smithsonian Institution Press.

Kruse, R. (2008). Fuzzy neural network. *Scholarpedia, 3*(11), 6043. doi:10.4249/scholarpedia.6043

Kucian, K., Loenneker, T., Dietrich, T., Dosch, M., Martin, E., & von Aster, M. (2006). Impaired neural networks for approximate calculation in dyscalculic children: A functional MRI study. *Behavioral and Brain Functions : BBF, 2*(1), 31. doi:10.1186/1744-9081-2-31 PMID:16953876

Kumar, A. V. Aruna, & Reddy, M. V. (2011). A Fuzzy Neural Network for Speech Recognition. *Journal of Systems and Software, 1*(9), 284–290.

Kunz, J. C., Fallat, R. J., McClung, D. H., Osborne, J. J., Votteri, R. A., & Nii, H. P. … Feigenbaum, E.A. (1978). A Physiological Rule-based System for Interpreting Pulmonary Function Test Results, Stanford University.

Lahiri, D. K., Sokol, D. K., Erickson, C., Ray, B., Ho, C. Y., & Maloney, B. (2013). Autism as early neurodevelopmental disorder: Evidence for an sAPPα-mediated anabolic pathway. *Frontiers in Cellular Neuroscience, 7,* 94. doi:10.3389/fncel.2013.00094 PMID:23801940

Laing, A., Royle, J. (2013). Bookselling Online: An Examination of Consume Behavioural Patterns, *Publishing. Research Quarterly, 29*(2), 110–129.

Lamere, P. (2008). Social tagging and music information retrieval. *Journal of New Music Research, 37*(2), 101–114. doi:10.1080/09298210802479284

LaPierre, A. (2004). Body Psychotherapy. *The USA Body Psychotherapy Journal, 3*(2).

Laplante, A., & Downie, J. S. (2006). Everyday life music information seeking behaviour of young adults.*Proceedings of the 7th International Conference of the Society for Music Information Retrieval (ISMIR'06)*. Victoria, British Columbia, Canada. ISMIR.

Laplante, A., & Downie, J. S. (2011). The utilitarian and hedonic outcomes of music information seeking in everyday life. *Library & Information Science Research*, *33*(3), 202–210. doi:10.1016/j.lisr.2010.11.002

Lash, S. (2002). *Critique on Information*. London: Sage Publications.

Laudon, K., & Laudon, J. (2011). Essentials of management information systems [9th Edition]. New Jearey: Pearson.

Lau, E. F., Gramfort, A., Hämäläinen, M. S., & Kuperberg, G. R. (2013). Automatic semantic facilitation in anterior temporal cortex revealed through multimodal neuroimaging. *The Journal of Neuroscience*, *33*(43), 17174–17181. doi:10.1523/JNEUROSCI.1018-13.2013 PMID:24155321

Law, E. L. C., Roto, V., Hassenzahl, M., Vermeeren, A. P., & Kort, J. (2009). Understanding, scoping and defining user experience: A survey approach. In *Proceedings of the SIGCHI Conference on Human Factors in Computing Systems, CHI '09*. Boston, USA. ACM. doi:10.1145/1518701.1518813

Lazarsfeld, P. F., & Henry, N. W. (1968). *Latent Structure Analysis*. Boston: Houghton Mifflin.

Ledermann, F., & Schmalstieg, D. (2005, March 12-16). APRIL: a high-level framework for creating augmented reality presentations. Paper presented at the Proceedings of VR 2005 Virtual Reality 2005. IEEE.

Ledoux, J. (1998). *The Emotional Brain: The Mysterious Underpinnings of Emotional Life*. Simon & Schuster.

Lee, A., & Berge, Z. L. (2011). *Second Life in Healthcare Education: Virtual Environment's Potential to Improve Patient Safety* (Publication). Knowledge Management & E-Learning. *International Journal (Toronto, Ont.)*, *3*(1).

Lee, H. J. J., Messom, C., & Yau, K. L. A. (2013). Can an electronic textbooks be part of K-12 Education? *The Turkish Online Journal of Educational Technology*, *12*(1), 32–44.

Lee, J. H. (2010). Analysis of user needs and information features in natural language queries seeking music information. *Journal of the American Society for Information Science and Technology*, *61*(5), 1025–1045. doi:10.1002/asi.21302

Lee, J. H., Downie, J. S., & Jones, M. C. (2007). Preliminary analyses of information features provided by users for identifying music.*Proceedings of the 8th International Conference of the Society for Music Information Retrieval (ISMIR'07)*. Vienna, Austria. ISMIR.

Leiva, J., Guevara, A., Rossi, C., & Aguayo, A. (2014). Augmented reality and recommendation systems for groups. A new perspective on tourist destinations systems. *Estudios y Perspectivas en Turismo*, *23*(1), 40–59.

Leku.pl. (n. d.). Retrieved from http://www.leku.pl

Levine, A. J., Hinckley, C. A., Hilde, K. L., Driscoll, S. P., Poon, T. H., Montgomery, J. M., & Pfaff, S. L. (2014). Identification of a cellular node for motor control pathways. *Nature Neuroscience*, *17*(4), 586–593. doi:10.1038/nn.3675 PMID:24609464

Levitin, D. (2008). *The world in six songs*. New York, NY: Plume Publishers Group.

Levy, M., & Sandler, M. (2009). Music information retrieval using social tags and audio. *IEEE Transactions on Multimedia*, *11*(3), 383–395. doi:10.1109/TMM.2009.2012913

Liem, C. C. S., Müller, M., Eck, D., Tzanetakis, G., & Hanjalic, A. (2011). The need for music information retrieval with user-centered and multimodal strategies.*Proceedings of the 1st International ACM Workshop on Music Information Retrieval with User-Centered and Multimodal Strategies (MIRUM'11)*. Scottsdale, Arizona, USA. ACM Press. doi:10.1145/2072529.2072531

Liem, C. C. S., Rauber, A., Lidy, T., Lewis, R., Raphael, C., & Reiss, J. D. et al. (2012). Music information technology and professional stakeholder audiences: Mind the adoption gap. In M. Müller, M. Goto, & M. Schedl (Eds.), *Multimodal Music Processing, Dagstuhl Follow-Ups* (Vol. 3, pp. 227–246). Dagstuhl, Germany: Schloss Dagstuhl-Leibniz-Zentrum für Informatik.

Lieser, W. (2009). *Digital Art*. Königswinter (Germany): h.f. ullmann / Tandem.

Liljander, V. (1994). Modeling perceived service quality using different comparison standard. *Journal of Consumer Satisfaction and Dissatisfaction*, *7*, 126–142.

Lindgren, S. (2012). The Sociology of Media and Information Technologies. In G. C. Aakvaag, M. Hviid Jacobsen, & T. Johansson (Eds.), *Introduction to Sociology: Scandinavian Sensibilities*. London: Pearson.

Lippincott, A. (2002). Issues in content-based music information retrieval. *Journal of Information Science*, *28*(2), 137–142. doi:10.1177/016555150202800205

Li, T., & Ogihara, M. (2003). Detecting emotion in music. In *Proceedings of 4th International Symposium on Music Information Retrieval*. U.S.A.

Lo, M. Y. (2012). Evolving Cellular Automata for Music Composition with Trainable Fitness Functions [Doctoral dissertation]. University of Essex, Essex.

Lohr, S. L. (1999). *Sampling: Design and Analysis. California, CA: Duxbury Press*. Pacific Grove: Brooks/Cole Thomson Learning.

Lombardo, V., & Damiano, R. (2012). Semantic annotation of narrative media objects. *Multimedia Tools and Applications*, *59*(2), 407–439. doi:10.1007/s11042-011-0813-2

Long, M., Chei Sian, L., & Goh, D. H. L. (2012, April 16-18). *Sharing in Social News Websites: Examining the Influence of News Attributes and News Sharers*. Paper presented at the Ninth International Conference of Information Technology: New Generations (ITNG).

López, J., Pérez, D., Santos, M., & Cacho, M. (2013). GuideBot. A Tour Guide System Based on Mobile Robots. *International Journal of Advanced Robotic Systems*, *10*.

Lowry, M. (1979). *The world of Aldus Manutius. Business and Scholarship in Renaissance Venice.* Cornell University Press.

Lüders, H., & Comair, Y. G. (2001). *Epilepsy Surgery*. California: Lippincott Williams & Wilkins.

Lu, L., Liu, D., & Zhang, H.-J. (2006). Automatic mood detection and tracking of music audio signals. *IEEE Transactions on Audio, Speech, and Language Processing*, *14*(1), 5–18. doi:10.1109/TSA.2005.860344

Lundquist, B., & Szego, C. K. (Eds.), (1998). Musics of the world's cultures. Perth, Australia: Callaway.

Lundström, S., & Särndal, C. E. (2005). *Estimation in Surveys with No response*. John Wiley and Sons, Ltd.

Lynette, K., & Eileen, M. T. (2002). *The Digital Divide at Work and Home: The Discourse about Power and Underrepresented Groups in the Information Society*: Kluwer, B.V.

Lynn, B. C. (2012, 04). The real bad guy in the e-Book price fixing case: Amazon's continued domination of the publishing industry will hurt the book market. *Slate*. Retrieved from www.slate.com/articles/technology/future_tense/2012/04/e_book_price_fixing_amazon_is_the_real_bad_guy_.html

MacLuhan, M. (1997). *Understanding Media. The Extensions of Man, fifth printing*. Cambridge Massachusetts – London: MIT Press.

MacWilliam, A. (2013). The engaged reader. A human centred evaluation of ebook user experience. *Publishing Research Quarterly, 29*(1), 1–11. doi:10.1007/s12109-013-9305-8

Madge, C., Meek, J., Wellens, J., & Hooley, T. (2009). Facebook, social integration and informal learning at university: 'It is more for socialising and talking to friends about work than for actually doing work'. *Learning, Media and Technology, 34*(2), 141–155. doi:10.1080/17439880902923606

Maes, P. (1997). On Software Agents: Humanizing the Global Computer. *IEEE Internet Computing, 1*(4), 10–19. doi:10.1109/MIC.1997.612209

Maffesoli, M. (1996). *The time of the tribes*. London, GB: Sage.

Mahadev, M. M., & Kulkarni, R. (2013). A Review: Role of Fuzzy Expert System for Prediction of Election Results. *Reviews of Literature, 1*(2). http://doi.org/2347-2723

Mahona, K., Burdicka, K. E., & Szeszkoa, P. R. (2010). A Role for White Matter Abnormalities in the Pathophysiology of Bipolar Disorder. *Neurosci Biobehav, 34*(4), 533–554. doi:10.1016/j.neubiorev.2009.10.012 PMID:19896972

Manaris, B., Roos, P., Machado, P., Krehbiel, D., Pellicoro, L., & Romero, J. (2007). A corpus-based hybrid approach to music analysis and composition.*Proceedings of 22nd International conference on Artificial intelligence*. Vancouver, British Columbia, Canada. AAAI Press.

Manovich, L. (2001). *The Language of New Media*. Cambridge: MIT Press.

Manovich, L. (2011). Trending: The Promises and the Challenges of Big Social Data. In M. K. Gold (Ed.), *Debates in the Digital Humanities*. Minneapolis, MN: The University of Minnesota Press.

Margounakis, D., & Politis, D. (2010). Implementation and Interaction Issues in Digital Music Libraries, *WSEAS Transactions on Systems, 9*(2), 146-155.

Marsh, K. (2002). Children's song acquisition: an ethnomusicological perspective. In C. Stephens, D. Burnham, G. McPherson, E. Schubert & J. Renwick (Eds.) Proceedings of the 7th International Conference of Music Perception and Cognition (pp. 256-268). Adelaide: Causal Productions.

Martin, S., & Grosenick, U. (Eds.). (2006). *Video Art*. London: Taschen.

Mather, G. (2011). *Sensation and Perception*. Taylor & Francis.

Matthen, M., & Stephens, C. (2007). *Philosophy of Biology*. Oxford: Elsevier.

Matthews, D. (2006). Book Review: How People Learn Brain, Mind, Experience, and School. In J. D. Bransford, A. L. Brown, & R. R. Cocking (Eds.), Learning Committee on Developments in the Science of Learning, Gifted Children: 1(1).

Maturana, H. R., & Varela, F. J. (1987). *The Tree of Knowledge: The Biological Roots of Human Understanding*. Boston: Shambhala Publications.

McCutcheon, A. L. (1987). Latent class analysis. Quantitative Applications in the Social Sciences Series No. 64. California: Thousand Oaks.

McDermott, J., & O'Reilly, U.-M. (2011). An executable graph representation for evolutionary generative music. *Proceedings of the 13th Annual Conference on Genetic and Evolutionary Computation, GECCO '11.* Dublin, Ireland. ACM. doi:10.1145/2001576.2001632

McGonigal, J. (2007). *Why I Love Bees: A Case Study in Collective Intelligence Gaming.* Paper.

McLean, A. (2011). *Artist-Programmers and Programming Languages for the Arts* [Unpublished PhD Thesis]. University of London, United Kingdom.

McLean, R., Oliver, P. G., & Wainwright, D. W. (2010). The myths of empowerment through information communication technologies: An exploration of the music industries and fan bases. *Management Decision, 48*(9), 1365–1377. doi:10.1108/00251741011082116

McLoughlin, C., & Lee, M. J. (2007). *Social software and participatory learning: Pedagogical choices with technology affordances in the Web 2.0 era.* Paper presented at the ICT: Providing choices for learners and learning. Proceedings ascilite Singapore 2007.

McLoughlin, C., & Lee, M. J. (2007). *Social software and participatory learning: Pedagogical choices with technology affordances in the Web 2.0 era.* Paper presented at the ICT: Providing choices for learners and learning. Proceedings ascilite Singapore.

McLuhan, M. (1964). *Undersstanding Media: The Extentions of Man.* New York: McGraw Hill.

McMahon, M., & Ojeda, C. (2008). *A Model of Immersion to Guide the Design of Serious Games.* Paper presented at the World Conference on E-Learning in Corporate, Government, Healthcare, and Higher Education, Las Vegas, Nevada, USA.

Mehrotra, K., Mohan, C. K., & Ranka, S. (1996). *Elements of Artificial Neural Networks.* Chester: Bradford Book CO Inc.

Melucci, M., & Orio, N. (1999). Musical information retrieval using melodic surface. *Proceedings of the 4th ACM conference on Digital libraries (DL'99).* San Francisco, California, USA. ACM Press. doi:10.1145/313238.313293

Menachemi, N., & Brooks, R. G. (2006). EHR and other IT adoption among physicians: results of a largescale statewide analysis. *J Healthc Inf Manag.* Retrieved from http://www.ncbi.nlm.nih.gov/pubmed/16903665

Menachemi, N., Perkins, R. M., van Durme, D. J., & Brooks, R. G. (2006). Examining the adoption of electronic health records and personal digital assistants by family physicians in Florida. *Inform Prim Care.* Retrieved from http://www.ncbi.nlm.nih.gov/pubmed/16848961

Menary, R. (Ed.). (2010). Special issue on 4E Cognition: Embodied, Embedded, Enacted, Extended. *Phenomenology and the Cognitive Sciences, 9*(4).

Merriman, N. (2000). *Beyond the Glass Case: The Past, the Heritage and the Public.* London, UK: Institute of Archaeology.

Meyer, B. (2013). Transporting and Preserving Interactive New Media Exhibits through Time. *Exhibitionist-. National Association for Museum Exhibition, 32*(2), 46–53.

Microsoft Flight Simulator (n. d.). Retrieved from: http://www.microsoft.com/Products/Games/FSInsider/

Miller, H., Witherow, D. S., & Carson, S. (2011). *Oxford Handbook of Clinical and Laboratory Investigation* (3rd ed.). New York, NY: Oxford University Press (USA).

Miller, L. J. (2007). *Reluctant Capitalists. Bookselling and the Culture of Consumption.* Chicago, London: The University of Chicago Press.

Milton, L. M., & Jorge Reina, S. (2001). Universal service from the bottom up: a study of telephone penetration in Camden, New Jersey The digital divide: facing a crisis or creating a myth? (pp. 119-146). MIT Press

Ministerstwo Administracji i Cyfryzacji. (2012). *Do lekarza z PESELem, czyli e-WUŚ*. Retrieved from http://mac.gov.pl/dzialania/e-administracja/do-lekarza-z-peselem/

Ministerstwo Spraw Wewnętrznych. (2013). *Nowa odsłona projektu pl.ID*. Retrieved from https://msw.gov.pl/pl/aktualnosci/11600,Nowaodslona-projektu-plID.html

Mistilis, N. (2012). Challenges and potential of the Semantic Web for tourism. *E-Review of Tourism Research, 10*(2), 51–55.

Mödinger, W. (Ed.). (2011). *Marketing 3.0 – New Issues in Marketing: From Integrated Marketing Communication to the Marketing of Sustainable Leaders*. Stuttgart: Stuttgart Media University.

Mondloch, K. (2010). *Screens – Viewing Media Installation Art*. Minneapolis: University of Minnesota press.

Moore, J., & Zouridakis, G. (2004). *Biomedical Technology and Devices Handbook*. New York: CRC Press.

Morgan, M., Lugosi, P., & Ritchie, J. R. (Eds.). (2010). *The tourism and leisure experience* (pp. 117–136). Bristol, GB: Channel View Publications.

Mossberger, K., Tolbert, C. J., & Stansbury, M. (2003). *Virtual Inequality: Beyond the Digital divide*. Washington, DC: Georgetown University Press.

Mossberg, L. (2008). Extraordinary Experiences through Storytelling. *Scandinavian Journal of Hospitality and Tourism, 8*(3), 195–210. doi:10.1080/15022250802532443

Moussouri, T. (1997). Family Agendas and the Museum Experience. In G. T. Denford (Ed.), *Museums for the 21st century* (pp. 20-30). Liverpool: Society of Museum Archaeologists.

Moussouri, T., Nikiforidou, A. & Gazi, A. (2004). What Can Museums Learn from their Visitors: the Role of Evaluation in Exhibition Development. *IMEros 4*(2), FHW, 192-206.

Moussouri, T., Nikiforidou, A., & Gazi, A. (2003). Front- end and formative evaluation of an exhibition on Greek Mathematics. American Association of Museums, 42-47.

Moussouri, T. (2003). Negotiated Agendas: Families in Science and Technology Museums. *International Journal of Technology Management, 25*(5), 477–489. doi:10.1504/IJTM.2003.003114

Mulawka, J. J. (1996). *Systemy ekspertowe*. Warszawa: Wydawnictwo Naukowo-Techniczne.

Muller, L., Edmonds, E. and Connell, M. (2006, December 4). Living Laboratories for Interactive Art. *CoDesign, 2,* 195-207.

Munakata, Y., Casey, B. J., & Diamond, A. (2004). Developmental cognitive neuroscience: Progress and potential. *Trends in Cognitive Sciences, 8*(3), 122–128. doi:10.1016/j.tics.2004.01.005 PMID:15301752

Muntean, C. I. (2011). Raising engagement in e-learning through gamification, *Proceedings of the 6th International Conference on Virtual Learning* (pp. 323-329). Bucharest.

Murphy, T. (1992). *Music and Song*. Oxford: Oxford University Press.

Nadel, L., & Piattelli-Palmarini, M. (2002). What is Cognitive Science? In L. Nadel (Ed.), The Encyclopedia of Cognitive Science. John Wiley & Sons.

Nanopoulos, A., Rafailidis, D., Ruxanda, M. M., & Manolopoulos, Y. (2009). Music search engines: Specifications and challenges. *Information Processing & Management, 45*(3), 392–396. doi:10.1016/j.ipm.2009.02.002

Nardelli, E. (2010). *A classification framework for interactive digital artworks.* Paper presented at the International ICST Conference on User Centric Media, Palma, Mallorca.

Nardelli, E. (2010). *A classification framework for interactive digital artworks.* Paper presented at the International ICST Conference on User Centric Media. Palma, Mallorca.

Narodowy Fundusz Zdrowia. (2013). Karta Ubezpieczenia Zdrowotnego. Retrieved from http://www.nfzkatowice.

National Library of Medicine. (n.d.). Medline Plus. Retrieved from http://www.nlm.nih.gov/medlineplus

National Research Council. (2003). Information technology, productivity, and creativity. In W. J. Mitchell, A. S. Inouye, & M. S. Blumenthal (Eds.), *Beyond Productivity: Information, Technology, Innovation, and Creativity* (pp. 15–29). Washington, District of Columbia, USA: The National Academies Press.

Nauck, D., & Kruse, R. (1993). A fuzzy neural network learning fuzzy control rules and membership functions by fuzzy error backpropagation. Proceedings of *IEEE International Conference on Neural Networks* (pp. 1022–1027). http://doi.org/ doi:10.1109/ICNN.1993.298698

Neogi, P., & Brocca, J. (2012). Broadband Adoption and Use in Canada and the US: Is the Digital Divide Closing? Nick, C. (2003). Digital divide or discursive design? On the emerging ethics of information space. *Ethics and Information Technology, 5*(2), 89–97.

Nesamalar, E. K., & Ganesan, G. (2012). An introduction to virtual reality techniques and its applications. *International Journal of Computing Algorithm, 1*(2), 59–62.

NHS.uk. (n.d.). The NHS in the 1990s. Retrieved from http://www.nhs.uk/NHSEngland/thenhs/nhshistory/Pages/NHShistory1990s.aspx

Nichols, B., & Honig, A. (1997). Music Teaches Children about Themselves and Others. *Early Childhood Education Journal, 24*(4), 213–216. doi:10.1007/BF02354834

Niedermeyer, E., & Lopes da Silva, F. (2004). *Electroencephalography: Basic Principles, Clinical Applications, and Related Fields.* Philadelphia: Lippincott Williams & Wilkins.

Nieuwenhuisen, M., & Behnke, S. (2013). Human-like interaction skills for the mobile communication robot Robotinho. *International Journal of Social Robotics, 5*(4), 549–561. doi:10.1007/s12369-013-0206-y

Nikolaidou, G. N., Hadjileontiadou, S. J., & Hadjileontiadis, L. J. (2004). On modeling children's non-verbal interactions during computer mediated music composition: A case study in primary school peers. Proceedings of the *4th IEEE International Conference on Advanced Learning Technologies (ICALT'04)* (pp. 756-758). Joensuu, Finland. IEEE. doi:10.1109/ICALT.2004.1357647

Nilsen, T., Linton, S., & Looser, J. (2004). Motivations for augmented reality gaming. *Proceedings of FUSE, 4,* 86–93.

Noble, J. (2012). *Programming Interactivity.* Sebastopol, CA: O'Reilly Media.

Noë, A. (2004). *Action in Perception.* Cambridge, MA: MIT Press.

Noe, F. P., & Uysal, M. (1997). Evaluation of outdoor recreational settings. A problem of measuring user satisfaction. *Journal of Retailing and Consumer Services, 4*(4), 223–230. doi:10.1016/S0969-6989(96)00030-6

Notess, M. (2004). Three looks at users: a comparison of methods for studying digital library use. *Information Research, 9*(3). Retrieved from http://www.informationr.net/ir/9-3/paper177.html

Notess, M., & Swan, M. B. (2003). Predicting user satisfaction from subject satisfaction. In *Proceedings of the CHI 2003 Conference on Human Factors in Computing Systems (CHI'03)*. Fort Lauderdale, Florida. ACM Press.

Nozaki, K., Ishibuchi, H., & Tanaka, H. (1996). Adaptive Fuzzy Rule-Based Classification System. *IEEE Transactions on Fuzzy Systems, 4*(3), 238–250. doi:10.1109/91.531768

Nyland, B., Ferris, J., & Deans, J. (2010). Young children and music: Constructing meaning through a performance. *Australian Journal of Music Education, 10*(1), 5–17.

O'Neill, S. A. (2012). Becoming a music learner: Towards a theory of transformative music engagement. In G. E. McPherson & G. Welch (Eds.), *The Oxford handbook of music education* (Vol. 1, pp. 163–186). New York, NY: Oxford University Press.

O'Regan, J. K., & Noë, A. (2001). A sensorimotor account of vision and visual consciousness. *Behavioral and Brain Sciences, 24*(05), 939–1031. doi:10.1017/S0140525X01000115 PMID:12239892

O'Sullivan, E. L., & Spangler, K. J. (1998). *Experience marketing. Strategies for the new millennium*. State College: Venture Publishing.

Oliver, J. (2011). Multimedia systems: Tools for learning. Proceedings of INTED 2011 (pp. 4633-4635).

Oliver, R. (1999). Value as Excellence in the Consumption Experience. In M. Holbrook (Ed.), Consumer Value: A Framework for Analysis and Research (pp. 43-62). New York: Routledge. doi:10.4324/9780203010679.ch2

Oliver, R. L. (1997). *Satisfaction: A Behavioral Perspective on the Consumer*. NewYork: Irwin/McGraw-Hill.

Omondi, A. R., & Ralapakse, J. C. (2006). *FPGA Implementations of Neural Networks. Springer*. Dordrecht: Springer. doi:10.1007/0-387-28487-7

Opoka, J. (2008). Multimedia w edukacji. *Studia i Materiały Centrum Edukacji Przyrodniczo-Leśnej, 10*, 1[17], p. 120.

Orio, N. (2006). Music retrieval: A tutorial and review. *Foundations and Trends in Information Retrieval, 1*(1), 1–90. doi:10.1561/1500000002

Ortony, A., & Turner, T. J. (1990). What's basic about basic emotions? *Psychological Review, 97*(3), 315–331. doi:10.1037/0033-295X.97.3.315 PMID:1669960

Overview of the U.S. Comic Book & Graphic Novel Market 2010-2011 . (2010). Simba Information. Retrieved from http://www.simbainformation.com/Overview-Comic-Book-2523144/

Ozcan, E., & Eral, T. (2008). A genetic algorithm for generating improvised music (pp. 266–277). In Monmarch, N., Talbi, E.-G., Collet, P., Schoenauer, M., & Lutton, E. (Eds.). Artificial Evolution, volume 4926 of Lecture Notes in Computer Science. Berlin/Heidelberg: Springer.

Pal, S. K., De, R. K., & Basak, J. (2002). Unsupervised feature evaluation: A neuro-fuzzy approach. *Elsevier. Fuzzy Sets and Systems, 126*, 277–291. doi:10.1109/TFUZZ.2002.1006431

Panayiotopoulos, C. (2005). *Optimal Use of the EEG in the Diagnosis and Management of Epilepsies*. Oxfordshire, UK: Bladon Medical Publishing.

Pankowska, M. (2004). Value-driven management in e-healthcare. *Studies in Health Technology and Informatics, 105*, 3–11. PMID:15718588

Papachristopoulos, L., Tsakonas, G., & Papatheodorou, C. (2008). Enforcement of information seeking behaviour through digital library services. *Proceedings of the Libraries in the Digital Age Conference (LIDA'08)*. Dubrovnik and Mljet, Croatia. E-LIS.

Papadopoulos, G., & Wiggins, G. (1998). A Genetic Algorithm for the Generation of Jazz Melodies.*Proceedings of Finnish Conference on Artificial Intelligence (STeP)*. Jyväskylä.

Papatheodorou, C., Kapidakis, S., Sfakakis, M., & Vassiliou, A. (2003). Mining User Communities in Digital Libraries. *Information Technology and Libraries, 22*(4), 152–157.

Paramythis, A., Weibelzahl, S., & Masthoff, J. (2010). Layered evaluation of interactive adaptive systems: Framework and formative methods. *User Modeling and User-Adapted Interaction, 20*(5), 383–453. doi:10.1007/s11257-010-9082-4

Partridge, H. L. (2007). Establishing the human perspective of the information society.

Pascale, L. (2005). The power of simply singing together in the classroom. *Music Education Research, 9*(1), 1–15.

Pasternak, T., Bisley, J. W., & Calkins, D. (2003). Visual processing in the primate brain. In B. Weiner (Ed.), Handbook of Psychology (Vol. I). Hoboken, NJ, USA: John Wiley & Sons, Inc.

Paszkiel, S. (2014). Augmented Reality of Technological Environment in Correlation with Brain Computer Interfaces for Control Processes. Recent Advances in Automation, Robotics and Measuring Techniques (pp. 197-203). Springer.

Patan, K. (2008). *Artificial Neural Networks for the Modelling and Fault Diagnosis of Technical Processes*. Springer; doi:10.1007/978-3-540-79872-9

Patil, S., Balar, A., Malviya, N., & Prasad, S. (2013, December). Innovation in Shopping Experience using augmented reality and integration with social networking. *International Journal of Scientific & Engineering Research, 4*(12), 2154–2156.

Paul, C. (2008). *New Media in the White Cube and Beyond*. London, Berkeley, Los Angeles: University of California press.

Paulesu, E., Harrison, J., Baron-Cohen, S., Watson, J. D. G., Goldstein, L., & Heather, J. … Frith, C. D. (1995). The physiology of coloured hearing A PET activation study of colour-word synaesthesia. Brain - Oxford University Press, 118, 661–676.

Pavlik, J. V., & Bridges, F. (2013). The Emergence of Augmented Reality (AR) as a Storytelling Medium in Journalism. *Journalism & Communication Monographs, 15*(1), 4–59.

Pearce, P. L. (1982). *The Social Psychology of Tourist Behavior*. Oxford: Pergamon Press.

Petrantonakis, P. C., & Hadjileontiadis, L. J. (2012). Adaptive Emotional Information Retrieval from EEG Signals in the Time-Frequency Domain. *IEEE Transactions on Signal Processing, 60*(5), 2604–2616. doi:10.1109/TSP.2012.2187647

Phon-Amnuaisuk, S., Law, E., & Kuan, H. (2007). Evolving music generation with som-fitness genetic programming. In M. Giacobini (Ed.), Lecture Notes in Computer Science: Vol. 4448. *Applications of Evolutionary Computing* (pp. 557–566). Berlin, Germany: Springer. doi:10.1007/978-3-540-71805-5_61

Picard, D., & Robinson, M. (Eds.). (2012). *Emotion in Motion. Tourism, Affect and Transformation*. Farnham: Ashgate.

Pine, B., & Gilmore, J. (1999). The experience economy: work is theatre & every business a stage. Boston, Harvard: Harvard Business School Press.

Ping, Y., Teng, L., Jingsheng, L., & Weimin, H. (2011). Synchronization of Fuzzy High-order Cohen-Grossberg Neural Networks with Reaction-diffusion Term and Time-varying. *Journal of Computer Information Systems, 7*(11), 4145–4152.

Pino, C., & Di Salvo, R. (2011). *A survey of semantic multimedia retrieval systems*.

Playseat Redbull Racing F1 (n. d.). Retrieved from: http://www.playseat.com/en/playseat-rbr-1-seat

Plerou, A. (2012). Artificial Neural Networks Simulating Human Brain | Antonia Plerou - Academia.edu. *Open Education - The Journal for Open and Distance Education and Educational Technology, 8*(1).

Plerou, A., Vlamos, P., & Kourouthanasis, P. (2014). Screening Dyscalculia and Algorithmic Thinking Difficulties. In *Difficulties 1st International Conference on New Developments in Science and Technology Education.*

Plerou, A. (2014). Dealing with Dyscalculia over time. In *International Conference on Information Communication Technologies in Education.*

Polaine, A. (2005). *The flow principle in interactivity.* Paper presented at the Proceedings of the second Australasian conference on Interactive entertainment, Sydney, Australia.

Pollard, S. E., Neri, P. M., Wilcox, A. R., Volk, L. A., Williams, D. H., & Schiff, G. D. ... Bates, D.W. (2013). How physicians document outpatient visit notes in an electronic health record. Retrieved from http://www.ncbi.nlm.nih.gov/pubmed/22542717

Poole, D. L., & Mackworth, A. K. (2010). *Artificial Intelligence - Foundations of Computational Agents.* New York, NY: Cambridge University Press. doi:10.1017/CBO9780511794797

Poon, E. G., Wright, A., Simon, S. R., Jenter, C. A., Kaushal, R., & Volk, L. A. ... Bates, D.W. (2010). Relationship between use of electronic health record features and health care quality: results of a statewide survey. *Med Care.* Retrieved from http://www.ncbi.nlm.nih.gov/pubmed/20125047

Popescu, F., Fazli, S., Badower, Y., Blankertz, B., & Müller, K.-R. (2007). Single trial classification of motor imagination using 6 dry EEG electrodes. *PLoS ONE, 2*(7), e637. doi:10.1371/journal.pone.0000637 PMID:17653264

Pople, H. E. Jr., Myers, R.D., Miller, R.A. (1975). DIALOG: A Model of Diagnostic Logic for Internal Medicine. *International Joint Conferences on Artificial Intelligence* 4.

Poulos, M., Deliyannis, I., & Floros, A. (2012). Audio Fingerprint Extraction using an Adapted Computational Geometry Algorithm. *Computer and Information Science, 5*(6), 88–97. doi:10.5539/cis.v5n6p88

Poulos, M., Deliyannis, I., & Floros, A. (2013). Efficient Audio Fingerprint Application Verification Using the Adapted Computational Geometry Algorithm. *Computer and Information Science, 6*(1), 70–82. doi:10.5539/cis.v6n1p70

Poznaj system e-Recepta (2012). *Poznaj system e-recepta.* Retrieved from http://e-recepta.gov.pl/web/sim/poznaj-system-e-recepta

Prahalad, C. K., & Krishnan, M. S. (2008). *The New Age of Innovation: Driving Co-created Value through Global Networks.* New York, NY: Mc Graw-Hill.

Prata, A. (2009). Interactive Television Evolution. In M. Pagani (Ed.), Encyclopedia of Multimedia Technology and Networking (2nd ed., pp. 757-762). Hershey, PA: IGI Global doi:10.4018/978-1-60566-014-1.ch102

Prata, A., Chambel, T., & Guimarães, N. (2012). Personalized Content Access in Interactive TV-Based Cross Media Environments. In Y. Kompatsiaris, B. Merialdo, & S. Lian (Eds.), *TV content analysis: techniques and applications.* Taylor & Francis.

Preece, J., Rogers, Y., & Sharp, H. (2011). *Interaction Design: Beyond. Human-Computer Interaction* (3rd ed.). Hoboken, NJ: John Wiley & Sons.

Pritzker, L., & Hanson, R. (1962). Measurement Errors in the 1960 Census of Population. *Proceedings of the Section on Survey Research Methods. American Statistical Association.*

Proctor, N. (2011). The Google Art Project: A New Generation of Museums on the Web? *Curator: The Museum Journal*, *54*(2), 215–221. doi:10.1111/j.2151-6952.2011.00083.x

Przelaskowski, A. (2011). *Techniki multimedialne*. Warszawa: PW OKNO (pp. iii, 3).

Putnam, J. B. (1994). Genetic programming of music. Retrieved from ftp://ftp.cs.bham.ac.uk/pub/tech-reports/1997/CSRP-97-07.ps.gz

Qzdrowiu.pl. (n. d.). Retrieved from http://www.qzdrowiu.pl

Raichle, M. E. (2009). A brief history of human brain mapping. *Trends in Neurosciences*, *32*(2), 118–126. doi:10.1016/j.tins.2008.11.001 PMID:19110322

Raimond, Y., & Sandler, M. (2008). A web of musical information.*Proceedings of the 9th International Conference of the Society for Music Information Retrieval (ISMIR'08)*. Philadelphia, Pennsylvania, USA. ISMIR.

Raitamaki, J. (1998). Improving the performance of fuzzy systems by using local partitioning. Proceedings of *EURO-MICRO Conference* (Vol. 2, pp. 745–752). IEEE Comput. Soc. http://doi.org/ doi:10.1109/EURMIC.1998.708097

Rak, M. (2003). *Immagine e scrittura. Sei studi sulla teoria e la storia dell' imagine nella cultura del barocco a Napoli*. Napoli: Liguori.

Ramirez, M., Ramos, E., Cruz, O., Hernandez, J., Perez-Cordoba, E., & Garcia, M. (2013). *Design of interactive museographic exhibits using Augmented reality*. Paper presented at the Electronics, Communications and Computing (CONIELECOMP), 2013 International Conference. doi:10.1109/CONIELECOMP.2013.6525747

Ransburg, M., Timmerer, C., & WHellwagner, H. (2008). *Dynamic and Distributed Multimedia Content Adaptation based on the MPEG-21 Multimedia Framework* (Vol. 101/2008). Berlin: Springer.

Rashmi, N., Halse, S. V., & Teli, D. (2015). Research Article non Linear Load Simulation for Power Quality Control using Fuzzy Controller. *International Journal of Recent Scientific Research Research*, *6*(1), 2608–2612.

Rautaray, S., & Agrawal, A. (2012). Vision based hand gesture recognition for human computer interaction: A survey. *Artificial Intelligence Review*, 1–54. doi:10.1007/s10462-012-9356-9

Reddin, J., McDermott, J., & O'Neill, M. (2009). Elevated pitch: Automated grammatical evolution of short compositions. In M. Giacobini, I. De Falco, & M. Ebner (Eds.), *Applications of Evolutionary Computing, EvoWorkshops2009* (Vol. 5484, pp. 579–584). Tubingen, Germany. Springer Verlag. doi:10.1007/978-3-642-01129-0_65

Reed, C. (2004). *Internet Law: Text and Materials*. Cambridge: Cambridge University Press. doi:10.1017/CBO9780511808791

Reply of the Secretary. (2013). Reply of the Secretary of State Zbigniew Podraza in Health Ministry – on behalf of the Minister – to the question no 9353 concerning resigning from introducing a medical services register 02.03.2005. Retrieved from http://orka2.sejm.gov.pl/IZ4.nsf/main/7719F1C7

Rhee, B. T., & Kim, D. J. (2013). Summative evaluation of children's creative engagement through interactive exhibits: a case study on the participatory exhibition of masterpieces in South Korea. *International Journal of Advanced Science and Technology*, *59*, 1–12. doi:10.14257/ijast.2013.59.01

Rhodes, N., & Sadway, J. (Eds.). (2000). *The Renaissance Computer. Knowledge Technology in the First Age of Print*. London, New York: Routledge.

Rice, J. (2007). Assessing Higher Order Thinking in Video Games. *Journal of Technology and Teacher Education*, *15*(1), 87–100.

Richard Taylor, M. J. (2001). *Asian Technology Parks: Lessons For The "Digital Divide".* Pacific Telecommunications Council.

Richards, J. T., & Hanson, V. L. (2004). *Web accessibility: a broader view.* New York, NY, USA: ACM Press. doi:10.1145/988672.988683

Richardson, B. (1999). *Typography, Writers and Readers in Renaissance Italy.* Cambridge: Cambridge University Press.

Rincón, J. (2012). *XML y Web semántica: Bases de datos en el contexto de la Web semántica.* Universitat Oberta de Catalunya, 1-63.

Robertson, I. H., Manly, T., Andrade, J., Baddeley, B. T., & Yiend, J. (1997). `Oops!': Performance correlates of everyday attentional failures in traumatic brain injured and normal subjects. *Neuropsychologia, 35*(6), 747–758. doi:10.1016/S0028-3932(97)00015-8 PMID:9204482

Rodowick, D. N. (2001). *Reading the Figural, or Philosophy After the New Media.* London: Duke University press. doi:10.1215/9780822380764

Ronchi, A. M. (2009). *Games and Edutainment Applications eCulture* (pp. 375–378). Springer Berlin Heidelberg.

Roos, P., & Manaris, B. (2007). A music information retrieval approach based on power laws.*Proceedings of the 19th IEEE International Conference on Tools with Artificial Intelligence (ICTAI'07).* Patras, Greece. IEEE. doi:10.1109/ICTAI.2007.170

Rose, F. (2011). *The Art of Immersion: How the Digital Generation Is Remaking Hollywood, Madison Avenue, and the Way We Tell Stories.* New York: W.W. Norton & Co.

Rosen, L. (2014). Augmented Reality and the Future of Publishing, *Publishing Perspectives.* Retrieved from http://publishingperspectives.com/2014/08/augmented-reality-and-the-future-of-publishing/

Rosen, E. (2000). *The anatomy of buzz: how to create word-of-mouth marketing.* New York: Doubleday.

Roshandeh, A. M., Puan, O. C., & Joshani, M. (2009). Data Analysis Application for Variable Message Signs Using Fuzzy Logic in Kuala Lumpur. *International Journal of Systems Applications, Engineering & Development, 3*(1).

Rotzer, S., Kucian, K., Martin, E., von Aster, M., Klaver, P., & Loenneker, T. (2008). Optimized voxel-based morphometry in children with developmental dyscalculia. *NeuroImage, 39*(1), 417–422. doi:10.1016/j.neuroimage.2007.08.045 PMID:17928237

Rouf, E., Chumley, H. S., & Dobbie, A. E. (2008). Electronic health records in outpatient clinics: perspectives of third year medical students, *BMC Med Educ.* Retrieved from http://www.ncbi.nlm.nih.gov/pubmed/18373880

Roussou, M. (2006). Οι τάσεις στο χώρο των νέων τεχνολογιών για την έρευνα και την ανάδειξη της πολιτιστικής κληρονομιάς. *Tetradia Mouseiologias, 3,* 56–61.

Rowan, J., & Tolunsky, E. (2003). *Primer of EEG: With A Mini-Atlas. Neuroscience.* Oxford, UK: Butterworth-Heinemann Ltd. doi.

Rowles, D. (2013). *Mobile Marketing: How Mobile Technology is Revolutionizing Marketing, Communications and Advertising.* Kogan Page Publishers.

Rozpędowska-Matraszek, D. (2012). e-Zdrowie w kształtowaniu zatrudnienia w opiece zdrowotnej. In Zieliński Z. (Ed.), Rola informatyki w naukach ekonomicznych i społecznych. Innowacje i implikacje interdyscyplinarne, Tom 1/2012, Kielce: Wydawnictwo Wyższej Szkoły Handlowej w Kielcach.

Rubenstein, W. B. (1987). A database design for musical information. *Proceedings of the 1987 ACM SIGMOD International Conference on Management of Data (SIGMOD '87)*. San Francisco, California, USA. ACM Press. doi:10.1145/38713.38762

Rugg, M. D., & Yonelinas, A. P. (2003). Human recognition memory: A cognitive neuroscience perspective. *Trends in Cognitive Sciences*, *7*(7), 313–319. doi:10.1016/S1364-6613(03)00131-1 PMID:12860190

Rush, M. (1999). *New Media in Late 20th- century Art*. London: Thames & Hudson.

Russell, S., & Norvig, P. (2002). Artificial Intelligence: A Modern Approach (2nd ed.). London: Prentice Hall Series in Artificial Intelligence.

Russell, J. A. (1980). A circumplex model of affect. *Journal of Personality and Social Psychology*, *39*(6), 1161–1178. doi:10.1037/h0077714

Russell, S., & Norvig, P. (2007). *Artificial Intelligence - A modern Approach* (2nd ed.). Upper Saddle River, NJ: Prentice Hall.

Ryan, M. (2014). *The Digital Mind: An Exploration of artificial intelligence*. Michael Ryan.

Rynek i Opinia, A. R. C. (2012a). *Internet leczy skutecznie*. Retrieved from http://www.arc.com.pl/internet_leczy_skutecznie-40999450-pl.html

Rynek i Opinia, A. R. C. (2012b). *Lekarz online poszukiwany*. Retrieved from http://www.arc.com.pl/lekarz_online_poszukiwany-41999453-pl.html

Salmon, C. (2008). *Storytelling. La fabbrica delle storie*. Roma: Fazi Editore.

Sanger, T. D. (1989). Optimal unsupervised learning in a single-layer linear feedforward neural network. *Neural Networks*, *2*(6), 459–473. doi:10.1016/0893-6080(89)90044-0

Sassoon, J. (2012). *Web Storytelling. Costruire storie di marca nei social media*. Milano: Franco Angeli.

Sauvé, L. (2009). *Design Tools for Online Educational Games: Concept and Application Transactions on Edutainment II* (pp. 187–202). Springer-Verlag.

Savolainen, R. (1995). Everyday life information seeking: Approaching information seeking in the context of "way of life". *Library & Information Science Research*, *17*(3), 259–294. doi:10.1016/0740-8188(95)90048-9

Sawers, P. (2013, January 28). Anne Frank for iPad and Nook reimagines The Diary of a Young Girl for the digital age. *TheNextWeb*. Retrieved from http://thenextweb.com/apps/2013/01/28/anne-franks-diary-for-ipad/

Schallauer, P., Bailer, W., Troncy, R., & Kaiser, F. (2011). Multimedia Metadata Standards. *Multimedia Semantics*, 129-144.

Schianchi, A. (2013). Location-based virtual interventions. *Leonardo Electronic Almanac*, *19*(2), 112–135.

Schmidt, C. (2004). The Analysis of Semi- structured Interviews. In Flick et al. (Eds.), *A Companion to Qualitative Research* (pp. 253–258). Australia: Sage Publications.

Schmidt, E. M., Turnbull, D., & Kim, Y. E. (2010). Feature selection for content-based, time-varying musical emotion regression. *Proceedings of International Conference on Multimedia Information Retrieval, MIR '10*. Philadelphia, PA, USA. ACM. doi:10.1145/1743384.1743431

Schmitt, B. (1999). *Experiential Marketing*. New York: The Free Press.

Schmitt, B. (2003). *Customer Experience Management. New Jersey*. Hoboken: John Wiley & Sons.

Schmitt, B., & Simonson, A. (1997). *Marketing aesthetics. The strategic management of brands, identity, and image.* New York: The Free Press.

Schober, M. F., & Conrad, F. G. (1998). Response Accuracy When Interviewers Stray from Standardization. *Proceedings of the American Statistical Association, Section on Survey Methods Research.* Alexandria, VA. American Statistical Association.

Schober, M. F., Conrad, F. G., & Fricker, S. S. (1999). Further explorations of conversational interviewing. How gradations of flexibility affect cost. *Paper presented at the54th Annual Conference of the American Association for Public Opinion Research.* St. Petersburg, FL.

Schober, M. F., & Conrad, F. G. (1997). Does Conversational Interviewing Reduce Survey Measurement Error? *Public Opinion Quarterly, 61*(4), 576–602. doi:10.1086/297818

Schraffenberger, H., & Heide, E. (2012). Interaction Models for Audience-Artwork Interaction: Current State and Future Directions. In A. Brooks (Ed.), *Arts and Technology* (Vol. 101, pp. 127–135). Springer Berlin Heidelberg. doi:10.1007/978-3-642-33329-3_15

Schuller, B., Hantke, S., Weninger, F., Han, W., Zhang, Z., & Narayanan, S. (2012). Automatic recognition of emotion evoked by general sound events.*Proceedings of IEEE International Conference on Acoustics, Speech and Signal Processing (ICASSP).* Kyoto, Japan. IEEE doi:10.1109/ICASSP.2012.6287886

Schuman, H., & Presser, S. (1981). *Questions and Answers in Attitude Surveys: Experiments on Question Form, Wording, and Context.* San Diego, California: Academic Press.

Schwarz, N., Hippler, H., Deutsch, B., & Strack, F. (1985). Response Order Effects of Category Range on Reported Behavior and Comparative Judgments. *Public Opinion Quarterly, 49*(3), 388–395. doi:10.1086/268936

Scolari, A. (2009). Transmedia Storytelling: Implicit Consumers, Narrative Worlds, and Branding in Contemporary Media Production. *International Journal of Communication, 3,* 586–606.

Segaran, T. (2007). *Programming Collective Intelligence: Building Smart Web 2.0 Applications.* Sebastopol, CA: O'Reilly Media.

Serrell, B., & Adams, R. (1998). *Paying Attention: Visitors and Museum Exhibitions.* Washington, D.C., USA: American Association of Museums.

Servon, L. J. (2002). *Bridging the Digital Divide: Technology, community and Public Policy.* Oxford: Blackwell Publishing. doi:10.1002/9780470773529

Sesame Street. (2011). *The Monster at the End of This Book...starring Grover!* Retrieved from https://itunes.apple.com/us/app/monster-at-end-this-book...starring/id409467802?mt=8

Shafritz, K. M., Gore, J. C., & Marois, R. (2002). The role of the parietal cortex in visual feature binding. *Proceedings of the National Academy of Sciences of the United States of America, 99*(16), 10917–10922. doi:10.1073/pnas.152694799 PMID:12149449

Shanken, E. A. (2011). *Contemporary Art and New Media: Toward a Hybrid Discourse?* Retrieved from: http://hybridge.files.wordpress.com/2011/02/hybrid-discourses-overview-4.pdf

Sharma, A. kumar, & Badri, V. P. (2013). Fuzzy logic based systems in management and business applications. *International Journal of Innovative Research in Engineering & Science, 1*(2), 1–6.

Shaw, I. S. (1998). *Fuzzy Control of Industrial Systems.* Boston, MA: Springer US; doi:10.1007/978-1-4757-2813-2

Shea, G. (2008). *Art, design, education and research in pursuit of interactive experiences.* Paper presented at the Proceedings of the 7th ACM conference on Designing interactive systems, Cape Town, South Africa. doi:10.1145/1394445.1394482

Shegog, R., Lazarus, M., M., Murray, N., G., Diamond, P., M., Sessions, N., & Zsigmond, E. (2011). *Virtual Transgenics: Using a Molecular Biology Simulation to Impact Student Academic Achievment and Attitudes.* Springer Science+Business Media.

Shekelle, P. G., Morton, S. C., & Keeler, E. B. (2006). Costs and benefits of health information technology.[Full Rep]. *Evid Rep Technol Assess,* (132): 1–71. Retrieved from http://www.ncbi.nlm.nih.gov/pubmed/17627328 PMID:17627328

Shillingsburg, P. (2006). *From Gutenberg to Google: Electronic Representations of Literary Texts.* Cambridge: Cambridge University Press. doi:10.1017/CBO9780511617942

Sidorko, A. (2012). *Druk RMUA co miesiąc tylko na wyraźne żądanie pracownika.* Retrieved from http://serwisy.gazetaprawna.pl/praca-i-kariera/artykuly/613096,druk_rmua_co_miesiac_tylko_na_wyrazne_zadanie_pracownika.html

Silva, B. S. d., & Barbosa, S. D. J. (2012). *A conceptual model for HCI design cases.* Paper presented at the Proceedings of the 11th Brazilian Symposium on Human Factors in Computing Systems. Cuiaba, Brazil.

Silverman, D. (2005). *Doing qualitative research.* London, UK: Sage Publications Ltd.

Simões, M. G., & Farret, F. A. (2014). *Modeling and Analysis with Induction Generators* (3rd ed.). Taylor & Francis.

Siskos, Y., Grigoroudis, E., Zopounidis, C., & Saurais, O. (1998). Measuring Customer Satisfaction Using a Collective Preference Disaggregation Model. *Journal of Global Optimization, 12*(2), 175–195. doi:10.1023/A:1008262411587

Sittig, D. F., & Singh, H. (2012). *Electronic Health Records and National Patient-Safety Goals.* Retrieved from http://www.ncbi.nlm.nih.gov/pmc/articles/PMC3690003/#!po=50.0000

Sittig, D. F., Wright, A., Meltzer, S., Simonaitis, L., Evans, R. S., & Nichol, W. P. ... Middleton B. (2011). Comparison of clinical knowledge management capabilities of commercially-available and leading internally-developed electronic health records. *BMC Med Inform Decis Mak.* Retrieved from http://www.ncbi.nlm.nih.gov/pubmed/21329520

Skeels, M. M., & Grudin, J. (2009). *When social networks cross boundaries: a case study of workplace use of facebook and linkedin.* Paper presented at the Proceedings of the ACM 2009 international conference on Supporting group work, Sanibel Island, Florida, USA. doi:10.1145/1531674.1531689

Skinner, R. E. (2012). *Building the Second Mind: 1956 and the Origins of Artificial Intelligence Computing.* California: Smashwords.

Slack, J. D., & Wise, J. M. (2005). Culture and Technology. A Primer. New York: Peter Lang.

Smith, J. O. (2010). *Physical audio signal processing: for virtual musical instruments and audio effects.* Stanford: W3K Publishing.

Smith, K. (2012). *The Publishing Business. From pbooks to ebooks.* Lausanne: Ava Publishing.

Smith, M. (2000). *The Title-Page. Its Early Development. 1460-1510.* London – Newcastle Delaware: Oak Knoll Press.

Smith, M., & Richards, G. (2013). *Routledge Handbook of Cultural Tourism.* Routledge.

Snelgrove, W. X., & Baecker, R. M. (2010). A system for the collaborative reading of digital books with the partially sighted: project proposal. Paper presented at the *Proceedings of the third workshop on Research advances in large digital book repositories and complementary media.* Toronto, ON, Canada. doi:10.1145/1871854.1871870

Sole, D., & Gray-Wilson, D. (1999). *Storytelling in Organizations: The power and traps of using stories to share knowledge in organizations. LILA*. Harvard University.

Solée, R. V., Valverde, S., Casals, M. R., Kauffman, S. A., Farmer, D., & Eldredge, N. (2013). The evolutionary ecology of technological innovations. *Complexity*. doi: 10.1002/cplx.21436

Soltész, F., Szucs, D., Dékány, J., Márkus, A., & Csépe, V. (2007). A combined event-related potential and neuropsychological investigation of developmental dyscalculia. *Neuroscience Letters, 417*(2), 181–186. doi:10.1016/j.neulet.2007.02.067 PMID:17367929

Sołtysik-Piorunkiewicz, A. (2009). Kontroling w organizacji i zarządzaniu. Koncepcja informatyzacji. Sosnowiec: Oficyna Wydawnicza „HUMANITAS", 2009, p. 177.

Sołtysik-Piorunkiewicz, A. (2014c). The management of patient information in Polish health care system. International Journal Information Theories and Applications, 21(2).

Sołtysik-Piorunkiewicz, A. (2015b): The evaluation method of Web 2.0/3.0 usability in e-health knowledge management system. *Online Journal of Applied Knowledge Management*, 3(2), 168-180.

Sołtysik-Piorunkiewicz, A. (2012). Implementation of IT system in health protection. In R. Knosala (Ed.), *Innovations in management and production engineering* (pp. 568–576). Opole: Oficyna Wydawnicza Polskiego Towarzystwa Zarządzania Produkcją.

Sołtysik-Piorunkiewicz, A. (2014a, June 24). The Telecom Business Strategies: a Comparative Study of Corporate Blogs.*Proceedings of the 2014 Multimedia, Interaction, Design and Innovation International Conference on Multimedia, Interaction, Design and Innovation* (pp. 1-11). ACM. doi:10.1145/2643572.2643592

Sołtysik-Piorunkiewicz, A. (2014b). Technologie mobilne w zarządzaniu organizacją opartą na wiedzy. In R. Knosala (Ed.), *Komputerowo Zintegrowane Zarządzanie. Część VIII. Zarządzanie wiedzą, transfer wiedzy, systemy wspomagania podejmowania decyzji* (pp. 263–274). Opole: Oficyna Wydawnicza Polskiego Towarzystwa Zarządzania Produkcją.

Sołtysik-Piorunkiewicz, A. (2015a). Knowledge management impact of information technology Web 2.0/3.0. The case study of agent software technology usability in knowledge management system. *AIP Conference Proceedings, 1644*(1), 219–227. doi:10.1063/1.4907840

Song, T., & Jiashan, L. (2013). *Application Research of Augmented Reality Technology in Jingju Art Dissemination.* Paper presented at the Proceedings of the 2013 International Conference on Business Computing and Global Informatization.

Song, S., Moustafa, H., & Afifi, H. (2012). A Survey on Personalized TV and NGN Services through Context-Awareness. *ACM Computing Surveys, 44*(1), 1–18. doi:10.1145/2071389.2071393

Spector, L., & Alpern, A. (1994). Criticism, culture, and the automatic generation of artworks. In *Proceedings of the twelfth national conference on Artificial intelligence(*vol. 1*), AAAI '94*. Seattle, Washington, USA. American Association for Artificial Intelligence.

Spector, L., & Alpern, A. (1995). Induction and recapitulation of deep musical structure.*Proceedings of the IFCAI-95 Workshop on Artificial Intelligence and Music*. Montreal, Quebec, Canada.

Spector, L., Klein, J., & Harrington, K. (2005). Selection songs: Evolutionary music computation. *YLEM Journal, 25*(6 & 8), 24–26.

Spillman, R. (2011, December 6). *Inside the geeky, revolutionary world of "Minecraft"*. SALON. Retrieved from: http://www.salon.com/2011/12/06/inside_the_geeky_revolutionary_world_of_minecraft/

Stamboulis, Y., & Skayannis, P. (2003). Innovation strategies and technology for experience-based tourism. *Tourism Management, 24*(1), 35–43. doi:10.1016/S0261-5177(02)00047-X

Stamou, S., & Christodoulakis, D. (2005). Retrieval Efficiency of Normalized Query Expansion. *Proceedings of the 6th International Conference on Computational Linguistics and Intelligent Text Processing (CICLing'05)*. Mexico City, Mexico. Springer-Verlag. doi:10.1007/978-3-540-30586-6_64

Stamou, S., Kozanidis, L., Tzekou, P., & Zotos, N. (2008). A Recommendation Model based on Site Semantics and Usage Mining. *International Journal of Digital Information Management, 6*(3), 244–256.

Stanescu-Cosson, R. (2000). Understanding dissociations in dyscalculia: A brain imaging study of the impact of number size on the cerebral networks for exact and approximate calculation. *Brain, 123*(11), 2240–2255. doi:10.1093/brain/123.11.2240 PMID:11050024

State, L., Cocianu, C., Stefanescu, V., & Vlamos, P. (2004). A Neural Network Framework for Implementing the Bayesian Learning. In *International Conference on Informatics in Control, Automation and Robotics* (pp. 328–331). Setúbal,Portugal.

Stavrakantonakis, I., Gagiu, A., Toma, I., & Fensel, D. (2013). Towards Online Engagement via the Social Web (pp. 26-31). Proceedings of *WEB 2013: The First International Conference on Building and Exploring Web Based Environments*.

Steele, C. F. (2009). *Inspired Teacher*. Alexandria, VA: ASCD.

Stellaki, P. (2010) *Οικογένειες και μάθηση στο χώρο του μουσείου: μελέτη περίπτωσης για τον "Ελληνικό Κόσμο", πολιτιστικό κέντρο του Ιδρύματος Μείζονος Ελληνισμού.* [Unpublished master's thesis]. Panteion University, Athens, Greece.

Stephanidis, C. (2001). Adaptive Techniques for Universal Access. *User Modeling and User-Adapted Interaction, 11*(1-2), 159–179. doi:10.1023/A:1011144232235

Stephanidis, C. (2003, February). Towards Universal Access in the Disappearing Computer Environment. *UPGRADE, IV*, 53–59.

Stevens, C. (2010, April 10). *Making Alice for the iPad*. Retrieved from The Literary Platform: http://www.theliterary-platform.com/2010/04/making-the-alice-for-the-ipad/

Stiles, J., Akshoomoff, N., & Haist, F. (2013). The Development of Visuospatial Processing. *Comprehensive Developmental Neuroscience: Neural Circuit Development and Function in the Brain, 3*, 271–296.

Stobbe, A., Just, T., Heng, S., Kaiser, S., & Walter, N. (2006). The dawn of technological convergence. *Deutsche Bank. Research in Economics*, 56.

Storn, R., & Price, K. (1997). Differential evolution – a simple and efficient adaptive scheme for global optimization over continuous spaces. *Journal of Global Optimization, 11*(4), 341–359. doi:10.1023/A:1008202821328

Stoyanova, J., Gonçalves, R., Brito, P. Q., & Coelho, A. (2013). Real-time Augmented Reality Pemo Platform for Exploring Consumer Emotional Responses with Shopping Applications. *International Journal of Online Engineering*.

Strapatsakis, M. (2008, November). Invisible Places - Immense White [Sensor-Based Interactive Video Installation]. Strasbourg.

Stromer-Galley, J. (2004). Interactivity-as-Product and Interactivity-as-Process. *The Information Society Journal, 20*(5), 391–394. doi:10.1080/01972240490508081

Strover, S. (2003). Remapping the Digital Divide. *The Information Society Journal, 19*(4), 275–277. doi:10.1080/01972240309481

Stuss, D. T., & Knight, R. T. (2012). *Principles of Frontal Lobe Function*. New York: Oxford University Press.

Suchman, L. (1987). *Plans and Situated Actions: The Problem of Human-machine Communication*. New York: Cambridge University Press.

Suchman, L. (2007). *Human-Machine Reconfigurations: Plans and Situated Actions*. New York: Cambridge University Press.

Sugimoto, T., Legaspi, R., Ota, A., Moriyama, K., Kurihara, S., & Numao, M. (2008). Modeling affective-based music compositional intelligence with the aid of ANS analyses. *Knowledge-Based Systems*, *21*(3), 200–208. doi:10.1016/j.knosys.2007.11.010

Sujan, M., Bettam, J., & Baumgartner, H. (1993). Influencing judgments using autobiographical memories: A self-referencing perspective. *JMR, Journal of Marketing Research*, *30*(4), 422–436. doi:10.2307/3172688

Sumathi, S., & Paneerselvam, S. (2010). *Computational Intelligence Paradigms: Theory & Applications using MATLAB*. CRC Press.

Sundar, S. S. (2004). Theorizing Interactivity's Effects. *The Information Society Journal*, *20*(5), 385–389. doi:10.1080/01972240490508072

Sutton, G. (2004). Exhibiting New Media Art. Retrieved from: http://kris.constantvzw.org/?p=20

Suzuki, K. (2011). *Artificial Neural Networks-Methodological Advances and Biomedical Applications*. Rijeka, Croatia: InTech. doi:10.5772/644

System Zdrowotny Informator Pacjenta. (2013). System: Zdrowotny Informator Pacjenta. Retrieved from https://zip.nfz.poznan.pl/ap-zip-user/

Szepe, H. (1997). Artistic Identity in the Poliphilo. *Papers of the Bibliographical Society of Canada.*, *35*(1), 39–73.

Tahir, M. (2012). *Reality Technologies and Tangible Interaction: A brief guide to tangible user interfaces, augmented reality and related technologies*. LAP Lambert Academic Publishing.

Takacs, G., Chandrasekhar, V., Gelfand, N., Xiong, Y., Chen, W.-C., Bismpigiannis, T., et al. (2008). *Outdoors augmented reality on mobile phone using loxel-based visual feature organization*. Paper presented at the Proceedings of the 1st ACM international conference on Multimedia information retrieval, Vancouver, British Columbia, Canada. doi:10.1145/1460096.1460165

Thakur, S., Pawar, S., & Rajput, S. (2014). Electroencephalography: A Wide Approach. *International Journal of Innovative Research in Technology*, *1*(6).

Thatcher, M. (2013). IT Governance in Acute Healthcare: A Critical Review of Current Literature. In C. George, D. Whitehouse, P. Duquenoy (Eds.), *eHealth: Legal, Ethical and Governance Challenges* (pp. 349-370). Retrieved from http://link.springer.com/chapter/10.1007/978-3-642-22474-4_15

The Castle. (2010). *Zuuka!* Retrieved from http://download.cnet.com/The-Castle/3000-20412_4-75304654.html

Thompson, E. (2005). Sensorimotor subjectivity and the enactive approach to experience. *Phenomenology and the Cognitive Sciences*, *4*(4), 407–427. doi:10.1007/s11097-005-9003-x

Thompson, E. (2007). *Mind in Life: Biology, Phenomenology, and the Sciences of Mind*. Cambridge, MA: Harvard University Press.

Thompson, J. B. (2010). *Merchants of Culture. The Publishing Business in the Twenty-First Century*. Cambridge: Polity Press.

Thurman, L., & Welch, G. (Eds.). (2000). *Bodymind and Voice: foundations of voice education* (revised Edition). Iowa City, Iowa: National Center for Voice and Speech.

Tian, X., & Martin, B. (2013). Value Chain Adjustments in Educational Publishing, *Publishing. Research Quarterly*, *29*(1), 12–25.

Timmerer, C., Waltl, M., Rainer, B., & Hellwagner, H. (2012). Assessing the quality of sensory experience for multimedia presentations. *Signal Processing Image Communication*, *27*(8), 909–916. doi:10.1016/j.image.2012.01.016

Torrance, S., & Froese, T. (2001). An Inter-Enactive Approach to Agency: Participatory Sense-Making, Dynamics, and Sociality. *Humana. Mente*, *15*, 21–53.

Torrente, J., Mera, P. L., Moreno-Ger, P., & Fernández-Manjón, B. (2009). Lecture Notes in Computer Science: Vol. 5660. *The Relationship between Game Genres, Learning Techniques and Learning Styles in Educational Computer Games. Transactions on Edutainment II* (pp. 1–18). Doi:10.1007/978-3-642-03270-7_1

Torrey, E. F. (2007). Schizophrenia and the inferior parietal lobule. *Schizophrenia Research*, *97*(1-3), 215–225. doi:10.1016/j.schres.2007.08.023 PMID:17851044

Tourangeau, R., & Smith, T. W. (1998). Collecting Sensitive Information with Different Modes of Data Collection. In M. P. Couper, R. P. Baker, J. Bethlehem, C. Z. F. Clark, J. Martin, W. L. Nicholls II, and J. M. O'Reilly (Eds.), Computer Assisted Survey Information Collection (pp. 431-453). New York: Wiley

Tourangeau, R., Rips, L., & Rasinski, K. (2000). *The Psychology of Survey Response*. Cambridge, UK: Cambridge University Press. doi:10.1017/CBO9780511819322

Train, K. E. (2003). *Discrete Choice Methods with Simulation*. Cambridge, UK: Cambridge University Press. doi:10.1017/CBO9780511753930

Trifonova, A., Ahmed, S. U., & Jaccheri, L. (2009). In C. Barry, M. Lang, W. Wojtkowski, K. Conboy, & G. Wojtkowski (Eds.), *SArt: Towards Innovation at the Intersection of Software Engineering and Art Information Systems Development* (pp. 809–827). Springer, US.

Trifonova, A., Jaccheri, L., & Bergaust, K. (2008). *Software engineering issues in interactive installation art. International Journal of Arts and Technology* (Vol. 1, p. 1). IJART.

Trifonova, A., Jaccheri, L., & Bergaust, K. (2008). Software engineering issues in interactive installation art. *Int. J. Arts and Technology*, *1*(1), 43–65. doi:10.1504/IJART.2008.019882

Tsai, W. H., & Wang, H. M. (2005). On the extraction of vocal-related information to facilitate the management of popular music collections.*Proceedings of the 5th ACM/IEEE-CS Joint Conference on Digital Libraries (JCDL'05)*. Denver, Colorado, USA. IEEE. doi:10.1145/1065385.1065432

Tsakonas, G., & Papatheodorou, C. (2006). Analyzing and Evaluating Usefulness and Usability in Electronic Information Services. *Journal of Information Science*, *32*(5), 400–419. doi:10.1177/0165551506065934

Tsiridou, T., Zannos, I., & Strapatsakis, M. (2011). An interactive windscape. *Technoetic Arts: A Journal of Speculative Research, 9*(2), 153–162.

Tsiridou, T., Zannos, I., & Strapatsakis, M. (2012). An interactive windscape. *Thechnoetic Arts*, *9*(2-3), 153–162. doi:10.1386/tear.9.2-3.153_1

Tussyadiah, I. P., & Fesenmaier, D. R. (2009). Mediating tourist experiences. Access to places via shared videos. *Annals of Tourism Research*, *36*(1), 24–40. doi:10.1016/j.annals.2008.10.001

Typke, R., Wiering, F., & Veltkamp, R. C. (2005). A Survey of music information retrieval systems. *Proceedings of the 6th International Conference of the Society for Music Information Retrieval (ISMIR'05)*. London, United Kingdom. ISMIR.

Uehara, T. (2011). *Psychiatric Disorders – Trends and Developments*. Rijeka: InTech. doi:10.5772/2330

Ujejski, M. (2011). Funkcje karty ubezpieczenia zdrowotnego realizowane w elektronicznym dowodzie osobistym. Proceedings of *Materiały konferencyjne "IT w służbie zdrowia GigaCon"*, Warszawa. Retrieved from http://sdcenter.pl/system/lectures/attachment1s/1729/original/Funkcje_KUZ_w_pl.ID_23.03.2011_final_pdf?1301043192

Ursu, M. F., Thomas, M., Kegel, I., Williams, D., Tuomola, M., & Lindstedt, I. et al. (2008). Interactive TV narratives: Opportunities, progress, and challenges. *ACM Trans. Multimedia Comput. Commun. Appl.*, *4*(4), 1–39. doi:10.1145/1412196.1412198

Vaidyanathan, P. P., & Hoang, P.-Q. (1988). Lattice structures for optimal design and robust implementation of two-channel perfect-reconstruction QMF banks. *IEEE Transactions on Acoustics, Speech, and Signal Processing*, *36*(1), 81–94. doi:10.1109/29.1491

van Dijck, J. (2013). *The Culture of Connectivity: A Critical History of Social Media*. OUP USA. doi:10.1093/acprof:oso/9780199970773.001.0001

Van Krevelen, D., & Poelman, R. (2010). A survey of augmented reality technologies, applications and limitations. *International Journal of Virtual Reality*, *9*(2), 1.

Vanderstoep, S., & Johnston, D. (2008). *Research Methods for Everyday Life: Blending Qualitative and Quantitative Approaches*. San Francisco, CA: John Wiley & Sons.

Varela, F. J., Thompson, E., & Rosch, E. (1991). *The Embodied Mind: Cognitive Science and Human Experience*. Cambridge, MA: MIT Press.

VARIATIONS2. (2003). VARIATIONS2: the Indiana University Digital Music Library Project. Retrieved from http://variations2.indiana.edu/research/

Venkatesh, V., Morris, M. G., Davis, G. B., & Davis, F. D. (2003). User acceptance of information technology: Toward a unified view. *Management Information Systems Quarterly*, *27*, 425–478.

Veryard, R. (2005). Technology Hype Curve [blog post]. Retrieved from http://demandingchange.blogspot.co.uk/2005/09/technology-hype-curve.html

Vieira, J., Dias, F. M., & Mota, A. (2004). Neuro-Fuzzy Systems: A Survey. Proceedings of *International Conference on Neural Networks and Applications*.

Viel, C. C., Melo, E. L., Godoy, A. P., Dias, D. R. C., Trevelin, L. C., & Teixeira, C. A. C. (2012). *Multimedia presentation integrating interactive media produced in real time with high performance processing*. Paper presented at the Proceedings of the 18th Brazilian symposium on Multimedia and the web. São Paulo, Brazil. doi:10.1145/2382636.2382664

Viharos, Z. J., & Kis, K. B. (2014). Fuzzy Systems and their Applications in Technical Diagnostics. Proceedings of *Workshop on Technical Diagnostics Advanced measurement tools in technical diagnostics for systems' reliability and safety*. Warsaw, Poland.

Vinciarelli, A., Pantic, M., & Bourlar, H. (2009). Social signal processing: Survey of an emerging domain. *Image and Vision Computing*, *27*(12), 1743–1759. doi:10.1016/j.imavis.2008.11.007

Vlist, B., Niezen, G., Rapp, S., Hu, J., & Feijs, L. (2013). Configuring and controlling ubiquitous computing infrastructure with semantic connections: A tangible and an AR approach. *Personal and Ubiquitous Computing, 17*(4), 783–799. doi:10.1007/s00779-012-0627-x

Vuckovic, A. (2006). *Singing the tunes of the world: preschool children responses to songs in diverse languages* [Unpublished master thesis]. LaTrobe University, Bundoora, Victoria, Australia.

Wagner, A. D., Shannon, B. J., Kahn, I., & Buckner, R. L. (2005). Parietal lobe contributions to episodic memory retrieval. *Trends in Cognitive Sciences, 9*(9), 445–453. doi:10.1016/j.tics.2005.07.001 PMID:16054861

Waltl, M., Rainer, B., Timmerer, C., & Hellwagner, H. (2012). A toolset for the authoring, simulation, and rendering of sensory experiences. Proceedings of ACM international conference on Multimedia - MM '12 (p. 1469). New York, USA. ACM Press. doi:10.1145/2393347.2396522

Waltl, M., Rainer, B., Timmerer, C., & Hellwagner, H. (2012a). An end-to-end tool chain for Sensory Experience based on MPEG-V. *Signal Processing Image Communicatio*n. doi:10.1016/j.image.2012.10.009

Wang, R., & Mei, K. (2010). Analysis of Fuzzy Membership Function Generation with Unsupervised Learning Using Self-Organizing Feature Map. Proceedings of *2010 International Conference on Computational Intelligence and Security* (pp. 515–518). IEEE. http://doi.org/ doi:10.1109/CIS.2010.118

Wang, I. (2013). Globalization and Theater Spectacles in Asia. *CLCWeb: Comparative Literature and Culture, 15*(2), 22.

Wang, J., Deng, H., Yan, Q., & Wang, J. (2008). A collaborative model of low-level and high-level descriptors for semantics-based music information retrieval.*Proceedings of the 2008 IEEE/WIC/ACM International Conference on Web Intelligence and Intelligent Agent Technology (WI-IAT'08)*. Sydney, New South Wales, Australia. IEEE. doi:10.1109/WIIAT.2008.27

Wang, T., Kim, D. J., Hong, K. S., & Youn, J. S. (2009). Music information retrieval system using lyrics and melody information.*Proceedings of the 2009 Asia-Pacific Conference on Information Processing (APCIP'09)*. Shenzhen, China. IEEE. doi:10.1109/APCIP.2009.283

Waraich, A. (2004). *Using narrative as a motivating device to teach binary arithmetic and logic gates*. Paper presented at the Proceedings of the 9th annual SIGCSE conference on Innovation and technology in computer science education, Leeds, United Kingdom. doi:10.1145/1007996.1008024

Weedon, A., Miller, D., Franco, C. P., Moorhead, D., & Pearce, S. (2014). Crossing media boundaries: Adaptations and new media forms of the book. *Convergence (London)*, 1354856513515968.

Weigl, D. M., & Guastavino, C. (2011). User studies in the music information retrieval literature.*Proceedings of the 12th International Conference of the Society for Music Information Retrieval (ISMIR'11)*. Miami, Florida, USA. ISMIR.

Weiss, S. M., Kulikowski, C. A., & Safir, A. (1978). A Model-Based Consultation System the Long-term Management Glaucoma. *International Joint Conferences on Artificial Intelligence, 5*.

Welch, G. F. (2005). Singing as Communication. In D. Miell, R. Mac- Donald, & D. Hargreaves (Eds.), Musical Communication (pp. 239-259). New York: Oxford University Press. doi:10.1093/acprof:oso/9780198529361.003.0011

Weninger, F., Eyben, F., Schuller, B. W., Mortillaro, M., & Scherer, K. R. (2013). On the acoustics of emotion in audio: What speech, music and sound have in common. *Frontiers in Psychology*, 4. PMID:23750144

Weyns, D., Malek, S., & Andersson, J. (2012). FORMS. *ACM Transactions on Autonomous and Adaptive Systems, 7*(1), 1–61. doi:10.1145/2168260.2168268

Weyns, D., Malek, S., Andersson, J., & Schmerl, B. (2012). Introduction to the special issue on state of the art in engineering self-adaptive systems. *Journal of Systems and Software*, *85*(12), 2675–2677. doi:10.1016/j.jss.2012.07.045

Whitehead, A. N. (1929). *Process and Reality*. New York: The Macmillan Company.

Wieczorkowska, A., Synak, P., Lewis, R., & Ra, W. Z. (2005). Extracting emotions from music data. In Hacid, M.-S., Murray, N., Ra, Z., & Tsumoto, S. (Eds.), Foundations of Intelligent Systems (LNCS) (Vol. 3488, pp. 456–465). Berlin Heidelberg: Springer.

Wieczorkowska, A. A., & Ras, Z. W. (2003). Editorial-Music information retrieval. *Journal of Intelligent Information Systems*, *21*(1), 5–8. doi:10.1023/A:1023543016136

Wiering, F. (2006). Can humans benefit from music information retrieval?*Proceedings of the 4th international conference on Adaptive multimedia retrieval: user, context, and feedback (AMR'06)*. Geneva, Switzerland. Springer-Verlag.

Wilkolaski, S., & DiCamillo, K. (2014). Publishing Picasso in the Infinite Real Estate of Digital. *Publishing Perspectives*. Retrieved from http://publishingperspectives.com/2014/07/publishing-picasso-in-the-infinite-real-estate-of-digital/

Willingham, D. T. (2009). *Why don't students like school?* San Francisco: Jossey-Bass.

Wilson, R. S. (2002). First steps towards violin performance extraction using genetic programming. In J. R. Koza (Ed.), *Genetic Algorithms and Genetic Programming at Stanford 2002*. Stanford, California, USA: Stanford Bookstore.

Wilson, T. D. (2006). Revisiting user studies and information needs. *The Journal of Documentation*, *62*(6), 680–684. doi:10.1108/00220410610714912

Wolton, D. (1997). *Penser la communication*. Paris: Flammarion.

Wood, R. (1996). Families. In G. Durbin (Ed.), *Developing Museum Exhibitions for Lifelong Learning* (pp. 77–82). London: The Stationery Office.

Woodruff, R. B., & Gardial, S. F. (1996). *Know Your Customer: New Approaches to Understanding Customer Value and Satisfaction*. Cambridge, Massachusetts: Blackwell.

Wooldridge, M. (2009). *An Introduction to MultiAgent Systems*. New York: John Wiley and Sons.

Wu, C.-H., Chuang, Z.-J., & Lin, Y.-C. (2006). Emotion recognition from text using semantic labels and separable mixture models.[TALIP]. *ACM Transactions on Asian Language Information Processing*, *5*(2), 165–183. doi:10.1145/1165255.1165259

Wu, S., & Er, M. J. (2000). Dynamic fuzzy neural networks-a novel approach to function approximation. *IEEE Transactions on Systems, Man, and Cybernetics. Part B, Cybernetics : A Publication of the IEEE Systems. Man, and Cybernetics Society*, *30*(2), 358–364. doi:10.1109/3477.836384

Wu, Y., & Ren, F. (2010). Improving emotion recognition from text with fractionation training.*Proceedings of International Conference on Natural Language Processing and Knowledge Engineering (NLP-KE)*. Beijing, China. IEEE. doi:10.1109/NLPKE.2010.5587800

Wylin, B., & Desmet, P. (2005). *How to integrate games or game elements in educational multimedia: a typology of educational game use*. Paper presented at the World Conference on Educational Multimedia, Hypermedia and Telecommunications 2005, Montreal, Canada.

Xiao, Z., Dellandrea, E., Dou, W., & Chen, L. (2008). What is the best segment duration for music mood analysis? *Proceedings of* International Workshop on *Content-Based Multimedia Indexing (CBMI 2008)*. London, U.K. IEEE.

Xia, S. (2011). Interactive Design Research of Multimedia Courseware in Teaching. *Advanced Materials Research*, *271*, 1472–1477. doi:10.4028/www.scientific.net/AMR.271-273.1472

Yang, X. H., Chen, Q. C., & Wang, X. L. (2010). Dictionary based inverted index for music information retrieval. *Proceedings of the 2010 International Conference on Machine Learning and Cybernetics (ICMLC'10)*. Qingdao, China. IEEE. doi:10.1109/ICMLC.2010.5580673

Yang, Y. H., Lin, Y. C., Cheng, H. T., & Chen, H. H. (2008). Mr. emo: music retrieval in the emotion plane. *Proceedings of 16th ACM international conference on Multimedia*. Vancouver, Canada: ACM. doi:10.1145/1459359.1459550

Yegnarayana, B. (1994). Artificial neural networks for pattern recognition. *Scidhanci*, *19*(2), 189–238.

Yeh, C. H., Lin, H. H., & Chang, H. T. (2009). An efficient emotion detection scheme for popular music. *Proceedings of IEEE International Symposium on Circuits and Systems (ISCAS 2009)*. Taipei, Taiwan. IEEE. doi:10.1109/ISCAS.2009.5118126

Yin, R. (2011). *Qualitative research from start to finish*. New York, NY: The Guilford Press.

Youngblood, G. (1970). *Expanded Cinema*. New York: Dutton.

Yourdon, E. (1989). *Modern Structured Analysis*. Upper Saddle River, NJ: Yourdon Press.

Zafeiropoulos, V. (2008). *Adventure Game Implementation under the Prolog Programming Language*. Master Thesis. Mälardalen University.

Zdrowie publiczne (n. d.). Retrieved from http://www.ec.europa.eu/health-eu/care_for_me/e-health/index_pl.htm

Zhang, P. (2008). *Industrial Control Technology: A Handbook for Engineers and Researchers*. William Andrew.

Zhang, S., Tian, Q., Jiang, S., Huang, Q., & Gao, W. (2008). Affective mtv analysis based on arousal and valence features. *Proceedings of IEEE International Conference on Multimedia and Expo (ICME 2008)*. Hanover, Germany. IEEE. doi:10.1109/ICME.2008.4607698

Zhou, Z., Cheok, A. D., Pan, J. H., & Li, Y. (2004, June). Magic Story Cube: An Interactive Tangible Interface for Storytelling. *ACE*, 3–5.

Zhu, H., Wang, S., & Wang, Z. (2008). Emotional music generation using interactive genetic algorithm. *Proceedings of International Conference on Computer Science and Software Engineering* (volume 1). Wuhan, Hubei, China. IEEE. doi:10.1109/CSSE.2008.1203

Zichermann, G., & Cunningham, C. (2011). Introduction. In G. Zichermann, & C. Cunningham (Eds.), Gamification by Design: Implementing Game Mechanics in Web and Mobile Apps (p. xiv). Sebastopol, CA: O'Reily Media, Inc.

Zichermann, G., & Linder, J. (2013). The Gamification Revolution: How Leaders Leverage Game Mechanics to Crush the Competition. McGraw Hill.

Zintegrowany Informator Pacjenta. (n.d.). *Zintegrowany Informator Pacjenta*. Retrieved from https://zip.nfz.gov.pl

Ziuziański, P., Furmankiewicz, M., & Sołtysik-Piorunkiewicz, A. (2014). E-health artificial intelligence system implementation: Case study of knowledge management dashboard of epidemiological data in Poland. *International Journal of Biology and Biomedical Engineering*, *8*, 164–171.

About the Contributors

Ioannis Deliyannis is an appointed Lecturer in the field of "Interactive Multimedia and Digital Technology" at the Department of Audiovisual Arts at Ionian University, Corfu, Greece since 2010. His research interests include the application of Interactive and Multimedia Communication Technologies in the area of Audiovisual Arts. He is the author of a series of journal and conference publications in the above fields, followed by a series of books targeting the experimental and creative aspects of the technologies involved. He completed his undergraduate studies (B.Sc.) and was subsequently offered a scholarship to pursue a Ph.D degree in the field of Interactive Multimedia at the University of Wales Swansea. He holds a Computer Science Degree (1997, University of Wales Swansea) and a Ph.D in the field of Interactive Multimedia (2002, University of Wales Swansea). He worked within the Computational Fluid Dynamics research team as a research student under the supervision of Professors P. Townsend and M. F. Webster. His research work was largely related with multi-media applications, visualisation and web-based technologies applied to complex scientific fields such as Computational Rheology and the development of Educational Systems for Research and Interactive Learning. This work was truly groundbreaking in the field forming a highly respected thesis on the subject. It led to wide public exposure and a deeper understanding of the systems involved. This work is actively utilised and extended under the Institute for Non-Newtonian Fluid Mechanics and Swansea CFD research group. Today he is a founding member of the inArts Research Laboratory (inArts.eu) and a member of the faculty of Music and Audiovisual Arts at Ionian University.

Petros A. Kostagiolas is Assistant Professor of information services management in the Department of Archive, Library Science and Museology, Faculty of Information Science and Informatics at Ionian University, Corfu, Greece. He is also a visiting lecturer at Robert Gordon's University, Aberdeen, U.K. He holds a Ph.D. in the field of quality and reliability management from the University of Birmingham, U.K. and he has published his work in international journals and conference proceedings. He has been co-author of four management books in Greek and author of a book titled "Managing Intellectual Capital in Libraries: beyond the balance sheet" published in Chandos-Elsevier publisher. His research interests include the theory and practice of information services management, healthcare management, intellectual capital management, quality management, as well as information seeking behaviour in various settings with emphasis in healthcare.

Christina Banou is Assistant Professor in Book Policy and Publishing in the Department of Archives, Library Science & Museology, Faculty of Information Science and Informatics, Ionian University, Corfu, Greece. Banou studied at the National and Kapodistrian University of Athens, Dep. of Phililogy, she holds a Ph.D. on the ornamentation and illustration of Greek books printed in Italy during the Renaissance and the early Baroque era (Dep. of History, Ionian University, 2002). She has been a visiting lecturer in autumn 2014 at the Robert Gordon University, Aberdeen, Business School, Dep. of Information Management. Her main areas of research interests include publishing, book policy, current trends of the publishing industry, history of the book publishing industry, aesthetics of the printed book, reading policy, development of the publishing policy and of promotion strategies, art history of the printed book, and the impact of new technologies on the book publishing activity. She has presented papers in refereed journals and has participated at international conferences. Two monographs of her concerning the publishing industry have been published in Greek: Banou, Christina (2012), *Gutenberg's Next Step: the Publishing Companies in Greece at the Beginning of the 21ˢᵗ century*, Athens: Papazisis Publishers. Banou, Christina (2008), *Diachronic Features of the Publishing Industry in the Western World*, Athens: Kotinos Publications.

***

Eleanor Dare is a computer scientist and a fine artist with a PhD in Arts and Computational Technology from Goldsmiths, Department of Computing, University of London. Her doctorate was concerned with artificial intelligence and e-books, she developed an intelligent book that used a multi-agent system to respond uniquely to each reader. She was reputedly the first fine artist to be awarded a full doctoral studentship from the Engineering and Physical Sciences Research Council. Eleanor is currently an associate academic at the University of Derby where she authors and delivers modules for the School of Computing and Mathematics, she is widely published and continues to develop and write about computational systems for collaboration and creativity.

Zoe Dionyssiou is Assistant Professor in Music Education at the Department of Music, Ionian University. Her main research interests include early childhood music education, Greek folk music in education, children's playsongs and games, music teachers' education, etc. She is co-ordinator of the Project "Euterpi - Digital Music Anthology," a project designed upon the receipt of ISME - Gibson 2012 award to both the Greek Society for Music Education and Lilian Voudouri Music Library of Greece, with the support of the National Documentation Centre of Greece. She is partner to the programme «MusiChild - Mediterranean Early Childhood Music Education: raising children's musicality, evaluating music learning and enabling teachers' preparation» (Erasmus+, 2014-16). She is co-editor of the scientific journal "Musical Pedagogics". She coordinates a series of community music educational activities organised by Ionian University, such as music education courses for babies and toddlers, interdisciplinary music-based educational activities in museums, art galleries and libraries, concerts for babies, etc.

Konstantinos Drossos holds a BEng equivalent on Sound and Musical Instruments Technology with distinction from the Technological Educational Institute of Ionian Islands. In 2007 he received his MSc from ISVR, University of Southampton. Currently he is a PhD candidate at the Dept. of Audiovisual Arts of Ionian University. His main research interests are emotion recognition from sound events, affective acoustic ecology, audio processing, audio perception and audio interfaces. He has also worked as an acoustic consultant and as an Adjunct Lecturer at the dept. of Sound and Musical Instruments Technology of the Technological Educational Institute of Ionian Islands. Mr. Drossos is a student member of the Audio Engineering Society and of Hellenic Institute of Acoustics.

Sonia Ferrari Sonia Ferrari is associate professor of Tourism Marketing and Place Marketing at the University of Calabria, Italy. She has been a researcher in the same University since 1993. She has also taught Management, Service Management, Event Marketing, Marketing of Museums, and Tourism Management at the University of Calabria. At the same university she is President of the Tourism Science Degree Course and President of Valorizzazione dei Sistemi Turistico Culturali Degree Course. Her main fields of study and research are: services management, tourism and place marketing, web marketing, event marketing, and wellness tourism.

Andreas Floros holds an engineering and Ph.D. degree in the area of digital audio technology from the dept. of electrical and computer engineering, University of Patras. In 2001, he joined the semiconductors industry, leading projects in the area of digital audio delivery over PANs and WLANs, Quality-of-Service, mesh networking, wireless VoIP technologies and lately with audio encoding and compression in embedded processors. During 2003 - 2005 he was a member of IEEE Tasks Groups 802.11e, .11k and .11s. For a period of three years (2005 - 2008), he was an adjunct professor at the dept. of informatics, Ionian University, teaching also at the postgraduate (MSc) program ``Arts and Technologies of Sound'' organized by the dept. of Music Studies. Since 2009 he is an Assistant Professor at the dept. of Audiovisual Arts, Ionian University. His current research interests focus on analysis, processing and conversion of digital audio signals, digital audio coding and distribution techniques, digital audio technologies for multimedia and networking applications, audio systems for consumer and professional applications, wireless technologies for multimedia applications (with emphasis on Quality of Service for Wireless LANs) and high-quality audio streaming over packet networks. Dr. Floros is a member of ACM, the Audio Engineering Society (currently serving as the Secretary of the AES Greek Section) and the treasurer of the Hellenic Institute of Acoustics.

Małgorzata Furmankiewicz, M.Sc. in Informatics and Econometrics at Faculty of Informatics and Communication at the University of Economics in Katowice (Poland), currently an honorary member of Student's Research Group for knowledge engineering "Scientia Ingenium" at the Department of Knowledge Engineering at the University of Economics in Katowice. Author of publications mainly connected with informatics applications in health care. Major Fields of scientific research and interests: e-health, artificial intelligence and expert systems, implementation of information systems and human role in this process, project management and knowledge management

Dalila Honorato was born in Portugal where she graduated in Communication and Media Studies at the University of Lisbon in Portugal. She has been living in Greece since 1997 where she obtained her MA and Ph.D degrees by the Department of Communication and Mass Media at the National and Kapodistrian University of Athens as a scholarship holder. Since 2005, she has been teaching courses on Media Aesthetics and Semiotics at the Department of Audio and Visual Arts part of the Faculty of Music and Audiovisual Arts of the Ionian University in Corfu, Greece currently as an Assistant Professor. Until the present date, she has supervised, co-advised and participated in the examination committee of a large number of BA theses and undergraduate individual projects. As a staff member, she has developed administrative activities such as students' mentoring and internships' supervision and she is currently the Departmental Erasmus coordinator. She was a member of the organizing committee of the symposia "Art and Interculturality in the Mediterranean region" (2013) and "Metamorphoses of corporeality: Art-Body-Technology" (2014). She has been appointed president of the organizing committee of the 10th Audiovisual Arts Festival for the academic year 2015-16. One of the founding members of the Interactive Arts Lab, her research focus is on embodiment in the intersection of performing arts and new media. She is also co-advising doctoral students developing their PhD Arts Practice. Her publications include: "The Symbolic Aesthetics of Shadow Play or the perseverance of puppet theater in the digital age" presented at the 18th International Congress of Aesthetics, ISBN: 9787516129401 (2013) and "Bullfight: embracing the animal, performing the god" presented at the 2nd International Conference on Consciousness, Theatre, Literature and the Arts, ISBN: 9781847184184 (2008). At the beginning of 2014 she was a Visiting Fellow at the Center of Philosophy of Sciences of the University of Lisbon and since 2013 she participates in a research program by COST Appearance matters: Tackling the Physical & Psychological Consequences of Dissatisfaction with Appearance (Action IS1210) running until 2017.

Panayotis K. Ioannou is an Assistant Professor in Art History, Department of History and Archaeology, University of Crete. Dr. Ioannou received a BA in History and Archaeology from the University of Athens and a MA in History of Western Art from the University of Athens. Dr. Ioannou received his PhD from the University of Crete, with a thesis on the work of the painter Belisario Corenzio, 1558-1646. From 1993-1997 he was a member of the editing board of the "Dictionary of Greek Artists" (16-20 cent.), vol. 1-4, Athens, Melissa Publishers, 1997-2000. From 1997-2004, he completed research in various Italian archives, mainly Venice, Naples, and Rome. From 1999-2000 Dr. Ioannou was a researcher at Hellenic Institute of Venice. Since 2005, he has been a Lecturer of Art History in the University of Crete, and assistant professor since 2011. Since 2007, Dr. Ioannou is a researcher at the Institute of Mediterranean Studies / Foundation for Research and Technology.

Maximos Kaliakatsos-Papakostas is currently a postdoc researcher in the Music Department of Aristotle University of Thessaloniki. He holds a PhD in Computational Intelligence methods for music analysis and generation, an MSc in Computational Intelligence and a Bachelor's degree in Mathematics, from the Department of Mathematics, University of Patras. Among his research interests are automated music generation and information retrieval, as well as conceptual blending on multiple domains for generating novel musical concepts.

Dimitris Kalles is an Assistant Professor on Artificial Intelligence with the Hellenic Open University. He holds a PhD in Computation from UMIST and is actively researching artificial intelligence and e-learning. He has taught several courses and supervised numerous dissertations and theses, both undergraduate and postgraduate, at the Hellenic Open University and at other universities. He has worked as a researcher with Computer Technology Institute (Greece), as a Technical Director and member of BoD with Ahead Relationship Mediators SA (Greece), and as an evaluator for the European Commission, for the Corallia Clusters Initiative and for several other organisations. He was a member of the Organising Committee of ECAI-08 and ICTAI-12 and he co-chaired SETN-14. He has served as Chairperson and Secretary General of the Hellenic Society for Artificial Intelligence. He has published over 60 papers in journals and conferences and he is a skilled programmer.

May Kokkidou (M.Ed, Ph.D.) is a music education specialist and researcher. She is author of three books and of the monograph "European Music Curricula: Philosophical Orientations, Trends, and Comparative Validation", and co-author of four book on Aesthetic Education. She is member of the Project "Euterpi - Digital Music Anthology" which is designed upon the receipt of ISME - Gibson 2012 award.

She has given many lectures and held seminars and workshops in Greece and abroad. Her recent work focuses on the areas of the semiotics of music, the music literacy, the meaning and value of music for young people, and the multi-modal music perception. At present, she teaches within the field of Musical Semiotics and Aesthetics in the Post-Graduate Course "Semiotics and Communication", University of Western Macedonia. She is co-editor of the scientific journal "Musical Pedagogics" and member of Scientific Committee in several international and Greek journals. She served as president of the Greek Society for Music Education (2007-2012).

Charilaos Lavranos is a PhD candidate in the Department of Music Studies, Ionian University, Greece. He holds BA from the Department of Music Studies, Ionian University, and M.Sc. from the Department of Archives and Library Science, Ionian University, Greece. He also holds degree in the trumpet and music theory (fugue and instrumentation) from the Conservatory of Corfu, Greece. His research interests include music information seeking behaviours in relation to creativity. Since 2004 he works as a secondary school music teacher in Greece.

Elena Papadaki is an art historian and cultural theorist. Her doctoral research (Goldsmiths, University of London – Centre for Cultural Studies, Arts and Computational Technology), titled: "Curating Screens: Art, Performance and Public Spaces", has examined the curation of screen media in diverse physical environments. Her research interests lie in the intersection of screen-based arts, architecture and audience reception. She is a lecturer in Creative Professions and Digital Arts at University of Greenwich, London, and a founder of Incandescent Square, a collaborative meeting point for research and design. She is a voting member of the International Council of Museums (ICOM) and a Fellow of the Higher Education Academy (HEA).

Joseph Papadatos is a Professor of musical composition in the Department of Music Studies, Ionian University, Greece. He teaches composition, orchestration and music theory. He holds the position of president of the Department of Music Studies of Ionian University, as well as the position of vice president of the Greek Composers Union.

Vasil Papadopoulos is a Professor of Mathematics and Statistics at the Democritus University of Thrace, Section of Mathematics, Civil Engineering Department. His research focuses on Point-Set Topology, Mathematical Modeling and Fuzzy Logic with Applications in Engineering, Statistics and Theory of Economics & Finance. His publications include over eighty papers and books in various journals in all the above topics, both as a single author and as co-author. He holds a Diploma in Mathematics - Aristotle University of Thessaloniki, 1977 and a Ph. D. His Doctoral Thesis is entitled: "A Study of the Isbell Topology on Function Spaces" 1985 awarded by the Democritus University of Thrace.

Georgios Papaioannou was born in Ioannina, Greece. At an early age he was exposed to scholarship and international travel. His life has reflected this. After gaining his BA degree at Ioannina University, he went to Britain where he completed an MA Degree in Archaeology and IT at University College London. He then went on to take a PhD at King's College London in classics, archaeology, cultural heritage and IT. After spending time in Spain and conducting archaeological work in Jordan, Syria and Oman, he joined the staff of the Ionian University in Corfu, Greece, where he now is an Assistant Professor at the Department of Archives, Library Sciences and Museology. The focus of his research interests lies in museums, archaeology, education (including distance learning) and IT applications, including augmented reality and mobile applications. He has set-up archaeological exhibitions at the Lowest Place on Earth in Jordan and ethnographic exhibitions at various museums in Greece. He has led and coordinated multi-partner cross border research and innovation projects. Dr Papaioannou is General-Secretary of the Hellenic Society for Near Eastern Studies and a member of ICOM. He has lectured widely, excavated and led tours to the UK, Greece, Cyprus, Spain, Syria, Oman, Turkey, Yemen and Saudi Arabia.

Antonia Plerou is a PhD candidate at the Department of Informatics of the Ionian University in Corfu and a collaborator of the Laboratory of Bioinformatics and Human Electrophysiology (BiheLab) of the Ionian University. She studied Applied Mathematics at the Faculty of Sciences in Aristotle University of Thessaloniki and obtained her Master Degree in Mathematics from the Faculty of Sciences and Technology of the Greek Open University. She has published several articles in international conferences and journals and her research interests are mainly related with the fields of Cognitive Science and Learning Difficulties, Dyscalculia and Algorithmic Thinking Difficulties, Artificial Neural Networks and Algorithms, Artificial Intelligence and Pattern Recognition, Neuronal Disorders using Neuroinformatics, Neurodegenerative Diseases and Educational Neuroscience.

Argyro Sgourou holds a PhD in "Molecular Biology and Genetics" obtained from Medical School (2001), University of Patras, under the funding of the "States Scholarship Foundation" of Greece. She has acquired the know-how of molecular biology emerging techniques during 2 EMBO research fellowships to the Laboratory of Gene Structure and Expression National Institute for Medical Research, UK and the Dept. of Medical and Molecular Genetics, King's College, London and her postdoctoral studies (2003-5) on Gene Therapy Biotechnology issues at the Dept. of Medical and Molecular Genetics, King's College, London, funded by a Marie Curie Individual Fellowship. Between 2005-2008 she has been serving the Pathology Division, University Hospital, Rion-Patras, on specialized molecular diagnostic tests. She has gained 4 years teaching experience as a tutor at the Molecular Biology and Genetics Dept., Democritus University of Thrace (2002-3), Dept. of Pharmacy (2006-8) and Dept. of Materials Science (2008), University of Patras. Currently, she offers research activities and technical assistance at the Biology laboratory of HOU. She has published 14 original papers (PubMed), 17 papers in International conference proceedings and 15 in Greek, of which 3 have been awarded.

Anna Sołtysik-Piorunkiewicz, Ph.D. is employed at the University of Economics in Katowice as lecturer at Faculty of Informatics and Communication, at Department of Informatics, Katowice, Poland. Major Fields of Scientific Research: business information systems, knowledge management, knowledge based organization, mobile enterprise, ICT, UX, user acceptance of information technology, computer science, systems analysis and computer system design, management information systems, e-business, e-health and public informatics.

Panagiota Stellaki holds a degree of Archaeology & History of Art from the University of Athens and a Master's degree in Cultural Management from Panteion University, Athens. For more than 10 years, she has worked as a museum educator at "Hellenic Cosmos", the cultural centre of the Foundation of the Hellenic World, designing and performing guided tours and educational activities, virtual reality walkthroughs, seminars etc. She is also a licensed tour guide with specialization in ancient Greek history and culture. Her research interests include educational programmes for museums and cultural institutions, exhibitions with the use of new media and visitor's studies.

Roxana Theodorou holds a PhD in Academic Electronic Publishing from the Ionian University in Greece, an MA degree in Electronic Publishing and Communication from UCL in London and a BA in Archive and Library Science from the Ionian University. Her research has been published in several scientific journals (i.e. Journal of Academic Publishing, Libraries Management ets) and major conferences (IFLA, LIBER, QQML etc). In the past she has been teaching Librarianship for several years at the Ionian University, at the department of Archive and Library Science as an Adjunct Lecturer (Introduction to Information Science, Preservation and Conservation, Collection Management, Information Literacy and Resources etc) and has worked as a freelancer on several research projects (Modernization of the Central Library of the Ionian University, Books+ etc). At the Hellenic American University she teaches Information Literacy and Technology Basics and is also the Head Librarian of the University's Library.

Panayiotis Vlamos is an Associate Professor and Head of the Department of Informatics at the Ionian University. He received his Diploma in Mathematics from the University of Athens and his Ph.D. degree in Mathematics from the National Technical University of Athens, Greece. He has (co-) authored more than 130 papers in international journals, conferences and book chapters. He is director of "Computational Modeling Lab" at the Department of Informatics, Ionian University. He is also (co-) author of more than 16 educational books and creator of several educational materials. He has been member or principal investigator of several research projects on Mathematical Modeling and Simulation. His research interests mainly concern mathematical modeling in Bioinformatics, algorithms on recent advances in Neuroinformatics, image restoration problems and physical- chemical engineering problems, discrete mathematics and mathematical modeling in Education.

Elena Vlamou is at the moment a Ph.D Candidate at Democritus University of Thace at the Department of Civil Engineering. She has a diploma in mathematics and is a graduate of the School Chrysostomos of Smyrna. She is the owner of a private education centre and works as a mathematician. Her research interests focuses in fuzzy logic methods. She has published articles in national and international conferences.

Vasilis Zafeiropoulos is a PhD candidate in Artificial Intelligence at Hellenic Open University (HOU) with his PhD thesis being "Computer-Human Learning Interaction in Laboratory Environments". He is also a member of Hellenic Artificial Intelligence Society (EETN). He holds a BSc in Mathematics from University of Patras, Greece and a MSc in Computer Engineering from Mälardalen University of Västerås, Sweden. He has also been educated in the Instruction of Students with Learning Disabilities at the Association for the Psychosocial Health of Children and Adolescents of Greece (APHCA). His work experience includes having worked as a Mathematics and Computer Programming teacher for High School and University students in private education, as an Architectural Engineer at "KYMA" structural engineering office and as a Journalist and Science Editor at "Ethnos" newspaper. His research interests involve, among others, Educational Game Design and Implementation, Ontology Engineering and Machine Learning.

Stelios Zimeras holds a BSc. (Hons) on Statistics and Insurance Sciences from University of Piraeus (5fth in the rank) and Ph.D. on Statistics from the University of Leeds, U.K. He had received a full scholarship (fees and maintenance) during his research studies (1993-1997) from the University of Leeds. Since 2008, he is a full time staff member (Assistant Prof) on statistics and probabilities at the

Department of Mathematics, Division of Statistics and Financial-Actuarial Mathematics, University of the Aegean, Samos, Greece. He had worked as post-doc at University of Leeds, Department of Electrical Engineering (funded by EPSRC), at IRISA/INRIA-VISTA PROJECT institute, France (funded by EUMETSAT-ESA) and at MedCom GmbH, Germany (funded by Marie-Curie grants). Finally from 2011-2012 he had worked during his sabbatical in University of Piraeus, Department of Digital Systems, in computer virus modelling. In 2011 he has nominated the Best Paper for the 5th International Conference on Energy and Development - Environment - Biomedicine 2011 (EDEB '11) with title "Spatial Uncertainty", pp. 203-208, by S. Zimeras, Y. Matsinos. He has been involved in national and international projects (FP7, ESPA, Marie-Curie). His published material and presentations are on a number of topics of Data Processing, Statistical Simulations, Image analysis, Medical Image analysis, Spatial Statistics, Telemedicine, and Statistical Modelling with applications in biology, ecology, and medicine, statistical epidemiology, and Bayesian statistics. He has been a member of a number of professional and scientific societies and associations; while he is a reviewer for a number of conferences.

Piotr Ziuziański, M.Sc. in Informatics and Econometrics at Faculty of Informatics and Communication at the University of Economics in Katowice (Poland), currently honorary member of Student's Research Group for knowledge engineering "Scientia Ingenium" at the Department of Knowledge Engineering at the University of Economics in Katowice. Author of publications mainly connected with informatics applications in health care. Major Fields of scientific research and interests: e-health, data visualization and performance dashboards, Business Intelligence, survey methodology and knowledge management

Index

Become an IRMA Member

Members of the **Information Resources Management Association (IRMA)** understand the importance of community within their field of study. The Information Resources Management Association is an ideal venue through which professionals, students, and academicians can convene and share the latest industry innovations and scholarly research that is changing the field of information science and technology. Become a member today and enjoy the benefits of membership as well as the opportunity to collaborate and network with fellow experts in the field.

IRMA Membership Benefits:

- **One FREE Journal Subscription**

- **30% Off Additional Journal Subscriptions**

- **20% Off Book Purchases**

- Updates on the latest events and research on Information Resources Management through the IRMA-L listserv.

- Updates on new open access and downloadable content added to Research IRM.

- A copy of the Information Technology Management Newsletter twice a year.

- A certificate of membership.

IRMA Membership $195

Scan code to visit irma-international.org and begin by selecting your free journal subscription.

Membership is good for one full year.

Printed in the United States
By Bookmasters